T0189670

Lecture Notes in Artificial Intelligence   12798

Subseries of Lecture Notes in Computer Science

Series Editors

Randy Goebel
    University of Alberta, Edmonton, Canada
Yuzuru Tanaka
    Hokkaido University, Sapporo, Japan
Wolfgang Wahlster
    DFKI and Saarland University, Saarbrücken, Germany

Founding Editor

Jörg Siekmann
    DFKI and Saarland University, Saarbrücken, Germany

More information about this subseries at http://www.springer.com/series/1244

Hamido Fujita · Ali Selamat ·
Jerry Chun-Wei Lin · Moonis Ali (Eds.)

Advances and Trends
in Artificial Intelligence

Artificial Intelligence Practices

34th International Conference
on Industrial, Engineering and Other Applications
of Applied Intelligent Systems, IEA/AIE 2021
Kuala Lumpur, Malaysia, July 26–29, 2021
Proceedings, Part I

 Springer

Editors
Hamido Fujita 🆔
i-SOMET Incorporate Association
Morioka, Japan

Jerry Chun-Wei Lin 🆔
Western Norway University
of Applied Sciences
Bergen, Norway

Ali Selamat 🆔
Universiti Teknologi Malaysia
Kuala Lumpur, Malaysia

Moonis Ali
Texas State University San Marcos
San Marcos, TX, USA

ISSN 0302-9743   ISSN 1611-3349   (electronic)
Lecture Notes in Artificial Intelligence
ISBN 978-3-030-79456-9   ISBN 978-3-030-79457-6   (eBook)
https://doi.org/10.1007/978-3-030-79457-6

LNCS Sublibrary: SL7 – Artificial Intelligence

This Springer imprint is published by the registered company Springer Nature Switzerland AG
The registered company address is: Gewerbestrasse 11, 6330 Cham, Switzerland

Preface

Artificial Intelligence innovations in recent decades have entered a sophisticated stage in providing intelligent interaction between humans and machines, solving problems, and providing advice in many different infrastructures. Machines in different disciplines have become ubiquitous in all aspects of life, including education, governance, science, healthcare, warfare, and industry. Computing machinery has become smaller and faster, and the costs of data storage and communication have greatly decreased. Consequently, big data of vast dimensionality is being intelligently collected and stored in smart databases for use in decision making and prediction for applications such as security and health care, amongst others. Moreover, novel and improved computing architectures have been designed for efficient large-scale data processing, such as big data frameworks, FPGAs and GPUs. Thanks to these advancements and recent breakthroughs in artificial intelligence, researchers and practitioners have developed more complex and effective artificial intelligence-based systems. This has led to a greater interest in artificial intelligence to solve complex real-world problems, and the proposal of many innovative applications.

This volume contains the proceedings of the 34th International Conference on Industrial, Engineering and other Applications of Applied Intelligent Systems (IEA/AIE 2021), which was held online during July 26–29, 2021, in Kuala Lumpur, Malaysia. The IEA/AIE conference is an annual event that emphasizes applications of applied intelligent systems to solve real-life problems in all areas including engineering, science, industry, automation and robotics, business and finance, medicine and biomedicine, bioinformatics, cyberspace, and human-machine interactions. This year, 145 submissions were received. Each paper was evaluated by three to four reviewers from an International Program Committee consisting of 196 members from 37 countries. Based on the evaluation, 87 papers were selected as full papers and 19 as short papers, which are presented in two volumes. We are grateful to all the reviewers for the time spent writing detailed and constructive comments for the authors, and also the authors for the proposal of so many high-quality papers.

The program of IEA/AIE 2021 included eight special sessions:

- Special Session on Data Stream Mining: Algorithms and Applications (DSMAA2021)
- Special Session on Intelligent Knowledge Engineering in Decision Making Systems (IKEDS2021)
- Special Session on Knowledge Graphs in Digitalization Era (KGDE2021)
- Special Session on Spatiotemporal Big Data Analytics (SBDA2021)
- Special Session on Big Data and Intelligence Fusion Analytics (BDIFA2021)
- Special Session on AI in Healthcare (AIH2021)
- Special Session on Intelligent Systems and e-Applications (iSeA2021)
- Special Session on Collective Intelligence in Social Media (CISM2021).

Moreover, two keynote talks were given by Professor Francisco Herrera, from the University of Granada, Spain, and Director of the Andalusian Research Institute "Data Science and Computational Intelligence", and Professor Vincent S. Tseng from the Department of Computer Science, National Yang Ming Chiao Tung University, Taiwan.

We would like to thank everyone who has contributed to the success of this year's edition of IEA/AIE, that is the authors, Program Committee members, reviewers, keynote speakers, organizers and participants.

May 2021

Hamido Fujita
Ali Selamat
Jerry Chun-Wei Lin
Moonis Ali

Organization

General Chairs

Hamido Fujita, Japan
Moonis Ali, USA

Organizing Chairs

Ali Selamat, Malaysia
Jun Sasaki, Japan

Program Chairs

Ali Selamat, Malaysia
Jerry Chun-Wei Lin, Norway

Special Session Chairs

Philippe Fournier-Viger, China
Nor Azura Mohd Ghani, Malaysia

Publicity Chairs

Mohd Hazli Mohamed Zabil, Malaysia
Lim Kok Cheng, Malaysia

Program Committee

Abidalrahman Moh'D, USA
Adel Bouhoula, Tunisia
Adrianna Kozierkiewicz, Poland
Ahmed Tawfik, Egypt
Alban Grastien, Australia
Alexander Ferrein, Germany
Artur Andrzejak, Germany
Ayahiko Niimi, Japan
Barbara Pes, Italy
Bay Vo, Vietnam
Dariusz Krol, Poland
Dinh Tuyen Hoang, Korea
Du Nguyen

Contents – Part I

Artificial Intelligence and Machine Learning

Sematic, Topology, and Ontology Models

Medical and Health-Related Applications

Graphic and Social Network Analysis

Signal and Bioinformatic Processing

Evolutionary Computation

Attack and Security

Natural Language and Text Processing

Fuzzy Inference and Theory

Sensor and Communication Networks

Contents – Part II

Data Management, Clustering and Classification

Robotics

Knowledge Based and Decision Support Systems

Multimedia Applications

Innovative Applications of Intelligent Systems

CPS and Industrial Applications

Defect, Anomaly and Intrusion Detection

Financial and Supply Chain Applications

Bayesian Networks

BigData and Time Series Processing

Information Retrieval and Relation Extraction

Knowledge Discovery and Pattern Mining

Fast Mining of Top-k Frequent Balanced Association Rules

Xiangyu Liu[✉], Xinzheng Niu, Jieliang Kuang, Shenghan Yang,
and Pengpeng Liu

School of Computer Science and Engineering, University of Electronic
Science and Technology of China, Chengdu, China
xinzhengniu@uestc.edu.cn

Abstract. Association rule mining (ARM), as a basic data mining task, aims to find association rules that satisfy predefined parameters from a given database. However, traditional ARM algorithms always generate a huge number of rules in many cases, which will greatly limit the usefulness of the mining results. Considering the unintuitiveness of setting parameters, algorithms have been designed to mine the top-k rules with the highest support that meet a minimum confidence. But it is not comprehensive to evaluate the strength of rules only by support and confidence. In some specific applications, the balance of rules also plays a decisive role in the actual effect. To address this issue, this paper proposes a top-k frequent balanced association rule mining algorithm named TFBRM (Top-k Frequent Balanced Rule Miner), which uses support, kulczynski (kulc) and imbalance ratio (IR) as measures. The algorithm employs three effective pruning strategies to reduce the search space. Experiments were conducted to evaluate the efficiency of TFBRM, and TFBRM has good scalability, which can be used in many applications.

Keywords: Association rule mining · Top-k rules · Rule expansion · Imbalance ratio

1 Introduction

Association rule mining (ARM) is an important branch in the field of data mining. It aims to extract interesting associations or various frequent patterns from different data repositories. Association rules are widely used in market and risk management, inventory control, fraud detection, telecommunication and many other fields [17]. Traditional ARM task mainly consists of two steps. Frequent patterns with support not less than the minimum support threshold ($minsup$) are first mined from a database in step one, and then in step two, all the rules that meet the minimum confidence threshold ($minconf$) are generated from the obtained frequent patterns.

A serious problem is that the parameter setting is not intuitive for users, and most of the time traditional ARM will generate many rules, which greatly

© Springer Nature Switzerland AG 2021
H. Fujita et al. (Eds.): IEA/AIE 2021, LNAI 12798, pp. 3–14, 2021.
https://doi.org/10.1007/978-3-030-79457-6_1

limits the usefulness of the mining results. Therefore, the TopKRules algorithm was proposed [7], which uses an intuitive parameter k to replace the unintuitive parameter $minsup$ to mine the top-k rules with the highest support. Although TopKRules can complete the mining task, its search space is huge. To solve this problem, the ETARM (Efficient Top-k Association Rule Miner) algorithm combining two effective pruning strategies was recently proposed [14].

However, it is not comprehensive to evaluate the strength of rules only by support and confidence. In some specific applications, such as in various decision-making aspects, the balance of rules also plays a decisive role in the actual effect. To address this issue, this paper presents an efficient top-k frequent balanced ARM algorithm named TFBRM (Top-k Frequent Balanced Rule Miner). Based on the extension of ETARM through three pruning strategies, TFBRM uses support, kulczynski (kulc) and imbalance ratio (IR) as measures to more comprehensively evaluate the strength of the rules.

The rest of this paper is organized as follows. Section 2 conducts a survey of related work. The problem statement and basic definitions are introduced in Sect. 3. Section 4 describes the details of the TFBRM algorithm. Section 5 shows the experimental results. Finally, Sect. 6 summarizes the study and discusses future work.

2   Relation Work

With the rapid explosion of information, the analysis process designed to mine data becomes more complex and difficult. ARM, which is an important branch of the data mining field, also faces this problem.

Since the concept of ARM was proposed in 1993, many approaches have been designed to improve the performance of this task from different angles. Some efficient data structures have been used to improve the efficiency of rule mining algorithms. For instance, Wang et al. [19] introduced a novel framework for mining temporal association rules by discovering itemsets with frequent itemsets tree. Mai et al. [12] used a lattice to quickly mine rules. Anand et al. [1] presented a novel ARM algorithm using treap. Besides, combining the ARM algorithm with different optimization techniques can also effectively improve the mining performance. Sharmila et al. [15] introduced a rule mining method using fuzzy logic and whale optimization algorithm. In [13], Moslehi et al. presented a novel GA-PSO framework for mining quantitative association rules. Wen et al. [22] introduced a hybrid temporal ARM algorithm that can be used for traffic congestion prediction. More related work can be found in [2,5,11,18].

As a sub-problem of ARM, frequent itemset mining (FIM) has also received extensive attention from researchers. Since its concept was put forward, different problem variants have been generated [4,8,9], and many efforts have been made to improve its mining performance. Sohrabi et al. [16] proposed a method underpinned upon cellular learning automata for mining frequent itemsets. A novel algorithm using hashing and lexicographic order for FIM was proposed in [3]. Han et al. [10] presented an efficient FIM algorithm to compute the frequent itemsets quickly on massive data. And Djenouri et al. [6] presented a novel FIM method that can be used to extract useful information in logs.

In view of the fact that in some practical applications, users only want to obtain the strongest rules, the idea of top-k ARM was proposed. And algorithms were designed to mine the strongest rules such as k-optimal rules [21] and filtered top-k association rules [20]. They are efficient but limit the consequence of the rule to be mined to contain only one item. The proposal of the TopKRules algorithm solves this problem [7]. It replaces the traditional *minsup* parameter with a k parameter, and the most important thing is that there is no limit to the size of the final mining rules. To further improve the performance of Top-KRules, the ETARM algorithm using two novel pruning strategies was recently proposed [14]. Experiments have verified that the ETARM algorithm is efficient and significantly better than the TopKRules algorithm.

Top-k association rules have been widely used in various practical applications. But for the top-k frequent rules, sometimes they cannot meet actual needs, because the balance of rules also greatly affects the actual effect in some applications, such as decision-making. Therefore, in combination with practical application needs, this paper proposes an efficient top-k frequent balanced association rule mining algorithm named TFBRM, which extends ETARM with three effective pruning strategies, and uses kulc and IR instead of confidence as measures to evaluate the strength of rules more comprehensively.

3   Problem Formulation

In this section, the traditional ARM problem is described first, and then the top-k frequent balanced ARM problem.

3.1   Traditional ARM

Let $I = \{i_1, i_2, i_3, ..., i_m\}$ be a set of items, and $DB = \{T_1, T_2, T_3, ..., T_n\}$ be a set of transactions, where each transaction $T_j \subseteq I$ $(1 \leq j \leq n)$, and has a transaction identifier (tid) j. For a rule $X \rightarrow Y$, X is called the antecedent and Y is called the consequent. They are both sets of items and $X \cap Y = \emptyset$. The strength of association rules can be measured in terms of support and confidence, and the goal of traditional ARM is to mine all rules that meet *minsup* and *minconf* from the database.

Definition 1. *Transaction identifier set (Tidset):* *For a rule $r : X \rightarrow Y$, its tidset can be defined as $tids(r) = tids(X \cup Y) = tids(X) \cap tids(Y)$. And for an itemset X, its tidset is defined as $tids(X) = \{j | T_j \in DB \wedge X \subseteq T_j\}$.*

Definition 2. *Support:* *For a rule $r : X \rightarrow Y$, its support $sup(r)$ describes the proportion of transactions in DB that contain all items in rule r. And the support $sup(X)$ of an itemset X is defined in the same way.*

$$sup(r) = \frac{|tids(X) \cap tids(Y)|}{|DB|} \tag{1}$$

Definition 3. *Confidence:* *For a rule* $r : X \to Y$, *its confidence* $conf(r)$ *is defined as the probability that a transaction contains itemset* Y *under the condition that it contains itemset* X.

$$conf(r) = \frac{|tids(X) \cap tids(Y)|}{|tids(X)|} \qquad (2)$$

Definition 4. *Kulczynski (Kulc):* *For a rule* $r : X \to Y$, *its kulczynski* $kulc(r)$ *is defined as the average of two conditional probabilities.*

$$kulc(r) = \frac{P(X|Y) + P(Y|X)}{2} \qquad (3)$$

Definition 5. *Imbalance ratio (IR):* *For a rule* $r : X \to Y$, IR *is used to evaluate the degree of imbalance between itemset* X *and itemset* Y.

$$IR(r) = \frac{|sup(X) - sup(Y)|}{sup(X) + sup(Y) - sup(X \cup Y)} \qquad (4)$$

3.2 Top-k Frequent Balanced ARM

Considering that top-k frequent association rules sometimes cannot meet actual needs, the concept of top-k frequent balanced ARM is proposed, using support, kulc and IR as measures to more comprehensively evaluate the strength of the rules. Given an integer k, the minimum kulc threshold ($minkulc$) and the maximum IR threshold ($maxIR$), the task of top-k frequent balanced ARM is to mine a set L containing k rules from the database such that for each rule $r \in L|kulc(r) \geq minkulc \wedge IR(r) \leq maxIR$, and there is no rule $s \notin L|kulc(s) \geq minkulc \wedge IR(s) \leq maxIR \wedge sup(s) \geq sup(r)$ [7].

Definition 6. *Candidate item:* *An item can be regarded as a candidate item if it is larger than all items on the expanded side in the total order, and it does not appear on the non-expanded side.*

Definition 7. *Left expansion:* *For any association rule* r, *left expansion refers to adding an item* i *to its antecedent, where item* i *belongs to the candidate item set of its antecedent.*

Definition 8. *Right expansion:* *For any association rule* r, *right expansion refers to adding an item* i *to its consequent, where item* i *belongs to the candidate item set of its consequent.*

Property 1. Whether a rule r is expanded left or right, the support of the new rule r' obtained must not be greater than the support of r.

Property 2. If a rule r is left expanded, the confidence of the new rule r' obtained may be less than, equal to, or greater than the confidence of r.

Property 3. If a rule r is right expanded, the confidence of the new rule r' obtained must not be greater than the confidence of r.

4   The Proposed TFBRM

In this section, the novel propositions used by TFBRM is first introduced, followed by the detailed design of the proposed algorithm.

4.1   The Novel Propositions

Proposition 1. *In the process of generating a rule with a size of 1*1, only rules whose item in the antecedent is smaller in total order than that in the consequent are generated.*

Rationale. For two rules $r : X \rightarrow Y$ and $r' : Y \rightarrow X$, their corresponding values are the same on the three measures (support, kulc and IR). Then in the mining process, only one of the rules r and r' needs to be generated, and whether the rules r and r' are the top-k frequent balanced rules that need to be mined from the database can be simultaneously determined according to the specific values of the three measures.

Proposition 2. *For any association rule r, if its confidence satisfies $conf(r) < minkulc * 2 - 1$, then it should not be considered for right expansion, because the new rule obtained by right expansion must not be a top-k frequent balanced association rule.*

Rationale. From Property 3, for a rule $r : X \rightarrow Y$ and a rule r' obtained by right expansion of r, they satisfy $conf(r) \geq conf(r')$, that is, the confidence of the new rule r' must be less than or equal to the confidence of r. From Definition 4, $kulc(r) = (P(X|Y) + P(Y|X))/2 = (conf(X \rightarrow Y) + conf(Y \rightarrow X))/2$, where the maximum possible value of $conf(Y \rightarrow X)$ is 1, so if $kulc(r) \geq minkulc$, then $conf(X \rightarrow Y)$ must be greater than or equal to $minkulc * 2 - 1$. Otherwise, if $conf(X \rightarrow Y)$ is less than $minkulc * 2 - 1$, then $kulc(r)$ must be less than $minkulc$, and $kulc(r')$ must also be less than $minkulc$, which means that in this case, the new rule r' obtained by right expansion of r must not be a top-k frequent balanced association rule.

Proposition 3. *For an association rule $r : X \rightarrow Y$, if $sup(X) \geq sup(Y)$ and $(sup(X) - sup(Y))/(sup(X) + sup(Y) - sup(X \cup Y)) > maxIR$, then the rule r should not be considered for right expansion.*

Rationale. Given a rule $r : X \rightarrow Y$, assume that the support of X is greater than or equal to the support of Y. According to Definition 5, the IR of the rule $r : X \rightarrow Y$ is $IR(r) = |sup(X) - sup(Y)|/(sup(X) + sup(Y) - sup(X \cup Y))$, then in the process of right expansion of rule r, the numerator part will increase or remain unchanged, and the denominator part will remain unchanged or decrease. The IR of the new rule r' obtained by right expansion of rule r must not be less than that of the original rule r, that is, $IR(r') \geq IR(r)$. Therefore, if $IR(r) > maxIR$, then there must be $IR(r') > maxIR$, and the rule r' must not be a top-k rule.

4.2   The TFBRM Algorithm

To mine the top-k frequent balanced association rules faster, the proposed TFBRM algorithm extends the ETARM algorithm and adopts three pruning strategies to reduce the search space. It should be noted that because TFBRM uses support, kulc and IR as measures to evaluate the strength of a rule, the pruning strategy of rule confidence in the ETARM algorithm is not suitable for mining the top-k frequent balanced association rules, so it has not been applied to the TFBRM algorithm.

Algorithm 1. TFBRM($DB,k,minkulc,maxIR$)

1: $R := \emptyset$. $L := \emptyset$. $minsup := 0$.
2: **if** k is an even number **then** $k := k/2$. **else** $k := (k+1)/2$.
3: Scan the database DB to get the tidset of each item.
4: **for** each pair of items (i,j) such that $sup(i) \geq minsup$ and $sup(j) \geq minsup$ **do**
5:     **if** item i is smaller than item j **then** Generate rule $p : \{i\} \rightarrow \{j\}$.
6:     **else** Generate rule $p : \{j\} \rightarrow \{i\}$.
7:     **if** $sup(p) \geq minsup$ **then**
8:         **if** $kulc(p) \geq minkulc$ and $IR(p) \leq maxIR$ **then SAVE**$(p, L, k, minsup)$.
9:         **if** the largest item in the antecedent of rule p is equal to $MaxItem$ **then**
10:             **if** $conf(p) \geq minkulc * 2 - 1$ **then**
11:                 **if** $sup(p.\text{antecedent}) \geq sup(p.\text{consequent})$ **then**
12:                     **if** $IR(p) \leq maxIR$ **then** Set flag $expandLR$ to false. $R := R \cup \{p\}$.
13:                     **else** Set flag $expandLR$ to false. $R := R \cup \{p\}$.
14:             **else** Set flag $expandLR$ to true. $R := R \cup \{p\}$.
15: **while** $\exists$ $rule \in R$ and its support is greater than or equal to $minsup$ **do**
16:     Select the rule r with the highest support in the set R.
17:     **if** $r.expandLR = $ true **then**
18:         **EXPAND_L**$(r, L, R, k, minsup, minkulc, maxIR)$.
19:         **EXPAND_R**$(r, L, R, k, minsup, minkulc, maxIR)$.
20:     **else EXPAND_R**$(r, L, R, k, minsup, minkulc, maxIR)$.
21:     Remove r from R.
22:     Remove rules with support less than $minsup$ from the set R.
23: $T := \emptyset$.
24: **for** each rule q in set L **do**
25:     Exchange the antecedent and the consequent of q to obtain rule q'.
26:     $T := T \cup \{q'\}$.
27: $L := L \cup T$.
28: Return L.

As shown in Algorithm 1, the mining process can be divided into two major stages. In the first stage, the parameter k is re-assigned, and then only rules with a size of 1*1 where the item on the left is smaller than the item on the right are generated (based on Proposition 1). And the rules of size 1*1 that satisfy the certain conditions are added to the sets L and R, respectively. Among them, R is a set of candidate rules, and L is used to store the top-k frequent balanced association rules. The second stage is to loop to select the rule r with the highest support from R to expand it. If the flag $expandLR$ of r is true, then r can be expanded from either side. Otherwise, r cannot be expanded left. After the expansion operations are completed, for the set R, the rule r and the rules whose support is less than the current $minsup$ will be removed. When R is empty, the expansion process ends, and another rule $q' : Y \to X$ corresponding to each rule $q : X \to Y$ in the set L is also added to L, and then return L.

Algorithm 2. SAVE(r,L,k,$minsup$)

1: $L := L \cup \{r\}$.
2: **if** $|L| > k$ **then**
3:     Record the number of rules with support equal to $minsup$ in the current set L into a variable sum.
4:     **if** $|L| - sum \geq k$ **then**
5:         Remove all rules in the set L with support equal to $minsup$.
6:         Set $minsup$ to the lowest support of rules in the set L.

The SAVE procedure (Algorithm 2) is mainly used to update $minsup$ and set L. It initially adds the rule r to the set L. If L contains more than k rules, then the procedure records the number of rules in L whose support is equal to $minsup$ to a variable sum. If $|L| - sum \geq k$, all rules in L whose support is equal to $minsup$ will be removed, and then $minsup$ will be updated to the lowest support of the current rules in L.

Algorithm 3. EXPAND_L(r,L,R,k,$minsup$,$minkulc$,$maxIR$)

1: Scan the transaction tid to obtain the candidate item set I_l of the antecedent of r, where $tid \in tids(r)$.
2: **for** each item $i \in I_l$ **do**
3:     Add item i to the antecedent of rule r to obtain rule r'.
4:     **if** $sup(r') \geq minsup$ **then**
5:         **if** $kulc(r') \geq minkulc$ and $IR(r') \leq maxIR$ **then SAVE**($r', L, k, minsup$).
6:         **if** the largest item in the antecedent of rule r' is equal to $MaxItem$ **then**
7:             **if** $conf(r') \geq minkulc * 2 - 1$ **then**
8:                 **if** $sup(r'.\text{antecedent}) \geq sup(r'.\text{consequent})$ **then**
9:                     **if** $IR(r') \leq maxIR$ **then** Set flag $expandLR$ to false. $R := R \cup \{r'\}$.
10:                **else** Set flag $expandLR$ to false. $R := R \cup \{r'\}$.
11:            **else** Set flag $expandLR$ to true. $R := R \cup \{r'\}$.

Rule expansion is the key step to generate candidate rules, which ensures that the algorithm can mine all the top-k rules that meet the conditions in a given database. The execution details of **EXPAND_L** can be found in Algorithm 3. For the rule r to be expanded, **EXPAND_L** first constructs the candidate item set I_l of its antecedent, and then individually adds each item in the set I_l to the antecedent of rule r to obtain a new rule r'. If $sup(r') \geq minsup$ and $kulc(r') \geq minkulc$ and $IR(r') \leq maxIR$, r' will be added to L. Under the premise of $sup(r') \geq minsup$, if $MaxItem$ is not equal to the largest item in the antecedent of rule r', then the $expandLR$ of r' will be set to true, and r' will be added to the set R. Otherwise, the procedure will judge whether r' satisfies $conf(r') \geq minkulc * 2 - 1$, if so, the $expandLR$ of r' will be set to false. At this time, if $sup(r'.\text{antecedent}) < sup(r'.\text{consequent})$, r' is added to R, otherwise rule r' must satisfy $IR(r') \leq maxIR$ to be added to R (based on Propositions 2 and 3).

EXPAND_R (Algorithm 4) mainly expands the rules to the right. It first constructs the candidate item set I_r of the consequence of rule r, and then adds each item in I_r to the consequence of r individually to obtain rule r'. Similarly, if the rule r' satisfies the corresponding conditions, it is added to the set L. Then according to Propositions 2 and 3, the rules obtained by right expansion that meet the conditions are added to the set R. The difference between **EXPAND_R** and **EXPAND_L** is that **EXPAND_R** only considers whether the rule r' can continue to be expanded right, and does not consider whether it can continue to be expanded left.

Algorithm 4. EXPAND_R($r,L,R,k,minsup,minkulc,maxIR$)

1: Scan the transaction tid to obtain the candidate item set I_r of the consequent of
    r, where $tid \in tids(r)$.
2: **for** each item $i \in I_r$ **do**
3:    Add item i to the consequent of rule r to obtain rule r'.
4:    **if** $sup(r') \geq minsup$ **then**
5:       **if** $kulc(r') \geq minkulc$ and $IR(r') \leq maxIR$ **then** **SAVE**($r', L, k, minsup$).
6:       **if** the largest item in the consequent of rule r' is not equal to $MaxItem$ **then**
7:          **if** $conf(r') \geq minkulc * 2 - 1$ **then**
8:             **if** $sup(r'.\text{antecedent}) \geq sup(r'.\text{consequent})$ **then**
9:                **if** $IR(r') \leq maxIR$ **then** Set flag $expandLR$ to false. $R := R \cup \{r'\}$.
10:            **else** Set flag $expandLR$ to false. $R := R \cup \{r'\}$.

---

5   Experimental Evaluation

This section mainly evaluates the performance of the proposed TFBRM algorithm from different perspectives. Section 5.1 first introduces the experimental environment. Then detailed experimental results and corresponding discussions are in Sect. 5.2.

5.1 Experimental Environment

The proposed TFBRM algorithm was implemented in Java, and all experiments were performed on a Windows 10 operating system equipped with Intel Core i7 CPU@3.7 GHz and 8 GB of RAM. The experiments were conducted 20 times in each case, and the average results were recorded. Six standard benchmark datasets that can be downloaded from http://www.philippe-fournier-viger.com/spmf/ were used for testing. They are widely used in the field of association rule mining to evaluate the performance of algorithms due to their different transaction numbers, item numbers and densities. The specific characteristics of these datasets can be found in Table 1.

Table 1. Characteristics of the datasets

Dataset	Transaction number	Item number	Density
Mushrooms	8,416	119	0.193
T25i10d10k	9,976	929	0.027
Pumsb	49,046	2,113	0.035
Connect	67,557	129	0.333
OnlineRetail	541,909	2,603	0.002
USCensus	1,000,000	396	0.172

5.2 Experimental Results

The experiments were divided into two cases to comprehensively evaluate the performance of the proposed TFBRM algorithm, the parameter k is changed and the database size is varied.

Case 1: minkulc and maxIR were set to 0.8 and 0.2, respectively, and k was changed from 2000 to 16000.

Figure 1 shows the running time of the TFBRM algorithm for different parameter values and datasets. As the value of k increases, the running time of TFBRM on different datasets varies differently. For instance, on the Connect dataset, the running time of TFBRM changes significantly. When $k = 2000$, the time used by TFBRM is 7.31 s, and when k increases to 16000, the time required for TFBRM mining rules reaches 44.32 s. However, on the OnlineRetail dataset, the time used by TFBRM tends to be stable. When $k = 2000$, the time used by TFBRM is 52.16 s, and when $k = 16000$, the time used by TFBRM is 59.82 s. The memory usage of the TFBRM algorithm under the same experimental conditions can be seen in Fig. 2. Similarly, with the increase of k, the memory usage required by TFBRM to mine the corresponding number of rules on different datasets increases. The experimental datasets have different transaction numbers, item numbers and densities, which makes the memory usage of

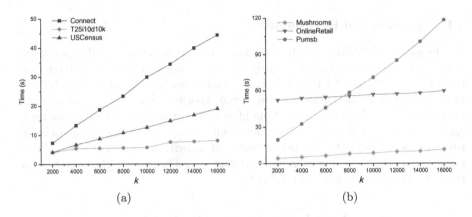

Fig. 1. Performance analysis in term of time in case 1.

TFBRM differ greatly when mining rules. For example, for the Pumsb dataset, when $k = 2000$, the memory usage of TFBRM exceeds 4500 MB, while for the USCensus dataset, when $k = 2000$, TFBRM mining rules only need to use no more than 300 MB of memory.

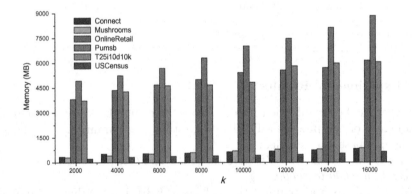

Fig. 2. Performance analysis in term of memory usage in case 1.

Case 2: minkulc, maxIR and k were set to 0.8, 0.2 and 16000, respectively, and the database size was changed from 20% to 100%.

Scalability experiments on sparse and dense datasets were conducted to evaluate the performance of the TFBRM algorithm. In terms of running time, as shown in Fig. 3a, as the database size increases, the running time of the TFBRM algorithm shows an upward trend. For memory usage (Fig. 3b), it is the same as running time. As the database size increases, the memory required by TFBRM mining rules also gradually increases. In general, whether the proposed algorithm is on sparse or dense datasets, as the size of the database increases, the running

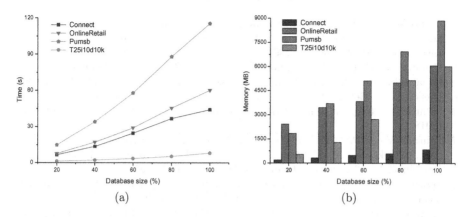

Fig. 3. Scalability analysis in term of time and memory usage in case 2.

time and memory usage of TFBRM basically increase linearly, indicating that the proposed algorithm has good scalability.

6   Conclusion and Future Work

This paper proposed a top-k frequent balanced association rule mining algorithm named TFBRM, which is different from other top-k mining algorithms in that it uses support, kulc and IR as measures to more comprehensively evaluate the strength of the rules. Based on the properties of the measures, three effective pruning strategies are designed in the TFBRM algorithm to reduce the search space. Experimental results show that the proposed algorithm has good performance and scalability, and can be used in many practical applications. For future work, it is an interesting topic to combine TFBRM with parallel strategies to reduce the time required to mine rules. In addition, to meet the needs of different applications, other measures can also be used to mine the top-k rules.

Acknowledgments. This research is sponsored by the Science and Technology Planning Project of Sichuan Province under Grant No. 2020YFG0054, and the Joint Funds of the Ministry of Education of China.

References

1. Anand, H.S., Vinodchandra, S.S.: Association rule mining using treap. Int. J. Mach. Learn. Cybern. **9**(4), 589–597 (2016). https://doi.org/10.1007/s13042-016-0546-7
2. Aqra, I., Ghani, N.A., Maple, C., Machado, J., Safa, N.S.: Incremental algorithm for association rule mining under dynamic threshold. Appl. Sci. **9**(24), 5398 (2019)
3. Bustio-Martínez, L., Letras-Luna, M., Cumplido, R., Hernández-León, R., Feregrino-Uribe, C., Bande-Serrano, J.M.: Using hashing and lexicographic order for frequent itemsets mining on data streams. J. Parallel Distrib. Comput. **125**, 58–71 (2019)

4. Chun-Wei Lin, J., Gan, W., Fournier-Viger, P., Hong, T.P., Tseng, V.S.: Fast algorithms for mining high-utility itemsets with various discount strategies. Adv. Eng. Inform. **30**(2), 109–126 (2016)
5. Czibula, G., Czibula, I.G., Miholca, D.L., Crivei, L.M.: A novel concurrent relational association rule mining approach. Expert Syst. Appl. **125**, 142–156 (2019)
6. Djenouri, Y., Belhadi, A., Fournier-Viger, P.: Extracting useful knowledge from event logs: a frequent itemset mining approach. Knowl.-Based Syst. **139**, 132–148 (2018)
7. Fournier-Viger, P., Wu, C.-W., Tseng, V.S.: Mining top-k association rules. In: Kosseim, L., Inkpen, D. (eds.) AI 2012. LNCS (LNAI), vol. 7310, pp. 61–73. Springer, Heidelberg (2012). https://doi.org/10.1007/978-3-642-30353-1_6
8. Fournier-Viger, P., Zhang, Y., Chun-Wei Lin, J., Fujita, H., Koh, Y.S.: Mining local and peak high utility itemsets. Inf. Sci. **481**, 344–367 (2019)
9. Gan, W., Lin, J.C.W., Fournier-Viger, P., Chao, H.C., Hong, T.P., Fujita, H.: A survey of incremental high-utility itemset mining. Wiley Int. Rev. Data Min. Knowl. Disc. **8**(2), e1242 (2018)
10. Han, X., Liu, X., Chen, J., Lai, G., Gao, H., Li, J.: Efficiently mining frequent itemsets on massive data. IEEE Access **7**, 31409–31421 (2019)
11. Huang, M.-J., Sung, H.-S., Hsieh, T.-J., Wu, M.-C., Chung, S.-H.: Applying data-mining techniques for discovering association rules. Soft. Comput. **24**(11), 8069–8075 (2019). https://doi.org/10.1007/s00500-019-04163-4
12. Mai, T., Vo, B., Nguyen, L.T.T.: A lattice-based approach for mining high utility association rules. Inf. Sci. **399**, 81–97 (2017)
13. Moslehi, F., Haeri, A., Martínez-Álvarez, F.: A novel hybrid GA-PSO framework for mining quantitative association rules. Soft. Comput. **24**(6), 4645–4666 (2020)
14. Nguyen, L.T.T., Vo, B., Nguyen, L.T.T., Fournier-Viger, P., Selamat, A.: ETARM: an efficient top-k association rule mining algorithm. Appl. Intell. **48**(5), 1148–1160 (2017). https://doi.org/10.1007/s10489-017-1047-4
15. Sharmila, S., Vijayarani, S.: Association rule mining using fuzzy logic and whale optimization algorithm. Soft. Comput. **25**(2), 1431–1446 (2020). https://doi.org/10.1007/s00500-020-05229-4
16. Sohrabi, M.K., Roshani, R.: Frequent itemset mining using cellular learning automata. Comput. Hum. Behav. **68**, 244–253 (2017)
17. Telikani, A., Gandomi, A.H., Shahbahrami, A.: A survey of evolutionary computation for association rule mining. Inf. Sci. **524**, 318–352 (2020)
18. Varol Altay, E., Alatas, B.: Intelligent optimization algorithms for the problem of mining numerical association rules. Physica A: Stat. Mech. Appl. **540**, 123142 (2020)
19. Wang, L., Meng, J., Xu, P., Peng, K.: Mining temporal association rules with frequent itemsets tree. Appl. Soft Comput. J. **62**, 817–829 (2018)
20. Webb, G.I.: Filtered-top-k association discovery. Wiley Interdisc. Rev.-Data Mining Knowl. Discov. **1**(3), 183–192 (2011)
21. Webb, G.I., Zhang, S.: K-optimal rule discovery. Data Min. Knowl. Disc. **10**(1), 39–79 (2005)
22. Wen, F., Zhang, G., Sun, L., Wang, X., Xu, X.: A hybrid temporal association rules mining method for traffic congestion prediction. Comput. Ind. Eng. **130**(6), 779–787 (2019)

Towards Increasing Open Data Adoption Through Stream Data Integration and Imputation

Robert Kunicki[1,2] and Maciej Grzenda[1(✉)]

[1] Faculty of Mathematics and Information Science, Warsaw University
of Technology, ul. Koszykowa 75, 00-662 Warszawa, Poland
{R.Kunicki,M.Grzenda}@mini.pw.edu.pl
[2] Digitalisation Department, The City of Warsaw, pl. Bankowy 2,
00-095 Warszawa, Poland

Abstract. Open data portals are used to make a growing number of government data resources public. However, difficulties in preprocessing and integrating multiple possibly incomplete open data resources hinder the potential of open data re-use for software development. While incomplete data sets can be imputed in an offline process, this is not the case for data streams expected to be published in an online manner.

In this work, we propose a novel data stream preprocessing method aimed at simplifying open data stream re-use through the unification of time resolution and imputation of incomplete instances. The method relies on stream mining methods to predict categorical values to be imputed. A separate online learning model is built for every incomplete feature. The method we propose allows the model to benefit from both inter-feature similarities and temporal dependencies present in data streams. We validate the proposed method with public transport data streams.

Keywords: Data preprocessing · Stream mining · Open data

1 Introduction

Smart city solutions are largely dependent on the availability of sensor data. To promote their development, numerous IoT platforms are deployed. Irrespective of the IoT platforms involved, it is the data collected by these platforms that is of particular value both for the cities and the providers of novel software. To promote civic engagement and foster the development of novel applications and services, open data portals have been started by numerous cities [10], which make urban data available to the general public. In the case of data sets, the data supposed to be made public could be prepared in an *off-line* process prior to their publication. Hence, some data sets such as those made public at the *Find Open Data* portal (http://data.gov.uk) contained in-filled data in cases where no observed data was available[1].

---

[1] Highways Agency network journey time and traffic flow data was an example of such a data set.

© Springer Nature Switzerland AG 2021
H. Fujita et al. (Eds.): IEA/AIE 2021, LNAI 12798, pp. 15–27, 2021.
https://doi.org/10.1007/978-3-030-79457-6_2

More recently, growing interest in online analytics (rather than periodic batch processing of the data), when coupled with the growing availability of sensors operated by the cities, has resulted in data streams shared through open data platforms. Many such data streams come from IoT sensors, whereas the data from IoT platforms are known to be noisy, and incomplete. There can be many reasons for such quality issues including the inability to transmit data, breakdowns of data collection platforms, and failures of metering devices. Low quality data requires even higher technical abilities to overcome its deficiencies. At the same time, insufficient technical abilities were observed to hinder the actual use of open data [8].

As many IoT data resources such as bus location data are of limited value if not published online, improving in an online manner the quality of the data, including the elimination of gaps resulting from missing and delayed sensor readings, turns out to be of the utmost importance for the actual software development. Not surprisingly, machine learning methods can be used for this purpose. In particular, rapid growth of stream mining methods [2,4], i.e. machine learning methods focused on data streams rather than data sets, has been observed in the recent period. However, in spite of the developments in classification and regression techniques for data streams [2–5], many issues still have to be addressed, such as the development of stream imputation techniques.

In this study, we focus on the provisioning of open data streams while increasing their quality in an on-line manner. The primary objective is to simplify the use of the data by software developers. This is done by proposing a novel stream-oriented data preprocessing method, which can be used to develop in an online manner instances integrating a number of the most recent preprocessed readings from IoT sensors with standardised time resolution and context data. Importantly, when gaps in raw time series of readings are observed, we propose a novel imputation method for data streams which relies on data stream classification methods and aims to substitute missing categorical values with estimated predicted values. As a consequence, the augmented data stream includes imputed instances with standardised time resolution.

Furthermore, to assess the performance of the data imputation method we propose, we ran a number of experiments with real data streams and stream mining techniques. The main motivation for these studies was to investigate how preprocessed data affects the accuracy of predictions of deviations from the planned arrival time of public transport vehicles. Since the true but missing values are not known in real scenarios, we focused on checking whether imputed data does not hinder prediction of delays, which is one of the key applications of the reference data streams we used in this study.

The remainder of this work is organised as follows. In Sect. 2, we provide an overview of stream data imputation in relation to stream mining methods, which is followed by Sect. 3, discussing the reference problem of incomplete location data streams. In Sect. 4, we propose a stream data preprocessing method, and discuss the results of applying it for a number of reference data streams in Sect. 5. Finally, conclusions and possible future works are outlined in Sect. 6.

2   Related Works

Streaming data is characterised by infinite size and speed of data growth. This makes the use of traditional methods of data set processing inappropriate. It is then necessary to use special techniques and algorithms that process data at the time of inflow while taking into account time and memory constraints. Hence, stream mining methods [2] have been developed. The most important requirements for the stream mining methods are [2]: to process every instance at most once, rely on constrained used of memory and processing power, and adapt to temporal changes.

There are three possible reasons for missing values in data [11]: missing completely at random (MCAR) - the occurrence of missing value in the instances does not depend on either the observed data or the missing value, missing at random (MAR) - the occurrence of the absence depends on the available data but not on the missing value, and not missing at random (NMAR) - the occurrence of the absence is related to the missing value. As gaps and delays in IoT-originated data acquisition are frequently due to device or transmission failures, they can be classified as being largely due to MCAR reasons. Handling of incomplete data can rely on one of three methods [7]: simple deletion, data imputation or special treatment. The first method involves removing all instances that contain missing entries, and the third involves dealing with deficiencies by choosing methods capable of processing incomplete data. The second category, i.e. data imputation, includes methods based on both statistical and machine learning approaches. Not surprisingly, it is the data imputation approach that is of particular value in the case of the provisioning of preprocessed open data accompanying the provisioning of raw open data.

Until now, in Massive Online Analysis (MOA) [2] i.e. the key stream mining platform, data imputation methods based on both statistical features of the attribute values observed so far in a stream (such as mean and median value) and the last known value of an attribute have been proposed. These methods include imputation with last known value (LKV) of an attribute, mean, maximum and minimum value for numerical attributes, and mode (MOD) for categorical data.

Another approach is to use machine learning methods to predict the actual value of an attribute and use it in place of the missing value [9]. Importantly, due to the characteristics of streaming data, there are special requirements for machine learning methods applicable for data streams [2], including periodic updates of a model, and its adaptation to nonstationary processes (concept drift) [4]. Hence, batch machine learning methods such as MLP networks can not be directly applied to impute data streams rather than data sets. As a consequence, works on stream mining are largely focused on the processing of the streams of complete instances [2–4]. In particular, in [5] i.e. a related study on prediction models for IoT public transport data streams, only complete instances were used for the prediction of the delay status of public transport vehicles.

3 Motivation

Open data portals are used to make public a growing number of data resources, including data sets and data streams. As of the time of writing this article, Greater London Authority (https://data.london.gov.uk) had published 1489 data sets, while San Francisco had published 1209 data sets (https://datasf.org). Importantly, open data is an enabler for the development of innovative software applications [6]. However, lack of validity and completeness of data, and lack of technical interoperability were already observed to be some of the most commonly identified barriers that hinder the generation of value from open data [8]. At the same time, open time series data were among these open data resources, which were most frequently accessed by software developers, as pointed out in the analysis of applications developed with open data [6]. Hence, increasing the quality and usability of open data streams, including IoT data streams is of particular importance. However, with this large number of data sets made public, data preprocessing methods should ideally be automated.

Let us discuss a sample use case of the imputation of public transport location data streams i.e. the location of vehicles. Similarly to other IoT sensor readings, the time between consecutive GPS sensor readings received by IoT platforms and made available as open data varies. This situation is illustrated in Fig. 1. It can be observed that the period $t(v_{i+1}) - t(v_i)$ between two consecutive sensor readings v_i and v_{i+1} acquired from the GPS sensor varies. In some cases $t(v_{i+1}) - t(v_i)$ exceeds 30 s. The second situation includes a lack of data due to the fact that the readings do not reach the server-side IoT platform in the assumed time. This is because the time between reading the data at a sensor and receiving these data in the system collecting data such as an open data portal is non-negligible.

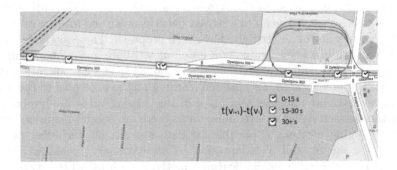

Fig. 1. Different times of recording the GPS location. Based on location data stream for Warsaw trams from 5th Jan. 2020.

This illustrates the fact that making raw IoT data streams available for online processing results in major data preprocessing burden for third-party software developers, who frequently have to try to skip excessive readings at some periods and perform the imputation of gaps at other periods. The key need to be answered is to provide sensor readings for standardised time resolution e.g. one minute time resolution, possibly combined with context data and with imputed values, when needed.

4   Data Integration and Imputation Method

To overcome the problem of incomplete IoT data streams affected by varied time resolution, we propose integrating raw sensor readings into instances containing a number of recent consecutive sensor readings with unified time resolution and context data, including imputed feature values in case the raw ones were not available within the expected time resolution. The Unified Time-Resolution Integration and Imputation of Data Streams (UTRIIDS) method proposed in this work consists of two stages: the unification of time resolution and integration stage, and the data imputation stage.

Input: $I(i)$ - raw stream of sensor readings, Δ_R - acceptance time, N - the number of previous instances that we aim to integrate with the current reading while taking into account Δ_R, δ - time resolution of output instance, $\Delta_\mathrm{P} \geq 0$ - prediction horizon

Output: D - merged data stream composed of $\mathcal{S}_i$ instances

begin

    `/* for every received sensor reading                      */`

    for $i = 1, \ldots$ **do**

        $\mathcal{S}_i.\mathbf{x} = I(i)$;

        $\mathcal{S}_i.\mathbf{x} = \mathcal{S}_i.\mathbf{x}.Append\_Additional\_Features(I(i))$;

        `/* Find N readings closest to` $t - \delta, t - 2\delta, \ldots, t - N\delta$ `*/`

        for $k = 1, \ldots, N$ **do**

            if $Exists\ I(j) :\mid t(I(j)) - k\delta \mid \leq \frac{\Delta_\mathrm{R}}{2}$ **then**

                $\tilde{I}_k = I(m) :\mid t(I(m)) - k\delta \mid = min\big(\{\mid t(I(j)) - k\delta \mid, j < i\}\big)$;

                $\tilde{I}_k.Append\_Additional\_Features(\tilde{I}_k)$;

            else

                $\tilde{I}_k = \mathrm{NULL}$;

            $\mathcal{S}_i.\mathbf{x} = \mathcal{S}_i.\mathbf{x}.append(\tilde{I}_k)$;

        end

        `/* Add` $\mathcal{S}_i$ `to output stream                          */`

        $D.Submit(\mathcal{S}_i)$;

        `/* Add now known true label values for` Δ_P `prediction horizon`

            `for previously processed instances                      */`

        $D.Submit(\mathcal{S}_j.\mathbf{y}) : j < i, t(\mathcal{S}_j) < t(\mathcal{S}_i) - \Delta_\mathrm{P} + \frac{\Delta_\mathrm{R}}{2}$;

    end

end

Algorithm 1: UTRIIDS method: the unification of time resolution and data integration stage.

Unlike standard methods of data stream imputation, which rely on simple statistics of attribute value such as the aforementioned methods available in the MOA environment, the method we propose relies on machine learning methods to impute missing values. Importantly, taking into account the unbounded number of instances of a data stream, we propose the use of stream mining methods for data imputation. The applicable methods include the streaming version of Naive Bayes, Hoeffding Trees (HT) [3], Hoeffding Adaptive Tree (HAT) [1] and the recently proposed adaptation of the random forest method to stream processing needs i.e. Adaptive Random Forest (ARF) [4].

The first stage of the UTRIIDS method is defined in Algorithm 1. The objective of this stage is to develop from raw sensor readings $I(i)$, the instances $\mathcal{S}_i$ of the output stream D. Every instance $\mathcal{S}_i$ includes the current sensor reading and N previous readings separated by approximately δ seconds. One of the key settings of UTRIIDS is acceptance time Δ_R. If no sensor reading acquired from a sensor in the period $[t - k\delta - \frac{\Delta_R}{2}, t - k\delta + \frac{\Delta_R}{2}]$, $k = 1, \ldots, N$ exists in $I(i)$, readings for both the k-th preceding time step and dependent data such as vehicle delay status of a vehicle for the k-th step will be considered missing. Otherwise, sensor readings from the time closest to $t - k\delta$ will be placed in the $\mathcal{S}_i$ instance. It is important to note that the dependent data such as delay status calculated based on location readings can be even more important in practical cases. Moreover, Δ_R controls the precision of time resolution; a low value results in an increased proportion of missing entries.

Furthermore, context data for a stream of interest, such as the tram line the vehicle is serving now, which can be appended to instance data based on schedule data for location data streams, can be added to every instance $\mathcal{S}_i$ developed in Algorithm 1. Finally, the algorithm can be used to develop instances, which can be used next to predict future values for the stream of interest i.e. predict the $\mathcal{S}(j).\mathbf{y}$ labels before they are available. As an example, the location of a vehicle or delay status of the vehicle in approx. Δ_P seconds can be predicted. Hence, every time a new reading is received from a sensor, the true label(s) to previous instance(s) can be added to be used to verify the quality of such predicted labels.

A data stream produced in Algorithm 1 is typically incomplete. This is because of possibly major time differences between consecutive sensor readings, i.e. raw $I(i)$ readings periodically not matching the time resolution and acceptance levels, defined by δ and Δ_R, respectively. Hence, the second stage of the UTRIIDS method, which we defined in Algorithm 2, can be used to impute incomplete instances and add predicted labels $\tilde{y}_i$. For every input feature j of $\mathcal{S}_i$ instances, which may be incomplete, a prediction model is developed with a stream mining method. Based on the remaining features of an instance and the data of U previous instances and U previous instances for which the value of this attribute was known, the attribute model M_j is built. Hence, the attribute model can learn both the relation between attributes of the current instance and possibly preceding instances and the attribute of interest to possibly exploit temporal dependencies present in the data.

Input: $\mathcal{S}_1, \mathcal{S}_2, \ldots$ - a data stream, E - ML method used to train models performing data imputation, M - ML method used to train models used to predict future values, U - the number of previous instances used to predict attribute values to be imputed

Data: $L_j, j = 1, \ldots, J$ - sliding windows of U most recent instances with known value of attribute j, $P = [\mathcal{S}_{i-1}, \mathcal{S}_{i-2}, ..., \mathcal{S}_{i-U}]$ - sliding window of U previous instances, I_m - merged instance, A_i - imputed instance

begin

    /* For every instance in stream   */

    for $i = 1, \ldots$ **do**

        $A_i = \mathcal{S}_i.\mathbf{x}$;

        /* For every attribute of the instance   */

        for $j = 1, \ldots$ **do**

            $I_m = [\mathcal{S}_i.\mathbf{x}, P_1, \ldots, P_U, L_j[1], \ldots, L_j[U]]$;

            if $A_i[j]\ != NULL$ **then**

                /* If the attribute is not empty update list with the instance   */

                $L_j.Insert(\mathcal{S}_i)$;

            if $A_i[j] = NULL$ **then**

                /* Perform imputation   */

                $A_i[j] = M_j.Predict(I_m)$;

            else

                /* Update model using merged instance as an input and known value of j-th attribute as a true label   */

                $M_j = E.Update(M_j, I_m, A_i[j])$

        end

        $P.Insert(A_i)$; $\tilde{y}_i = \mathcal{M}.predict(A_i)$; $Publish([A_i, \tilde{y}_i])$;

        $\mathcal{M} = M.Update(\mathcal{M}, A_i, \mathcal{S}_i.y)$;

    end

end

Algorithm 2: UTRIIDS method: data imputation stage

When the value of an attribute j is known, the model M_j is updated in an incremental manner to learn the dependencies between other attributes of the current instance and previously observed attributes and the value of attribute j. Otherwise, the $M_j()$ model is used to predict the value to be imputed and used instead of the missing attribute value.

Let us note that each of the possibly incomplete attributes necessitates a separate model. However, all M_j models are stream mining models i.e. models with limited memory and computational cost. Their number is no larger than the constant $J = dim(\mathcal{S}.\mathbf{x})$ i.e. the number of all attributes in an instance. Moreover, the question of how to evaluate the quality of imputed instances arises, taking into account that the missing attribute values are not known. We propose that, since every instance $\mathcal{S}_i$ can include a label $\mathcal{S}_i.y$, the quality of imputed $\mathcal{S}_i$ instances can be assessed by evaluating their impact on the performance of the $\mathcal{M}$ models predicting the $\mathcal{S}_i.y$ labels, while using imputed instances as an input. This performance can be compared to the performance of the models predicting the $\mathcal{S}_i.y$ labels while using incomplete data as input data.

5 Results

To analyse the UTRIIDS method, reference data streams were selected. We focused on tram location data from the City of Warsaw to verify the method. These data streams are available via the Open Data portal of the City of Warsaw and were used *inter alia* in [5,6]. Raw data include vehicle identification such as tram line and brigade number, location and GPS timestamp. Once integrated with schedule data, they can be extended with additional features such as vehicle delay. All the data streams described here were processed with the UTRIIDS method. For each reading I, $N = 5$ preceding readings were sought as defined in Algorithm 1, assuming $\delta = 60\,$s resolution. In this way, merged instances S_i spanning the period of the last 5 mins., and including location data and dependent data from $N + 1 = 6$ time steps, were developed. In addition, tram delay status in $\Delta_{\mathrm{P}} = 60\,$s was denoted as $S_i.y$. Five vehicle statuses were adopted: `accelerated` (delay of $[-\infty, -60]\,$s), `on time` - delay of $(-60, 60)\,$s, `small delay`, `delay`, and `major delay` for delays in the range of $[60, 120)$, $[120, 240)$, and $[240, \infty)$, respectively. The acceptance time Δ_{R} was set to different values, as described in Table 1, which describes all data streams developed with Algorithm 1. The streams collected in different time periods were used. The tram line (L) and brigade numbers (B) for every stream are given in the L/B column. Different Δ_{R} settings were applied to analyse the impact of the acceptance level on the proportion of missing attribute values in S instances. The decreasing Δ_{R} value affects the number of stream instances. This is due to the necessity to have a true label $S.y$ for a $[t(I(i)) + \Delta_{\mathrm{P}} - \frac{\Delta_{\mathrm{R}}}{2}, t(I(i)) + \Delta_{\mathrm{P}} + \frac{\Delta_{\mathrm{R}}}{2}]$ period. Let us note that this is only because of developing ground truth labels that will be used to evaluate the merits of imputed values by analysing the accuracy of predicted labels $\tilde{y}_i$. Otherwise, the number of instances for varied Δ_{R}, but the same line, brigade and period would be the same. Furthermore, the proportion of I readings that arrived to server platform collecting data from GPS sensors after Δ_t is reported. It follows from Table 1 that for every data stream, over 90% of readings arrived after more than 5 s, which confirms the limited timeliness of the data. Moreover, the small Δ_{R} values show the tradeoff between unifying time resolution and completeness of S_i instances.

Table 1. Data streams used for the evaluation of UTRIIDS method.

Data stream	Δ_{R}	L/B	Data period	Records	Missing data [%]	Late data for Δ_t of 5,10,15,20,30 s [%]
W6_A_20	6	23/1	1st Jan.–30th Jun.2020	112,722	14.40	94, 49, 5, 1, 1
W6_B_20	6	24/2	2nd Feb.–1st May 2020	50,407	14.68	91, 36, 5, 1, 1
W10_B_20	10	24/2	2th Feb.–1st May 2020	83,454	10.02	91, 37, 5, 1, 1
W6_C_20	6	26/1	1st Mar.–1st Jun.2020	83,780	14.01	91, 36, 5, 1, 1
W10_C_20	10	26/1	1st Mar.–1st Jun.2020	155,932	8.82	91, 37, 5, 1, 1
W16_C_20	16	26/1	1st Mar.–1st Jun.2020	191,927	4.44	93, 43, 7, 2, 1

The question arises of how to evaluate the quality of data imputed by stream mining methods. As we focused on the imputation of categorical features such as tram delay status, we performed a number of experiments with standard imputation techniques i.e. mode and LKV of an attribute. The results of the imputation performed using these methods were compared with the results of applying stream mining methods to provide imputed values, as defined in Algorithm 2. In the experiments performed with Algorithm 2 and the data described in Table 1, ARF, Naive Bayes, kNN, HT and HAT methods were used as the M method, while ARF and Naive Bayes were used as the E method and $U = 1$ was used in Algorithm 2. In this way, probabilistic, instance-based, tree-based and ensemble models were included. Furthermore, the simple strategies of re-using the last known label as a prediction for the next instance i.e. the NoChange (NC) method and Majority Class (MC), i.e. the use of the most frequent label as a predicted label, were used as the M method. Notably, the two latter techniques produce labels $\tilde{y}_i$, which do not depend on the $\mathcal{S}_i.\mathbf{x}$ features i.e. the $\tilde{y}_i$, labels, which are the same irrespective of what missing features values were replaced with. Hence, the results for these two techniques are reported in Table 2. MOA was extended in this study to provide the implementation of Algorithm 2. All results were obtained with standard implementation of the M methods available in MOA.

Table 2. The accuracy of predicted labels for two simple M methods.

M Method	W6_A_20	W6_B_20	W10_B_20	W6_C_20	W10_C_20	W16_C_20
NC	89.88	88.80	92.48	89.98	94.01	94.73
MC	68.66	64.01	63.75	67.96	67.88	67.71

It follows from Table 2 that the majority of the y labels ranging between 63.75% and 68.66% can be predicted by using the most frequent class as a prediction. An even higher proportion of labels can be predicted with NoChange i.e. by re-using the previous label in a stream, which illustrates the temporal dependencies frequently observed in IoT data streams. The accuracy of the predictions made with imputed data by the remaining M methods is presented in Table 3. As far as imputation methods are concerned, NOT denotes no imputation, whereas LKV and MOD denote the use of the last known value, and the mode of the attribute for the imputation, respectively. The UTRIIDS used with ARF and Naive Bayes, denoted by U_ARF and U_NB, was used to predict the missing attribute values to be imputed. Let us note that when a method such as NoChange is used as the E method, we get the same results for U_NCH as when using LKV for the imputation, which we show in Table 3.

It follows from Table 3 that for highly correlated consecutive labels, the simple NoChange strategy can yield superior accuracy of M predictions, irrespective of whether data imputation is performed or not. This shows that even largely

Table 3. Accuracy of predicted labels i.e. vehicle delay statuses for M and E methods.

Data stream	Main method M	Imputation method E					
		LKV	MOD	U_ARF	U_NB	U_NCH	NOT
W6_A_20	Naive Bayes	54.52	53.85	53.70	**55.15**	54.52	54.03
	ARF	87.83	87.83	87.84	87.84	87.83	87.73
	kNN	77.74	74.26	76.43	**78.34**	77.74	75.87
	Hoeffding Tree	87.70	87.78	87.78	87.78	87.70	87.60
	HAT	86.77	87.38	**87.38**	86.53	86.77	86.68
W6_B_20	Naive Bayes	44.46	43.24	43.71	**45.02**	44.46	44.16
	ARF	86.51	86.50	86.51	86.49	86.51	86.40
	kNN	75.59	71.16	73.64	**75.87**	75.59	72.77
	Hoeffding Tree	86.46	86.41	86.42	86.41	86.46	85.90
	HAT	86.28	85.87	86.25	86.30	86.28	85.89
W10_B_20	Naive Bayes	**44.26**	43.26	43.73	43.86	**44.26**	43.91
	ARF	86.12	86.14	86.19	86.11	86.12	85.97
	kNN	**77.50**	74.66	74.66	76.99	**77.50**	75.16
	Hoeffding Tree	86.10	86.14	86.13	86.13	86.10	85.90
	HAT	83.92	83.47	83.87	**85.05**	83.92	84.97
W6_C_20	Naive Bayes	36.95	34.75	**37.26**	35.55	36.95	35.43
	ARF	86.12	**86.15**	86.14	86.14	86.12	85.94
	kNN	**75.61**	73.02	75.35	75.31	75.61	73.18
	Hoeffding Tree	86.04	86.04	86.03	86.03	86.04	85.81
	HAT	**86.03**	85.84	85.84	85.84	86.03	85.95
W10_C_20	Naive Bayes	**35.00**	33.29	34.58	34.16	**35.00**	33.93
	ARF	**86.46**	86.37	86.40	86.35	**86.46**	86.31
	kNN	**77.98**	77.32	76.37	77.54	**77.98**	76.48
	Hoeffding Tree	85.96	85.96	85.95	85.96	85.96	85.94
	HAT	84.92	84.33	84.90	85.22	84.92	85.42
W16_C_20	Naive Bayes	**34.55**	33.65	34.35	33.70	**34.55**	34.20
	ARF	87.00	86.97	86.97	87.00	87.00	86.98
	kNN	**80.11**	79.45	79.84	79.91	**80.11**	79.54
	Hoeffding Tree	86.28	86.30	86.30	86.27	86.28	86.16
	HAT	**85.61**	85.52	85.44	85.20	**85.61**	84.74

incomplete instances could be accepted from the prediction performance point of view. However, this would not answer the need for imputed open data.

Still, even under highly correlated consecutive labels, the use of imputation can yield a slight increase in the accuracy of prediction. What follows from Fig. 2 is that even though the overall accuracy of predicted labels attained with

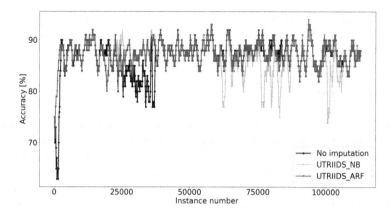

Fig. 2. Prediction accuracy for W6_A_20 data. Main method M: HAT.

Table 4. The average κ coefficient of predicted labels for different M and E methods

Main prediction method M	Imputation method E					
	LKV	MOD	U_ARF	U_NB	U_NCH	NOT
Naive Bayes	24.44	23.39	23.75	23.93	24.44	23.85
ARF	74.20	74.18	74.23	74.18	74.20	73.95
NoChange	82.91	82.91	82.91	82.91	82.91	82.91
Majority Class	0.02	0.02	0.02	0.02	0.02	0.02
kNN	45.00	34.29	41.34	47.17	45.00	39.41
Hoeffding Tree	71.60	71.60	71.60	71.61	71.60	71.22
HAT	69.00	68.97	69.17	69.33	69.00	69.22

imputed data may be similar, lack of imputation may result in major periodic degradation of accuracy, which can be avoided when UTRIIDS_ARF is used. In addition to the increase in the accuracy of prediction, a significant benefit itself is the imputed data stream, which makes software development with the imputed data stream much easier.

The question remains of how to evaluate the quality of the imputed data stream in the presence of highly correlated consecutive true labels making NC the best prediction method. In order to answer this question, we propose using the values of Cohen's κ coefficient [2] provided in Table 4 for the scenarios already described in Table 3. Importantly, κ shows the scale of improvement that a model $\mathcal{M}$ provides over a random prediction method. It follows from Table 4 that UTRIIDS compared to NOT yields the same or higher performance of prediction models built with different methods. The largest performance gains are observed when U_NB imputes data used with kNN. This can be explained by the fact that tree-based models can overcome incomplete data in one attribute by using the data from other attributes. At the same time, kNN explicitly aims to use the data of all attributes, which makes it particularly vulnerable to incomplete data. Hence, the quality of the imputed data stream can be assessed with the κ measure calculated for distance-based classifiers.

6   Conclusions

Modern IoT platforms provide growing volumes of sensor data, which enable novel software services. However, this raises the question of the quality of the data shared in the open data model. In this study, we addressed one of the main features of IoT data streams, i.e. their limited quality. The method we propose provides integrated instances with unified time resolution, making it possible to obtain a number of the most recent sensor readings, features based on them, and the value of a predicted feature. An important part of the method is the imputation of missing attribute values. Experiments with a number of data streams developed under different quality settings show that the method not only provides imputed instances, but also increases the quality of the data compared to no imputation. Importantly, as IoT data streams frequently exhibit temporal dependencies, it is the κ measure rather than accuracy that can be used to evaluate the quality of imputed data by analysing its impact on the performance of prediction models. Moreover, in the future, the development of stream mining methods combining data imputation with exploiting temporal dependencies in the data is planned.

Acknowledgements. The project was funded by the POB Research Centre for Artificial Intelligence and Robotics of Warsaw University of Technology within the Excellence Initiative Program - Research University (ID-UB).

References

1. Bifet, A., Gavaldà, R.: Adaptive learning from evolving data streams. In: Adams, N.M., Robardet, C., Siebes, A., Boulicaut, J.-F. (eds.) IDA 2009. LNCS, vol. 5772, pp. 249–260. Springer, Heidelberg (2009). https://doi.org/10.1007/978-3-642-03915-7_22
2. Bifet, A., Gavaldà, R., Holmes, G., Pfahringer, B.: Machine Learning for Data Streams with Practical Examples in MOA. MIT Press, Cambridge (2018)
3. Domingos, P., Hulten, G.: Mining high-speed data streams. In: Proceedings of the Sixth ACM SIGKDD International Conference on Knowledge Discovery and Data Mining, KDD 2000, pp. 71–80. ACM, New York (2000)
4. Gomes, H.M., et al.: Adaptive random forests for evolving data stream classification. Mach. Learn. **106**(9), 1469–1495 (2017)
5. Grzenda, M., Kwasiborska, K., Zaremba, T.: Hybrid short term prediction to address limited timeliness of public transport data streams. Neurocomputing **391**, 305–317 (2020). https://doi.org/10.1016/j.neucom.2019.08.100
6. Grzenda, M., Legierski, J.: Towards increased understanding of open data use for software development. Inf. Syst. Front. **23**(2), 495–513 (2019). https://doi.org/10.1007/s10796-019-09954-6

7. Grzymala-Busse, J.W., Grzymala-Busse, W.J.: Handling missing attribute values. In: Maimon, O., Rokach, L. (eds.) Data Mining and Knowledge Discovery Handbook, pp. 37–57. Springer, Boston (2005). https://doi.org/10.1007/978-0-387-09823-4_3

8. Jetzek, T., Avital, M., Bjorn-Andersen, N.: Data-driven innovation through open government data. J. Theor. Appl. Electron. Commer. Res. **9**(2), 100–120 (2014). https://doi.org/10.4067/S0718-18762014000200008

9. Miao, X., Gao, Y., Guo, S., Liu, W.: Incomplete data management: a survey. Front. Comput. Sci. **12**(1), 4–25 (2018). https://doi.org/10.1007/s11704-016-6195-x

10. Thorsby, J., Stowers, G.N., Wolslegel, K., Tumbuan, E.: Understanding the content and features of open data portals in American cities. Gov. Inf. Q. **34**(1), 53–61 (2017)

11. Yu, Q., Miche, Y., Eirola, E., van Heeswijk, M., Séverin, E., Lendasse, A.: Regularized extreme learning machine for regression with missing data. Neurocomputing **102**(C), 45–51 (2013)

Towards Efficient Discovery of Periodic-Frequent Patterns in Columnar Temporal Databases

Ravikumar Penugonda[1,2(✉)], Likhitha Palla[1], Uday Kiran Rage[2],
Yutaka Watanobe[2], and Koji Zettsu[3]

[1] IIIT-RK Valley, RGUKT, Vempalli, AP, India
[2] The University of Aizu, Aizuwakamatsu, Fukushima, Japan
[3] National Institute of Information and Communications Technology, Tokyo, Japan
zettsu@nict.go.jp

Abstract. Finding periodic-frequent patterns in temporal databases is a challenging problem of great importance in many real-world applications. Most previous studies focused on finding these patterns in row temporal databases. To the best of our knowledge, there exists no study that aims to find periodic-frequent patterns in columnar temporal databases. One cannot ignore the importance of the knowledge that exists in very large columnar temporal databases. It is because the real-world big data is widely stored in columnar temporal databases. With this motivation, this paper proposes an efficient algorithm, Periodic Frequent-Equivalence CLass Transformation (PF-ECLAT), to find periodic-frequent patterns in a columnar temporal database. Experimental results on sparse and dense real-world databases demonstrate that PF-ECLAT is not only memory and runtime efficient but also highly scalable. Finally, we present the usefulness of PF-ECLAT with a case study on air pollution analytics.

Keywords: Pattern mining · Periodic-frequent patterns · Columnar databases

1 Introduction

The big data generated by real-world applications is naturally stored in row databases or columnar databases. The row databases store the data in a horizontal layout, while the columnar databases store the data in a vertical layout. Since there exists no universally accepted best data layout for any application, selecting an appropriate database layout depends on the user and/or application requirements. Row databases help the user write the data quickly, while the columnar databases facilitate the user to execute fast (aggregate) queries. In other words, row databases are suitable for Online Transaction Processing

---

First three authors have equally contributed to 90% of the paper. Remaining author has contributed to 10% of the paper.

© Springer Nature Switzerland AG 2021
H. Fujita et al. (Eds.): IEA/AIE 2021, LNAI 12798, pp. 28–40, 2021.
https://doi.org/10.1007/978-3-030-79457-6_3

(OLTP), while columnar databases are suitable for Online Analytical Processing (OLAP). In this context, the support move has been made in this paper to find periodic-frequent patterns in columnar databases.

Periodic-frequent pattern mining is an important model in data mining with many real-world applications. It involves discovering all patterns in a temporal database that satisfy the user-specified *minimum support (minSup)* and *maximum periodicity (maxPer)* constraints. The *minSup* controls the minimum number of transactions that a pattern must cover in the database. The *maxPer* controls the maximum time-interval within which a pattern must reoccur in the data. A classical application of periodic-frequent pattern mining is air pollution analytics. It involves identifying the geographical areas in which people were regularly exposed to air pollutants' harmful levels, say PM2.5. A periodic-frequent pattern discovered in our air pollution database is as follows:

$$\{433, 1613, 1988\} \quad [support = 50\%, \ periodicity = 2 \ hrs].$$

The above pattern indicates that the people living close to the sensors, 433, 1613, and 1988, were frequently and regularly (i.e., at least once every 2 h) exposed to harmful levels of PM2.5. The produced information may help the users for various purposes, such as finding high polluted areas on which day of the week or particular time interval of a day.

Several algorithms (e.g., PFP-growth [7], PFP-growth++ [5], and PS-growth [4]) have been described in the literature to find periodic-frequent patterns in a row database. To the best of our knowledge, there exists no algorithm that can find periodic-frequent patterns in a columnar temporal database. We can find periodic-frequent patterns by transforming a columnar temporal database into a row database. However, we must avoid such a naïve transformation process due to its high computational cost. With this motivation, this paper makes an effort to find periodic-frequent patterns in a columnar temporal database effectively.

Zaki et al. [8] first discussed the importance of finding frequent patterns in columnar databases. Besides, a depth-first search algorithm, called Equivalence CLass Transformation (ECLAT), was also described to find frequent patterns in a columnar database. Unfortunately, this algorithm cannot be directly used to find periodic-frequent patterns in a columnar temporal database. It is because the ECLAT algorithm completely disregards the temporal occurrence information of an item in the database. This paper proposes a variant of the ECLAT algorithm, called Periodic Frequent-Equivalence CLass Transformation (PF-ECLAT), to find all periodic-frequent patterns in a columnar temporal database. Experimental results demonstrate that our algorithm is not only memory and runtime efficient but also scalable.

The rest of the paper is organized as follows. Section 2 reviews the work related to our method. Section 3 introduces the model of periodic-frequent pattern. Section 4 presents the proposed algorithm. Section 5 shows the experimental results. Section 6 concludes the paper with future research directions.

2 Related Work

Agrawal et al. [2] introduced the concept of frequent pattern mining to extract useful information from the transactional databases. It has been used in many domains, and several other algorithms have been developed [1]. Luna et al. [6] conducted a detailed survey on frequent pattern mining and presented the improvements that happened in the past 25 years. However, frequent pattern mining is inappropriate for identifying patterns that are regularly appearing in a database.

Tanbeer et al. [7] introduced the idea of periodic-frequent pattern mining. A highly compacted periodic frequent-tree (PF-tree) was constructed and applied a pattern growth technique to generate all periodic-frequent patterns in a database based on the user-specified $minSup$ and $maxPer$ constraints. Amphawan et al. [3] designed an efficient depth-first search based algorithm named as mining top-K periodic-frequent patterns without using the user specified $minSup$ constraint. Uday et al. [5] introduced a novel greedy approach to discover periodic-frequent patterns. Authors have designed a two phase architecture named as expanding phase and shrinking phase to store all the patterns with support and periodicity efficiently. Where these phases have effectively utilized the newly introduced local periodicity concept. Finally, created a PF-tree++ and applied pattern growth technique to generate periodic-frequent patterns in a database based on the user-specified $minSup$ and $maxPer$. Anirudh et al. [4] introduced a novel concept of periodic-summaries to find the periodic-frequent patterns in temporal databases. Authors have introduced a novel concept called periodic summaries-tree to maintain the time stamp information of the patterns in a database and designed a pattern growth algorithm to generate complete set of periodic-frequent patterns. Unfortunately, all of the above algorithms have used the concept of a row database. As a result, these algorithms cannot be directly applied to a columnar database.

3 Proposed Model

Let I be the set of items. Let $X \subseteq I$ be a **pattern** (or an itemset). A pattern containing β, $\beta \geq 1$, number of items is called a β-**pattern**. A **transaction**, $t_k = (ts, Y)$ is a tuple, where $ts \in \mathbb{R}^+$ represents the timestamp at which the pattern Y has occurred. A **temporal database** TDB over I is a set of transactions, i.e., $TDB = \{t_1, \cdots, t_m\}$, $m = |TDB|$, where $|TDB|$ can be defined as the number of transactions in TDB. For a transaction $t_k = (ts, Y)$, $k \geq 1$, such that $X \subseteq Y$, it is said that X occurs in t_k (or t_k contains X) and such a timestamp is denoted as ts^X. Let $TS^X = \{ts_j^X, \cdots, ts_k^X\}$, j, $k \in [1, m]$ and $j \leq k$, be an **ordered set of timestamps** where X has occurred in TDB.

Example 1. Let $I = \{a, b, c, d, e, f\}$ be the set of items. A hypothetical row temporal database generated from I is shown in Table 1. Without loss of generality, this row temporal database can be represented as a columnar temporal database as shown in Table 2. The temporal occurrences of each item in the

Table 1. Row database

ts	Items	ts	Items
1	abcf	6	abcd
2	bcde	7	ab
3	abcd	8	cdf
4	abce	9	abcd
5	cef	10	bcdf

Table 2. Columnar database

ts	a	b	c	d	e	f	ts	a	b	c	d	e	f
1	1	1	1	0	0	1	6	1	1	1	1	0	0
2	0	1	1	1	1	0	7	1	1	0	0	0	0
3	1	1	1	1	0	0	8	0	0	1	1	0	1
4	1	1	1	0	1	0	9	1	1	1	1	0	0
5	0	0	1	0	1	1	10	0	1	1	1	0	1

Table 3. List of ts of an item

Item	TS-list
a	1, 3, 4, 6, 7, 9
b	1, 2, 3, 4, 6, 7, 9, 10
c	1, 2, 3, 4, 5, 6, 8, 9, 10
d	2, 3, 6, 8, 9, 10
e	2, 4, 5
f	1, 5, 8, 10

entire database is shown in Table 3. The set of items 'c' and 'b', i.e., $\{c, b\}$ is a pattern. For brevity, we represent this pattern as 'cb'. This pattern contains two items. Therefore, it is 2-pattern. The pattern 'cb' appears at the timestamps of 1, 2, 3, 4, 6, 9, and 10. Therefore, the list of timestamps containing 'cb', i.e., $TS^{cb} = \{1,\ 2,\ 3,\ 4,\ 6,\ 9,\ 10\}$.

Definition 1. *(**The** support **of** X.) The number of transactions containing X in TDB is defined as the **support** of X and denoted as $sup(X)$. That is, $sup(X) = |TS^X|$.*

Example 2. The support of 'cb,' i.e., $sup(cb) = |TS^{cb}| = 7$.

Definition 2. *(**Frequent pattern** X.) The pattern X is said to be a **frequent pattern** if $sup(X) \geq minSup$, where minSup refers to the user-specified minimum support value.*

Example 3. If the user-specified $minSup = 5$, then cb is said to be a frequent pattern because of $sup(cb) \geq minSup$.

Definition 3. *(Periodicity **of** X.) Let ts_q^X and ts_r^X, $j \leq q < r \leq k$, be the two consecutive timestamps in TS^X. The time difference (or an inter-arrival time) between ts_q^X and ts_r^X is defined as a **period** of X, say p_a^X. That is, $p_a^X = ts_r^X - ts_q^X$. Let $P^X = (p_1^X,\ p_2^X, \cdots,\ p_r^X)$ be the set of all periods for pattern X. The **periodicity** of X, denoted as $per(X) = maximum(p_1^X,\ p_2^X, \cdots,\ p_r^X)$.*

Example 4. The periods for this pattern are: $p_1^{cb} = 1 \ (= 1 - ts_{initial})$, $p_2^{cb} = 1 \ (= 2 - 1)$, $p_3^{cb} = 1 \ (= 3 - 2)$, $p_4^{cb} = 1 \ (= 4 - 3)$, $p_5^{cb} = 2 \ (= 6 - 4)$, $p_6^{cb} = 3 \ (= 9 - 6)$, $p_7^{cb} = 1 \ (= 10 - 9)$, and $p_8^{cb} = 0 \ (= ts_{final} - 10)$, where $ts_{initial} = 0$ represents the timestamp of initial transaction and $ts_{final} = |TDB| = 10$ represents the timestamp of final transaction in the database. The periodicity of cb, i.e., $per(cb) = maximum(1,\ 1,\ 1,\ 1,\ 2,\ 3,\ 1,\ 0) = 3$.

Definition 4. *(Periodic-frequent pattern X.) The frequent pattern X is said to be a **periodic-frequent pattern** if $per(X) \leq maxPer$, where maxPer refers to the user-specified maximum periodicity value.*

Example 5. If the user-defined $maxPer = 3$, then the frequent pattern '*cb*' is said to be a periodic-frequent pattern because $per(cb) \leq maxPer$.

Definition 5. *(**Problem definition.**) Given a temporal database (TDB) and the user-specified minimum support (minSup) and maximum periodicity (maxPer) constraints, the aim is to discover the complete set of periodic-frequent patterns that have support no less than minSup and periodicity no more than the maxPer constraints.*

4   Proposed Algorithm

In this section, we first describe procedure for finding one length periodic-frequent patterns (or 1-patterns), along with transforming row database to columnar database. Next, we will explain the PF-ECLAT algorithm to discover complete set of periodic-frequent patterns in columnar temporal databases. PF-ECLAT algorithm employs Depth-First Search (DFS) and the *downward closure property* (see Property 1) of periodic-frequent patterns to reduce the huge search space effectively.

Property 1. (**The downward closure property** [7].) If Y is a periodic-frequent pattern, then $\forall X \subset Y$ and $X \neq \emptyset$, X is also a periodic-frequent pattern.

4.1   PF-ECLAT Algorithm

Finding One Length Periodic-Frequent Patterns. Algorithm 1 describes the procedure to find 1-patterns using PFP-list, which is a dictionary. We now describe this algorithm's working using the row database shown in Table 1. Let $minSup = 5$ and $maxPer = 3$.

We will scan the complete database once to generate 1-patterns and transforming the row database to columnar database. The scan on the first transaction, "1 : *abcf*", with $ts_{cur} = 1$ inserts the items a, b, c, and f in the PFP-list. The timestamps of these items is set to 1 $(= ts_{cur})$. Similarly, Per and TS_l values of these items were also set to 1 and 1, respectively (lines 5 and 6 in Algorithm 1). The PFP-list generated after scanning the first transaction is shown in Fig. 1(a). The scan on the second transaction, "2 : *bcde*", with $ts_{cur} = 2$ inserts the new items d and e into the PFP-list by adding 2 $(= ts_{cur})$ in their TS-list. Simultaneously, the Per and TS_l values were set to 2 and 2, respectively. On the other hand, 2 $(= ts_{cur})$ was added to the TS-list of already existing items b and c with Per and TS_l set to 1 and 2, respectively (lines 7 and 8 in Algorithm 1). The PFP-list generated after scanning the second transaction is shown in Fig. 1(b). A similar process is repeated for the remaining transactions in the database. The final PFP-list generated after scanning the entire database is shown in Fig. 1(c). The pattern e and f are pruned (using the Property 1) from the PFP-list as its *support* value is less than the user-specified $minSup$ value (lines 10 to 15 in Algorithm 1). The remaining patterns in the PFP-list are considered periodic-frequent patterns and sorted in descending order of their *support* values. The final PFP-list generated after sorting the periodic-frequent patterns is shown in Fig. 1(d).

Finding Periodic-Frequent Patterns Using PFP-list. Algorithm 2 describes the procedure for finding all periodic-frequent patterns in a database. We now describe the working of this algorithm using the newly generated PFP-list.

We start with item c, which is the first pattern in the PFP-list (line 2 in Algorithm 2). We record its *support* and *periodicity*, as shown in Fig. 2(a). Since c is a periodic-frequent pattern, we move to its child node cb and generate its TS-list by performing intersection of TS-lists of c and b, i.e., $TS^{cb} = TS^c \cap TS^b$ (lines 3 and 4 in Algorithm 2). We record *support* and *periodicity* of cb, as shown in Fig. 2(b). We verify whether cb is periodic-frequent or uninteresting pattern (line 5 in Algorithm 2). Since cb is periodic-frequent pattern, we move to its child node cba and generate its TS-list by performing intersection of TS-lists of cb and a, i.e., $TS^{cba} = TS^{cb} \cap TS^a$. We record *support* and *periodicity* of cba, as shown in Fig. 2(c) and identified it as a periodic-frequent pattern. We once again, move to its child node $cbad$ and generate its TS-list by performing intersection of TS-lists of cba and d, i.e., $TS^{cbad} = TS^{cba} \cap TS^d$. As *support* of $cbad$ is less than the user-specified $minSup$, we will prune the pattern $cbad$ from the periodic-frequent patterns list as shown in Fig. 2(d). A similar process is repeated for remaining nodes in the set-enumeration tree to find all periodic-frequent patterns. The final list of periodic-frequent patterns generated from Table 1 are shown in Fig. 2(e). The above approach of finding periodic-frequent patterns using the downward closure property is efficient, because it effectively reduces the search space and the computational cost.

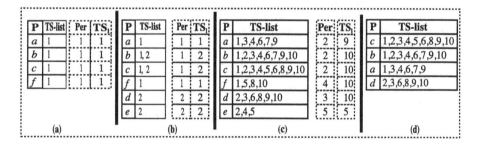

P	TS-list	Per	TS$_l$	P	TS-list	Per	TS$_l$	P	TS-list	Per	TS$_l$	P	TS-list
a	1	1	1	a	1	1	1	a	1,3,4,6,7,9	2	9	c	1,2,3,4,5,6,8,9,10
b	1	1	1	b	1,2	1	2	b	1,2,3,4,6,7,9,10	2	10	b	1,2,3,4,6,7,9,10
c	1	1	1	c	1,2	1	2	c	1,2,3,4,5,6,8,9,10	2	10	a	1,3,4,6,7,9
f	1	1	1	f	1	1	1	f	1,5,8,10	4	10	d	2,3,6,8,9,10
				d	2	2	2	d	2,3,6,8,9,10	3	10		
				e	2	2	2	e	2,4,5	5	5		
(a)				(b)				(c)				(d)	

Fig. 1. Finding periodic-frequent patterns. (a) after scanning the first transaction, (b) after scanning the second transaction, (c) after scanning the entire database, and (d) final list of periodic-frequent patterns sorted in descending order of their *support* (or the size of TS-list)

5 Experimental Results

In this section, we first compare the PF-ECLAT against the state-of-the-art algorithms (E.g., PFP-growth [7], PFP-growth++ [5], and PS-growth [4]) and show that our algorithm is not only memory and runtime efficient, but also high

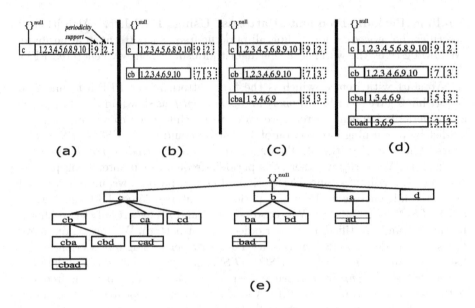

Fig. 2. Mining periodic-frequent patterns using DFS.

Algorithm 1. PeriodicFrequentItems(Row database (TDB), minimum support ($minSup$), maximum periodicity ($maxPer$):

1: Let $PFP\text{-}list = (X, TS\text{-}list(X))$ be a dictionary that records the temporal occurrence information of a pattern in a TDB. Let TS_l be a temporary list to record the *timestamp* of the last occurrence of an item in the database. Let Per be a temporary list to record the *periodicity* of an item in the database. Let *support* be another temporary lists to record the *support* of an item in the database.

2: **for** each transaction $t_{cur} \in TDB$ **do**

3:    Set $ts_{cur} = t_{cur}.ts$;

4:    **for** each item $i \in t_{cur}.X$ **do**

5:      **if** i does not exit in PFP-list **then**

6:        Insert i and its timestamp into the PFP-list. Set $TS_l[i] = ts_{cur}$ and $Per[i] = (ts_{cur} - ts_{initial})$;

7:      **else**

8:        Add i's timestamp in the PFP-list. Update $TS_l[i] = ts_{cur}$ and $Per[i] = max(Per[i], (ts_{cur} - TS_l[i]))$;

9: **for** each item i in PFP-list **do**

10:    $support[i] = length(TS\text{-}list(i))$

11:    **if** $support[i] < minSup$ **then**

12:      Prune i from the PFP-list;

13:    **else**

14:      Calculate $Per[i] = max(Per[i], (ts_{final} - TS_l[i]))$;

15:      **if** $Per[i] > maxPer$ **then**

16:        Prune i from the PFP-list.

17: Sort the remaining items in the PFP-list in ascending order or descending order of their *support*. Call PF-ECLAT(PFP-List).

Algorithm 2. PF-ECLAT(PFP-List)

1: **for** each item i in PFP-List **do**
2:    Set $pi = \emptyset$ and $X = i$;
3:    **for** each item j that comes after i in the PFP-list **do**
4:        Set $Y = X \cup j$ and $TS^Y = TS^X \cap TS^j$;
5:        **if** $sup(TS^Y) \geq minSup$ and $per(TS^Y) \leq maxPer$ **then**
6:            Add Y to pi and Y is considered as periodic-frequent itemset;
7:    $PF\text{-}ECLAT(pi)$

---

scalable as well. Next, we describe the usefulness of our algorithm with a case study on air pollution data.

5.1 Experimental Setup

The algorithms, PFP-growth, PFP-growth++, PS-growth and PF-ECLAT, were developed in Python 3.7 and executed on an Intel i5 2.6 GHz, 8 GB RAM machine running Ubuntu 18.04 operating system. The experiments have been conducted on real-world (Congestion, Pollution, BMS-WebView-2, and Kosarak) databases.

The **Congestion** database is a high dimensional real-world sparse database provided by JApan Road Traffic Information Center (JARTIC) for Kobe, Japan. The database contains 1,414 items and 8,928 transactions. The *minimum*, *average*, and *maximum* transaction lengths are 1, 57.73, and 338, respectively. The **Pollution** database contained 1600 items (or stations) with 720 transactions. It is a high dimensional dense database with *minimum*, *average*, and *maximum* transaction lengths equal to 11, 460 and 971, respectively. The **BMS-WebView-2** is a real-world sparse database containing 77,512 transactions and 3,340 items. The *minimum, average*, and *maximum* transaction lengths of this database are 2, 5, and 161. The **Kosarak** is a real-world very large sparse database containing 990,000 transactions and 41,270 items. The *minimum*, *average*, and *maximum* transaction lengths of this database are 2, 9, and 2499. In this paper, we employ this database to evaluate the scalability of PFP-growth, PFP-growth++, PS-growth, and PF-ECLAT algorithms.

5.2 Evaluation of PFP-growth, PFP-growth++, PS-growth, and PF-ECLAT Algorithms by Varying *minSup* Constraint

In this experiment, we evaluate PFP-growth, PFP-growth++, PS-growth, and PF-ECLAT algorithms performance by varying only the *minSup* constraint in each of the databases. The *maxPer* in Congestion, Pollution, and BMS-WebView-2 databases is fixed at 35%, 50%, and 30%, respectively.

Figure 3(a), 3(b), and 3(c) respectively show the number of periodic-frequent patterns generated in Congestion, Pollution and BMS-WebView-2 databases at different *minSup* values. It can be observed that, increase in *minSup* has a negative effect on the generation of periodic-frequent patterns. It is because many patterns fail to satisfy the increased *minSup*.

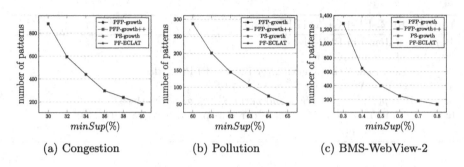

Fig. 3. Number of periodic-frequent patterns generated by various algorithms

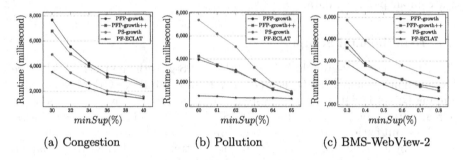

Fig. 4. Runtime evaluation of various algorithms

Figure 4(a), 4(b), and 4(c) respectively show the runtime requirements of PFP-growth, PFP-growth++, PS-growth, and PF-ECLAT algorithms in Congestion, Pollution and BMS-WebView-2 databases at different $minSup$ values. It can be observed that even though the runtime requirements of all the algorithms decrease with the increase in $minSup$, PF-ECLAT algorithm completed the mining process much faster than the remaining algorithms in both sparse and dense databases at any given $minSup$. In BMS-WebView-2 database, PF-ECLAT algorithm was an order of magnitude time faster than remaining algorithms. More importantly, PF-ECLAT algorithm was several times faster than remaining algorithms, especially at low $minSup$ values.

Figure 5(a), 5(b), and 5(c) respectively show the memory requirements of PFP-growth, PFP-growth++, PS-growth, and PF-ECLAT algorithms in Congestion, Pollution and BMS-WebView-2 databases at different $minSup$ values. It can be observed that though an increase in $minSup$ resulted in the decrease of memory requirements for all the algorithms, PF-ECLAT algorithm has consumed relatively very little memory in all databases at different $minSup$ values. More importantly, PS-growth has taken huge amount of memory at low $minSup$ values in all of the databases.

5.3 Evaluation of PFP-growth, PFP-growth++, PS-growth, and PF-ECLAT Algorithms by Varying *maxPer* Constraint

Figure 6(a) shows the number of periodic-frequent patterns generated in the Congestion database at different *maxPer* values. The *minSup* has been fixed at 30%. It can be observed that an increase in *maxPer* has increased the number of periodic-frequent patterns.

Figure 6(b) shows the runtime requirements of PFP-growth, PFP-growth++, PS-growth, and PF-ECLAT algorithms in the Congestion database at different *maxPer* values. It can be observed that though the runtime requirements of all the algorithms increase with the increase in *maxPer* value, PF-ECLAT algorithm consumes relatively less runtime than the remaining algorithms.

Figure 6(c) shows the memory requirements of PFP-growth, PFP-growth++, PS-growth, and PF-ECLAT algorithms in the Congestion database at different *maxPer* values. It can be observed that though the memory requirements of all the algorithms increase with *maxPer*, PF-ECLAT algorithm consumes very less memory than the remaining algorithms.

Similar results were obtained during the experimentation on remaining databases. However, we have confined this experiment to the Congestion database due to page limitations.

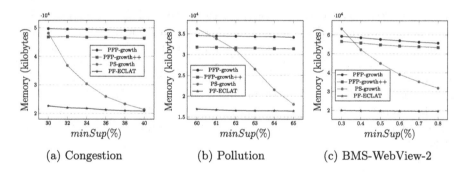

(a) Congestion   (b) Pollution   (c) BMS-WebView-2

Fig. 5. Memory evaluation of various algorithms

5.4 Scalability Test

The Kosarak database was divided into five portions of 0.2 million transactions in each part. Then we investigated the performance of PFP-growth, PFP-growth++, PS-growth, and PF-ECLAT algorithms after accumulating each portion with previous parts. Figure 7(a) and 7(b), respectively show the runtime and memory requirements of all algorithms at different database sizes when $minSup = 0.09$ (%) and $maxPer = 0.1$ (%). The following two observations can be drawn from these figures: (i) Runtime and memory requirements of PFP-growth, PFP-growth++, PS-growth, and PF-ECLAT algorithms increase almost

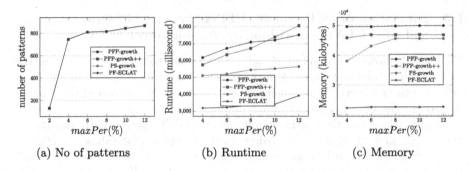

Fig. 6. Evaluation of different algorithms in Congestion database by varying $maxPer$.

linearly with the increase in database size. (ii) At any given database size, PF-ECLAT consumes less runtime and memory as compared against the remaining algorithms.

5.5 A Case Study: Finding Areas Where People Have Been Regularly Exposed to Hazardous Levels of PM2.5 Pollutant

The spatial locations of interesting patterns generated from the **Pollution** database are shown in Fig. 8. It can be observed that most of the sensors in this figure are situated in south-east of Japan. Thus, it can be inferred that people working or living in the south-east parts of Japan were periodically exposed to high levels of PM2.5. Such information may be found very useful to the Ecologists in devising policies to control pollution and improve public health. Please note that more in-depth studies, such as finding high polluted areas on weekends or particular time intervals of a day, can also be carried out with our algorithm efficiently.

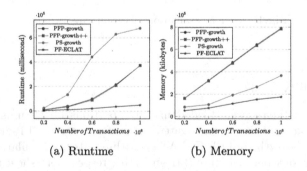

Fig. 7. Scalability of PFP-growth, PFP-growth++, PS-growth, and PF-ECLAT

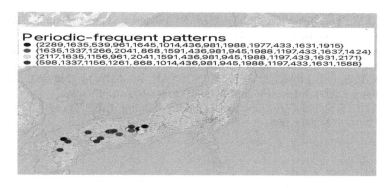

Fig. 8. Areas where people have been regularly subjected to unhealthy levels of PM2.5 concentrate

6   Conclusions and Future Work

This paper has proposed an efficient algorithm named Periodic Frequent-Equivalence CLass Transformation (PF-ECLAT) to find periodic-frequent patterns in columnar temporal databases. The performance of the PF-ECLAT is verified by comparing it with other algorithms on different real-world databases. Experimental analysis shows that PF-ECLAT exhibits high performance in periodic-frequent pattern mining and can obtain all periodic-frequent patterns faster and with less memory usage against the state-of-the-art algorithms. We have also presented a case study to illustrate the usefulness of generated patterns in a real-world application.

As part of future work, we would like to investigate parallel algorithms to find periodic and fuzzy periodic-frequent patterns in very large temporal databases.

References

1. Aggarwal, C.C.: Applications of frequent pattern mining. In: Aggarwal, C.C., Han, J. (eds.) Frequent Pattern Mining, pp. 443–467. Springer, Cham (2014). https://doi.org/10.1007/978-3-319-07821-2_18
2. Agrawal, R., Imieliński, T., Swami, A.: Mining association rules between sets of items in large databases. In: SIGMOD, pp. 207–216 (1993)
3. Amphawan, K., Lenca, P., Surarerks, A.: Mining top-k periodic-frequent pattern from transactional databases without support threshold. In: Papasratorn, B., Chutimaskul, W., Porkaew, K., Vanijja, V. (eds.) IAIT 2009. CCIS, vol. 55, pp. 18–29. Springer, Heidelberg (2009). https://doi.org/10.1007/978-3-642-10392-6_3
4. Anirudh, A., Kiran, R.U., Reddy, P.K., Kitsuregawa, M.: Memory efficient mining of periodic-frequent patterns in transactional databases. In: 2016 IEEE Symposium Series on Computational Intelligence, pp. 1–8 (2016)
5. Kiran, R.U., Kitsuregawa, M.: Novel techniques to reduce search space in periodic-frequent pattern mining. In: Bhowmick, S.S., Dyreson, C.E., Jensen, C.S., Lee, M.L., Muliantara, A., Thalheim, B. (eds.) DASFAA 2014. LNCS, vol. 8422, pp. 377–391. Springer, Cham (2014). https://doi.org/10.1007/978-3-319-05813-9_25

6. Luna, J.M., Fournier-Viger, P., Ventura, S.: Frequent itemset mining: a 25 years review. Wiley Interdiscip. Rev. Data Min. Knowl. Discov. **9**(6) (2019)
7. Tanbeer, S.K., Ahmed, C.F., Jeong, B.-S., Lee, Y.-K.: Discovering periodic-frequent patterns in transactional databases. In: Theeramunkong, T., Kijsirikul, B., Cercone, N., Ho, T.-B. (eds.) PAKDD 2009. LNCS (LNAI), vol. 5476, pp. 242–253. Springer, Heidelberg (2009). https://doi.org/10.1007/978-3-642-01307-2_24
8. Zaki, M.J.: Scalable algorithms for association mining. IEEE Trans. Knowl. Data Eng. **12**(3), 372–390 (2000)

Data-Driven Simulation of Ride-Hailing Services Using Imitation and Reinforcement Learning

Haritha Jayasinghe, Tarindu Jayatilaka$^{(\boxtimes)}$, Ravin Gunawardena,
and Uthayasanker Thayasivam

University of Moratuwa, Moratuwa 10400, Sri Lanka
{haritha.16,tarindu.16,ravinsg.16,rtuthaya}@cse.mrt.ac.lk
http://www.cse.mrt.ac.lk/

Abstract. The rapid growth of ride-hailing platforms has created a highly competitive market where businesses struggle to make profits, demanding the need for better operational strategies. However, real-world experiments are risky and expensive for these platforms as they deal with millions of users daily. Thus, a need arises for a simulated environment where they can predict users' reactions to changes in the platform-specific parameters such as trip fares and incentives. Building such a simulation is challenging, as these platforms exist within dynamic environments where thousands of users regularly interact with one another. This paper presents a framework to mimic and predict user, specifically driver, behaviors in ride-hailing services. We use a data-driven hybrid reinforcement learning and imitation learning approach for this. First, the agent utilizes behavioral cloning to mimic driver behavior using a real-world data-set. Next, reinforcement learning is applied on top of the pre-trained agents in a simulated environment, to allow them to adapt to changes in the platform. Our framework provides an ideal playground for ride-hailing platforms to experiment with platform-specific parameters to predict drivers' behavioral patterns.

Keywords: Ride-hailing simulation · Driver behavior patterns · Imitation learning · Reinforcement learning

1 Introduction

Within less than a decade, internet-based ride-hailing platforms have managed to penetrate all global markets. However, all of these platforms are struggling with low or negative profit margins, implying that these platforms must be able to fine-tune parameters within their control to maximize profits. These parameters include surge pricing [5], commissions, service fees, driver incentives, discounts, information available to the driver before accepting a trip (trip distance, payment method), and so on.

H. Jayasinghe, T. Jayatilaka and R. Gunawardena—Equal contribution.

© Springer Nature Switzerland AG 2021
H. Fujita et al. (Eds.): IEA/AIE 2021, LNAI 12798, pp. 41–52, 2021.
https://doi.org/10.1007/978-3-030-79457-6_4

Experimenting with such parameters in a live platform is unrealistic due to; the high cost of running such trials, the in-adaptability of findings from one region to another, the exceedingly large number of trials required to search through combinations of multiple parameters, and the negative reactions from riders or drivers towards the changes and inconsistencies in the platform.

However, as these platforms begin to scale and offer more complex features, simulating them is essential to predict the behavior of agents—drivers and riders— under different pricing and incentive strategies. Thus, the necessity arises for a simulated platform where such experiments can be conducted. The simulation should precisely predict how the agents react to different combinations of the above-mentioned parameters.

Unfortunately, realistically simulating the driver and passenger behavior within the platform is challenging as these platforms exist within highly volatile environments susceptible to change from external factors such as weather, traffic, or fuel prices. Existing simulations fail to capture precise driver behavior as they either utilize analytical models [1] or attempt to simplify the objective function of drivers into simple reward functions [4,9]. Furthermore, any simulation requires the selection of certain parameters for precise modeling at the cost of abstracting away remaining parameters. The selection of the ideal parameter set for modeling within the simulation is a non-trivial task as it directly affects the accuracy of the predictions offered by the system.

This paper presents a novel approach to realistically mimic and predict the trip acceptance behavior of drivers on ride-hailing platforms. We propose a data-driven imitation learning approach to mimic driver behaviors which overcomes the aforementioned challenges of modeling driver behavior. Our model is portable across platforms as it can be adapted by merely changing the data set. Furthermore, deep reinforcement learning allows us to predict how agents change their behavior when the platform-specific parameters are changed using the reward function. Our prescriptive framework predicts the probability distribution of driver behavior on a macro scale in response to such changes.

We make the following contributions in this paper.

- We present a data-backed framework to simulate ride-hailing platforms and their users.
- We demonstrate how imitation learning can be utilized to mimic drivers' behaviors in a ride-hailing platform.
- We show how reinforcement learning agents pre-trained with behavioral cloning can be used to predict changes in driver behaviors in response to changes in the platform.

2   Related Work

The earliest efforts in modeling taxi-cab services were based on concepts such as linear programming and statistical modeling. To investigate the relationship between the demand and the number of cabs to dispatch while overcoming the limitations in the previous methodologies, Bailey and Clark [1] introduced the concept of simulated environments in ride modeling. The same researchers developed an event-based simulation [2] to simulate taxi dispatching to reinforce the idea behind fleet size and performance. Despite the efforts, due to the lack of computational power during the era, the developed models were confined to use a minimal amount of data and resources, limiting their performance.

Machine learning is a more modern approach to model taxi cab services. Rossi et al. [12] used RNNs to predict the next location of taxi drivers. Lin et al. [9] worked on capturing the complicated stochastic demand-supply of taxi service variations in high-dimensional space using reinforcement learning. Gao et al. [4] also used reinforcement learning to optimize taxi driving strategies to discover new operations decisions. Shou et al. [13] used an imitation learning approach to optimize passenger seeking behavior in ride-hailing platforms. However, all of the above primarily focus on mobility or demand and fleet size management compared to the drivers' trip acceptance decisions, which is the primary focus of our work.

In terms of reinforcement learning, there are value-based and policy-based reinforcement learning algorithms. A prime example of a value-based algorithm is deep Q learning [11], a model-free reinforcement learning approach commonly used in practical applications. There are also additional variations on DQ networks such as Categorical DQN [3], which increases training stability. In contrast to value-based approaches that attempt to maximize cumulative reward, a policy-based approach such as the REINFORCE algorithm [14] attempts to learn the best policy or set of actions to follow. In addition, there are also policy + action-based approaches such as actor-critic networks [8] and A2C networks [10] which combines both of these strategies.

A major challenge of reinforcement learning is reward engineering. To solve this, we turn to imitation learning, particularly behavioral cloning, where the agent learns from real observations rather than through a reward function. Torabi et al. [15] use observations first to learn a model and then use the learned model to infer the missing actions to improve the imitation policy. Goecks et al. [6] take this further by following behavioral cloning with reinforcement learning to take advantage of both approaches. It allows to capture the behavior of the agent and then improve the policy without additional observations. We adopt a similar approach in this paper.

3 Methodology

We propose a data-driven framework consisting of driver agents and a reinforcement learning environment (Fig. 1). The driver agents are initially trained through imitation learning. Next, they are trained to adapt to varying platform parameters through a reinforcement learning approach, through interactions with the reinforcement learning environment.

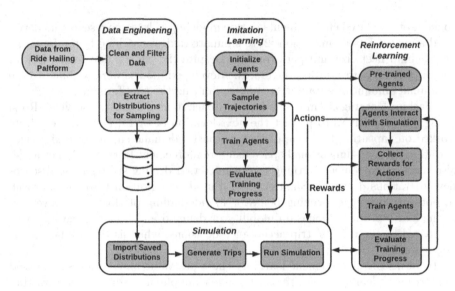

Fig. 1. System architecture

3.1 Data

For our work, we use a data set provided to us by a privately owned ride-hailing platform based in Sri Lanka. The data set consists of all the rides generated from 1st February 2020–29th February 2020 in the Colombo Metropolitan Area—a sprawling region with a population of approximately 6 million people occupying 1,422 square miles. Within the period, nearly 6.7 million trip requests have been prompted to the 28,982 drivers on the platform. Each trip is represented as a vector with the fields: driver id, trip id, trip created time, driver assigned time, trip accept/reject time, pickup time, pickup latitude, pickup longitude, drop latitude, drop longitude, distance to pick up, trip distance, status, and payment method. We only consider trips that occur in the busiest urban areas of Colombo. We also eliminate data that were duplicated, or erroneous, including trips with missing values. Around 5.6 million trips remained after cleaning, selection, and pre-processing of the data set.

For our simulation to accurately reflect the real world, the above data set is incorporated into the system using sampling techniques. We treat the coordinates of each location as two random variables L_x and L_y distributed across our region. Each random variable is described using its own cumulative distribution function: F_{L_x} and F_{L_y}. We assume that the number of data points we have is a sufficient approximation for the actual CDF of the distribution. Finally, we use the *inverse transformation method* to generate values for L_x and L_y. We can sample values for L using F_L^{-1}, where F_L is a common representation of F_{L_x} and F_{L_y}. Similarly, we create another random variable D to sample trip distances.

3.2   Simulation Framework

The simulation framework is composed of driver agents and the reinforcement learning environment.

Reinforcement Learning Environment. The RL environment comprises the interactions between drivers, riders, and the ride-hailing platform. The ability of the simulation to reflect reality directly affects the performance of the agents. Hence, the primary goal of building this environment is to incorporate real-world information and replicate the operations taking place within the ride-hailing platform.

From here on, we abstract the behavior of riders and refer to them as rides for modeling purposes. A ride is a vector, $R = (r_x^p, r_y^p, r_x^d, r_y^d, r_d)$, of variables sampled from the distributions we extract from the data set. Each ride has pickup and drop coordinates $([r_x^p, r_y^p], [r_x^d, r_y^d])$ and a ride distance (r_d). All the geographic coordinates are in a rectangular grid of size $M_h \times M_w$.

We only simulate a fraction of the total available rides to increase the throughput of the system and to optimize the training time of the agents. We use a scaling factor of 35 to scale down the number of rides generated per week to around 20,000. To maintain the distribution coherent when the scaled ride count per minute is below 1, which accounts for 25–30% of the total time, a probabilistic approach is taken instead of naively rounding off the decimal places, for better accuracy. The scaled ride count is rounded up with a probability equivalent to its fractional part. Consequently, the expected value of the number of trips per minute becomes equal to the scaled ride count.

Ride Generation Algorithm. A ride (R) is described using the pickup/ drop coordinates and the ride distance. The time of day (t_d) decides the frequency of the rides being generated. For each minute, the number of trips per minute (N_t) is sampled from the time distribution (T) using the time of day (t_d). Using the number of trips per minute (N_t), location distribution (L), and distance distribution (D), Algorithm 1 generates trips for the simulation.

The vector $[r_x^p, r_y^p]$ which is sampled from L (*line 4*), represents the latitude and longitude (x, y) coordinates of the pickup location. We add a small amount of random noise uniformly distributed between $(-\epsilon, \epsilon)$ to make the location different every time (*line 5*). The coordinates have an upper bound of M_h or M_w, and a lower bound of 0. The trip distance t_d is sampled from D (*line 8*). Now, we can draw a circle of radius t_d having the center as $[r_x^p, r_y^p]$. A random point on the circumference of this circle is selected as the drop location, $[r_x^d, r_y^d]$. If all possible locations are outside the grid, t_d is halved and the process is restarted (*lines 10–12*). Once the drop location is identified, the ride is initialized and pushed to a queue to be processed by the simulation.

Agent Modelling Approach. We model the ride accept/reject decision for each driver in the simulation using an agent trained using a combination of

Input: Map Size $[M_h, M_w]$
        Random Variables L_x, L_y, D
        Number of Rides Per Minute N_t
        Output: Queue of Ride Objects $\langle r_1, r_2, \ldots, r_n \rangle$
1 $rides \leftarrow [\ \ ]$
2 $ride\_no \leftarrow 0$
3 **while** $ride\_no < N_t$ **do**
4 $\quad (r_x^p, r_y^p) \leftarrow (L_x(\omega), L_y(\omega))$ for $\omega \in \Omega$
5 $\quad (r_x^p, r_y^p) \leftarrow (r_x^p, r_y^p) + (\mathcal{U}(-\epsilon, \epsilon), \mathcal{U}(-\epsilon, \epsilon))$
6 $\quad r_x^p \leftarrow max(0, min(M_w, r_x^p))$
7 $\quad r_y^p \leftarrow max(0, min(M_h, r_y^p))$
8 $\quad r_d \leftarrow D(\omega)$ for $\omega \in \Omega$
9 $\quad (r_x^d, r_y^d) \leftarrow$ calculate drop location
10 $\quad$ **while** $not\ 0 < r_x^d < M_w\ and\ 0 < r_y^d < M_h$ **do**
11 $\quad\quad r_d \leftarrow \frac{r_d}{2}$
12 $\quad\quad (r_x^d, r_y^d) \leftarrow$ calculate drop location
13 $\quad$ **end**
14 $\quad r_i \leftarrow (r_x^p, r_y^p, r_x^d, r_y^d, r_d)$
15 $\quad rides.insert(r_i)$
16 $\quad ride\_no \leftarrow ride\_no + 1$
17 **end**
18 **return** $rides$

Algorithm 1: GENERATERIDES Generates Rides for the Simulation

imitation learning and deep reinforcement learning. Specifically, we use a two-step approach. We first train the agent to clone the behavior demonstrated by the drivers in our data-set, allowing the agent to learn the inherent behavioral patterns of the drivers. Next, we add a layer of reinforcement learning, utilizing rides generated from our simulation, thereby adapting the agent to the platform-specific parameters we define within the simulation. This approach is described in detail below.

We initially utilize the data-set to generate demonstrations, which are treated as independent and identically distributed (i.i.d.) samples, to follow a behavioral cloning approach. We utilize a deep Q network [7] for training purposes, and provide the demonstrations gathered above as trajectories for the training process.

A single training trajectory $[s, a, s', r]$ consists of; 1. environment state immediately before the action (s), 2. action (a), 3. environment state immediately after the action (s'), 4.reward associated with the action (r).

We expose the environment state to our agent via the following observations; 1. the distance to pick-up location from current driver location, 2. the trip distance, 3. the time of day (useful to infer information regarding peak / off-peak time and demand patterns), 4. the number of trips to complete till weekly reward is achieved, 5. trip destination, 6. the idle time since last completed trip (useful for inferring the opportunity cost of remaining idle).

We posit that by providing observations such as *Trips Left till Weekly Reward*, we can overcome limitations imposed by the i.i.d. assumption of behavioral cloning approaches in simulating Markov Decision Processes (MDP), as such observations can provide an agent a rudimentary understanding of its state history.

Secondly, we move to a reinforcement learning approach to train the agent on the simulation with a set of platform parameters. These parameters include various reward factors, which can be adjusted as required. During this step, the agent interacts directly with the simulation. We utilize a relatively lower exploration rate and early stopping to ensure that the agent retains the patterns learned during the imitation learning phase.

The basic process of the reinforcement learning system is as follows.

- Whenever a trip is generated and offered to a driver(agent), the agent is provided with a set of observations that describe the environment.
- Based on the observations the agent is required to make a decision. (accept/reject trip)
- The agent is given a reward for the action taken.

Drivers take actions to maximize their rewards according to the concepts of Game Theory. Thus, a key factor required for realistic simulation of driver behavior is the ability to accurately represent the reward function of the driver. Ideally, the reward function should be capable of representing the fact that human agents are not perfectly rational, however using traditional reinforcement learning, we are restricted to representations of rational behavior only. The reward used for training the agents is calculated as a function of trip distance(td), pickup distance(pd), opportunity cost (oc), and weekly reward(wr).

$$Q(s,a) := Q(s,a) + \alpha(r + \gamma max_{a'} Q(s',a') - Q(s,a)) \qquad (1)$$
$$r = w * (fare/km * td) - x * (cost/km * (td + pd)) - y * oc + z * wr \qquad (2)$$

The opportunity cost is a penalty calculated based on the driver's active time, which represents the value of the time invested into the platform by the driver, and the weekly reward is an additional reward present in the platform to motivate drivers. Each driver is given a weekly goal based on his past performance, which he must meet to gain this reward. w, x, y, and z represent weights that scale an agent's preference for different types of rewards. The agent attempts to select actions that maximize the overall expected value of the decisions taken. This is achieved by iteratively updating the expected value (Q value) for each training example, as given in the below equation. γ represents a discounting factor for future rewards, and s represents the state (sequence of actions and observations), while a' and s' denote all actions and the resultant state of all actions respectively [7].

While the most obvious method to model individual drivers would be to use separate DQN agents to represent each driver, this is impractical due to the large number of training examples required for each agent. For simplicity, we train a single agent for all drivers and utilize an experiment setup with 50 drivers.

For improved stability, we utilize a categorical deep Q network [3] instead of a vanilla DQN, where a Q value distribution is learned as opposed to a single Q value, which results in a more stable learning process due to reduced chattering, state aliasing, etc.

4   Experimental Setup

Our experimental setup consists of two main sections. The simulation environment is evaluated based on the accuracy of the generated rides in their ability to reflect real-world data. The agent learning method is evaluated by both the agent's ability to mimic driver behavior, as well as the agent's ability to adapt to platform parameters. This is achieved by comparing the behavioral changes of the drivers in response to changes in parameters. Our results reflect the success of the system in predicting the agent behavior at a macroscopic level.

In our setup, we train a single imitation learning agent using around 4.2 million trips, for 150 iterations with a replay buffer containing 1000 trajectories. A single trajectory represents all trip acceptance/rejection actions of a given driver over three weeks, as the final week of the data set was excluded for evaluation purposes.

During the reinforcement learning setup, we train for a further 50 iterations, where a single iteration consists of all trajectories collected in a single run of our simulation. A single run involves a 1 week run time. We evaluate the adaptive behavior of the agent through the following experiment setup. The agent is first trained through the imitation learning process. Subsequently, copies of the agent are trained on variations of the simulation with different platform parameters. Post-training, we observe the behavior of the agents to understand behavioral changes induced by the parameter changes during the reinforcement learning phase.

5   Results

For the purpose of evaluating the efficacy of our simulation, Table 1 compares the predicted number of trips for the final week by the simulation, against the actual number of trips from the data-set.

We observe that the simulation is successful in predicting the demand of the economy to a significant extent. However, it is not perfect. This could be due to other factors we did not take into consideration: weather, traffic, special events, holidays, etc. The notable gap between the predicted and actual ride count on Thursday reflects this notion. Since the following Friday was a public holiday in Sri Lanka, the demand for rides increased on Thursday evening.

Figure 2 shows the distribution of the actual demand for rides against the predicted demand for each day of the week. It can be seen that the simulation is successful in identifying the underlying demand patterns of the ride-hailing platform sufficiently.

Table 1. Comparison of predicted trip count against the actual trip count. The upper and lower bounds are the intervals of 95% confidence level.

Day	Predict. (mean)	Lower bound	Upper bound	Actual	$\delta(\%)$
Mon	110,852	110,162	111,542	100,905	+9.858
Tue	106,807	106,141	107,473	108,280	−1.360
Wed	115,947	115,487	116,407	122,377	−5.254
Thu	116,370	115,589	117,151	127,664	−8.847
Fri	149,515	148,561	150,469	145,924	+2.461
Sat	83,263	82,746	83,780	88,365	−5.774
Sun	57,442	57,054	57,830	58,734	−2.200

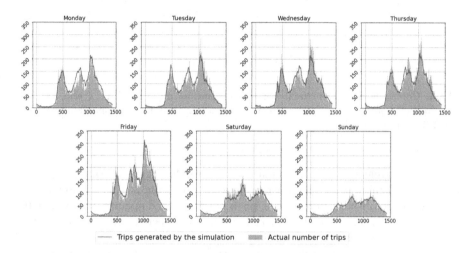

Fig. 2. Distribution of the predicted number of trips generated by the simulation (red) against the actual number of trips (blue) for each day of the week in the last week of February (Color figure online)

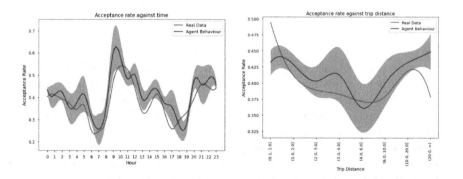

Fig. 3. Comparison of the actual driver behavior and the agent behavior after training using Imitation Learning

To compare the behavior of the drivers trained through imitation learning against the behavior of drivers from the real-world dataset, we compute the correlation between their acceptance rates. Figure 3 shows that our imitation agents' behavior strongly correlates with the actual driver behavior with a Pearson correlation coefficient of 0.875.

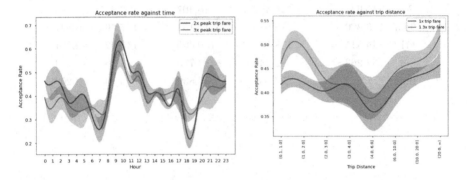

Fig. 4. Comparison of agent behavior against time of day (h) with 2× and 3× peak trip fare(left), and Comparison of agent behavior against trip distance(km) with 1× and 1.3× trip fare(right)

When evaluating the performance of the reinforcement learning approach, Fig. 4 (left) demonstrates the contrast between providing 2× vs 3× trip fare (per km, relative to off-peak rate) during peak hours, plotted against time of day. (6–8 h and 16–19 h are defined as peak hours). As expected, the acceptance rate during peak hours has increased, however with the caveat of a slightly reduced acceptance rate during off-peak hours. Crucially, in practice, these parameters do not operate in isolation, and the gap between peak and off-peak rates can also be controlled through other parameters such as weekly rewards. Figure 4 (right) depicts the effect of increasing trip fare (per km) by 1.3×, where it can be observed that the acceptance rates increase noticeably, across all distances, as the trips become more profitable.

Fig. 5 demonstrates the contrast between setting the weekly reward target at 1× vs 1.3× the previous week's performance. A notable increase can be observed in the general acceptance rates when reward targets are increased, particularly for trips with lower distances, as the profitability of these trips now increase. Interestingly, the higher reward target does not cause a notable increase in the lower acceptance rate during peak hours, implying that the drivers can cherry-pick trips and still maintain their goal.

The above are two of the various platform parameters that can be tweaked. Since the behavioral response of drivers become more complicated as these parameters interact with one another, complicated behavioral patterns can be monitored by tweaking them in tandem, to identify parameters that maximize the KPIs of the platform.

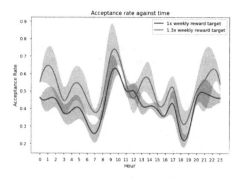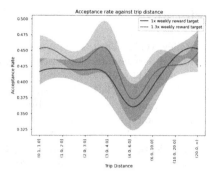

Fig. 5. Comparison of agent behavior against time of day (h) (left) and agent behavior against trip distance(km) (right) with weekly 1× and 1.5× reward targets

6 Conclusion

We present a novel data-driven simulation framework that uses imitation learning and Categorical Deep Q-Networks to model driver behaviors in ride-hailing platforms. Our simulation successfully manages to predict the economy at a macroscopic level. We achieve a margin of error of less than 10% in predicting the demand through the week and the total revenue generated by the platform. The quantitative results prove the ability of the DQN agent to imitate the behavior of drivers with a strong correlation coefficient of 0.875, against observations such as trip distance and time of day. Furthermore, we can observe how the agent behavior changes using reinforcement learning when we tweak the platform-specific parameters using in the simulated environment. Our framework demonstrates that any ride-hailing service, where assets and services are shared between a large number of individuals interacting with one another, can be simulated using imitation learning.

7 Future Work

While our approach utilizes behavioral cloning to learn driver behavior, Inverse Reinforcement Learning presents a more advanced method to potentially capture a reward function that depicts driver behavior more effectively. Furthermore, we currently allow users to manually tweak a parameter and observe driver behavior. Zheng et al. [16] utilize multi-agent reinforcement learning to simulate the behavior of participants as well as a rule-setting agent, demonstrating a method to create a system that can automatically determine the ideal rule set to maximize the utility of the system. This approach can be adapted to our use case, where an additional RL agent can be designed to tweak the parameters of the platform (incentives, information available to the driver at decision time, etc.) in between simulation episodes. Once trained, such a system could automatically identify the ideal set of parameters to maximize the revenue of the ride-hailing platform.

References

1. Bailey, W.A., Clark, T.D.: A simulation analysis of demand and fleet size effects on taxicab service rates. In: Proceedings of the 19th Conference on Winter Simulation, pp. 838–844 (1987)
2. Bailey, W.A., Clark, T.D.: Taxi management and route control: a systems study and simulation experiment. In: Proceedings of the 24th Conference on Winter Simulation, pp. 1217–1222 (1992)
3. Bellemare, M.G., Dabney, W., Munos, R.: A distributional perspective on reinforcement learning. In: Proceedings of the 34th International Conference on Machine Learning, vol. 70, pp. 449–458 (2017)
4. Gao, Y., Jiang, D., Xu, Y.: Optimize taxi driving strategies based on reinforcement learning. Int. J. Geogr. Inf. Sci. **32**, 1677–1696 (2018)
5. Garg, N., Nazerzadeh, H.: Driver surge pricing. arXiv:1905.07544 (2021)
6. Goecks, V.G., Gremillion, G.M., Lawhern, V.J., Valasek, J., Waytowich, N.R.: Integrating behavior cloning and reinforcement learning for improved performance in dense and sparse reward environments. In: AAMAS, pp. 465–473 (2020)
7. Hausknecht, M.J., Stone, P.: Deep recurrent Q-learning for partially observable MDPs. In: AAAI Fall Symposia (2015)
8. Konda, V.R., Tsitsiklis, J.N.: Actor-critic algorithms. In: Solla, S.A., Leen, T.K., Müller, K. (eds.) Advances in Neural Information Processing Systems 12, pp. 1008–1014 (2000)
9. Lin, K., Zhao, R., Xu, Z., Zhou, J.: Efficient large-scale fleet management via multi-agent deep reinforcement learning. In: Proceedings of the 24th ACM SIGKDD International Conference on Knowledge Discovery & Data Mining, pp. 1774–1783 (2018)
10. Mnih, V., et al.: Asynchronous methods for deep reinforcement learning. In: Proceedings of the 33rd International Conference on International Conference on Machine Learning, vol. 48, pp. 1928–1937 (2016)
11. Mnih, V., et al.: Human-level control through deep reinforcement learning. Nature **7540**, 529–533 (2015)
12. Rossi, A., Barlacchi, G., Bianchini, M., Lepri, B.: Modelling taxi drivers' behaviour for the next destination prediction. IEEE Trans. Intell. Transp. Syst. **21**(7), 2980–2989 (2019)
13. Shou, Z., Di, X., Ye, J., Zhu, H., Zhang, H., Hampshire, R.: Optimal passenger-seeking policies on e-hailing platforms using Markov decision process and imitation learning. Transp. Res. Part C Emerg. Technol. **111**, 91–113 (2020)
14. Sutton, R.S., McAllester, D., Singh, S., Mansour, Y.: Policy gradient methods for reinforcement learning with function approximation. In: Proceedings of the 12th International Conference on Neural Information Processing Systems, pp. 1057–1063 (1999)
15. Torabi, F., Warnell, G., Stone, P.: Behavioral cloning from observation. In: Proceedings of the 27th International Joint Conference on Artificial Intelligence (IJCAI) (2018)
16. Zheng, S., Trott, A., Srinivasa, S., Naik, N., Gruesbeck, M., Parkes, D.C.: The AI economist: improving equality and productivity with AI-driven tax policies (2020)

Discovering Spatial High Utility Itemsets in High-Dimensional Spatiotemporal Databases

Sai Chithra Bommisetty[1], Ravikumar Penugonda[1,2(✉)], Uday Kiran Rage[2,3], Minh Son Dao[3], and Koji Zettsu[3]

[1] IIIT-RK Valley, RGUKT-AP, Vempalli, India
[2] The University of Aizu, Fukushima, Japan
[3] National Institute of Information and Communications Technology, Tokyo, Japan
{dao,zettsu}@nict.go.jp

Abstract. Finding spatial high utility itemsets (SHUIs) in a quantitative spatiotemporal database is a challenging problem of great importance in many real-world applications. Most previous studies have focused on the efficient discovery of SHUIs in a low-dimensional database. This paper advances the state-of-the-art by introducing an efficient algorithm to find SHUIs in a high-dimensional spatiotemporal database. Two novel concepts, 'spatially closed utilities of an itemset' and 'spatially non-closed utilities of an itemset,' were explored to tackle the predicament caused by the violation of downward closure property of SHUIs. The performance study shows that our algorithm is efficient and is about an order of magnitude faster than the state-of-the-art algorithm.

Keywords: Data mining · Pattern mining · Spatiotemporal database

1 Introduction

Spatial High Utility Itemset Mining (SHUIM) [3] is an important data mining model with many real-world applications. It involves finding all spatially interesting itemsets having high value (or *utility*) in a quantitative spatiotemporal database. A classic application for finding SHUIs in a database is traffic congestion analytics. It involves identifying the sets of neighboring road segments that have witnessed long traffic congestions in the data. An SHUI found in our traffic congestion database is as follows:

$$\{264, 170, 253, 177, 153, 169\} \quad [utility = 352, 312\,m].$$

The above pattern conveys that a set of neighboring road segments whose identifiers were 264, 170, 253, 177, 153, and 169 were witnessing long traffic congestions

---

S. C. Bommisetty, R. Penugonda and U. K. Rage—Equally contributed to 90% of the paper. M. S. Dao and K. Zettsu—Equally contributed to 10% of the paper.

H. Fujita et al. (Eds.): IEA/AIE 2021, LNAI 12798, pp. 53–65, 2021.
https://doi.org/10.1007/978-3-030-79457-6_5

Table 1. Spatial database

Items	Location
a	(0,0)
b	(3,4)
c	(3,-4)
d	(6,0)
e	(3,0)
f	(9,0)
g	(12,0)

Table 2. Temporal database

ts	Items
1	a,c,d
2	a,c,e,g
3	a,b,c,d,e,f
4	b,c,d,e
5	b,c,e,g
6	a,c,d
7	a,b,c,d,f
8	a,b,c,e,f

Table 3. Utility database (in 100's of mts)

ts	a	b	c	d	e	f	g
1	5	0	1	2	0	0	0
2	10	0	6	0	6	0	5
3	5	4	1	12	3	5	0
4	0	8	3	6	3	0	0
5		4	2	0	3	0	2
6	15	0	3	6	0	0	0
7	5	2	1	4	0	3	0
8	5	4	2	0	3	3	0

Table 4. SHUIs

Itemset	Utility
db	3600
dbe	3600
dc	3900
a	4500
aec	4100
ac	5900

of length 352, 312 meters in the data. Such information may be beneficial to the users for various purposes, such as monitoring the traffic, suggesting police patrol routes, and developing intelligent navigation systems.

The model of spatial high utility itemset is as follows [3]: Let $I = \{i_1, i_2, \cdots, i_m\}$, $m \geq 1$, be a set of items. A **spatial database** SD is a collection of items and their coordinates. That is, $SD = \{(i_1, C_{i_1}), (i_2, C_{i_2}), \cdots, (i_m, C_{i_m})\}$, where $C_{i_j} = \{(x_1, y_1), (x_2, y_2), \cdots, (x_p, y_p)\}, p \geq 1$, denote the set of coordinates for an item $i_j \in I$. Let $X = \{i_1, i_2, \cdots, i_k\}$, $k \geq 1$, be an **itemset**. An itemset containing k number of items is called as k-**itemset**. An itemset X is said to be an interesting **spatial itemset** if the maximum distance between any two of items is no more than the user-specified *maximum distance* ($maxDist$) constraint. That is, X is a spatial itemset if $max(Dist(i_a, i_b)|\forall i_a, i_b \in X) \leq maxDist$, where $Dist()$ is a distance function. A **temporal database**, $D = \{T_1, T_2, \cdots, T_n\}, n \geq 1$, where $T_{ts} \subseteq I$ is a transaction. Each transaction T_{ts} is associated with a timestamp $ts \in (1, n)$. Let $u(i_j, T_{ts})$ denote the **utility** of an item i_j in a transaction whose timestamp is ts. The **utility database**, UD, is the set of utility values of all items in a database. That is, $UD = \bigcup_{i_j \in I} \bigcup_{ts=1}^{n} u(i_j, T_{ts})$. The utility of an itemset X in the database D, denoted as $u(X) = \Sigma_{T_{ts} \in D^X} u(X, T_{ts})$, where $D^X \subseteq D$ represent a sub-database containing X in D. A spatial itemset X is said to be a **spatial high utility itemset** if $u(X) \geq minUtil$, where $minUtil$ represents the user-specified *minimum utility* constraint. Given a temporal database D, spatial database SD, and a utility database UD, the **problem definition of SHUIM** is to find all itemsets that have *utility* no less than the $minUtil$ and the maximum distance between its items is no more than the $maxDist$.

Example 1. Let $I = \{a, b, c, d, e, f, g\}$ be the set of items (or road segments). The spatial database of all road segments in I is shown in Table 1. The set of items a and c, i.e., $\{a, c\}$ (or ac, in short) is an itemset. This is a 2-itemset as it contains 2 items. Let Euclidean be the distance function. The distance between the items a and c, i.e., $Dist(a, c) = 5$. If the user-specified $maxDist = 5$, then ac is an interesting spatial itemset as $Dist(a, c) \leq maxDist$. A temporal database generated from I is shown in Table 2. The utility database of this table is shown in Table 3. The *utility* of an itemset ac in T_1 (or the total length of congestion observed on the neighboring road segments a and c at T_1), i.e.,

$u(ac, T_1) = u(a, T_1) + u(c, T_1) = 500 + 100 = 600$ m. The *utility* of itemset ac in the entire database (or the total length of congestion observed on the neighboring road segments a and c in the entire database), i.e., $u(ac) = u(ac, T_1) + u(ac, T_2) + u(ac, T_3) + u(ac, T_6) + u(ac, T_7) + u(ac, T_8) = 600 + 1600 + 600 + 1800 + 600 + 700 + 300 = 5900$ m. If the user-specified $minUtil = 3500$ m, then ac is considered as a SHUI because $Dist(a, c) \leq maxDist$ and $u(ac) \geq minUtil$. All SHUIs generated from Table 2 are shown in Table 4.

Uday et al. [3] described the SHUI-Miner algorithm to find all SHUIs in a database. It is a depth-first search algorithm that finds SHUIs using *projected databases*. A projected database represents a subset of a database containing a particular itemset. Constructing a projected database is a computationally expensive step concerning both memory and runtime. Consequently, finding SHUIs using SHUI-Miner is costly (or impracticable) for high-dimensional databases containing several hundred or thousands of items per transaction.

This paper aims to advance the state-of-the-art by presenting an efficient algorithm to find SHUIs in a high-dimensional quantitative spatiotemporal database. Our key contributions are as follows: First, we introduce the High Dimensional Spatial High Utility Itemset-Miner (HDSHUI-Miner) algorithm to find desired itemsets in a database. HDSHUI-Miner is inspired by HMiner [4] as it also uses a compact utility list structure to efficiently store utility information. We present the notion of 'spatially closed utility' and 'spatially non-closed utility' of an itemset to store utility values compactly. Second, the paper presents a method to determine duplicate transactions using the concept of spatial virtual hyperlink structure. Third, the article applies several pruning strategies for efficiently mining SHUIs. Rigorous experimental evaluation is performed on real-world databases to demonstrate the utility of the proposed algorithm. We also made a comparative assessment of HDSHUI-Miner against the state-of-the-art SHUI-Miner algorithm. HDSHUI-Miner has shown significant improvement in memory consumption and execution performance on most of the datasets studied.

The rest of this paper is organized as follows. Section 2 describes the related work. Section 3 introduces HDSHUI-Miner. Section 4 reports the experimental results. Finally, Sect. 5 concludes the paper with future research directions.

2   Related Work

Frequent itemset mining [1] is an important model in data mining with many applications [5]. However, this model's successful industrial application has been hindered by its inability to discover interesting patterns that exist in a quantitative transactional database. When confronted with this problem in real-world applications, researchers [6,7] have exploited the notion of *utility* (or value) to discover high utility itemsets in a quantitative transactional database. A recent survey on high utility itemset mining algorithms may be found in [2]. Although the high utility itemset model considers the item's *utility* values, it completely disregards the items' spatiotemporal characteristics in the database.

Consequently, the basic model of high utility itemset is inadequate to discover only those high utility itemsets whose items are close to each other in a coordinate system.

Uday et al. [3] presented a generic SHUI model to discover regularities in a spatiotemporal database. A depth-first search algorithm, called SHUI-Miner, was also introduced to find all SHUIs in a database. We have observed that SHUI-Miner suffers from performance issues while dealing with high-dimensional databases. To tackle this problem, we present HDSHUI-Miner to find SHUIs in a high-dimensional spatiotemporal database effectively.

3   Proposed Algorithm

3.1   Basic Idea: Pruning Techniques to Reduce the Search Space

High utility itemsets discovered using *utility* measure do not satisfy the apriori property. Thus, increasing the search space and the overall computational cost of finding the desired itemsets. When confronted with this problem in the real-world applications, researchers have employed *utility* upper-bound measures, namely *non-closed utility*, *non-closed remaining utility* and *non-closed prefix utility* [4], to prune the search space and reduce the computational cost of finding the high *utility* itemsets. Since these *utility* upper-bound measures completely ignore the items' spatial information in the database, they were inadequate to reduce the search for finding SHUIs effectively. In this context, we have introduced tighter *utility* upper-bound measures, namely *spatially non-closed utility*, *spatially non-closed remaining utility*, and *spatially non-closed prefix utility*, by exploiting the spatial information of the items in the database. We found that the proposed measures reduce the search space effectively. We now describe these *utility* upper-bound measures.

Definition 1. (Probable maximum utility of an item i_j in a database. [3]*)* Let N_{i_j} denote the neighbors of an item $i_j \in I$, i.e., $\forall i_k \in N_{i_j}, dist(i_j, i_k) \leq maxDist$. The probable maximum utility *(pmu)* of an item in a database, denoted as $pmu(i_j) = \sum_{T_{ts} \in D^{i_j}} (u(i_j, T_{ts}) + \sum_{i_k \in T_{ts} \cap i_k \in N_{i_j}} u(i_k, T_{ts}))$.

Example 2. The neighbors for the item a in Table 1 are b, c, and e. Thus, $N_a = \{bce\}$. The *probable maximum utility* of a in the first transaction T_1, i.e., $pmu(a, T_1) = u(a, T_1) + u(c, T_1) = 500 + 100 = 600$ m. Similarly, $pmu(a, T_2) = 2200$ m, $pmu(a, T_3) = 1300$ m, $pmu(a, T_6) = 1800$ m, $pmu(a, T_7) = 800$ m, and $pmu(a, T_8) = 1400$ m. The pmu of a in the database, i.e., $pmu(a) = pmu(a, T_1) + pmu(a, T_2) + pmu(a, T_3) + pmu(a, T_6) + pmu(a, T_7) + pmu(a, T_8) = 8100$ m.

Definition 2. (Candidate items.) *An item $i_j \in I$ is said to be a candidate item (or 1-itemset) if $pmu(i_j) \geq minUtil$. Let CI denote the set of candidate items in pmu ascending order.*

Example 3. The pmu values for the items a, b, c, d, e, f, and g in Table 2 are 8100, 7100, 11200, 6700, 9000, 2500, and 700, respectively. If $minUtil = 3500$, then a, b, c, d, e, and f are considered as candidate items because their pmu value is no less than the $minUtil$ value. In contrast, item g is not a candidate item because $pmu(g) < minUtil$. Thus, we prune the item g from the database. The complete set of candidate items in ascending order of pmu values, i.e., $CI = \{d, b, a, e, c\}$.

Definition 3. (*Spatially closed utility of* X.) Let $\bar{D} \subseteq D$ represents a sorted temporal database containing candidate items in CI order. Let $\widehat{D} \subseteq \bar{D}$ be a (sub-)database such that $\forall T_{ts} \in \widehat{D}$, $T_{ts} \supseteq N_X$, where $N_X = \cup_{\forall i_j \in X} N_{i_j}$ denote the set of neighboring items of all items in X. The spatially closed utility of an itemset X in the database D is denoted as $SCU(X)$, and is computed as follows:

$$SCU(X) = \sum_{\forall T_{ts} \in \widehat{D}} u(X, T_{ts}) = \sum_{\forall T_{ts} \in \widehat{D}} \sum_{\forall i_j \in X} u(i_j, T_{ts}). \qquad (1)$$

Example 4. The sorted temporal database constituting of candidate items is shown in Table 6. Consider the itemset db in Table 6. The set of neighbors of d and b, i.e., $N_{db} = N_d \cup N_b = \{d, a, e\} \cup \{b, c, e\} = \{d, b, a, e, c\}$. In Table 6, the set of items in N_{db} appear only in the transaction whose timestamp is 3. Therefore, $\widehat{D} = \{T_3\}$. The spatially closed utility of an itemset db in D, i.e., $SCU(X) = \sum_{T_{ts} \in \widehat{D}} \sum_{i_j \in X} u(i_j, T_{ts}) = u(d, T_3) + u(b, T_3) = 1600 \ m$.

Definition 4. (*Spatially closed remaining utility of an itemset* X.) The spatially closed remaining utility of an itemset X in a database D is denoted as $SCRU(X)$, and is computed as follows:

$$SCRU(X) = \sum_{\forall T_{ts} \in \widehat{D}} \sum_{\forall i_j \in (T_{ts} \cap E(X))} u(i_j, T_{ts}) \qquad (2)$$

where, $E(X)$ represent the set of items that can extend an itemset.

Example 5. The items that can extend an itemset db, i.e., $E(db) = CI - \{d, b\} = \{a, e, c\}$. The $\widehat{D}$ contains only one transaction, which is T_3. The common items in $T_3 \cap E(db) = \{d, b, a, e, c\} \cap \{a, e, c\} = \{a, e, c\}$. Thus, the spatially closed remaining utility of an itemset db in the database D, i.e., $SCRU(db) = \sum_{i_j \in \{a, e, c\}} u(i_j, T_3) = u(a, T_3) + u(e, T_3) + u(c, T_3) = 500 + 100 + 300 = 900 \ m$.

Definition 5. (*Spatially closed prefix utility of an itemset* X.) The spatially closed prefix utility of an itemset X in a database D is denoted as $SCPU(X)$, and is computed as follows:

$$SCPU(X) = \sum_{\forall T_{ts} \in \widehat{D}} \sum_{j=1}^{|X|-1} u(i_j, T_{ts}). \qquad (3)$$

Example 6. The spatially closed prefix utility of an itemset db in D, i.e., $SCPU(db) = \sum_{T_{ts} \in \widehat{D}} \sum_{j=1}^{|db|-1} u(i_j, T_{ts}) = u(d, T_3) = 1200 \ m$.

Definition 6. *The remaining utility [7] of an itemset X in a transaction T_{ts} is denoted as $RU(X, T_{ts})$ and is computed as,*

$$RU(X, T_{ts}) = \sum_{i_j \in T_{ts} \cap E(X)} u(i_j, T_{ts}) \qquad (4)$$

Example 7. The *remaining utility of db in T_3, i.e., $RU(db, T_3) = U(a, T_3) + U(c, T_3) + U(e, T_3) = 500 + 100 + 300 = 900$ m. Similarly, $RU(db, T_4) = 600$ m and $RU(db, T_7) = 600$ m.*

Definition 7. *The remaining utility of an itemset X in a database D is defined as $RU(X)$ and is computed as,*

$$RU(X) = \sum_{X \subseteq T_{ts} \in D} RU(X, T_{ts}). \qquad (5)$$

Example 8. Continuing with the previous example, the remaining utility of an itemset db in the entire database, i.e., $RU(db) = RU(db, T_3) + RU(db, T_4) + RU(db, T_7) = 900 + 600 + 600 = 2100\,m.$

Definition 8. *The spatially non-closed utility (SNU), spatially non-closed remaining utility (SNRU) and the spatially non-closed prefix utility (SNPU) of an itemset X in the database D are respectively defined as follows:*

$$SNU(X) = U(X) - SCU(X) \qquad (6)$$
$$SNRU(X) = RU(X) - SCRU(X) \qquad (7)$$
$$SNPU(X) = PU(X) - SCPU(X) \qquad (8)$$

Property 1. **(Pruning technique 1.)** Given two itemsets X and Y if $SCU(X) + SCRU(X) + SNU(X) + SNRU(X) - \sum_{\forall T_{ts} \in D, X \in t_{ts} \text{ and } Y \notin t_{ts}} \text{-} \forall Y' \supseteq Y$ and $\forall X' \supseteq X$, $X'Y' \notin SHUI$.

Property 2. **(Pruning technique 2.)** Given two itemsets X and Y if $SCU(X) + SCRU(X) + \sum_{XY \subseteq T_{ts} \in D} SNU(X, T_{ts}) + SNRU(X, T_{ts}) \leq minUtil$, then $\forall Y' \supseteq Y$ and $\forall X' \supseteq X$, $\bar{X}'Y' \notin SHUI$.

In addition to the above pruning techniques, we also employ other pruning techniques discussed in SHUI-Miner.

Property 3. **(Pruning technique 3 [3].)** If $pmu(X) \leq minUtil$, then neither X nor its supersets can be SHUIs.

Property 4. **(Pruning technique 4 [7].)** Let X and Y be two patterns such that $Y \subset X$. If $u(X) + RU(X) < minUtil$, then neither X nor Y can be SHUIs.

Property 5. **(Pruning technique 5 [4].)** Estimated Utility Co-occurrence Structure (*EUCS*) is a triangular matrix and is defined as $EUCS[i, j] = TWU(X = \{i, j\})$. If *EUCS* of a 2-itemset X is less than $minUtil$, then none of the supersets of X can be *SHUIs*.

3.2 HDSHUI-Miner

The procedure for finding SHUIs in a database using HDSHUI-Miner is presented in Algorithms 1, 2, 3, 4 and 5. Before we describe each of these algorithms, we describe the structure of Compressed Spatial Utility List (CSUL), which is used for finding all SHUIs in the database.

Table 5. Neighboring items of an item in Table 1

Item	Neighbours	Item	Neighbours
a	b,c,e	e	a,b,c,d
b	a,d,e	f	d,g
c	a,d,e	g	f
d	b,c,e,f		

Table 6. Sorted temporal database of Table 2 containing only candidate items

ts	Items	ts	Items
1	d,a,c	5	b,e,c
2	a,e,c	6	d,a,c
3	d,b,a,e,c	7	d,b,a,c
4	d,b,e,c	8	b,a,e,c

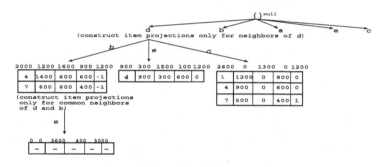

Fig. 1. Mining lists in HDSHUI-Miner for item d

Construction of CSUL for Each Candidate Item. The CSUL of an item-set $X = \{i_1, i_2, \cdots, i_k\}$ is a data structure that stores itemset information in a compact form. CSUL maintains (1) aggregated information such as $SNU(X)$, $SNRU(X)$, $SCU(X)$, $SCRU(X)$, $SCPU(X)$, and (2) transaction level information using transaction stamp list (or ts-list). Each tuple or entry in the ts-list is a quintuple $\langle ts, SNU(X, T_{ts}), SNRU(X, T_{ts}), SNPU(X, T_{ts}), PPOS(X, T_{ts})\rangle$. The term PPOS refers to previous item's ts-list position of the same transaction and is defined as follows:

$$PPOS(X, T_{ts}) = \begin{cases} |CSUL[Prev(X_k, T_{ts}).ts\text{-}list]|, & \text{if } Prev(X_k)! = -1 \\ -1, & \text{otherwise} \end{cases}$$

CSUL Generation for 1-Itemset: Algorithm 1 describes the construction of CSUL for each candidate item. First, we calculate the *pmu* values for each item by scanning the database. The items having *pmu* less than *minUtil* will be pruned from the database (line 2 in Algorithm 1). The remaining candidate items

---

Algorithm 1. Main(temporalDatabase (D), spatialDatabase (SD), minimum utility $(minUtil)$, maximum distance $(maxDist)$)

1: Let $CSUL^X = \{ts, snu, snru, snpu, ppos\}$ represent the compressed spatial utility list of an itemset X.
2: Scan D and compute pmu for all 1-itemsets. Prune the items that have pmu value less than $minUtil$ and sort the remaining items in ascending order of their pmu value. Let CI denote this sorted list of candidate items. Initialize, CSUL for each candidate item. Initialize a hash table HT to record distinct transactions constituting of only candidate items.
3: **for all** $i_j \in CI$ **do**
4:     **for all** $i_k \in CI$, $j \neq k$ **do**
5:         **if** $Dist(i_j, i_k) \leq maxDist$ **then**
6:             add i_k as neighbor of i_j;
7: **for** each transaction T_p in D **do**
8:     Construct $\widehat{T_p} \subseteq T_p$ with candidate items in CI order. Set remaining utility $RU = 0$. Let i_k be the last time in $\widehat{T_j}$.
9:     **if** $\widehat{T_p} \notin HT$ **then**
10:         HT.add($\widehat{T_p}, CSUL^{i_k}.size()$);
11:         **for** each item $i_j \in reverseOrder(\widehat{T_p})$ **do**
12:             $CSUL^{i_j}.add(p, u(i_j, \widehat{T_p}), ru, 0, PPOS(i_j, \widehat{T_p}))$;
13:             Update $ru+ = u(i_j, \widehat{T_p})$
14:     **else**
15:         Set $pos = HT.get(\widehat{T_p})$
16:         **for** each item $i_j \in reverseOrder(\widehat{T_p})$ **do**
17:             Update $CSUL^{i_j}.snu[pos]+ = u(i_j, \widehat{T_p})$ and $CSUL^{i_j}.ru[pos]+ = ru$;
18:             Update $pos = CSUL^{i_j}[HT.get(\widehat{T_p})][pos].PPOS$
19:     build EUCS
20:     HUI = Explore-Search-Tree(ϕ, CSUL, $minUtil$,all promising items)

Algorithm 2. Explore-Search-Tree(R the itemset prefix, CSULs, $minUtil$, Npx:neighbours of Prefix Itemset.)

1: **for** each utility position i in CSULs **do**
2:     $X = CSULs[i]$
3:     **if** X.item not in Npx **then**
4:         continue
5:     **if** $u(X) \geq minUtil$ **then**
6:         SHUI = $\{SHUI \cup X\}$
7:     **if** $u(X) + RU(X) \geq minUtil$ **then**
8:         NewCSUL=CSUL which are Neighbours of X.
9:         exCSULs = ConstructCSUL(X,NewCSUL, $minUtil$)
10:         R = $\{R \cup X\}$ //update prefix with extension
11:         Explore-Search-Tree(R, exCSULs, $minUtil$,Npx $\cap$ $Neighbours of X.item$)

Algorithm 3. ConstructCSUL(X, CSULs, $minUtil$)

1: $sz = |CSULs|$, $extSz = sz$ //if a transaction has all extensions
2: **for** each position j in sz **do**
3:     **if** $EUCS[X, CSULs[j]] < minUtil$ **then**
4:        Set $exCSULs[j] = NULL$ and $--extSz$;
5:     **else**
6:        exCSULs[j]={}, ey[j] = 0 //track ts position in CSULs
7:        LAU[j]=$SCU(X)+SCRU(X)+SNU(X)+SNRU(X)$ {$Pruning technique 1$}

8:        CUTIL[j]=$SCU(X)+SCRU(X)$ {$Pruning technique 2$}
9: Initialize a hash table HT = {}
10: **for** each tslist element ex in X **do**
11:     newT = ϕ
12:     **for** each j in sz **do**
13:        **if** exCSULs[j] == NULL **then**
14:           go to step 12
15:        eylist = CSULs[j].tslist
16:        **while** $ey[j] \langle |eylist|$ and $eylist[ey[j]].ts \rangle ex.ts$ **do**
17:           increment ey[j]
18:        **if** $ey[j] < |eylist|$ and $eylist[ey[j]] = ex.ts$ **then**
19:           newT={ $newT U j$ }
20:        **else**
21:           $LAU = LAU - SNU(X, ex.ts) - SNRU(X, ex.ts)$
22:           **if** $(LAU < minUtil)$ **then**
23:              $exCSULs[j] = NULL$ and $---extSz$;
24:     **if** $|newT| == extSz$ **then**
25:        Update-Closed(X, CSULs, st, exCSULs, newT, ex.ts)
26:     **else**
27:        $dupPos = HT.get(newT)$//check if a duplicate exists
28:        **if** dupPos == NULL **then**
29:           $HT[newT] = |CSULs[xk].tslist|$ //xk is the last item in newT
30:           Insert new entries in exCSULs for each newT
31:        **else**
32:           Update-Element(X, CSULs, st, exCSULs, newT, ex.ts,dupPos)
33:     **for** each j in sz **do**
34:        increment CUTIL[j] by $SNU(X, ts) + nru$
35: filter exCSULs where $CUTIL[j] < minUtil$ or $exCSULs[j] = NULL$
36: return exCSULs

Algorithm 4. Update-Closed(X, CSUL, st, exCSULs, newT, ts)

1: set $nru = 0$
2: **for** each element j in reverseOrder(newT) **do**
3:     Set $ey = CSUL[st + j]$;
4:     Set $exCSUL[j].SCU+ = SNU(X, ts) + SNU(ey, ts) - SNPU(X, ts)$
5:     Set $exCSUL[j].SCRU+ = nru$, and $exCSULs[j].SCPU+ = SNU(X, ts)$
6:     Set $nru+ = (SNU(ey, ts) - SNPU(X, ts))$

Algorithm 5. Update-Element(X, CSUL, st, exCSUL, newT, ts, pos)

1: set $nru = 0$
2: **for** each element j in reverseOrder(newT) **do**
3:     Set $ey = CSUL[st + j]$
4:     $update exCSUL[j].tslist$ at pos with$\langle \_, SNU(X, ts) \quad + \quad SNU(ey, ts) \quad - SNPU(X, ts), nru, SNU(X, ts), \_\rangle$
5:     $nru = nru + SNU(ey, ts) - SNPU(X, ts)$
6:     $pos = [ey.tslist, pos].PPOS$ //previous item position

---

are sorted in pmu ascending order. Let CI denote the sorted list of candidate items. Next, find neighbors for each candidate item by scanning the spatial database. The neighbors for each candidate item are shown in Table 5 (lines 3 to 6 in Algorithm 1). Now, we scan the database the second time and construct $CSUL$ for each item as follows. Let us consider first transaction, i.e., T_1, containing the items d, a, and c in CI order. Choosing the last item c, we construct its CSUL by adding an element $\langle 1, 100, 0, 0, 0 \rangle$. Next, we create $CSUL$ for item a by adding an element $\langle 1, 500, 100, 0, 0 \rangle$. Finally, the CSUL is created for item d by adding an element $\langle 1, 200, 600, 0, -1 \rangle$ (lines 9 to 13 in Algorithm 1). Similar process is repeated for the remaining transactions in Table 6, and CSUL for each item are updated accordingly. To achieve memory efficiency, CSUL were updated when identifications transactions are encountered (lines 15 to 18 in Algorithm 1). Next, we construct a triangular matrix known as PUCS (line 19 in Algorithm 1). Next, Explore-Search-Tree method is called to find spatial high utility k-itemsets (line 20 in Algorithm 1).

Tree Exploration Process: Algorithms 2, algo:Main3, algo:Main4 and algo:Main5 describe the tree exploration process to find all SHUIs in a database. It involves recursively exploring the search path in the depth-first search manner to mine $SHUIs$. The pruning techniques described in Properties 1, 2, 32, 4 and 5 were applied as part of the utility construction process to limit the search space and computational cost of finding the SHUIs.

Utility List Construction: In the Utility list construction we are going to process each element in the prefix of X. For each element ex there are two sub stages. In the first stage, we determine all CSULs that contain transaction ex.tslist. If a particular CSUL does not contain ex.tslist then we invoke pruning Property 1, otherwise all items are inserted into new transaction newT. In the second stage, the algorithm check's whether the transaction is closed or not if so, we update the utility values of SCU, SCRU and SCPU. Otherwise we check whether it is a duplicate transaction (similar as above), at last we invoke pruning Property 2. We repeat the process till all the tslist elements in X are processed. The recursive mining of HDSHUI-Miner is shown in Fig. 1.

4   Experimental Results

In this section, we show that the HDSHUI-Miner outperforms the SHUI-Miner with respect to both memory and runtime. More important, we show that HDSHUI-Miner is order of magnitude times faster than the SHUI-Miner in high-dimensional and dense databases.

Both SHUI-Miner and HDSHUI-Miner algorithms were written in Java and executed on an Ubuntu 18.04 machine with a 2.6 GHz processor and 8 GB RAM. The experiments have been conducted on the real-world (**BMS-WebView-1**, *Congestion* and **Chess**) databases. The BMS-WebView-1 is a sparse database containing 497 items and 59,602 transactions. The minimum, average, and maximum transaction lengths of this database are 1, 2.5, and 267, respectively. The Congestion database is a high-dimensional database containing 287 items and 1,045 transactions. The minimum, average, and maximum transaction lengths of this database are 40, 133, and 344, respectively. The Chess is a dense database containing 75 items and 3,196 transactions. The minimum, average, and maximum transaction lengths of this database are 37, 37, and 37, respectively.

Figure 2 shows the number of SHUIs generated in BMS-WebView-1, Congestion, and Chess databases at different $minUtil$ values. We can observe that increase in $minUtil$ decreases the number of SHUIs. It is because of the reason that many itemsets have failed to satisfy the increased $minUtil$ value. Please note that both SHUI-Miner and HDSHUI-Miner generate the same set of SHUIs in a database.

Figure 3 shows the runtime requirements of SHUI-Miner and HDSHUI-Miner algorithms in BMS-WebView-1, Congestion, and Chess databases at different $minUtil$ values. We can observe that increase in $minUtil$ decreases the runtime requirements of both algorithms. However, HDSHUI-Miner was faster than SHUI-Miner at any given $minUtil$ in all of the databases. More important, at low $minUtil$ values, HDSHUI-Miner is faster than SHUI-Miner by order of magnitude in dense and high-dimensional databases.

Figure 4 shows SHUI-Miner and HDSHUI-Miner algorithms' memory requirements in BMS-WebView-1, Congestion, and Chess databases at different

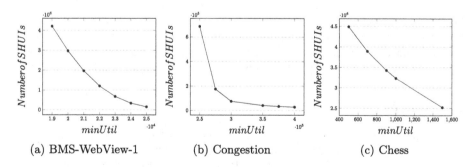

(a) BMS-WebView-1   (b) Congestion   (c) Chess

Fig. 2. SHUIs generated by both algorithms

minUtil values. We can observe that increase in *minUtil* decreases the algorithms' memory requirements; however, HDSHUI-Miner consumes less memory than SHUI-Miner at any given *minUtil* in all of the databases.

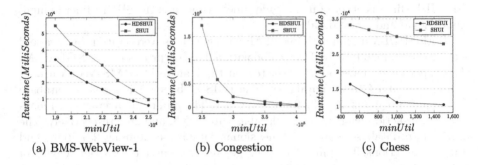

Fig. 3. Runtime requirements of HDSHUI and SHUI algorithms

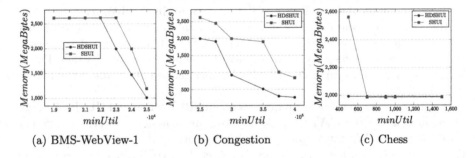

Fig. 4. Memory requirement of HDSHUI and SHUI algorithms

5   Conclusions and Future Work

In this paper, we have proposed a novel algorithm to discover SHUIs in a quantitative spatiotemporal database. We have also introduced new utility upperbound measures to reduce the search space and the computational cost of finding the SHUIs. Experimental results demonstrate that our algorithm is both memory and runtime efficient over the state-of-the-algorithm. As part of future work, we would like to extend our study to find top-k SHUIs in a database.

References

1. Agrawal, R., Imieliński, T., Swami, A.: Mining association rules between sets of items in large databases. In: ACM SIGMOD Record. **22**, 207–216 (1993)
2. Gan, W., Lin, J.C.W., Fournier-Viger, P., Chao, H.C., Hong, T.P., Fujita, H.: A survey of incremental high-utility itemset mining. Wiley Interdiscip. Rev. Data Min. Knowl. Discov. **8**(2), e1242 (2018)

3. Kiran, R.U., Zettsu, K., Toyoda, M., Fournier-Viger, P., Reddy, P.K., Kitsuregawa, M.: Discovering spatial high utility itemsets in spatiotemporal databases. In: SSDBM, pp. 49–60. ACM (2019)
4. Krishnamoorthy, S.: HMiner:: Efficiently mining high utility itemsets. xpert Syst. Appl. **90**, 168–183 (2017)
5. Luna, J.M., Fournier-Viger, P., Ventura, S.: Frequent itemset mining: A 25 years review. Wiley Interdiscip. Rev. Data Min. Knowl. Discov. 9(6), e1329 (2019)
6. Uday Kiran, R., Yashwanth Reddy, T., Fournier-Viger, P., Toyoda, M., Krishna Reddy, P., Kitsuregawa, M.: Efficiently finding high utility-frequent itemsets using cutoff and suffix utility. In: Yang, Q., Zhou, Z.-H., Gong, Z., Zhang, M.-L., Huang, S.-J. (eds.) PAKDD 2019. LNCS (LNAI), vol. 11440, pp. 191–203. Springer, Cham (2019). https://doi.org/10.1007/978-3-030-16145-3_15
7. Yao, H., Hamilton, H.J., Butz, C.J.: A foundational approach to mining itemset utilities from databases. In: SIAM. pp. 482–486 (2004)

A Single-Stage Tree-Structure-Based Approach to Determine Fuzzy Average-Utility Itemsets

Tzung-Pei Hong[1,2(✉)], Meng-Ping Ku[2], Hsiu-Wei Chiu[1], Wei-Ming Huang[3], Shu-Min Li[2], and Jerry Chun-Wei Lin[4]

[1] National University of Kaohsiung, Kaohsiung 811, Taiwan
tphong@nuk.edu.tw, fuvu7620250@gmail.com
[2] National Sun Yat-Sen University, Kaohsiung 804, Taiwan
peter0617ku@gamil.com, smli@cse.nsysu.edu.tw
[3] China Steel, Inc., Kaohsiung 806, Taiwan
granthill168@gmail.com
[4] Western Norway University of Applied Science, 5063 Bergen, Norway
jerrylin@ieee.org

Abstract. Fuzzy utility mining (FUM) techniques are used to mine high fuzzy utility itemsets for market analysis. They consider items that include purchase quantities, unit profits, and linguistic terms representing quantity information. Although FUM facilitates market analysis, it has the measurement problem in which the fuzzy utility value for an itemset may be higher than that for its subset. In the past, a tree-based mining method was proposed to find fuzzy average-utility itemsets using a two-stage strategy tree-based method with an average-utility measure. It was, however, computationally expensive because two-stage processing was needed. To handle this, we propose a single-stage tree-structure-based method that uses an external list for each node in the tree to find fuzzy average-utility itemsets efficiently. Experimental results show that the proposed method outperforms the former approach in terms of execution time.

Keywords: FP-growth · Fuzzy theory · Fuzzy average-utility mining · Tree structure

1 Introduction

Pattern mining is an active subfield of data mining used to find interesting knowledge patterns in a large database, where mined rules are used for decision support. The Apriori algorithm [1, 2] considers item frequencies in a binary database, but the number of items sold or their importance is ignored. Utility mining (UM) was thus proposed [3], where items in a database include the purchase quantities and relative importance indicating unit profits or weights. Its goal is to find high-utility itemsets, which indicate potential importance; however, the downward closure (DC) property does not hold in UM. Two-stage mining is used to improve mining efficiency [4]. In the UM mining process, larger itemsets in a transaction tend to have a greater utility value than that of their sub-itemsets.

© Springer Nature Switzerland AG 2021
H. Fujita et al. (Eds.): IEA/AIE 2021, LNAI 12798, pp. 66–72, 2021.
https://doi.org/10.1007/978-3-030-79457-6_6

Hence using the same threshold to evaluate itemsets, regardless of their length, is an unfair strategy. The average-utility mining algorithm is used to normalize itemset lengths [6]. In contrast to UM, FUM jointly considers the characteristics of UM and fuzzy reasoning to identify high fuzzy utility itemsets and handle quantity information better via its transformed linguistic terms [5]. However, as with UM, the DC property does not hold for FUM either. Thus, two-stage [9] and two-stage tree-structure [8] based approaches were proposed to find desired itemsets using an average-utility measurement. However, their two-stage nature makes these methods computationally expensive. To efficiently extract fuzzy average-utility itemsets, a single-stage tree structure method based on FP-tree [7] is proposed, in which each node in the tree has an external array list to store mined information. Experiments demonstrate improved execution times with respect to [8]. However, adding list information for each node also increases memory consumption compared to [8].

2 Related Work

The frequent itemset mining, named Apriori [1, 2], is used to find knowledge patterns in which their frequency counting is executed by scanning multiple databases. To account for the performance, the FP-Growth [7] is then proposed by applying tree structure to store mined information, reducing the database scans. The Apriori is useful, but it does not take into account item quantities or unit profits for items. To overcome this, relative importance based on profit and item quantity is considered using utility mining [3]. The utility values of itemsets are used to evaluate whether they are useful. One phenomenon of UM is that since the utility value of an itemset in a transaction may be larger than those of its subsets, it is unfair to use the same threshold to determine different itemsets. Average-utility measurement accounts for those [6, 11–13]. FUM [5] is superior to UM in that it efficiently explains quantitative information. By using the membership function of items, item quantities are transformed into fuzzy terms where they possess semantic meaning in item amounts. The FUM process derives actual itemsets with their fuzzy utility values satisfying the threshold along with the quantitative values of items, profits, and semantic meaning in item amounts. However, FUM shares the limitation of UM: the actual value for a larger itemset may be higher than that of a smaller itemset. Two fuzzy average-utility methods for FUM have thus been proposed [8, 9]. An over-estimation model is used to avoid information loss and a two-stage algorithm with this model is designed for efficient mining [9]. To improve the efficiency in [9], Hong et al. consider a two-stage tree-based method [8]. Here, we propose an alternative with shorter execution times than [8]. An external list containing mined information is embedded within each node in the tree, performing for single-stage operation.

3 Definition

Let D be a transaction database, and the items in D are represented as $I = \{i_1, i_2, ..., i_Q\}$, where each item i_n has its own profit, denoted as $p(i_n)$. The database is the set of transactions denoted as $D = \{t_1, t_2, ..., t_P\}$. Each t_m in D contains purchased item i_n with quantities v_{mn}. A set of membership functions (MFs) is given in advance, which represents the membership degree of each item. Given the *MF* for an item, each quantity value v_{mn} in D is converted into a fuzzy set $f_{mn} = (\frac{f_{mn1}}{R_{n1}} + \frac{f_{mn2}}{R_{n2}} + \cdots + \frac{f_{mnl}}{R_{nl}} + \frac{f_{mnh}}{R_{nh}})$, where h is the number of membership functions for i_n, R_{nl} is the l-th fuzzy term of i_n, and f_{mnl} is the fuzzy membership value of v_{mn} in R_{nl}.

Shown in Table 1 is a transaction database that contains the items and the item quantities for each transaction. Table 2 is the utility table, which records the unit profit of each item. The membership functions are shown in Fig. 1, where we assume that the *MFs* of all the items are the same. We use the *MFs* to divide the quantities into fuzzy regions L, M, and H. The above information is used as an example of the definition.

Table 1. A transaction database

Transaction	(Item, quantity)
t_1	$(A, 2)$, $(B, 6)$, $(C, 2)$, $(D, 6)$
t_2	$(A, 4)$, $(B, 5)$, $(C, 5)$, $(D, 4)$
t_3	$(B, 1)$, $(C, 8)$, $(D, 4)$

Table 2. A utility table

Item	Profit
A	5
B	6
C	2
D	4

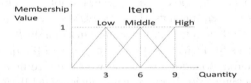

Fig. 1. Membership functions

Definition 1. The fuzzy average utility of a fuzzy item R_{nl} in i_n in t_m is $fau_{mnl} = f_{mnl} * v_{mn} * p(i_n)$, where v_{mn} is the quantity of i_n in t_m, f_{mnl} is the fuzzy value of R_{nl} according to the *MF* of i_n, and $p(i_n)$ is the individual profit for i_n. According to the *MF* in Fig. 1, $\{A\}$ with quantity 4 in t_2 in Table 1 is converted to $\{0.33/A.L, 0.67/A.M\}$, yielding a *fau* value of $0.67 * 4 * 5 (= 13.4)$ for $\{A.M\}$. All fuzzy items from Table 1 are calculated and shown in Table 3.

Definition 2. The fuzzy average utility of each fuzzy itemset S in t_m is $fau_{mS} = \frac{1}{|S|} *$ $f_{mS} * \sum_{R_{nl} \in S} \left[v_{mn} * p(i_n) \right]$, where $|S|$ is the number of R_{nl} and f_{mS} is the minimum fuzzy value for R_{nl}, where $R_{nl} \in S$. Take $\{A.L, B.M\}$ in t_1 as an example. According to the MF in Fig. 1, its integrated fuzzy value is $min\{0.67, 1\}$, which is 0.67. Thus, its $fau_{1,\{A.L, B.M\}}$ is $\frac{1}{2} * 0.67 * (2 * 5 + 6 * 6) = 15.41$.

Table 3. Fuzzy average utility values

Tid.	(Fuzzy item, fuzzy average utility value)	$mtfau_m$
t_1	$(A.L, 6.67)$, $(B.M, 36)$, $(C.L, 2.67)$, $(D.M, 24)$	36
$t2$	$(A.L, 13.33)$,$(A.M, 6.67)$,$(B.L, 10)$,$(B.M, 20)$,$(C.L, 3.33)$,$(C.M, 6.67)$, $(D.L, 1.33)$	20
$t3$	$(B.L, 2)$, $(C.M, 5.33)$, $(C.H, 10.67)$, $(D.L, 10.67)$, $(D.M, 5.33)$	10.67

Definition 3. The actual fuzzy average utility of each fuzzy itemset S in D is expressed as $afau_S = \sum_{S \subseteq t_m \cap t_m \in D} fau_{mS}$. For example, the $afau_{\{A.L, B.M\}}$ in D is $fau_{1,\{A.L, B.M\}} +$ $fau_{2,\{A.L, B.M\}} = 0.5 * 0.67 * (2 * 5 + 6 * 6) + 0.5 * 0.67 * (4 * 5 + 5 * 6) = 32.16$.

Definition 4. Let $MinFAUtil$ be the given threshold. A fuzzy itemset S is considered a high fuzzy average-utility itemset $HFAUI$ and $afau_S \geq MinFAUtil$ holds. Let $MinFAUtil$ = 30. Since the $afau_{\{A.L, B.M\}}$ is 32.16, $\{A.L, B.M\}$ is an $HFAUI$. However, $afau_{\{A.L\}}$ is $0.67 * 10 + 0.67 * 20 = 20.1$, so $\{A.L\}$ is not a $HFAUI$, because the DC in fuzzy average-utility mining does not hold.

To take this into account, we use the over-estimation model [8] for fuzzy average-utility mining. The definitions for this model are given below.

Definition 5. The maximum fuzzy average utility of an item i_n in t_m is $mfau_{mn} =$ $\max_{R_{nl} \subseteq i_n \cap i_n \in t_m} \{fau_{mn1}, fau_{mn2}, \ldots, fau_{mnh}\}$. For example, the $mfau_A$ in t_2 is 13.33.

Definition 6. The maximum transaction fuzzy average utility in t_m is $mtfau_m =$ $\max_{i_n \subseteq t_m} mfau_{mn}$. For example, the $mtfau_2$ is 20.

Definition 7. The fuzzy average-utility upper bound of a fuzzy itemset S is $fauub_S =$ $\sum_{S \subseteq t_m \cap t_m \in D} mtfau_m$. Since $\{A.L\}$ exists in t_1 and t_2, its $fauub_{\{A.L\}}$ is 56.

Definition 8. The fuzzy itemset S is considered the high fuzzy average-utility upper-bound itemset $HFAUUBI$ and $fauub_S \geq MinFAUtil$ holds. For example, $fauub_{\{A.L\}}$ is 56, which is greater than $MinFAUtil$, so $\{A.L\}$ is an $HFAUUBI$.

4 Proposed FHFAUIM Algorithm

This algorithm, called Fast High Fuzzy Average-Utility Itemset Mining (FHFAUIM), enhances the performance for fuzzy average-utility mining compared to High Fuzzy Average-Utility Itemset Mining (HFAUIM) [8]. An external list that stores fuzzy item's transaction ID, fuzzy value, and utility value is added to the tree node. Thus, the mined process can be performed directly in a single phase. Below we list the steps of the algorithm:

Step 1. Based on the *MFs* for all items, convert the quantities in *D* into a fuzzy set.

Step 2. Calculate the *mfau* value of each item in each transaction.

Step 3. Find the *mtfau* value of each transaction.

Step 4. Initialize the candidate 1-table ($HFAUUBI_1$) table into an empty table with three attributes: fuzzy itemset *S*, its *fauub_S* value, and its frequency.

Step 5. Store fuzzy items in *D* into the $HFAUUBI_1$ table and get the *fauub_S* for each.

Step 6. Filter each fuzzy itemset *S* in the $HFAUUBI_1$ table: if *fauub_S* is not less than *MinFAUtil*, keep it in the table; otherwise, remove it.

Step 7. Calculate the frequency of the fuzzy items in the $HFAUUBI_1$ table. Sort all fuzzy items in the table by decreasing frequency; this is the header table.

Step 8. Trim fuzzy items in *D* that do not appear in the $HFAUUBI_1$ table as *UD*.

Step 9. Build a tree structure similar to an FP-tree. Each node in the tree stores a fuzzy item and its *mtfau* value. In addition, each node contains an external list that stores the identifier transaction, the fuzzy value of the fuzzy item, and its utility value. According to the *UD*, each fuzzy item in a transaction is inserted into the tree structure from the first transaction to the end, one by one.

Step 10. The $HFAUUBI_1$ table is considered the header table. All fuzzy items in the $HFAUUBI_1$ table are directed to the nodes of the tree's corresponding fuzzy items.

Step 11. After completing the tree structure, find *HFAUI*s. First, each fuzzy item in the $HFAUUBI_1$ table is used to establish its conditional FP-tree by traversing the tree from the bottom up. After going through the conditional FP-tree with each fuzzy item's node, the *afau* values of the fuzzy itemsets are calculated using the nodes' external lists for fuzzy itemsets. If their *afau* ≥ *MinFAUtil*, they are considered *HFAUI*s.

Step 12. Output all *HFAUI*s.

5 Experiments

We compared the previous *HFAUIM* [8] with the proposed *FHFAUIM* on the test datasets, T25I2N1KD10K and T24I2N1KD10K [10]. Two methods were implemented in Java, and experiments were conducted on a computer with an Intel CPU at 3.00GHz and 8GB of RAM. Various thresholds were used to evaluate the performance of the two methods, with the execution time and the memory consumption results shown in Figs. 2 and 3. Moreover, to evaluate the execution time, the *FHFAUIM* uses a single-stage strategy to reduce the number of candidates generated compared to *HFAUIM*. Execution times decrease as *MinFAUtil* is increased. Also, when *MinFAUtil* = 0.01, the single-stage strategy in *FHFAUIM* generally yields significantly reduced computation times in comparison with *HFAUIM*. Therefore, the maximum efficiency improvement rate of execution time is 95.39%. In memory strategy, given different thresholds: the memory usage of *HFAUIM* is less than that of *FHFAUIM*, because *FHFAUIM* accelerates the runtimes by using an external list for each node to store mined data, which requires extra memory.

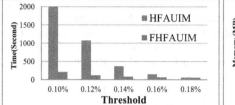 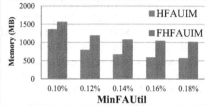

Fig. 2. Execution times and memory consumption in database T25I2N1KD10K

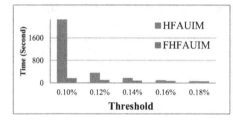 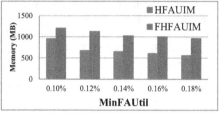

Fig. 3. Execution times and memory consumption in database T24I2N1KD10K

6 Conclusion

We propose a fast method for mining fuzzy average-utility itemsets. The proposed algorithm integrates a single-stage strategy with a tree structure to reduce the search space by storing information in node-level external lists. Experimental results show that the method requires far less computation time than the previous approach [8].

References

1. Agrawal, R., Imielinski, T., Swami, A.: Mining association rules between sets of items in large databases. In: The ACM SIGMOD International Conference on Management of Data, pp. 207–216 (1993)
2. Agrawal, R., Srikant, R.: Fast algorithms for mining association rules. In: The 20th International Conference on Very Large Data Bases, pp. 487–499 (1994)
3. Yao, H., Hamilton, H., Butz, C.: A foundational approach to mining itemset utilities from databases. In: The 4th SIAM International Conference on Data Mining, pp. 211–225 (2004)
4. Liu, Y., Liao, W.-K., Choudhary, A.: A two-phase algorithm for fast discovery of high utility itemsets. In: Ho, T.B., Cheung, D., Liu, H. (eds.) PAKDD 2005. LNCS (LNAI), vol. 3518, pp. 689–695. Springer, Heidelberg (2005). https://doi.org/10.1007/11430919_79

5. Lan, G.C., Hong, T.P., Lin, Y.H., Wang, S.L.: Fuzzy utility mining with upper-bound measure. Appl. Soft Comput. **30**, 767–777 (2015)
6. Hong, T.P., Lee, C.H., Wang, S.L.: Effective utility mining with the measure of average-utility. Expert Syst. Appl. **38**(7), 8259–8265 (2011)
7. Han, J., Pei, J., Yin, Y.: Mining frequent patterns without candidate generation. In: The ACM SIGMOD International Conference on Management of Data, vol. 29, pp. 1–12 (2000)
8. Hong, T.P., Ku, M.P., Huang, W.M., Li, S.M., Lin, J.C.W.: A tree-based fuzzy average-utility mining algorithm. In: IEEE International Conference on Data Mining (2020)
9. Hong, T.P., Ku, M.P., Huang, W.M., Li, S.M., Lin, J.C.W.: Mining high fuzzy average-utility itemsets. In: The International Conference on System Science and Engineering (2020)
10. IBM Quest Data Mining Projection, Quest synthetic data generation code (1996). http://www.almaden.ibm.com/cs/quest/syndata.htm
11. Wu, J.M.-T., Teng, Q., Lin, J.C.-W., Fournier-Viger, P., Cheng, C.-F.: Maintenance of prelarge high average-utility patterns in incremental databases. In: Fujita, H., Fournier-Viger, P., Ali, M., Sasaki, J. (eds.) IEA/AIE 2020. LNCS (LNAI), vol. 12144, pp. 884–895. Springer, Cham (2020). https://doi.org/10.1007/978-3-030-55789-8_75
12. Truong, T.C., Duong, H.V., Le, B., Fournier-Viger, P.: Efficient high average-utility itemset mining using novel vertical weak upper-bounds. Knowl. Based Sys. **183**, (2019). https://doi.org/10.1016/j.knosys.2019.07.018
13. Yildirim, I., Celik, M.: An efficient tree-based algorithm for mining high average-utility itemsets. IEEE ACCESS **7**, 144245–144263 (2019). https://doi.org/10.1109/ACCESS.2019.2945840

Mining Episode Rules from Event Sequences Under Non-overlapping Frequency

Oualid Ouarem[1], Farid Nouioua[1,2(✉)], and Philippe Fournier-Viger[3]

[1] Department of Computer Science, University of Bordj Bou Arréridj,
El-Anasser, Algeria
`oualid.ouarem@univ-bba.dz`
[2] LIS, UMR-CNRS 7020, Aix-Marseille University, Marseille, France
`farid.nouioua@lis-lab.fr`
[3] Harbin Institute of Technology (Shenzhen), Shenzhen, China
`philfv@hit.edu.cn`

Abstract. Frequent episode mining is a popular framework for retrieving useful information from an event sequence. Many algorithms have been proposed to mine frequent episodes and to derive episode rules from them with respect to a given frequency function and its properties such as the anti-monotony. However, the interpretation of these rules is often difficult as their occurrences are allowed to overlap. To address this issue, this paper studies the novel problem of mining episode rules using non-overlapping occurrences of frequent episodes. The proposed rules have the form $\beta \Rightarrow \alpha$ where α and β are frequent episodes and β is a prefix of α. This kind of rules is well adapted for prediction tasks where a phenomenon is predicted from some observed event(s). An efficient algorithm named NONEPI (NON overlapping EPIsode rule miner) is presented and experiments have been performed to compare its performance with state-of-the-art algorithms.

Keywords: Frequent episode mining · Event sequence · Episode rules

1 Introduction

Frequent Episode Mining (FEM) is an active subfield of data mining, which aims at retrieving important knowledge from temporal data [1–4,13]. The input of that process is a single event sequence, which may encode various types of data such as user clicks of web sessions [10], alarms in a telecommunication network [13], and network intrusion data [16]. The objective of FEM is to find partially or totally ordered sets of events that occur frequently in an input sequence.

FEM algorithms have been designed to find frequent episodes using various frequency functions to count their occurrences (how many times each episode appears). The first type, called **dependent frequency functions**, consider that occurrences of an episode may overlap (share some common events). The

H. Fujita et al. (Eds.): IEA/AIE 2021, LNAI 12798, pp. 73–85, 2021.
https://doi.org/10.1007/978-3-030-79457-6_7

main functions of this type are the *window-based frequency, minimal occurrence-based frequency* [13], *head frequency* [7], *total frequency* [7] and *non-interleaved frequency* [8]. The second type are the **independent frequency functions**, which do not allow episode occurrences to overlap. Some functions of this type are the *non-overlapped occurrence-based frequency* [9] and the *distinct occurrence-based frequency* [12].

Since the seminal work of Mannila et al. in 1997 [13], many algorithms were proposed to efficiently extract all frequent episodes. The first algorithms are MINEPI and WINEPI [13]. WINEPI applies a level-wise search to find large episodes using a sliding window, and counts the number of windows that contains each target episode, while MINEPI searches for minimal windows containing each target episode. Then, episode rules can be derived from the obtained frequent episodes. A drawback of MINEPI and WINEPI is the duplicate counting of episode occurrences. To overcome this problem, Huang and Chang proposed two novel frequency functions called the head frequency and total frequency, and two algorithms [5]. The first one, called MINEPI+, adopts a depth-first strategy inspired by MINEPI while the second one, called EMMA, avoids the huge number of duplication and unnecessary duplicate checks of MINEPI using the head frequency. Unfortunately, under the head frequency function, an episode may have a higher frequency than its sub-episodes, which makes the result difficult to interpret. The total frequency function avoids this issue. That study also showed how to generate an episode rule using that frequency function.

Some other FEM algorithms use other types of constraints. For instance, 2PEM [11] and FCEMiner [6] find closed episodes. However, in general, dependent frequency functions suffer from over counting the number of episode occurrences to calculate an episode's frequency. Therefore, they consume too much time and memory space compared to independent frequency functions. Contrarily, an algorithm that relies on an independent frequency function can calculate the set of frequent episodes with minimal resources. The non-overlapped occurrence-based frequency is an independent frequency function used in many applications such as manufacturing [9].

To find strong relationships between events in a complex event sequence, FEM was extended to mine episode rules satisfying some minimum confidence constraint. Several algorithms where proposed [5] to find episode rules that first find frequent episodes using the head frequency to then generate rules from them. Algorithms such as WinMiner [14] and PPER [2] apply the minimal occurrence-based frequency to find episode rules with optimal window size. To the best of our knowledge, no studies deal with the problem of mining episode rules using the non-overlapped occurrence-based frequency function, although this frequency function can be argued to be more adequate for real applications due to not over counting occurrences. This paper addresses this research gap by proposing an efficient algorithm named NONEPI (NON overlapping EPIsode rule miner) for mining episode rules using non-overlapped occurrence-based frequency, by extending a depth-first search FEM algorithm proposed by Wan et al. [17].

The remaining of this paper in organized as follows. Section 2 explains preliminaries of FEM. Section 3 states the problem solved in this paper. The details of the proposed algorithm are given in Sect. 4. Experimental results are presented and discussed in Sect. 5. Finally, a conclusion is drawn in Sect. 6.

2 Frequent Episode and Episode Rule Mining

This section briefly defines the main concepts used in episode mining and episode rule mining. An event sequence is defined as follows.

Definition 1 (Event sequence). . *Let E be a set of event types. An event is a pair (e_i, t_i) where $e_i \in E$ is an event type and t_i is an integer that represents its occurrence time. An event sequence S on event types E is an ordered set of events $S = < (e_1, t_1), (e_2, t_2), ..., (e_n, t_n) >$ where t_1 and t_n are the starting time and ending time of S respectively, and for any integers i, j if $i < j$ then $t_i < t_j$.*

For instance, an example event sequence is presented in Fig. 1. This sequence contains 13 events on 6 different event types: $E = \{A, B, C, D, M, N\}$. It starts at time $t_1 = 52$ and ends at time $t_{13} = 67$.

Fig. 1. An event sequence with 13 timestamps

The general definition of an episode is the following:

Definition 2 (Episode). *An episode α is a triple $(V, <_\alpha, g_\alpha)$ where V is a set of nodes $\{v_1, v_2, ..., v_n\}$, $<_\alpha$ is an order on V and $g_\alpha : V \to E$ is a mapping that associate each node with an event type.*

The integer n is the length of episode α. There are several particular types of episodes: when the order $<_\alpha$ is total, episode α is a *serial* episode. In this case, α is simply denoted as $\alpha = A_1 \to A_2 \to ... \to A_n$ where each A_i is an event type. When the order $<_\alpha$ is trivial, episode α is called *parallel* and it is denoted as $\alpha = A_1 A_2 ... A_n$. Episode α is said to be **injective** if it does not contain any repeated event types, i.e., for any $1 \leq i, j \leq n$, if $i \neq j$ then $g(v_i) \neq v(v_j)$.

This paper focuses on discovering injective serial episodes. Thus, in the subsequent sections, any serial injective episode is simply called an episode. In the example sequence of Fig. 1, the event A is followed by event N, then followed by B, forming an episode with 3 events ($\alpha = A \to N \to B$) as they appear in that order in the sequence. The notion of sub-episode is formally defined as follows:

Definition 3 (Sub-episode). *Let $\alpha = A_1 \to \cdots \to A_n$ and $\beta = B_1 \to \cdots \to B_m$ be two episodes. β is said to be a **sub-episode** of α (denoted as $\beta \sqsubseteq \alpha$) if and only if: $\exists k, 1 \leq k \leq n - m + 1$ such that $\forall j, 1 \leq j \leq m, B_j = A_{k+j-1}$.*

In other words, β is a sub-episode of α if β is a part of α. Notice that if β is a sub-episode of α then it is easy to see that every occurrence of α contains an occurrence of β [13]. If $\beta \sqsubseteq \alpha$, we also say that α is a **super-episode** of β.

Two particular cases are distinguished: If $k = 1$ then β is located at the beginning of α and is called a **prefix** of α. In contrast, if $k = n - m + 1$ then β is situated at the end of α and is called a **suffix** of α.

Returning to the running example, the episode $\beta = A \rightarrow N$ is a sub-episode of the episode $\alpha = A \rightarrow N \rightarrow B$, denoted as $\beta \sqsubseteq \alpha$. Moreover, β is a *prefix* of α.

The notion of episode occurrence in a sequence and that of non-overlapped occurrences are formally defined as follows:

Definition 4 (Occurrence of an episode). *An occurrence of an episode α in an event sequence S is a vector $h = [t_1 t_2 ... t_n]$ where each t_i is an integer that represents the occurrence time (timestamp) of the ith node of episode α.*

Given two occurrences $h = [t_1 t_2 ... t_n]$ and $h' = [t'_1 t'_2 ... t'_n]$, h and h' are said to be non-overlapped occurrences of episode α iff either $t_n < t'_1$ or $t'_n < t_1$.

In general, different sets of non-overlapped occurrences can be obtained for a given episode. We are in particular interested in maximal sets, i.e., containing a maximal number of non-overlapped occurrences:

Definition 5 (Maximal set of non-overlapped occurrences of an episode). *Given a set H of non-overlapped occurrences of an episode α, H is said to be a maximal set of non-overlapped occurrences iff for every other set H' of non-overlapped occurrences of α, it holds that: $|H| \geq |H'|$. We denote by $no(\alpha)$ the maximal set of non-overlapped occurrences of the episode α.*

For instance, consider the example sequence S of Fig. 1 and the episode $\alpha = A \rightarrow N \rightarrow B$. The set $H = \{[52\ 54\ 55], [56\ 59\ 61], [62\ 66\ 67]\}$ is the maximal set of non-overlapped occurrences of α in S, and hence $no(\alpha) = H$.

Definition 6 (Support of an episode). *The support of an episode α (denoted by $support(\alpha)$) is the cardinality of the maximal set of non-overlapped occurrences, i.e., $support(\alpha) = |no_\alpha|$.*

An episode α is frequent under non-overlapped occurrence-based support, if $support(\alpha) \geq minsup$ where $minsup$ is a user-defined support threshold.

In the previous example, we can see that the support of the episode α is 3.

To go further, episode rules captures binary relationships between couples of frequent episodes. An episode rule is an expression of the form $\beta \Rightarrow \alpha$ where α and β are two frequent episodes. An episode rule is said to be valid if the probability that its consequent occurs when its antecedent occurs is sufficiently high. This conditional probability associated to a rule defines the so-called confidence of this rule. It is given by : $conf(\beta \Rightarrow \alpha) = \frac{support(\beta \sqcup \alpha)}{support(\beta)}$ where $\beta \sqcup \alpha$ means the occurrence of β and α together. The exact interpretation of the $\sqcup$ operator depends on the kind of used rules and frequency. In our work, β is a sub-episode of α and hence $\beta \sqcup \alpha = \alpha$ (see Sect. 3). If the confidence of a rule is greater or equals to a user-defined confidence threshold $minconf$, then the rule is valid.

In general, different types of rules capturing different relationships between an antecedent and a consequence may be defined according to the application domain. This paper focuses on one particular type of episode rules which may be useful for prediction tasks.

3 Problem Definition

The proposed NONEPI approach uses the non-overlapped occurrence-based frequency to capture how often a rule is frequent. An episode rule is defined as follows:

Definition 7 (Episode rule). *An episode rule is an implication of the form: $\beta \Rightarrow \alpha$ where α and β are two frequent episodes (under non-overlapping frequency) and β is a prefix of α.*

The meaning of such episode rule is that if prefix β appears in the sequence, then its events or actions will strongly trigger all the remaining events necessary to form an occurrence of α. This may be helpful in understanding the root of a given phenomenon or to predict the future evolution of a set of ordered events.

Therefore, the confidence of an episode rule $\beta \Rightarrow \alpha$ is the ratio between $support(\alpha)$ and $support(\beta)$:

$$conf(\beta \Rightarrow \alpha) = \frac{support(\alpha)}{support(\beta)} \tag{1}$$

The main task of an episode rule mining algorithm is to efficiently find all valid episode rules at low cost (time and memory consumption). Thus, the problem to be resolved in this paper is formulated as follows: Given an event sequence S, a support threshold $minsup$ and a confidence threshold $minconf$, the task is to mine the set of valid episode rules, i.e., rules of the form $\beta \Rightarrow \alpha$ such that $conf(\beta \Rightarrow \alpha) \geq minconf$.

4 The Proposed Episode Rule Mining Approach

This section presents the proposed NONEPI approach to mine the set of frequent episode rules based on non-overlapped occurrences. The approach is divided into two steps: the first one consists in mining frequent episodes and the second one consists in mining the set of valid episode rules.

4.1 Extracting Frequent Episodes

The first step consists in mining frequent episodes according to their non-overlapped occurrences. This function (Algorithm 1) is inspired by the approach of Wan et al. [17], where the input is the minimum frequency threshold $minsup$.

To avoid considering all the search space, the frequent episode generation under the non-overlapped occurrence-based support count utilizes the following anti-monotony property.

Algorithm 1: Mining Frequent Episodes

    Input: *minsup* - minimum support threshold

    Output: F - the set of all frequent serial episodes

 1 $P = \{\}, F = \{\}, \alpha = \emptyset$

 2 **for** *each individual event $e \in E$* **do**

 3     $no_e = \{\}$

 4 **for** $k = 1$ *to* n **do**

      % scan the sequence S

 5     $e =$ the event found at time t_k

 6     $no_e = no_e \cup \{[t_k, t_k]\}$

 7 **for** *each individual event $e \in E$* **do**

 8   **if** $|no_e| \geq minsup$ **then**

 9        $P = P \cup \{(e)\}$

10 $F = P$

11 **for** *each individual episode $\alpha \in F$* **do**

12   **for** *each individual episode $\beta \in P$* **do**

13        $no_{\alpha \sqcup \beta} = Occurrence\_Recognition(\alpha, \beta)$

14   **if** $|no_{\alpha \sqcup \beta}| \geq minsup$ **then**

15           $F = F \cup \{\alpha \sqcup \beta\}$

16           $\alpha = \alpha \sqcup \beta$

17 **return** F

Proposition 1. *Let α and β two episodes such that $\beta \sqsubseteq \alpha$, if episode α is frequent then episode β is also frequent. Equivalently, if episode β is infrequent then episode α is infrequent.*

Proof. Since $\beta \sqsubseteq \alpha$ it follows that each occurrence of α in S includes an occurrence of β in S. The inverse is not necessarily true since it is possible to find an occurrence of β with a continuation which does not necessarily reach an occurrence of α. Hence, the number of occurrences of α is at most equal to the number of occurrences of β, i.e. $support(\alpha) \leq support(\beta)$.

    Then if α is frequent, $support(\alpha) \geq minsup$. But since $support(\alpha) \leq support(\beta)$ it follows that : $support(\beta) \geq minsup$. We show in a similar manner that if β is infrequent then α is infrequent. ∎

    Algorithm 1 is applied as follows: First, it computes the frequent episodes of size one by scanning the event sequence S and for each event e occurring at time t_k in S, the time interval $[t_k , t_k]$ is added to the set no_e of occurrences of e (lines 4–6). Then, the algorithm checks the support of these single event episodes to constitute the first frequent episodes (lines 7–9). After that, the function performs a depth-first search to find larger frequent episodes by successive calls of the *occurrence recognition* function which given an arbitrary episode α and an episode of size 1 β looks for the occurrences of $\alpha \sqcup \beta$ obtained by adding β to the end of α (lines 11–16). Notice that thanks to Proposition 1, the depth-first exploration continues only for nodes corresponding to frequent episodes (line

14). In other words, if an episode is not frequent, all the episodes that extend it will not be frequent and the corresponding search sub-space is pruned.

Algorithm 2 shows the details of the occurrence recognition function. This algorithm is inspired from [17] but thanks to the particularities of our context, the proposed algorithm avoids performing multiple sequence accesses to obtain the set of occurrences of new episodes. The input is an episode to grow α and a single event episode β to grow α by. We get as output the occurrences of the new episode $\alpha \sqcup \beta$. For each occurrence of α, $O_i \in no_\alpha$, the algorithm browses the set no_β of occurrences of β to obtain an occurrence $O_j \in no_\beta$ which starts after the end O_i, i.e., $O_j.start > O_i.end$ where $O_j.start$ is the starting time of the jth occurrence of β and $O_i.end$ is the ending time of the ith occurrence of α. Then, we obtain a new occurrence $[O_i.start, O_j.end]$ of $\alpha \sqcup \beta$ (line(1–5)). To overcome the problem of overlapping occurrences, the function also removes any occurrences of α that overlaps with the new one of the new episode (line 6–7)).

Algorithm 2: Occurrence Recognition

Input: episode α - an episode to grow
episode β - a single event episode to grow α by.
Output: $no_{\alpha \sqcup \beta}$ - set of non-overlapped occurrences of new episode $\alpha \sqcup \beta$

1 **for** $each\ O_i \in no_\alpha$ **do**
2   **for** $each\ O_j \in no_\beta$ **do**
3   **if** $O_j.start > O_i.end$ **then**
4   update $O_i.end = O_j.start$
5             $O_i.timestamps = O_i.timestamps \cup O_j.start$
6   **for** $each\ O_k\ in\ no_\alpha\ s.t.\ i < k \leq m \wedge O_k.start < O_i.end$ **do**
7   remove O_k from no_α
8             $no_{\alpha \sqcup \beta} = no_{\alpha \sqcup \beta} \cup O_i$
9 **return** $no_{\alpha \sqcup \beta}$

4.2 Extracting Episode Rules

The second phase of the process is to mine all valid episode rules of the form $\beta \Rightarrow \alpha$ where α and β are two frequent episodes under non-overlapping frequency and β is a prefix of α. Recall that valid rules are those having a confidence which is no less than a minimum confidence threshold $minconf$. The confidence of a rule is calculated according to Eq. 1. The consideration of all possible combinations of α and β to form an episode rule leads to a huge search space. To reduce this search space two techniques are used: (1) For a given episode α as a rule consequent, only its prefixes are candidates to be antecedents of that rule. This follows from the very definition of an episode rule; (2) For a rule consequent α, it can be shown that some prefixes may not be tested at all as antecedents of this rule because they surely lead to invalid rules. This is obtained by using the anti-monotony property at the rule level (see Proposition 2).

Proposition 2. *Let α and β be two frequent episodes such that β is a prefix of α. If the rule $\beta \Rightarrow \alpha$ is invalid then: (1) the rule $\beta' \Rightarrow \alpha$ is invalid for every episode β' which is a prefix of β ($\beta' \sqsubseteq \beta$), and (2) $\beta \Rightarrow \alpha'$ is invalid for every episode α' such that α is a prefix of α' ($\alpha \sqsubseteq \alpha'$).*

Proof. Let us prove the part (1) of the proposition. Let α and β be two frequent episodes such that $\beta \sqsubseteq \alpha$ and suppose that the rule $\beta \Rightarrow \alpha$ is invalid. Let $\beta' \sqsubseteq \beta$. From Proposition 1 we have: $support(\beta') \geq support(\beta)$. It follows that: $conf(\beta' \Rightarrow \alpha) = \frac{support(\alpha)}{support(\beta')} \leq conf(\beta \Rightarrow \alpha) = \frac{support(\alpha)}{support(\beta)}$. But, since $\beta \Rightarrow \alpha$ is invalid we have: $\frac{support(\alpha)}{support(\beta)} \leq minconf$. It follows that: $\frac{support(\alpha)}{support(\beta')} \leq minconf$, which means that $\beta' \Rightarrow \alpha$ is invalid.

The part (2) of the proposition can be proved in a similar way. ∎

Based on Proposition 2, Algorithm 3 generates all valid episode rules from an input sequence S.

Algorithm 3: Extracting Episode rules

Input: S: sequence of events on E (event types set), $minsup$: support threshold, $minconf$: confidence threshold
Output: R: complete set of episode rules.
1   $F = FrequentEpisodes(minsup)$
2   $R = \emptyset$
3   **for** *each episode $\alpha \in F$* **do**
4      $stop =$ false
5      $\beta = pred(\alpha)$/* returns the predecessor of episode α*/
6   **while** ***not** stop **and** $\beta \neq NULL$* **do**
7   **if** $\frac{|no_\alpha|}{|no_\beta|} \geq minconf$ **then**
8            $R = R \cup \{\beta \Rightarrow \alpha\}$
9            $\beta = pred(\beta)$
        else
10            $stop =$ true
11 **return** R

The algorithm takes as input the sequence of events S on the event types E, the user-defined frequency threshold $minsup$ and confidence threshold $minconf$. The output is the complete set of valid episode rules of the form $\beta \Rightarrow \alpha$. Hereafter, for an episode α of length l, we denote by $pred(\alpha)$ (predecessor of α) the largest prefix of α, i.e., the prefix of α of length $l - 1$.

Initially, the algorithm starts by extracting all frequent episodes with $minsup$ as a minimum support threshold (by a call of Algorithm 1). Then, for each frequent episode α the algorithm produces all the valid rules having α as consequent. Starting by $\beta = pred(\alpha)$ as a potential antecedent, the algorithm computes the confidence of $\beta \Rightarrow \alpha$. If this rule is valid it is added to the set of output rules and the algorithm passes to the next shorter prefix. The algorithm stops the exploration of prefixes of α as soon as it finds a prefix β such that $\beta \Rightarrow \alpha$ is invalid. Indeed, from Proposition 2, any further prefix β' will lead to an invalid rule too.

5 Experimental Results

As the proposed form of episode rules is introduced for the first time in this paper, there is no existing works about the same form that may be used for comparison with the performance of our algorithm. That is why the aim of this section is rather to understand some aspects of the behaviour of our algorithm. This section describes the experimental results obtained from two experiments carried out on synthetic sequences generated randomly. To randomly generate a sequence we specify : (1) its length, i.e., the number of events occurring in the sequence, (2) the number of event types and (3) the maximal duration between two consecutive events. We have used three types of sequences : large, medium and small. More information about the used sequences is given in Table 1.

Table 1. Information about used sequences

	Large	Medium	Short
1st sequence	40 event types	50 events types	20 event types
	500000 events	100000 events	29000 events
2nd sequence	80 event types	20 event types	100 event types
	600000 events	130000 events	350000 events
3^{d} sequence	100 event types	100 event types	50 event types
	700000 events	160000 events	390000 events

5.1 Frequent Episode Mining

In this experiment, we have compared the proposed NONEPI algorithm with three well-known frequent episode mining algorithms that are implemented in Java and available in the SPMF library [15]: MINEPI which is a breadth-first algorithm using the minimal occurrence-based frequency as well as MINEPI+ and EMMA that are depth-first algorithms using the head frequency.

The comparison considers the variation, according to the support threshold, of (1) the number of found frequent episodes, (2) the maximal size of found frequent episodes as well as (3) the execution time. For each type of sequences we take the average value of the three used sequences (see Fig. 2).

Figures 2(a), (d) and (g) show the influence of $minsup$ on the number of discovered frequent episodes in sequences of large, medium and short size, respectively. We can see that the number of generated frequent episodes in NONEPI is relatively more sensible to the variation of support threshold than in the other

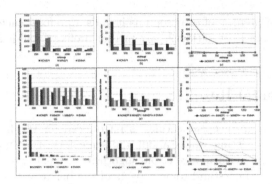

Fig. 2. Influence of *minsup* on the number of frequent episodes, the maximum episode size and the execution time for sequences of large, medium and short size.

algorithms, where the number of generated frequent episode tends to remain stable for several successive values of *minsup*. We can also notice that for medium and large sequences, NONEPI generates less frequent episodes than the other algorithms. Indeed, as the size of a sequence increases, the episode occurrences that do not overlap tend to be less numerous than the overlapping occurrences.

Figures 2(b), (e) and (h) show the influence of the support threshold *minsup* on the maximal size of frequent episodes in sequences of large, medium and short size, respectively. We can see that as *minsup* increases, the maximum size of the discovered episodes by NONEPI decreases. However, that of MINEPI and MINEPI+ remains almost stable regardless of the value of support threshold. This means that the maximum size of frequent episodes is more sensible to support threshold in NONEPI than in the other algorithms. This is because NONEPI considers independent occurrences. Indeed, large episodes give rise to large and non overlapped occurrences that are naturally less frequent than overlapped occurrences or occurrences of small episodes. Thus, the large episodes that are frequent for small support thresholds become non frequent as soon as the support threshold increases.

Figures 2(c), (f) and (i) show the runtime comparison of the algorithms for different support thresholds in sequences of large, medium and short size, respectively. It is clear that the runtime of NONEPI and EMMA are significantly lower than that of the two other algorithms. MINEPI+ obtained the worst performance among all the tested algorithms for all types of sequences. For large sequences MINEPI+ fails to terminate before 800 s, that is why it is not represented in Figures (a), (b) and (c) of large sequences. The very good performance of NONEPI is explained by the fact that it scans the event sequence only once to extract timestamps of single event episodes and then joins them to obtain larger episodes occurrences while MINEPI and MINEPI+ scan the sequence more than once to find the occurrences of the newest episodes using the window width. This also shows the efficiency of the pruning strategy used in NONEPI and based on the anti-monotony property presented in Proposition 2.

5.2   Episode Rules

This experiment shows the proposed NONEPI for episode rule generation. It presents the variations of the execution time and the number of generated rules according to the minimum confidence threshold. We have represented the average values of the execution time and the number of generated rules, obtained in the nine tested sequences, and we have fixed the support threshold to $minsup = 100$ in order to focus on the confidence effect.

Figure 3(a) and Fig. 3(b) show the influence of $minconf$ on execution time and the number of mined episode rules respectively. As the confidence threshold increases, the number of rules decreases slowly which means that generally, valid episode rules generated by NONEPI have high confidence values. By contrast, As the confidence threshold increases, the runtime decreases rapidly. This means that one may obtain the main valid episode rules even by using a relatively high value of confidence threshold which ensures a short runtime.

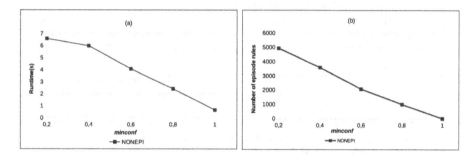

Fig. 3. Influence of $minconf$ on (a) execution time and (b) number of episode rules

6   Conclusion

This paper has proposed a new type of episode rules based on the non-overlapped occurrence-based support where an efficient algorithm, named NONEPI was presented. To the best of our knowledge, this is the only work that uses this support definition to mine all episode rules.

We have shown that our episode rules enjoy an anti-monotony property that allowed us to propose a pruning strategy that stops the generation of episode rules having a given episode α as consequent as soon as we find the largest prefix of α, say β such that $\beta \Rightarrow \alpha$ is invalid.

There are several possibilities of future work on NONEPI such as (1) extending it to process uncertain data using a probabilistic model or to mine episode rules with partially ordered events (2) considering more complex event sequences like streams and (3) building a sequence prediction model based on this algorithm.

References

1. Achar, A., Ibrahim, A., Sastry, P.S.: Pattern-growth based frequent serial episode discovery. Data Knowl. Eng. **87**, 91–108 (2013)
2. Ao, X., Luo, P., Wang, J., Zhuang, F., He, Q.: Mining precise-positioning episode rules from event sequences. IEEE Trans. Knowl. Data Eng. **30**(3), 530–543 (2018)
3. Ao, X., Shi, H., Wang, J., Zuo, L., Li, H., He, Q.: Large-scale frequent episode mining from complex event sequences with hierarchies. ACM Trans. Intell. Syst. Technol. (TIST) **10**(4), 1–26 (2019)
4. Fournier-Viger, P., Yang, Y., Yang, P., Lin, J.C.-W., Yun, U.: TKE: mining top-K frequent episodes. In: Fujita, H., Fournier-Viger, P., Ali, M., Sasaki, J. (eds.) IEA/AIE 2020. LNCS (LNAI), vol. 12144, pp. 832–845. Springer, Cham (2020). https://doi.org/10.1007/978-3-030-55789-8_71
5. Huang, K.Y., Chang, C.H.: Efficient mining of frequent episodes from complex sequences. Inf. Syst. **33**(1), 96–114 (2008)
6. Huisheng, Z., Wang, P., Wang, W., Shi, B.: Discovering frequent closed episodes from an event sequence. In: The 2012 International Joint Conference on Neural Networks (IJCNN), Brisbane, QLD (2012)
7. Iwanuma, K., Takano, Y., Nabeshima, H.: On anti-monotone frequency measures for extracting sequential patterns from a single very-long data sequence. In: Proceedings of 7th IEEE Conference on Cybernetics and Intelligent Systems, pp. 213–217. IEEE (2004)
8. Laxman, S.: Discovering frequent episodes: fast algorithms, connections with HMMs and generalizations. Indian Institute of Science, Bangalore, PhD thesis (2006)
9. Laxman, S., Sastry, P.S., Unnikrishnan, K.P.: Discovering frequent episodes and learning hidden Markov models: a formal connection. IEEE Trans. Knowl. Data Eng. **17**(11), 1505–1517 (2005)
10. Laxman, S., Sastry, P.S., Unnikrishnan, K.P.: A fast algorithm for finding frequent episodes in event streams. In: Proceedings of 13th ACM SIGKDD International Conference on Knowledge Discovery and Data Mining, pp. 410–419. ACM, New York (2007)
11. Liao, G., Yang, X., Xie, S., Yu, P.S., Wan, C.: Two-phase mining for frequent closed episodes. In: Cui, B., Zhang, N., Xu, J., Lian, X., Liu, D. (eds.) WAIM 2016. LNCS, vol. 9658, pp. 55–66. Springer, Cham (2016). https://doi.org/10.1007/978-3-319-39937-9_5
12. Mahesh, J., Karypis, G., Kumar, V.: A Universal formulation of sequential patterns. Technical report 99–021, University of Minnesota (1999)
13. Mannila, H., Toivonen, H., Verkamo, I.: Dicovery of frequent episodes in event sequences. Data Mining Knowl. Discov. **1**(3), 259–289 (1997)
14. Méger, N., Rigotti, C.: Constraint-based mining of episode rules and optimal window sizes. In: Boulicaut, J.-F., Esposito, F., Giannotti, F., Pedreschi, D. (eds.) PKDD 2004. LNCS (LNAI), vol. 3202, pp. 313–324. Springer, Heidelberg (2004). https://doi.org/10.1007/978-3-540-30116-5_30
15. SPMF Homepage. http://www.philippe-fournier-viger.com/spmf/. Accessed 01 Dec 2020
16. Su, M.-Y.: Discovery and prevention of attack episodes by frequent episodes mining and finite state machines. J. Netw. Comput. Appl. **2**(33), 156–167 (2010)

17. Wan, L., Chen, L., Zhang, C.: Mining dependent frequent serial episodes from uncertain sequence data. In: Proceedings IEEE 13th International Conference on Data Mining, pp. 1211–1216. IEEE (2013)
18. Zhu, H., Chen, L., Li, J., Zhou, A., Wang, P., Wang, W.: A general depth-first-search based algorithm for frequent episode discovery. In: Proceedings 14th International Conference on Natural Computation, Fuzzy Systems and Knowledge Discovery, pp. 890–899 (2018)

Distributed Mining of High Utility Time Interval Sequential Patterns with Multiple Minimum Utility Thresholds

Sumalatha Saleti[✉], Jaya Lakshmi Tangirala,
and Ragunathan Thirumalaisamy

SRM University AP, Andhra Pradesh, India
sumalatha.s@srmap.edu.in

Abstract. In this paper, the problem of mining high utility time interval sequential patterns with multiple utility thresholds in a distributed environment is considered. Mining high utility sequential patterns (HUSP) is an emerging issue and the existing HUSP algorithms can mine the order of items and they do not consider the time interval between the successive items. In real-world applications, time interval patterns provide more useful information than the conventional HUSPs. Recently, we proposed distributed high utility time interval sequential pattern mining (DHUTISP) algorithm using MapReduce in support of the BigData environment. The algorithm has been designed considering a single minimum utility threshold. It is not convincing to use the same utility threshold for all the items in the sequence, which means that all the items are given the same importance. Hence, in this paper, a new distributed framework is proposed to efficiently mine high utility time interval sequential patterns with multiple minimum utility thresholds (DHUTISP-MMU) using the MapReduce approach. The experimental results show that the proposed approach can efficiently mine HUTISPs with multiple minimum utility thresholds.

Keywords: High utility sequential pattern mining · Time interval sequential patterns · Multiple minimum utility

1 Introduction

Sequential pattern mining (SPM) [1,2] is considered to be important as it predicts the frequent sequences from transactional databases. For example, a person who has purchased a book "Data Mining Concepts and Techniques" would like to visit the store again to purchase an "Advanced Data Mining" book. Knowing this information, market analyst can come up with new marketing strategies such as cross selling the products and promotional activities. Traditional approaches to SPM considers the frequency based framework and they are not considered to be informative because they cannot mine highly profitable sequences. In view of this, utility based framework [3–5] has been introduced and it considers both

© Springer Nature Switzerland AG 2021
H. Fujita et al. (Eds.): IEA/AIE 2021, LNAI 12798, pp. 86–97, 2021.
https://doi.org/10.1007/978-3-030-79457-6_8

the quantity (internal utility) and profit (external utility) of the items being purchased. Even though the existing HUSP [6–9] algorithms are able to generate highly profitable sequences, they could not predict the time gap between the successive visits of customers to the store [10–12].

Finding the high utility sequences of the form $\langle X, 2, Y, 4, Z \rangle$, which means that a customer visited a store to purchase item X and after 2 months visited the store to purchase item Y and later after 4 months visited the store to purchase item Z, allows the market analyst to predict the future needs of the items along with the time gap. This issue of high utility time interval sequential patterns is introduced in [10] and the authors proposed UTMining algorithm. Later it was modified and a new version namely, $UTMining\_A$ [11] was proposed. However, these are centralized algorithms and not suitable for handling big data. In view of this, recently, we proposed DHUTISP [12] algorithm that works in a distributed MapReduce environment. It not only mines highly profitable sequences but also the time interval in between the items. However, it considers a single minimum utility threshold to derive HUTISPs. In case of real time applications, all the items do not have the same unit profit and it is unfair to consider all the items with equal importance. For example, sales of "diamond ring" generates more profit compared to sales of "cricket bat". Thus, assessing the utility of items using a single threshold is not adequate and fails to consider the inherent nature of the items. Hence, in this paper, we propose a new framework called distributed mining of high utility time interval sequential patterns with multiple minimum utility thresholds (DHUTISP-MMU). The rest of the paper is organized as follows. A brief review of related work is given in Sect. 2. Preliminaries and problem statement are defined in Sect. 3. The proposed algorithm is described in Sect. 4. The experimental results of proposed algorithm are presented in Sect. 5. Finally, Sect. 6 presents the concluding remarks.

2   Related Work

In this section, we review the related literature of high utility itemset mining and high utility sequential pattern mining with multiple minimum utility thresholds. High utility itemset mining with multiple minimum utility thresholds (HUIM-MMU) was initially proposed in [13]. The user can specify varying thresholds for each item. Based on the HUIM-MMU framework, two algorithms were designed, namely, HUI-MMU and HUI-MMU$_{TID}$. The former is a baseline approach with a generate-and-test strategy. It follows sorted downward closure property (SDC) to prune the search space. However, it generates a large number of candidates due to the generate-and-test strategy. The later is an improved version of HUI-MMU that makes use of an additional TID-index strategy. To avoid repeated scanning of the database and generating candidates, Lin et al. [14] proposed high-utility itemsets with multiple minimum utility thresholds (HIMU). The authors proposed a multiple item utility set-enumeration tree (MIU-tree) structure. Also, global downward closure property (GDC) and conditional downward closure property (CDC) have been introduced for speeding up the mining process. The authors proposed two algorithms, namely HIMU and $HIMU_{EUCP}$. The later algorithm proved to be more efficient than the HIMU algorithm and the other two approaches - HUI-MMU and $HUI-MMU_{TID}$. However, $HIMU_{EUCP}$ sorts the items in the transaction based on the items minimum utility threshold. Any changes in the preference of items can affect the performance of the algorithm. MHUI algorithm proposed in [15] overcomes this limitation of item ordering. The authors introduced the concept of suffix minimum utility (SMU) and four pruning properties, namely TWU-M-Prune, U-M-Prune, EUCS-M-Prune, and LA-M-Prune for better mining efficiency. All these four pruning properties are used at different stages of the MHUI algorithm and proved to be efficient compared to the existing approaches. All the aforementioned algorithms involve multiple utility thresholds and not related to the problem of HUSP.

Recently, Gan et al. [16] proposed USPT framework for mining HUSPs with individual thresholds for each item. The authors introduced a compact utility-tree structure and proposed various upper bounds and pruning strategies to improve the efficiency of mining. To the best of our knowledge, [16] and [17] ([17] is an earlier version of [16]) are the only approaches to HUSP mining with multiple minimum utility thresholds. Moreover, the above mentioned approaches do not find the time interval between successive items [18–21]. Finding the time interval between the items is required in the real time applications to satisfy the future demands of the customer. The problem of mining time interval sequential patterns with high utility is initiated by Wang et al. [10,11]. As an extension of the centralized approach proposed in [11], we recently proposed a distributed algorithm for HUTISP [12] using MapReduce paradigm that best suits the big data environment. However, our approach in [12] is based on a single minimum utility threshold. Since each item possess different nature, using a single minimum utility is difficult to fairly measure the utility of sequences. Hence, in this paper, we propose an efficient MapReduce algorithm for mining high utility time interval sequential patterns with multiple minimum utility thresholds.

3   Preliminaries and Problem Statement

Definition 1. Let I be a set of items and $TI = \{I_0, I_1, I_2, \ldots, I_r\}$ be a set of predefined time intervals. A time interval sequence dataset is a set of n sequences $TSD = \{S_1, S_2, \ldots, S_n\}$. Each sequence is represented as an ordered list of triplets, where each triplet denoted as (i, iu, ts), includes an item $i \in I$, internal utility of item iu and the time stamp ts. Each item in the itemset I is associated with an external utility or profit of the item and is denoted as eu. For example, consider the sequence dataset shown in Table 1. The dataset consists of five sequences $(S_1, S_2, \ldots, S_5)$ and $TI = \{I_0, I_1, I_2, I_3\}$, where $I_0 : ts = 0$, $I_1 : 0 < ts \leq 5$, $I_2 : 5 < ts \leq 10$ and $I_3 : ts > 10$. The external utilities of items are as follows: $a : 2, b : 1, c : 1, d : 8, e : 1, f : 1, g : 3, h : 2$.

Table 1. Sample sequence dataset.

SID	Sequence	Sequence utility
S_1	$((a, 5, 8), (b, 2, 8), (c, 1, 8), (c, 1, 15), (d, 3, 15), (c, 2, 17), (h, 1, 17))$	42
S_2	$((a, 1, 10), (b, 3, 10), (a, 2, 20), (d, 1, 20), (f, 1, 20), (c, 3, 25), (d, 1, 25), (g, 2, 25))$	35
S_3	$((c, 2, 5), (e, 1, 5), (a, 2, 15), (g, 2, 15), (h, 1, 15))$	15
S_4	$((c, 2, 8), (a, 5, 15), (d, 3, 15), (g, 3, 15))$	45
S_5	$((d, 3, 16), (g, 5, 16))$	39

Definition 2. A Time Interval sequence (TI-sequence) is denoted as $\langle a_1, I_1, a_2, I_2, \ldots I_{s-1}, a_s \rangle$, where $a_i \in I$ for $1 \le i \le s$ and I_i is the purchased time interval between the successive items such that $I_i \in TI$ for $1 \le i \le s - 1$. The number of items in the TI-sequence defines the length of the sequence. TI-sequence of length 1 is denoted as $\langle a \rangle$, where $a \in I$. For example, $\langle a, I_1, b, I_0, d \rangle$ is a TI-sequence of length 3.

Definition 3. Given a sequence B and a TI-sequence $A = \langle a_1, I_1, a_2, I_2, \ldots, I_{s-1}, a_s \rangle$, A is said to be contained in a sequence $B = ((b_1, iu_1, ts_{b_1}), (b_2, iu_2, ts_{b_2}), \ldots, (b_m, iu_m, ts_{b_m}))$ at (ts_s, ts_e), if there exist integers such that $1 \le i_1 < i_2 < \cdots < i_s \le m$ and $a_1 = b_{i_1}, a_2 = b_{i_2}, \ldots a_s = b_{i_s}$ and $ts_{b_{i_j}} - ts_{b_{i_{j-1}}} = I_{j-1}$, where $2 \le j \le s$ and ts_s, ts_e are the start and end timestamps of A such that ts_s and ts_e are the timestamps of first and last items of A. For example, TI-sequence $\langle a, I_0, c, I_2, c, I_0, d \rangle$ is contained in the sequence $((a, 5, 8)(b, 2, 8)(c, 1, 8)(c, 1, 15)(d, 3, 15))$ at $(8, 15)$.

Definition 4. The minimum utility threshold of an item i in a time interval sequence dataset TSD is denoted as $mu(i)$ in percentage, and the multiple minimum utility threshold table (MMU-table) consists of the minimum utility threshold of each item in TSD. MMU-table is defined as: $MMU\text{-}table = \{mu(i_1), mu(i_2), \ldots mu(i_m)\}$. The MMU-table for the items in Table 1 is defined as $\{mu(a), mu(b), mu(c), mu(d), mu(e), mu(f), mu(g), mu(h)\{85\%, 57\%, 80\%, 85\%, 85\%, 57\%, 85\%, 57\%\}$.

Definition 5. The minimum utility threshold of a TI-sequence A is defined as the least minimum utility value among all the items in A and it is denoted as $MIU(A)$.

Definition 6. The utility of an item i at any timestamp ts in a sequence S is denoted as ui_t and defined as $ui_t(i, ts, S) = iu(i, ts, S) \times eu(i)$. The utility of an item i in a sequence S is denoted as $ui_s(i, S)$ and is defined as the maximum utility of i among all the timestamps in S.

Definition 7. Given a TI-sequence A and a sequence B, the utility of A in B at (ts_s, ts_e) is denoted as us_t and defined as

$$us_t(A, (ts_s, ts_e), B) = \sum_{i=1}^{s} ui_s(a_i, ts_i, B). \tag{1}$$

where ts_s and ts_e are the respective timestamps of first and last items in A. A may be contained in B more than once with varying ts_s and a fixed ts_e. In such cases the utility of A at ts_e is the maximum value among the varying ts_s and is denoted as $us_{te}(A, ts, B)$.

Definition 8. Given a TI-sequence A and a sequence B, the utility of A in B is denoted as $us_s(A, B)$ and defined as the maximum utility among multiple utility values of A in B at multiple timestamps.

The basic terminology of DHUTISP-MMU related to MapReduce environment (Refer to [22] for more details on MapReduce programming) is given from Definition 9 to Definition 15. Let TSD be a sequence dataset stored in the Hadoop Distributed File System (HDFS) and $T_1, T_2, \ldots, T_n$ be the nonempty disjoint input splits of TSD such that $TSD = \{T_1 \cup T_2 \cup \cdots \cup T_n\}$. For example, consider the dataset given in Table 1. It is divided into two input splits, $T_1 = \{S_1, S_2\}$ and $T_2 = \{S_3, S_4, S_5\}$.

Definition 9. The local utility of a TI-sequence A in an input split T_i is denoted as $LU(A, T_i)$ and defined as

$$LU(A, T_i) = \sum_{B \in T_i} u(A, B). \tag{2}$$

Definition 10. The global utility of a TI-sequence A in a time interval sequence dataset TSD is denoted as $GU(A, TSD)$ and defined as

$$GU(A, TSD) = \sum LU(A, T_i), \forall T_i \in TSD. \tag{3}$$

Definition 11. The utility of an input sequence $S = ((a_1, iu_1, ts_{a_1}), (a_2, iu_2, ts_{a_2}), \ldots, (a_m, iu_m, ts_{a_m}))$ also called sequence utility is denoted as $su(S)$ and defined as

$$su(S) = \sum_{i=1}^{m} u(a_i, ts_{a_i}, S). \tag{4}$$

Definition 12. The utility of an input split T_i is defined as

$$u(T_i) = \sum_{j=1}^{m} su(S_j). \tag{5}$$

where m represents the total number of input sequences in input split T_i.

Definition 13. The utility of a time interval sequence dataset TSD is defined as:

$$u(TSD) = \sum_{i=1}^{n} u(T_i). \tag{6}$$

where n represents the number of partitions.

Definition 14. A TI-sequence A is defined as a local high utility time interval sequential pattern (LHUTIS) in an input split T_i if its local utility is no less than the minimum utility threshold of A.

$$LU(A, T_i) \geq MIU(A) \times u(T_i) \tag{7}$$

Definition 15. A TI-sequence A is defined as a global high utility time interval sequential pattern (GHUTIS) in a time interval sequence dataset TSD if its global utility is no less than the minimum utility threshold of A.

$$GU(A, TSD) \geq MIU(A) \times u(TSD) \tag{8}$$

Problem Statement. Given a time interval sequence dataset TSD stored in the Hadoop distributed file system, external utility table and MMU-table, the problem of high utility time interval sequential pattern mining with multiple minimum utility thresholds is to find all the time interval sequential patterns whose utility are no less than their MIU values.

4   Distributed Approach for Mining High Utility Time Interval Sequential Patterns with Multiple Minimum Utility Thresholds

4.1   Utility Upper Bound

The downward closure property of minimum support framework do not hold for the current problem. Hence, we apply a downward closure property TI-SWDC [12] which is an upper bound for a TI-sequence and all its supersequences. The details are given below:

Definition 16. From the definition of sequence weighted utility (SWU) [7], the upper bound of a TI-sequence A in an input split T_i is defined as local time interval sequence weighted utility (LTSWU) and is given below:

$$LTSWU(A, T_i) = \sum su(S), \forall S \in T_i. \tag{9}$$

where A is a subsequence of S

Definition 17. The upper bound of a TI-sequence A in a time interval sequence dataset TSD is defined as a global time interval sequence weighted utility (GTSWU) and is given below:

$$GTSWU(A, TSD) = \sum LTSWU(A, T_i), \forall T_i \in TSD. \tag{10}$$

For Example, $LTSWU(\langle a \rangle, T_2) = su(S_3) + su(S_4) = 15 + 45 = 60$, $GTSWU(\langle a \rangle, TSD) = LTSWU(\langle a \rangle, T_1) + LTSWU(\langle a \rangle, T_2) = 77 + 60 = 137$. The $GTSWU$ of all the items in Table 1 are as follows: $\{a : 137, b : 77, c : 137, d : 161, e : 15, f : 35, g : 134, h : 57\}$. From the upper bound defined in 17, the downward closure property is given below:

Property 1 (Time Interval Sequence Weighted Downward Closure Property (TI-SWDC)). Given a time interval sequence dataset TSD and two TI-sequences A and B, where A is a subsequence of B, then $GTSWU(A, TSD) \geq GTSWU(B, TSD)$. (Please refer [12] for proof.)

From Property 1, if $GTSWU$ of an item i is no less than the $MIU(i)$, then it is said to be a promising item, otherwise it is called unpromising. All the unpromising items can be pruned from the TSD. From definitions 4, 5 and 17, the promising items in our sample dataset are $\{a, c, d, g\}$.

Definition 18. The remaining utility of a given TI-sequence A in an input sequence B at a timestamp ts is denoted as $ru(A, ts, B)$ and defined as the sum of the item utilities those occur after the last item of A to the end item of B. The remaining sequence is denoted as $rs(B/(A, ts))$. For example, $ru(\langle c, I_2, a \rangle, 15, S_4)$ $= u(d, 15, S_1) + u(g, 15, S_1) = 24 + 9 = 33$.

Definition 19. Given a TI-sequence A, the potential minimum utility threshold of A in an input split T_i is denoted as $PMIU(A)$ and defined as:

$$PMIU(A) = min\{mu(i) | i \in A \vee i \in rs(B/(A, ts)) \forall B \in T_i\} \qquad (11)$$

Definition 20. Given a TI-sequence A and an input sequence B, the Remaining Utility Upper Bound (RUUB) of A in B at timestamp ts is denoted as $RUUB(A, ts, B)$ and defined as:

$$RUUB(A, ts, B) = \begin{cases} u(A, ts, B) + ru(A, ts, B) & \text{if } ru(A, ts, B) > 0, \\ 0 & \text{otherwise.} \end{cases} \qquad (12)$$

Definition 21. Given a TI-sequence A and an input sequence B, the RUUB of A in B is denoted as $RUUB(A, B)$ and defined as:

$$RUUB(A, B) = max(RUUB(A, ts, B)) \forall\ ts \text{ in } B. \qquad (13)$$

Definition 22. Given a TI-sequence A, the RUUB of A in an input split T_i is denoted as $RUUB(A, T_i)$ and defined as:

$$RUUB(A, T_i) = \sum_{B \in T_i \wedge A \subseteq B} RUUB(A, B). \qquad (14)$$

4.2   Time Interval Utility Linked List

In the proposed algorithm, a time interval utility linked list data structure is built inorder to store the TI-sequence and its details for efficient calculation of utility. TIUL of a TI-sequence S is of the form $(sid, lseq)$, where sid is the sequence id and $lseq = (ts, u, ru, link)$ contains the following data:

– ts is the timestamp of S.
– u is the maximum utility of S at timestamp ts.

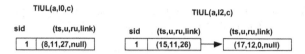

Fig. 1. Time interval utility linked strcture after scanning modified sequence S_1

Fig. 2. TIUL of sequences $\langle a, I_0, c \rangle$ and $\langle a, I_2, c \rangle$

- ru is the remaining utility of S.
- $link$ is the link to next $lseq$.

Figure 1 shows the TIUL data structure built for 1-sequences after scanning the modified input sequence S_1 (the sequence obtained after pruning the unpromising items from S_1). For example, S_1 contains the items a, c, and d. $\langle a \rangle$ occurs only once at timestamp 8 and its utility and remaining utility are 10 and 28 respectively, where as $\langle c \rangle$ occurs thrice at timestamps 8, 15, and 17. Its utility and remaining utility at timestamp 8 are 1, 27, at timestamp 15 they are 1, 26 and 2, 0 at timestamp 17. Similarly, TIUL of $\langle d \rangle$ is built as shown in Fig. 1. Figure 2 shows the TIUL data structure built for the sequences $\langle a, I_0, c \rangle$ and $\langle a, I_2, c \rangle$ in T_1. $\langle c \rangle$ occurs at three timestamps 8, 15 and 17 in S_1 and the time interval between $\langle a \rangle$ and $\langle c \rangle$ at timestamp 8 is I_0 $(8 - 8 = 0)$, at timestamp 15 is I_2 $(15 - 8 = 7)$ and at timestamp 17 is I_2 $(17 - 8 = 9)$. The utility of $\langle a, I_0, c \rangle$ in $S1$ is found by calculating the sum of the utilities i.e. $u(a, 8, S_1) + u(c, 8, S_1) = 10 + 1 = 11$. Similarly, the utility of $\langle a, I_2, c \rangle$ is found by calculating the $max((u(a, 8, S_1) + u(c, 15, S_1)), (u(a, 8, S_1) + u(c, 17, S_1))) = max(10 + 1, 10 + 2) = max(11, 12) = 12$. Hence, $(15, 11, 26, link)$ and $(17, 12, 0, null)$ are the two elements in TIUL of $\langle a, I_2, c \rangle$.

4.3 Itemset-Extension and Sequence-Extension

Given a TI-sequence A and an item i, the itemset-extension of A with i is to append i to the last itemset of A and the time interval is same as the last time interval in A. The sequence-extenison of A with i is to add i as a new itemset at the end of A and the time interval is found by scanning the TIUL of last item in A and i. For example, given a TI-sequence $\langle a, I_0, c \rangle$ and an item d, the itemset-extension would be $\langle a, I_0, c, I_0, d \rangle$ and the sequence-extension would be $\langle a, I_0, c, TI, d \rangle$, where TI is the new time interval between c and d.

4.4 Proposed Algorithm

Based on the concepts defined in Sect. 3, Sect. 4.1, Sect. 4.2 and Sect. 4.3, MapReduce algorithm is proposed and it consists of three phases. The first phase generates all the promising items of the dataset and is described in Algorithm 1.

The second phase mapper finds all the local high utility time interval sequential patterns (LHUTISPs) and is described in Algorithm 2. All the LHUTISPs generated by the second phase mapper in an input split may not be of high utility with respect to the entire dataset. Hence, in the third MapReduce phase as shown in Algorithm 3, the local utilities of all LHUTISPs are added to find the global utility and they are treated as global high utility sequential patterns (GHUTISPs) only if the global utility satisfies the MIU.

Algorithm 1. The first phase of DHUTISP-MMU.

Input:
  TSD_i ▷ Time interval sequence dataset of the input split T_i
  EU ▷ External utilities
  $MMU\text{-}table$ ▷ Minimum utility thresholds of each item
Output:
  $\langle item, global\_utility \rangle$ ▷ Promising item and its global utility
1: **function** MAP(key $offset$, value S)
2:    Scan the items in S and find the local utility of each item and sequence utility
3:    output($item$,($local\_utility$,$sequence\_utility$))
4: **end function**
5: **function** REDUCE(key $item$, values $\langle local\_utility, sequence\_utility \rangle$)
6:    Read each item and its associated values
7:    Calculate the global utility of item by adding its local utilities.
8:    Calculate the GTSWU of each item by adding the sequence utilities.
9:    **if** $GTSWU \geq MIU(item)$ **then**
10:       output($item$,$global\_utility$)
11:    **end if**
12: **end function**

---

5   Experimental Results

We have evaluated the proposed algorithm on a Hadoop cluster with 1 master node and 8 data nodes. Each node runs on a CentOS 6.5 server with Hadoop 2.9.1. The experiments have been conducted on 2 real datasets. More information related to data sets and the time interval generation can be refered in [12]. The setting of different minimum utility thresholds can be referred from [17]. To the best of our knowledge, there is no algorithm either centralized or distributed approach to solve the problem mentioned in the paper. Hence, we evaluated the baseline algorithm, DHUTISP-MMU-Baseline and the proposed algorithm, DHUTISP-MMU. The baseline approach do not include the upper bounds PMIU and RUUB. Figure 3 shows the run time performance of the proposed algorithms under different least minimum utilities (LMU). From Fig. 3, it is observed that the runtime performance of DHUTISP-MMU is more efficient compared to the baseline approach. This is because of the proposed upper bounds PMIU and RUUB. The run time tends to increase with the decrease in LMU. This is due to the increase in number of candidates for low values of LMU.

Algorithm 2. The second map-only phase.

Input:

TSD_i ▷ Time interval sequence dataset of the input split T_i

$pitems$ ▷ Distributed cache file containing promising items

$MMU\text{-}Table$ ▷ Minimum utility threshold of each item

Output:

$\langle LHUTIS, LU \rangle$ ▷ Local high utility TI-sequence and its local utility

1: **function** MAP(key $offset$, value S)
2:     Read $pitems$ and modify the sequence S by pruning unpromising items.
3:     **for** each promising item t **do**
4:        Read the projected database of t and find its itemset-extension list t'_i and sequence extension list t'_s.
5:        **for** each item i in t'_i **do**
6:           Build the TIUL of new sequence t'.
7:           **if** $LTSWU(t') \geq PMIU(t')$ and $LU(t') \geq MIU(t')$ **then**
8:             output(t',$LU(t')$)
9:           **end if**
10:          **if** $RUUB(t') \geq PMIU(t')$ **then**
11:             Repeat the steps 4 and 5 for t'
12:          **else**
13:             return
14:          **end if**
15:        **end for**
16:        Repeat the loop at step 5 for t'_s
17:     **end for**
18: **end function**

Algorithm 3. The third phase of DHUTISP-MMU.

Input:

$Lseq$ ▷ Distributed cache file containing local high utility time interval sequences

$TIUL_{T_i}$ ▷ Time interval utility linked list of partition T_i

$MMU\text{-}table$ ▷ Minimum utility thresholds of each item

Output:

$\langle S, global\_utility \rangle$ ▷ Global high utility time interval sequence and its global utility

1: **function** MAP(key $offset$, value $TIUL_{T_i}$)
2:     **for** each sequence S in $Lseq$ **do**
3:        Find the $local\_utility$ of S in partition T_i
4:        output(S,$local\_utility$)
5:     **end for**
6: **end function**
7: **function** REDUCE(key S, values $local\_utility(S)$)
8:     Calculate the $global\_utility$ of sequence by adding its local utilities
9:     **if** $global\_utility \geq MIU(S)$ **then**
10:        output(S,$global\_utility$)
11:     **end if**
12: **end function**

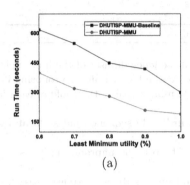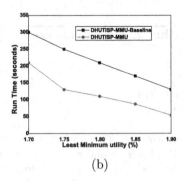

(a)   (b)

Fig. 3. Run time performance with different values of least minimum utility (a) Kosarak (b) BMSWebView2

6   Conclusion

This paper presents a novel idea of mining high utility time interval sequential patterns with multiple minimum utility thresholds in a distributed environment. We proposed a three phase MapReduce algorithm as a solution that deals with the current idea. The proposed downward closure property and remaining utility upper bound prunes the search space to find the HUTISPs. Also, the TIUL data structure has been used to find the utility and upper bound values in an efficient manner. The experimental results reveal that the proposed approach is efficient in terms of run time compared to the baseline approach. As a future work, we would like to extend the problem by providing more efficient pruning strategies. Also, more experimental results need to be done to prove the scalability of the approach.

References

1. Agrawal, A. Srikant, R.: Fast algorithms for mining association rules. In: Proceedings of the 20th International Conference on Very Large Databases, pp. 487–499. ACM, Santiago, Chile (1994)
2. Agrawal, A. Srikant, R.: Mining sequential patterns. In: Proceedings of the 11th International Conference on Data Engineering, pp. 3–14. IEEE, Taipei, Taiwan (1995)
3. Yao, H., Howard, J.H., Cory, J.B.: A foundational approach to mining itemset utilities from databases. In: Proceedings of the 2004 SIAM International Conference on Data Mining, pp. 482–486 (2004)
4. Yao, H., Howard, J.H., Liqiang, G.: A unified framework for utility based measures for mining itemsets. In: Proceedings of ACM SIGKDD 2nd Workshop Utility-Based Data Mining, pp. 28–37 (2006)
5. Hong, Yao., Howard J.H.: Mining itemset utilities from transaction databases. Data Knowl. Eng. **59**(3), 603–626 (2006)
6. Ahmed, C.F., Tanbeer, S.K., Jeong, B.-S.: A novel approach for mining high- utility sequential patterns in sequence databases. ETRI J. **32**(5), 676–686 (2010)

7. Yin, J., Zheng, Z., Cao, L.: USpan: an efficient algorithm for mining high utility sequential patterns. In: Proceedings of the 18th ACM SIGKDD International Conference on Knowledge Discovery and Data Mining, pp. 660–668 (2012)
8. Alkan, O.K., Karagoz, P.: Crom and huspext: improving efficiency of high utility sequential pattern extraction. IEEE Trans. Knowl. Data Eng. **27**(10), 2645–2657 (2015)
9. Wang, J.-Z., Huang, J.-L., Chen, Y.-C.: On efficiently mining high utility sequential patterns. Knowl. Inf. Syst. **49**(2), 597–627 (2016). https://doi.org/10.1007/s10115-015-0914-8
10. Wang, W.-Y., Huang, A. Y.-Q.: Considering high utilities for time interval sequential pattern mining. In: Proceedings of 2015 Conference on Technologies and Applications of Artificial Intelligence, pp. 412–418 (2015)
11. Wang, W.-Y., Huang, A.Y.-Q.: Mining time-interval sequential patterns with high utility from transaction databases. J. Adv. Comput. Intell. Intell. Inform. **20**(6), 1018–1026 (2016)
12. Sumalatha, S., Subramanyam, RBV.: distributed mining of high utility time interval sequential patterns using mapreduce approach. Expert Syst. Appl. **141**, 1–25 (2019)
13. Lin, J.C.-W., Gan, W., Fournier-Viger, P., Hong, T.-P.: Mining high-utility itemsets with multiple minimum utility thresholds. In: Proceedings of the 8th International Conference on Computer Science & Software Engineering, pp. 9–17 (2015)
14. Lin, J.C.-W., Gan, W., Fournier-Viger, P., Hong, T.-P., Zhan, J.: Efficient mining of high-utility itemsets using multiple minimum utility thresholds. Knowl. Based Syst. **113**, 100–115 (2016)
15. Srikumar, K.: Efficient mining of high utility itemsets with multiple minimum utility thresholds. Eng. Appl. Artif. Intell. **69**, 112–126 (2018)
16. Gan, W., Lin, J.C.-W., Zhang, J., Fournier-Viger, P.: Utility mining across multi-sequences with individualized thresholds. ACM/IMS Trans. Data Sci. **1**(2), (2020)
17. Lin, J.C.-W., Zhang, J., Fournier-Viger, P.: High-utility sequential pattern mining with multiple minimum utility thresholds. In: Chen, L., Jensen, C.S., Shahabi, C., Yang, X., Lian, X. (eds.) APWeb-WAIM 2017. LNCS, vol. 10366, pp. 215–229. Springer, Cham (2017). https://doi.org/10.1007/978-3-319-63579-8_17
18. Chen, Y.-L., Chiang, M.-C., Ko, M.-T.: Discovering time-interval sequential patterns in sequence databases. Expert Syst. Appl. **25**(3), 343–354 (2003)
19. Chen, Y.-L., Huang, T.C.-K.: Discovering fuzzy time-interval sequential patterns in sequence databases. IEEE Trans. Syst. Man Cybern. Part B: Cybern. **35**(5), 959–972 (2005)
20. Yen, S.-J., Lee, Y.-S.: Mining time-gap sequential patterns. In: Proceedings of Advanced Research in Applied Artificial Intelligence, pp. 637–646, Springer, Berlin, Heidelberg (2012)
21. Yen, S.-J., Lee, Y.-S.: Mining non-redundant time-gap sequential patterns. Appl. Intell. **39**(4), 727–738 (2013). https://doi.org/10.1007/s10489-013-0426-8
22. Dean, J., Ghemawat, S.: Mapreduce: simplified data processing on large clusters. Commun. ACM **51**(1), 107–113 (2008)

Artificial Intelligence and Machine Learning

Emergency Analysis: Multitask Learning with Deep Convolutional Neural Networks for Fire Emergency Scene Parsing

Jivitesh Sharma[✉], Ole-Christoffer Granmo, and Morten Goodwin

Center for Artificial Intelligence Research (CAIR), University of Agder,
Kristiansand, Norway
{jivitesh.sharma,ole.granmo,morten.goodwin}@uia.no

Abstract. In this paper, we introduce a novel application of using scene semantic image segmentation for fire emergency situation analysis. To analyse a fire emergency scene, we propose to use deep convolutional image segmentation networks to identify and classify objects in a scene based on their build material and their vulnerability to catch fire. We introduce our own fire emergency scene segmentation dataset for this purpose. It consists of real world images with objects annotated on the basis of their build material. We use state-of-the-art segmentation models: DeepLabv3, DeepLabv3+, PSPNet, FCN, SegNet and UNet to compare and evaluate their performance on the fire emergency scene parsing task. During inference time, we only run the encoder (backbone) network to determine whether there is a fire or not in the image. If there is a fire, only then the decoder is activated to segment the emergency scene. This results in dispensing with unnecessary computation, i.e. the decoder. We achieve this by using multitask learning. We show the importance of transfer learning and the difference in performance between models pretrained on different benchmark datasets. The results show that segmentation models can accurately analyse an emergency situation, if properly trained to do so. Our fire emergency scene parsing dataset is available here: https://github.com/cair.

Keywords: Scene parsing · Semantic segmentation · Image segmentation · Multitask learning · Fire dataset · Emergency analysis · Deep convolutional neural networks · DeepLabv3+ · DeepLabv3 · PSPNet · FCN · SegNet · UNet

1 Introduction

Emergency management and response pertains to situations that interrupt normal behaviour and warrant immediate, strict and swift actions to control the state of the situation and avoid turning it into a disaster. Every environment must have an integrated emergency management unit that deals with unforeseen

© Springer Nature Switzerland AG 2021
H. Fujita et al. (Eds.): IEA/AIE 2021, LNAI 12798, pp. 101–112, 2021.
https://doi.org/10.1007/978-3-030-79457-6_9

---

and hazardous circumstances. Emergency management is crucial as it tries to prevent, prepare and respond to threatening circumstances and mitigate human and economic losses.

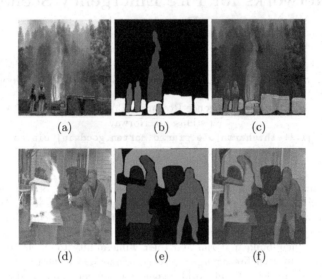

Fig. 1. Fire Images: (a), (d) are the source images, (b), (e) are the segmentation masks and (c), (f) are the annotated images

Emergency management and response consists of three stages: detection, analysis and response/evacuation. The analysis stage is one of the most important steps of the emergency management process. It consists of gathering and analysing as much information about the predicament as possible. Missing information at this stage can be fatal to the victims of the emergency as well as the search and rescue (SAR) personnel.

The analysis step usually shouldn't require risking search and rescue personnel. So, the only reliable way of extracting important information from the environment is through means that do not require human intervention. So, in this work, we focus on the vital stage of emergency analysis. In order to extract relevant information about the emergency situation, we require visual, verbal or audible data. We focus on computer vision for emergency analysis. The advantage of using computer vision for the analysis stage is that, data can be easily gathered and there are well established methods to extract precise and relevant information.

In [16], the Institute of Medicine, US, gave an extensive review on data collection capabilities and information resources in disaster management. It discusses some interesting guidelines like having a central repository of data, a national emergency information system and improving data collection techniques.

In this paper, we propose a novel solution to the above problem of emergency analysis. It is not only a data collection technique, but also consists of data analysis. Many such guidelines and proposals [8] elaborate on efficient data collection and information management, while lacking the crucial step of data analysis.

An analysis of information systems and efficiency in communication during disasters was presented in [21]. It consists of detailed analysis of previous disasters by the Pan-American health organization under the World Health Organization (WHO). It also enlists guidelines for efficient information gathering and communication for emergencies.

Since there is no dataset that consists of annotation based on build material, we build our own dataset which will be freely available to use. We train state-of-the-art segmentation models like U-Net, SegNet, FCN, PSPNet, DeepLabv3 and DeepLabv3+ on our dataset and compare their results. We use multitask learning to train the encoder to recognize whether there is a fire in an image and simultaneously train the decoder to segment the image. During inference, the decoder is activated to segment an image only if the encoder detects fire in an image. We also show the importance of transfer learning by fine-tuning and testing pretrained PSPNet on our dataset. We also compare different pretrained PSPNet models that are trained on different benchmark datasets.

The rest of the paper has been organized in the following manner: Sect. 2 describes our approach in detail with our dataset and segmentation models; Sect. 3 describes the experiments and shows the results; And finally Sect. 4 concludes our work.

2   Fire Emergency Analysis System

In this paper, we propose semantic scene parsing as an approach to emergency situation analysis. To the best of our knowledge, this is the first time emergency analysis has been performed using image segmentation. Specifically, we consider the case of fire related emergencies. For analysing such situations, we propose to identify and classify objects based on their build material in order to determine their vulnerability to catch fire and thereby obtaining useful information about potential fire spread. For example, a wooden object is more likely to catch fire than a plastic object, which can reveal a potential direction of fire spread.

Along with objects, the fire itself is also segmented. The area covered by the segmented fire can show whether the fire has recently been ignited or is it full-blown. Since all pixels of a fire are segmented, it could also give information on the direction of the fire, i.e. are the flames bent towards a particular direction (due to wind or any other factor). Apart from fire, smoke is also identified and segmented. Before the fire erupts, smoke provides the first signs of an impending fire hazard. Segmenting smoke could also provide necessary information about the epicentre of fire and its spread direction.

Also, people and other living beings are identified and classified in the environment, which helps in getting head count. Including this information, fire fighters have crucial details about the environment which can result in better evacuation planning. Priority could be given to areas which contain more people for swift evacuation.

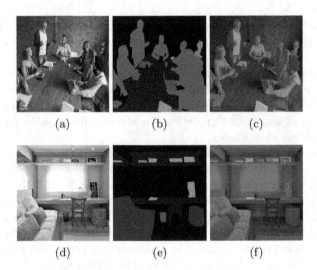

Fig. 2. Normal Images: (a), (d) are the source images, (b), (e) are the segmentation masks and (c), (f) are the annotated images

Note that the information gained from the analysis stage is readily available to the fire fighters even before they enter the hazardous environment, which not only results in better planning but also reduces the risk for fire fighters themselves, since they enter an unseen and unexplored environment with some important information.

In order to achieve this, we train and test several state-of-the-art segmentation models on our own dataset. We use the DeepLabv3, DeepLabv3+, PSPNet, FCN, SegNet and UNet with multitask learning. To the best of our knowledge, this is the first time semantic segmentation has been used to analyse an emergency situation. The following subsections illustrate the design of our emergency analysis system by describing our fire emergency scene parsing dataset and the segmentation models benchmarked on the dataset.

2.1 The Fire Emergency Scene Parsing Dataset

We uniquely design our dataset consisting of fire and normal images. We use images from our previous fire detection dataset which was used in [18,19]. We add more images consisting of many different objects in order to properly train the models. The dataset consists of 2065 images which are annotated on the basis of object material, fire and living beings. The fire emergency scene parsing dataset consists of nine categories (+1 for background), which are:

Wood: It is arguably the most vulnerable object during a fire emergency. It can catch fire more easily than other objects and thus spread fire more rapidly.

Plastic: It is one of the less vulnerable objects to catch fire. It can hinder the spread of fire, which makes it an important object material to identify.

Cloth: It is also one of the objects that is vulnerable to catch fire. It is abundant in most environments, which makes it important to identify.

Plants: Trees and vegetation are one of the most vulnerable objects in a fire hazard, which is evident from forest fires. They can be found in indoor as well as outdoor environments. Since forest fires are one of the most common and devastating disasters, it is imperative to identify such objects.

Stone: Identifying and classifying stone objects makes the analysis model generalize well over indoor and outdoor environments. Also, like plastic, usually stone based objects are less vulnerable to catch fire.

Fire: Identifying fire is the central idea behind a fire emergency analysis stage. Segmenting fire can provide information about the nature of fire as well as the magnitude of the fire hazard.

Smoke: One of the first signs of fire, sometimes revealed even before the fire starts, is smoke. It is one of the most important objects to identify since it can act as a signal for an impending fire hazard.

Person: Identifying people and their location is the most important task of the analysis phase. Segmenting people in the environment reveals head count and the distribution of people in the environment.

Other: This object class consists of the objects that can't be identified accurately only through visual data.

Some examples of images with fire from our dataset are shown in Fig. 1. However, in our dataset, we also have images displaying normal circumstances as well. It allows the models trained on the dataset to have better generalization performance. Some examples of such images are shown in Fig. 2.

To the best of our knowledge, this is the first scene parsing or segmentation dataset that is based on emergency analysis and segmenting objects based on build material. The dataset is imbalanced as the number of instances of each class vary a lot. Keeping this in mind, we also calculate the frequency weighted mean intersection over union metric to compare models.

As the results of state-of-the-art segmentation models suggest, this dataset is difficult to classify since objects of the same shape might belong to different classes (different build material) and the shape of fire is usually highly irregular with different colour properties. That's why we choose to employ state-of-the-art segmentation models instead of a small custom model.

2.2 The Segmentation Models

For the task of fire emergency scene parsing, we employ four state-of-the-art segmentation models. Namely, U-Net [17], SegNet [2], FCN [15], PSPNet [25], DeepLabv3 [5] and DeepLabv3+ [6]. We train these networks from scratch on our dataset. We also fine-tune pretrained versions on the PSPNet to show the effect of transfer learning. Here, we briefly describe each of the segmentation models used in our work.

U-Net. U-Net is a Deep CNN that was first developed for medical image segmentation [17]. It was one of the first fully convolutional networks for image segmentation. It consists of contraction and expansion blocks connected via skip connections resulting in a 'U' shaped architecture. The remarkable aspect about U-Net was its ability to achieve good performance by training on very few annotated images. It was also able to segment a 512×512 image in less than a second.

SegNet. Another end-to-end trainable, fully convolutional network for scene parsing and understanding, called SegNet, was proposed in [2]. SegNet consists of an encoder-decoder structure. The VGG16 [20] acts as the encoder to extract features from the input images. The decoder is almost a mirror image of the encoder and is designed to output a pixel-level classification map. The novelty of the model lies in upsampling feature maps using the saved indices of the max-pooled features in the corresponding encoder layers. This produces a sparse 'unpooled' feature map. Convolutional filters are used to produce dense feature maps from these unpooled features. Using unpooling layers dispenses with using trainable upsampling layers. This results in reduced memory consumption and computation.

FCN. In [15], a family of fully connected network architectures for semantic image segmentation was proposed. The adaptation of contemporary classification models like VGG net [20], AlexNet [14], GoogleNet [22] etc. into fully convolutional networks for segmentation was proposed. The dense predictions from classification models were used as image features. Upsampling layers were changed to backward strided convolutions, also called transposed convolutions. In this way, the whole networks consisted of convolutional layers only and hence the name Fully Convolutional Networks. Features from different depths and strides were combined to produce rich segmentation masks. 32, 16 and 8 strided features were combined, pooled and upsampled (using transposed convolutions) to get the final predictions. In this way, the model encompassed coarse as well as fine features to produce accurate predictions.

PSPNet. The PSPNet, proposed in [25], held the state-of-the-art model in the segmentation task in 2016. The main idea behind this model was the Pyramid Pooling module. The features extracted from a backbone network (like the ResNet-50 and ResNet-101 [11] classification models) were used as input to the pyramid pooling module. The module consists of different levels of pooling sizes like 1×1, 2×2, 3×3 and 6×6. These pooled features were followed by a convolutional layer. Finally, the outputs of different levels were upsampled, concatenated and fed to a convolutional classifier to produce the final predictions. The pyramid pooling module enabled the model to capture both local and global context information. The model was trained with deep supervision with auxiliary loss for ResNet-based FCN network.

DeepLabv3 and DeepLabv3+. In 2017, the DeepLabv3 segmentation model, proposed in [5], outperformed the PSPNet to set a new state-of-the-art for semantic segmentation. In [5], the usage of atrous convolutions, also called dilated convolutions, for semantic segmentation was advocated. The main advantage of using atrous convolutions was the increase in the receptive field of the network and it allowed to control the spatial density of feature maps. These atrous convolutions, with different dilation rates, were laid out in a spatial pyramid pooling module, like in the PSPNet, called atrous spatial pyramid pooling (ASPP). This model was further improved in [6], by proposing a novel decoder module to morph the DeepLabv3 model into an encoder-decoder structure. This improved model is called the DeepLabv3+. The decoder consists of sequential convolutions and upsampling layers with a skip connection from the ASPP module. In order to reduce computation, depthwise separable convolutions were also employed.

All the above models have shown exemplary performance on the image segmentation task. Each one has some advantages and disadvantages over the other models. To see which of these models is best suited for the task of emergency analysis, we train and test all the above models on our fire emergency scene parsing dataset and present our findings in Sect. 3.

2.3 Multitask Learning

In order to avoid unnecessarily executing the decoder part of the segmentation model for every image during inference, we propose to use the encoder/backbone network as a first stage classifier to distinguish between fire and normal images. If a fire is detecting, only then the decoder is activating to segment the image. So, instead of training the backbone network and segmentation decoder separately, we use multitask learning [4] to train the whole model in an end-to-end manner.

This is done by adding a classifier with a sigmoid activation at the end of the backbone network for binary classification between fire and normal images. However, the decoder stage receives the output of the last convolutional feature map of the encoder/backbone network. The end-to-end training of the whole model is performed using a multitask loss which is the combined loss of fire detection and segmentation.

We use per-image binary cross entropy as the classification loss denoted by L_{cls}:

$$L_{cls} = -y\log(p) + (1-y)\log(1-p) \tag{1}$$

For the segmentation loss, we use the per-pixel cross entropy, denoted by L_{seg}:

$$L_{seg} = -\frac{1}{N}\sum_{i=1}^{N}\sum_{c=1}^{M} y_{i,c}\log(p_{i,c}) \tag{2}$$

where, N is the number of pixels in the image and M are the number of classes. The total loss is simply the sum of the above two losses, denoted by L_{total}:

$$L_{total} = L_{cls} + L_{seg} \tag{3}$$

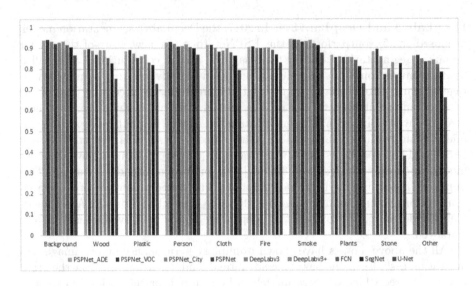

Fig. 3. Class-wise IOU distribution

The classification loss is calculated at the end of the encoder/backbone stage, while the segmentation loss is calculated at the end of the decoder stage. The gradients for the segmentation loss flow from the decoder to the encoder as well, but we keep a very small learning rate associated with the segmentation loss for the encoder. So, the task of segmentation depends on the decoder.

Note that, this way of multitask learning to reduce computation is only effective at inference time when the model is deployed in the real world. For unbiased comparison, we run the whole model on all the test images.

3   Experiments and Results

We test the performance of the above mentioned segmentation models on our fire emergency scene parsing dataset. For a fair comparison, we split our dataset into training and testing sets which is kept the same for all the models. Out of the 2065 images, we use 1665 images for training and 400 images for testing.

We train all the models for 250 epochs on our dataset. To effectively compare the performance of the segmentation models, we use the same backbone/encoder network for all models. We set the ImageNet pretrained ResNet-50 [11] as the backbone network. Since the encoder/backbone is the same for all segmentation models, the fire image classification accuracy is also relatively the same, i.e. around 94.5%. However, to evaluate the segmentation models independently of the encoder/backbone fire detection accuracy, we run the whole model on all test images. The main purpose of multitask learning is to optimize computations during inference.

We have tested the models while conditionally running the decoder conditioned on the backbone classifier, which produced similar final results since all models have the same ResNet-50 backbone network that achieves high fire detection accuracy (94.5%).

Also, to better understand the segmentation results of these models on our unique dataset, we also calculate the frequency weighted mIOU of each model. The frequency weighted mIOU weighs the IOU score by taking into account the number of data points in each class [23]. It can be calculated as:

$$(\sum_{i=1}^{k} t_i)^{-1} \sum_{i=1}^{k} \frac{t_i.n_{ii}}{t_i - n_{ii} + \sum_{j=1}^{k} n_{ij}} \in [0,1] \tag{4}$$

where, t_i are the number of pixels belonging to class i in the ground truth segmentation mask. n_{ii} are the number of pixels belonging to class i and are predicted as class i and n_{ij} are the number of pixels belonging to class i and are predicted as class j.

The dataset consists of images of different sizes in the RGB format, so we resize all images to 473×473, which are fed as the input to the models. We train the models using the Adam optimizer [13]. The batch-size is set to 16 images per batch. We use standard data augmentation techniques to improve generalization performance on the test set, such as random scaling, gaussian blur, random rotation and horizontal flipping. The scaling factor ranges from $[0.75, 1.0, 1.25, 1.5]$ with the randomness of scaling, rotation and flipping set to 0.5.

We implement the segmentation models using Keras [7] and Tensorflow [1] with the help of the Keras segmentation library [24]. The images are preprocessed using [3] and the image augmentations are implemented using the imgaug library [12].

The performance of the segmentation models on our dataset is shown in Table 1. SegNet, FCN-8, PSPNet, DeepLabv3 and DeepLabv3+ achieve high mIOU scores, with the DeepLabv3+ scoring the highest, nearing 88% mIOU. The U-Net scored a moderate mIOU of 74.8%. However, the U-Net achieves a competitive frequency weighted mIOU of 82.2%. Table 1 shows that all the segmentation models achieve expected performance results according to their results on the benchmark datasets of Cityscapes [9], MIT ADE20K [26] and Pascal VOC 2012 [10].

We also test the effect of transfer learning on the task of emergency analysis with fire emergency scene parsing dataset. We use pretrained versions of the PSPNet with trained weights of the Cityscapes, MIT ADE20K and Pascal VOC 2012 datasets. Then, we fine-tune these pretrained models on our fire emergency scene parsing dataset. We use the same experimental setup for these pretrained models. We test different pretrained models to compare their performance and find out whether pretraining on some benchmark datasets yields better performance than others.

Our findings are shown in Table 2. All the pretrained models give relatively the same performance in terms of mIOU and frequency weighted mIOU scores,

Table 1. Performance evaluation of segmentation models

Model	Frequency weighted mIOU	mIOU
U-Net	0.822	0.748
SegNet	0.876	0.852
FCN-8	0.891	0.862
PSPNet	0.899	0.871
DeepLabv3	0.909	0.879
DeepLabv3+	0.913	0.884

with some minute differences. The PSPNet pretrained on the Cityscapes dataset give slightly better performance compared to the other two pretrained models. However, the performance comparison of these pretrained models is highly dependent on the experimental setup and training methodology. So, we believe that the results shown in Table 2 should be taken with a grain of salt.

Table 2. Performance evaluation of pre-trained segmentation models

Model	Pretrained on	Frequency weighted mIOU	mIOU
PSPNet	MIT ADE20K	0.918	0.901
PSPNet	CityScapes	0.921	0.903
PSPNet	PASCAL VOC 2012	0.912	0.892

We plot the class-wise IOU distribution shown in Fig. 3. As we can see from Fig. 3, the pretrained models score slightly higher than other models in most of the classes. But, the major difference in performance can be seen in the 'Stone', 'Wood', 'Plastic' and 'Cloth' classes. Especially in the 'Stone' class, the U-Net performs poorly, since the 'Stone' class has the lowest number of instances in our dataset (that's why U-Net scores higher in frequency weighted mIOU and low on the mIOU scores).

Other than that, we can see the same trend in all class IOU scores: Pretrained models > Other models and DeepLabv3+ > DeepLabv3 > PSPNet > FCN > SegNet > U-Net, with the exception of the 'Stone' class, where the SegNet scores higher. This could be because SegNet can deal with class imbalance problem better than other models. Overall, the models score less on the classes 'Plants', 'Stone' and 'Other'. This is because the classes 'Stone' and 'Plants' have the least number of instances. However, the 'Others' class has one of the higher number of class instances, but since it contains many different types of objects (where the build material cannot be determined with high confidence), it becomes difficult to classify accurately.

4 Conclusion

We have proposed a new approach towards fire emergency analysis using image segmentation. For this purpose, we built our own fire scene parsing dataset consisting of 10 object classes in 2065 images. To segment images based on object build materials, we employed state-of-the-art segmentation models: U-Net, SegNet, FCN, PSPNet, DeepLabv3 and DeepLabv3+. Comparison between these models shows that SegNet, FCN-8, PSPNet, DeepLabv3 and DeepLabv3+ give good performance, with DeepLabv3+ scoring slightly more than others. To reduce computation during inference, we use multitask learning to use th encoder/backbone as a preliminary classifier. If it detects fire in an image, only then the decoder is activated to segment the image. We also showed the importance of transfer learning by fine-tuning pretrained PSPNet models on our dataset. We also compared pretrained models based on the benchmark dataset that they have been trained on. Results show that the PSPNet pretrained on the Cityscapes dataset gives slightly better performance compared to the model trained on MIT ADE20K and Pascal VOC 2012. However, we would like to point out that since there is a very small difference in performance, the results might differ for different training sets and schemes.

References

1. Abadi, M., Agarwal, A., Barham, P., et al.: TensorFlow: large-scale machine learning on heterogeneous systems (2015). https://www.tensorflow.org/, software available from tensorflow.org
2. Badrinarayanan, V., Kendall, A., Cipolla, R.: Segnet: a deep convolutional encoder-decoder architecture for image segmentation. IEEE Trans. Pattern Anal. Mach. Intell. **39**(12), 2481–2495 (2017). https://doi.org/10.1109/TPAMI.2016.2644615
3. Bradski, G.: The OpenCV library. Dr. Dobb's J. Softw. Tools **25**, 120–125 (2000)
4. Caruana, R.: Multitask learning. Mach. Learn. **28**(1), 41–75 (1997)
5. Chen, L., Papandreou, G., Schroff, F., Adam, H.: Rethinking atrous convolution for semantic image segmentation. CoRR abs/1706.05587 (2017). http://arxiv.org/abs/1706.05587
6. Chen, L., Zhu, Y., Papandreou, G., Schroff, F., Adam, H.: Encoder-decoder with atrous separable convolution for semantic image segmentation. CoRR abs/1802.02611 (2018). http://arxiv.org/abs/1802.02611
7. Chollet, F.: Keras (2015). https://github.com/fchollet/keras
8. Columb, M.O., Haji-Michael, P., Nightingale, P.: Data collection in the emergency setting. Emerg. Med. J. **20**(5), 459–463 (2003). https://doi.org/10.1136/emj.20.5.459, https://emj.bmj.com/content/20/5/459
9. Cordts, M., et al.: The cityscapes dataset for semantic urban scene understanding. In: Proceedings of the IEEE Conference on Computer Vision and Pattern Recognition (CVPR) (2016)
10. Everingham, M., Van Gool, L., Williams, C.K.I., Winn, J., Zisserman, A.: The PASCAL Visual Object Classes Challenge (2012) (VOC2012) Results. http://www.pascal-network.org/challenges/VOC/voc2012/workshop/index.html

11. He, K., Zhang, X., Ren, S., Sun, J.: Deep residual learning for image recognition. In: The IEEE Conference on Computer Vision and Pattern Recognition (CVPR), June 2016
12. Jung, A.B.: imgaug. https://github.com/aleju/imgaug (2018), [Online; accessed 30-Oct-2018]
13. Kingma, D.P., Ba, J.: Adam: A method for stochastic optimization. CoRR abs/1412.6980 (2014). http://arxiv.org/abs/1412.6980
14. Krizhevsky, A., Sutskever, I., Hinton, G.E.: Imagenet classification with deep convolutional neural networks. In: Pereira, F., Burges, C.J.C., Bottou, L., Weinberger, K.Q. (eds.) Advances in Neural Information Processing Systems 25, pp. 1097–1105. Curran Associates, Inc. (2012). http://papers.nips.cc/paper/4824-imagenet-classification-with-deep-convolutional-neural-networks.pdf
15. Long, J., Shelhamer, E., Darrell, T.: Fully convolutional networks for semantic segmentation. In: Proceedings of the IEEE Conference on Computer Vision and Pattern Recognition, pp. 3431–3440 (2015)
16. Megan Reeve, T.W., Altevogt, B.: Improving Data Collection Capabilities and Information Resources. National Academies Press (US), April 2015. https://doi.org/10.17226/18967
17. Ronneberger, O., Fischer, P., Brox, T.: U-Net: convolutional networks for biomedical image segmentation. In: Navab, N., Hornegger, J., Wells, W.M., Frangi, A.F. (eds.) MICCAI 2015. LNCS, vol. 9351, pp. 234–241. Springer, Cham (2015). https://doi.org/10.1007/978-3-319-24574-4_28
18. Sharma, J., Granmo, O.-C., Goodwin, M., Fidje, J.T.: Deep convolutional neural networks for fire detection in images. In: Boracchi, G., Iliadis, L., Jayne, C., Likas, A. (eds.) EANN 2017. CCIS, vol. 744, pp. 183–193. Springer, Cham (2017). https://doi.org/10.1007/978-3-319-65172-9_16
19. Sharma, J., Granmo, O.-C., Goodwin, M.: Deep CNN-ELM hybrid models for fire detection in images. In: Kůrková, V., Manolopoulos, Y., Hammer, B., Iliadis, L., Maglogiannis, I. (eds.) ICANN 2018. LNCS, vol. 11141, pp. 245–259. Springer, Cham (2018). https://doi.org/10.1007/978-3-030-01424-7_25
20. Simonyan, K., Zisserman, A.: Very deep convolutional networks for large-scale image recognition. CoRR abs/1409.1556 (2014). http://arxiv.org/abs/1409.1556
21. Arroyo Barrantes, S., Martha Rodriguez, R.P. (ed.): Information management and communication in emergencies and disasters. World Health Organization (WHO) (2009)
22. Szegedy, C., et al.: Going deeper with convolutions. CoRR abs/1409.4842 (2014). http://arxiv.org/abs/1409.4842
23. Thoma, M.: A survey of semantic segmentation. CoRR abs/1602.06541 (2016). http://arxiv.org/abs/1602.06541
24. Yakubovskiy, P.: Segmentation models. https://github.com/qubvel/segmentation_models (2019)
25. Zhao, H., Shi, J., Qi, X., Wang, X., Jia, J.: Pyramid scene parsing network. In: Proceedings of the IEEE Conference on Computer Vision and Pattern Recognition, pp. 2881–2890 (2017)
26. Zhou, B., Zhao, H., Puig, X., Fidler, S., Barriuso, A., Torralba, A.: Scene parsing through ade20k dataset. In: Proceedings of the IEEE Conference on Computer Vision and Pattern Recognition (2017)

Comparison of Consolidation Methods for Predictive Learning of Time Series

Ryoichi Nakajo[✉] and Tetsuya Ogata

Waseda University, Tokyo, Japan
nakajo@idr.ias.sci.waseda.ac.jp, ogata@waseda.jp

Abstract. In environments where various tasks are sequentially given to deep neural networks (DNNs), training methods are needed that enable DNNs to learn the given tasks continuously. A DNN is typically trained by a single dataset, and continuous learning of subsequent datasets causes the problem of catastrophic forgetting. Previous studies have reported results for consolidation learning methods in recognition tasks and reinforcement learning problems. However, those methods were validated on only a few examples of predictive learning for time series. In this study, we applied elastic weight consolidation (EWC) and pseudo-rehearsal to the predictive learning of time series and compared their learning results. Evaluating the latent space after the consolidation learning revealed that the EWC method acquires properties of the pre-training and subsequent datasets with the same distribution, and the pseudo-rehearsal method distinguishes the properties and acquires them with different distributions.

Keywords: Consolidation learning · Predictive learning · Recurrent neural network

1 Introduction

Deep neural networks (DNNs) can acquire features from training datasets collected in advance and show high performance in fields such as recognition, translation, and autonomous driving. DNNs are typically trained with a single dataset, and when DNNs are trained by multiple datasets continuously, this inevitably results in the problem of catastrophic forgetting, in which trainable weights accrue to the subsequent datasets. In environments where training data are successively given to the DNNs, DNNs require the capability to learn successive datasets continuously but retain knowledge from previous datasets.

To overcome the catastrophic forgetting problem, elastic weight consolidation (EWC) proposed by [6] has been attracting attention. EWC is an algorithm that computes Fisher information matrices of the trainable weights as the metrics of importance for previous datasets. The Fisher information matrices are applied as a regularization term when training new datasets. Methods have been proposed that use transfer learning [9] and knowledge distillation [4,11] and that generate pseudo training data by rehearsal [1,8]. These methods are different from EWC, as they try to store the properties of a network trained by previous datasets.

© Springer Nature Switzerland AG 2021
H. Fujita et al. (Eds.): IEA/AIE 2021, LNAI 12798, pp. 113–120, 2021.
https://doi.org/10.1007/978-3-030-79457-6_10

It has been suggested that the stored properties describe representative information about previous datasets, and the network can learn new data more efficiently than when learning the previous datasets again. Results have been reported for the previously proposed consolidation learning methods in recognition and reinforcement learning tasks. However, few examples are available for the field of predictive learning of time series, and the effects of consolidation learning methods in this field remain unclear.

Therefore, the aim of this study was to apply the proposed consolidation learning methods to the predictive learning of time series and compare their learning results. In this study, we applied EWC and pseudo-rehearsal to training of sketch-rnn for drawing tasks [2]. After training sketch-rnn, sketches drawn by the trained network and the latent spaces of the network were evaluated, and the difference between the two consolidation learning methods and conventional learning was compared.

2   Sketch-rnn: Consolidation Learning for Drawing Tasks

For the consolidation learning tasks in predictive learning, we chose the sketch-rnn drawing task. Sketch-rnn [2] generates drawings with a DNN trained with sketches drawn by humans. The DNN is a sequence-to-sequence network with a variational autoencoder, and is composed of encoder-decoder recurrent neural networks (RNNs) and a latent vector between the encoder and decoder. Each RNN receives a time series that includes the pen distance in the x and y directions between the previous and current points, representing three pen states at each time step. Sketch-rnn is trained to reconstruct the given time series and minimize the Kullback-Leibler divergence of the latent vector $z \sim \mathcal{N}(\boldsymbol{\mu}, \boldsymbol{\sigma})$.

3   Comparison of Two Consolidation Learning Methods

In this study, we compared two consolidation learning methods, EWC [6] and pseudo-rehearsal [8]. EWC realizes consolidation learning by mathematical restriction. During the training phase of subsequent datasets, EWC regularizes the trainable weights using Fisher information matrices. In the pseudo-rehearsal method, the trained network generates a dataset itself. Both the generated dataset and the subsequent datasets are given to the network for consolidation learning.

3.1   Elastic Weight Consolidation

The EWC algorithm applies a Bayesian approach to consolidation learning. The main idea of EWC is that the information of a given task can be involved in the posterior distribution without catastrophic forgetting; thus, finding the most probable parameters for subsequent tasks requires no explicit data for the old tasks. Because the true posterior distribution is intractable for neural networks,

EWC introduces a Gaussian approximation. In the regularization term, EWC uses the diagonals of the Fisher information matrices, which approximate the posterior distribution of old tasks. Fisher information matrices are metrics that can measure the importance of current trainable parameters against those of old tasks. Then the EWC algorithm restricts the trainable parameters to retain the information on old tasks. For example, after training for the first task A, the objective loss $L(\theta)$ when the second task B is continuously trained is written as follows:

$$L(\boldsymbol{\theta}) = L_{\mathrm{B}}(\boldsymbol{\theta}) + \sum \frac{\lambda}{2} \boldsymbol{F}_i(\theta_i - \boldsymbol{\theta}_{\mathrm{A}})^2, \tag{1}$$

where $\boldsymbol{\theta}_{\mathrm{A}}$ and $\boldsymbol{\theta}$ are the current trainable parameters and those after training task A, respectively; λ is the strength of regularization; and $\boldsymbol{F}_i$ is the diagonal of a Fisher information matrix.

In the original EWC algorithm proposed in [6], the number of Fisher information matrices needed to compute regularization terms grows linearly with the number of tasks. Then, this growth becomes a bottleneck in consolidation learning and restricts scalability for a large number of tasks. In this study, therefore, we applied the online EWC introduced by [11], which avoids growth in the number of regularization terms by accumulating old Fisher information matrices with a stochastic parameter.

3.2 Pseudo-rehearsal

Pseudo-rehearsal is a consolidation learning method in which the network generates pseudo-data after training, and both the pseudo-data and the subsequent datasets are given to the network during the consolidation learning phase [8]. Properties of previous tasks are stored in the generated pseudo-data. By feeding the network pseudo-data, the pseudo-rehearsal can avoid reuse of the previous dataset during the consolidation phase and thus reduce the amount of training data. In [8], it is suggested that the consolidation learning progresses more efficiently compared to the case of reusing the previous datasets because the pseudo-data capture the properties of the previous tasks. In the field of DNNs, Atkinson and his colleagues [1] introduced the generative adversarial network to generate pseudo-data and conducted consolidation learning for image recognition.

4 Experiment

To compare the performance of the consolidation learning methods for the predictive learning of time series, we conducted an experiment in which the network was trained with sketch data. Three classes of sketch data, *cat*, *laptop*, and *cake*, were prepared from *Quick, Draw!* [5]. Each class had 70,000 sketches for network training and 2,500 sketches for testing. The numbers of neural units of the encoder RNN, the decoder RNN, and the latent variables in sketch-rnn were

256, 512, and 128, respectively. In this experiment, we set the strength of regularization by EWC as $\lambda = 1.0 \times 10^3$. The trained network generated 210,000 pseudo-data sketches for the rehearsal method. At each stage of consolidation learning, we updated the trainable parameters of the network for 100,000 epochs. We used Adam optimization for training, the initial learning rate was set to 0.001. We also trained sketch-rnn in a conventional way by feeding it all three training sketch classes (*cat*, *laptop*, and *cake*) at once.

After consolidation learning by EWC or pseudo-rehearsal, we applied the trained network to the drawing of sketches. The drawn sketches are shown in Fig. 1. Sketches shown in Fig. 1(b) were drawn by the network that was simultaneously trained with all training data. Sketches shown in Fig. 1(c) to (f) were drawn by the network after consolidation learning. Comparing sketches Fig. 1(b) with (c) to (f), it appears that the sketches drawn after consolidation learning lost characteristics of the original sketches. Sketches drawn by the network using the EWC method tended to be affected by the subsequent sketch training. As shown in Fig. 1(c) and (e), the drawn sketches come close to the subsequent sketches for *laptop* and *cake*. Sketches drawn by the network trained by the pseudo-rehearsal method appear to maintain some of characteristics of the pre-training sketches, like *cat* shown in Fig. 1(d). However, as shown in Fig. 1(f), the network after consolidation of three sketch classes could not capture the subsequent training data, such as *cake*, and the pre-trained characteristics were also lost. The reconstruction costs after consolidation learning of three sketch classes are shown in Table 1. The costs of reconstructed sketches after EWC training were lower than those after pseudo-rehearsal training. In addition, the network trained with EWC showed better performance than the network that was simultaneously trained by three classes of training data.

Table 1. Reconstruction costs after consolidation learning. The "no consolidation" method means that the network was simultaneously trained by all three sketch classes, and consolidation learning was not applied.

Consolidation method	*Cat*	*Laptop*	*Cake*
No consolidation	1.40 ± 0.04	1.06 ± 0.03	1.33 ± 0.02
EWC	$\mathbf{1.34 \pm 0.03}$	$\mathbf{0.99 \pm 0.02}$	$\mathbf{1.11 \pm 0.03}$
Pseudo-rehearsal	2.35 ± 0.05	1.89 ± 0.02	1.97 ± 0.04

We conducted linear discriminant analysis of the parameter μ of the latent variable $z \sim \mathcal{N}(\mu, \sigma)$ after consolidation learning with the three sketch classes. Figure 2 shows the results for each consolidation learning method. Figure 2 shows that both the EWC and pseudo-rehearsal methods have similar feature spaces, and the clusters obtained in the EWC method are slightly closer than those obtained in pseudo-rehearsal. After sketches were generated, we applied the trained network to encode the drawn sketches again, and transform the encoded variables into the feature space. The basis of the linear discriminant analysis

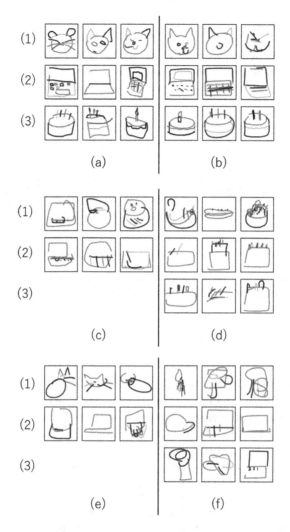

Fig. 1. Sketches of (1) *cat*, (2) *laptop*, and (3) *cake*. Sketches in (a) are training data. Sketches in (b) were generated by a single network trained with (1), (2), and (3). Sketches in (c–f) were generated by the network trained by consolidation learning. EWC was applied as the consolidation learning method in (c) and (d), and pseudo-rehearsal was applied in (e) and (f). In (c) and (e), the networks were trained by sketches (1) and (2). In (d) and (f), the networks were trained by sketches (1)–(3).

applied to obtain Fig. 2 was used to reduce the dimensions of the encoded mean parameter μ. The transformed features of drawn sketches are plotted in Fig. 3. The left graph in Fig. 3 reflects features after training with EWC. In this graph, the features of drawn *cat* sketches, on which the network was trained first, are placed in the cluster of the original *cat* sketches. Features of subsequent sketches, *laptop* and *cake*, crowd into the cluster of original *cake* sketches, which were the final stage of training. The right graph in Fig. 3 reflects features after training with pseudo-rehearsal. In this graph, features of *laptop* sketches broaden the cluster of *laptop*. Most features of drawn sketches are gathered to the center of the three training clusters.

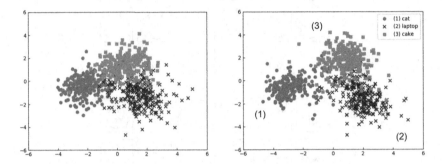

Fig. 2. Linear discriminant analysis of the mean parameter μ of the latent variable $z \sim \mathcal{N}(\mu, \sigma)$. The left graph is the result of EWC, and the right is the result of pseudo-rehearsal.

5   Discussion

The results in Fig. 3 and the sketches in Fig. 1 suggest that the consolidation learning method affects the encoder in sketch-rnn, which recognizes the class of a sketch. However, catastrophic forgetting occurred in the sketch generation phase of the sketch-rnn decoder in both the EWC and pseudo-rehearsal methods. Comparison of EWC with pseudo-rehearsal shows that both consolidation methods acquired similar features from the consolidation learning. During sketch generation, the EWC method tended to produce sketches that were similar to the first or last training data, as shown in Fig. 3. Sketch-rnn trained with pseudo-rehearsal appeared to extract the common characteristics from the whole training dataset, and then most of the features of drawn sketches were encoded in the center of the class clusters in Fig. 3.

From the perspective of an optimization process, the EWC method outperforms the pseudo-rehearsal method because EWC directly restricts trainable parameters in the network. However, the objective losses in the optimization process are generally not consistent with the metrics that humans would apply, and some sketches are unrecognizable. In this study, sketch-rnn was applied to optimize the direction and offset of strokes at each time step, after which the objective losses cannot reflect the whole shape of a sketch. Thus, to avoid catastrophic forgetting during sketch drawing training, other metrics should have been introduced to losses around the reconstruction of sketches by the decoder. For metric learning, triplet loss [10] and Siamese networks [7] have attracted attention in the field of image categorization. These schemes can measure the distance to training targets in embedding space; thus, to generate human-like

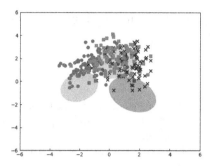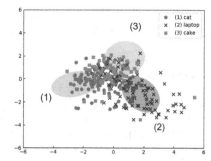

Fig. 3. Latent variables of sketches generated by trained networks. After consolidation learning, the trained networks encoded drawn sketches again and transformed the encoded variables according to the linear discriminant analysis shown in Fig. 2. The left graph is the feature space of EWC, and the right is that of pseudo-rehearsal. The ellipses in the graphs indicate the distribution of the original sketches shown in Fig. 2. The features obtained from the drawn sketches are plotted by symbols.

data, these metrics should be introduced in future work on network learning. Furthermore, the latent variables z approximated the normal distribution, causing the sketches drawn by the network trained via pseudo-rehearsal to crowd into the center of the three class clusters. These latent variables would restrict the variety of sketches in pseudo-data, and promote extraction of the common characteristics of the whole training dataset. To maintain the variety of pseudo-data, a uniform distribution might store the characteristics of each class more effectively. For instance, the generative adversarial imitation learning (GAIL) method [3] includes a uniform distribution in its learning schema. For pseudo-rehearsal, we might compare the normal distributions with the uniform distribution in a method such as GAIL.

6   Conclusion

In this study, we applied two consolidation learning methods, namely, EWC and pseudo-rehearsal, for predictive learning of time-series data and compared the results. For the predictive learning task, we chose sketch drawing by sketch-rnn [2] and conducted sequential training with sketches. After the consolidation, the sketches drawn by the trained network appeared to lose characteristics of the pre-trained sketches in both of the consolidation learning methods. From the perspective of reconstruction cost, the EWC method outperformed the pseudo-rehearsal method. The encoded information about sketches was similar between the EWC and pseudo-rehearsal methods.

In this work, the networks included latent spaces along the normal distribution, and it was suggested that this normal distribution restricted the variety of pseudo-data. Thus, in future work, we should conduct consolidation learning on a network with a uniform distribution, such as GAIL [3]. In addition, we will explore the application of consolidation learning to different types of time-series data. For example, learning for robotic control in a living environment requires the ability to sequentially learn given tasks.

References

1. Atkinson, C., McCane, B., Szymanski, L., Robins, A.: Pseudo-rehearsal: achieving deep reinforcement learning without catastrophic forgetting. Neurocomputing **428**, 291–307 (2021). https://doi.org/10.1016/j.neucom.2020.11.050
2. Ha, D., Eck, D.: A neural representation of sketch drawings. In: International Conference on Learning Representations (2018)
3. Ho, J., Ermon, S.: Generative adversarial imitation learning. In: Lee, D., Sugiyama, M., Luxburg, U., Guyon, I., Garnett, R. (eds.) Advances in Neural Information Processing Systems, vol. 29. Curran Associates, Inc. (2016)
4. Hou, S., Pan, X., Loy, C.C., Wang, Z., Lin, D.: Lifelong learning via progressive distillation and retrospection. In: Proceedings of European Conference on Computer Vision, pp. 437–452 (2018)
5. Jongejan, J., Rowley, H., Kawashima, T., Kim, J., Thomson, R., Fox-Gieg, N.: Quick, Draw! (2016). https://quickdraw.withgoogle.com
6. Kirkpatrick, J., et al.: Overcoming catastrophic forgetting in neural networks. Proc. Natl. Acad. Sci. **114**(13), 3521–3526 (2017). https://doi.org/10.1073/pnas.1611835114
7. Koch, G., Zemel, R., Salakhutdinov, R.: Siamese neural networks for one-shot image recognition. In: ICML Deep Learning Workshop, vol. 2 (2015)
8. Robins, A.: Catastrophic forgetting, rehearsal and pseudorehearsal. Connect. Sci. **7**(2), 123–146 (1995). https://doi.org/10.1080/09540099550039318
9. Rusu, A.A., et al.: Progressive neural networks. arXiv preprint arXiv:1606.04671 (2016)
10. Schroff, F., Kalenichenko, D., Philbin, J.: FaceNet: a unified embedding for face recognition and clustering. In: 2015 IEEE Conference on Computer Vision and Pattern Recognition (CVPR), pp. 815–823 (2015). https://doi.org/10.1109/CVPR.2015.7298682
11. Schwarz, J., et al.: Progress & compress: a scalable framework for continual learning. In: 35th International Conference on Machine Learning (ICML 2018), vol. 10, pp. 7199–7208 (2018)

Evolutionary Optimization of Convolutional Neural Network Architecture Design for Thoracic X-Ray Image Classification

Hassen Louati[1][(✉)] , Slim Bechikh[1] , Ali Louati[2] , Abdulaziz Aldaej[2] ,
and Lamjed Ben Said[1]

[1] SMART Lab, University of Tunis, ISG, Tunis, Tunisia
hassen.louati@stud.acs.upb.ro,slim.bechikh@fsegn.rnu.tn,
lamjed.bensaid@isg.rnu.tn
[2] Department of Information Systems, College of Computer Engineering and
Sciences, Prince Sattam bin Abdulaziz University, Al-Kharj 11942, Saudi Arabia
{a.louati,a.aldaej}@psau.edu.sa

Abstract. Chest X-Ray images are among the most used tools in medical diagnosis of various hearts and lung abnormalities and infections that could cause pneumonia, severe acute respiratory syndrome, septic shock, failure of multiple organs, and even death. Although such kind of images could be obtained at low cost, the lacking of qualified radiologists limits the exploitation of the X-Ray imaging technology. For these reasons, researchers have proposed the use of deep learning techniques to develop computer-assisted diagnosis systems. Among the most used techniques that have shown great performance in image classification, we find the Convolutional Neural Network (CNN). According to the literature, a good number of CNN architectures already exist. Unfortunately, there are no guidelines to design a specific architecture for a particular task; therefore, such design is still very subjective and mainly depends on the expertise and knowledge of data scientists. Motivated by these observations, we propose in this paper an automated method of CNN design for X-Ray image classification. We demonstrate that the CNN design can be seen as an optimization problem and we propose an Evolutionary algorithm (EA) that evolves a population of CNN architectures, with the aim to output an optimized one. Thanks to the ability of the EA to vary the graphs topologies of convolution blocks, the architecture search space is intelligently sampled approximating the optimal possible CNN architecture. Our proposed evolutionary method is validated by means of a set of comparative experiments with respect to relevant state-of-art architectures coming from three-generation approaches, namely: manual crafting, reinforcement learning-based design, and evolutionary optimization. The obtained results show the merits of our proposal based on the detection of the thoracic anomalies in the X-Ray images.

Supported by the Deanship of Scientific Research at Prince Sattam bin Abdulaziz University through the research project No. 2020/01/13222.

© Springer Nature Switzerland AG 2021
H. Fujita et al. (Eds.): IEA/AIE 2021, LNAI 12798, pp. 121–132, 2021.
https://doi.org/10.1007/978-3-030-79457-6_11

Keywords: Deep CNN architecture design · Evolutionary algorithms · Thorax disease · Chest X-Ray

1 Introduction

Chest X-Ray is one of the most commonly available radiological tests for the diagnosis of several lung diseases. Actually, there are a huge number of X- ray imaging studies stored and accumulated in many image archiving and communication systems of many modern hospitals. An open question is that how can a database containing invaluable image information be used to facilitate data-starved deep learning models in building computer-assisted diagnostic systems. There are a few research efforts reported in the literature for identifying the chest radiograph image view [1]. The rapid and tremendous progress has been evidenced in a range of computer vision problems via deep learning. Recently, COVID-19 infection could cause pneumonia, respiratory syndrome, septic shock, multiple organ failure, and even death. The earlier the detection of contamination is the lower the danger and negative effects will be. To deal with the pandemic, many companies around the world are investing in developing fast diagnosis tools.

During the last decade, deep learning has made great inroads in computer vision applications [2], including the classification of natural and medical images. This success has led many researchers to diagnose chest diseases in chest radiography using deep convolutional neural networks (DCNNs). Despite the very interesting performance of CNNs, their architecture design is still so far, a major challenge for researchers and practitioners. CNN has a high number of hyper-parameters that define its architecture and hence they should be well-tuned to optimize such architecture. During the last years, many CNN architectures have been proposed by expert engineers from well-known companies such as Google. Among them, we cite ResNet [3], AlexNet [4], DenseNet [5], and VGGNet [6].

As these architectures were designed manually, researchers in the areas of optimization and learning suggested that better architectures could be found by automated methods, some researchers suggested to model the design of the architecture as a process of Reinforcement Learning (RL) and others have proposed to model this task as an optimization problem and then solve it using an appropriate search algorithm.

Indeed, for any architecture there exist a topology of convolution within each block of a CNN corresponds to an optimization problem with a large search space as showed in Fig. 1. According to the literature, a large number of CNN architectures already exist. Unfortunately, there are no guidelines for designing a specific architecture for a particular task; therefore, such design is still very subjective and very much depends on the expertise of data scientists.

The main idea that we propose is the evolutionary work, consisting of proposing an effective evolutionary approach for CNN architecture design for Chest X-Ray Image Classification. In fact, any CNN architecture is a sequence of convolution and pooling layers followed by a SoftMax aggregation layer. However, the design heavily depends on: (a) the hyper-parameters settings, (b) the graph topologies of convolution nodes. All these settings could be progressively optimized on the X-Ray images data sets of patients. In this way, at the end of the evolutionary process, the user could be provided with a high-performing CNN architecture that is able to detect different thoracic diseases including COVID-19 with high enough precision and recall.

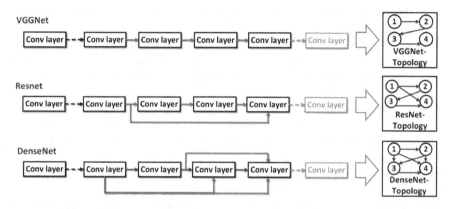

Fig. 1. Illustration of block topologies of three sample CNNs: VGGNet [6], ResNet [3], and DenseNet [5].

2 Related Works

Manual optimization is the first deep architectures designed by expert researchers and practitioners. Since 2012, these architectures have gained popularity thanks to their interesting performance in image classification competitions at that time [26]. Krizhevsky et al. [4] proposed an architecture stacking more layers than LeNet-5 called AlexNet. It is composed of eight layers: five convolutional layers and three fully-connected ones. It is the first architecture that uses the Rectified Linear unit (ReLu) activation function. Szegedy et al. [7] proposed Inception-v1 1, which is the first architecture grouping convolution layers into blocks and makes use of batch normalization. It starts by an inception layer that uses different sizes and types of convolutions for the same input while stacking all the outputs. He et al. [3] proposed an architecture called ResNet, that increased the number of layers to 152. It uses a residual block that includes a series of two convolutional layers whose output is added to the input of the residual block. Lin et al. [8] proposed an architecture known as ResNeXt-50, It is an extension of ResNet that replaces the standard residual block with one that leverages a "split-transform-merge" strategy (i.e., branched paths within a cell) used in the Inception models. The manual architectures have shown their promising performance in many learning tasks. However, these architectures are locally optimal as the search space of the hyper-parameters defining the architecture is huge. This observation recalls us the new research field of Evolutionary Machine Learning (EML) [9] where evolutionary computation techniques have been successfully applied to many learning tasks.

Evolutionary optimization has been successfully applied to many learning tasks. This success could be explained by the global search ability of population-based metaheuristics that allows escaping local optima and coming up with a (near) globally-optimal solution [22]. Shinozaki et al. [13] used GA to optimize the structure and the parameters of a DNN. While GA works on the binary vectors representing the structure of a DNN as a directed acyclic graph, CMA-ES which is inherently a continuous optimizer uses an indirect encoding to convert discrete structural variables to real numbers. Xie et al. [8] represented the network structure as a binary string and optimized the recognition accuracy. The main issue was the high computational cost which pushed the authors to perform the experiments only on small-scale data sets. Sun et al. [14] developed an evolutionary approach to automatically optimize the architectures and initialize the weights of CNNs for image classification problems. This goal has been successfully achieved by proposing a new strategy for weight initialization, a new encoding scheme for variable-length chromosomes, a slacked binary tournament selection, and an efficient fitness evaluation technique. Lu et al. [15] proposed for the first time a multi-objective modeling of the architecture search problem by minimizing two possibly conflicting objectives that are the classification error rate and the computational complexity, which were defined by the number of floating-point operations (FLOPS). They adapted the Non-dominated Sorting GA-II (NSGA-II) as a multi-objective EA.

Many computational intelligence methods have been proposed to detect different thoracic diseases using chest X-Ray images. Wang et al. [16] proposed a weakly supervised multi-label unified classification framework considering various DCNN multi-label losses and different pooling strategies. Islam et al. [17] have defined a set of multiple advanced network architectures to increase classification performance. Rajpurkar et al. [18] demonstrated that a common DenseNet architecture can surpass the accuracy of radiologists in detecting pneumonia. Yao et al. [19] have developed an approach which makes more use of the dependencies of statistical labels and thus improved performance. Irvin et al. [20] designed a deep learning model called CheXNet and used dense connections and batch normalization to make the optimization of this model treatables. Prabira et al. [21] used nine pre-trained CNN models to extract a set of deep features that are subsequently sent to the Support Vector Machines (SVM) classifier. Eleven manually designed deep CNN architectures were considered in the comparative experiments and the proposed method has been shown to have better detection accuracy on X-Ray images.

3   The Proposed Method

Our approach is motivated by the following question:

– **RQ:** There is a very large number of possible CNN convolution blocks' graphs' topologies defining the relationships between nodes. How to find the optimal sequence of block topologies for X-Ray images ?

To answer this research question, we need to look for the best graph topology sequence to classify X-Ray images and detect the possible thoracic anomalies and infections.

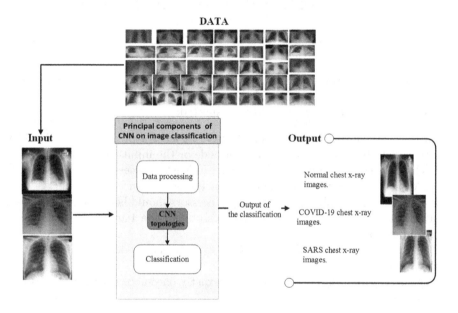

Fig. 2. Illustration of the working principal of CNN on X-Ray images classification based on EAs

We propose an approach called **CNN-XRAY** to find an efficient evolutionary approach for the design of the CNN architecture by looking for the optimal sequence of block topologies to detect different thoracic diseases. In fact, any CNN architecture is a sequence of convolution and pooling layers followed by a SoftMax aggregation layer. Figure 2 presents our approach of CNN architecture optimization that will be detailed in the following subsections.

3.1   CNN Topologies

The solution encoding is a sequence of squared binary matrices each of which represents a possible directed graph. An element value equal to 1 means that

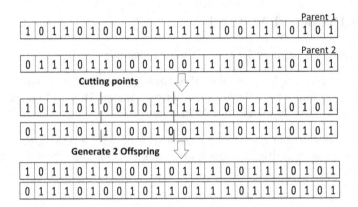

Fig. 3. Crossover operator

the row node is a predecessor of the column node; while a value of zero means that there is no connection between the two nodes.

The following constraints should be respected:

- Each active convolution node should have at least a predecessor node. The latter could be a previous convolution node or the input convolution node.
- Each active convolution node should have at least a successor node. The latter could be a successor convolution node or the output successor node.
- For any active convolution node, its predecessors should belong to its previous layers. For example, the possible predecessors of node 4 are nodes 3, 2, 1, and the input node.
- The first convolution node should have exactly one predecessor node that is the input node.
- The last convolution node should have exactly one successor node that is the output node.

Crossover Operator: To vary the population at the lower level, we use the two-point crossover operator [9] as it allows varying all parts of the chromosomes as showed in Fig. 3. To be able to apply such operator, each parent solution is a set of binary strings. In the two-point crossover process, two cutting points are applied to each parent and then the bits between the cuts are swapped to obtain two offspring solutions. Eventually, infeasible solutions produced by the crossover are repaired by local changes to meet the five above described feasibility constraints.

Mutation Operator: Similar to the crossover operator, the solution is first transformed into a binary string using Gray encoding and then the one-point mutation is applied [9].

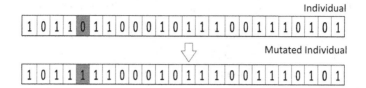

Fig. 4. Mutation operator

4   Experiments

4.1   Benchmarks

Chest X-Ray14 database consists of 112,120 frontal-view radiographs X-Ray images from 30,805 unique patients. The database was compiled using natural language processing techniques from associated radiological reports stored in hospital image archiving and communication systems. Each image may have one or more common chest conditions (one or many common thoracic diseases), or "Normal" otherwise.

Table 1. Summary of parameter settings.

Categories	Parameters	Value
Gradient descent	Batch size	128
	Epochs	50/350
	SGD Learning rate	0.1
	Momentum	0.9
	Weight decay	0.0001
Search strategy	# of generation	40
	Population size	60
	Crossover probability	0.9
	Mutation probability	0.1

Chest X-Ray of COVID-19 patients were obtained from the opensource GitHub repository shared by Dr. Joseph Cohen https://github.com/ieee8023/covid-chestxray-dataset. This repository consists of chest X-Ray images from a number of patients with acute respiratory distress syndrome, severe acute respiratory syndrome, COVID-19, and pneumonia. Our experiment is based on the a database containing chest radiographic images divided into two categories which are: images of normal patients and images of COVID-19 ones. The dataset used was randomly splitted into two independent datasets with 80% and 20% for training and testing respectively.

Table 2. Obtained *AUROC and #Params,* results on ChestX-Ray14.

Method	Search method	Test AUROC (%)	#Params
Yao et al. [19]	Manual	79.8	–
Wang et al. [16]	Manual	73.8	–
CheXNet [18]	Manual	84.4	7.0M
Google AutoML [23]	RL	79.7	–
LEAF [24]	EA	84.3	–
NSGANet-X [25]	EA	84.6	2.2M
CNN-XRAY	EA	87.12	5.1M

Table 3. Obtained *Acc* values on Chest X-Ray images.

Detection method	Reference	Test Acc (%)	Sensitivity	Specificity
Deep features-based SVM	[21]	95.4	97.29	93.47
ResNet101		89.26	91.23	87.29
Inceptionv3		91.08	91.11	91.05
GoogleNet		91.44	89.82	93.05
VGG16		92.76	97.47	88.05
VGG19		92.91	95.11	90.70
XceptionNet		93.92	94.76	93.05
Inceptionresnetv2		93.32	94.76	93.05
AlexNet		93.32	93.41	93.23
DenseNet201		93.88	94.35	93.41
CNN-XRAY	Our work	96.12	97.45	94.27

4.2 Comparative Results

CNN-XRAY is compared to the most representative works from the three categories of CNN architecture generation methods. Table 1 summarizes the parameters settings used in our experiments.

Tables 2 summarizes the obtained comparative results of the different architectures outputted by the confronted CNN design methods on X-Ray images. In fact, the AUROC of manual methods is lying between 79.8% and 84.6%. Google AutoML corresponds to the worst method among non-manual ones and provides an AUROC 79.7%. Always in terms of classification AUROC, the evolutionary ones provide an AUROC values of 84.3% for LEAF (2019) [24] and 84.6% for NSGANet-X [25]. We observe that **CNN-XRAY** is able to automatically design a CNN architecture that achieves better AUROC values than the considered peer methods.

These results could be explained by the following arguments. The manual design of CNNs is a very complex and tedious task that requires a lot of expertise from the user. Even with a high expertise, coming up with a good architecture is

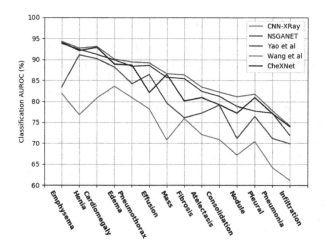

Fig. 5. CNN-XRAY multi-label classification performance on ChestX-Ray14, the class-wise mean test AUROC comparison with peer works.

not easy at all because the number of possible architectures is huge. To automate this design task, RL-based methods and evolutionary ones were proposed and have shown superior performance over manual design thanks to their ability to search over the huge search space of possible architectures in an automated way. Evolutionary methods have shown in this study and previous ones the best performance because RL-based methods have a greedy behavior that maximizes the AUROC over the search process. In fact, evolutionary methods have the capability to escape local optima and to cover the whole search space thanks to their global search ability in addition to the probabilistic acceptance of less-performing architectures by means of the mating selection operator.

Furthermore, Table 2 shows **CNN-XRAY** is the best performing method with an AUROC value of 87.12%. More detailed results showing the disease curve of **CNN-XRAY** and the comparison AUROC by a disease with other peer methods are provided in Fig. 5. These results further validate the capacity of our proposed algorithm to automatically generate task-dependent architectures. In Table 3, we observe that **CNN-XRAY** is able to automatically design a CNN architecture that achieves better accuracy values than the considered peer methods. This could be explained by the fact that CNN design is not easy at all, even in the presence of a high level of expertise. Automatic design methods outperform manually designed architectures for radiographic images. The reason behind this is that the number of possible architectures is enormous.

To sum up, the network topology optimization process has a great impact on the classification performance as each topology defines the relationships between the neural network nodes. To the best of our knowledge, **CNN-XRAY** is the first EAs based system in the literature capable of detecting COVID-19 infection. It has been tested against several architectures.

4.3   Brief Analysis of Best Architectures

It would be interesting to study the common features of the best obtained architectures. After the mining process, we have deduced the following observations:

– Kernel size has a direct impact on the classification. Through our analysis, we noticed that the best architectures mostly include conv3×3 kernels in addition to some conv5×5 ones.
– Some operations are shared by the best architectures as it seems that they reduce the network complexity. Mainly, these operations are non-parametric and correspond to average pooling and skip connections. On the one hand, the skip connection allows learning deviation from the identity layer. On the other hand, average pooling reduces the misclassification rate especially at the last layers.

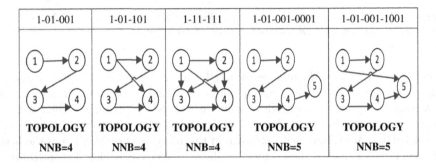

Fig. 6. Example of five convolution blocks' topologies encoded as binary strings.

– **Parallel operations** are more effective than sequential ones in terms of AUROC. In fact, using different filters with various sizes at the same level makes the network "wider" rather than "deeper" at that level. We believe that the concatenation of multiple inputs has a beneficial effect on the classification performance.
– **The internal graph topologies** seem to have a crucial effect on the network performance. During the evolutionary search, we have mined also some architectures having poor AUROC values. Surprisingly, some of them share some characteristics with the good architectures' those, but their convolution blocks' topologies are very different from those of the good architectures. We believe that the topology factor plays a principal role in the classification task.

5   Conclusion

In this work, we have proposed an efficient evolutionary approach for the design of the CNN architecture by looking for the optimal sequence of block topologies to detect different thoracic diseases, including COVID-19 data set. Based on the analysis of the obtained results, our approach **CNN-XRAY** has shown its effectiveness and outperformance on the X-Ray images benchmarks data set with respect to several representative architectures in addition to some others that are generated by recent prominent reinforcement learning and evolutionary approaches.

Acknowledgements. This project was supported by the Deanship of Scientific Research at Prince Sattam bin Abdulaziz University through the research project No. 2020/01/13222.

A   Solution Encoding

As described in Sect. 3.1, The solution encoding is a sequence of squared binary matrices each representing a possible directed graph. Figure 6 details an example of five convolution blocks' topologies encoded as binary strings.

References

1. Becker, A.S., et al.: Detection of tuberculosis patterns in digital photographs of chest X-ray images using Deep Learning: feasibility study. Int. J. Tuberc. Lung Dis. **22**(3), 328–335 (2018)
2. Louati, A., Louati, H., Li, Z.: Deep learning and case-based reasoning for predictive and adaptive traffic emergency management. J. Supercomput. **77**(5), 4389–4418 (2020). https://doi.org/10.1007/s11227-020-03435-3
3. He, K., Zhang, X., Ren, S., Sun, J.: Deep residual learning for image recognition. In: IEEE conference on Computer Vision and Pattern Recognition, pp. 770–778 (2016)
4. Krizhevsky, A., Sutskever, I., Hinton, G.E.: ImageNet classification with deep convolutional neural networks. Adv. Neural Inf. Process. Syst. **25**, 1097–1105 (2012)
5. Huang, G., Liu, Z., van der Maaten, L., Weinberger, K.Q.: Densely 750 connected convolutional networks. In: The IEEE Conference on Computer Vision and Pattern Recognition, pp. 4700–4708 (2017)
6. Simonyan, K., Zisserman, A.: Very deep convolutional networks for large-scale image recognition. CoRR arXiv:1409.1556 (2014)
7. Szegedy, C. et al.: Going deeper with convolutions. In: IEEE Conference on Computer Vision and Pattern Recognition, p. 19 (2015)
8. Xie, S., Girshick, R., Dollar, P., Tu, Z., He, K.: Aggregated residual transformations for deep neural networks. In: IEEE conference on Computer Vision and Pattern Recognition, pp. 1492–1500 (2017)
9. Louati, H., Bechikh, S., Louati, A., Hung, C.C., Ben Said, L.: Deep convolutional neural network architecture design as a bi-level optimization problem. Neurocomputing **439**, 44–62 (2021). https://doi.org/10.1016/j.neucom.2021.01.094
10. Zoph, B., Le, Q.V.: Neural architecture search with reinforcement learning. In: 2017 International Conference on Learning Representations, Toulon, France. arXiv:1611.01578 (2016)

11. Zhong, Z., Yan, J., Wu, W., Shao, J., Liu, C.-L.: Practical block-wise neural network architecture generation. In: IEEE conference on Computer Vision and Pattern Recognition, pp. 2423–2432 (2018)
12. Baker, B., Gupta, O., Naik, N., Raskar, R.: Designing neural network architectures using reinforcement learning. MedRxiv (2016) https://doi.org/10.1101/2020.02.14.20023028
13. Shinozaki, T., Watanabe, S.: Structure discovery of deep neural network based on evolutionary algorithms. In: 2015 IEEE International Conference on Acoustics, Speech and Signal Processing, pp. 4979–4983 (2015)
14. Sun, Y., Xue, B., Zhang, M., Yen, G.G.: Completely automated CNN architecture design based on blocks. IEEE Trans. Neural Netw. Learn. Syst. **33**(2), 1242–1254 (2019)
15. Lu, Z., et al.: NSGA-Net: neural architecture search using multi-objective genetic algorithm. In: Genetic and Evolutionary Computation Conference, pp. 419–427 (2019)
16. Wang, X., Peng, Y., Lu, L., Lu, Z., Bagheri, M., Summers, R.M.: ChestX-ray8: hospital-scale chest x-ray database and benchmarks on weakly-supervised classification and localization of common thorax diseases. In: IEEE Conference on Computer Vision and Pattern Recognition, pp. 3462–3471 (2017)
17. Islam, M.T., Aowal, M.A., Minhaz, A.T., Ashraf, K.: Abnormality detection and localization in chest X-rays using deep convolutional neural networks. CoRR arXiv:1705.09850 (2017)
18. Rajpurkar, P., et al.: Deep learning for chest radiograph diagnosis: a retrospective comparison of the CheXNeXt algorithm to practicing radiologists. PLoS Med. **15**(11), 1–17 (2018)
19. Yao, L., Poblenz, E., Dagunts, D., Covington, B., Bernard, D., Lyman, K.: Learning to diagnose from scratch by exploiting dependencies among labels. CoRR arXiv:1710.1050 (2017)
20. Irvin, J., et al.: CheXpert: a large chest radiograph dataset with uncertainty labels and expert comparison. In: Thirty-Third AAAI Conference on Artificial Intelligence, pp. 590–597 (2019)
21. Sethy, P.K., Behera, S.K.: Detection of coronavirus disease (COVID-19) based on deep features. Int. J. Math. Eng. Manag. Sci. **5**(4), 643–651 (2020)
22. Said, R., Bechikh, S., Louati, A., Aldaej, A., Ben Said, L.: Solving combinatorial multi-objective bi-level optimization problems using multiple populations and migration schemes. IEEE Access **8**, 141674–141695 (2020). https://doi.org/10.1109/ACCESS.2020.3013568
23. Blog, G.R.: AutoML for large scale image classification and object detection. Google Research (2017) https://research.googleblog.com/2017/11/automl-for-large-scaleimage.html
24. Liang, J., Meyerson, E., Hodjat, B., Fink, D., Mutch, K., Miikkulainen, R.: Evolutionary neural autoML for deep learning (2019). https://doi.org/10.1145/3321707.3321721
25. Lu, Z., et al.: Multi-criterion evolutionary design of deep convolutional neural networks. arXiv arXiv:1912.01369 (2019)
26. Louati, A., Louati, H., Nusir, M., hardjono, B.: Multi-agent deep neural networks coupled with LQF-MWM algorithm for traffic control and emergency vehicles guidance. J. Ambient Intell. Hum. Comput. **11**(11), 5611–5627 (2020). https://doi.org/10.1007/s12652-020-01921-3

Understanding the Effects of Mitigation on De-identified Data

Andrew Chester[1]([✉]), Yun Sing Koh[1], and Junjae Lee[2]

[1] The University of Auckland, Auckland, New Zealand
ache968@aucklanduni.ac.nz, ykoh@auckland.ac.nz
[2] Orion Health, Auckland, New Zealand
Junjae.Lee@orionhealth.com

Abstract. Machine learning algorithms can play a significant role in peoples lives. The data used in these algorithms often contains sensitive information and can have inherent biases. We investigate the effects of the interaction between mechanisms designed to preserve privacy and to mitigate biases. The mechanisms employed for this investigation were k-anonymity for de-identification and re-weighting for bias mitigation. The experiments were threefold. First, we investigated the effects of mitigation on de-identified data. Second, we measured the effects of three data parameters: class imbalance ratio, privileged positive outcome ratio and unprivileged positive outcome ratio. Third, we assessed the utility of the mitigation mechanism in a healthcare context. Using real-world data, we tested the effects of different levels of de-identification. We primarily utilised three measures to indicate the procedures' effects. First, for accuracy, we analysed simple accuracy and balanced accuracy rate. Second, we measured the number of positive outcomes for the privileged and unprivileged class and the disparate impact for fairness. Third, for utility, we measured the recall rate as well as a novel metric; recall ratio. We display these two metrics based on the classification threshold to indicate the trade-off between achieving high true positives while limiting overall positive outcomes. This trade-off is analogous to a medical testing scenario where the objective is to have high accuracy of true positives and minimise cost given overall percent positives.

Keywords: De-identification · Mitigation · Machine learning bias

1 Introduction

Machine learning algorithms are being used more and more frequently in fields which directly influence peoples lives. Institutions use these algorithms to determine matters including which students to choose for admission, and which patients to receive further treatment. The significant impact these decisions can have has led to provisions in legislation such as the General Data Protection Regulation (GDPR) in the E.U. and Health Insurance portability and Accountability Act (HIPAA), in the U.S which governs the disclosure of specific sensitive

© Springer Nature Switzerland AG 2021
H. Fujita et al. (Eds.): IEA/AIE 2021, LNAI 12798, pp. 133–144, 2021.
https://doi.org/10.1007/978-3-030-79457-6_12

demographic data, *i.e.*, ethnicity, gender, and age [15]. These restrictions led to the need to develop methods to accurately predict outcomes and meet the various equity objectives of users. The field of fairness in machine learning employs bias mitigation to address this challenge.

The issue of privacy has long been a significant concern in many human-centric applications of machine learning due to the sensitive data involved [5]. The protection of individuals' privacy is another aspect controlled by legislation, *i.e.*, the GDPA and HIPPA. One of the primary mechanisms to achieve this is through de-identification procedures. There are various procedures, but all present additional challenges when attempting to use or publish sensitive data.

Due to the growing concern over privacy and fairness, de-identification and mitigation processes have become more prevalent [14]. This leads to the question of how these processes interact with one another. This paper conducts a novel investigation into the effects of applying bias mitigation to de-identified data. Additionally, Isofidis et al. [10] discuss the effects of high class imbalance on the accuracy and fairness of models. Given that imbalance is a possible source of bias, we conduct further investigations to understand the implications data characteristics have on the mitigation procedure.

The contributions of this paper are three-fold. First, we investigate the combined effects of employing bias mitigation to de-identified data. Second, we analyse how class imbalance and positive outcome levels affect the mitigation process. Third, we discuss the utility of the mitigation procedure in a medical diagnostic scenario.

2   Related Work

The related work falls into three categories fairness, privacy, and the interaction between the two.

Fairness in machine learning seeks to address inherent or introduced biases that are present a model [14]. Bias refers to the difference in positive outcomes between similar individuals or between certain groups, for example, male and female. Positive outcomes can refer to loan approval, college acceptance, or recommendation for further medical treatment. We refer to the class with uneven positive outcomes as the protected class. The individuals who receive the higher proportion of positive outcomes are the privileged class, and the individuals with the lower percentage are the unprivileged class.

The difference in outcomes can be measured in various ways based on performance characteristics of the model, such as accuracy or percentage of positive outcomes. As such, fairness is a diverse topic which can be approached from many different perspectives and can have equally varied objectives. Due to the subjective nature of fairness, different metrics of fairness can oppose one another, *i.e.*, group and individual fairness [2].

To improve fairness, mitigation procedures can be applied during the machine learning process. Mitigation procedures are categorised into three types based on when they are performed. They are pre-processing, in-processing and post-processing. Regardless of the stage, these mitigation procedures implement some kind of transformation to the data or model to alter the final outcome based on the parameters set in the mitigation procedure [2].

For our tests, we implemented the Re-weighing procedure [11]. This is an explainable process which takes in a dataset with one attribute set as the target and with one attribute on which the target outcomes differ, the protected class. The re-weighting procedure divides the dataset into four groups privileged positive, privileged negative, unprivileged positive, and unprivileged negative. Then, weights are applied based on frequency counts of each group to partially or fully mitigate the existing bias. These weights can then be used during the classification process [11].

Privacy preservation can be achieved through numerous methods. However, all methods perform some kind of transformation on the data to hide the identity of individuals [9]. These processes take two broad forms. Suppressing and generalisation, where direct identifiers, *i.e.*, name and drivers license number are suppressed; and quasi-identifiers (QIDs), *i.e.*, age and gender are generalised into broader groups. Alternatively, the entire dataset can be perturbed, producing a distribution of the original dataset.

For these experiments, we implemented Mondrian a k-anonymity algorithm from [13]. k-anonymity asserts that each individual record must have at least k other records with the same QID values. This is a top-down approach which iteratively splits the data into partitions based on their attribute values; as long as all partitions are greater than size k. The attributes are chosen in order of cardinally.

Interaction of fairness and privacy is an emerging field. However, the concept has been investigated in a few recent works [4,5,8,15]. Zemel et al. [16] first discussed the similarity between the concept of fairness mitigation transformations and differential privacy transformations. Subsequent works investigating privacy and fairness have predominantly focused on this relationship and therefore employed differential privacy over other de-identification methods.

3   Research Procedures

This research tackles the problem of applying mitigation to improve fairness while maintaining accuracy on de-identified data. The nature of the transformations that occur with both the de-identification and mitigation create constraints on these procedures. Certain de-identification techniques based on differential privacy [7] mechanisms produce statistical distributions rather than altered version of the original dataset. This makes it ineffective to apply certain mitigation methods to these distributions. For this reason, we chose the Mondrian method [13], which produces a transformed version of the original dataset.

The focus of this research is on data publishing, hence the mitigation methods investigated were limited to prepossessing techniques. Some mitigation techniques transform the dataset into a distribution in latent space [16]. Other mitigation methods perform a splitting on all attribute values [3] which produced a process which was computationally infeasible in this context. Thus we chose the re-weighting mechanism [11].

We applied de-identification to well-known datasets through the Mondrian algorithm at different k-anonymity levels. After this, we performed bias mitigation using the re-weighting algorithm. Then, we used a logistic regression classifier to create target predictions. Following this, we recorded various metrics to assess the effects of the mitigation process on the different data at the different levels of de-identification. These metrics assessed measures of accuracy, fairness, and utility. Further, we performed stratified sampling on the Adult dataset to create datasets with specific characteristics of imbalance and positive outcome percentages. We performed the same test on these datasets as with the real datasets (Fig. 1).

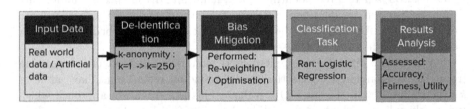

Fig. 1. Data processing pipeline

4 Experiments

The objectives of the experiments were three-fold. First, we investigated the effects of the re-weighting mechanism on de-identified data. Second, we investigated the impact of different levels of class imbalance, different positive outcome ratios, and the positive outcome difference between privileged and unprivileged groups. Third, we assessed the utility of the mitigation procedure from a medical diagnosis context.

4.1 Datasets

Three real-world datasets were used in the tests specifically the Adult, German Credit Scoring, and MEPS.

- **Adult** [12] The task here is to predict whether the income is above or below 50K per year. We use gender as protected attributes.
- **German Credit Scoring** [6] This dataset contains an imbalanced class learning task used to determine if the person has good or bad credit. In this dataset, there are 20 attributes, and gender was the protected attribute.

– **MEPS** [1] This dataset is used to determine the level of health services utilisation. The pre-processing of this data is performed based on [2] and results in 39 attributes, 8 of these are used to form the QID set; race, separated by white and non-white, is used as the protected attribute.

In addition to these standardised datasets, we utilised a Synthetic Data Generator developed in [4]. This data generator creates datasets by selectively sampling from the adult dataset. The size of the datasets is 8000 records. The imbalance ratio between male and female range from $[1 : 1, 2 : 1, 5 : 1, 20 : 1, 50 : 1, 100 : 1]$. The privileged positive percentage (PPP) ranges from $[50, 40, 20, 10]$ and the unprivileged positive percentages (UPP) ranges from $[40, 20, 10, 5]$. This process resulted in 280 unique datasets.

4.2 Effects of Mitigation Due to De-identification

To understand the effects of mitigation resulting from de-identification, we utilised three standard datasets; the Adult, German, and MEPS. Initially, we processed each dataset similar to the methods used in the AIF360 [2] experiments. For the Adult dataset, the feature set contains gender, race, age, and education years. Income is the target. All of the features form part of the QID set. We implemented Mondrian [13] such that the dataset is split first along the protected attribute. This implementation ensures different protected values are not generalised into the same partition. We performed this procedure using 14 different de-identification levels of $\{1, 2, 4, 6, 8, 10, 12, 14, 16, 32, 64, 128, 256\}$. We chose this range to represent a broad scope of possible privacy requirements and to show high granularity of effects.

We performed the re-weighting procedure following the experiments in AIF360 [2]. First, the data was split using a 70 : 30 train test split; then the test set was split 50 : 50 into validation and test sets. We performed ten splits using random seeds and took the mean. The seeds and standard deviations are available in the supplemental material (https://github.com/andrewj-rc/Understanding-the-Effects-of-Mitigation-on-De-identified-Data). Then the re-weight mitigation model is trained using the training set. This model is used to create transformed versions of the training and test datasets.

Following this, a logistic regression model was trained using the original training dataset. The classifier was then run on the original training, validation and test datasets to create predictions for each dataset. The original validation set and models predictions from it were used to find the optimal classification threshold from $0.0 - 1.0$ using increments of 0.01. The optimal threshold is at the highest balanced accuracy. A second logistic regression model was created on the transformed training dataset. Then the classifier is run on the transformed training data and the original test data.

We recorded eight metrics from the results of the original and transformed logistic regression models. The first two metrics recorded were: accuracy and balanced accuracy to set a benchmark for effectiveness of the classifier given the mitigation and de-identification. The next three metrics recorded were: PPP,

UPP, and disparate impact. These metrics assess the fairness of the outcomes concerning the opportunity of outcomes. The last three metrics recorded were chosen to equate to a medical testing scenario. The first metric, percentage of positive outcomes represents the cost in terms of how many patients will receive further testing. The second metric, recall, describes the percentage of true cases accurately caught. The final metric is the novel recall ratio (RR), the percent of true positives for the unprivileged class over the percent of true positives in the privileged class. This measure indicates the differential in cases caught between the privileged and unprivileged classes.

4.3   Effects of Mitigation Due to Data Characteristics

This investigation aimed to understand the effects that data characteristics have on the efficacy of the mitigation method. We investigated three factors, class imbalance, PPP, and UPP. To measure the efficacy of the methods, we measured three metrics: accuracy, fairness, and utility. We employed the same metrics in these test as with the previous tests.

For these tests, we used the synthetic data generated. We performed ten random splits for each combination of imbalance ratio and positive percentages, and we took the mean. However, given the high imbalance ratios and low positive percentage outcomes, some splits lead to no positive outcomes in the minority class. This is not compatible with some metrics; specific random seeds were chosen to ensure that in all datasets had at least one individual in the minority class with a positive outcome. These seeds are available in the supplementary material. The pre-processing was performed as in AIF360 [2]. Five attributes were selected they were; gender, race (binarised to white and non-white), age (binned to ten-year increments), gender, and education years. Education years was between 1–13 with less than six and greater then 12 each binned together. The target was income per year binarised to above 50 thousand per year or not. We performed the same mitigation and classification procedures for these tests on the synthetic data as real data.

4.4   Utility of Mitigation Mechanism in Medical Context

The concept of utility can vary depending on the context. In this context, the utility measures the improvement in the RR compared to the loss in overall recall and the cost of overall positive outcomes. These metrics imply a scenario such as a healthcare setting where the objective is to identify as many individuals requiring further treatment as possible while dealing with limited resources and trying to meet the aim of even identification rates between the protected groups.

We performed the same mitigation and classification procedures for these tests on the synthetic data as real data. However, we display the results on a range of classification thresholds. The classification threshold shows the contrast in the metrics between using mitigated and non-mitigated data.

5 Results

The experiments were conducted on real-world and synthetic data.

5.1 Real-World Data

The experiments using real data had a two-fold purpose. First, to investigate the accuracy and fairness trade-off of the mitigation procedure with different levels of de-identification. Second, to investigate the cost in regards to overall positive outcomes in relation to recall with respect to different de-identification levels.

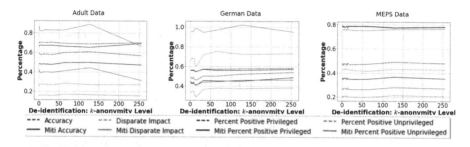

Fig. 2. Results for accuracy, class positive percentages and disparate impact with and without mitigation on different levels of de-identified data.

Figure 2 presents the results for the three data sets comparing the accuracy, disparate impact and positive percentages to the level of de-identification. On the original Adult dataset, initially, with $k = 1$ the PPP is 0.59 and the UPP is 0.15 thus the disparate impact is 0.25 while the accuracy is 0.69. Whereas on the transformed Adult dataset the PPP is 0.48 and the UPP is 0.42 thus the disparate impact is 0.87 and accuracy remains 0.66. As the level of de-identification increases, there is some variation; however, the most significant effect is apparent at high levels of de-identification. With an extreme case of $k = 250$ the original PPP is 0.56 and UPP is 0.15. After mitigation, the PPP decreases to 0.47 while the UPP only increases to 0.31.

These results indicate a reduction in the efficiency of the mitigation process with high de-identification levels. However, with the German and MEPS dataset, this pattern is not as clear. The reduction in PPP and the increase in UPP have some variation with de-identification level; however, the efficacy of the mitigation does not consistently decrease and accuracy for mitigated data only decreases by 0.01 even at the highest de-identification level. On the MEPS dataset, there is very little variation through different levels of de-identification. The reduction in PPP and the increase in UPP remain consistent at all levels of de-identification as well. These results could be due to the number of attributes included in the QID set for each dataset. With the adult dataset, all four attributes were included in the QID set, whereas, with the German dataset, only 2/4 features were in the

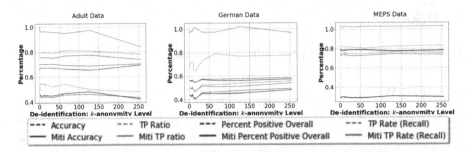

Fig. 3. Results for accuracy, overall positive rate, class true positive rates, and true positive ratio difference on different levels of de-identified data.

QID set. With the MEPS dataset, 8/39 of the attributes were included in the QID set.

Figure 3 displays the results for the overall percent positive, the recall rate and the RR. Initially, at $k = 1$ the recall is 0.79 while the RR is 0.48 and the overall percent positive is 0.44. After re-weighting, the recall reduces to 0.76, and the RR reaches 0.99. The overall positive percentage only increases from 0.44 to 0.46. As the de-identification level increases the effect of mitigation on the loss in recall remains almost constant. However, with high levels of de-identification, the improvement in the RR is less significant. At $k = 250$ the original recall is 0.78 and the RR is still 0.48. After re-weighting, the recall reduces to 0.74, and the RR reaches 0.83. The percent positive overall decreases from 0.43 to 0.42. In comparison, with the non-de-identified data, the recall reduces by 0.03 to improve the RR by 0.51. Whereas with de-identification at $k = 250$ the recall reduces by 0.04 and only improves the RR by 0.35.

These results indicate the percent of positive outcomes is not significantly affected by mitigation on the de-identified data. However, with high de-identification levels, the mitigation process becomes less efficient at improving the RR compared to the reduction in recall. These results are similar but less significant on the German and MEPS data sets.

5.2 Synthetic Data

The purpose of using the synthetic data was to investigate the efficacy and robustness of mitigation method when dealing with data which is: imbalanced, has low positive target outcomes, or has high differential between group target outcomes. In addition, to compare the utility of the mitigation process we compared it to non-mitigated data in which the classification threshold has been independently optimised.

The pre-processing methodology employed by Bellamy et al. [2], generalises and performs binning on many of the QID attributes, where the de-identification process was largely obfuscated. As a result, the effects of de-identification in these test were, in most cases, negligible. Throughout the 280 datasets 210 were de-identified using four different levels of de-identification $k = \{1, 4, 8, 16\}$. In 144 cases, the de-identification reduced the accuracy with an average reduction of -0.015 and a highest reduction of -0.049. In 66 cases, the de-identification increased the accuracy with an average of 0.017 and a highest increase of 0.06.

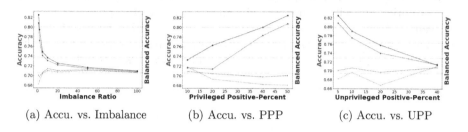

(a) Accu. vs. Imbalance   (b) Accu. vs. PPP   (c) Accu. vs. UPP

Fig. 4. Results for accuracy and balanced accuracy on synthetic data.

Accuracy: The effects of the mitigation process on accuracy on average are minimal. Of the 280 datasets in 240 cases, the mitigation process leads to a decrease in accuracy with an average reduction of -0.023%. In 39 cases, the mitigation process leads to an increase in accuracy with an average increase of 0.005%. However, in certain cases, the process of mitigation can lead to significant reductions in accuracy.

Figure 4 presents the results of three tests. Figure 4a compares the accuracy and balanced accuracy of the original and mitigated data with respect to the imbalance ratio. The PPP was set to 50%, and the UPP was set at 5%. Initially, with an imbalance ratio of 1 : 1 there is a reduction in accuracy of 15%, this continually decrease to 1% at a ratio of 100 : 1. With higher imbalance ratios, the decrease in accuracy and balanced accuracy is lessened. High imbalance ratio means there are fewer unprivileged examples, thus the re-weighting process must augment the outcomes on fewer examples. Therefore it has a lower impact on the overall accuracy.

Figure 4b presents accuracy and balanced accuracy in relation to the PPP. The imbalance ratio is set to 1 : 1 and the UPP is set to 5%. To start with the PPP is at 10% with no loss in accuracy and a 3% loss in balanced accuracy. As the PPP increases, we see a continuous increase in the accuracy lost up to 15% when the PPP is at 50%. Figure 4c presents the accuracy and balanced accuracy in relation to the UPP. The imbalance ratio is set to 1 : 1 and PPP is set to 50%. To start with the PPP is 5% and the loss to accuracy is 15%. As the UPP increases, there is a reduction in the accuracy loss. Figures 4b and 4c show that it is not the high or low values of the PPP and UPP that affect the accuracy. Thus, the indication is that the differential between the privileged and unprivileged positive outcomes is what causes a loss to accuracy. Since the re-weighting mechanism is designed to balance the difference in outcomes, the higher the difference in outcomes the more significant the weights the mechanism must apply and thus the more significant the effect the process has on the outcomes and the accuracy.

These results indicate that the significant factors which determine the change in accuracy are the size of the minority class as a ratio of the whole dataset and the percentage difference in the target outcome of the privileged and unprivileged groups. Intuitively this results from the underlying objective to align the positive outcomes of the privileged and unprivileged groups. Thus with higher differential, the weights must be altered more and thus introduces a greater opportunity for error. Additionally, with high class imbalance, if the minority population is the disadvantaged population, then the number of instances that need to have the outcome changed to align the positive outcomes is much lower. As a result, the weights can be less, so the impact on the overall accuracy is lessened.

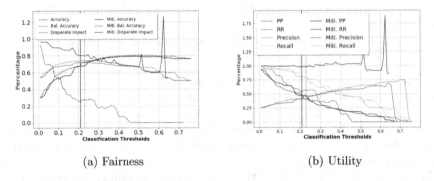

(a) Fairness   (b) Utility

Fig. 5. Fairness trade-off and utility trade-off on classification threshold.

Figure 5 shows the results of tests performed using a classification threshold from 0.01–0.8. These tests had two objectives. First, to analyse the effects the mitigation mechanism has on disparate impact and accuracy. Second, to analyse RR compared to the loss in overall recall and the cost in overall percentage of positive outcomes. The graphs compare the mitigated data to the original data.

Fairness: In Fig. 5a the original data initially starts with a classification threshold of 0.01 the disparate impact metric is high meaning the percentage of positive outcomes between groups are similar. As the threshold increases, there is a steep drop in the disparate impact. With the re-weighted data, the decease in disparate impact is significantly lessened with high classification thresholds. This indicates the mitigation mechanism is effectively increase fairness over non-mitigated data. With increases classification threshold, the change in accuracy and balanced accuracy varies slightly; however, the result is always a reduction from the original dataset. This reduction to accuracy and balanced accuracy appears to generally be minimal compared to the gain in fairness.

Utility: Figure 5b displays that initially, for both the original and re-weighted datasets, the recall rate is 1.0, the RR is also 1.0, and the overall positive percentage is 0.95. Thus, the precision is 0.25. This indicates the situation is completely equal between the groups and that all necessary positive cases have been captured. However, with the positive percentage at 0.95 the cost would be extremely high. As the classification threshold increases, the RR for the original data varies; however, in general, it decreases significantly. With the re-weighted data, the RR generally remains at or above 1.0 up to a threshold of 0.53. Specifically, at the optimal balanced accuracy threshold, for the original data the recall rate 0.77, the RR is 0.55, the overall positive percentage is 0.4, and the precision is 0.46. At the optimal threshold for the re-weighted data, the recall rate is 0.8, the RR is 0.98, the overall positive percentage is 0.46, and the precision is 0.4. Due to the differing optimal thresholds, the transformation results in an increase in RR of +0.43 and an increase in recall of +0.03 while there is only an increase of +0.06 in the overall positive percentage and a decrease of −0.06 in the precision.

The tests indicate the re-weighting mitigation mechanism is effective at reducing the fairness bias while only marginally effecting the accuracy and balanced accuracy. Additionally, when set to an appropriate threshold, the overall positive outcomes and the precision can be minimally affected when improving the RR and recall.

6 Conclusion

We briefly outlined some of the recent work on the issues of both fairness and privacy in machine learning. We also discussed the motivation to understand the effects of the interaction between these to concepts. The experiments we performed empirically tested the effects of this interaction using three main concepts. First, we investigated the effects of mitigation of different levels of de-identified data using real-world data. Second, we used synthetic data to measure the effects of mitigation, given different data characteristics. Third, we assessed the utility of the re-weighting mitigation mechanism based on the improvement in fairness compared to the loss to accuracy and to the increased cost of positive outcomes. These experiments indicate that the effects of mitigation become less effective with higher levels of de-identification and that this is dependent on how significant the QID set is on determining the outcome of a classifier. Additionally, we found that the re-weighting mechanism is more efficient on detests with higher imbalance. Additionally, we found that the higher the differential between the PPP and UPP, the less efficient the re-weighting mechanism is. Finally, we found that given an optimally derived threshold, the re-weighting mechanism is effective at improving fairness while having minimal effect on the accuracy and cost in terms of overall positive outcomes.

Future investigation into other mitigation and de-identification methods would help to improve the understanding of the complex interaction and to possibly standardise procedures for optimisation of mitigation and de-identification approaches.

Acknowledgments. This research was supported by Precision Driven Health (PDH).

References

1. Medical expenditure panel survey (MEPS) (2017). http://archive.ics.uci.edu/ml
2. Bellamy, R.K., et al.: AI fairness 360: an extensible toolkit for detecting and mitigating algorithmic bias. IBM J. Res. Dev. **63**(4–5), 4-1 (2019). https://doi.org/10.1147/JRD.2019.2942287
3. Calmon, F., Wei, D., Vinzamuri, B., Ramamurthy, K.N., Varshney, K.R.: Optimized pre-processing for discrimination prevention. In: Advances in Neural Information Processing Systems, pp. 3992–4001 (2017)
4. Chester, A., Koh, Y.S., Wicker, J., Sun, Q., Lee, J.: Balancing utility and fairness against privacy in medical data. In: 2020 IEEE Symposium Series on Computational Intelligence (SSCI), pp. 1226–1233. IEEE (2020)
5. Cummings, R., Kimpara, D., Gupta, V., Morgenstern, J.: On the compatibility of privacy and fairness. In: ACM UMAP 2019 Adjunct - Adjunct Publication of the 27th Conference on User Modeling, Adaptation and Personalization (FairUMAP), pp. 309–315 (2019). https://doi.org/10.1145/1122445.1122456
6. Dua, D., Graff, C.: UCI machine learning repository (2017). https://www.meps.ahrq.gov/mepsweb/
7. Dwork, C., McSherry, F., Nissim, K., Smith, A.: Calibrating noise to sensitivity in private data analysis. In: Halevi, S., Rabin, T. (eds.) TCC 2006. LNCS, vol. 3876, pp. 265–284. Springer, Heidelberg (2006). https://doi.org/10.1007/11681878_14
8. Ekstrand, M.D., Joshaghani, R., Mehrpouyan, H.: Privacy for all: ensuring fair and equitable privacy protections. Mach. Learn. Res. **81**, 1–13 (2018)
9. Fung, B.C.M., Wang, K.E., Chen, R.U.I., Yu, P.S.: Privacy-preserving data publishing : a survey of recent developments. ACM Comput. Surv. (Csur) **42**(4), 1–53 (2010). https://doi.org/10.1145/1749603.1749605
10. Iosifidis, V., Ntoutsi, E.: Fabboo-online fairness-aware learning under class imbalance. In: Discovery Science (2020)
11. Kamiran, F., Calders, T.: Data preprocessing techniques for classification without discrimination. Knowl. Inf. Syst. **33**(1), 1–33 (2012)
12. Kohavi, R.: Scaling up the accuracy of Naive-Bayes classifiers: a decision-tree hybrid. In: KDD, vol. 96, pp. 202–207 (1996)
13. LeFevre, K., DeWitt, D.J., Ramakrishnan, R.: Mondrian multidimensional K-anonymity. In: International Conference on Data Engineering, p. 25 (2006)
14. Mehrabi, N., Morstatter, F., Saxena, N., Lerman, K., Galstyan, A.: A survey on bias and fairness in machine learning. arXiv (2019)
15. Pujol, D., McKenna, R., Kuppam, S., Hay, M., Machanavajjhala, A., Miklau, G.: Fair decision making using privacy-protected data. In: Proceedings of the 2020 Conference on Fairness, Accountability, and Transparency, pp. 189–199 (2020)
16. Zemel, R., Wu, Y., Swersky, K., Pitassi, T., Dwork, C.: Learning fair representations. In: International Conference on Machine Learning, pp. 325–333 (2013)

Combining Siamese Network and Correlation Filter for Complementary Object Tracking

Kosuke Honda[1]($\boxtimes$)(ID) and Hamido Fujita[2](ID)

[1] Faculty of Software and Information Science, Iwate Prefectural University, Iwate, Japan
[2] Regional Research Center, Iwate Prefectural University, Iwate, Japan

Abstract. Fully-Convolutional Siamese Network (SiamFC) is convolutional neural networks (CNNs) model-based tracking method. This method learns a similarity map from the cross-correlation between the feature representations of the search image and the target image extracted using CNNs, and tracks based on it. The tracking performance of SiamFC tends to degrade when there are similar distractors to the object or when the target object is deformed. On the other hand, recent object tracking methods using the correlation filter (CF) drift under some scenarios such as fast motion and complete occlusion. The analysis showed that although these two approaches have very different structures, they tend to have complementary characteristics. In this work, we propose a complementary tracking framework that parallel connects SiamFC with the CF-based tracker. In the proposed framework, to detect tracking failures, we evaluate the response map output from SiamFC using the confidence score defined in this paper. When a tracking failure is detected, the CF-based tracker provides relative correlated correction. Experiments on the OTB2015 show that our tracker obtains up to more than 5.7%/5.5% (precision score/success score) relative improvements over the original SiamFC and CF-based tracker on the OTB2015, and competitive performance with advanced trackers.

Keywords: Computer vision · Object tracking · Siamese network · Correlation filter

1 Introduction

Visual object tracking is one of the most important problems in the field of computer vision [1], which aims to track moving and changing objects in a video. Recently, object tracking is applied to a wide range of fields such as surveillance cameras, automatic driving, human-computer interaction, and the military [3]. In general, after an arbitrary object position is specified in the first frame of a video, how to precisely estimate its position in the subsequent frames is the main task of object tracking. Although significant progress in recent years, it

H. Fujita et al. (Eds.): IEA/AIE 2021, LNAI 12798, pp. 145–157, 2021.
https://doi.org/10.1007/978-3-030-79457-6_13

has still been commonly recognized as a very challenging task due to numerous factors such as deformation, occlusion, illumination variations, and scale change. Therefore, designing a robust and accurate object tracking model is of important value.

In recent challenges [1,2], correlation filter (CF)-based discriminative trackers [10–13] and Siamese network-based deep object tracker [15,16] have achieved high performance. Among the Siamese network-based methods, SiamFC [15] has superior performance and speed, and many SiamFC based follow-up studies have been conducted. SiamFC [15] considers object tracking as a similarity learning problem between target and search region. It uses a large dataset to train a complete end-to-end network offline to obtain high discriminability. SiamFC achieves state-of-the-art performance while running at over 80FPS on the GPU without online model updates. However, since the first frame target is always used as a template without the model update, tracking often fails when the target is heavily deformed or when there is a confusing object (distractor) that looks like the target.

Most CF-based object trackers use samples extracted from the current tracking video and use online learning to model the appearance of the target. Besides, while SiamFC uses features extracted from convolutional neural networks (CNNs), most CF-based trackers use manually created features (e.g., HOG features [9]) to spatially locate the target. This tends to make them more robust to relatively distractor situations and slow appearance changes. However, these trackers can only train relatively simple models because they use only the tracking video as training data. As a result, they sometimes fail to track in situations such as fast motion, occlusion, etc.

As analyzed in a previous study [17], SiamFC and CF-based trackers are complementary in some of the following aspects, even though they are different algorithms.

- CF-based tracker is an approach to acquire a target-specific tracking model through online learning. SiamFC is trained offline, tracking with fixed weights and no learning during tracking.
- Handcrafted features (e.g. HOG features [9]) are used in CF-based trackers to locate them spatially. In SiamFC, features are extracted from CNNs to locate them semantically. Features extracted from CNNs are low resolution and therefore semantic, but relatively coarse for location information.
- CF-based trackers have a narrow search area, while SiamFC has a relatively wide search area, so it can handle high-speed motion and camera movement.

In addition to the above, SiamFC and the CF-based tracker Staple [10] have some complementary results in OTB2015 [2], as shown in Fig. 1. Staple is one of the CF-based trackers, which combines a correlation filter using HOG features and a global color histogram to train online as two independent ridge regression problems. It is relatively robust to color changes and deformations, complementary to SiamFC, and fast, making it a highly real-time method.

Inspired by the results of these analyses, this paper proposes a complementary tracking framework by combining SiamFC with a CF-based tracker. In the proposed framework, SiamFC is used as the main tracker, and Staple is used as the sub-tracker. Then, we consider the state in which the response map of SiamFC is contaminated as a tracking failure and select Staple when the tracking is failed. In addition, the search area of each of Staple and SiamFC in the next frame is corrected to avoid losing sight of the target and searching the wrong area. We experiment with OTB2015 [2], a popular benchmark for single object tracking tasks, and compare it to previous studies compared to some correlated filter trackers and Siamese Network-based trackers our tracker runs at 40 fps and achieves better performance.

━━ SiamFC ━━ STAPLE ━━ Groundtruth

Fig. 1. Tracking results of SiamFC and Staple in the Basketball sequence and Motor-Rolling sequence of the OTB2015 [2] dataset. One of the examples Staple correctly tracking when SiamFC drifts, and SiamFC correctly tracking when Staple fails in tracking.

2 Related Work

2.1 Correlation Filter Based Trackers

In general, CF-based trackers are trained online using tracking video as training data to acquire target-specific tracking models. It samples positive and negative samples from the target template and trains a discriminator from it. Then, the tracking model trains to get a large value when it filters the location of the object in the search region. The traditional tracking methods, such as using Boosting [4] or SVM [5] for identification, sample randomly, whereas the CF-based tracker first shifts pixel by pixel and samples densely. The sampled images are computed as a circulant matrix by circular convolution using the discrete Fourier transform. This in practice provides good speed. Besides, the extension to multiple feature channels [6–8], and HOG features [9] has enabled this method to achieve high performance on previous benchmarks such as an OTB2013 [1]. Staple [10] proposed combines a CF with a global color histogram to achieve robustness against both deformation and color change. SRDCF [11] introduces a spatial regularization factor into the learning process to weaken the filter response near the edges of the image and to enhance the filter response in the center of the image.

Despite the above achievements, these approaches do not work well in some hard-to-track situations such as deformation, occlusion, etc. One of the reasons for this is that it is designed for special applications and uses hand-crafted features. From this point of view, methods to replace the hand-crafted features used in CF-based trackers with features extracted from CNNs models [12] and methods to combine them [13] have been proposed, using automatic feature extraction by CNNs models. In [12], the hand-crafted features of SRDCF are replaced by deep features using CNNs, which shows that the framework achieves accurate performance. In [13], the hand-crafted features and deep features by CNNs are combined to reduce the redundancy of the algorithm. Although these approaches have been able to significantly improve the tracking performance, they come at the cost of a significant reduction in tracking speed due to the computational complexity of handling the great quantity of CNNs deep features online.

2.2 Siamese Network Based Trackers

In recent years, CNNs have greatly improved many computer vision techniques such as image classification [20–22], object detection [19], and pose estimation [23]. Similarly, the field of object tracking has benefited a lot from CNNs, including the aforementioned method that combines a CF and CNNs [12,13]. Recently, the Siamese network architecture, which utilizes the capabilities of CNNs for object tracking, has been attracting much attention [14–16]. SINT [14] adopts the siamese network and extracts hierarchical convolutional features of the template and search region, respectively. SINT aims to identify candidate image locations that match the target object's appearance. Candidates are randomly selected from the search region, each of which is compared with the search region to acquire the match one. However, SINT runs at 4FPS due to the huge amount of computation, sacrificing real-time performance. SiamFC [15] uses the Siamese network structure to train a robust similarity function between target and search regions end-to-end. It uses deep CNNs as feature extractors and adopts fully convolutional layers. SiamFC trains a similarity function from the cross-correlation between feature representations extracted from CNNs in the target and search regions, respectively. It also inputs a larger search region to the network than previous correlation filter trackers. The weights of this network are always fixed during tracking. It is simple in structure, yet it achieves state-of-the-art of performance in benchmarks. SiamRPN [16] is a follow-up study of SiamFC, which greatly improves discriminability by adding the region proposal network (RPN) used in Faster R-CNN, an object detection method.

Two major factors are preventing SiamFC from tracking. The first is the low-resolution semantic feature. The similarity map trained by SiamFC is a very low-resolution score map because CNNs decrease the resolution and extract features semantically. Deep CNNs reduce the resolution, the output loses the positional information of the image. Therefore, this low-resolution feature alone is not sufficient to identify the exact location of the object. This problem applies not only to object tracking but also to research in the field of object detection. Siamese trackers and recent object detection methods [19] use AlexNet [20], VGG [21], ResNet [22], etc. for feature extraction, however, these CNNs models are designed for image classification in the first place. Semantic features extracted from these CNNs models are considered important for image classification, but not sufficient for the localization tasks of tracking and detection. This problem can be seen from the fact that the accuracy of tracking of SiamFC decreases as it becomes a CNNs model with deeper layers, as analyzed by Zhang et al. [24]. Secondly, SiamFC is vulnerable to distractors. SiamFC continues using the target of the first frame as a template without updating the model. Meanwhile, semantic features extracted from deep CNNs cannot distinguish spatial details of appearance. As a result, SiamFC cannot clearly distinguish between distractors and targets, as shown in Fig. 2.

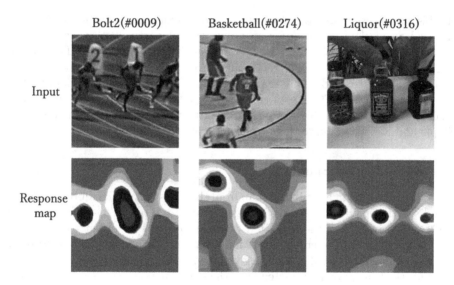

Fig. 2. Input search regions and SiamFC response maps for several sequences in the OTB2015 dataset [2]. SiamFC generates the same high score for distractor regions as for targets, and cannot clearly distinguish between them.

2.3   Combining Siamese Network and Correlation Filter

In the Real-time complementary tracker (RCT) [17], the CF-based tracker and SiamFC [15] are combined in series connection to take advantage of their complementary properties. In this framework, the first step is to coarsely but robustly position the target using SiamFC. In the second stage, the coarse position is refined using a CF to achieve higher accuracy. However, since RCT [17] connects the two methods in series, if SiamFC fails to track, the CF-based tracker also fails to track. Therefore, MFCFSiam [18] fixes this problem by combining SiamFC and the CF-based tracker by parallel connection. In this method, the two methods are parallelized and work independently. The uniquely designed correlation filter tracker guides SiamFC using HOG features and color name (CN) functions. MFCFSiam [18] uses a validity evaluation filter to evaluate the two trackers and output better evaluation tracking results.

Based on these research results, in this work, we connect SiamFC [15] and a relatively fast CF-based tracker in parallel. We use SiamFC as the main tracker and output the tracking results of the CF-based tracker when SiamFC fails to track. This method uses simpler metrics using the confidence score to evaluate the accuracy of tracking with less computation, thus maintaining real-time performance.

3   Proposed Framework

In this paper, we take advantage of the complementary features of SiamFC [15] and Staple [10] and propose an object tracking framework that combines both methods. Figure 3 shows an overall view of the framework. The framework consists of SiamFC main-tracker and Staple sub-tracker. First, both Staple and SiamFC make predictions against the input frame. It then adopts Staple's prediction when SiamFC has lower tracking confidence and tracks it in a complementary manner. In this section, we describe the mechanism of SiamFC and Staple and how to evaluate them to detect tracking failures.

3.1   Main-Tracker SiamFC

SiamFC aims to train a similarity map from the cross-correlation of target image z and search region x. The target image z and search region x are input to the CNN respectively, and the extracted two feature maps are input to the cross-correlation layer. In the cross-correlation layer, the feature map extracted from the target image z is used as a sliding window, and the similarity score is calculated for the feature map extracted from the search region x in a convolution-like manner as given in formula (1),

$$f(z, x) = \varphi z * \varphi x + b\mathbb{1}, \tag{1}$$

where $f(z, x)$ is the real number score of similarity between target image z and search region x as a pair, and $b\mathbb{1}$ denotes a signal that takes the value $b \in \mathbb{R}$ in every position. The network is pre-trained offline using a logistic loss function as shown in formula (2),

$$\ell(y, v) = log(1 + exp(-yv)), \tag{2}$$

where y is the ground truth and v is the output response map. The ground truth is defined as a binary label score map where each pixel is labeled with -1 or $+1$ depending on the distance of the center pixel. The final loss denoted by $L(y, v)$

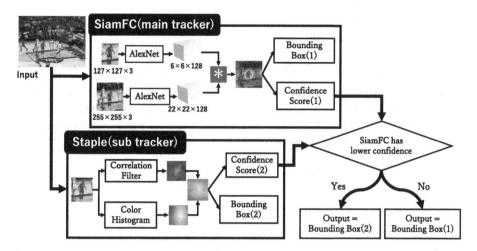

Fig. 3. Schematic of a complementary object tracking framework combining Staple and SiamFC.

between the ground truth y and output score map v is the average of the logistic loss of each pixel as shown in formula (3),

$$L(y, v) = \frac{1}{\|D\|} \sum_{u \in D} \ell(y[u], v[u]). \tag{3}$$

Here, D is the score map and u is each position in D. The parameters using CNN φ are optimized by Stochastic Gradient Descent (SGD) as shown in formula (4),

$$\arg \min_{\theta} \mathbb{E}_{(z,x,y)} L(y, v(z, x, \theta)). \tag{4}$$

During tracking, the target image uses the target of the first frame of the video and calculates the similarity with the search region x of all subsequent frames. The peak point of the output similarity map is used as the center point of the target. To cope with changes in scale, the target is searched from the three scale candidates and the scale is updated by linear completion with a factor of 0.35 to provide damping.

3.2 Sub-Tracker Staple

In the proposed framework, Staple [10] is used as a sub-tracker to support SiamFC when it fails to track. In this section, we formulate the mechanism of Staple, referring to D. Li et al. [17]. Staple combines a CF using HOG features with a global color histogram to increase robustness to color changes and deformations. To maintain real-time performance, it uses the inherent structure of each representation and solves them as two independent ridge regression problems. Staple [10] aims to maximize a score that is a linear combination of template and histogram scores as given formula (5),

$$f(x) = \gamma \cdot f_{tmpl}(x) + (1 - \gamma) \cdot f_{hist}(x), \tag{5}$$

where f_{tmpl} is a template score, f_{hist} is a histogram score, and γ is an interpolation parameter. A template model that uses a CF denoted as h is trained using least-squares and quadratic regularization. It aims to learn h that minimizes the following objective function.

$$\min \| \sum_{d=1}^{D} f^d * h^d - y \|^2 + \lambda \sum_{d=1}^{D} \| h^d \|^2. \tag{6}$$

Here, d is the number of dimensions, f^d is a feature of dimension d, and $*$ is the circular convolution operation. The output of y is a scalar-valued function containing the label of each position. λ is the regularization scalar, which adjusts the effect of regularization. Formulas (6) is computed efficiently for each channel by Fast Fourier Transform (FFT) without the need for iterative processing.

On the other hand, the histogram model computes the object likelihood for each pixel in the target object region. It derives the normalized object histogram and background histogram from the target region T and the surrounding background region B in the input search region I, respectively. The foreground likelihoods $P(x \in T|I)$ and background likelihoods $P(x \in B|I)$ can be calculated directly from these two histograms. From the two calculated likelihoods, the object likelihood P of pixel x in the input search region I can be obtained as shown in formula (7),

$$P(x \in T|I, x) = \frac{P(x \in T|I)}{P(x \in T|I) + P(x \in B|I)}. \tag{7}$$

From the calculated likelihood function, the score of the histogram is defined as given in formula (8),

$$f_{hist}(c) = \sum_{x} P(x \in T). \tag{8}$$

Here, c is the center point of the bounding box and x is a pixel in the bounding box.

3.3   Tracking Evaluation Based on Confidence Score

We evaluate whether the tracking of SiamFC [15] is successful or not based on the confidence score. Two metrics are used for the confidence score: peak-to-sidelobe ratio (PSR) and average peak-to-correlation energy (APCE) [25]. The PSR is the ratio of the peak intensity of the main lobe to the peak intensity of the side lobes. It is defined as shown in formula (9),

$$PSR(y) = \frac{\max(y) - \mu(y)}{\sigma(y)}, \tag{9}$$

where y is the response map output from the tracker, μ is the mean value, and σ is the standard deviation. Similarly, the APCE, which indicates the fluctuated degree of the response map and the confidence level of the detected target, is defined as given in formula (10),

$$APCE = \frac{|F_{max} - F_{min}|^2}{mean(\sum_{w,h}(F_{w,h} - F_{min})^2)}, \tag{10}$$

where $|-|$ denotes the Euclidean distance, $F_{max}, F_{min}, F_{w,h}$, mean the maximum, minimum, and w-th row h-th column element of the filter response matrix of size $W \times H$, respectively. The response map with large APCE and PSR has higher tracking confidence. On the other hand, a low value indicates that the response map has lower confidence due to severe deformation, heavy occlusion, and distractors.

Assess tracking based on a confidence score that combines two metrics, PSR and APCE [25], to determine if SiamFC [15] is failing to track. The confidence score is defined as given in formula (11),

$$Score = \alpha \cdot APCE + (1 - \alpha) \cdot PSR, \tag{11}$$

where α is a hyperparameter that adjusts the ratio of PSR and APCE [25]. In the framework, if the confidence score of the response map of SiamFC [15] is less than the threshold and at the same time less than the confidence score of the response map of Staple [10] during tracking, it is considered as tracking failure. It then outputs the bounding box inferred from Staple.

4 Experiment

The proposed framework is implemented using the Pytorch library. The PC used is equipped with an Intel Core i7-9700k CPU and two NVIDIA GeForce RTX2070super GPUs in parallel. To evaluate the performance of the tracker, we conduct experiments on the OTB2015 benchmark dataset [2]. On our runtime environment, the proposed framework runs at 40FPS. All the source code of this method is released at https://github.com/danho47/CSCF.

OTB2015 [2] consists of 100 videos containing several different tracking scenarios such as illumination variation (IV), scale variation (SV), occlusion (OCC), deformation (DEF), low resolution (LR), motion blur (MB), out-of-plane rotation (OPR), out of view (OV), background cluttered (BC), fast motion (FM), and in-plane rotation (IPR). For evaluation in the benchmark, we use the One-Pass Evaluation (OPE) protocol, which evaluates the performance of a tracker by performing the tracker process only once, from start to finish. We use the Center Location Error (CLE) and Intersection over Union (IoU) of the bounding boxes as evaluation metrics. CLE is the distance between the center of the prediction and the ground truth, and IoU is the percentage of overlap between the two bounding boxes. CLE is defined as precision plots, and IoU is defined as success plots. Precision plots score is the percentage of frames whose center position error is less than the threshold of 20, and success plots score is the percentage of frames whose IoU is greater than the threshold of 0.5. In the experiments, we compare the proposed method with nine other methods: SiamFC [15], Staple [10], SiamRPN [16], BACF [27], CSRDCF [28], KCF [26], CFML [29], TRBACF [30], and MFCFSiam [18]. The precision and success performance are shown in Fig. 4. Table 1 illustrates success performance in 11 different scenarios on OTB2015.

The experimental results show that the proposed framework outperforms the original SiamFC [15] and Staple [10]. Compared with the state-of-the-art methods, our tracker scores near the top in precision score ranks third and ranks fifth in success score. This proves the effectiveness and competitiveness of the proposed algorithm in overall performance. In the comparison of performance per scenario, our tracker ranks in the top three in 7 out the 11 scenarios. This proves proposed method has a competitive performance with the latest methods and able to handle difficult tracking scenarios.

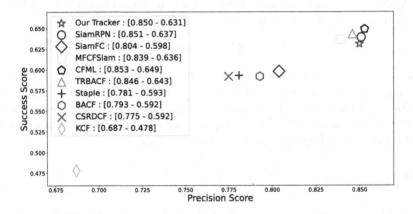

Fig. 4. Precision and success score on OTB2015 [2].

Table 1. Comparison of success scores in 11 different scenarios on OTB2015. The first, second and third best scores are highlighted in red, blue and green, respectively.

Tracker	FM	BC	MB	DEF	IV	IPR	LR	OCC	OPR	OV	SV
OurTracker	0.609	0.600	0.618	0.592	0.612	0.608	0.641	0.577	0.601	0.558	0.607
SiamRPN [16]	0.609	0.605	0.612	0.615	0.657	0.644	0.593	0.576	0.614	0.560	0.619
SimaFC [15]	0.577	0.534	0.588	0.555	0.605	0.578	0.623	0.547	0.562	0.493	0.584
MFCFSiam [18]	0.585	0.601	0.607	0.591	0.632	0.611	0.535	0.608	0.619	0.549	0.591
CFML [29]	0.619	0.662	0.614	0.622	0.662	0.604	0.531	0.620	0.622	0.564	0.610
TRBACF [30]	0.602	0.634	0.609	0.626	0.638	0.585	0.513	0.611	0.617	0.543	0.599
Staple [10]	0.558	0.609	0.541	0.555	0.630	0.582	0.525	0.554	0.566	0.497	0.556
BACF [27]	0.554	0.635	0.565	0.564	0.620	0.542	0.451	0.555	0.561	0.519	0.521
CSRDCF [28]	0.571	0.568	0.583	0.575	0.595	0.529	0.505	0.556	0.542	0.507	0.540
KCF [26]	0.458	0.505	0.461	0.441	0.477	0.467	0.281	0.433	0.452	0.360	0.393

5   Conclusions

In this paper, we proposed an object tracking framework that combines SiamFC with Staple. We also proposed an algorithm to detect tracking failures based on confidence scores. By taking advantage of the complementary features of the two methods, it was shown that the proposed framework can track objects with higher accuracy than the original method. However, the threshold of confidence score that deciding which method to select is not yet optimal. Therefore, it is necessary to select the best tracker for the appropriate situation in an optimal way. Such a problem is considered as future work to optimize the threshold and to select the best tracker using a classifier from confidence scores and response maps as features.

Acknowledgements. This study is supported by JSPS/JAPAN KAKENHI (Grants-in-Aid for Scientific Research) #JP20K11955.

References

1. Wu, Y., Lim, J., Yang, M.H.: Online object tracking: a benchmark. In: Proceedings of the Computer Vision and Pattern Recognition, pp. 2411–2418, 23–28 June 2013
2. Wu, Y., Lim, J., Yang, M.H.: Object tracking benchmark. TPAMI **37**(9), 1834–1848 (2015)
3. Yilmaz, A., Javed, O., Shah, M.: Object tracking: a survey. ACM Comput. Surv. **38**(4), 1–45 (2006)
4. Babenko, B., Yang, M.-H., Belongie, S.: Robust object tracking with online multiple instance learning. TPAMI **33**(8), 1619–1632 (2011)
5. Hare, S., et al.: Struck: structured output tracking with kernels. IEEE Trans. Pattern Anal. Mach. Intell. **38**(10), 2096–2109 (2016). https://doi.org/10.1109/TPAMI.2015.2509974
6. Boddeti, V.N., Kanade, T., Kumar, B.V.K.: Correlation filters for object alignment. In: IEEE Computer Society Conference on Computer Vision and Pattern Recognition (CVPR) (2013). https://ieeexplore.ieee.org/document/6619141
7. Henriques, J.F., Carreira, J., Caseiro, R., Batista, J.: Beyond hard negative mining: efficient detector learning via block-circulant decomposition. In: IEEE International Conference on Computer Vision (ICCV) (2013)
8. Kiani Galoogahi, H., Sim, T., Lucey, S.: Multi-channel correlation filters. In: IEEE International Conference on Computer Vision (ICCV) (2013)
9. Dalal, N., Triggs, B.: Histograms of oriented gradients for human detection. In: 2005 IEEE Computer Society Conference on Computer Vision and Pattern Recognition (CVPR), vol. 1, pp. 886–893, June 2005
10. Bertinetto, S., Valmadre, J., Golodetz, S., Miksik, O., Torr, P.H.S.: Staple: complementary learners for real-time tracking. In: 2016 IEEE Conference on Computer Vision and Pattern Recognition (CVPR), pp. 1401–1409, June 2016
11. Danelljan, M., Hger, G., Khan, F.S., Felsberg, M.: Learning spatially regularized correlation filters for visual tracking. In: 2015 IEEE International Conference on Computer Vision (ICCV), pp. 4310–4318, December 2015

12. Danelljan, M., Robinson, A., Shahbaz Khan, F., Felsberg, M.: Beyond correlation filters: learning continuous convolution operators for visual tracking. In: Leibe, B., Matas, J., Sebe, N., Welling, M. (eds.) ECCV 2016. LNCS, vol. 9909, pp. 472–488. Springer, Cham (2016). https://doi.org/10.1007/978-3-319-46454-1_29

13. Danelljan, M., Bhat, G., Khan, F.S., et al.: ECO: efficient convolution operators for tracking. In: IEEE Conference on Computer Vision and Pattern Recognition (CVPR), Honolulu (2017). https://ieeexplore.ieee.org/document/8100216

14. Tao, R., Gavves, E., Smeulders, A.W.M.: Siamese instance search for tracking. In: IEEE Conference on Computer Vision and Pattern Recognition (CVPR), Las Vegas (2016)

15. Bertinetto, L., Valmadre, J., Henriques, J.F., Vedaldi, A., Torr, P.H.S.: Fully-convolutional siamese networks for object tracking. In: Hua, G., Jégou, H. (eds.) ECCV 2016. LNCS, vol. 9914, pp. 850–865. Springer, Cham (2016). https://doi.org/10.1007/978-3-319-48881-3_56

16. Li, B., Yan, J., Wu, W., Zhu, Z., Hu, X.: High performance visual tracking with siamese region proposal network. In: Proceedings of the IEEE Conference on Computer Vision and Pattern Recognition (CVPR), pp. 8971–8980 (2018)

17. Li, D., Porikli, F., Wen, G., Kuai, Y.: When correlation filters meet siamese networks for real-time complementary tracking. IEEE Trans. Circuits Syst. Video Technol. **30**(2), 509–519 (2019)

18. Li, C., Xing, Q., Ma, Zang, K.: MFCFSiam: a correlation-filter-guided siamese network with multifeature for visual tracking. Wirel. Commun. Mobile Comput. 2020, 19 (2020)

19. Ren, S., He, K., Girshick, R., Sun, J.: Faster R-CNN: towards real-time object detection with region proposal networks. In: International Conference on Neural Information Processing Systems, pp. 91–99 (2015)

20. Krizhevsky, A., Sutskever, I., Hinton, G.E.: ImageNET classification with deep convolutional neural networks. In: Advances in Neural Information Processing Systems, pp. 1097–1105 (2012)

21. Simonyan, K., Zisserman, A.: Very deep convolutional networks for large-scale image recognition. arXiv preprint, arXiv:1409.1556 (2014)

22. He, K., Zhang, X., Ren, S., Sun, J.: Deep residual learning for image recognition. In: Proceedings of the IEEE Conference on Computer Vision and Pattern Recognition (CVPR), pp. 770–778 (2016)

23. Newell, A., Yang, K., Deng, J.: Stacked hourglass networks for human pose estimation. In: Leibe, B., Matas, J., Sebe, N., Welling, M. (eds.) ECCV 2016. LNCS, vol. 9912, pp. 483–499. Springer, Cham (2016). https://doi.org/10.1007/978-3-319-46484-8_29

24. Zhang, Z., Peng, H.: Deeper and wider siamese networks for real-time visual tracking. In: Proceedings of the IEEE/CVF Conference on Computer Vision and Pattern Recognition (CVPR), pp. 4591–4600 (2019)

25. Wang, M.M., Liu, Y., Huang, Z.Y.: Large margin object tracking with circulant feature maps. In: Proceedings of the Computer Vision and Pattern Recognition (CVPR), pp. 4800–4808 (2017)

26. Henriques, J.F., Caseiro, R., Martins, P., Batista, J.: High-speed tracking with kernelized correlation filters. IEEE Trans. Pattern Anal. Mach. Intell. **37**(3), 583–596 (2015)

27. Kiani Galoogahi, H., Fagg, A., Lucey, S.: Learning background-aware correlation filters for visual tracking. In: Proceedings of the IEEE International Conference on Computer Vision, Venice Italy, pp. 1135–1143 (2017)

28. Lukezic, A., Vojir, T., Zajc, L.C., Matas, J., Kristan, M.: Discriminative correlation filter with channel and spatial reliability. In: IEEE, Conference on Computer Vision and Pattern Recognition, vol. 1, pp. 4847–4856 (2017). 10.1109
29. Yuan, D., Kang, W., He, Z.: Robust visual tracking with correlation filters and metric learning. Knowl. Syst. **195** (2020). https://doi.org/10.1016/j.knosys.2020. 105697
30. Yuan, D., Shu, X., He, Z.: TRBACF: Learning temporal regularized correlation filters for high performance online visual object tracking. J. Vis. Commun. Image Represent. **72** (2020). https://doi.org/10.1016/j.jvcir.2020.102882

Closed-Form Expressions for Global and Local Interpretation of Tsetlin Machines

Christian D. Blakely[1,2]([✉]) and Ole-Christoffer Granmo[2] [ID]

[1] PwC Switzerland, Zurich, Switzerland
[2] Centre for AI Research, University of Agder, Grimstad, Norway

Abstract. Tsetlin Machines (TMs) capture patterns using conjunctive clauses in propositional logic, thus facilitating interpretation. However, recent TM-based approaches mainly rely on inspecting the full range of clauses *individually*. Such inspection does not necessarily scale to complex prediction problems that require a large number of clauses. In this paper, we propose closed-form expressions for understanding why a TM model makes a specific prediction (local interpretability). Additionally, the expressions capture the most important features of the model overall (global interpretability). We further introduce expressions for measuring the importance of feature value ranges for continuous features making it possible to capture the role of features in real-time as well as during the learning process as the model evolves. We compare our proposed approach against SHAP and state-of-the-art interpretable machine learning techniques.

Keywords: Tsetlin Machines · Interpretable machine learning · Artificial intelligence

1 Introduction

Motivations. Computational predictive modelling is becoming increasingly complicated in order to handle the deluge of high-dimensional data in machine learning and data science-driven industries. With rising complexity, not understanding why a model makes a particular prediction is becoming one of the most significant risks [7]. To overcome this risk and to give insights into how a model is making predictions given the underlying data, several efforts over the past few years have provided methodologies for explaining so-called black-box models[1]. The purpose is to offer performance enhancements over more simplistic, but transparent and interpretable models, such as linear models, logistic regression, and decision trees. Prominent efforts include SHAP [4], LIME [9], and modifications or enhancements to neural networks, such as in Neural Additive Models

---

[1] We will understand black-box models as models which lack intrinsic interpretability features, such as ensemble approaches, neural networks, and random forests.

© Springer Nature Switzerland AG 2021
H. Fujita et al. (Eds.): IEA/AIE 2021, LNAI 12798, pp. 158–172, 2021.
https://doi.org/10.1007/978-3-030-79457-6_14

[2]. Typical approaches either create *post hoc* approximations of how models make a decision or build local surrogate models. As such, they require additional computation time and are not intrinsic to the data modelling or learning itself.

Apart from increased trust, attaining interpretability in machine learning is essential for several reasons. For example, it can be useful when forging an analytical driver that provides insight into how a model may be improved, from both a feature standpoint and also a validation standpoint. It can also support understanding the model learning process and how the underlying data is supporting the prediction process. Additionally, interpretability can be used when reducing the dimensionality of the input features.

This paper introduces an alternative methodology for high-accuracy interpretable predictive modelling. Our goal is to combine competitive accuracy with closed-form expressions for both global and local interpretability, without requiring any additional local linear explanation layers or inference from any other surrogate models. That is, we intend to provide accessibility to feature strength insights that are intrinsic to the model, at any point during a learning phase. To this end, the methodology we propose enhances the intrinsic interpretability of the recently introduced Tsetlin Machines (TMs) [3], which have obtained competitive results in terms of accuracy, memory footprint, and learning speed, on diverse benchmarks.

Contributions. Interpretability in all of the above TM-based approaches relies on inspecting the full range of clauses *individually*. Such inspection does not necessarily scale to complex pattern recognition problems that require a large number of clauses, e.g., in the thousands. A principled interface for accessing different types of interpretability at various scales is thus currently missing. In this paper, we introduce closed-form expressions for local and global TM interpretability. We formulate these expressions at both an overall feature importance level and a feature range level, namely, which ranges of the data yield the most influence in making predictions. Secondly, we evaluate performance on several industry-standard benchmark data sets, contrasting against other interpretable machine learning methodologies.

2   Tsetlin Machine Basics

Classification. A TM takes a vector $X = (x_1, \ldots, x_o)$ of Boolean features as input (Fig. 1), to be classified into one of two classes, $y = 0$ or $y = 1$. Together with their negated counterparts, $\bar{x}_k = \neg x_k = 1 - x_k$, the features form a literal set $L = \{x_1, \ldots, x_o, \bar{x}_1, \ldots, \bar{x}_o\}$. In the following, we will use the notation I_j to refer to the indexes of the non-negated features in L_j and $\bar{I}_j$ to refer to the indexes of the negated features.

A TM pattern is formulated as a conjunctive clause C_j, formed by ANDing a subset $L_j \subseteq L$ of the literal set:

$$C_j(X) = \bigwedge_{l_k \in L_j} l_k = \prod_{l_k \in L_j} l_k. \tag{1}$$

E.g., the clause $C_j(X) = x_1 \wedge x_2 = x_1 x_2$ consists of the literals $L_j = \{x_1, x_2\}$ and outputs 1 iff $x_1 = x_2 = 1$.

The number of clauses employed is a user set parameter m. Half of the clauses are assigned positive polarity. The other half is assigned negative polarity. In this paper, we will indicate clauses with positive polarity with odd indices and negative polarity with even indices[2]. The clause outputs, in turn, are combined into a classification decision through summation and thresholding using the unit step function $u(v) = 1$ if $v \geq 0$ else 0:

$$\hat{y} = u\left(\sum_{j=1,3,\ldots,m-1} C_j(X) - \sum_{j=2,4,\ldots,m} C_j(X) \right). \tag{2}$$

Namely, classification is performed based on a majority vote, with the positive clauses voting for $y = 1$ and the negative for $y = 0$. The classifier $\hat{y} = u\left(x_1 \bar{x}_2 + \bar{x}_1 x_2 - x_1 x_2 - \bar{x}_1 \bar{x}_2\right)$, e.g., captures the XOR-relation.

Learning. A clause $C_j(X)$ is composed by a team of Tsetlin Automata [8], each Tsetlin Automaton deciding to *Include* or *Exclude* a specific literal l_k in the clause (see Fig. 1). Learning which literals to include is based on reinforcement: Type I feedback produces frequent patterns, while Type II feedback increases the discrimination power of the patterns.

A TM learns on-line, processing one training example (X, y) at a time.

Type I feedback is given stochastically to clauses with positive polarity when $y = 1$ and to clauses with negative polarity when $y = 0$. An afflicted clause, in turn, reinforces each of its Tsetlin Automata based on:

1. The clause output $C_j(X)$;
2. The action of the targeted Tsetlin Automaton – *Include* or *Exclude*; and
3. The value of the literal l_k assigned to the automaton.

Two rules govern Type I feedback:

- *Include* is rewarded and *Exclude* is penalized with probability $\frac{s-1}{s}$ if $C_j(X) = 1$ and $l_k = 1$. This reinforcement is strong (triggered with high probability) and makes the clause remember and refine the pattern it recognizes in X.
- *Include* is penalized and *Exclude* is rewarded with probability $\frac{1}{s}$ if $C_j(X) = 0$ or $l_k = 0$. This reinforcement is weak (triggered with low probability) and coarsens infrequent patterns, making them frequent.

---

[2] Any systematic division of clauses can be used as long as the cardinality of the positive and negative polarity sets are equal.

Above, s is a hyperparameter that controls the frequency of the patterns produced.

Type II feedback is given stochastically to clauses with positive polarity when $y = 0$ and to clauses with negative polarity when $y = 1$. It penalizes *Exclude* with probability 1 **if** $C_j(X) = 1$ **and** $l_k = 0$. This feedback is strong and produces candidate literals for discriminating between $y = 0$ and $y = 1$.

Resource allocation dynamics ensure that clauses distribute themselves across the frequent patterns, rather than missing some and overconcentrating on others. That is, for any input X, the probability of reinforcing a clause gradually drops to zero as the clause output sum

$$v = \sum_{j=1,3,\ldots,m-1} C_j(X) - \sum_{j=2,4,\ldots,m} C_j(X) \tag{3}$$

approaches a user-set target T for $y = 1$ (and $-T$ for $y = 0$). To exemplify, Fig. 1 plots the probability of reinforcing a clause when $T = 4$ for different clause output sums v, per class y. If a clause is not reinforced, it does not give feedback to its Tsetlin Automata, and these are thus left unchanged. In the extreme, when the voting sum v equals or exceeds the target T (the TM has successfully recognized the input X, no clauses are reinforced. Accordingly, they are free to learn new patterns, naturally balancing the pattern representation resources. See [3] for further details.

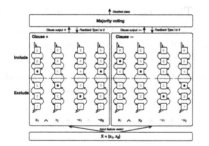 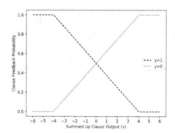

Fig. 1. (left) Two TA teams, each producing a conjunctive clause. Classification is based on majority voting. (right) Clause feedback probability for $T = 4$

3 Tsetlin Machine Interpretability

Because the TM represents patterns as self-contained conjunctive clauses in propositional logic, the method naturally leads to straightforward interpretability. However, as is the consensus in the machine learning literature, a model is fully interpretable only if it is possible to understand how the underlying data features impact the predictions of the model, both from a global perspective (entire model) and at the individual sample level. For example, a model that predicts housing prices in California should give much emphasis on specific latitude/longitude coordinates, as well as the age of the neighbouring houses (and perhaps other factors such as proximity at the beach). For individual sample data points, the model interpretation should show which features (such as house age, proximity to the beach) had the most positive (or negative) impact in expression the prediction. Before we present how closed-form expressions for both global and local interpretability can be derived intrinsically from any TM model, we first define some basic notation on the encoding of the features to a Boolean representation and feature inclusion sets, a critical first step in TM modeling.

3.1 Boolean Representation

We first assume that the input features to any TM can be booleanized into a bit encoded representation. Each bit represents a Boolean variable that is either False or True (0 or 1). To map continuous values to a Boolean representation, we use the encoding scheme adapted as follows. Let $I_u = [a_u, b_u]$ be some interval on the real line representing a possible range of continuous values of feature f_u. Consider $l > 0$ unique values $u_1, \ldots, u_l \in I_u$. We encode any $v \in I_u$ into an l-bit representation $[\{0,1\}]^l$ where the ith bit is given as 1 if $v \geq u_i$, and 0 otherwise. We will denote $v \in I_u$ of a feature f_u as $X_{f_u} := [x_1, \ldots, x_l]$ where any $x_i := v \geq u_i$. For example, suppose $I_u = [0, 10]$ with $u_1 = 1, u_2 = 2, \ldots, u_{10} = 10$. Then $v = 5.5$ is encoded as $[1, 1, 1, 1, 1, 0, 0, 0, 0, 0]$, while any $v \leq 0$ becomes $[0, 0, 0, 0, 0, 0, 0, 0, 0, 0]$, and any $v \geq 10$ becomes $[1, 1, 1, 1, 1, 1, 1, 1, 1, 1]$. The choice of $l > 0$ and the values $u_1, \ldots, u_l \in I_u$ should typically be chosen according to the properties of the empirical distribution of the underlying feature. If the values of feature f_u are relatively uniform across I_u, then a uniform choice of $u_1, \ldots, u_l \in I_u$ would seem appropriate. Otherwise the grid should be chosen to accompany the underlying density of the data, with a finer grid choice near higher densities.

3.2 Global Interpretability

Global interpretability is interested in understanding the most salient (important) features of the model, namely to what degree and strength a certain feature impacts predictions overall. We now introduce multiple output variables $y^i \in \{y^1, y^2, \ldots, y^n\}$, $y^i = \{0, 1\}$ and the upper index i, which refers to a particular output variable. For simplicity in exposition, we assume that the corresponding literal index sets $I_j^i, \bar{I}_j^i$, for each output variable, $i = 1, \ldots, n$, and clause, $j = 1, \ldots, m$, have been found under some performance criteria of the learning procedure, described in Sect. 2. With these sets fixed, we can now assemble the closed form expressions.

Global Feature Strength. For global feature strength we make direct use of the indexed inclusion sets $I_j^i, \bar{I}_j^i$, which are governed by the actions of the Tsetlin Automata. Specifically, we compute positive (negative) feature strength for a given output variable y^i and kth bit of feature f_u as follows:

$$g[k] \leftarrow \frac{1}{m} \sum_{j \in \{1,3,\ldots,m-1\}} \{1 \text{ if } k \in I_j^i\}, \quad \bar{g}[k] \leftarrow \frac{1}{m} \sum_{j \in \{1,3,\ldots,m-1\}} \{1 \text{ if } k \in \bar{I}_j^i\}.$$

(4)

In other words, for any given feature index $k \in [1,\ldots,o]$, the frequency of its inclusion across all clauses, restricted to positive polarity, governs its global importance score $g[k]$. This score thus reflects how often the feature is part of a pattern that is important to making a certain class prediction y^i. Notice that we are only interested in indices pertaining to the positive polarity clauses $C_j^i(X)$ since these are the clauses that contain references to features that are beneficial for predicting the ith class index.

The $g[k]$ and $\bar{g}[k]$ scores give positive and negative importance at the bit level for each feature. To get the total strength for a feature f_u itself, we simply aggregate over each bit k based on Eq. 4, restricted to the given feature f_u:

$$\phi(f_u) \leftarrow \sum_{k|x_k \in X_{f_u}} g[k], \quad \bar{\phi}(f_u) \leftarrow \sum_{k|x_k \in X_{f_u}} \bar{g}[k].$$

(5)

Above, X_{f_u} should be understood as the bit encoded features representing feature f_u. The functions $\phi(\cdot)$ accordingly measure the general importance of a feature when it comes to predicting a given class label y^i. As we shall see empirically in the next section, this measure defines the most relevant features of a model.

Remark: Due to the fact that the above expression can be trivially computed given any inclusion sets derived from the clauses, the feature importance can be observed in real-time during the online training procedure of TMs, to see how the feature importance evolves with new unseen date training samples. Such a feature is not available in typical batch machine learning methodologies utilizing frameworks such as SHAP.

Global Continuous Feature Range Strength. One additional global feature importance representation that we can derive for continuous input feature ranges is measuring the importance of a feature in terms of ranges of values. To do this, we can make use of the inclusion of features and negated features to construct a mapping of the important ranges for a given class. Based on our Boolean representation of continuous features, we define the allowable range for f_u as follows:

$$R(f_u) := [\min_{k \in \bar{I}_j^i} f_u(x_k), \max_{k \in I_j^i} f_u(x_k)].$$

(6)

Notice that according to the literal x_k, $\max_{k \in I_j^i} f_u(x_k)$, gives the largest $u_k \in I_u$ such that $v \geq u_k$ was an influential feature for an input v. Similarly, $\min_{k \in \bar{I}_j^i} f_u(x_k)$ yields the smallest $u_k \in I_u$ such that $\neg(v \geq u_k)$, or $v < u_k$, was a relevant feature for y^i.

So now do we not only know the most salient features in making a certain prediction, but we know the range of the influential values as well for every feature f_u given prediction class y^i. Again, these can all be computed in real-time during the learning of the model, giving full insight into the modeling procedure.

3.3   Local Interpretability

Local interpretability is interested in understanding to what degree features positively (or negatively) impact individual predictions. Due to the transparent nature of the clause structures, it is relatively straightforward to extract the driving features of a given input sample. If we assume again the bit representation $X = [x_1, x_2, \ldots, x_o]$ is a concatenation of the bit representation of all features f_{u_j}, and we suppose i is the predicted class index of X, then we define

$$l[k, X] \leftarrow \sum_{j \in \{1,3,\ldots,m-1\}} \{C_j^i(X) \mid x_k = 1, k \in I_j^i\} \tag{7}$$

which give positive importance at the bit level for each feature. To get the total predictive impact for each feature we again aggregate over the individual bits of the feature:

$$\phi(f_u, X) \leftarrow \sum_{k \mid x_k \in X_{f_u}} l[k, X], \quad \bar{\phi}(f_u, X) \leftarrow \sum_{k \mid x_k \in X_{f_u}} \bar{l}[k, X]. \tag{8}$$

In other words, for a given input, all the combined clauses act as a lookup table of important features, from which the strength of each feature in a prediction can be determined.

4   Empirical Evaluation and Applications

In order to evaluate the capability of our expressions for global and local TM interpretability, we will now consider two types of data sets: 1) Data sets which have an intuitive set of features which are already quite interpretable without model insight and 2) Data sets which will be more data driven, with features that are not necessarily understood by humans. We will further compare our results with other interpretable approaches to gain insight into the properties of our closed-form expressions. We further demonstrate that the TM can compete accuracy-wise with black-box methods, while simultaneously remaining relatively transparent. We will be using the Integer Weighted Tsetlin Machine (IWTM) proposed in [1], a recent extension of the classical TM summarized in Sect. 2 that has been shown to provide superior performance in both accuracy and training time by inducing weights on the clause structures. More details on motivation, formulation, and empirical studies are given in [1].

4.1 Comparison with SHAP

We first compare our feature strength scores, as defined in Eq. 5 and Eq. 6, with SHapley Additive exPlanations (SHAP) values, a popular methodology for explaining black-box models, considered as state-of-the-art. First published in 2017 by Lundberg and Lee [4], the approach attempts to "reverse-engineer" the output of any predictive algorithm by assigning each feature an importance value for a particular prediction. As it is first and foremost concerned with the local interpretability of a model, global interpretability of the SHAP approach can be viewed at the level of visualizing all the samples in the form of a SHAP value (impact on model output) by feature value (from low to high).

We use the Wisconsin Breast Cancer data set to compare the two approaches. This data set contains 30 different features extracted from an image of a fine needle aspirate (FNA) of a breast mass. These features represent different physical characteristics like the concavity, texture, or symmetry computed for each cell with various descriptive statistics such as the mean, standard deviation and "worst" (sum of the three largest values). Each sample is labelled according to the diagnosis, benign or malign.

Before comparing the results on the most influential features, we compare the performance metrics of the IWTMs with XGBoost. Table 1 shows the comparison in terms of mean and variance on accuracy and error types where the models were constructed 10 times each, with a training set of 70% randomly chosen samples. We see that the IWTM clearly competes in performance with XGBoost, albeit with a much higher variance in performance.

Table 1. Performance comparison of the IWTM and XGBoost models on the breast cancer data set

Method	Accuracy	AUC	Type I Error	Type II Error
IWTM	95.19 ± 0.52	98.10 ± 0.43	0.033 ± 0.021	0.053 ± 0.023
XGBoost	95.45 ± 0.15	98.02 ± 0.04	0.039 ± 0.01	0.054 ± 0.01

In the SHAP summary plot shown in Fig. 2, we observe that the most important features for the XGBoost model are perimeter_worst, concave points-mean, concave points-worst, texture_worst and area_se among others. Taking into account the feature value and impact on model output, the most impactful features for making a prediction tend to be perimeter_worst, concave points-worst, area_se, and area_worst, whereas texture_worst and concave points_mean prove to be the most effective in their lower value range.

Figure 2 also shows the corresponding results for the TM, providing the strength of the features when predicting benign cells, calculated based on Eq. 5. We can see that concave points_mean, concave points_worst, texture_worst, area_se, and concavity_worst seem to be the strongest contributors. Apart from feature perimeter_worst being the most effective for

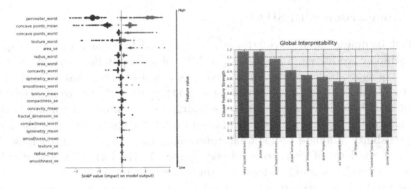

Fig. 2. SHAP value impact on model output against feature value plot and global feature importance for predicting output of benign, respectively

SHAP, it can clearly be seen that both methods yield very similar global feature strengths. Nearly all of the top 10 features in both sets agree in relative strength.

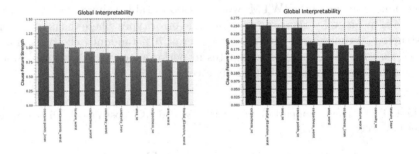

Fig. 3. Global positive and negated feature importance for predicting output of malign

Similarly, the scores of the most relevant features for the benign class are shown in Fig. 3. As seen, `concave points_mean`, `concave points_worst`, and `area_worst` have a non-trivial impact.

Finally, Fig. 3 also reports the global importance for the features negated, calculated using $\bar{\phi}(f_u)$ in Eq. 5 for the top features f_u. In essence, the strength of these features show that in general, the inclusion of their negated feature ranges had a positive impact on predicting the malign class of cells.

4.2   Comparison with Neural Additive Models

Recently introduced in [2], Neural Additive Models offer a novel approach to general additive models. In all brevity, the goal is to learn a linear combination of simple neural networks that each model a single input feature. Being trained jointly, they learn arbitrarily complex relationships between input features and outputs. In this section, we compare IWTM models to NAMs both in terms of AUC and interpretability. For convenience, we also show the performance against several other popular black-box type machine learning approaches.

We first investigate two classification tasks, continuing with a regression task to contrast interpretability against NAMs. All of the performance results, except for those associated with the IWTMs, are adapted directly from [2].

Credit Fraud. In this task, we wish to predict whether a certain credit card transaction is fraudulent or not. To learn such fraudulent transaction, we use the data set found in [6] containing 284,807 transactions made by European credit cardholders. The data set is highly unbalanced, containing only 492 frauds (or 0.172%) of all transactions.

The training and testing strategy is to sample 60% of the true positives of fraudulent transactions, and then randomly select an equal number of non-fraudulent transactions from the remaining 284k+ transactions. Testing is then done on the remaining fraudulent transactions.

The globally important features for the fraudulent class of transactions are shown in Fig. 4. With the exception of "time from first transaction" and "transaction amount", there is unfortunately no reference to other features names due to confidentiality. Thus, we cannot interpret features meaningfully. However, we can analyze how the ranges of the features vary according to predicting fraudulent or non-fraudulent transactions.

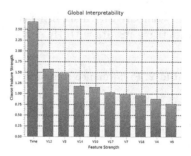

Fig. 4. Global feature importance in the credit card fraud detection data set. These are the 10 most influential features for predicting fraud from this data set.

Note that all plots concerning ranges have had the feature values normalized such that the minimal value for that feature is 0.0 and the maximal value is 1.0. We will use blue-colored bars to represent where the range with the most impact for the given class is located.

In applying the feature range expression from Eq. 6 to a batch of non-fraudulent samples, we see from Fig. 5 that the "time from first transaction" feature, while one of the most important, is important in its entire range for both classes of transactions. Namely there is no range that sways the model to predict either fraudulent or non-fraudulent. This is in accordance with the NAM [2], where their graph depicts no sway of contribution into either class for the entire range of values.

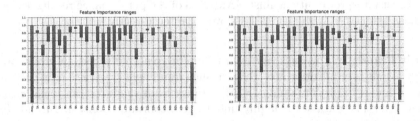

Fig. 5. Feature ranges when predicting non-fraudulent and fraudulent activity. Notice that time is unbiased when predicting fraud

The "transaction amount" feature can also be compared with NAMs, again considering feature value ranges. In Fig. 5, we see that most relevant range is from around 0 to 50 for the non-fraudulent class, but for fraudulent transaction class the most salient range shrinks to about 0–25. Indeed, for most of the other V-features, the value ranges tend to shrink, in particular for the higher value ranges. We can see that even though the visual representation of the model outputs in terms of feature and range importance are quite different, they can still be traced to yield similar conclusions.

In terms of performance compared with six other approaches, Table 2 shows IWTMs have yielded competitive results with those used in [2].[3]

Table 2. Performance comparison.

Method	Credit Fraud Accuracy
IWTM (w/out bias)	0.990 ± 0.005
Logistic regression	0.975 ± 0.010
Decision trees	0.956 ± 0.004
NAMs	0.980 ± 0.002
EBMs	0.976 ± 0.009
XGBoost	0.981 ± 0.008
DNNs	0.978 ± 0.003

---

[3] The choice of hyperparameters of the IWTM can be summarized as picking the number of clauses randomly three times, between 50 and 500 clauses, with a threshold of twice the number of clauses. The best model in terms of accuracy was chosen of the three configurations.

For a more in-depth study on IWTMs comparing with other methods on benchmark classification data sets, please refer to [1].

California Housing Price Data Set. In our last example, we investigate performance and interpretability on a regression task, using the California Housing data set. This data set appears in [5] where it is used to explore important features from a regression on housing price averages, offering features that are intrinsically interpretable and easy to validate in how they contribute to predictions. The data is comprised of one row per census block group, where a block group is the smallest geographical unit for which the U.S. Census Bureau publishes sample data, with a population typically between 600 to 3,000 people. The data set suggests we can derive and understand the influence of community characteristics on housing prices by predicting the median price of houses (in million dollars) in each California district.

We include results on both global and local interpretability, while also including results on influential ranges conditional on three tiers of prediction of housing prices (low, medium, high).

The global feature importance diagram measures the importance of each feature by how often if appears as a positive contribution in the clauses, per Eq. 5. In summary, the diagram indicates that both median income and house location are the most influential features to predicting housing prices. This also conforms with the features derived by the NAM approach in [2].

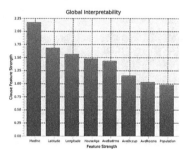 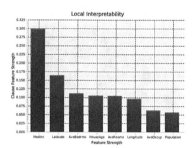

Fig. 6. Global feature importance output by the Integer Weighted Tsetlin Machine, and local feature importance showing median income and latitude (Bay Area) as the highest importance of such prediction

We now investigate local interpretability using a specific housing price instance. For our example, we take geographical region in the scenic hill area just east of Berkeley, known for its high real estate. Being from an affluent Bay Area zip code, it should be clear that with a high housing price predicted, both median income and location should be the main drivers.

Applying the local interpretability expression from Eq. 8 to this specific sample, we see that the top features concur with the assumption on the particular real estate area (Fig. 6). The location is sparsely populated with smaller occupancy per home, but hugely driven by the large median income and the Bay Area zip code. We also see that latitude achieves an exceptionally higher influence than longitude for this example, in comparison with their global importance, which could be from the fact that this particular latitude is aligned with northern California in the Bay Area and thus has more informative content to provide for a high housing cost prediction. Furthermore, housing age and number of bedrooms for this region in the Bay Area also seem to provide more information in making a prediction than longitude. This clearly exhibits how a local explanation can differ from a general global explanation of the model feature importance.

More insight can be gained by examining the feature value ranges that are important for certain levels of housing price predictions. Using the range importance expression Eq. 6, we look at some typical ranges of values that are attributed to lower prediction in the housing price. In Fig. 7, we note that Median income is low for this class of housing prices, while latitude and longitude values take on nearly the entire range of values. On the other hand, average number of rooms does not seem be a factor. We now apply the same approach to mid-tiered housing prices. Here we expect to see higher median income and maybe some changes in the location to accommodate more rural housing prices. In general, relatively all ranges of values for most features are important, with the exception of median income which takes on the upper 70% of values. Further, the number of bedrooms plays a larger part in the prediction. Lower population seems to have a positive impact as well, accounting for those rural census blocks.

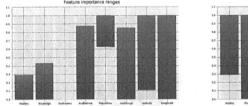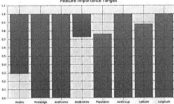

Fig. 7. Typical ranges which are influential when predicting lower-tiered and medium-tiered housing prices, respectively

Considering regression error, we compare techniques by means of average RMSE, obtaining the one-standard deviation figures via 5-fold cross validation. Table 3 show the results compared with those from [2], Sect. 3.2.1.

We see that IWTMs performs similarly to the other techniques, however, is outperformed by the DNNs. This can be explained by the low number of clauses employed, making it more difficult to exploit the large number of samples (20k), which gives the DNN[4] an advantage.

---

[4] DNN with 10 hidden layers containing 100 units each with ReLU activation and Adam optimizer.

Table 3. Comparison of performances of the regression IWTM with several other models

Method	California housing
IWTM	0.572 ± 0.044
Linear regression	0.728 ± 0.015
Decision trees	0.720 ± 0.006
NAMs	0.562 ± 0.007
EBMs	0.557 ± 0.009
XGBoost	0.532 ± 0.014
DNNs	0.492 ± 0.009

5   Conclusion

In this paper, we proposed closed-form expressions for understanding why a TM model makes a specific prediction and capturing the most important features of the model overall (global interpretability). We further introduced expressions for measuring the importance of feature value ranges for continuous features. The clause structures that we investigated revealed interpretable insights about high-dimensional data, without the use of additional *post hoc* methods or additive approaches. Upon comparing the interpretability results to a staple in machine learning interpretability such as SHAP and a more recent novel interpretable extension to neural networks in NAMs, we observed that the TM-based interpretability yielded similar insights. Furthermore, we validated the approach of range importance on California housing data which offer human interpretable features.

Current and future work in the closed-form expressions are being developed for the problem of unsupervised dimension reduction and clustering in large dimensional data, along with further adapting the approach for both learning in time-series data and images.

References

1. Abeyrathna, K.D., Granmo, O.C., Goodwin, M.: Extending the Tsetlin Machine with integer-weighted clauses for increased interpretability. IEEE Access **9**, 8233–8248 (2020)
2. Agarwal, R., Frosst, N., Zhang, X., Caruana, R., Hinton, G.E.: Neural additive models: interpretable machine learning with neural nets (2020)
3. Granmo, O.C.: The Tsetlin Machine - a game theoretic bandit driven approach to optimal pattern recognition with propositional logic (2018). https://arxiv.org/abs/1804.01508
4. Lundberg, S., Lee, S.I.: A unified approach to interpreting model predictions (2017)
5. Pace, K., Barry, R.: Sparse spatial autoregressions. Stat. Probab. Lett. **33**(3), 291–297 (1997)

6. Pozzolo, A.D., Bontempi, G.: Adaptive machine learning for credit card fraud detection (2015)
7. Rudin, C.: Stop explaining black box machine learning models for high stakes decisions and use interpretable models instead. Nat. Mach. Intell. **1**(5), 206–215 (2019)
8. Tsetlin, M.L.: On behaviour of finite automata in random medium. Avtomat. i Telemekh **22**(10), 1345–1354 (1961)
9. Tulio Ribeiro, M., Singh, S., Guestrin, C.: "Why should i trust you?": explaining the predictions of any classifier. arXiv e-prints arXiv:1602.04938 (February 2016)

Explainable Reinforcement Learning with the Tsetlin Machine

Saeed Rahimi Gorji[1]([⊠])[iD], Ole-Christoffer Granmo[1][iD], and Marco Wiering[2][iD]

[1] Centre for Artificial Intelligence Research, University of Agder, Grimstad, Norway
{saeed.r.gorji,ole.granmo}@uia.no
[2] University of Groningen, Groningen, Netherlands
mwiering@ai.rug.nl

Abstract. The Tsetlin Machine is a recent supervised machine learning algorithm that has obtained competitive results in several benchmarks, both in terms of accuracy and resource usage. It has been used for convolution, classification, and regression, producing interpretable rules. In this paper, we introduce the first framework for reinforcement learning based on the Tsetlin Machine. We combined the value iteration algorithm with the regression Tsetlin Machine, as the value function approximator, to investigate the feasibility of training the Tsetlin Machine through bootstrapping. Moreover, we document robustness and accuracy of learning on several instances of the grid-world problem.

Keywords: Tsetlin Machines · Explainable machine learning · Learning automata · Reinforcement learning

1 Introduction

The Tsetlin Machine (TM), introduced in [9], is a novel supervised learning algorithm. It combines learning automata and propositional logic to describe the frequent patterns present in training data. A TM takes a feature vector of propositional values as input, which it maps to a target output using conjunctive clauses. This representation allows for capturing non-linear patterns, leveraging Disjunctive Normal Form (DNF).

The relation to DNF makes the TM suited for interpretation. As articulated by Valiant [17]: *"Such expressions appear particularly easy for humans to comprehend. Hence we expect that any practical learning system would have to allow for them."* The main difference between a TM model and a DNF formula, however, is that the disjunction operator is replaced by a summation operator. This allows the TM to produce an ensemble of clauses, which jointly provides a multi-valued measure of output confidence. The resulting fine-grained output guides the learning process more robustly than simply employing the Boolean output of a DNF formula. Yet, interpretability is maintained because one can interpret the clauses individually due to the linear decomposition of a TM model. Indeed, a TM produces formula in DNF for certain hyper-parameter settings.

© Springer Nature Switzerland AG 2021
H. Fujita et al. (Eds.): IEA/AIE 2021, LNAI 12798, pp. 173–187, 2021.
https://doi.org/10.1007/978-3-030-79457-6_15

After its introduction, TM research has proceeded along several paths. A convolutional architecture was proposed in 2019 [10], which has provided competitive results, both in terms of accuracy and resource usage on different benchmarks (natural language understanding [5]). Further, the vanilla TM has been significantly extended, including the introduction of weighted clauses [3,11], regression architectures [2], and elimination of hyperparameters [14]. Furthermore, theoretical work on convergence has recently appeared [18], while scalable architectures have been proposed for CPU[1] [13] and GPU[2] [1].

This paper investigates the possibility of turning the TM, a fundamentally supervised learning algorithm, into an effective TM-based reinforcement learning algorithm. The idea of using supervised learning in the context of reinforcement learning is not new in the literature [6–8,15]. The authors of the latter papers tried to address the issue of slow or non-convergence of different reinforcement methods, due to incremental and online learning, with a supervised learning approach. For instance, [7] proposed a reinforcement learning algorithm where a training set is prepared in each iteration to enable training the model according to supervised learning principles. They reported faster and more reliable convergence using this combination of reinforcement and supervised learning. Nowadays, batch-learning methods such as experience replay are often used for training RL agents.

Our approach here is similar in the sense that we collected training data by interacting with the environment over several episodes, after which a regression TM is trained using reinforcement learning principles.

Contributions of this Paper. This paper provides a proof of concept on using the TM in a reinforcement learning context. We demonstrate the viability of using bootstrapping as the learning mechanism in the TM, despite the lack of a pre-labelled training set. In particular, we show that the TM is able to unlearn and recover from the misleading experiences that often occur at the beginning of training. A key challenge that we address is the mapping of the intrinsically continuous nature of RL state-value learning to the discrete nature of the TM, leveraging probabilistic updates. Finally, we propose how the class of models learnt by our TM for the grid-world problem can be translated into a more understandable graph structure. The graph structure captures the state value function approximation and the corresponding policy found by the TM.

The rest of the paper is organized as follows. Section 2 describes the TM, its learning process, and the regression variant that we use in this paper. Section 3 defines the reinforcement learning problem and the details of our proposed approach. The empirical results and their analysis are presented in Sect. 4, while Sect. 5 concludes the paper.

---

[1] https://github.com/cair/pyTsetlinMachine.
[2] https://github.com/cair/PyTsetlinMachineCUDA.

2   Tsetlin Machine

In this section, we first describe how the TM performs classification. Then we lay out the method TMs use to learn a classification model from a dataset. Finally, we examine how the TM can be adopted for solving regression problems.

2.1   Classification

A TM takes a vector $X = (x_1, \ldots, x_o)$ of Boolean features as input, to be classified into one of two classes, $y = 0$ or $y = 1$. Together with their negated counterparts, $\bar{x}_k = \neg x_k = 1 - x_k$, the features form a literal set $L = \{x_1, \ldots, x_o, \bar{x}_1, \ldots, \bar{x}_o\}$.

A TM pattern is formulated as a conjunctive clause C_j (Eq. 1), formed by ANDing a subset $L_j \subseteq L$ of the literal set:

$$C_j(X) = \bigwedge_{l \in L_j} l = \prod_{l \in L_j} l. \tag{1}$$

E.g., the clause $C_j(X) = x_1 \wedge x_2 = x_1 x_2$ consists of the literals $L_j = \{x_1, x_2\}$ and outputs 1 iff $x_1 = x_2 = 1$.

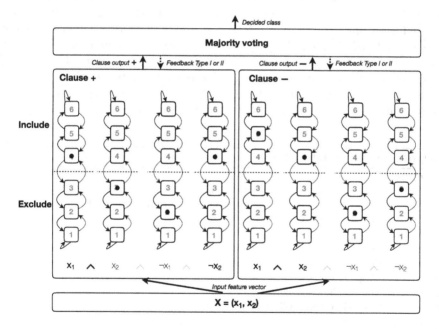

Fig. 1. The TM architecture. Each clause is constructed using Tsetlin Automata (TA) for each literal. The different TAs learn to include or exclude the different literals. The number of clauses is chosen beforehand. Here, only one positive and one negative clause are shown.

The number of clauses employed is a user set parameter n. Half of the clauses are assigned positive polarity. The other half is assigned negative polarity.

The clause outputs are combined into a classification decision through summation and thresholding using the unit step function $u(v) = 1$ **if** $v \geq 0$ **else** 0:

$$\hat{y} = u \left(\sum_{j=1}^{n/2} C_j^+(X) - \sum_{j=1}^{n/2} C_j^-(X) \right). \tag{2}$$

Namely, classification is performed based on a majority vote, with the positive clauses voting for $y = 1$ and the negative for $y = 0$. The classifier $\hat{y} = u\left(x_1 \bar{x}_2 + \bar{x}_1 x_2 - x_1 x_2 - \bar{x}_1 \bar{x}_2\right)$, e.g., captures the XOR-relation (illustrated in Fig. 1).

2.2 Learning Procedure

A clause j is composed by an attached team of Tsetlin Automata (TA), one TA per literal l_k in L. The TA for literal l_k has a state $a_{j,k}$, which decides whether l_k is included in clause j. Learning which literals to include is based on two types of reinforcement: Type I and Type II, as described in the following. Type I feedback produces frequent patterns, while Type II feedback increases the discrimination power of the patterns.

TMs learn on-line, processing one training example $(\mathbf{X}, y)$ at a time. In all brevity, after a forward pass through the layers as shown in Fig. 1, each clause is updated according to Algorithm 1. The first step is to decide whether the clause is to be updated (Lines 2–4). Here, resource allocation dynamics ensure that clauses distribute themselves across the frequent patterns, rather than missing some and over-concentrating on others. That is, for any input $\mathbf{X}$, the probability of reinforcing a clause gradually drops to zero as the voting sum v approaches a user-set target T for $y = 1$ (and $-T$ for $y = 0$).

Algorithm 1: UpdateClause($\mathbf{X}, v, c_j, p_j, T, s$)

Input:
> Training example $(\mathbf{X}, y)$, voting sum v, clause output c_j,
> positive polarity indicator $p_j \in \{0, 1\}$, voting target $T \in [1, \infty)$,
> pattern specificity $s \in [1.0, \infty)$

Output:
1 $v^c \leftarrow \text{clip}\,(v, -T, T)$
2 $e \leftarrow T - (2 \cdot y_i - 1) \cdot v_i^c$
3 **if** $rand() \leq \frac{e}{2T}$ **then**
4 $\quad$ **if** y_i **xor** p_j **then**
5 $\qquad$ **TypeIIFeedback**($\mathbf{X}, c_j$)
6 $\quad$ **else**
7 $\qquad$ **TypeIFeedback**($\mathbf{X}, c_j, s$)

8 **return**

As seen, if a clause is not reinforced, it does not give feedback to its TAs, and these are thus left unchanged. In the extreme, when the voting sum v equals or exceeds the target T (the TM has successfully recognized the input $\mathbf{X}$), no clauses are reinforced. They are then free to learn new patterns, naturally balancing the pattern representation resources [9].

If a clause is going to be updated, the updating is either of Type I or Type II:

Type I feedback is given to clauses with positive polarity when $y = 1$ and to clauses with negative polarity when $y = 0$ (Line 8). Each TA of the clause is then reinforced based on: (1) the clause output c_j; (2) the action of the TA – *include* or *exclude*; and (3) the value of the literal l_k assigned to the TA. Two rules govern Type I feedback:

- *Include* is rewarded and *exclude* is penalized with probability $\frac{s-1}{s}$ whenever $c_j = 1$ and $l_k = 1$. This reinforcement is strong (triggered with high probability) and makes the clause remember and refine the pattern it recognizes in $\mathbf{X}$.[3]
- *Include* is penalized and *exclude* is rewarded with probability $\frac{1}{s}$ whenever $c_j = 0$ or $l_k = 0$. This reinforcement is weak (triggered with low probability) and coarsens infrequent patterns, making them frequent.

Above, hyper-parameter s controls pattern frequency.

Type II feedback is given to clauses with positive polarity when $y=0$ and to clauses with negative polarity when $y=1$ (Line 6). It penalizes *exclude* with probability 1 if $c_j = 1$ and $l_k = 0$. If this happens, the corresponding TA state $a_{j,k}$ is increased by 1. Thus, this feedback introduces literals for discriminating between $y = 0$ and $y = 1$.

2.3 Regression

The regression TM (RTM) performs regression based on formulas in propositional logic [2]. Like the regular TM, the input to an RTM is a vector $\mathbf{X}$ of o Boolean features x_k, $\mathbf{X} \in \{0,1\}^o$. These are further augmented with their negated counterparts $\bar{x}_k = 1 - x_k$ to form a vector of literals: $\mathbf{L} = (x_1, \ldots, x_o, \bar{x}_1, \ldots, \bar{x}_o) = (l_1, \ldots, l_{2o})$. In contrast to a regular TM, the output of an RTM is real-valued, normalized to the domain $y \in [0, 1]$.

Prediction. The regression function of an RTM is simply a linear summation of products, where the products are built from the literals:

$$y = \frac{1}{T} \sum_{j=1}^{n} \prod_{l \in L_j} l. \tag{3}$$

In Eq. 3 above, the index j refers to one particular product of literals, defined by the subset L_j of literal indexes. If we e.g. have two propositional variables x_1 and x_2, the literal index sets $L_1 = \{1, 4\}$ and $L_2 = \{2, 3\}$ define the function: $y = \frac{1}{T}(x_1\bar{x}_2 + \bar{x}_1x_2)$. The user set parameter T decides the resolution of the regression function. Notice that each product in the summation either evaluates

---

[3] Note that the probability $\frac{s-1}{s}$ is replaced by 1 when boosting true positives.

to 0 or 1. This means that a larger T requires more literal products to reach a particular value y. Thus, increasing T makes the regression function increasingly fine-grained. Finally, note that the number of conjunctive clauses n in the regression function also is a user set parameter, which decides the expression power of the RTM.

Learning. The RTM employs two kinds of feedback, Type I and Type II, further defined below. Type I feedback triggers TA state changes that eventually make a clause output 1 for the given training example **X**. Conversely, Type II feedback triggers state changes that eventually make the clause output 0. Thus, overall, regression error can be systematically reduced by carefully distributing Type I and Type II feedback:

$$Feedback = \begin{cases} \text{Type I,} & \text{if } y < \hat{y}_i, \\ \text{Type II,} & \text{if } y > \hat{y}_i. \end{cases} \quad (4)$$

In effect, the number of clauses that evaluates to 1 is increased when the predicted output is less than the target output $(y < \hat{y}_i)$ by providing Type I feedback. Type II feedback, on the other hand, is applied to decrease the number of clauses that evaluates to 1 when the predicted output is higher than the target output $(y > \hat{y}_i)$.

3   Reinforcement Learning Tsetlin Machine

In this paper, we introduce a shift in TM research. Up until now, all the efforts in progressing the TM has been based on the supervised learning paradigm. By proposing a scheme for learning from reinforcement, we here address several challenges.

To form a foundation for further research, we limit ourselves to a basic reinforcement problem. That is, we propose a solution for learning a state-value function and solve simple grid-world problems. We first investigate how the supervised TM algorithm can form the basis for solving simple reinforcement learning problems. For this purpose, we use the vanilla regression TM [4] to learn state-value pairs and to act as the function approximator.

It has previously been reported that the RTM can learn a function approximation efficiently and with high accuracy, given a fixed training set [4]. Here, however, the challenge comes from learning the function approximation through bootstrapping based on other partially learned, and possibly inaccurate, state values. Furthermore, we propose a method to cope with the exploration-exploitation dilemma of reinforcement learning.

Our approach combines the vanilla RTM and a standard reinforcement learning algorithm (value iteration). We use deterministic instances of the grid-world problem and a model to infer the next state given the current state and an action (e.g., up, down, left, right for grid-worlds). The goal for the TM is to learn the state-value function for the whole state space by interacting with the environment.

3.1   The Grid-World Problem

For our testbed, we use the grid-world problem, which is a well-known environment for reinforcement learning. An instance of the problem consists of an $m \times n$ grid of cells, where some of the cells can contain a wall. The agent starts in a fixed starting cell in the grid and is to reach one of the predefined goal cells.

In each time step, the agent can choose one of the four available directions as its action: up, down, left, and right. Upon choosing an action the agent receives a reward of -1 and moves to the corresponding adjacent cell in that direction. In case that the move results in moving into a wall or off the grid, the agent's position does not change in that time step.

Figures 2, 3, 4 and 5 show the grid-worlds that we use as examples and for evaluation. The starting cells and the goal cells (also referred to as terminal cells) are marked with ○ and +, respectively. In addition, the gray cells represent walls where the agent cannot move.

Since the (regression) TM only accepts Boolean vectors as input, the first step is to encode the problem in Boolean form. To that end, we represent the position of the agent in an $m \times n$ grid by using a Boolean feature vector with $m + n$ elements. The vector one-hot encodes the position of the agent. That is, the first m elements are zero-valued, except for the element that corresponds to the row of the agent's cell in the grid, which is one-valued. Similarly, the n next elements are zero-valued as well, apart from the element that refers to the column of the agent's cell. For instance, in Fig. 4, the feature vector corresponding to the agent's current position is $(0, 0, 1, 1, 0, 0, 0, 0, 0)$ (numbering rows from top to bottom and columns from left to right). Note that the agent's position uniquely describes the current state in the corresponding Markov Decision Process (MDP), which is constructed by encoding all the possible locations for the agent on the grid. In the rest of the paper, we use the terms "cell" and "state" interchangeably, to refer to each tile in the grid.

The output of the regression TM is a real value between the minimum (Y_{min}) and the maximum (Y_{max}) values that the machine can represent. After successful training, the RTM should be able to approximate the state-value function for all the states of the MDP. With an accurate function approximator, the process of finding the optimal path from the starting state to the terminal state is straightforward. One can simply use the greedy policy of choosing the best action (corresponding to the highest state-value approximation) at each state.

3.2   TM Reinforcement Learning Approach

An RTM needs to know the smallest (Y_{min}) and largest (Y_{max}) output value to predict. These two values form the interval $[Y_{min}, Y_{max}]$, which is discretized uniformly into $T + 1$ bins. Each bin is associated with the mean of its values, and together the bins form the set of all the output values that the algorithm could possibly learn. Thus, the theoretical accuracy of learning a value in general is within the order of magnitude of the bin size $(Y_{max} - Y_{min})/T$, which we refer to as a discretization gap.

In the context of reinforcement learning, however, since there is no explicit training set, our RTM does not have access to any explicit upper or lower bounds beforehand. Ideally, the upper and lower bounds should be learnt as part of the learning process. However, in this paper, we defer tackling the challenge of learning Y_{min} and Y_{max} to future work. Instead, we manually select effective values by analysing each grid-world instance. For instance, in our 3×6 grid, we observe that the minimum value becomes -6 and the maximal value becomes 0. Accordingly, we used -10 and $+5$ as loose predefined limits.

Algorithm 2: MODIFIED VALUE ITERATION (OFF-POLICY)

Input: Learning rate α, threshold value T, the current state S, the current
        state-value function estimator $V(.)$

Output: The updated state-value function estimator $V(.)$

1 Initialize $V(S)$, for all states S arbitrarily except that $V(terminal) = 0$
2 $episode \leftarrow 1$
3 **while** $episode \leq max$ **do**
4 $\quad$ Generate an episode following $\pi_{\epsilon-greedy}$:
    $\quad S_0, A_0, S_1, A_1, ..., S_{T-1}, A_{T-1}, S_T = terminal$
5 $\quad step \leftarrow T - 1$
6 $\quad$ **while** $step \geq 0$ **do**
7 $\quad\quad V(S_{step}) \leftarrow V(S_{step}) + \alpha \cdot \max_a(R_{S,a} + V(S'_{S,a}) - V(S_{step}))$
8 $\quad\quad step \leftarrow step - 1$
9 $\quad episode \leftarrow episode + 1$
10 **return** $V(.)$

For our reinforcement learning approach, we replace the static training set used in a regular supervised learning scenario with a dynamic one. Then the actual examples and their corresponding values could change from one iteration to the next, according to the latest bootstrapping results. More specifically, in each iteration, the algorithm generates an episode (a path from the starting point to the terminal), following the ϵ-greedy policy with $\epsilon = 1$ (taking random actions at each state) as the behaviour policy. Then the target policy is learned implicitly by training the RTM on the training examples generated along the episode for each state visited. The value of each state comes from following the best action and bootstrapping on the next state (cf. Algorithm 2 and Algorithm 3). Equation 5 shows the updating formula for the value function approximation $V(.)$:

$$V(s) = V(s) + \alpha \cdot \max_a(R_{s,a} + V(s'_{s,a}) - V(s)) \tag{5}$$

Here, α, s and s', are the learning rate, the current state, and the next state after taking action a, respectively. Moreover, $R_{s,a}$ is the reward received, resulting from taking action a in state s, which is equal to -1 for all states and actions.

Algorithm 2 is a variation of the standard value iteration algorithm in reinforcement learning [16] where the updates take place asynchronously along an episode. Considering the random policy here, the value function for all the states have a non-zero probability of being updated in each episode and the TM has the chance of learning the state value function for the whole state space.

Moreover, since the policy for the episode generation is a random one, the online nature of the algorithm presented here is not essential and the algorithm could potentially use a set of fixed episodes where only the target values for training examples are updated for the next round of training. The only consideration is that this fixed set of episodes should be sufficiently diverse and cover the whole state space so that all the states could get updated frequently.

Algorithm 3: RTM TRAINING THROUGH BOOTSRAPPING

Input: Learning rate α, threshold value T, the current state S, the current state-value function estimator $V(.)$ (RTM)

Output: The updated state-value function estimator $V(.)$ (updated RTM)

1 $gap \leftarrow (Y_{max} - Y_{min})/T$
2 $target \leftarrow \max_a(R_{S,a} + V(S'_{S,a}))$
3 **if** $|target - V(S)| \cdot \alpha \geq gap$ **then**
4 $\quad$ RTMTrain($\mathbf{X}_S$, $V(S) + |target - V(S)| \cdot \alpha$)

5 **else**
6 $\quad$ **if** $rand() < |target - V(S)| \cdot \alpha/gap$ **then**
7 $\quad\quad$ RTMTrain($\mathbf{X}_S$, $V(S) + Sgn(target - V(S)) \cdot gap$)

8 **return**

Algorithm 3 shows the way that the updates for the value function (described in Algorithm 2), are applied to the RTM for a state S with the corresponding feature vector X_S. By comparing the two algorithms (2 and 3) we see a slight difference which relates to the discrete nature of the RTM in learning values. More specifically, when the target value for a state S (*target* at Line 2 in Algorithm 3) is far from the current estimation ($V(S)$), the discretization gap does not affect the update and RTM will be updated normally (line 4). When the target value is too close to the current estimation, however, the new value would fall into the gap of discretization and the normal update is ineffective. To counter this issue, we considered a minimum viable sized update to take place with the probability proportional to the size of the actual update that was supposed to be applied but was too small to have any effect (Lines 6 and 7 in Algorithm 3).

4   Empirical Results and Analysis

We use four grid-world instances of different sizes and difficulty levels to measure the performance of our approach. Two of the grids are without internal walls. These are of size 5×5 and 7×7 (empty grids). The two other grids contain walls and are of size 3×6 and 5×7 (see Figs. 2, 3, 4, 5). Empty grids correspond to simpler MDPs with multiple alternative paths. Internal walls, on the other hand, introduce more challenge because they block some paths, thus differentiating more distinctly between states.

We run three different sets of experiments with three different discretization gaps of 0.5, 0.25 and 0.1, on each of the four grids. Smaller gaps require higher thresholds, and accordingly more clauses. We therefore use $1.5 \times T$ clauses for each experiment. In general, everything else being similar, we expect higher accuracy with smaller discretization gaps. Therefore, there is a trade-off between the accuracy of the value function and the size of the TM.

To present the results, for each grid, and for each of the three gap sizes, we plot the average result for Mean Absolute Error (MAE) over 10 independent runs. Overall, the results show the effect of increasing the size of the RTM on both accuracy and consistency of the resulting function approximator (Table 1).

Table 1. Experiment configurations

Experiment	Grid size	Clauses			Threshold			Y_{min}	Y_{max}
		0.5	0.25	0.1	0.5	0.25	0.1		
1	5×5	75	150	375	50	100	250	−20	+5
2	7×7	90	180	450	60	120	300	−25	+5
3	3×6	45	90	225	30	60	150	−10	+5
4	5×7	60	120	300	40	80	200	−15	+5

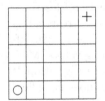 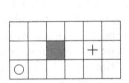 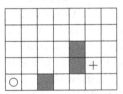

Fig. 2. The 5×5 (empty) grid   **Fig. 3.** The 7×7 (empty) grid   **Fig. 4.** The 3×6 grid   **Fig. 5.** The 5×7 grid

The output of a TM is a set of conjunctive clauses. These have the potential to provide us with a more understandable and insightful perspective of the problem solution. Here, we realize this potential by building a grid graph, in which we assign a number to each state representing the number of clauses that evaluate to 1 for that state. Moreover, between any two neighboring states, we put a directed edge from the state with a lower number (lower clause satisfaction) toward the state with a higher number (higher clause satisfaction).

Each grid graph reflects the relationship between clauses and states, which in turn corresponds to the state-value function that the algorithm has found.

Moreover, if for each state we only consider the edge toward the neighbor with the maximum number, these edges represent the policy that the TM found for the corresponding grid-world problem. Figures 10, 11, 12 and 13 show the grid graph for our four grids for the case of $gap = 0.25$. In all cases the policy is optimal except for occasional incorrect directions for some edges due to low accuracy in value function estimation (dashed edges). Using a smaller gap, effectively increases the accuracy of the learned value function and the final policy tends toward the optimal policy in all states.

As expected, in all grids, using a smaller gap (higher threshold) results in lower average error (Figs. 6, 7, 8 and 9). This is because the discretization error is amplified throughout the state space. Moreover, the average standard deviation also goes down when the gap decreases. This can be credited to the smoother transitions in TMs with more clauses, which in turn increases consistency and robustness across multiple runs.

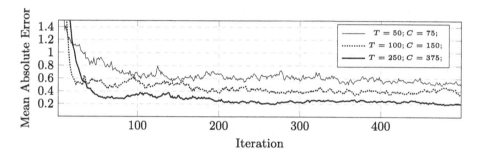

Fig. 6. MAE for the 5×5 grid

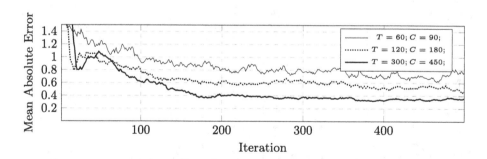

Fig. 7. MAE for the 7×7 grid

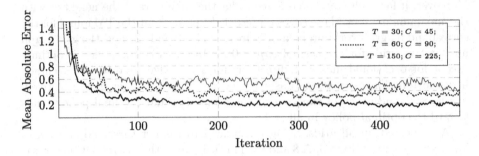

Fig. 8. MAE for the 3 × 6 grid

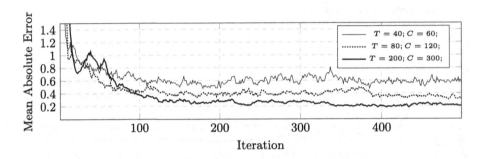

Fig. 9. MAE for the 5 × 7 grid

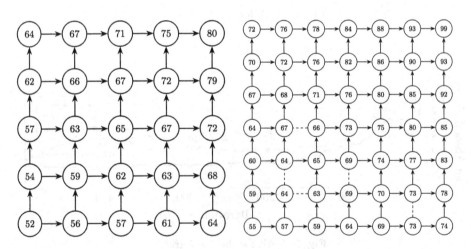

Fig. 10. The number of satisfied clauses at each state (5 × 5 grid)

Fig. 11. The number of satisfied clauses at each state (7 × 7 grid)

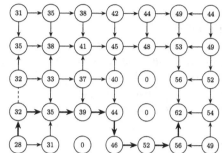

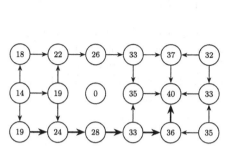

Fig. 12. The number of satisfied clauses at each state (3 × 6 grid)

Fig. 13. The number of satisfied clauses at each state (5 × 7 grid)

5   Conclusion and Future Work

The TM as a supervised learning algorithm has proven effective across various tasks, obtaining results comparable with other state-of-the-art algorithms. In this work, we addressed an open research question, namely, how to perform reinforcement learning with TMs.

By using bootstrapping instead of a training set in the learning process, we trained the TM to learn a state-value function for several instances of the grid-world problem. Despite the limitations of small-scale grid-worlds, these results act as a proof-of-concept for our proposed approach, being the first results on employing the TM as a reinforcement learning algorithm. While our focus was on learning the state-value function accurately for the entire state space, this is not necessary for finding the optimal path. Thus, our next step is to focus on finding the optimal path and using the value function to guide this search. To that end, the algorithm only needs to learn the value function for the relevant states. The rest of the state space can be safely ignored, which increases the scalability of the approach.

Moreover, another area of investigation is how to adaptively learn the output bounds needed by the RTM (i.e., Y_{min} and Y_{max}). When used in a supervised learning context, the RTM automatically uses the minimum and maximum values in the training set as the bounds, but without a given training set, these bounds also need to be learned during training. We here addressed this issue by providing the algorithm with a predefined interval. In our subsequent work, however, we plan to modify the approach so that it learns the bounds by itself during training.

Another issue that needs to be addressed in future work is convergence. In the literature, there are a few convergence results for the TM itself [9,18], but not for the RTM. While thre are convergence results for the value iteration and policy iteration algorithms [12], a convergence proof is needed for the RTM.

Further, the proofs must be integrated to comprehensively cover reinforcement with RTM.

Finally, we intend to investigate how our algorithm can scale up to larger problems. Such an investigation will include a comparison with the well-established methods in similar settings. For the small-scale problems we investigate here, however, our goal was to show how TMs, which previously only have been used for supervised learning, can be used for reinforcement learning.

References

1. Abeyrathna, K.D., et al..: Massively parallel and asynchronous Tsetlin Machine architecture supporting almost constant-time scaling. arXiv preprint arXiv:2009.04861 (2020)
2. Abeyrathna, K.D., Granmo, O.C., Zhang, X., Jiao, L., Goodwin, M.: The regression Tsetlin Machine - a novel approach to interpretable non-linear regression. Philos. Trans. R. Soc. A **378**, 20190165 (2019)
3. Abeyrathna, K.D., Granmo, O.-C., Goodwin, M.: A regression Tsetlin Machine with integer weighted clauses for compact pattern representation. In: 33rd International Conference on Industrial, Engineering and Other Applications of Applied Intelligent Systems (IEA/AIE 2020). Springer (2020)
4. Abeyrathna, K.D., Granmo, O.-C., Jiao, L., Goodwin, M.: The regression Tsetlin Machine: a Tsetlin Machine for continuous output problems. In: Moura Oliveira, P., Novais, P., Reis, L.P. (eds.) EPIA 2019. LNCS (LNAI), vol. 11805, pp. 268–280. Springer, Cham (2019). https://doi.org/10.1007/978-3-030-30244-3_23
5. Berge, G.T., Granmo, O.C., Tveit, T.O., Goodwin, M., Jiao, L., Matheussen, B.V.: Using the Tsetlin Machine to learn human-interpretable rules for high-accuracy text categorization with medical applications. IEEE Access **7**, 115134–115146 (2019). https://doi.org/10.1109/ACCESS.2019.2935416
6. Ernst, D., Geurts, P., Wehenkel, L.: Iteratively extending time horizon reinforcement learning. In: Lavrač, N., Gamberger, D., Blockeel, H., Todorovski, L. (eds.) ECML 2003. LNCS (LNAI), vol. 2837, pp. 96–107. Springer, Heidelberg (2003). https://doi.org/10.1007/978-3-540-39857-8_11
7. Ernst, D., Geurts, P., Wehenkel, L.: Tree-based batch mode reinforcement learning. J. Mach. Learn. Res. **6**, 503–556 (2005)
8. Ernst, D., Glavic, M., Geurts, P., Wehenkel, L.: Approximate value iteration in the reinforcement learning context. Application to electrical power system control. Int. J. Emerg. Electr. Power Syst. **3** (2005). https://doi.org/10.2202/1553-779X.1066
9. Granmo, O.C.: The Tsetlin Machine - a game theoretic bandit driven approach to optimal pattern recognition with propositional logic. arXiv preprint arXiv:1804.01508 (2018)
10. Granmo, O.C., Glimsdal, S., Jiao, L., Goodwin, M., Omlin, C.W., Berge, G.T.: The convolutional Tsetlin Machine. arXiv preprint, arXiv:1905.09688 (2019)
11. Phoulady, A., Granmo, O.C., Rahimi Gorji, S., Phoulady, H.A.: The weighted tsetlin machine: compressed representations with clause weighting. In: Ninth International Workshop on Statistical Relational AI (StarAI 2020) (2020)
12. Puterman, M.L., Shin, M.C.: Modified policy iteration algorithms for discounted Markov decision problems. Manag. Sci. **24**(11), 1127–1137 (1978). http://www.jstor.org/stable/2630487

13. Rahimi Gorji, S., Granmo, O.-C., Glimsdal, S., Edwards, J., Goodwin, M.: Increasing the inference and learning speed of Tsetlin Machines with clause indexing. In: Fujita, H., Fournier-Viger, P., Ali, M., Sasaki, J. (eds.) IEA/AIE 2020. LNCS (LNAI), vol. 12144, pp. 695–708. Springer, Cham (2020). https://doi.org/10.1007/978-3-030-55789-8_60

14. Rahimi Gorji, S., Granmo, O.-C., Phoulady, A., Goodwin, M.: A Tsetlin Machine with multigranular clauses. In: Bramer, M., Petridis, M. (eds.) SGAI 2019. LNCS (LNAI), vol. 11927, pp. 146–151. Springer, Cham (2019). https://doi.org/10.1007/978-3-030-34885-4_11

15. Rosenstein, M., Barto, A.: Supervised learning combined with an actor-critic architecture title2: Tech. rep., USA (2002)

16. Sutton, R.S., Barto, A.G.: Reinforcement Learning: An Introduction. A Bradford Book, Cambridge (2018)

17. Valiant, L.G.: A theory of the learnable. Commun. ACM **27**(11), 1134–1142 (1984). https://doi.org/10.1145/1968.1972

18. Zhang, X., Jiao, L., Granmo, O.C., Goodwin, M.: On the convergence of Tsetlin Machines for the identity-and not operators. arXiv preprint arXiv:2007.14268 (2020)

Sematic, Topology, and Ontology Models

Semantic Technologies Towards Missing Values Imputation

Iker Esnaola-Gonzalez[1]([✉]), Unai Garciarena[2], and Jesús Bermúdez[3]

[1] TEKNIKER, Basque Research and Technology Alliance (BRTA),
Iñaki Goenaga 5, 20600 Eibar, Spain
iker.esnaola@tekniker.es
[2] University of the Basque Country (UPV/EHU), Paseo Manuel Lardizabal 1,
20018 Donostia-San Sebastián, Spain
unai.garciarena@ehu.eus
[3] Eibar, Spain
jesus.bermudez@ehu.eus

Abstract. Missing values are a data quality problem affecting almost every type of real world datasets. Since poor data quality has a direct impact on organisational success, there is a dire need to eradicate missing values as a way to minimise costs and increase efficiency in companies. There are different methods to deal with missing values including the Imputation Methods, which try to compute an accurate estimation of missing values using the rest of the information available. This article devises the potential of Semantic Technologies towards the solution of the limitations of current Imputation Methods by proposing alternative approaches.

1 Introduction

Poor data quality has far-reaching effects and consequences [12]. It has a direct impact on organisational success as it is the primary reason for 40% of all initiatives failing to achieve their targeted benefits, and it affects overall labour productivity as much as 20% [3]. Therefore, it can be concluded that data quality influences the economic success of an organisation. Furthermore, as more business processes become automated, data quality is turning into the rate limiting factor for overall process quality.

Many different data quality problems can be found in literature such as noisy data or high data dimensionality. The focus of this paper is placed on Missing Values, that is, data quality problems that occur when values are empty or null in attributes where a value should have been recorded. Among the wide pool of strategies developed to manage missing values, Imputation Methods try to compute an accurate estimation of missing values using the rest of the information available [9]. This paper proposes the use of Semantic Technologies towards an alternative to avoid the existing limitations of current Imputation Methods. Furthermore, a set of experiments and assumptions are shown, which are expected to set the ground to guide future research.

© Springer Nature Switzerland AG 2021
H. Fujita et al. (Eds.): IEA/AIE 2021, LNAI 12798, pp. 191–196, 2021.
https://doi.org/10.1007/978-3-030-79457-6_16

The rest of this paper is structured as follows. Section 2 introduces the related work. Section 3 describes the foundation of the new proposed approach and finally, Sect. 4 discusses the possibilities of this approach.

2   Related Work

When it comes to analysing missing values, different categories can be identified, usually differentiated by the reason that caused the missing values themselves. Each of these originators can produce different patterns on the data that goes lost. The most common three patterns are [8]:

- Missing Completely At Random (MCAR): When there is no identifiable pattern to describe the missing values.
- Missing At Random (MAR): When there is a pattern that relates an observed variable and the missing values. MAR is a much broader class than MCAR.
- Missing Not At Random (MNAR): When a pattern exists, but it cannot be associated with any observed values. MNAR can also be referred to as NMAR (Not Missing At Random).

Different methods for handling missing values can be found in the literature [2,9]. A straightforward way of dealing with missing data is the deletion of incomplete observations or variables. This method is effective in some cases, such as when the quantity of incomplete observations or variables is low with respect to the dimension of the data, and when independence of the observations can be assumed. When this is not the case, however, the deletion strategy becomes a bad choice. Imputation Methods have been used in these scenarios.

In [5], a strategy attempting to maintain the imputed values quality while reducing the computing time complexity of the method for constructing the regression models was designed. This method reduced the set of observations used to build the regression model, thus saving time. However, the selection of the observations was performed using the euclidean distance between the observation being imputed and those available in the dataset, which added some extra computation time. Results obtained resembled those obtained with the common regression techniques, but could not improve them. This work shows a limitation on how the similar observations are found, as it adds computing time to the imputation procedure, and the obtained results were not optimal.

2.1   Semantic Technologies to Handle Missing Values

Even though it has been proved that data quality is a relevant aspect for process quality and organisational success, it has not received sufficient attention from the Semantic Web Community. In [4,7] methodologies for assessing the quality of Linked Data resources and the Semantic Web are presented. Even though existing work are an interesting example of how to make use of Semantic Technologies to deal with data quality issues, their full potential in this task is yet to be unlocked. In this article, we try to raise awareness of the prominent impact Semantic Technologies could have in both handling and imputing missing values.

3   Semantics-Based Imputation Approach

Recent articles argue that current machine learning methods perform poorly when they are required to act beyond the environment on which they have been trained [13]. In order to solve this situation, the idea that data-driven models should be complemented with knowledge-driven, reasoning based approaches is presented [10]. In this regard, Semantic Technologies and their capabilities to represent metadata can play a vital role and enable a range of possibilities to support the imputation of missing values. We believe that the a priori known information related to the problem could happen to be key in the design of new, improved imputation methods.

Representing data with appropriate ontological terms opens up new possibilities to define new contextual similarity criteria avoiding the use of simple metrics such as the euclidean distance and their consequent non-optimal imputation results. Moreover, the semantic annotation of raw data can be fundamental to enrich it, adding relevant contextual features, and enabling a more fine-grained selection of similar observations, which could be key to develop enhanced imputation methods.

3.1   Testing the Approach in a Real-World Office

This semantics-based imputation approach is validated on a real-world office. Figure 1 shows a simplified overview of the office where there are four temperature sensors (C021, C023, C026 and C029), two $CO2$ sensors (Z031, Z036), a luminosity sensor (Z033) and a humidity sensor (C028) installed. Let us consider that sensors register a measurement every hour and that, due to some unknown reason, temperature sensor C021 has suffered from a data loss of 30 consecutive data points.

In order to test the proposed semantics-based imputation approach, first of all, the office itself, the deployed devices, their capabilities and the measurements registered among others, need to be semantically represented. To do so, different ontologies have been reused. Among others, the office building topology has been represented using the Building Topology Ontology (BOT) [11], the deployed sensors and their measurements have been represented with the SOSA/SSN ontology [6], the properties observed by each sensor (e.g. temperature or humidity) have been represented using the Q4EEPSA ontology [1], and the units of measurement with the QUDT (Quantities, Units, Dimensions and Data Types) ontology.

Having this scenario annotated, different semantics-based imputation methods could be defined. Likewise, these imputation methods could be based on different contextual similarity criteria enabled by Semantic Technologies and the ontological representation. In this case, we propose imputing C021's missing values with measurements registered by the most similar temperature sensor. In this context, the similarity is understood in terms of distance and building element in which it is installed. The calculation of this similarity is enabled by the semantic representation of the office scenario.

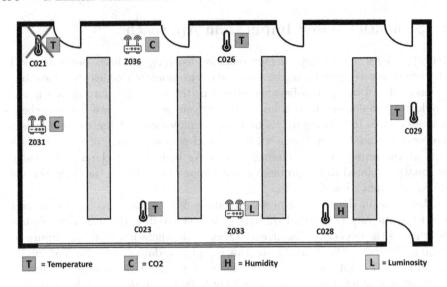

Fig. 1. Simplified representation of the use case office.

The approach proposed for this case has been divided into two phases: the first one, aimed at retrieving the most similar sensor, and the second one, aimed at retrieving its measurements for the specified period of time. After querying the knowledge base where the office is represented (via a SPARQL query), temperature sensor C026 is concluded to be the most similar one to C021. Therefore, the temperature measurements registered by this sensor are the values that have been used for replacing the missing values of sensor C021.

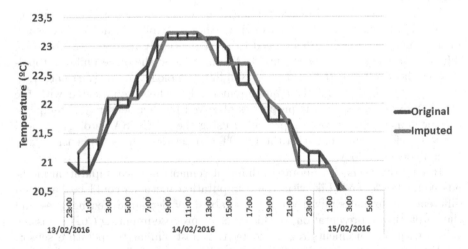

Fig. 2. Comparison between the original C021 measurements and the values imputed with the proposed Semantics-Based Imputation approach.

Figure 2 shows the comparison between the real C021 values and the values imputed after applying the proposed semantics-based imputation method. A RMSLE (Root Mean Squared Log Error) of -0.73 was obtained, which means that the difference between real and imputed values is less than $1\,°C$.

4 Discussion

Nowadays, datasets in general suffer from missing values, which leads to inevitable data quality issues, and the imputation of these values is of utmost importance for a variety of services and applications. In this article, Semantic Technologies have been proposed as an alternative to solve these issues.

The semantic representation of the scenario in which missing values occur enables the definition of new contextual similarity criteria rather than the classic distance-based ones (e.g. euclidean distance). In the scenario presented, contextual similarity has been specified based on the distance between sensors, their measurement capabilities and the building structure in which they are installed. However, there are countless possibilities, including the consideration of sensor manufacturer, their height or their orientation to name a few.

Furthermore, we believe that the potential of the Semantic Technologies is not limited to defining new imputation methods. If semantics are adequately complemented with tools that support the assistance of missing values handling, its usability and exploitation capabilities will be at hand. For instance, a system could exploit these resources to recommend data analysts the most suitable imputation methods for their datasets.

Although this article sets the base for the introduction of Semantic Technologies in the Missing Values handling problem, further investigation is necessary, such as the evaluation of performances from a time and resource consumption point of view.

Acknowledgement. This work has received funding from ELKARTEK project KK-2020/00049 3KIA of the Basque Government, REACT project from the European Union's Horizon 2020 research and innovation programme under grant agreement no. 824395, FEDER/TIN2016-78011-C4-2-R, TIN2016-78365-R (Spanish Ministry of Economy, Industry and Competitiveness) and IT-1244-19 (Basque Government). Unai Garciarena holds a predoctoral grant from the University of the Basque Country (ref. PIF 16/238).

References

1. Esnaola-Gonzalez, I., Bermúdez, J., Fernandez, I., Arnaiz, A.: EEPSA as a core ontology for energy efficiency and thermal comfort in buildings. Appl. Ontol. **16**(2), 193–228 (2021). https://doi.org/10.3233/AO-210245
2. Farhangfar, A., Kurgan, L.A., Pedrycz, W.: A novel framework for imputation of missing values in databases. IEEE Trans. Syst. Man Cybern.-Part A: Syst. Hum. **37**(5), 692–709 (2007)

3. Friedman, T., Smith, M.: Measuring the business value of data quality. Tech. Rep. G00218962 (2011). https://www.data.com/export/sites/data/common/assets/pdf/DS_Gartner.pdf

4. Fürber, C., Hepp, M.: Using semantic web resources for data quality management. In: Cimiano, P., Pinto, H.S. (eds.) EKAW 2010. LNCS (LNAI), vol. 6317, pp. 211–225. Springer, Heidelberg (2010). https://doi.org/10.1007/978-3-642-16438-5_15

5. Garciarena, U., Santana, R.: An extensive analysis of the interaction between missing data types, imputation methods, and supervised classifiers. Expert Syst. Appl. **89**, 52–65 (2017)

6. Haller, A., et al.: The modular SSN ontology: a joint W3C and OGC standard specifying the semantics of sensors, observations, sampling, and actuation. Semant. Web **10**(1), 9–32 (2019). https://doi.org/10.3233/SW-180320

7. Kontokostas, D., Zaveri, A., Auer, S., Lehmann, J.: TripleCheckMate: a tool for crowdsourcing the quality assessment of linked data. In: Klinov, P., Mouromtsev, D. (eds.) KESW 2013. CCIS, vol. 394, pp. 265–272. Springer, Heidelberg (2013). https://doi.org/10.1007/978-3-642-41360-5_22

8. Little, R.J., Rubin, D.B.: Statistical Analysis with Missing Data, vol. 793. Wiley, Hoboken (2002). https://doi.org/10.1002/9781119013563

9. Luengo, J., García, S., Herrera, F.: On the choice of the best imputation methods for missing values considering three groups of classification methods. Knowl. Inf. Syst. **32**(1), 77–108 (2012). https://doi.org/10.1007/s10115-011-0424-2

10. Marcus, G.: The next decade in AI: four steps towards robust artificial intelligence. arXiv preprint arXiv:2002.06177 (2020)

11. Rasmussen, M.H., Lefrançois, M., Schneider, G., Pauwels, P.: BOT: the building topology ontology of the W3C linked building data group. Semant. Web **12**, 143–161 (2021). https://doi.org/10.3233/SW-200385

12. Redman, T.C.: The impact of poor data quality on the typical enterprise. Commun. ACM **41**(2), 79–82 (1998)

13. Schmidt, J., Marques, M.R., Botti, S., Marques, M.A.: Recent advances and applications of machine learning in solid-state materials science. npj Comput. Mater. **5**(1), 1–36 (2019)

An Improved Integer Programming Formulation for Inferring Chemical Compounds with Prescribed Topological Structures

Jianshen Zhu[1]([✉]), Naveed Ahmed Azam[1], Kazuya Haraguchi[1], Liang Zhao[2], Hiroshi Nagamochi[1], and Tatsuya Akutsu[3]

[1] Department of Applied Mathematics and Physics, Kyoto University, Kyoto, Japan
{zhujs,azam,haraguchi,nag}@amp.i.kyoto-u.ac.jp
[2] Graduate School of Advanced Integrated Studies in Human Survivability
(Shishu-Kan), Kyoto University, Kyoto, Japan
liang@gsais.kyoto-u.ac.jp
[3] Bioinformatics Center, Institute for Chemical Research, Kyoto University,
Kyoto, Japan
takutsu@kuicr.kyoto-u.ac.jp

Abstract. Various intelligent methods have recently been applied to the design of novel chemical graphs. As one of such approaches, a framework using both artificial neural networks (ANNs) and mixed integer linear programming (MILP) has been proposed. The method first constructs an ANN so that a specified chemical property is predicted from a feature vector $f(G)$ of a chemical graph G. Next an MILP is formulated so that it simulates the construction of $f(G)$ from G and the computation process in the ANN. Then a novel chemical graph with a given target chemical property is inferred by solving the MILP. Based on the framework, the class of graphs to which the above MILP can be formulated has been extended from the graphs with cycle index 0 to the graphs with cycle index 1 and 2. Recently an MILP has been designed to deal with a graph with any cycle index and the computational results on a system with the MILP showed that chemical graphs with around up to 50 non-hydrogen atoms can be inferred. However, this MILP is computationally costly for some instances, e.g., it takes about 10 h to solve some instances with 50 atoms. One of the main reasons for this is that the number of constraints and variables in the MILP is relatively large. In this paper, we improve the MILP by reducing the number of constraints and variables. For this purpose, we drive and utilize a characterization of a chemical acyclic graph in terms of the frequency of some configurations of atom-pairs, by which we can omit part of the construction of $f(G)$ in the MILP. Our experimental results show that the improved MILP can be solved around 20 times faster than the previous MILP.

© Springer Nature Switzerland AG 2021
H. Fujita et al. (Eds.): IEA/AIE 2021, LNAI 12798, pp. 197–209, 2021.
https://doi.org/10.1007/978-3-030-79457-6_17

1   Introduction

Inference of chemical compounds from given chemical properties is an important application area of intelligent methods and systems due to its potential applications to the design of novel drugs. Indeed, design of novel chemical structures has become a hot topic in artificial neural network (ANN) studies, and various models and methods have been applied, which include variational autoencoders [6], recurrent neural networks [15,17], grammar variational autoencoders [10], generative adversarial networks [5], and invertible flow models [11,16].

Inference of chemical compounds has also been studied for several decades in the field of chemo-informatics, under the name of inverse quantitative structure activity/property relationships (inverse QSAR/QSPR). In this framework, chemical compounds are treated as undirected graphs and are often represented as vectors of real or integer numbers, which are called *descriptors* and correspond to *feature vectors* in machine learning. Various heuristic and statistical methods have been developed for finding chemical graphs having desired chemical properties [7,12,14], using these chemical descriptors. Such methods often need inference or enumeration of graph structures from a given set of descriptors, and various methods have been developed for that purpose [9,13]. However, enumeration in itself is a challenging task because the number of molecules (i.e., chemical graphs) with up to 30 atoms (vertices) C, N, O, and S, may exceed 10^{60} [4].

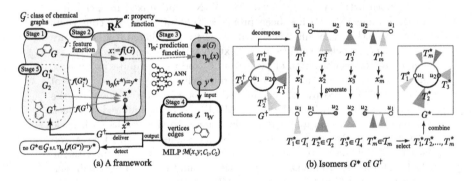

(a) A framework   (b) Isomers G^* of $G^\dagger$

Fig. 1. (a) An illustration of a framework for inferring a chemical graph G^*; (b) An illustration of generating a chemical isomer G^* of a chemical graph $G^\dagger$ in Stage 5.

A novel framework for inferring chemical graphs has been proposed [2,18] based on ANNs and mixed integer linear programming (MILP), as illustrated in Fig. 1(a). In the first phase of the framework, we choose a chemical property π, a class $\mathcal{G}$ of graphs and a data set D_π of chemical graphs in $\mathcal{G}$ in Stage 1, and introduce a feature function $f : \mathcal{G} \to \mathbb{R}^K$ for a positive integer K in Stage 2. In Stage 3, we construct a prediction function $\eta_{\mathcal{N}}$ with an ANN $\mathcal{N}$ that, given a vector $x \in \mathbb{R}^K$, returns a value $y = \eta_{\mathcal{N}}(x) \in \mathbb{R}$ so that $\eta_{\mathcal{N}}(f(G))$ serves as a predicted value to the real value of π for each $G \in D_\pi$. Given a target chemical value

y^*, the second phase infers chemical graphs G^* with $\eta_{\mathcal{N}}(f(G^*)) = y^*$ in the next two stages. In Stage 4, we formulate an MILP that simulates the construction of $f(G)$ from G and the computation process in the ANN so that, given a target value y^*, solving the MILP delivers a chemical graph $G^\dagger$ and a feature vector x^* such that $f(G^\dagger) = x^*$ and $\eta_{\mathcal{N}}(x^*) = y^*$. In Stage 5, we generate other chemical graphs G^* such that $\eta_{\mathcal{N}}(f(G^*)) = y^*$ based on the output chemical graph $G^\dagger$. For this purpose, we generate a family of acyclic chemical graphs whose feature vectors are same as that of some of the acyclic subgraphs of $G^\dagger$ which are then combined to generate G^* as illustrated in Fig. 1(b).

MILP formulations required in Stage 4 have been designed for chemical compounds with cycle index 0 (i.e., acyclic) [3,18], cycle index 1 [8], and cycle index 2 [20]. In particular, Azam et al. [3] introduced a restricted class of acyclic graphs that is characterized by an integer ρ, called a "branch-parameter" such that the restricted class still covers most of the acyclic chemical compounds in the database.

Recently Akutsu and Nagamochi [1] defined a restricted class of cyclic graphs, called "ρ-lean cyclic graphs" that covers most of the cyclic chemical compounds in the database. Based on this, they also proposed a method of inferring a chemical compound with any cycle index under a flexible specification of substructures of a target chemical graph. The method has been implemented by Zhu et al. [19] and their computational results showed that chemical graphs with around up to 50 non-hydrogen atoms can be inferred. Since the new method is adjustable to a complex requirement in a practical situation, it would be important to improve the computational efficiency. In this paper, we derive a mathematical characterization of a chemical acyclic graph in terms of the frequency of configurations of atom-pairs, by which we can omit part of the construction of $f(G)$ in an MILP formulation. We apply the mathematical result to the MILP by Akutsu and Nagamochi [1]. Our experimental results show that the improved MILP can be solved around 20 times faster than the previous MILP.

The paper is organized as follows. Section 2 defines ρ-lean cyclic graphs and a feature vector f and reviews a method of specifying a target chemical graph and an algorithm for generating chemical isomers of a given chemical graph. Section 3 derives a new characterization of a chemical acyclic graph. Section 4 reports the results on some computational experiments conducted for some chemical properties such as flash point, lipophylicity and solubility. Section 5 makes some concluding remarks. The proposed method is available at GitHub https://github.com/ku-dml/mol-infer.

2   Preliminary and Related Work

Let $\mathbb{R}$, $\mathbb{Z}$ and $\mathbb{Z}_+$ denote the sets of reals, integers and non-negative integers, respectively. For two integers a and b, let $[a, b]$ denote the set of integers i with $a \leq i \leq b$.

Graphs. Given a graph G, let $V(G)$ and $E(G)$ denote the sets of vertices and edges, respectively. The *rank* of graph G is defined to be the minimum number

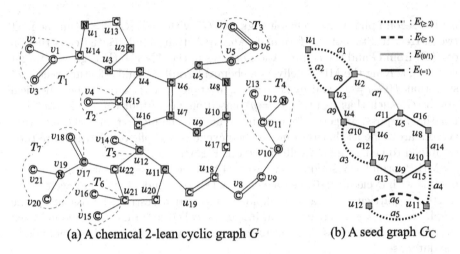

(a) A chemical 2-lean cyclic graph G   (b) A seed graph G_C

Fig. 2. (a) A chemical 2-lean cyclic graph G, where the seven 2-fringe-trees are enclosed with dotted circles; (b) A seed graph $G_C = (V_C, E_C = E_{(\geq 2)} \cup E_{(\geq 1)} \cup E_{(0/1)} \cup E_{(=1)})$.

of edges to be removed to make the graph a tree. A *rooted tree* is defined to be a tree where a vertex is designated as the *root*. The *height* ht(v) of a vertex v in a rooted tree T is defined to be the maximum length of a path from v to a leaf u, and the height ht(T) of T is defined to be the height ht(r) of the root r.

Core in Cyclic Graphs. Let H be a connected simple graph with rank at least 1. The *core* Cr(H) of H is defined to be an induced subgraph Cr(H) = ($V^{co} = V_1' \cup V_2', E^{co}$) such that V_1' is the set of vertices in a cycle of H and V_2' is the set of vertices each of which is in a path between two vertices $u, v \in V_1'$. A vertex (resp., an edge) in H is called a *core-vertex* (resp., *core-edge*) if it is contained in the core Cr(H) and is called a *non-core-vertex* (resp., *non-core-edge*) otherwise. The *core size* cs(H) is defined to be $|V^{co}|$. An *exterior-tree* T is defined to be a maximal induced subtree of H such that $V(T)$ contains exactly one core-vertex v of H, where T is regarded as a rooted tree rooted at v. The *core height* ch(H) is defined to be the maximum height ht(T) of an exterior-tree T of H.

Branch-parameter. Choose a positive integer ρ as a *branch-parameter* [3]. A non-core vertex v is called a *ρ-external vertex* (resp., *leaf ρ-branch*) if ht(v) $< \rho$ (resp., ht(v) $= \rho$). In the graph G in Fig. 2(a), the ρ-external vertices are $v_1, v_2, v_3, v_4, v_6, v_7, v_{11}, v_{12}, v_{13}, v_{14}, v_{15}, v_{16}, v_{18}, v_{19}, v_{20}$ and v_{21}, whereas the leaf 2-branches are v_5, v_{10} and v_{17}. An edge incident to a ρ-external vertex is called a *ρ-external edge*. A *ρ-fringe-tree* is defined to be a maximal subtree T' of an exterior-tree T such that the edge set of T' consists of ρ-external edges. The *ρ-branch-leaf-number* bl$_\rho$(H) of H is defined to be the number of leaf ρ-branches in H. An non-core vertex (resp., edge) that is not a ρ-external vertex (resp., edge) is called a *ρ-internal vertex* (resp., edge). We call a cyclic graph H *ρ-lean* if the set of ρ-internal edges in each exterior-tree T forms a single path. Figure 2(a) illustrates an example of a chemical 2-lean cyclic graph G with 43 vertices, where $cs(G) = 22$, $bl_2(G) = 3$, $V^{co} = \{u_1, u_2, \ldots, u_{22}\}$, and the 2-fringe-trees are $T_1, T_2, \ldots, T_7$. For $\rho = 2$, nearly 97% of cyclic chemical compounds with up to 100 non-hydrogen atoms in PubChem are 2-lean.

A Hydrogen-suppressed Model for Chemical Compounds

We represent the graph structure of a chemical compound as a graph H with labels on vertices and multiplicity on edges in a hydrogen-suppressed model. In a cyclic graph H, we regard each non-core-edge $uv \in E$ as a directed edge (u, v) from a vertex u to a child v of u in an exterior-tree of H in order to define a descriptor that exploits the direction of non-core-edges.

Let Λ be a set of labels each of which represents a chemical element. Let $mass(a)$ and $val(a)$ denote the mass and valence of a chemical element $a \in \Lambda$, respectively. We define an *adjacency-configuration* to be a tuple (a, b, m) with chemical elements $a, b \in \Lambda$ and a bond-multiplicity $m \in [1, \min\{val(a), val(b)\}]$; a *chemical symbol* to be a pair (a, d) of the chemical element $a \in \Lambda$ and the degree $d \in [1, 4]$, where Λ_{dg} denotes the set of all chemical symbols; and an *edge-configuration* to be a tuple (ai, bj, m) with $ai, bj \in \Lambda_{dg}$ and $m \in [1, 3]$. We choose a branch-parameter ρ and two sets Λ_{dg}^{co} and Λ_{dg}^{nc} of chemical symbols and three sets Γ^{co}, Γ^{in} and Γ^{ex} of edge-configurations.

Let $e = uv$ be an edge in a chemical graph G such that $a, b \in \Lambda$ are assigned to the vertices u and v, the degrees of u and v are i and j, respectively and the bond-multiplicity between them is m. When uv is a core-edge, the edge-configuration $\tau(e)$ of edge e is defined to be (ai, bj, m) if $ai \leq bj$ in a total order over Λ_{dg} (or (bj, ai, m) otherwise). When uv is a non-core-edge which is regarded as a directed edge (u, v) where u is the parent of v in some exterior-tree, the edge-configuration $\tau(e)$ of a ρ-internal (resp., ρ-external) edge e is defined to be $(ai, bj, m) \in \Gamma^{in}$ (resp., $(ai, bj, m) \in \Gamma^{ex}$).

Let $G = (H, \alpha, \beta)$ be a tuple with a cyclic graph $H = (V, E)$ and functions $\alpha : V \to \Lambda$ and $\beta : E \to [1, 3]$, where we use β_G to denote the function $V(H) \to [0, 12]$ such that $\beta_G(u) \triangleq \sum_{uv \in E(H)} \beta(uv)$ for each vertex $u \in V(H)$. A tuple $G = (H, \alpha, \beta)$ is called a *chemical cyclic graph* if (i) H is connected; (ii) $\beta_G(u) \leq val(\alpha(u))$ for each vertex $u \in V(H)$; and (iii) $\tau(e) \in \Gamma^{co}$, $\tau(e) \in \Gamma^{in}$ and $\tau(e) \in \Gamma^{ex}$ for each core-edge $e \in E(H)$, ρ-internal edge $e \in E(H)$ and ρ-external edge $e \in E(H)$, respectively.

Descriptors and Feature Vectors

A *feature vector* $f(G)$ of a chemical cyclic graph $G = (H = (V, E), \alpha, \beta)$ consists of the following 16 kinds of graph-theoretical descriptors.

- $n(G)$: the number $|V|$ of vertices; $cs(G)$: the core size of G; $ch(G)$: the core height of G; $bl_\rho(G)$: the ρ-branch-leaf-number of G;
- $\overline{ms}(G)$: the average mass of atoms in G; $ns_H(G)$: the number of hydrogen atoms suppressed in G;
- $dg_i^{co}(G)$, $dg_i^{nc}(G)$: the numbers of core-vertices and non-core-vertices of degree $i \in [1, 4]$ in G;
- $bd_m^{co}(G)$, $bd_m^{in}(G)$, $bd_m^{ex}(G)$: the numbers of core-edges, ρ-internal edges and ρ-external edges with bond multiplicity $m \in [2, 3]$ in G;

- $ns_\mu^{co}(G)$, $\mu \in \Lambda_{dg}^{co}$, $ns_\mu^{nc}(G)$, $\mu \in \Lambda_{dg}^{nc}$: the numbers of core-vertices and non-core-vertices v with a chemical symbol μ; and
- $ec_\gamma^{co}(G)$, $ec_\gamma^{in}(G)$, $ec_\gamma^{ex}(G)$: the numbers of core-edges $e \in E$ such that $\tau(e) = \gamma \in \Gamma^{co}$, ρ-internal edges $e \in E$ such that $\tau(e) = \gamma \in \Gamma^{in}$, and ρ-external edges $e \in E$ such that $\tau(e) = \gamma \in \Gamma^{ex}$ in G.

A Method of Specifying Target Chemical Graphs

We review the method of specifying a topological structure of a target chemical graph G [1]. We first prescribe a graph $G_C = (V_C, E_C)$, called a *seed graph*, from which a target chemical ρ-lean cyclic graph is required to be constructed as follows: (i) Replacing some edges $a_i = uv \in E_C$ with u, v-paths P_{a_i} (or remove some edges $a_i \in E_C$); (ii) Attach to some vertices u_i new paths Q_{u_i}; (iii) Attach some chemical rooted trees T with height at most ρ as ρ-fringe-trees; and (iv) Assign chemical elements and bond-multiplicities to the vertices and edges that are not in the ρ-fringe-trees.

The edge set E_C of a seed graph G_C has four types: $E_{(\geq 2)}$ (resp., $E_{(\geq 1)}$) consists of edges $a_i = uv \in E_{(\geq 2)}$ to be replaced with a u, v-path P_{a_i} of length at least 2 (resp., 1); $E_{(0/1)}$ consists of edges $a_i \in E_{(0/1)}$ that can be discarded; and $E_{(=1)}$ consists of edge $e \in E_{(=1)}$ that are always used in G.

For example, the chemical 2-lean cyclic graph G in Fig. 2(a) can be derived from the seed graph G_C in Fig. 2(b) by using the following choice of paths: paths $P_{a_1} = (u_1, u_{13}, u_2)$, $P_{a_2} = (u_1, u_{14}, u_3)$, $P_{a_3} = (u_4, u_{15}, u_{16}, u_7)$, $P_{a_4} = (u_{10}, u_{17}, u_{18}, u_{19}, u_{11})$ and $P_{a_5} = (u_{11}, u_{20}, u_{21}, u_{22}, u_{12})$ (edge a_7 is deleted) and paths $Q_{u_5} = (u_5, v_5)$, $Q_{u_{18}} = (u_{18}, v_8, v_9, v_{10})$ and $Q_{u_{22}} = (u_{22}, v_{17})$. Finally add the seven 2-fringe-trees $T_1, T_2, \ldots, T_7$ and assign chemical elements and bond-multiplicities to obtain G in Fig. 2(a).

The method also includes a specification that consists of upper and lower bounds on the following features of a target chemical graph: the length of path P_{a_i} or Q_{u_i}; the number of paths Q_{u_i}; the number of vertices with each chemical element and the number of edges with each edge-configuration. See [1] for details of the specification.

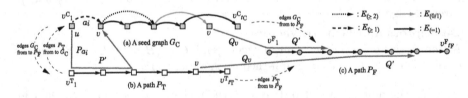

Fig. 3. (a) A seed graph G_C; (b) A path P_T for providing paths P_{a_i}; (c) A path P_F for providing paths Q_{v_i}.

An MILP for Inferring Chemical ρ-lean Graphs in Stage 4

We here give the idea of formulating an MILP that infers a chemical graph $G^\dagger$ for a given seed graph G_C (see [1] for the details). We consider a graph SG, called a *scheme graph* that consists of G_C and two paths P_T and P_F, directed edges from G_C to $P_T \cup P_F$ from P_T to P_F, as illustrated in Fig. 3. In an MILP, we introduce necessary integer variables for the vertices and edges in SG.

When we replace an edge $a_i = uv \in E_{(\geq 2)} \cup E_{(\geq 1)}$ with a u, v-path P_{a_i}, we choose a subpath P' of P_T together with an edge from u to the initial vertex of P' and an edge from the end vertex of P' to v to form a required u, v-path P_{a_i}. Similarly, when we add to a vertex v in G_C or P_T a new path Q_v, we choose a subpath Q' of P_F together with an edge from v to the initial vertex of Q' to form a required path Q_v.

In the previous MILP [1], a set of vertices and edges was required at each vertex v in G_C, P_T and P_F to choose a ρ-fringe-tree T_v rooted at v. However, by using Theorem 1 in Sect. 3, we do not need to introduce such a structure for choosing ρ-fringe-trees in our new MILP in this paper.

An Algorithm for Generating Chemical Isomers in Stage 5

We briefly review the method [1] for Stage 5. See Fig. 1(b) for this method.

1. Decompose a given chemical ρ-lean cyclic graph $G^\dagger$ into a collection of chemical trees $T_1^\dagger, T_2^\dagger, \ldots, T_m^\dagger$ such that each tree $T_i^\dagger$ contains at most two vertices in V_C of the seed graph $G_C = (V_C, E_C)$ of $G^\dagger$.
2. For each index $i \in [1, m]$, compute the feature vector $x_i^* = f(T_i^\dagger)$ and then generate a set $\mathcal{T}_i$ of all (or a limited number of) chemical acyclic graphs T_i^* such that $f(T_i^*) = x_i^*$ by using the dynamic programming algorithm [3].
3. Each combination of chemical trees $T_i^* \in \mathcal{T}_i, i \in [1, m]$ forms a chemical ρ-lean cyclic graph G^* such that $f(G^*) = f(G^\dagger)$.

3   A New Characterization of Chemical Trees

For the 2-fringe-tree T_7 with $\rho = 2$ in Fig. 2(a), the degree of the root v_{17} is $\deg_G(v_{17}) = 3$ in G and $\deg_{T_7}(v_{17}) = 2$ in T_7. We treat a degree Δ of the root r in G as a fictitious degree of a chemical rooted tree T and let T_Δ denote such a tree, where $\deg_{T_\Delta}(r) = \Delta$. Let $E(T_\Delta, i, \gamma)$ denote the set of edges $e \in E(T)$ with depth i such that the edge-configuration of e is $\gamma \in \Gamma$. Then we obtain the following characterization of a chemical acyclic graph in terms of the frequency of edge-configurations (we omit the proof due to a space limitation).

Theorem 1. *Let $\rho \geq 1$, $\Delta \geq d_r \geq 0$ and $m_r \geq 0$ be integers and $\mathsf{a}_r \in \Lambda$ be an element. A function* ec $: [1, \rho] \times \Gamma \to \mathbb{Z}_+$ *admits a fictitious tree T_Δ of a chemical rooted tree T such that $\deg_T(r) = d_r, \alpha(r) = \mathsf{a}_r, \mathrm{val}(\mathsf{a}_r) - m_r = \beta_T(r)$ and $|E(T_\Delta, i, \gamma)| = \mathrm{ec}(i, \gamma), i \in [1, \rho], \gamma \in \Gamma$ if and only if function* ec *satisfies the following, where we regard* $\mathrm{ec}(\rho + 1, \gamma) = 0, \gamma \in \Gamma$ *for a notational convenience:*

$$\sum_{\gamma \in \Gamma} \mathrm{ec}(1,\gamma) = \sum_{\gamma=(\mathrm{a}_r \Delta, \xi, m) \in \Gamma} \mathrm{ec}(1,\gamma) = d_r; \mathrm{val}(\mathrm{a}_r) - m_r = \sum_{\gamma=(\mathrm{a}_r \Delta, \xi, m) \in \Gamma} \beta(\gamma) \mathrm{ec}(1,\gamma);$$

$$\sum_{\gamma=(\xi,\mu,m)\in\Gamma} (d-1)\mathrm{ec}(i,\gamma) = \sum_{\gamma=(\mu,\xi,m)\in\Gamma} \mathrm{ec}(i+1,\gamma), \mu = \mathrm{ad} \in \Lambda_{\mathrm{dg}}, i \in [1,\rho];$$

$$\sum_{\gamma=(\xi,\mu,m)\in\Gamma} (\mathrm{val}(\mathrm{a})-m)\mathrm{ec}(i,\gamma) \geq \sum_{\gamma=(\mu,\xi,m)\in\Gamma} \beta(\gamma)\mathrm{ec}(i+1,\gamma), \mu=\mathrm{ad} \in \Lambda_{\mathrm{dg}}, i \in [1,\rho];$$

$$\sum_{\gamma=(\xi,\mathrm{a}2,1)\in\Gamma} \mathrm{ec}(i,\gamma) \geq \sum_{\gamma=(\mathrm{a}2,\xi,3)\in\Gamma} \mathrm{ec}(i+1,\gamma), \mathrm{a}2 \in \Lambda_{\mathrm{dg}}, i \in [1,\rho-1], \mathrm{val}(\mathrm{a})=4;$$

$$\sum_{\gamma=(\xi,\mathrm{a}2,m)\in\Gamma: m\leq 2} \mathrm{ec}(i,\gamma) \geq \sum_{\gamma=(\mathrm{a}2,\xi,m)\in\Gamma: m\geq 2} \mathrm{ec}(i+1,\gamma), \mathrm{a}2 \in \Lambda_{\mathrm{dg}}, i \in [1,\rho-1], \mathrm{val}(\mathrm{a})=4.$$

For example, the 2-fringe-tree T_7 in Fig. 2(a) can be constructed from a function ec such that $\mathrm{ec}(1,\gamma_1) = \mathrm{ec}(1,\gamma_2) = 1$, $\mathrm{ec}(2,\gamma_3) = 2$ $\mathrm{ec}(i,\gamma) = 0$ for the other pairs (i,γ), where $\gamma_1 = (\mathrm{C3}, \mathrm{O1}, 2)$, $\gamma_2 = (\mathrm{C3}, \mathrm{N3}, 1)$ and $\gamma_3 = (\mathrm{N3}, \mathrm{C1}, 1)$ by applying Theorem 1 to $\mathrm{a}_r = \mathrm{C}$, $\Delta = 3$, $d_r = 2$ and $m_r = 1$.

The previous MILP [1] contains an $O(|\Gamma|(d_{\max}-1)^\rho)$ number of variables to represent a chemical rooted tree T with height ρ. By Theorem 1, we can represent T implicitly with a frequency function ec with $O(|\Gamma|\rho)$ variables in our new MILP. Given a frequency function ec, we can easily find a chemical rooted tree T based on the algorithmic proof of Theorem 1.

4   Experimental Results of Stages 1 to 5

We conducted a computational experiment with a whole system of Stages 1 to 5 [19], wherein we compared our improved MILP with the previous MILP [1] in Stage 4. We executed the experiments on a PC with Processor: 3.0 GHz Core i7-9700 (3.0 GHz) Memory: 16 GB RAM DDR4.

Results on Phase 1

Stage 1. We set a branch-parameter ρ to be 2. We selected three chemical properties π: flash point (FP), lipophylicity (LP) and solubility (SL). For each property $\pi \in \{\mathrm{FP}, \mathrm{LP}, \mathrm{SL}\}$, we collected a data set D_π on chemical cyclic graphs provided by HSDB from PubChem, figshare and MoleculeNet.

Table 1 shows the size and range of data sets that we prepared for each chemical property π in Stage 1, where we denote the following: Λ: the set of selected chemical elements (hydrogen atoms are added at the final stage); $|D_\pi|$: the size of data set D_π; $|\Gamma^{\mathrm{co}}|$, $|\Gamma^{\mathrm{in}}|$, $|\Gamma^{\mathrm{ex}}|$: the number of different edge-configurations of core-edges, 2-internal edges and 2-external edges over the compounds in D_π; $[\underline{n}, \overline{n}]$: the minimum and maximum values of $n(G)$ over the compounds G in D_π.

Stage 2. We used a feature function f that consists of the descriptors defined in Sect. 2.

Stage 3. We used `scikit-learn` version 0.23.2 with Python 3.8.5, MLPRegressor and ReLU activation function to construct ANNs $\mathcal{N}$. We evaluated the resulting prediction function $\eta_\mathcal{N}$ with cross-validation over five subsets $D_\pi^{(i)}$,

$i \in [1, 5]$ of D_π. Table 1 shows the results on Stages 2 and 3, where we denote the following: Arch.: $(K, a, 1)$ (resp., $(K, a_1, a_2, 1)$) consists of an input layer with K nodes, a hidden layer with a nodes (resp., two hidden layers with a_1 and a_2 nodes, respectively) and an output layer with a single node, where K is equal to the number of descriptors in the feature vector $f(G)$; L-time: the average time (sec.) to construct ANNs for each trial; and test R^2 (ave.), test R^2 (best): the average value and the largest value of coefficient of determination over the five tests.

From Table 1, we see that the execution of Stage 3 was considerably successful, where the best of test R^2 is around 0.73 to 0.88 for all three chemical properties.

Table 1. Results of Stages 2 and 3 in Phase 1.

π	Λ	$|D_\pi|$	$|\Gamma^{co}|$	$|\Gamma^{in}|$	$|\Gamma^{ex}|$	$[\underline{n}, \overline{n}]$	Arch.	L-Time	Test R^2 ave.	Best
FP	C,O,N	178	20	17	32	[4, 32]	(104, 20, 10, 1)	0.32	0.618	0.858
FP	C,O,N,S,Cl	211	21	18	40	[4, 32]	(117, 40, 1)	1.99	0.481	0.737
LP	C,O,N	589	27	25	45	[6, 60]	(132, 40, 1)	0.36	0.838	0.845
LP	C,O,N,S,Cl	776	33	32	51	[6, 74]	(155, 20, 10, 1)	0.57	0.827	0.856
SL	C,O,N	454	24	20	39	[5, 55]	(118, 50, 1)	0.30	0.844	0.889
SL	C,O,N,S,Cl	638	27	29	54	[5, 55]	(149, 20, 10, 1)	0.47	0.864	0.885

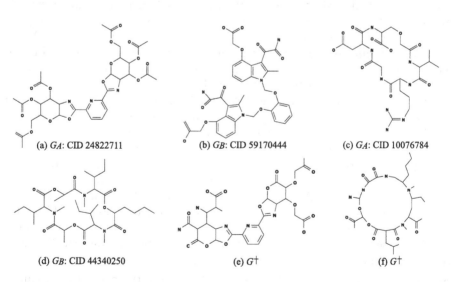

(a) G_A: CID 24822711   (b) G_B: CID 59170444   (c) G_A: CID 10076784

(d) G_B: CID 44340250   (e) $G^\dagger$ (f) $G^\dagger$

Fig. 4. An illustration of chemical compounds: (a) G_A: CID 24822711; (b) G_B: CID 59170444; (c) G_A: CID 10076784; (d) G_B: CID 44340250; (e) $G^\dagger$ inferred from I_c with $y^* = -2.23$ of LP; (f) $G^\dagger$ inferred from I_d with $y^* = -3.03$ of SL.

Results on Phase 2

To conduct experiments of Stages 4 and 5, we prepared test instances (a)–(d) with $\Lambda = \{C, O, N\}$ in a similar way of the experiment in [1,19]. We show a sketch of these instances (see [1,19] for the details).

(a) I_a: An instance with the seed graph G_C in Fig. 2(b) to infer a target chemical graph $G^\dagger$ with $n(G^\dagger) \in [30, 50]$ and $\mathrm{cs}(G^\dagger) \in [20, 28]$ using edge-configurations such that $|\Gamma^{co}| = 10$, $|\Gamma^{in}| = 5$ and $|\Gamma^{ex}| = 10$.

(b) I_b^i, $i = 1, 2, 3, 4$: An instance for inferring chemical graphs with rank at most 2. The seed graph G_C^1 of I_b^1 is a cycle with two vertices and the seed graphs G_C^i of I_b^i, $i = 2, 3, 4$ are given by three different types of rank-2 graphs G_C^i on a set of four vertices. Also $G^\dagger$ is required to satisfy $n(G^\dagger) = 38$ and $\mathrm{cs}(G^\dagger) = 6$ for $i = 1$ ($n(G^\dagger) = 50$ and $\mathrm{cs}(G^\dagger) = 30$ for $i = 2, 3, 4$) using edge-configurations such that $|\Gamma^{co}| = 28$, $|\Gamma^{in}| = 46$ and $|\Gamma^{ex}| = 74$.

(c) I_c: An instance aimed to infer a chemical graph $G^\dagger$ such that the core of $G^\dagger$ is equal to the core of the compound G_A: CID 24822711 in Fig. 4(a); the frequency of edge-configurations in the non-core of $G^\dagger$ is equal to that of the compound G_B: CID 59170444 in Fig. 4(b); and $G^\dagger$ satisfies $n(G^\dagger) = 46$ and $\mathrm{cs}(G^\dagger) = 24$ using edge-configurations such that $|\Gamma^{co}| = 8$, $|\Gamma^{in}| = 3$ and $|\Gamma^{ex}| = 7$.

(d) I_d: An instance aimed to infer a chemical monocyclic graph $G^\dagger$ whose frequency vector of edge-configurations is given by merging those of compounds G_A: CID 10076784 in Figure 4(c) and G_B: CID 44340250 in Figure 4(d); and $G^\dagger$ satisfies $n(G^\dagger) \in [40, 45]$ and $\mathrm{cs}(G^\dagger) = 18$ using $|\Gamma^{co}| = 7$, $|\Gamma^{in}| = 4$ and $|\Gamma^{ex}| = 11$.

Stage 4. To solve an MILP in Stage 4, we use CPLEX version 12.10. We solved the previous MILP and our new MILP for five target values y^* to measure their average running time. Table 2 shows the results of Stage 4, where we denote the following: y^*: the range of five target values. (For some cases, the MILP becomes infeasible for any target value in the range of observed values. In such a case, we selected target values out of the range to compare the computational performance of feasible instances of these MILPs.) #v (resp., #c): the average number of variables (resp., constraints) in the MILP of the previous method [19] and our new method in Stage 4; IP-time: the average time (sec.) to solve the MILPs of the previous method and our new method in Stage 4, where IP-time for our method includes the running time of constructing the 2-fringe-trees.

Figure 4(e) (resp., Fig. 4(f)) illustrates the chemical graph $G^\dagger$ inferred from instance I_c with $y^* = -2.23$ of LP (resp., I_d with $y^* = -3.03$ of SL).

From Table 2, we see that our MILP is solved always faster than the previous MILP, especially for instances with large size, where over 40 times faster for instances I_b^2 and I_b^4 in the experiment for SL. For the instances that required over 1000 (sec.) in the previous MILP, the running time by our MILP is 22.8 times shorter in average.

Stage 5. We selected one chemical graph $G^\dagger$ from the five target chemical graphs delivered by our MILP for each pair of an instance I and a property π. Then we generated all (or up to 100) chemical isomers of $G^\dagger$. We also evaluated a lower bound on the total number of all chemical isomers of $G^\dagger$. Table 2 shows

Table 2. Results of Stages 4 and 5 for properties FP, LP and SL.

			IP [19]			Ours					
π	I	y^*	#v	#c	IP-time	#v	#c	IP-time	G-LB	#G	DP-time
FP	I_a	[220, 280]	13940	11199	29.4	6604	9492	3.8	144	72	0.190
	I_b^1	[220, 280]	43098	11044	64.7	14786	9090	6.1	756	24	0.076
	I_b^2	[220, 280]	50487	16078	258.6	21307	14956	65.9	5.1×10^4	100	0.170
	I_b^3	[220, 280]	50556	16091	142.4	21376	14968	105.1	3.8×10^5	100	0.178
	I_b^4	[220, 280]	50625	16102	231.8	21445	14980	31.5	72	36	0.120
	I_c	[452, 460]	10270	9588	3.2	5441	8274	0.5	6	4	0.030
	I_d	[320, 400]	14033	11102	75.1	5980	8764	3.8	6.9×10^6	100	0.178
LP	I_a	[−2.25, −2.05]	13998	11297	112.0	6662	9590	21.5	2	2	0.115
	I_b^1	[−2.25, −2.05]	43156	11142	174.1	14844	9188	27.2	1.6×10^4	100	0.132
	I_b^2	[−2.25, −2.05]	50545	16176	441.3	21365	15054	299.2	2.9×10^6	100	0.184
	I_b^3	[−2.25, −2.05]	50614	16189	1691.4	21434	15066	254.8	3.7×10^5	100	0.187
	I_b^4	[−2.25, −2.05]	50683	16200	8444.7	21503	15078	396.5	6.0×10^5	100	0.026
	I_c	[−2.24, −2.20]	10328	9686	1.7	5499	8372	0.4	12	7	0.068
	I_d	[−2.25, −2.05]	14091	11200	287.1	6038	8862	21.5	1.3×10^6	100	0.119
SL	I_a	[−3.03, −2.83]	13797	11352	1597.4	6678	9646	80.1	12	4	0.115
	I_b^1	[−3.03, −2.83]	43172	11198	468.5	14860	9244	100.6	288	32	0.010
	I_b^2	[−3.03, −2.83]	50561	16232	36398.6	21381	15110	900.2	1.9×10^5	100	0.066
	I_b^3	[−3.03, −2.83]	50630	16245	2206.6	21450	15122	979.6	3.2×10^6	100	0.096
	I_b^4	[−3.03, −2.83]	50699	16256	11704.8	21519	15134	249.9	1.7×10^5	100	0.173
	I_c	[−3.03, −2.83]	10344	9742	2.2	5515	8428	0.5	2	2	0.066
	I_d	[−3.03, −2.83]	14107	11256	50.4	6054	8918	6.7	1.6×10^7	100	0.121

the results of Stage 5, where we denote the following: G-LB: a lower bound on the number of all chemical isomers G^* of $G^\dagger$; #G: the number of all (or up to 100) chemical isomers G^* of $G^\dagger$ generated in Stage 5; DP-time: the running time (sec.) to execute Stage 5 to compute G-LB and #G.

From Table 2, we see that the running time for Stage 5 is considerably smaller than that in Stage 4. This means that improving the computational efficiency for solving MILPs in Stage 4 is crucial to the entire system.

5 Concluding Remarks

In this paper, we derived a compact characterization of a chemical tree in terms of the frequency of edge-configurations, and used this to decrease the size of an MILP in the flexible inference method [1]. Our experimental results show that the method with the improved MILP runs around 20 times faster than the previous method in the case of branch-parameter $\rho = 2$. This will greatly increase the number of candidates of target chemical compounds in a limited running time in a practical situation.

References

1. Akutsu, T., Nagamochi, H.: A novel method for inference of chemical compounds with prescribed topological substructures based on integer programming. arXiv: 2010.09203 (2020)
2. Azam, N.A., Chiewvanichakorn, R., Zhang, F., Shurbevski, A., Nagamochi, H., Akutsu, T.: A method for the inverse QSAR/QSPR based on artificial neural networks and mixed integer linear programming. In: Proceedings 14th International Conference Biomedical Engineering Systems and Technologies, Malta, pp. 101–108 (2020)
3. Azam, N.A., et al.: A novel method for inference of acyclic chemical compounds with bounded branch-height based on artificial neural networks and integer programming, arXiv:2009.09646 (2020)
4. Bohacek, R.S., McMartin, C., Guida, W.C.: The art and practice of structure-based drug design: a molecular modeling perspective. Med. Res. Rev. **16**, 3–50 (1996)
5. De, N., Kipf, C.T.: MolGAN: an implicit generative model for small molecular graphs, arXiv:1805.11973 (2018)
6. Gómez-Bombarelli, R., et al.: Automatic chemical design using a data-driven continuous representation of molecules. ACS Central Sci. **4**, 268–276 (2018)
7. Ikebata, H., Hongo, K., Isomura, T., Maezono, R., Yoshida, R.: Bayesian molecular design with a chemical language model. J. Comput.-Aid. Mol. Des. **31**(4), 379–391 (2017). https://doi.org/10.1007/s10822-016-0008-z
8. Ito, R., Azam, N.A., Wang, C., Shurbevski, A., Nagamochi, H., Akutsu, T.: A novel method for the inverse QSAR/QSPR to monocyclic chemical compounds based on artificial neural networks and integer programming. In: Proceedings of 21st International Conference Bioinformatics and Computational Biology, Las Vegas, Nevada, USA, 27–30 July 2020
9. Kerber, A., Laue, R., Grüner, T., Meringer, M.: MOLGEN 4.0. Match Commun. Math. Comput. Chem. **37**, 205–208 (1998)
10. Kusner, M.J., Paige, B., Hernández-Lobato, J.M.: Grammar variational autoencoder. In: Proceedings of 34th International Conference Machine Learning-Volume **70**, 1945–1954 (2017)
11. Madhawa, K., Ishiguro, K., Nakago, K., Abe, M.: GraphNVP: an invertible flow model for generating molecular graphs. arXiv:1905.11600 (2019)
12. Miyao, T., Kaneko, H., Funatsu, K.: Inverse QSPR/QSAR analysis for chemical structure generation (from y to x). J. Chem. Inform. Model. **56** 286–299 (2016)
13. Reymond, J.-L.: The chemical space project. Acc. Chem. Res. **48**, 722–730 (2015)
14. Rupakheti, C., Virshup, A., Yang, W., Beratan, D.N.: Strategy to discover diverse optimal molecules in the small molecule universe. J. Chem. Inf. Model. **55**, 529–537 (2015)
15. Segler, M.H.S., Kogej, T., Tyrchan, C., Waller, M.P.: Generating focused molecule libraries for drug discovery with recurrent neural networks. ACS Central Sci. **4**, 120–131 (2017)
16. Shi, C., Xu, M., Zhu, Z., Zhang, W., Zhang, M., Tang, J.: GraphAF: a flow-based autoregressive model for molecular graph generation. arXiv:2001.09382 (2020)
17. Yang, X., Zhang, J., Yoshizoe, K., Terayama, K., Tsuda, K.: ChemTS: an efficient python library for de novo molecular generation. Sci. Technol. Adv. Mater. **18**, 972–976 (2017)

18. Zhang, F., Zhu, J., Chiewvanichakorn, R., Shurbevski, A., Nagamochi, H., Akutsu, T.: A new integer linear programming formulation to the inverse QSAR/QSPR for acyclic chemical compounds using skeleton trees. In: Fujita, H., Fournier-Viger, P., Ali, M., Sasaki, J. (eds.) IEA/AIE 2020. LNCS (LNAI), vol. 12144, pp. 433–444. Springer, Cham (2020). https://doi.org/10.1007/978-3-030-55789-8_38
19. Zhu, J., et al: Akutsu, a novel method for inferring of chemical compounds with prescribed topological substructures based on integer programming. IEEE/ACM Trans. Comput. Biol. Bioinform. (submitted) (2020)
20. Zhu, J., Wang, C., Shurbevski, A., Nagamochi, H., Akutsu, T.: A novel method for inference of chemical compounds of cycle index two with desired properties based on artificial neural networks and integer programming, Algorithms, **13**, 124 (2020)

Automatic Classification for Ontology Generation by Pretrained Language Model

Atsushi Oba, Incheon Paik[✉], and Ayato Kuwana

University of Aizu, Tsuruga Ikki-machi, Aizu-Wakamatsu City 965-8580, Fukushima, Japan
{paikic,m5241101}@u-aizu.ac.jp

Abstract. In recent years, for systemizing enormous information on the Internet, ontology that organizes knowledge through a hierarchical structure of concepts has received a large amount of attention in spatiotemporal information science. However, constructing ontology manually requires a large amount of time and deep knowledge of the target field. Consequently, automating ontology generation from raw text corpus is required to meet the ontology demand. As an initial attempt of ontology generation with a neural network, a recurrent neural N = network (RNN)-based method is proposed. However, updating the architecture is possible because of the development in natural language processing (NLP). In contrast, the transfer learning of language models trained by a large unlabeled corpus such as bidirectional encoder representations from transformers (BERT) has yielded a breakthrough in NLP. Inspired by these achievements, to apply transfer learning of language models, we propose a novel workflow for ontology generation consisting of two-stage learning. This paper provides a quantitative comparison between the proposed method and the existing methods. Our result showed that our best method improved accuracy by over 12.5%.

Keywords: Ontology · Automation · Natural Language Processing (NLP) · Pretrained model

1 Introduction

In recent years, the Internet has yielded various technological evolutions, and users have been required to collect and select information according to their purposes. In that situation, a data structure called ontology that organizes knowledge through a hierarchical structure, as shown in Fig. 1, has received a large amount of attention because ontology is required to systemize the vast knowledge on the Internet. In spatiotemporal information science, spatiotemporal ontology is used for geographic information [1] and establishing a general situation awareness framework [2]. However, when it is manually constructed, ontology requires a large amount of time and deep knowledge of the target field. Therefore, there is a need for a mechanism to support or substitute the ontology creation from unstructured text.

Automation by machine learning is indispensable in meeting ontology demand, and it is difficult to generate ontology directly from text by a single methodology. Ontology

© Springer Nature Switzerland AG 2021
H. Fujita et al. (Eds.): IEA/AIE 2021, LNAI 12798, pp. 210–221, 2021.
https://doi.org/10.1007/978-3-030-79457-6_18

is utilized by unique and sophisticated formats such as Ontology Web Language (OWL); it is quite different from typical language model outputs. In addition, the required configuration and scale of the ontology depends on the purpose. Therefore, we broke down the complex ontology generation task into the following three subtasks (Fig. 2):

1. Extracting key phrases from a target corpus
2. Generating a taxonomic structure consisting of a hypernym–hyponym relationship from the extracted phrase set
3. Creating detailed relationships between phrases according to the intended use of the ontology

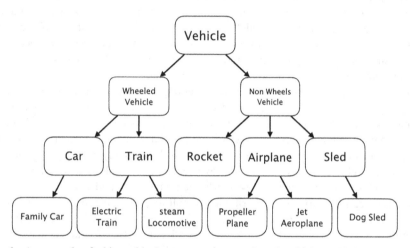

Fig. 1. An example of a hierarchical structure of an ontology in which a vehicle is a top class

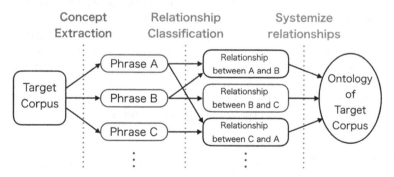

Fig. 2. The workflow of ontology generation

In this research, we focus on the automation of (2) and some cases of (3). Task (1) is a general problem in natural language processing (NLP), and sophisticated methods exist already [3, 4]. We can utilize those methods ideas for our task. However, (2) and

(3) are specific to this theme, and there is much room for research. In addition, these can be replaced with classification problems frequently used in machine learning.

As a classification method of phrase pair relationships, a model combining RNN and word embedding has been proposed in previous research [5]. The overall architecture is based on a traditional NLP model, and its input part is remodeled to twin text reader units to handle pairs of phrases. This method efficiently classifies phrase pair relationships, especially from the perspective of memory usage and calculation cost. Because of the rapid development of language models, we able to improve method. We describe two major problems of the current method in the next section.

The first problem is handling out-of-vocabulary (OOV) words. In the existing method, each word is encoded into a feature vector by pretrained vector representation before being entered into the model. At that time, if there are some OOV words in phrases, set zero vector space. For this reason, a large number of vocabularies and their vectors are required to improve model versatility; however, as the number of vocabularies increases, a larger memory is required. In particular, in tasks focused on specialized corpora such as ontology generation, rare domain-specific words appear frequently, and the OOV problem is directly linked to model performance.

The second problem is updating text processing architecture. Context information means additional information generated by word order and combination. The previous method uses RNN to handle context information; however, transformer architecture [6, 7] becomes standard in NLP. Many researchers have published papers using transformer architecture and have shown large progress. Empirically, we propose that using transformer architecture also yields improvement in our ontology generation area. In conclusion, our subjects handle OOV words and architecture updates.

Finally, we summarize our contribution as follows. To improve the weaknesses of our previous approach, we propose applying a PLM such as BERT [8] to taxonomically structure generation tasks. Recently, with the advent of BERT, transfer leaning has become a popular trend for language models, enabling extremely high performance by just fine-tuning on the target downstream tasks. Although various language processing techniques are used in this method, we focus on byte pair encoding (BPE) and transformer architecture. BPE is proposed as a simple data compression technique and has shown that it is also effective for NLP's subword tokenization [9]. Since BERT marked state-of-the-art scores in various tasks using transformers [6] as their core structure, many language models after BERT have adopted the transformer architecture at their base, also marking state-of-the-art results. In addition, it is expected that the processing units have high processing power for context information. From these features, we expect significant improvements both experimentally and functionally.

2   Related Work

2.1   Lexico-Syntactic Based Ontology Generation

The lexical-syntactic approach to extract the taxonomic relations of words is a famous traditional method of ontology generation [14]. The method uses the position of words and specific fixed phrase patterns in text, analyzes patterns scattered in sentences, and explores the taxonomical relationships available to the ontology. Combined with machine learning, it can help handle exceptional syntax patterns and improve accuracy.

2.2 Word Vectorization-Based Ontology Generation

As another method, the information amount and vectorization representation of words has been used for ontology's taxonomic relation classification. This method solves the problems that do not have super/sub relationships in a lexico-syntactic approach. The method handles words with numerical representation trained by word position in a sentence, and the relationships between them are determined using a machine learning model that takes a vector as input. The representative example of this approach is a combination of word embedding and support vector machine (SVM) [15].

2.3 RNN-Based Ontology Generation

RNN-based models were the first to solve the task of classifying relations between phrase pairs using grammatical semantic interpretation [5]. Prior to this model, models that combined word embedding and a simple classifier for ontology generation were the mainstream, and the disadvantage was that only one word could be compared. By using a neural network with the recurrent structure of RNN-base, it is now possible to classify compound words. This model follows the structure of the traditional sequential language model, and it is characterized by having two input layers for handling two input sentences. This model is roughly divided into four parts (embedding layer, RNN cells, concatenation process, and classification layers), Those processes are calculated in order.

3 Preliminaries

3.1 Relationship Classification Between Phrase Pair

To generate an ontology, it is necessary to automate the task of classifying relationships between phrases. The central element of ontology is the hierarchical structure of concepts, but it is difficult to build the hierarchical structure at once, and it is necessary to break down machine learning into easy-to-use tasks. Therefore, in ontology generation, the relationships between concepts (such as synonyms and hypernyms) are identified using a classification model. Then, it builds a hierarchical structure by organizing the acquired relationships. If the concept is interpreted as a set of phrases consisting of multiple words, it is possible to substitute it with a phrase instead of a concept. To summarize, ontology generation can be downsized into a classification problem that takes two phrases as the input and outputs the relationship between them.

To process two input text information and output relation labels, there are four essential factors in classifying relationships between concepts.

1. Word embedding: By converting words to their corresponding vectors, they are converted into a format that can be easily handled by neural networks. Also, because ontology generation often needs to deal with very rare words that are task-specific, learning those in advance in a large corpus is preferable.

2. Acquisition of context information: Phrases used in ontology generation often consist of a small number of words. However, the connection between words is stronger than general sentences, and it is necessary to process contextual information.
3. Concatenation: Because the input data for this task comprise two independent phrases, we need to combine the information at some stage in the process.
4. Classifier: We apply the information obtained in the presented steps to the classification model and calculate the final output label.

3.2   Encoding and Architecture for Pretrained Model

Byte Pair Encoding
As mentioned in the previous section, BPE is basically proposed as a data compression technique and is recognized for its versatility in the field of NLP [10–12]. This method is a variable-length encoding that displays text as a series of symbols and repeatedly merges the most frequent symbol pairs into a new symbol. Compared with regular word-based methods, the number of words and associated vectors in the dictionary can be significantly reduced while maintaining expressiveness. Words that do not exist in this dictionary can be expressed by subwords.

BERT
BERT [8] is an architecture of multiple layered transformer array to train deep bidirectional representations from unlabeled texts. It is pretrained from a large unsupervised text corpus such as Wikipedia using the two methods of "Masked Word Prediction" and "Next Sentence Prediction."

Unlike traditional sequential or recurrent models, the attention architecture processes the whole input sequence at once, enabling all input tokens to be processed in parallel. The layers of BERT are based on transformer architecture. The pretrained BERT model can be fine-tuned with just one additional layer to obtain state-of-the-art results in a wide range of NLP tasks.

ALBERT
A Lite BERT (ALBERT) [13] is a next-generation BERT-based architecture with an optimized configuration. The basic structure of ALBERT is the same as BERT. However, ALBERT reduces the parameters of the embedding layer and shares the transformer layers, improving the memory usage and the calculation time. ALBERT can use more layers and a larger hidden size if the same computational resources are available, allowing for a more complex and expressive model than BERT.

4   Proposed Method

4.1   Learning Procedure

The proposed PLM-based method uses fully divided two-stage learning: general learning and task-specific learning. In general learning, PLM is trained with tasks that require only an unlabeled corpus, making it possible to learn a large-scale corpus such as Wikipedia data. PLM acquires general and broad linguistic knowledge consisting of a large amount of sentence information. In task-specific learning, additional layers are appended at the bottom of the model for converting the output format. Then, the model is fine-tuned with labeled task-specific data. This research refers to the learning procedure, and we fine-tune PLM to taxonomic relation classification tasks.

This research utilizes a Hugging Face's transformer library [16] implemented in Python. The library provides the implementation of various language models and the model data that have acquired prior knowledge through the general learning process. It facilitates model comparison by collecting the latest models and generic pretraining models under a unified API. In this paper, we utilize this library to implement pre-training and general learning of the model.

4.2 Architecture

We use a simple architecture that appends the preprocessing unit, dropout regularization, and a softmax classification layer at each end of the language model. This is a standard configuration of PLMs when it is applied in classification tasks, indicating that the proposed method does not require a task-specific architecture. Figure 3. shows the overall architecture of our model in a task-specific ontology generation stage, and it consists of the following three main stages. In this section, we describe the details and the intention of each part individually.

Preprocess

The first stage of our architecture is the preprocessing step. In most cases, PLMs require a specific format of the input sentences to implement subword expressions and accept inputs for various tasks. In addition, relationship classification tasks require a pair of phrases as input data, and we perform the following preprocessing steps on the phrase pairs before entering them into the model (an example of these steps is shown in Table 1).

1. Concatenation & Special Token Insertion: First, the input phrase pair is concatenated into one sentence. At this time, a classifier token ([CLS]) is inserted at the front of the first phrase and separator tokens ([SEP]) are appended at the middle of the two phrases and the end of the second phrase.
2. Tokenization: The concatenated phrases are divided into subwords by a tokenizer corresponding to each language model. The number of divided subwords is equal to or greater than the number of words included in the phrase.

Pretrained Language Model

In this part, calculations for task-specific learning and actual ontology generation of some PLMs are performed. The concept of fine-tuning of the wiki-BERT has been done for ontology training with super-sub words set from wordnet. The number of outputs of PLMs corresponds to the number of input sequences. Because this study is a classification

Table 1. The architecture of the proposed pretraining-based method for taxonomic structure generation and the calculation process flow.

	Phrase A	Phrase B
Input	Airplane	Jet aeroplane
Concatenation	[CLS] airplane [SEP] jet aeroplane [SEP]	
Tokenization	[CLS] airplane [SEP] jet aero ##plane [SEP]	

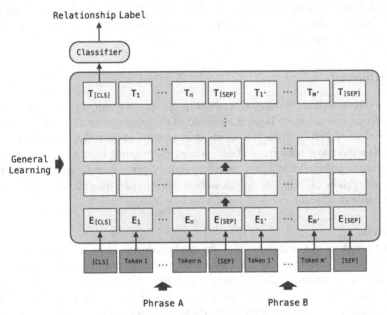

Fig. 3. The architecture of the proposed pretraining-based method for taxonomic structure generation and the calculation process flow.

problem, we extract only the head vector corresponding to the [CLS] token inserted in the preprocessing.

Classification Layers

This part classifies hidden vector (consist of two phrase relationship information) into four type of relationship labels. First, a single linear layer translates into as many vectors as class labels. Then, dropout with a probability factor of 0.1 is applied to regularize and prevent overfitting, and the dropout is only applied in the training phase and not in the inference phase. Finally, the softmax classification layer outputs the probabilities of the input text belonging to each of the class labels such that the sum of the probabilities is 1. The softmax layer is just a fully connected neural network layer with the softmax activation function.

5   Data Collection

5.1   Phrase Pair Relationship Datasets

As described in Sect. 1.1, ontology generation can be realized by the relationship classification between phrases. The proposed method using PLMs performs pretraining in the general learning process, and less data are required for task-specific learning than previous methods, but a large-scale dataset is still required for general ontology generation. Because the ultimate goal is to build an ontology, it is ideal to obtain it from a real ontology or something close to it. Therefore, in this study, we acquired data from WordNet [17], a large-scale concept dictionary and database that has a structure similar to that of ontology. The rest of this chapter provides an overview of WordNet and how to acquire phrase relationship datasets.

5.2   Overview of WordNet

In WordNet, to combine concepts that can be expressed in different notations with the same meaning into one object, a group of phrases called a synset is used as the smallest unit. All synsets on WordNet form a hierarchical structure; if synset A is a more abstract version of synset B, synset A is defined as a hypernym of the synset B. From the structure, WordNet can be viewed as a huge, multipurpose ontology that covers the entire language, and it can be used as teacher data in ontology generation.

Table 2. Details of dataset extracted from WordNet.

Relation label	Number of data
Synonym	208,068
Hypernym	191,255
Hyponym	191,255
Unrelated	500,000
Total	1,090,578

5.3   Dataset Extraction from WordNet

In this research, we extracted pairs of phrases and the four kinds of relationships (synonym, hypernym–hyponym, hyponym–hypernym, and unrelated) from the taxonomy structure of WordNet. The details of the datasets are shown in Table 2. First, for all noun synsets, all pairs of terms are registered in one synset as synonym pairs. Next, we extract hyponyms base on target synsets. It is labeled as hypernym-hyponym relations. Moreover, pairs of phrases where the order is reversed are labeled as hyponym–hypernym relations. Finally, we made many pairs of phrases randomly that do not have special relationships and labeled them as unrelated pairs.

6 Experiment

6.1 Training and Validation

In the experiment, we quantitatively compared the RNN-based and PLMs-based methods by observing the classification accuracy. To compare the BPE with the RNN method using the existing Word2vec, we investigated the combination of the embedding layer of the BERT-based model and RNN. Using the dataset acquired from WordNet described in Table 2, we trained the model and measured the classification performance after task-specific learning. At this time, the dataset of WordNet was randomly divided into three types: training data, validation data, and test data. Validation and Test datasets each have 10,000 data, and all other data are used for training.

Table 3. Configuration of pretrained language models used for comparison and learning parameters

	BERT		ALBERT	
	Base	Large	Base	Large
Optimizer	Adam			
Learning rate	1e−5			
Transformer layers	12	24	12	24
Hidden size	768	1024	768	1024
Embedding size	768	1024	128	128
Parameters	108M	334M	12M	18M

Table 4. Vocabulary size of word embedding methods

	Vocabulary size
Word2vec(previous)	297,141
BERT-embedding (subword representation)	30,522

6.2 Model Setup

To confirm the validity of PLMs for the relationship classification task, it is necessary to perform validation on many models. In addition, these language models have some configurable parameters, such as the number of layers and hidden size. Similar to the neural network models in other domains, verification of the effects of these parameters is also an important factor for PLMs. For these reasons, we compared the major PLMs architectures, and their configurations are summarized in Table 3. The vocabulary size of word embedding methods illustrated in the Table 4.

7   Evaluation

In this experiment, we compared the accuracy of the previous model, the proposed model, and the variation. These models were trained for any number of epochs by phrase pair relationship datasets extracted from WordNet. Then, this learning process was stopped based on the validation results after empirical measurement. Finally, the classification performance was evaluated by the test datasets. The accuracy results are summarized in Table 5. The calculation times required for learning one epoch were also compared, as also shown in Table 5.

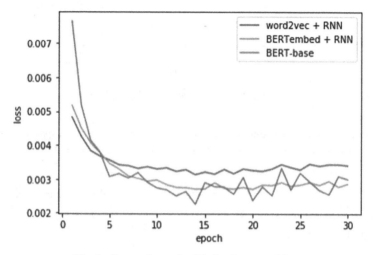

Fig. 4. Comparison of validation loss transitions

This experiment shows that the proposed PLM-based method has significantly better accuracy than existing methods. In particular, BERT-large reaches the highest accuracy of 98.6% among the models used for comparison. In contrast, the calculation time is much longer than the existing methods, and the calculation time of the minimum configuration ALBERT-base requires four times that of the RNN-based method. In comparison with the embedding method, the BERT-embed + RNN has better accuracy while keeping smaller vocabularies than the existing Word2vec + RNN method, indicating that BPE is an effective method for ontology generation. Figures 4 and 5 show that the PLM-based method can acquire better performance than RNN even in small epochs.

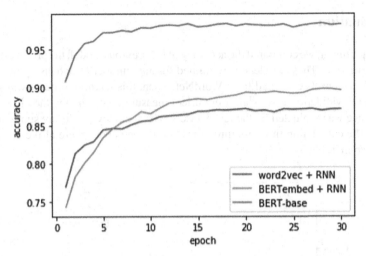

Fig. 5. Comparison of validation accuracy transitions

Table 5. Comparison of relationship classification accuracies between phrases, and the calculation time for learning is expressed as a ratio when the learning time of RNN is set to 1.0.

	Accuracy (four classes)	Ratio of calculation time
Word2vec + RNN(previous)	87.1%	1.00
BERT-embedding + RNN	89.6%	1.21
BERT-base	98.1%	6.26
BERT-large	98.6%	15.34
ALBERT-base	97.6%	4.23
ALBERT-large	98.3%	12.01

8   Conclusion and Future Work

In this paper, we applied the procedure of transfer learning and PLMs' technologies to ontology generation to improve the performance of relationship classification between phrase pairs. As a result, a dramatic improvement of + 12.4% was achieved in terms of accuracy without sophisticated architecture. The results also show that large model configurations provide better accuracy in PLM-based approaches. However, in terms of computational resources, the results show that ALBERT, a model with improved memory usage, fell short of existing methods. Combining learning processes such as DistilBERT [18] and TinyBERT [19] with knowledge distillation and optimizing models such as ALBERT to solve these weaknesses is an example of future work. Although the PLM-based method has succeeded in reproducing the hierarchical structure of general-purpose ontology such as WordNet, it does not support domain-specific ontologies. Therefore, creating an ontology that depends on purpose, quality, and uniqueness is also one of the issues to be addressed in the future.

The codes are available at "https://github.com/atshb/Text2ontology".

References

1. Bittner, T., Donnelly, M., Smith, B.: A spatio-temporal ontology for geographic information integration. Int. J. Geog. Inf. Sci. **23**, 765–798 (2009). https://doi.org/10.1080/136588107017 76767
2. Paik, I., Komiya, R., Ryu, K.: Customizable active situation awareness framework based on meta-process in ontology. In: Proceedings of International Conference on Awareness Science and Technology (iCAST) 2013, Aizu, Fukushima Japan, November 2013
3. Zhu, H., Paschalidis, I.C., Tahmasebi, A.: Clinical concept extraction with contextual word embedding (2018)
4. Brack, A., D'Souza, J., Hoppe, A., Auer, S., Ewerth, R.: Domain-independent extraction of scientific concepts from research articles (2020)
5. Oba, A., Paik, I.: Extraction of taxonomic relation of complex terms by recurrent neural network. In: 2019 IEEE International Conference on Cognitive Computing (ICCC), pp. 70–72, July 2019
6. Duan, S., Zhao, H.: Attention is all you need for Chinese word segmentation (2019)
7. Dowdell, T., Zhang, H.: Is attention all what you need? – an empirical investigation on convolution-based active memory and self-attention (2019)
8. Devlin, J., Chang, M.-W., Lee, K., Toutanova, K.: BERT: pre-training of deep bidirectional transformers for language understanding (2018)
9. García, I., Agerri, R., Rigau, G.: A common semantic space for monolingual and cross-lingual meta-embeddings (2020)
10. Sennrich, R., Haddow, B., Birch, A.: Neural machine translation of rare words with subword units (2015)
11. Bojanowski, P., Grave, E., Joulin, A., Mikolov, T.: Enriching word vectors with subword information. Trans. Assoc. Comput. Linguist. **5**, 135–146 (2017). https://www.aclweb.org/anthology/Q17-1010
12. Heinzerling, B., Strube, M.: BPEMB: tokenization-free pre-trained sub- word embeddings in 275 languages (2017)
13. Lan, Z., Chen, M., Goodman, S., Gimpel, K., Sharma, P., Soricut, R.: ALBERT: a lite BERT for self-supervised learning of language representations (2019)
14. Klaussner, C., Zhekova, D.: Lexico-syntactic patterns for automatic ontology building. In: Proceedings of the Second Student Research Workshop associated with RANLP 2011, Hissar, Bulgaria, pp. 109–114. Association for Computational Linguistics, September 2011. https://www.aclweb.org/anthology/R11-2017
15. Omine, K., Paik, I.: Classification of taxonomic relations by word embedding and wedge product
16. Wolf, T., et al.: Huggingface's transformers: state-of-the-art natural language processing (2019)
17. Miller, G.A., Beckwith, R., Fellbaum, C., Gross, D., Miller, K.J.: Introduction to WordNet: an on-line lexical database. Int. J. Lexicography **3**(4), 235–244 (1990). https://doi.org/10.1093/ijl/3.4.235
18. Sanh, V., Debut, L., Chaumond, J., Wolf, T.: DistilBERT, a distilled version of BERT: smaller, faster, cheaper and lighter (2019)
19. Jiao, X., et al.: TinyBERT: distilling BERT for natural language understanding (2019)

Deep Learning Architecture for Topological Optimized Mechanical Design Generation with Complex Shape Criterion

Waad Almasri[1,2]([✉]) [ID], Dimitri Bettebghor[1] [ID], Fakhreddine Ababsa[2] [ID], Florence Danglade[2] [ID], and Faouzi Adjed[1] [ID]

[1] Expleo France, Montigny-Le-Bretonneux, France
{waad.almasri,dimitri.bettebghor,faouzi.adjed}@expleogroup.com
[2] Laboratoire d'Ingénierie des Systèmes Physiques et Numériques (LISPEN),
Arts et Métiers, Cluny, France
{waad.almasri,fakhreddine.ababsa,florence.danglade}@ensam.eu

Abstract. Topology optimization is a powerful tool for producing an optimal free-form design from input mechanical constraints. However, in its traditional-density-based approach, it does not feature a proper definition for the external boundary. Therefore, the integration of shape-related constraints remains hard. It requires the experts' intervention to interpret the generated designs into parametric shapes; thus, making the design process time-consuming. With the growing role of additive manufacturing in the industry, developing a design approach considering mechanical and geometrical constraints simultaneously becomes an interesting way to integrate manufacturing and aesthetics constraints into mechanical design. In this paper, we propose to generate mechanically and geometrically valid designs using a deep-learning solution trained via a dual-discriminator Generative Adversarial Network (GAN) framework. This Deep-learning-geometrical-driven solution generates designs very similar to traditional topology optimization's outputs in a fraction of time.

Moreover, it allows an easy shape fine-tuning by a simple increase/decrease of the input geometrical condition (here the total-bar-count), a task that a traditional topology optimization cannot achieve.

Keywords: Topology Optimization (TO) · Deep Learning (DL) · Generative Adversarial Networks (GAN)

1 Introduction

In the late 20th century, the advent of additive manufacturing (AM) allowed the production of organic shapes that were costly and complex with conventional shaping processes. On the other hand, given a set of parameters such as loads, boundary conditions, and volume fraction (i.e. the percentage of material volume

© Springer Nature Switzerland AG 2021
H. Fujita et al. (Eds.): IEA/AIE 2021, LNAI 12798, pp. 222–234, 2021.
https://doi.org/10.1007/978-3-030-79457-6_19

used), topology optimization (TO) allows the generation of smooth and organic shapes. Its synergy with AM made it further attractive in the research areas. Despite the success of AM, not all the designs could be manufactured. Steep curvatures, overhanging patterns, the need for supports, and other geometrical constraints are still a hurdle [2]. Therefore, an engineer manually reconstructs a shape inspired by TO's suggestion, considering the geometric and manufacturing constraints implicitly. This re-interpretation phase is not straightforward, can compromise the initial design's optimality, and can be time-consuming; it depends on the engineer's experience and expertise. Moreover, a recent survey [26] has shown that half of TO practitioners regret the absence of geometric and manufacturing-related plug-ins in TO's software.

Thus, to accelerate the design process, [12,13,15,29,31] integrated overhangs and building directions into the formulation of TO to minimize the need for supports during manufacturing. Nevertheless, TO is an iterative, finite-element-based optimization method, hence computationally expensive. Its efficiency depends on the design space (mesh size), the complexity of the input conditions, and the resolution of discretized linear elasticity equations (e.g. Finite Elements). Consequently, other research has focused on accelerating the TO process via machine and Deep Learning (DL) techniques.

DL architectures have proven efficiency and robustness in learning complex spatial correlations and extracting high-level features (including geometrical or shape-related features) from real-world images [8,20,33].

The DL-TO methods found in the literature can be divided into two parts. The first part used DL to assist traditional finite-element-TO [11,17,25] while the second part tried to replace completely TO's formulation by DL [1,6,10,14,19,22,28,30]. None of these DL-based methods included any geometrical constraints; on the contrary, they were left to the re-interpretation phase.

In this work, the primary objective is not to accelerate TO via DL but to take advantage of DL's capability to learn spatial correlations to facilitate the integration of geometrical constraints at the conceptual level of TO. The geometrical constraint considered in this work is the total-bar-count referred to as the design's complexity. This DL-geometrical-driven TO paves the way to handle and tailor different complexities during design generation.

Our approach consists of a dual-discriminator Generative Adversarial Network (GAN) [7]. The generator (the DL-TO) encodes the mechanical and geometrical conditions and outputs the 2D design. The first discriminator penalizes the generator over the mechanical constraints, while the second penalizes it over the geometrical one. The GAN is chosen for its flexible training framework. New discriminators can be easily appended to pass new knowledge to the generator during training. For example, one can add a build-time predictor, a thermal distortion predictor, etc. as discriminators to generate designs accounting for a short build time, thermal distortion, etc. Besides, these discriminators can always be used separately (to predict the build-time of a design or its thermal distortion). To the best of our knowledge, related literature on automatic design generation only focuses on the generated designs' aesthetics. In our work, we developed an objective evaluation, which considers not only mechanical criteria (compliance, volume) but also an objective measure of complexity.

The major contributions of this paper can be summarized as follows: (1) The integration of mechanical and geometrical constraints simultaneously at the conceptual level via a DL-based TO. (2) The ability to easily tailor the geometry of a design by a simple change of the input geometrical condition (the total-bar-count in this case).

The rest of the paper is organized as follows: Sects. 2.1 and 2.2 provide a theoretical overview of TO and GANs respectively. In Sect. 3, the dual-discriminator GAN approach is explained. Section 4 details the consolidation of the training and test datasets used to train and evaluate the DL-TO. Generated designs are shown and evaluated in Sect. 5. Finally, Sect. 6 summarizes the methodology and its outcomes and discusses future works.

2   Theoretical Overview

2.1   Topology Optimization

Topology optimization seeks to find the optimal layout within a design space for a specific set of boundary conditions, load configurations, and volume fraction. It gained its success in the industrial world for its intrinsic characteristics: it allows effective use of the material and has a higher degree of freedom when addressing the topology, shape, and sizing problems altogether. In the literature, several approaches were developed to solve the TO problem: density-based [4], level-set [3] and others. The topmost common commercial approach is the Solid Isotropic Material with Penalization (SIMP) method [4]. SIMP is a density gradient-based iterative method that uses penalization of the intermediate non-binary values of density material to converge to an optimal binary design. SIMP represents a design as a distribution of discretized square material elements e (material properties are assumed constant within each element e). The variables are the element-relative-densities x_i such that $x_i = 1/0$ represents presence/absence of material at point i of the design domain.

A TO problem where the objective is to minimize the compliance $c(x)$ can be written as the following:

$$min_x = U^T K U = \sum_{e=1}^{N} x_e^p u_e^T k_0 u_e \ \ s.t. \ KU = F, \ \frac{V(x)}{V0} \leq f, \ 0 < x_0 \leq x \leq 1 \ \ (1)$$

where U and u_e are the global and element-wise displacements, F the forces vector, K and k_e are the global and element-wise stiffness matrices and N = number of elements used to discretize the design domain. x is the design variables vector i.e. the density material and x_0 the minimum relative densities (non-zero to avoid singularity), p penalization power (typically 3 for Poisson's ratio = 1/3 [5]). V_0 and $V(x)$ are the design domain volume and material volume respectively and f the volume fraction. To efficiently solve the problem stated above, several approaches were proposed: the Optimality Criteria (OC) methods, Sequential Linear Programming (SLP) methods, the Method of Moving Asymptotes (MMA), etc. In [23], Sigmund used the OC method and added a mesh-independency filter to ensure the existence of solutions to the problem and avoid checker-board patterns [24]. In this study, a modified Python version of the 99-line-of-code of the SIMP method written by Sigmund [23] is used to generate the training and test datasets of 2D designs (Sect. 4).

2.2 Generative Adversarial Networks

Generative adversarial network (GAN) was first introduced by Goodfellow [7]. This method learns to mimic any input data distribution. A GAN consists of two neural networks the generator $G(z, \theta_g)$ and the discriminator $D(x, \theta_d)$, where θ_g and θ_d are the parameters of the generator's and discriminator's networks respectively. $G(z, \theta_g)$ would like to generate from a latent space z (z follows a noise prior distribution p_z) samples with a distribution p_g similar to the original ones p_{data}. However, $D(x, \theta_d)$ tries to discriminate real sample (p_{data}) from synthesized ones (p_g). Both networks are trained in a minimax framework to improve the same loss function: the cross entropy loss $L(G, D)$. The optimization is successful when the generator starts to output data samples following the same distributions as the real sample (i.e. $p_g = p_{data}$). On the other hand, a conditional GAN (cGAN) [16] is an extension of the GAN network enabling the generation to be oriented by a specific input condition c. In this framework, the basics of cGAN become: the conditional generator as $G((z/c), \theta_g)$, the conditional discriminator as $D((x/c), \theta_d)$ and the loss function as:

$$L(G, D) = \min_G \max_D \mathbb{E}_{x \sim p_{data(x)}}[log(D(x/c))] + \mathbb{E}_{z \sim p_z(z)}[log(1 - D(G(z/c)))] \quad (2)$$

The approach adopted in this work is based on the cGAN framework.

3 Methodology

In this work, a conditional [16] convolutional [18] dual-discriminator GAN has been adopted. This approach consists of a deep ResUnet generator [32] (the DL-based TO), a Residual-based discriminator to differentiate between the real designs (SIMP-based) and the generated ones, and an inception-based [27] bar counter (the 2nd discriminator) to quantify the complexity of the generated/real designs. The training procedure is detailed in Fig. 1.

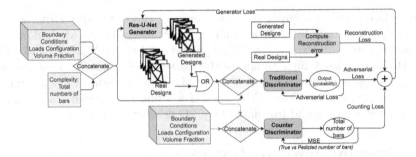

Fig. 1. Training procedure.

3.1 Architecture of the Generator

The generator is a deep ResUnet [32] network. It takes as input the mechanical and geometrical conditions and outputs the 2D design. It's an encoder-decoder convolutional architecture with residual and skip-connections between the outputs of encoder layers and the inputs of decoder layers or what is called U-Net. This architecture benefits from the U-Net [21] and residual [9] advantages. U-Net connections ensures that high-frequency details are not lost in the decoding phase, and residual connections allow a deeper network without any performance degradation (usually due to vanishing gradients). The network can be divided into three parts: an encoder, a bridge, and a decoder. The encoder is formed of 4 blocks, each consisting of a down-sampling layer (a convolution of stride 2) and a residual unit[1]. The bridge connection has the same architecture as an encoder's block and combines the encoder to the decoder. The decoder is formed of 5 blocks, each consisting of an up-sample layer (a transpose convolution of stride 2) and a residual unit, followed by a convolution of kernel size 1×1 and a sigmoid activation.

3.2 Architecture of the Discriminators

The first one, the traditional discriminator, takes as input the design along with the geometrical and mechanical conditions and outputs the probability that the design comes from the real data distribution. The second one is a regression inception-based DL counter. It takes as input the design and only its corresponding mechanical conditions and outputs the total number of bars present in the design.

The traditional discriminator's network consists of seven blocks of down-sample and residual units followed by a dropout, then a fully connected layer. It outputs a probability p regarding the design being real ($p \approx 1$) or fake ($p \approx 0$). It helps the generator improve the generated designs' quality and conformity to boundary conditions and load configurations.

---

[1] The architecture of the residual unit block used in this work is detailed in [32].

The counter network consists of a stem, an Inception/Reduction Resnet-v1-block-A, an Inception/Reduction Resnet-v1-block-B, an Inception Resnet-v1-block-C followed by an average pooling layer, a dropout layer, and a fully connected layer[2]. In this work, 4347 SIMP-designs were manually labeled (*we manually counted the total number of bars present in each design*). The counter-discriminator is pre-trained on these labeled SIMP designs before the full training of the GAN, for this procedure improves the generator's convergence.

The counter-discriminator is pre-trained using 3885 labeled designs and tested over the remaining 462 designs. The counter-discriminator predicts 94.9% of the time a total-bar-count within an error margin of ±2 bars. Additionally, even if we restrict further the error margin to ±1 bar, its accuracy slightly drops to 85.4%; knowing that the range of total-bar-count is very wide ([3, 31]).

This pre-trained counter is also used to predict the total-bar-count on unlabeled train designs to augment the training dataset.

3.3   Loss Function

This dual-discriminator GAN aims to train a generator embracing two aspects: the reconstructed 2D designs' quality and their conformity to the mechanical and geometrical conditions. Thus, the original adversarial loss function used to train the generator (Eq. 2) was altered to consider both aspects. A reconstruction loss (L_r) and a counting loss (L_{count}) were added to the generator's loss. The modified generator loss function L_G adapted in the training process is the following:

$$L_G = \lambda_1 L_r + \lambda_2 L_{adv} + \lambda_3 Acc_{count} L_{count} \tag{3}$$

where $L_r = \frac{1}{n}\sum_{i=1}^{n}(x_i - \hat{x}_i)^2$, $L_{count} = \frac{1}{n}\sum_{i=1}^{n}(\hat{y}_i - y_i)^2$, with x_i, $\hat{x}_i$ the true and predicted 2D design, y_i the input total bar-count, $\hat{y}_i$ the predicted total-bar-count in the generated designs and n the batch size. The accuracy of the counter discriminator $Acc_{count} = \frac{1}{N}\sum_{i=1}^{N}(\hat{t}_i == y_i)$ with y_i, $\hat{t}_i$ the true and predicted total-bar-count in the real designs and N the total number of training samples; this accuracy is updated at the end of each epoch. λ_1, λ_2 and λ_3 are the penalization weights of L_r, L_{adv} and L_{count} respectively. The adversarial loss ensures the generation of creative and varied 2D structures. The reconstruction loss boosts the aesthetics and the reproduction of high-frequency details in the generated samples. The counting loss penalizes the generator every time the geometrical constraint on the total number of bars is not respected.

In this work, stabilizing the loss function was a challenge, especially that it consists of different types of losses having different orders of magnitude: $0 \leq L_r \leq 1$, $0 \leq L_{adv} \leq 100$; due to Pytorch Implementation of the Binary Cross Entropy Loss, $0 \leq Acc_{count} \leq 1$ and $0 \leq L_{count} \leq 961$; in this work, the maximum total-bar-count is 31. Additionally, during training, L_r tends to decrease sharply after only few iterations ($0 \leq L_r \leq 0.1$). The same behavior is noticed with L_{adv} ($0 \leq L_{adv} \leq 1$). While $L_{count} \times Acc_{count}$ seems to vary

---

[2] The stem and inception/reduction blocks used defers from the original paper [27] only by the number of input/output feature maps.

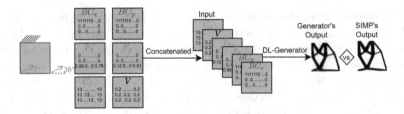

Fig. 2. Input of the DL-generator. Boundary conditions (BC_x, BC_y), load configurations (F_x, F_y), volume fraction V and complexity C_x (i.e. total-bar-count) are formulated as a six-channel image forming the generator's input.

between 0 and 30, especially that, as mentioned earlier, the counter discriminator is pre-trained before the training ($Acc_{count} \approx 0.8$). Thus, to ensure that the generator is equally penalized over the three losses, λ_1, λ_2 and λ_3 were set to 10, 1 and 0.1 respectively.

4   Data Generation

To train the model, 21 538 2D-designs of size 100×100 pixels were generated following the SIMP method explained in Sect. 2.1 via a modified Python version of the academic open-source TO code written by Sigmund [23][3]. The geometrical constraint (the complexity) is added by manual labeling over 4347 samples (which are used to pre-train the counter discriminator) and then the complexity of the remaining samples is predicted using the counter discriminator (Sect. 3.2).

A 2D structure of size $n_x \times n_y$ can be discretized into a mesh of $(n_x + 1) \times (n_y + 1)$ nodes and is subject to 2 major constraints: the boundary conditions i.e. the fixed nodes and the loads i.e. the loaded nodes. Boundary conditions BC are represented as $(n_x + 1) \times (n_y + 1)$ matrices with null values everywhere except for the fixed nodes set to 1.0; we only consider encastrated designs i.e. BC along the x axis (BC_x) and y axis (BC_y) are similar. Loads F_x and F_y are represented as $(n_x + 1) \times (n_y + 1)$ matrices with null values everywhere except for the loaded nodes[4]. Since BC and F are 101×101 matrices, hence, to concatenate the latter with the rest of the inputs altogether: the 2D design, the volume fraction, and the complexity are reshaped into a 101×101 image. An example of an input to the generator is shown in Fig. 2. The dataset was separated into train (17230 samples) and test (4308 samples). The test set is used to evaluate the generator's performance.

---

[3] This code is available on the GitHub repository: https://github.com/dbetteb/TOP_OPT.git.

[4] A loaded node n_e located at line i and column j tilted θ degrees has $F_x(i, j) = cos(\theta)$ and $F_y(i, j) = sin(\theta)$; the magnitude of the loads were set to 1.0 N.

Design	Original Design								
	Generated Design								
Metrics	$e_{V_\%}$	-3.9	-2.07	-3.64	-7.94	-1.58	2.37	-3.73	-1.11
	$e_{C_\%}$	20.12	12	2.41	39.27	9.39	6.94	44.24	37.7
	ΔC_x	0	0	0	+2	+1	-1	0	+1
	nT	1833	1017	14002	974	1903	3703	2838	3923

(a) Without Threshold

Design with Threshold	Original Design (Threshold =0.4)								
	Generated Design (Threshold =0.4)								
Metrics With Threshold	$e_{V_\%}$	-1.36	-0.16	-3.72	-7.16	-1.34	3.45	0.17	-3
	$e_{C_\%}$	3.75	-2	2.83	31.75	-2.53	0.48	4.31	21.1
	ΔC_x	0	0	0	+1	0	0	0	-1
	nT	1833	1017	14002	974	1903	3703	2838	3923

(b) With Threshold

Fig. 3. In this figure, we compare the aesthetics, volume fraction $(e_{V_\%})$, compliance $(e_{C_\%})$, complexity (ΔC_x) and generation speed (nT) of the original (SIMP-based) versus generated (DL-based) designs with and without Threshold. In both cases, DL-designs are barely indistinguishable, in terms of shape, from SIMP-designs, achieve lower Volume Fractions $(e_{V_\%} \leq 0)$, respect the Complexity constraint $(|\Delta C_x| \leq 2)$ and are generated thousand of times of faster than the SIMP-designs i.e. DL-TO generates the first design in Fig. 3a 1833 times faster than SIMP-TO. However, while the Compliance of DL-designs is higher than SIMP-designs before threshold, it is significantly reduced after threshold.

5   Experiments and Results

As mentioned above, TO finds the optimal material distribution in a design space that minimizes compliance and meets the boundary conditions, the loads, and the volume fraction constraint. Still, an optimal design for manufacturing is a compromise between mechanical performance and geometrical constraints. Thus, to evaluate the generated designs, we will examine their compliance values, volume fractions, and complexities (geometrical constraint). The metrics used for the volume fraction V and compliance C are the relative errors $e_{V_\%} = \frac{V_g - V_o}{V_o} \times 100$ and $e_{C_\%} = \frac{C_g - C_o}{C_o} \times 100$ respectively. The metric of Complexity C_x is the bar-count difference $\Delta C_x = C_{x_g} - C_{x_o}$. Where X_g, X_o refer to generated and original respectively and $\{X_g, X_o : X \in \{V, C, C_x\}\}$. The metric used to compare the generation speed between SIMP and DL-TO is $nT = \frac{\text{Generation Time of SIMP-TO}}{\text{Generation Time of DL-TO}}$, which refers to DL-TO is faster nT times than SIMP-TO.

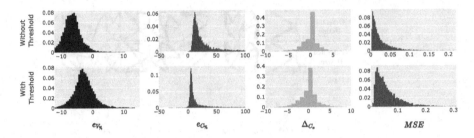

Fig. 4. Distributions of Volume Fraction ($e_{V\%}$), Compliance ($e_{C\%}$), Complexity (Total bar count, Δ_{C_x}) and Reconstruction error (MSE) between the original (SIMP-based) and generated (DL-based) designs with and without threshold in the Test Set. The generated designs show conformity with all constraints except for the compliance, which is improved with threshold.

Figure 3a displays a sample of original (i.e. SIMP-based) versus generated (i.e. DL-based) designs from the test set. It also shows their relative errors $e_{V\%}$, $e_{C\%}$ and bar-count differences ΔC_x.

The DL-designs are aesthetically plausible. The fixed and loaded bars[5] respect the input boundary conditions and load configurations.

In the majority of cases, $e_{V\%}$ is negative, e.g. the DL-TO (the generator) tends to find a lower volume fraction bound than that found by the traditional SIMP formulation. However, $e_{C\%}$ is relatively higher ($e_{C\%} \geq 10\%$ in most cases); showing that the DL-designs exhibit greater external stresses. It would be interesting to note here that SIMP-TO and DL-TO output continuous non-binary designs and the compliance is very sensitive to intermediate-density-pixel values. Hence, to account for this drawback, a threshold of 0.4 is applied to the test designs. This particular threshold improved the compliance of test designs globally compared to others. However, a better approach would be to choose an adapted global threshold per design. Results are reported in Fig. 3b. In most cases, the $e_{C\%}$ dropped significantly, $e_{C\%} \leq 5\%$, i.e. after threshold, DL and SIMP designs tend to have similar compliance values ($C_g \leq 1.05 \times C_o$). We point out that the application of threshold increased the volume fraction. Yet, the DL-designs still achieved lower volume fractions than the SIMP-designs. In other words, after threshold, in the majority of cases, DL-designs tend to present a better mechanical performance: lower volume fraction and similar compliance.

Additionally, the geometrical constraint is mainly respected. Complex DL-designs tend to display additional or fewer internal bars; the maximum bar-difference is more or less two bars (Fig. 3a, Fig. 3b).

Figure 4 summarizes the overall performance of the generator. The average reconstruction error (MSE) is 0.025, manifesting the aesthetic aspect of the DL-designs. The volume fraction constraint is respected with 94% of the DL-designs having a volume fraction lower than that achieved by SIMP. Moreover, 86% of

---

[5] A fixed bar is a bar where boundary conditions are applied. A loaded bar is a bar where a load is applied.

the DL-designs have, at most, 2 additional/fewer bars ($|\Delta C_x| \leq 2$). Nevertheless, the DL-designs tend to show higher external stresses. 50% of the DL-designs score a compliance greater than that computed over the SIMP designs ($e_{C_\%} \geq 20\%$). One of the reasons is that the generator was not penalized explicitly on the compliance during the training. The integration of a compliance predictor as a third discriminator into our GAN could improve the generated designs' compliance. We note that the DL-designs comply better with complexity and volume fraction constraints; the generator was penalized on the reconstruction error (it embeds the volume fraction constraint implicitly) and complexity error during training.

We also compare the designs after the application of threshold. As expected, the compliance dropped; ($e_{C_\%} \leq 20\%$) in 70% of the cases.

We underline that the design's mechanical and geometrical performance depends on the threshold-value's choice: the lower the threshold, the higher the volume fraction, the higher the threshold, the lower the bar-count, and possibly the appearance of discontinuities in the design. Consequently, we need to prioritize the constraints to find the best compromise.

To validate the generator's understanding of complexity (total-bar-count), we fixed the mechanical conditions of designs, changed the complexity and reported the generator's response to such change as shown in Fig. 5. The number of bars increases with the complexity. However, the additional bars are blurry. This is due to the volume fraction constraint. The volume fraction and complexity of a design are proportional. A better approach would be to increase/decrease the complexity and volume fraction together.

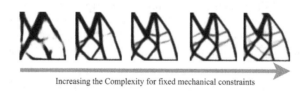

Increasing the Complexity for fixed mechanical constraints

Fig. 5. A sample of generated designs with similar mechanical constraints but different complexities. From left to right, the complexities are the following: 10, 18, 22, 25 and 30 bars.

Finally, in terms of computational time, it would be interesting to highlight that the DL-TO generates a 2D design in 0.047 s from specific mechanical conditions and an additional geometrical one (the total-bar-count in our case), while a SIMP-TO requires 221 s on average (i.e.$\approx$ 5000 times slower) for only the same mechanical conditions and needs supplementary post-processing to integrate the geometrical one. Moreover, a DL-TO's generation time and computational complexity are independent of the input constraints, unlike traditional TO approaches as shown in Table 1. For SIMP-TO, the computational time and complexity increase with the complexity of the input constraint (here, the number of loads) while they remain unchanged for DL-TO.

Table 1. Generation Time (in seconds s) and Computational Complexity (in Gega Floating Point Operations per Second $GFLOPS$) of SIMP (FE-based) versus DL-TO.

Input constraints	Generation time (s)		Computational complexity ($GFLOPS$)	
	SIMP	DL-TO	SIMP	DL-TO
1 Load	68	0.02	62.81	2.27
2 Loads	132	0.02	125.89	2.27
10 Loads	656	0.02	620.28	2.27

To sum up, the DL-TO proposed in this study generates mechanically valid designs, indistinguishable from those generated by SIMP-TO to the naked eye, and is a thousand times faster than SIMP-TO. Moreover, while SIMP-TO needs post-processing to account for a geometrical condition, DL-TO integrates it at the conceptual level. Finally, DL-TO enables TO users to easily tailor the design's complexity as the first step towards making it manufacturable.

6   Conclusion

In this paper, we build an original approach to generate topologically optimized designs with the help of advanced DL architectures. This DL-TO (generator) not only generates mechanical designs faster but also tailors the design's complexity (total-bar-count), as the first step towards making designs manufacturable. We demonstrate the DL-TO's ability to adjust the complexity, a task that is hardly feasible with conventional TO methods. Lastly, we leverage the generative capability of GANs; the DL-TO generates creative valid designs.

Moreover, the adopted training strategy enables the addition of future developed modules (as discriminators) to the generation approach such as: (a) a build-time module to identify structures rapidly manufactured, (b) a thermal distortion module, (c) and other complex modules to validate a design mechanically and geometrically. In future works, we will integrate more complex additive manufacturing constraints particularly, a build-time module, a geometry-evaluator (to check for overhangs, bar curvatures, minimum length/width, etc.), and supplementary mechanical validation modules into the generation process.

Acknowledgement. This work was supported by Expleo France.

References

1. Abueidda, D.W., Koric, S., Sobh, N.A.: Topology optimization of 2D structures with nonlinearities using deep learning. Comput. Struct. **237**, 106283 (2020)
2. Adam, G.A., Zimmer, D.: Design for additive manufacturing–element transitions and aggregated structures. CIRP J. Manuf. Sci. Technol. **7**(1), 20–28 (2014)

3. Allaire, G., Jouve, F., Toader, A.M.: A level-set method for shape optimization. Comput. R. Math. **334**(12), 1125–1130 (2002)
4. Bendsøe, M.P.: Optimal shape design as a material distribution problem. Struct. optim. **1**(4), 193–202 (1989)
5. Bendsøe, M.P., Sigmund, O.: Material interpolation schemes in topology optimization. Arch. Appl. Mech. **69**(9–10), 635–654 (1999)
6. Bi, S., Zhang, J., Zhang, G.: Scalable deep-learning-accelerated topology optimization for additively manufactured materials. arXiv preprint arXiv:2011.14177 (2020)
7. Goodfellow, I., et al.: Generative adversarial nets. In: Advances in Neural Information Processing Systems, pp. 2672–2680 (2014)
8. Guo, Y., Liu, Y., Oerlemans, A., Lao, S., Wu, S., Lew, M.S.: Deep learning for visual understanding: a review. Neurocomputing **187**, 27–48 (2016)
9. He, K., Zhang, X., Ren, S., Sun, J.: Deep residual learning for image recognition. In: Proceedings of the IEEE Conference on Computer Vision and Pattern Recognition, pp. 770–778 (2016)
10. Hoyer, S., Sohl-Dickstein, J., Greydanus, S.: Neural reparameterization improves structural optimization. arXiv preprint arXiv:1909.04240 (2019)
11. Kallioras, N.A., Kazakis, G., Lagaros, N.D.: Accelerated topology optimization by means of deep learning. Struct. Multi. Optim. **62**(3), 1185–1212 (2020)
12. Leary, M., Merli, L., Torti, F., Mazur, M., Brandt, M.: Optimal topology for additive manufacture: a method for enabling additive manufacture of support-free optimal structures. Mater. Des. **63**, 678–690 (2014)
13. Li, S., Yuan, S., Zhu, J., Wang, C., Li, J., Zhang, W.: Additive manufacturing-driven design optimization: building direction and structural topology. Add. Manuf. **36**, 101406 (2020)
14. Malviya, M.: A systematic study of deep generative models for rapid topology optimization (2020)
15. Mass, Y., Amir, O.: Topology optimization for additive manufacturing: accounting for overhang limitations using a virtual skeleton. Add. Manuf. **18**, 58–73 (2017)
16. Mirza, M., Osindero, S.: Conditional generative adversarial nets. arXiv preprint arXiv:1411.1784 (2014)
17. Nie, Z., Lin, T., Jiang, H., Kara, L.B.: Topologygan: topology optimization using generative adversarial networks based on physical fields over the initial domain. arXiv preprint arXiv:2003.04685 (2020)
18. Radford, A., Metz, L., Chintala, S.: Unsupervised representation learning with deep convolutional generative adversarial networks. arXiv preprint arXiv:1511.06434 (2015)
19. Rawat, S., Shen, M.H.H.: A novel topology optimization approach using conditional deep learning. arXiv preprint arXiv:1901.04859 (2019)
20. Rawat, W., Wang, Z.: Deep convolutional neural networks for image classification: a comprehensive review. Neural Comput. **29**(9), 2352–2449 (2017)
21. Ronneberger, O., Fischer, P., Brox, T.: U-Net: convolutional networks for biomedical image segmentation. In: Navab, N., Hornegger, J., Wells, W.M., Frangi, A.F. (eds.) MICCAI 2015. LNCS, vol. 9351, pp. 234–241. Springer, Cham (2015). https://doi.org/10.1007/978-3-319-24574-4_28
22. Sharpe, C., Seepersad, C.C.: Topology design with conditional generative adversarial networks. In: International Design Engineering Technical Conferences and Computers and Information in Engineering Conference, vol. 59186, p. V02AT03A062. American Society of Mechanical Engineers (2019)
23. Sigmund, O.: A 99 line topology optimization code written in matlab. Struct. Mult. Optim. **21**(2), 120–127 (2001)

24. Sigmund, O., Petersson, J.: Numerical instabilities in topology optimization: a survey on procedures dealing with checkerboards, mesh-dependencies and local minima. Struct. Optim. **16**(1), 68–75 (1998)
25. Sosnovik, I., Oseledets, I.: Neural networks for topology optimization. Russ. J. Numer. Anal. Math. Modell. **34**(4), 215–223 (2019)
26. Subedi, S.C., Verma, C.S., Suresh, K.: A review of methods for the geometric post-processing of topology optimized models. Journal of Computing and Information Science in Engineering, vol. 20, no. 6 (2020)
27. Szegedy, C., Ioffe, S., Vanhoucke, V., Alemi, A.A.: Inception-v4, inception-resnet and the impact of residual connections on learning. In: Thirty-First AAAI Conference on Artificial Intelligence (2017)
28. Ulu, E., Zhang, R., Kara, L.B.: A data-driven investigation and estimation of optimal topologies under variable loading configurations. Comput. Methods Biomech. Biomed. Eng. Imaging Vis. **4**(2), 61–72 (2016)
29. Wang, C., Qian, X.: Simultaneous optimization of build orientation and topology for additive manufacturing. Add. Manuf. **34**, 101246 (2020)
30. Yu, Y., Hur, T., Jung, J., Jang, I.G.: Deep learning for determining a near-optimal topological design without any iteration. Struct. Multi. Optim. **59**(3), 787–799 (2018). https://doi.org/10.1007/s00158-018-2101-5
31. Zhang, W., Zhou, L.: Topology optimization of self-supporting structures with polygon features for additive manufacturing. Comput. Methods Appl. Mech. Eng. **334**, 56–78 (2018)
32. Zhang, Z., Liu, Q., Wang, Y.: Road extraction by deep residual u-net. IEEE Geosci. Remote Sens. Lett. **15**(5), 749–753 (2018)
33. Zhao, Z.Q., Zheng, P., Xu, S.T., Wu, X.: Object detection with deep learning: a review. IEEE Trans. Neural Netw. Learn. Syst. **30**(11), 3212–3232 (2019)

Computational Ontology and BIM Technology in Data-Driven Indoor Route Planning

Barbara Strug[(⊠)] and Grażyna Ślusarczyk

Institute of Applied Computer Science, Jagiellonian University,
Lojasiewicza 11, 30-059 Kraków, Poland
{barbara.strug,grazyna.slusarczyk}@uj.edu.pl

Abstract. This paper deals with the problem of supporting the user in indoor route search. The application requires knowledge related to building structure and topology, and to functional and organizational structure of building spaces. The specified building ontology contains all concepts related to building elements enabling both vertical and horizontal communication and provided by Building Information Modeling (BIM). This ontology enables us to specify a graph, in which the required information (retrieved from the IFC file) representing the topology of the building is stored. The information about functional and organizational structure of building spaces is kept in the XML file. The knowledge stored in the graph and the XML file allows for generating the GUI of the application, where the start and end point of the search path together with personal preferences concerning this route, are specified. Then the modified Dijkstra algorithm is used to find the most appropriate route.

1 Introduction

This paper deals with the problem of supporting the user in indoor route search. The proposed application offers intelligent knowledge-based navigation, which supports moving around public buildings, taking into account the needs of people with disabilities. Therefore the information, which allows for finding different types of routes is needed. One type of knowledge necessary to generate an efficient application is the structure and topology of the building which is to be visited. The other one is related to semantics, i.e., the functional and organizational structure of building spaces together with positions, names and arrangements of people working in it. All this information together allows for specifying both complex criteria for a target place selection and for a required quality of a route.

Nowadays architectural building designs are often created with the use BIM technology. Such a project can be treated as a database that allows to record both technical information about building elements, and its purpose and history. Design data exchange is supported by the file format IFC (Industry Foundation Classes) [1] being an interoperable BIM standard for CAD applications. Although IFC is an open standard, its complex nature makes information retrieval difficult.

© Springer Nature Switzerland AG 2021
H. Fujita et al. (Eds.): IEA/AIE 2021, LNAI 12798, pp. 235–242, 2021.
https://doi.org/10.1007/978-3-030-79457-6_20

Therefore we provide the ontology, which includes BIM-specific concepts, their relations and attributes, and facilitates analysis of domain knowledge [2] as well as supports knowledge acquisition [3,4]. After determining concepts, relations and attributes, which are needed from the point of view of the problem being considered, like building spaces, their topology and accessibility between them, stairs, ramps, lifts and doors specification, this information can be retrieved from the appropriate IFC file.

This ontology enables us to specify a signature of a graph, in which the information retrieved from the IFC file is stored. A graph signature consists of node labels which correspond to ontology concepts, node attributes which correspond to ontology attributes and edge labels which describe relations between components. Giving such a signature, we can create a graph, where nodes represent building elements (spaces, rooms, stairs, lifts, ramps, etc.), while edges correspond to accessibility relations between these elements. Attributes assigned to graph nodes encode properties of building elements. Attributes of graph edges represent costs of moving between spaces, which can depend on existence of lifts, distances between spaces, and door types [5,6].

In order to create the building route searching application the information about functional and organizational structures of the building is needed. It is assumed that a file with an assignment of functional characteristics of building spaces, their organizational allocations and a register of persons working in them is given. Having such an assignment file and a graph containing semantic data about building constituent spaces and costs of moving between these spaces, any user-defined task related to path planning can be performed.

The proposed application is useful both for first-time visitors who want to find a specific place in an unknown building and for building occupants, building managers and maintenance operators who need support in their daily needs to move around the building. The interface of the application allows the user to specify the start and end point by selecting the space name, the room number, the organizational unit, or the person name. The user can also determine if the path which is looked for should/can contain lifts, stairs, ramps and heavy doors. Then the found path is shown on subsequent partial plans, on which the current place and the target place are marked.

2   Building Ontology

Before generation of UI of the application, the computational ontology related to buildings should be defined. This ontology provides a unified structure of concepts and relations possible between these concepts. The concepts are partially ordered according to a given specification hierarchy. Moreover, sets of attributes describing properties, are assigned to concepts.

The basic BIM-specific concepts, which are required in the ontology specified to support route searching tasks, are such building elements as floor, space, room, wall, opening, door, window, stair, lift, escalator and ramp. The concept *building* contains concepts *space* and *floor*. The concepts *stair, lift, escalator*

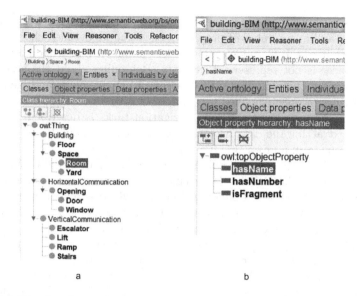

Fig. 1. (a) The class hierarchy in the building ontology in *Protègè* environment and (b) some of the properties defined for the classes depicted

and *ramp* are subconcepts of the concept *vertical_communication*. The concept *horizontal_communication* contains the concept *opening*, which in turn contains concepts *door* and *window*.

Two different relations between concepts are considered. The first one (denoted as *acc*) represents accessibility between spaces, while the second one (denoted as *isFragment*) specifies which building components constitute parts of the other concepts. Attributes, which specify areas, functional types, organizational and personal allocations, are assigned to the concepts *room* and *space*. To the concepts *stair, escalator* and *ramp* attributes specifying their sizes and slopes are assigned. The attributes which specify sizes and physical characteristics are assigned to *wall, door* and *window* concepts.

In Fig. 1a the concepts of the building domain are listed in the hierarchical structure. The ontology has been implemented using *Protègè* environment. In addition to the class hierarchy (taxonomy) presented in Fig. 1a there is a number of relations (properties) defined within the ontology (Fig. 1b). The property *hasName* is defined for all individuals belonging to the *Floor* class, which is the domain of this class. The property *hasNumber* is defined for all individuals belonging to the class *Room*. Moreover the property *isFragment* is used to relate the spaces and communication elements to the floors.

3   IFC File

The IFC file format [1] provides an object-oriented semantic data model for storing and exchanging building information. An IFC model is composed of IFC entities arranged in a hierarchical manner [7]. Each entity includes a fixed number of attributes and any number of properties encoding its detailed characteristics.

Hovewer, in an IFC model information about neighborhood or vicinity between spaces is not represented explicite. Reasoning about the accessibility between spaces requires finding walls common to these spaces and having non-closed openings or openings filled with a door or a window. The analysis of BIM and IFC building models for indoor navigation tasks is described in [8]. The method of extracting the data necessary to construct a graph-based model of a building layout from a given IFC file is presented in [5,6].

On the basis on the defined building ontology, the part of data which should be extracted from the IFC file is specified. The extracted semantic information concerning properties of building elements, which is related to route planning tasks, like room dimensions, types of doors, slopes of stairs, escalators and ramps, is stored in graph node attributes. The building entities extracted from the IFC file are IfcBuilding, IfcBuildingStorey, IfcSpace, which correspond to the ontology concepts representing places that can be visited, IfcWall, IfcOpening, IfsDoor, IfcWindow, which correspond to the ontology concepts representing elements allowing for communication on the same floor, IfcStair, IfcRamp, IfcTransportElement, which correspond to the ontology concepts representing elements allowing for communication between different floors. The accessibility between rooms or spaces is established by analyzing relations between the extracted elements. Two rooms or spaces are accessible from each other if they share a common transition element in the form of an opening or a door, in case of a horizontal transition, or in the form of stairs, a lift, an elevator or a ramp, in case of a vertical transition.

4   A Graph Based on the Ontology and IFC Files

The defined building ontology enables us to specify a signature of a graph, in which the information retrieved from the IFC file is stored. This signature consists of sets of node labels, node attributes and edge labels. A set of node labels contains functional types of spaces and rooms (like laboratory or work room) and names of elements allowing for vertical and horizontal communication. A set of node attributes contains attributes specified for ontology concepts, while edge labels describe relations between components specified in the ontology. Giving such a signature, we create an attributed, labelled and edge-directed graph, where nodes represent building elements extracted from the IFC data model (spaces, rooms, stairs, lifts, ramps, elevators), while edges correspond to vertical (openings or doors) or horizontal (stairs, lifts, ramps, elevators) accessibility and/or adjacency relations between these elements. Attributes assigned to graph nodes encode properties of building elements. Attributes of graph edges represent costs of moving between and through spaces, which depend on existence of lifts or ramps, distances between spaces, and door types. As the cost of passing the same path but in different direction may not be the same, due to slopes of stairs and ramps, and unalike forces needed for opening different types of doors, the graph is directed with two edges representing passing spaces in both directions.

For each IfcSpace, IfcStairs, IfcRamp or IfcTransportElement element, a node representing this elements is created. Then for each space all its bounding IfcWall elements are found and their openings are collected. If there exists an IfcDoor element filling the opening, then the door type and the direction of opening are stored in node attributes assigned to the same node. For each space with more than one door or opening costs of passing this space from any entry to any leaving point are stored in an attribute called lookup table. If two spaces share a common wall with an opening or door in it, the edges representing accessibility between spaces in both directions are added. The cost of passing between spaces is calculated on the basis of the cost of opening a door between them.

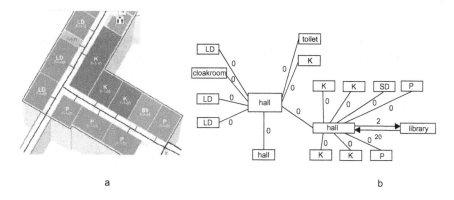

a   b

Fig. 2. (a) A plan of the first floor of the building (b) A graph with costs of passing between spaces of this layout

A fragment of the plan of the first floor of a building is shown in Fig. 2a. The doors of rooms are projected on the central line of the corridor in order to facilitate the calculation of the Euclidean distance between them. This space layout is represented by a graph shown in Fig. 2b. Graph nodes labelled P represent work rooms, nodes labelled K represent computer rooms, nodes labelled LD represent laboratories, the node labelled SD represents a classroom. Edges connecting nodes representing the right-hand side hall and library have the cost 2 and 20, as they represent the effort needed to push and pull, respectively, the fire doors between *hall* and *library*. The cost of opening the standard doors is set to 0 as there is no possibility to avoid them.

5   Path Finding Application

The UI of the an application supporting the user in finding routes is generated on the basis of an IFC file containing information about building elements and an XML file which contains the information on the function, organizational allocation and occupancy of each space in the building. The file is generated in a semi-automatic way, i.e. the list of possible spaces/rooms and their association with buildings and floors is obtained from the IFC file. The list of possible functions and organizational hierarchy within a given institution using a building is derived from the instantiation of the ontology. The other elements of the file, like persons names and their association with actual rooms are introduced manually.

On the basis of the BIM ontology and its instance together with the IFC file an XML file is created. Then the XML file is used as the data for the UI generator. The UI is used to select start and end points in the building. These points in turn are passed back to the graph, on which a path searching algorithm is run and the resulting route is passed back to the UI for the user to present. As the user does not have to know the number of a room he is searching for, the user interface provides different search criteria.

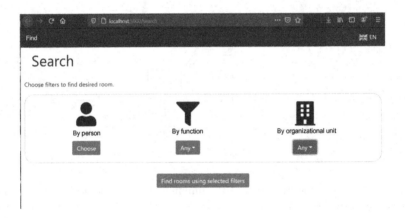

Fig. 3. The main search screen of the UI

A web-based application based on the proposed approach has been implemented and tested [9]. The screenshots of the user interface based on the data describing the FAIS building are presented in Figs. 3, 4 and 5. In Fig. 3 the main search screen is depicted. It allows the user to select filters for finding a start or target room. The filters are based on person names, function of rooms or their assignment to a particular unit within the faculty. Figure 4 top depicts a window showing the possible choices within the search by function of the space and Fig. 4 bottom shows the search result for a room with a function *classroom* and located within the main faculty unit. The numbers of found rooms are shown. Figure 5a depicts a window showing the combination of selections where a *workroom* has been selected as the function, and the *ZTG* as an organizational unit. Figure 5b shows the search result window for the workroom located within the main *ZTG* unit. The result shows the numbers of all found rooms as well as the persons assigned to them.

Fig. 4. (a) The search window for selecting room by function and (b) the result window for the room function "classroom" search

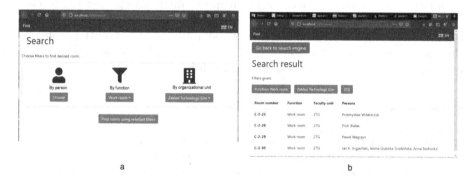

Fig. 5. (a) The search window for the combined search on function and organizational unit and (b) the result window.

When the user is presented with several rooms matching the search conditions (as many spaces located in different parts of the building can have the same functions, like toilets, entrances/exits or cloakrooms) he can select a single room. In the next step, both selected rooms are converted into a pair of numbers representing path source and target points, which is then passed to the graph. Then the modified Dijkstra algorithm, where costs of passing through different spaces and between them are considered, is used to find the most appropriate route for the user. At the end the obtained path is shown on subsequent partial plans, on which the current place and the target one are marked.

6   Conclusions

In this paper the problem of extracting knowledge required for creating the application supporting the building route search is considered. The computational building ontology, which determines concepts, relations and attributes needed to support route searching tasks, is specified. Then the instance ontology for the considered building is created. This ontology enables to retrieve from the building IFC file elements representing spaces and elements enabling both vertical and horizontal communication. The obtained data is stored in the graph representing the topology of the building. The proposed user interface of the application is derived from the knowledge stored in the graph and additional information about functional and organizational structure of building spaces kept in the XML file. It enables the user to specify source and target points of the searched path by selecting the space name, the room number, the organizational unit, or the person name. Personal preferences concerning the communication way, like the necessity to use lifts or ramps, can also be specified.

It should be noted that the proposed ontology can be easily extended to contain other concepts useful for task-specific requirements. For example in case of searching for routs which would be helpful for people responsible for electrical installation maintenance, the ontology should contain concepts related to electrical appliances, sockets, switches, distributions boards, etc. In future we plan to extend the approach by adding more possibilities for search options, offering the user some choices over how the route is generated. Also selecting several points through which the path should lead will be considered.

References

1. Building SMART International: IFC introduction. https://www.buildingsmart.org/about/what-is-openbim/ifc-introduction/. Accessed 10 Dec 2019
2. Noy, N.F., McGuinness, D.L.: Ontology Development 101: A Guide to Creating Your First Ontology. Stanford, Technical report KSL-01-05 (2001)
3. Milton, N.R.: Knowledge Acquisition in Practice: A Step-by-step Guide. Springer, London (2007)
4. Munir, K., Anjum, M.: The use of ontologies for effective knowledge modelling and information retrieval. Appl. Comput. Inform. **14**, 116–126 (2018)
5. Strug, B., Ślusarczyk, G.: Reasoning about accessibility for disabled using building graph models based on BIM/IFC. J. Vis. Eng. **5**, 1–12 (2017)
6. Ismail, A., Strug, B., Ślusarczyk, G.: Building knowledge extraction from BIM/IFC data for analysis in graph databases. In: Rutkowski, L., Scherer, R., Korytkowski, M., Pedrycz, W., Tadeusiewicz, R., Zurada, J.M. (eds.) ICAISC 2018. LNCS (LNAI), vol. 10842, pp. 652–664. Springer, Cham (2018). https://doi.org/10.1007/978-3-319-91262-2_57
7. Ismail, A., Nahar, A., Scherer, R.: Application of graph databases and graph theory concepts for advanced analysing of BIM models based on IFC standard. In: Proceedings of the 24th EG-ICE International Workshop. Nottingham, UK (2017)
8. Isikdag, U., Zlatanova, S., Underwood, J.: A BIM-oriented model for supporting indoor navigation requirements. Comput. Environ. Urban Syst. **41**, 112–123 (2013)
9. Lebioda, R.: Generating user interfaces based on XML files. Master Thesis. Jagiellonian University (2020)

Collaborative Maintenance of EDOAL
Alignments in VocBench

Armando Stellato[(⊠)] [ID], Manuel Fiorelli [ID], Tiziano Lorenzetti [ID],
and Andrea Turbati [ID]

Department of Enterprise Engineering, University of Rome "Tor Vergata", Via del Politecnico 1,
00133 Rome, Italy
stellato@uniroma2.it, {fiorelli,turbati}@info.uniroma2.it

Abstract. Ontology Alignment, intended in its broadest meaning of alignment
between datasets of different nature – thesauri, ontologies, and even mere instance
data – is a well-known practice aiming at realizing semantic links between datasets
on the (Semantic) Web. Considerable investigation has been carried on the automatic computation of alignments and on how to assess the quality of such process.
This is indeed a critical aspect, considering the non-trivial size of many datasets.
However, since human intervention is in any case essential, no less care should
be paid on scalability both in terms of distribution of work and of maintenance
of achieved results within the lifecycle of the aligned resources. In this paper
we guide the reader through the diverse solutions that have been implemented
in VocBench, a collaborative editing platform for RDF datasets, under a holistic
approach to collaborative alignment development and maintenance.

1 Introduction

The Semantic Web [1] has offered a powerful stack of standard languages and protocols for modeling, sharing and reuse of knowledge on the Web. However, the advantages brought by metadata standards and infrastructures for shareability of information
cannot avoid (but can support) the reconciliation work needed on the information content. Different, domain-overlapping, redundant to different extents, ontologies, thesauri,
vocabularies, datasets etc. are expected to emerge on the Web to satisfy specific needs
and exigencies and, at different points in time, are expected as well to be – somehow
– "reconciled" out of their heterogeneities, for interoperability's sake.

This "reconciliation" takes the form of alignments, that is, sets of correspondences
between the different entities that populate lexical and semantic resources on the Web.
The expression "ontology alignment" is often used in a broader sense than the one that
the first word of the term would suggest. "Ontology" is in this case a synecdoche for
ontologies, thesauri, lexicons and any sorts of knowledge resources modeled according
to core knowledge modeling languages for the Semantic Web, which were shared and
made available on the Web itself. The expression ontology alignment thus defines the task
of discovering and assessing alignments between ontologies and other data models of the
RDF family; alternative expressions are *ontology mapping* or *ontology matching* (as the
produced alignments are also referred to as *matches*). In the RDF jargon, and following

© Springer Nature Switzerland AG 2021
H. Fujita et al. (Eds.): IEA/AIE 2021, LNAI 12798, pp. 243–254, 2021.
https://doi.org/10.1007/978-3-030-79457-6_21

the terminology adopted in the VoID metadata vocabulary [2], a set of alignments is also called a *Linkset*.

The production of alignments is an intensive and error prone-task; for this reason, several approaches for automating the task have been devised [3] since the early years of the Semantic Web. An Ontology Alignment Evaluation Initiative[1] [4] is also held every year since 2004 with the intent of evaluating available tools against benchmarks consisting in well-assessed alignments between notable semantic resources (mostly ontologies, and some thesauri). The task are also divided into T-Box/Schema matching, dealing – as the name suggests – with the alignment of ontology vocabularies (i.e. world models including classes and properties), and instance matching, involving the creation of links between domain objects represented in different datasets.

In this work we present our approach for holistic management of alignments within our collaboration platform called VocBench [5]. The proposed solution is characterized by a multitude of tools, features and functionalities, all interconnected within a more general platform for collaborative management of RDF vocabularies and datasets.

2 Related Work

Even if shadowed for the most by research on automatic computation of alignments, the importance of alignment maintenance and of collaboration on their evolution has not been underestimated.

Limiting our overview to ontologies (as there is a large literature on database schema matching), one of the first, if not the first, collaborative platforms for alignment maintenance is probably Chimaera [6], a web based tool for merging ontologies and checking the correctness of ontologies. Chimera mixes automatic procedures (integrated with the platform) with interfaces for displaying the knowledge content and allowing for users to validate the produced mappings.

Another relevant work is represented by the MAFRA toolkit [7], a mapping framework for distributed ontologies that introduced the concept of transformation. In MAFRA, the objective is not just to find correspondences, rather being able to transform content objects that are specified in one dataset into their corresponding version (which may vary in the structure) on the aligned dataset. MAFRA is antecedent to the release of SPARQL as a query and update language for the Semantic Web, hence the need for expressing these transformations through a dedicated language.

The Alignment API [8] provided several contributions to the community, as other than representing, as their name suggest, a reusable set of API for managing alignments, they come together with an Alignment Server – an online service for alignment manipulation (creation, modification, display) – and a dedicated language, EDOAL, which has become a standard de-facto interchange format for representing alignments as first-class citizens i.e. they are not just triples using alignment predicates from OWL and SKOS to map resources from a source and a target dataset, rather resources themselves containing links and providing further information such as the strength of the alignment. Thanks to the reification of the alignments, it is possible to attach to them further

---

[1] http://oaei.ontologymatching.org/.

metadata. VocBench adopts EDOAL and indeed extends it with a vocabulary of further information for both storing the progress in the validation of alignments and, conversely, exploiting the data for evaluating the quality of automatic alignment tools.

More recently, the Agreement Maker [9] platform capitalized the experiences of past approaches, specifically in the geospatial domain, with a visual software tool for creating mappings between two ontologies, generating an agreement document.

Nowadays, support, at different levels, for collaborative alignments is also provided by most collaborative editing platforms, such as Semantic Web Company's PoolParty [10] and TopQuadrant's TopBraid Enterprise Data Governance (EDG).[2]

3   The VocBench Collaborative Editing Platform

VocBench 3 is a free and open-source advanced collaboration environment for creating and maintaining ontologies, thesauri, code lists, authority tables, lexicons, link sets and datasets, in compliance with Semantic Web standards recommended by the W3C.

VocBench 3 (from now on, VocBench or simply VB) is used to maintain vocabularies and ontologies in a wide number of domains, including the agrifood sector (e.g. [11, 12], see also [13] for a more thorough overview), government data, thesauri, ontologies (e.g. the Teseo thesaurus[3] of the Italian Senate of the Republic or EU's multilingual thesaurus EuroVoc[4] and many other semantic resources managed by the European Commission, such as the Common Metadata Model [14] ontology, thus exploiting the widened support of VB3 for OWL ontologies) and several others.

The user community's main point of interaction and support is the VocBench discussion group[5]. The group (as of 20th January 2021) counts 213 members.

The VocBench 3 project is funded by Action 1.1 of the ISA2 Programme of the European Commission for "Interoperability solutions for public administrations, businesse"'s and citizens". The VocBench site[6] contains documentation, download links and other references. VocBench supports different user profiles in fulfilling their job by providing different functionalities tailored for their roles. As a software suite, many of the tools offered by VocBench are available as separate components that can be integrated in other software. Depending on the standard being adopted and the type of user, the system provides several user-tailored facilities for easily modeling the needed resource and toggles or makes optional (with properly conceived default settings) various features. Quality checking is provided by dedicated Integrated Constraint Validation tools (ICVs) and by support for SHACL shapes.

---

[2] https://www.topquadrant.com/products/topbraid-enterprise-data-governance/.

[3] http://www.senato.it/tesauro/teseo.html.

[4] https://data.europa.eu/euodp/data/dataset/eurovoc.

[5] http://groups.google.com/group/vocbench-user.

[6] http://vocbench.uniroma2.it.

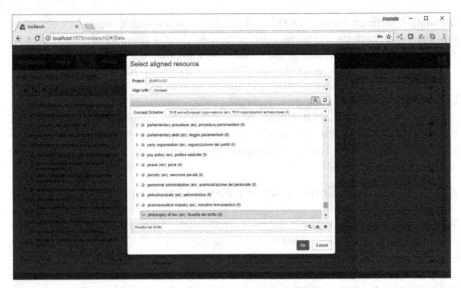

Fig. 1. On-the-fly manual alignment of concepts from the TESEO thesaurus to concepts from EuroVoc.

4 Alignment Support in VocBench at Large

VocBench does not provide a single entry point for addressing alignment development, rather alignment support is a pervasive aspect appearing in diverse points of the user experience. Roughly, we can identify the following entry points for performing/maintaining alignments:

- Alignment from within the resource-view
- Manual alignment (search based)
- Semi-automatic (search keywords based on available labels)
- Alignment Validation
- Input coming from a static EDOAL file
- Input coming from the invocation of an automatic alignment system
- EDOAL projects

4.1 Alignment from within the Resource View

The first possibility represents the quickest and most flexible choice, as it is embodied by an action that can be performed from within any kind of project (i.e. for any nature of the dataset, be it an ontology, thesaurus, lexicon or mere data), linking to both internally managed datasets (i.e. other projects within the same VocBench installation) and datasets on the Web (by exploiting well known practices for discovering them and exploiting available metadata for knowing how to inspect the content and what to look for), without any prior preparation/setup. From within the resource view, the panel that shows all the details of a selected resource, it is possible to select an option for aligning it to an external resource from another dataset, then the user is prompted for three possible choices:

Fig. 2. Alignment through assisted search of concepts from the TESEO thesaurus to concepts from EuroVoc directly from the SPARQL endpoint of the original dataset on the Web.

- Aligning to a resource from a project, by browsing the content of the project
- Aligning by means of assisted search; this option is available for both projects and external datasets hosted on the Web
- Manually enter the value of an aligned resource

In the first option, a list of projects generated by filtering those that can be accessed by the project being managed (depending on the ACL, see later) is shown to the user: the selected one will be the "target project" for choosing the aligned resource. After the user selects the target project, a dialog such as the one in Fig. 1 is prompted to the user, who can then explore the resources through convenient browsing panels (i.e. class/property/concept/collection trees for owl classes, SKOS concepts/collections or RDF properties in general, lists for concept schemes and class tree and related lists of instances for each class in the case of owl individuals). The ACL (Access Control List) is an access matrix in VocBench telling which projects can access the content of other projects. This access is indeed a delegation to users, so that if project A grants access to project B, this means that any user that has been granted access to project B, no matter their relationship with project A, may access the content of this latter by means of the permission from A to B and the delegation of all users of B.

The second option for alignment exploits dataset's metadata in order to automatically select the search keywords for the target dataset. The keywords basically come from the labels of the resource to be aligned (the one from the source dataset). What is interesting is the choice of the language of the labels (Fig. 2). To reduce the complexity of the query, which would imply (in case the source is characterized by lexicalizations

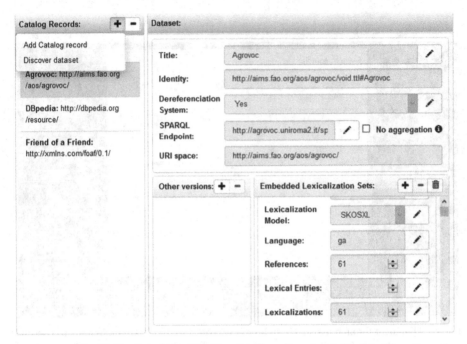

Fig. 3. User interface of the Metadata Repository inside VocBench3

in many languages) an OR clause of several terms, the system presents the lexicalization languages that are common to both the datasets and ranks them according to an average of the quality of their related lexicalizations for both datasets. This quality is mainly measured in terms of coverage of the dataset (the percentage of resources that are lexicalized in that given language) and, on a second order, on the lexical richness in that language (the overall number of lexicalizations, thus revealing the presence of alternative expressions, synonyms etc.).

Finally, dealing with the trivial case of already assessed alignments only needing to be added to a dataset, it is possible to manually add a link to a resource by explicitly expressing that resource through its IRI.

4.2 The Metadata Registry

The way the lexicalization metadata (used to power the semi-automatic alignment) is obtained is another peculiar characteristic of the VocBench platform, which tries to exploit Semantic Web principles to their full potential. VocBench features, among its diverse components, a *metadata registry* [15]. This registry contains metadata related.

The dataset metadata's model is a combination of different vocabularies (among these: DCAT [16], VoID [2] and LIME [17]), enriched with some system-specific information. In particular, LIME (LInguistic MEtadata vocabulary), developed by these same authors in the context of the OntoLex community group, and based on previous research

Fig. 4. The Alignment Validation interface of VocBench 3to both the datasets edited within the platform and other datasets on the Web, and supports different strategies to acquire it.

on automatic coordination for alignments [18, 19], provides rich statistical and qualitative information about the lexical asset of datasets and drives the coordination of resources and algorithms for performing alignments between heterogeneous sources.

The description of local projects combines information found in some configuration files with metadata generated through a profiler provided by our LIME API [20], while the description of remote projects may come directly from their metadata files exposed on the web or can be profiled as well (at least for the statistical part). A discovery mechanism allows for finding metadata files on the Web starting from just the IRI of any single resource belonging to the dataset, by following well known principles for publishing datasets[7]. An editor for the registry (Fig. 3) allows for the modification of the metadata gathered through the above different way and for grouping diverse datasets as different versions and/or distributions of a same one.

4.3 Alignment Validation

VocBench features an Alignment Validation page, providing several instruments (indeed, due to the later evolutions, this page is soon to be renamed "Alignment Management") for building and validating alignments.

Once the page has been accessed, the first option being prompted is whether to load an already available alignment document – i.e. a set of mappings between two datasets expressed according to the EDOAL [8] vocabulary – or to produce one by means of an external alignment system.

In the first case, a set of alignments (also referred as *linkset*) to another dataset is loaded in the validation interface (see Fig. 4). The alignment interface shows a list of

---

[7] http://linkeddatabook.com/editions/1.0/.

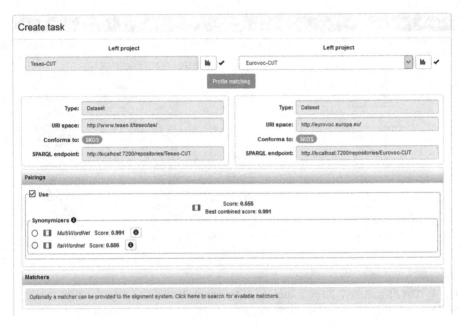

Fig. 5. Defining an alignment scenario through the MAPLE UI of VB3

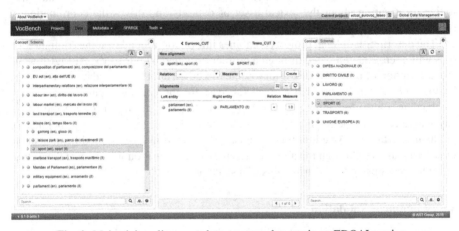

Fig. 6. Maintaining alignments between two datasets in an EDOAL projec

aligned resources. For each alignment, a resource from the source dataset (the one being managed within the active project) and one from the target dataset are linked to each other. A "relation" expressed, according to the EDOAL vocabulary, the nature of this link. EDOAL provides an (extensible) set of relations providing shallow semantics for the concept of broader/narrower/equivalent. The "strength" of the relation is expressed by a quantity (in the range of 0..1) representing how reliable the link is. Each link can be accepted or rejected; in the former case, it is possible to define a mapping property from the OWL or SKOS vocabulary that will instantiate the relation. We have extended the EDOAL standard by allowing for storing both the progress in the validation and the mapping property that has been selected. The use of stored alignments is twofold: it can be simply used to restore an incomplete validation process in order to finish the job or, even when completed, could be used as an oracle for evaluating the quality of automatically produced alignments.

4.4 External Alignment Systems

A second option for alignment validation enables communication with external alignment systems in order to produce fresh new alignments to be validated. This communication is managed by a dedicated component in VocBench called MAPLE. Given a matching task, MAPLE first analyzes the context of the alignment by inspecting the metadata of the two datasets (if the metadata is missing, dedicated profilers can produce this metadata on the fly and store it in the metadata registry of VocBench) and establishing the best matching lexicalizations from the two involved datasets, the requirements for their analysis (e.g. being able to read a certain lexical model, such as SKOS-XL or OntoLex) and other boundary conditions. MAPLE can also produce information about known lexical datasets (e.g. wordnets) that can be used as supporting resources for expanding the available lexical knowledge and provide a better bridge between the lexical description of the two datasets to be aligned. The result of this analysis is then compiled into a task report (Fig. 5) that is communicated to a downstream matching system, which executes the matching process. It is worth noticing that, as such, the system has no specific performance but completely demands the computation of the alignments to the external, connected, alignment systems.

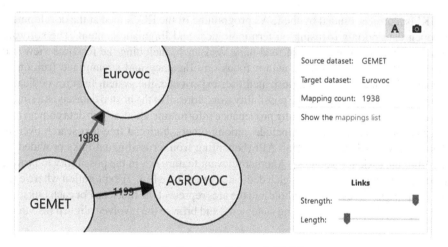

Fig. 7. Browsing linksets in PMKI

The principle of communication with MAPLE is realized through an open API for alignment[8] [21] that external systems may comply with. Currently, there are two systems adopting this API: Genoma [22], a simple yet highly configurable alignment system developed by part of the same team that developed VocBench, and NAISC[9] [23], an alignment tool created by the SFI Insight Centre for Data Analytics in the context of the Horizon 2020 ELEXIS project (grant agreement No 731015).

4.5 EDOAL Projects

The last (also in temporal terms, as it has been introduced in version 7 of VocBench, released on the first quarter of 2020) addition to VocBench for supporting development of alignments is the introduction of EDOAL projects. EDOAL projects have alignment as their first-class citizens. The typical scenario for this kind of project is collaborative development of alignments, independent from the maintenance of the aligned datasets. For instance, two organizations maintaining their own datasets may decide to collaborate on the development of a common linkset among their datasets. Obviously, neither of the two organizations want to give the other access to their maintained copy of the dataset, they thus setup an independent project, linked in read-only mode to a copy of the (or even the originally maintained) datasets. There data can be created, evolved, in an alignment-centric way: there is no source/target dataset; alignments are reified and equally maintained by both parties and observed by comparing the two datasets side-by-side (Fig. 6), who can then export them as simple mapping triples, placing their own resources as subject.

5 Hosting an Open Data Portal [PMKI]

PMKI is a project funded by the ISA2 programme of the EU, aimed at the development of open data portals focusing on terminological and linguistic content. The software powering the portal is a sort of read-only VocBench, including the resource view and much of the browsing views, with a focus on efficiency and streamlined fruition of content. Besides the browsing-oriented user experience, the system features dedicated capabilities mostly based on the possibility to explore all of the hosted datasets as a single, large, resource, while still keeping provenance information about which data comes from which project. These features include, among others, a global free-text search over all datasets and machine translation API (benefiting from cross-lingual links provided by multilingual lexical resources). Another relevant feature lies in the possibility to browse linksets between datasets through a dedicated graph (see Fig. 7) exploration where each node represents a dataset as a whole and the arcs represent the linksets. For each linkset, it is then possible to list its mapping statements and browse the involved aligned resources.

---

[8] https://bitbucket.org/art-uniroma2/maple/src/master/maple-alignment-services-api/src/main/openapi/alignment-services.yaml.

[9] https://elex.is/new-out-now-naisc-1-0/.

6 Conclusions

In this paper we have detailed, through the example of the VocBench platform, several supporting features that we consider of primary importance for the maintenance of alignments during their whole lifetime. The described features have been developed through a few years, across different iterations of the platform, however they all were part of a single design that aims at conceiving alignments as fundamental building blocks of the Semantic Web architecture, needing not only to be discovered and developed, but also maintained in a continuous lifecycle, kept alive by the same resources they link. Future work will focus even more on this latter aspect, improving the coordination between projects in order to keep alignments up-to-date with the evolution of the aligned datasets. There are still some functionalities for reporting broken links, but we plan to go further in exploring and exploiting the available alignments and the aligned content in order to automatically provide suggested actions to perform.

References

1. Berners-Lee, T., Hendler, J.A., Lassila, O.: The semantic web: a new form of web content that is meaningful to computers will unleash a revolution of new possibilities. Sci. Am. **279**(5), 34–43 (2001)
2. Alexander, K., Cyganiak, R., Hausenblas, M., Zhao, J.: Describing linked datasets with the VoID vocabulary (W3C interest group note). In: World Wide Web Consortium (W3C). http://www.w3.org/TR/void/.Accessed 3 March 2011
3. Euzenat, J., Shvaiko, P.: Ontology Matching,vol. 18, 2nd edn. Springer-Verlag Berlin, Heidelberg (2013)
4. Dragisic, Z., et al.: Results of the ontology alignment evaluation initiative. In: 9th International Workshop on Ontology Matching, vol. 1317, pp. 61–104. Riva del Garda, Trentino, Italy, 20 October 2014
5. Stellato, A., et al.: VocBench 3: a collaborative semantic web editor for ontologies, thesauri and lexicons. Semantic Web **11**(5), 855–881 (2020)
6. McGuinness, D.L., Fikes, R., Rice, J., Wilder, S.: The Chimaera ontology environment. In: Proceedings of AAAI, pp. 1123–1124 (2000)
7. Maedche, A., Motik, B., Silva, N., Volz, R.: Mafra a mapping framework for distributed ontologies. In: International Conference on Knowledge Engineering and Knowledge Management, pp. 235–250 (2002)
8. David, J., Euzenat, J., Scharffe, F., Trojahn dos Santos, C.: The Alignment API 4.0. Semantic Web Journal, **2**(1), 3–10 (2011)
9. Cruz, I.F., Sunna, W., Makar, N., Bathala, S.: A visual tool for ontology alignment to enable geospatial interoperability. J. Vis. Lang. Comput. **18**(3), 230–254 (2007)
10. Schandl, T., Blumauer, A.: PoolParty: SKOS thesaurus management utilizing linked data. In: Aroyo, L., Antoniou, G., Hyvönen, E., ten Teije, A., Stuckenschmidt, H., Cabral, L., Tudorache, T., eds. : The Semantic Web: Research and Applications (Lecture Notes in Computer Science) 6089. Springer, Berlin, Heidelberg, pp. 421-425 (2010)
11. Caracciolo, C., et al.: The AGROVOC Linked Dataset. Sem. Web J. **4**(3), 341–348 (2013)
12. Anibaldi, S., Jaques, Y., Celli, F., Stellato, A., Keizer, J.: Migrating bibliographic datasets to the Semantic Web: the agris case. semantic web ISSN for online version, vol. 6, pp. 2210–4968 (2015)

13. Caracciolo, C., et al.: 39 Hints to facilitate the use of semantics for data on agriculture and nutrition. Data Sci. J. **19**(1), 47 (2020)

14. Francesconi, E., Küster, M.W., Gratz, P., Thelen, S.: The ontology-based approach of the publications office of the eu for document accessibility and open data services. In : International Conference on Electronic Government and the Information Systems Perspective (EGOVIS 2015), Valencia, Spain (2015)

15. Fiorelli, M., et al.: Metadata-driven semantic coordination. In: Garoufallou, E., Fallucchi, F., William De Luca, E. (eds.) MTSR 2019. CCIS, vol. 1057, pp. 16–27. Springer, Cham (2019). https://doi.org/10.1007/978-3-030-36599-8_2

16. World Wide Web Consortium (W3C): Data Catalog Vocabulary (DCAT). In: World Wide Web Consortium (W3C). http://www.w3.org/TR/vocab-dcat/.Accessed 16 Jan 2014

17. Fiorelli, M., Stellato, A., Mccrae, J.P., Cimiano, P., Pazienza, M.T.: LIME: the metadata module for ontolex. In: Gandon, F., Sabou, M., Sack, H., d'Amato, C., Cudré-Mauroux, P., Zimmermann, A. (eds.) : The Semantic Web. Latest Advances and New Domains (Lecture Notes in Computer Science). Proceedings of the 12th Extended Semantic Web Conference (ESWC 2015), 9088, pp. 321-336, Portoroz, Slovenia, May 31-4 June 2015. Springer International Publishing (2015)

18. Pazienza, M.T., Sguera, S., Stellato, A.: Let's talk about our "being": a linguistic-based ontology framework for coordinating agents. Appl. Ontology Spec. issue Formal Ontologies Commun. Agents **2**(3–4), 305–332 (2007)

19. Pazienza, M.T., Stellato, A., Turbati, A.: Linguistic watermark 3.0: an RDF framework and a software library for bridging language and ontologies in the Semantic Web. In: 5th Workshop on Semantic Web Applications and Perspectives (SWAP2008), Rome, Italy, CEUR Workshop Proceedings, FAO-UN, Rome, Italy, vol. 426, pp. 11, 15–17 December 2008

20. Fiorelli, M., Pazienza, M.T., Stellato, A.: An API for OntoLex LIME datasets. In: OntoLex-2017 1st Workshop on the OntoLex Model (co-located with LDK-2017), Galway (2017)

21. Fiorelli, M., Stellato, A.: A lime-flavored RESTAPI for alignment services. In: Ionov, M., McCrae, J.P., Chiarcos, C., Declerck, T., Bosque-Gil, J., Gracia, J., (eds.) Proceedings of the 7th Workshop on Linked Data in Linguistics (LDL-2020). European Language Resources Association, pp. 52–60 (2020)

22. Enea, R., Pazienza, M.T., Turbati, A.: GENOMA: GENeric ontology matching architecture. In: Gavanelli, M., Lamma, E., Riguzzi, F. (eds.) AI*IA 2015. LNCS (LNAI), vol. 9336, pp. 303–315. Springer, Cham (2015). https://doi.org/10.1007/978-3-319-24309-2_23

23. McCrae, J.P., Buitelaar, P.: Linking datasets using semantic textual similarity. Cybern. Inf. Technol. **8**(1), 109–123 (2018)

DIKG2: A Semantic Data Integration Approach for Knowledge Graphs Generation from Web Forms

Rahma Dandan$^{(\boxtimes)}$ (ID) and Sylvie Despres

Sorbonne Paris Nord University, 93000 Bobigny, France
{rahma.dandan,sylvie.despres}@univ-paris13.fr

Abstract. Over the last two decades, semantic-based data integration has become one of the major data challenges. The use of semantic Web standards and Linked Open Data (LOD), especially knowledge graphs (KGs), provides support to address issues related to data access and integration. In this paper, we propose the approach DIKG2 to structure semi-structured data from Web forms and stored in a RDB and to facilitate the dynamic data integration in the KGs. By exploiting a common vocabulary between the Web forms and the entities of our domain ontology, OAFE, we describe the mapping process performed between RDB schema and the ontology's conceptual schema.

Keywords: Semantic data integration · Knowledge Graph · Ontology based data integration · User profiling · Personalized recommendation

1 Introduction

Over the past two decades, semantic-based data integration has become one of the major data challenges. The concept of Knowledge Graph (KG), adopted by the Semantic Web community, is one of the ways to aggregate knowledge from different domains and quickly and easily find new information about entities. However, creating knowledge graphs, from structured or unstructured data, is not an obvious task. When the data interoperability issue is not taken into account, data integration becomes a real challenge. Thus, the implementation of a strategy for structuring data, regardless of its source, facilitates the management of this problem. To make sense of the data and ensure consistency between the data to be integrated and the domain knowledge, ontologies are fundamental. They allow to represent and formally define the knowledge (concepts and relations between these concepts) of the studied domain. The use of ontologies for the KGs generation allow to link and improve the results expected by information systems, particularly recommendation systems.

The application context of this work is that of sedentary lifestyle prevention. Indeed, in recent years, demographic ageing and sedentary lifestyle have become one of the main public health problems in France. Because recommendations are

© Springer Nature Switzerland AG 2021
H. Fujita et al. (Eds.): IEA/AIE 2021, LNAI 12798, pp. 255–260, 2021.
https://doi.org/10.1007/978-3-030-79457-6_22

not specific, the development of a recommendation system based on individual data is becoming an unavoidable need. The work presented in this paper is based on a preliminary work carried out for the design of an ontological resource, OAFE (Ontology Activity For Elderly), needed to develop a personalized activity recommendation based on the profile of elderly.

The objective of this paper is to present the approach DIKG2 allowing the structuring of semi-structured data from Web forms stored in a relational database (RDB), and facilitating the dynamic and semantic integration of data in KGs. By exploiting a common vocabulary between Web forms and OAFE entities, we describe in this approach the mapping achieved between the database schema and the conceptual schema of the domain ontology. The knowledge graph built and enriched with the knowledge of OAFE is used for the elderly profile construction leading to personalized recommendation elaboration.

In the following section, we present the context related to the integration of data from RDB. Before concluding, we present in Sect. 3 the approach DIKG2 leading to their structuring and integration into knowledge graph.

2   Related Works

2.1   Ontologies and Data Integration

The work presented in this paper falls within a broad area of data integration. Data integration must be able to provide uniform and transparent access to manipulate multiple, stand-alone, heterogeneous, structured or semi-structured sources of data. The heterogeneity of format, structure, access mode, models, schema, semantics and data processing capacity make this task difficult to apply. Despite the considerable efforts made, various interoperability issues remain unresolved. To achieve data interoperability, the problem of data heterogeneity must be eliminated. In this paper, we address the problem of structural heterogeneity and semantic data integration. This process requires using the conceptual representation of data and their relationships to eliminate possible heterogeneities.

Currently, a large amount of data is stored in RDB. A multitude of approaches and techniques have been proposed in recent years for mapping data from RDB to RDF. The RDB2RDF working group of the W3C proposed, a few years ago, two standard recommendations: R2RML mapping language and Direct Mapping. Since then, Direct Mapping has become the most dominant approach in most studies which uses simple rules to convert RDB data into RDF format. However, instance generation from this approach does not take into account the semantics of the data. Because the conceptual schema of the data is not considered, using this approach to create a knowledge graph complicates the task of mapping process to the RDB and the ontology schema. Some studies have appeared lately [2,7] to adapt approaches based on the RDB2RDF method. However, the majority of tools using this type of approach are not available or not usable as such. This shows the need to adapt existing mapping approaches between the two heterogeneous systems that are RDB and ontologies.

3   Presentation of Approach DIKG2

Semantic data integration requires structuring the data collected and stored in RDB. This step is essential to facilitate data integration into KG. The different steps leading to the KG construction are represented in Fig. 1 and are detailed in the following sections.

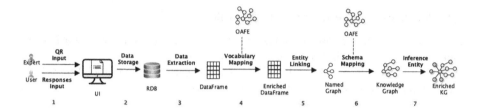

Fig. 1. Overview of data integration process leading to KG generation

3.1   Data Collection, Extraction and Structuring

The data collection step (step 1 of Fig. 1) is a fundamental component of any KG construction pipeline. It allows to acquire a maximum of information on user that is essential for building his profile and developing a personalized recommendation. This step consists of integrating questionnaires (unofficial and official) from a Web interface designed for this purpose and collecting, via a Web interface, the users' responses. From the questionnaires selected by the domain expert and presented to the user via Web forms, the user's answers are stored in a RDB (step2).

To get away from the constraints related to the RDB structure, the data are extracted and then structured in DataFrames (step 3) to then be merged into a single DataFrame (DataFrame 1) (Fig. 2). The advantage of the DataFrame is that it offers a two-dimensional structure in which the data can be stored in objects, which facilitates the manipulation of the data, in particular thanks to the indexes. The data structuring into the DataFrame 1, mainly depends on the questionnaires structure. A questionnaire is made up of a set of questions. Depending on question type (text field, checkbox, etc.), each question is associated with one or a set of propositions and the user provides or chooses the corresponding answer(s). The construction of RDF triple will thus consist in associating an answer to its user (Fig. 3).

Fig. 2. Steps to structure data from an RDB in a single DataFrame.

Fig. 3. Generating RDF triples from the Web form structure

3.2 Data Enrichment and Entity Linking

The KG generation requires to rely on the OAFE vocabulary to enrich the collected data. For this purpose, the elements of interest of OAFE (Classes, Object and Data Properties (OP/DP) and their corresponding labels) have been extracted and structured in DataFrames (Fig. 4).

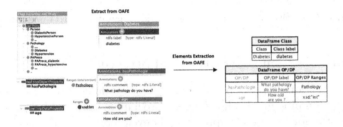

Fig. 4. Extraction of elements of interest from OAFE in DataFrames

To allow the data integration and modeling in a graph, a series of tabular treatments and mappings between the vocabulary of the questionnaires and that of OAFE were carried out on the DataFrame 1. Steps 4, 5 and 6 of Fig. 1 leading to the KG generation are detailed in the Fig. 5. Firstly, two alignments are performed: - between questions label and the OP and DP label (step 4a); - and between the responses label and the Classes label (step 4b). For example, as a result of this mapping, the question "What pathology do you have?" was associated to the OP label "hasPathology" and the question "How old are you?" was associated to the DP label "Age". At the end of this step, DataFrames (2a, 2b and 2c) enriched by the OAFE vocabulary are obtained and gather all the entities allowing the creation of triples between the user and his data, such as the triple: hasPathology (john, diabetes). Finally, to link a user to his recommendation, the OPs containing the string "reco" (OP reco) (step 4d) have been gathered in same DataFrame (2c). This step allows to create the triplet: hasPAPreco (john, john-papreco).

Following this data enrichment process, the different entities of the enriched DataFrames are used in step 5 and 6 to link the data to their users. The structured data in these DataFrames are then used in step 6 to generate a first KG. The following section presents the evolution of this KG representing a graph structure facilitating its mapping with the OAFE schema.

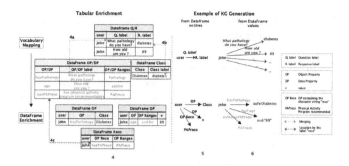

Fig. 5. Tabular enrichment process with the OAFE vocabulary (step 4), and entities linking of DataFrame 2 to each other (step 5) leading to the KG generation (step 6).

3.3 Knowledge Graph Evolution and Profiling Generation

The data integration and the knowledge graph evolution require the exploitation of the OAFE axioms. Based on the presented approach, a common data schema linking the user to his data and to his recommendations could be defined in which blank nodes represented are used to schematize an existential variable in the common data model.

The individuals instantiation and the property assertions creation at the A-Box level (blue arrows) allow the population of OAFE. Figure 6 shows the relations obtained after reasoning (red arrows) between the data schema and the OAFE schema. Therefore, the reasoning on this new structure allows to infer new relations (red arrows) between the created instances (previously schematized by blank nodes) and the classes of OAFE. In this example, these inferences allow to associate the recommendations of physical activity programs (PAPreco) to the person according to his profile obtained by reasoning.

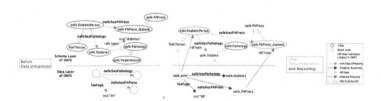

Fig. 6. Example of reasoning on the data to generate the recommendation (Color figure online)

4   Discussion and Conclusion

In this paper, we address the problem of data integration through knowledge graphs generation applied to the field of physical activity recommendation. To facilitate this task, we propose an approach that facilitates the semantic data integration from Web forms into knowledge graph. From this approach, we show, the interest of defining a common data schema to facilitate the mapping between the data schema and the schema of a domain ontology. As a result, semantic data integration becomes easier to address.

The approach DIKG2 is based on the principles of the W3C RDB2RDF standard, namely, the application of simple rules adapted for RDB data. However, in our approach, the semantic data integration process is independent of the RDB structure, which makes the approach DIKG2 generalizable to any information system using Web forms for data collection. Because the presented approach is generic, adding new questionnaires and changing the user profile will not affect the data processing and their integration in knowledge graph. Furthermore, the fact that the processing required for data integration is separated from the processing of data management facilitates its adoption regardless of the data source. Finally, the presented approach separates data storage from the processing required for data integration. Therefore, the modification of the collected data will not affect the processing necessary for the knowledge graph generation.

To conclude, it is therefore essential to keep in mind the interoperability issues to facilitate data integration and exploitation. Indeed, when information sources have not been designed to consider data interoperability issues, it becomes difficult to map the models and data structures with the ontology schema and the knowledge graph generation becomes a major challenge.

References

1. Dandan, R., et al.: OAFE: an ontology for the description of elderly activities. In: 14th International Conference on Signal-Image Technology & Internet-Based Systems, SITIS 2018, Gran Canaria, pp. 396–403. IEEE (2018)
2. Oldakowski, R., et al.: D2RQ platform – treating non-RDF databases as virtual RDF graphs. Nat. Precedings 2(5) (2011)
3. Collarana, C.: Semantic data integration for knowledge graph construction at query time. In: 11th International Conference on Semantic Computing (ICSC) (2017)
4. Calvanese, D., et al.: Ontology-Based Data Access and Integration. Springer, Cham (2018)
5. Kadadi, A., et al.: Challenges of data integration and interoperability in big data. In: International Conference on Big Data (Big Data). IEEE (2014)
6. Ehrlinger, L.: Towards a definition of knowledge graphs. In: Joint Proceedings of the Posters and Demos Track of the 12th International Conference on Semantic Systems. CEUR-WS.org (2010)
7. Zhao, Z., Han, S.K., Kim, J.R.: R2LD: schema-based graph mapping of relational databases to linked open data for multimedia resources data. Multimedia Tools Appl. 78(20), 28835–28851 (2019). https://doi.org/10.1007/s11042-019-7281-5

Ontology-Based Resume Searching System for Job Applicants in Information Technology

Tung T. Phan[1,2], Vinh Q. Pham[1,2], Hien D. Nguyen[1,2(✉)], Anh T. Huynh[1,2], Dung A. Tran[1,2], and Vuong T. Pham[3]

[1] University of Information Technology, Ho Chi Minh City, Vietnam
{16521399,16521446}@gm.uit.edu.vn, {hiennd,anhht,
dungta}@uit.edu.vn
[2] Vietnam National University, Ho Chi Minh City, Vietnam
[3] Sai Gon University, Ho Chi Minh City, Vietnam
vuong.pham@sgu.edu.vn

Abstract. In recruitment industry nowadays, the selection of best curriculum vitae (CV) for a particular job description (JD) among thousands of CVs is really challenging. The goal of this paper is to optimize job recruitment process by automatically matching skill graph extracted from CV and JD. Ontologies for contents of CVs and JDs are proposed to represent information of them. The screening system is worked based on built ontologies and solve matching problems between them. Some problems for matching the content of CVs and JDs are used by using natural language processing and machine learning techniques. The system has been tested on job domains about information technology (IT). Dataset is collected from TopCV, Dice and Indeed which are large IT labor markets on internet. Through testing results, the proposed method is effective to search CVs being appropriate with a determined JD in IT domain.

Keywords: Resume screening · Recruitment · Job skill · Job description · Ontology · Ontology matching · Machine learning

1 Introduction

In Information Technology (IT) domain, recruiters have to run up against a problem for finding appropriate candidates of recruitment jobs by their experiences. They may not have enough technical knowledge to know if the skills of a candidate are fit or not fit jobs' requirements. In addition, recruiters spend just a few seconds to look at a curriculum vitae (CV) before deciding who to "weed out" [1]. Unlike traditional method, the intelligent resume screening systems help recruiters to find appropriate candidates for the requirements in job descriptions (JD) faster and more efficiently.

The job matching between CVs and JDs is a task using several techniques in machine learning and natural language processing (NLP). In particular, the task is presented as follows: Given a job description, which were collected from several job seeking sites, and a set of candidate's CVs [2]. The problem is ranking of CVs for the given JD.

© Springer Nature Switzerland AG 2021
H. Fujita et al. (Eds.): IEA/AIE 2021, LNAI 12798, pp. 261–273, 2021.
https://doi.org/10.1007/978-3-030-79457-6_23

Ontology approach is a useful method to represent and search data with their semantic. This method is used in many domains [3–5]. In this paper, the structures of ontology representing CVs and JDs is proposed, called Job-Onto. This ontology is used to search CVs with their job skills matching requirements of JDs. The machine learning techniques and natural language processing are applied to solve the problem of candidate ranking in an automated recruitment system. This ranking is studied based the matching candidate's skills and job's requirements. The weights for each kind of matched skills can be controlled by the recruiter. The proposed method is applied to build a resume searching system for job applicants in IT.

The next section presents some related works about the methods for CV filter problem. Section 3 describes the structures of ontologies which were used to represent contents of resume applicants and JD posted by recruiters. Section 4 presents the architecture of a resume searching system for job applicants in IT domain. This system is worked as a system to recommend top k-CVs ranking for a given JD based on matching extracted skills from CVs and JDs. Experimental results of the built resume searching system are shown in Sect. 5. The last section concludes the paper and gives some future works.

2 Related Work

There are several studies for solving the problem about CV screening for a job description. They proposed many automated systems with different approaches. In [6], authors used ontology mapping to build an automated system for intelligent screening of candidates for recruitment. Their research focused on constructing ontology documents for candidates' problem to recommend the most suitable resumes for the job post using similarity measurement. They used concept linking to connect data/documents by identifying commonly shared concept, where data models are ontologies. Through that, they used ontology mapping to classify semantic interactions between related elements of various ontologies. They constructed their ontology for the features of candidates to match information between CV and JD. However, the ability to extract skills from text of this study is quite limited. It does not extract necessary information exactly to build ontology in the practice.

Another approach is building an integrated e-recruitment system for automated personality mining and applicant ranking. The study in [7] presented an e-recruitment system implementing automated applicant rankings based on a collection of credible requirements which make it easier for companies to integrate with their current human resources (HR) management infrastructure. That built system implemented automated candidate ranking based on objective parameters obtained from LinkedIn profile of candidates. The ranking of candidate profile is calculated by individual selection criteria using analytical hierarchy process (AHP), while their relative significance (weight) is controlled by the recruiter. Although, this study shown a useful system for mining personality of candidate, it cannot extract skills from profile information of candidates. Thus, it is very hard to apply in IT recruitment, because IT candidates usually have some necessary characteristic skills for job development in the future.

Transfer learning is a useful machine learning technique to process language problems [8–10], especially extracting main words in documents. The study in [10] used ontology and word embedding to extract skills from candidates. They proposed a theory on matching of candidate with the culture of organization to give a better candidate who fit for the company. In [31], an approach using of Policy Gradient through reinforcement learning was used to simulate the controlling of an autonomous car. However, those methods cannot use to automatic screen CV and their results are not effective to apply for build a real-world recruitment system.

The research in [11] generated taxonomy of job skills for recruitment systems automatically by using recurrent neural network models for capturing the context of skill words. This study also implemented some methods for the system, such as Bidirectional Long Short-Term Memory (BiLSTM), Long Short-Term Memory (LSTM), and Conditional Random Field (CRF). Besides, a few rule-based methods were used to extract skills appearing in front of the previous phrases indicating the start of the skills from JD. Nonetheless, because their Part-of-speech (POS) tagger labeled those skills as another tags, this approach misses lots of skills, and it cannot detect skills from unstructured JDs. Besides, that method is not effective to extract skills in CV because the structure of a CV is different from JD.

3 Ontology for Representing the Job Applicants and Job Recruitments

Ontology is the fundamental model to organize information delighting requirements of a recruitment system [12]. Ontology is used to address the meaning of target data, information or knowledge in Semantic Web model [13]. Moreover, ontology overcomes the most basic understanding of the Semantic Web by providing capabilities for standard reasoning, normally based on the specification of inference rules. In the resume screening system, ontology is used to represent the information extracted from CVs of applicants and JDs of recruiters.

Definition 3.1: The structure of ontology representing job applicants and job recruitments, called *Job-Onto*, is a triple:

$$(A, JD, R)$$

In which, A is the set of resume of applicants, JD is the set of job descriptions, and R is the set of relations between job applicants and job descriptions Ontology documents are created based on using standard languages, such as RDF and OWL.

3.1 The Structure of a Resume Applicant (CV)

Each a curriculum vitae c of an applicant in A has a structure as follows:

$$c = (Profile, Work\_history, Education, Course, Skills, Pos, Others)$$

where,

- *Profile*: store personal information of the applicant.

- *Work_history:* there are positions at previous companies of the applicant.
- *Education*: educational information of the applicant.
- *Courses:* It includes some supporting training courses which were learned by the applicant. Those courses supply more the information about understanding and self-studying of candidate.
- *Skills*: the information of skills. There are two kinds of skills:

  - *Technical skills:* they perform major skills of the applicant in IT. They include two kinds of skills: skills on programming environments, and general programming skills.
  - *Soft skills:* they perform some soft skills of the applicant, such as communication skill, team work, logical and critical thinking.

- *Pos:* the apply position of the applicant.
- *Others:* other information of the applicant.

3.2 The Structure of a Job Description (JD)

Each a job description $d \in \mathcal{JD}$ has a structure as follows:

$$d = (Information, Descriptions, Required, Skills)$$

In which,

• *Information*: general information about the recruitment position.
• *Descriptions* = $\{s_1, s_2, ..., s_m\}$: set of sentences describing the working at the recruitment position. Each sentence s_i $(1 \leq i \leq m)$ is a tube [*text, keywords*], where *text* is a description sentence as text, *keywords* is a set of main words extracted from *text*.
• *Required*: there are detailed requirements for a candidate.
• *Skills:* the information skills for the recruitment position. The kinds of skills are similarly to the structure of CV. This component can be inputted from the recruiter of extracted from the information in *Descriptions* and *Required* components automatically by the searching system.

3.3 CSO Classifier

The CSO Classifier is an unsupervised approach to automatically classify documents based on their content according to an ontology [14]. This approach uses well-known NLP technologies making it easily generalizable. It consists of two primary components: (i) the syntactic module and (ii) the semantic module. In this study, CSO classifier is applied to represent the information content of CVs and JDs which were represented by ontology Job-Onto. Figure 1 represents the workflow of this classifier:

- *Syntactic module:* The syntactic module maps n-gram chunks in the text to concepts. The algorithm removes stop words and collects unigrams, bigrams and trigrams chunks. Then for each *n*-gram, it computes the Levenshtein distance similarity [14] with the labels of topic in ontologies. The minimum similarity level can be set manually and it has been set to 0.94. This value allows us to recognize many variations between concept and ontologies.

- *Semantic module:* The semantic module was design to find topics that are semantically related to the text. These topics are explicitly not mentioned in the text. Here it required word embedding produced by Word2Vec to compute the semantic similarity between the terms in the text and the ontologies.

The word embedding model was created by CSO using the Word2Vec model [15]. The model is trained text collected from the CVs and JDs in the domain of IT.

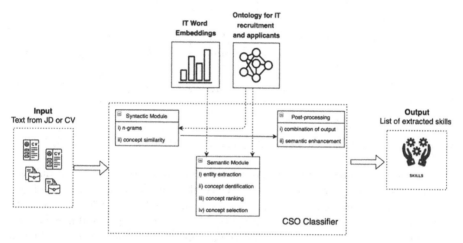

Fig. 1. The architecture of CSO Classifier applying in the IT recruitment system.

Through [16], for using CSO Classifier effectively in other domains, such as IT fields, we have collected Job Posting from Dice.com [17], answers, related tags, questions from Stackoverflow [18], alternative name and skill description from ESCO [19], and finally 50K sentences containing extracted skills has been preprocessed from the Job Post in the dataset at [20]. The training and data processing will be described in more detail in Sect. 4.2.

4 The Resume Searching System for Job Applicants in Information Technology

4.1 The Architecture of the Resume Searching System

The proposed recruitment system implements automated CV ranking based on a collection of criteria, and the ranking is calculated by their weight, which is controlled by the recruiter. In this study, there are four complementary selection criteria being focused: Education (candidate's highest level of education), General Technical Skills (skills of all domains extracted from candidate's CV), Domain Technical Skills (skills of domain that

JD is looking for), and Soft Skills. The architecture of this system consists of following components as Fig. 2:

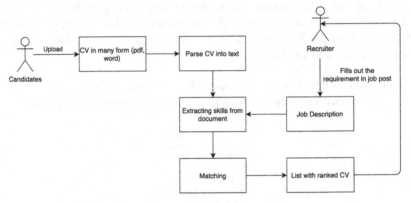

Fig. 2. The architecture of the resume searching system.

- *Resume parser* module: It takes CV uploaded by candidates and parses this file into text.
- *Extracting skills* module: From JDs which were filled by the recruiter, this module will extract a list of skills through four criteria: General Technical Skills, Domain Skills and Soft Skills. This module also extracts corresponding skills from CVs of applicants. It is worked by using CSO-Classifier [14], which is an unsupervised approach for automatically classifying papers according to Job-Onto filter. The working of CSO-filter was presented in the Sect. 3.3.
- *Matching* module: It takes the candidate's selection criteria to derive the relevance score of each criteria for the applied position. The grading function is implemented by calculated similarity of skill graph, which is result of Extracting skills module. The matching processing of the system is presented in the Sect. 4.2.

The information of candidates extracted from their CVs, including their relevance scores, are stored in the system as well as his/her. At the end of process, a recruiter can supply weights of requirement skills, and the system shows a list of candidate's CVs which are ranked by overall scores.

4.2 The Method for Matching CV and JD

Data Collecting

There are several data set existing in the internet, but choosing a set of data that could be fit our intent is extremely difficult. First, we collected a large number of job posts from multiple career websites, such as Dice.com, Indeed, etc. From each job post, we take its job description and cleaned those raw data to feed it into our word2vec model which is explained further later in this section.

In order to perform a good skills extraction, we collected and prepared a huge dictionary of skill as proposed in [21]. This skill dictionary is generated by mining several websites for data sources rich in skill phrases and field terminologies (ESCO [19], Stack-Share [22]). After cleaning and processing these skill-terms, we achieved a dictionary with over 30,000 skill-terms.

Data Processing

a) Extract text from CV
At the very first, we thought that it is fairly simple to parse a CV from pdf or word to raw text, but it turns out that we were wrong. In order to build a parser for CV is really tough, because CV is unstructured document, there are so many kinds of layout of an CV that you could imagine.

We have tried with several packages available to parse PDF formats into text, such as PyPDF2, PDFMiner, PDFtoTree. One common mistake that all above packages made is that sometimes they place extracted text in incorrect positions. Hence, the proposed method uses optical character recognition (OCR) [23]. In this approach, we attempted to parse CV into text with following steps:

- Convert CV into images, each image represents a single page in CV.
- Create a threshold image with OpenCV [24]
- Parse text from threshold image with tesseract OCR [25]

This approach still has some cons, such as it takes a bit longer than extract text directly from original file or quality of extracted data is unsatisfactory if the scanned pages are blurred. But after testing in around 1000 CV, this approach gives positive results which can apply in the practice.

b) Preprocess data for Word2Vec model
The data are collected from different sources, so they have different structures. Therefore, the preprocessing will be slightly different. However, in general, data will be processed sequentially through the following steps:

- Remove HTML tags if any
- Separate paragraphs into sentences
- Remove special characters; however, keep some of the characters that usually appear in programming languages such as "+", "#" in "C++", "C#"
- Remove stop words (eg: *and, or, it, the, if, a*) often appear in English text without giving meaning to skill-terms.
- Lemmatization each sentences

After sentence separating and word processing we have dataset of 1.8M sentences ready for training Word2Vec model.

Create Ontologies
In order to create an ontology to feed into the CSO Classifier, based on its documentation, the domain specific ontology of IT was manually created from the crawled job posts.

For each field of IT, such as frontend developer, there are collected 10000 job posts and got all keywords of each job post. After filter all stop words and nonrelated keywords, a set of skills from all keywords is created through combining with collected skills from Stackshare [22].After exploring all the skills, the domain specific ontology was created by using the Protégé software.

Extract Skills from CV and JD

When processing a document, the CSO Classifier needs to retrieve the top 10 similar words for all tokens, and compare them with CSO topics, which is a quite expensive in terms of time. To overcome this problem, a cached model for each specified domain is used. That cached model plays as a dictionary which directly connects all token available within the vocabulary of the model with skill-terms in the ontology. This thing helps to quickly retrieve all the skill-terms inferred by a particular token.

After that, the cached models are organized into a dictionary. To extract skill-terms from text, the user of this extract module should pick the specified domain, then the specified domain CSO Classifier will be created and used for extraction. Figure 3 briefly depicts the process of extracting skill-terms.

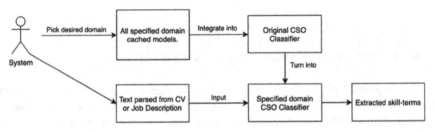

Fig. 3. The extracting skill-terms for specified domain process.

Skill Graph Generation

For the purpose of feature matching, the skill graph is generated from the extracted skill list. The edges between nodes are determined by the domain ontology and drawn by NetworkX graph library. The generated graph has tree form, which its root is the name of the domain ontology and nodes are related skills.

Matching the Information of CV and JD

Our approach to matching feature is graph edit distance (GED) which is a measure of similarity between two graphs. In details, the graph generated from CV by insert/update/delete actions to match with the graph from JD is will be improved. The

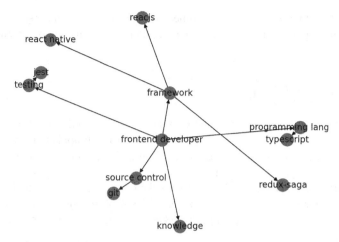

Fig. 4. The graph generated from the extracted skill list of a JD for frontend developer and the frontend ontology.

more actions it takes to transform, the more different the graphs are. In this step, Gmatch4py, a library dedicated to graph matching, is used. Its calculating follows the algorithm of graph edit distance by combining Hausdorff matching and greedy assignment [26]. The graph structures were stored in NetworkX graph as objects.

Table 1. The number of CVs and JDs entering into the system for testing

Order	IT fields	Number of CVs	Nums of JDs
1	iOS Developer	25	20
2	Android Developer	25	20
3	Frontend Developer	25	20
4	Backend Developer	25	20
5	Fullstack Developer	25	20
6	Devops Engineer	25	20
7	AI Engineer	25	20
8	Data Science	25	20
	Total	**200**	**160**

After matching step, the score of each criterion between CV and JD is got. There are several sorting algorithms to rank list of CVs for each JD. In reality, recruiters may have their own idea in mind of which aspects they want to favor depending on the situation, and the needs of their company at that time. Thus, our resume searching system for job applicants gives that sorting by letting the recruiters to modify the parameters as they want.

5 Experimental Results

Job-Onto is used to represent a set of CVs and JDs collected from TopCV [27] and Indeed [28]. From that, a resume searching system for job applicants in Information Technology is designed by using Reactjs and Flask. Table.1 shows amount of CVs and JDs which are assuming entered into our system.

For each posted JD, the system calculates the correlation score of each candidate's CV, which is overall of domain skill, general skill, soft skill matching scores. For example, Fig. 5 and Table 2 shows a list of ranked CV with overall scores for the JD of Front-end engineer.

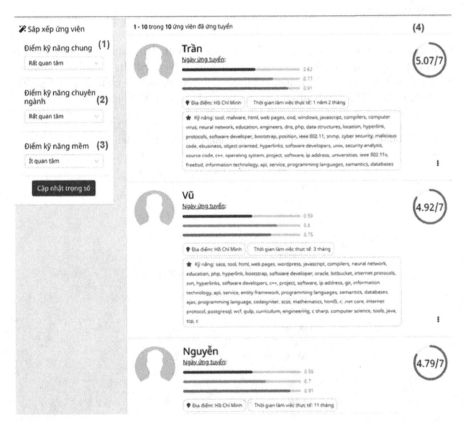

Fig. 5. The page of list of ranked CVs for the JD of Front-end engineer. (1) General score (2) Domain score (3) Soft skill score (4) List of emerging CV.

Table 2. The matching results of Frontend CVs and Front-end engineer job description. Input weights: Domain 3, General 3, Soft Skill 1.

ID	Domain score	General score	Soft Skill score	Overall score
CV_2	0.7692	0.6193	0.9091	5.0746
CV_8	0.8033	0.5899	0.75	4.9296
CV_1	0.7049	0.5899	0.9091	4.7935
CV_6	0.6897	0.5829	0.9	4.778
CV_9	0.7344	0.5924	0.5455	4.5259
CV_5	0.6607	0.5795	0.7	4.4206
CV_0	0.619	0.509	0.6364	4.0204
CV_3	0.6316	0.506	0.5455	3.9583
CV_4	0.5714	0.521	0.5455	3.8227
CV_7	0.5091	0.506	0.5455	3.5908

6 Conclusion and Future work

In this paper, the structure of ontology for representing of curriculum vitaes (CV) and job descriptions (JD) of a resume searching system for job applicants is presented. The designed system has the function of extracting information from collected CVs and JDs, classifying of extracted information. Besides, the system also can evaluate the matching between CVs and JDs. This system is built based on an ontology about IT domain, called Job-Onto.

Moreover, the designed system is implemented as a recruitment website which allows candidates to find the most suitable job, and recruiters can easily find the right candidate easily, thereby helping candidates and employers optimized their recruitment process as well as find jobs.

In the future, some methods to enrich Ontology automatically will be studied more to collect data more effectively. From that, with the huge of collected data, the improvement of some techniques for extracting information from the CV will be useful in the practice. Moreover, beside the ability to deploy on other platforms, the proposed method is emerging to apply intelligent educational systems for searching of course intellectual [29, 30].

Acknowledgement. This research is funded by Vietnam National University HoChiMinh City (VNU-HCM) under grant number DSC2021-26-07.

References

1. Faliagka, E., Iliadis, L., Karydis, I., et al.: On-line consistent ranking on e-recruitment: seeking the truth behind a well-formed CV. Artif. Intell. Rev. **42**, 515–528 (2014)

2. Cannella-Malone, H.I., Bumpus, E.C., Sun, X.: Using a job-matching assessment to inform skills to target with video prompting. Adv. Neurodevelopmental Disord. **4**(4), 471–479 (2020). https://doi.org/10.1007/s41252-020-00182-7

3. Do, N., Nguyen, H., Hoang, L.: Some techniques for intelligent searching on ontology-based knowledge domain in E-learning. In: Proceedings of 12th International Joint Conference on Knowledge Discovery, Knowledge Engineering and Knowledge Management (IC3K 2020), KEOD, Budapest, Hungary, vol. 2 (2020)

4. Dumontier, M., Baker, C.J., Baran, J., et al.: The Semanticscience Integrated Ontology (SIO) for biomedical research and knowledge discovery. J. Biomed. Semant. **5**, 14 (2014)

5. Do, N., Nguyen, H.D., Mai, T.: A method of ontology integration for designing intelligent problem solvers. Appl. Sci. **9**(18), 3793 (2019)

6. Senthil Kumaran, V., Sankar, A.: Towards an automated system for intelligent screening of candidates for recruitment using ontology mapping (EXPERT). Int. J. Metadata Semant. Ontologies (IJMSO) **8**(1), 56–64 (2013)

7. Faliagka, E., Tsakalidis, A., Tzimas, G.: An integrated e-recruitment system for automated personality mining and applicant ranking. Internet Res. **22**(5), 551–568 (2012)

8. Pillai, R., Sivathanu, B.: Adoption of artificial intelligence (AI) for talent acquisition in IT/ITeS organizations. Benchmarking. Int. J. **27**(9), 2599–2629 (2020)

9. Nguyen, H.D., Huynh, T., Hoang, S., Pham, V., Zelinka, I.: Language-oriented sentiment analysis based on the grammar structure and improved self-attention network. In: Proceedings of 15th International Conference on Evaluation of Novel Approaches to Software Engineering (ENASE 2020), Prague, Czech Public (2020)

10. Mishra, R., Rodriguez, Portillo, V.: An AI based talent acquisition and benchmarking for job. https://arxiv.org/abs/2009.09088

11. Baad, D.: Automatic job skill taxonomy generation for recruitment systems. Master's Thesis in ICT Innovation, Aalto University (2019)

12. Chandrasekaran, B., Josephson, J., Benjamins, V.: What are ontologies, and why do we need them? IEEE Intell. Syst. Appl. **14**(1), 20–26 (1999)

13. Calaresu, M., Shiri, A.: Understanding semantic web: a conceptual model. Libr. Rev. **64**(1/2), 82–100 (2015)

14. Salatino, A.A., Osborne, F., Thanapalasingam, T., Motta, E.: The CSO classifier: ontology-driven detection of research topics in scholarly articles. In: Doucet, A., Isaac, A., Golub, K., Aalberg, T., Jatowt, A. (eds.) TPDL 2019. LNCS, vol. 11799, pp. 296–311. Springer, Cham (2019). https://doi.org/10.1007/978-3-030-30760-8_26

15. Tomas Mikolov, T., Chen, K., Corrado, G.S., Dean, J.: Efficient estimation of word representations in vector space. In: Proceedings of the International Conference on Learning Representations (ICLR 2013), AZ, USA (2013)

16. Salatino, A., Osborne, F.: How to use the CSO Classifier in other domains. Zenodo (2019). http://doi.org/10.5281/zenodo.3459286

17. Dice: https://www.dice.com/. Accessed 25 Jan 2021

18. Stackoverflow: https://stackoverflow.com/. Accessed 25 Jan 2021

19. ESCO: https://ec.europa.eu/esco/portal. Accessed 25 Jan 2021

20. Skill2Vec Dataset: https://github.com/duyet/skill2vec-dataset. Accessed 25 Jan 2021

21. Gugnani, A., Kasireddy, V., Karthikeyan. P.: Generating unified candidate skill graph for career path recommendation. In: Proceedings of 2018 IEEE International Conference on Data Mining Workshops (ICDMW 2018), Singapore (2018)

22. Stackshare: https://www.stackshare.io. Accessed 25 Jan 2021

23. OCR: https://en.wikipedia.org/wiki/Optical_character_recognition

24. OpenCV: https://opencv.org/. Accessed 25 Jan 2021

25. Tesseract OCR: https://github.com/tesseract-ocr/tesseract. Accessed 25 Jan 2021

26. Fischer, A., Riesen, K., Bunke, H.: Improved quadratic time approximation of graph edit distance by combining Hausdorff matching and greedy assignment. Pattern Recogn. Lett. **87**, 55–62 (2017)
27. TopCV: https://www.topcv.vn/. Accessed 25 Jan 2021
28. Indeed: https://vn.indeed.com/?r=us. Accessed 25 Jan 2021
29. Pham, X.T., Tran, T.V., Nguyen, V., et al.: Build a search engine for the knowledge of the course about Introduction to Programming based on ontology Rela-model. In: Proceedings of 12th International Conference on Knowledge and Systems Engineering (KSE 2020), Can Tho, Vietnam, pp. 207–212 (2020)
30. Nguyen, H., Tran, D., Pham, H., Pham, V.: Design an intelligent system to automatically tutor the method for solving problems. Int. J. Integr. Eng. (IJIE) **12**(7), 211–223 (2020)
31. Huynh, A., Nguyen, B.T., Nguyen, H.T, Vu, S., Nguyen, H.: A method of deep reinforcement learning for simulated autonomous vehicle control. In: Proceedings of 16th International Conference on Evaluation of Novel Approaches to Software Engineering (ENASE 2021), Online streaming, pp. 372–379 (2021)

An Approach to Expressing Metamodels' Semantics in a Concept System

Marcin Jodłowiec[(✉)] and Marek Krótkiewicz

Department of Applied Informatics, Wrocław University of Science and Technology,
Wybrzeże Stanisława Wyspiańskiego 27, 50-370 Wrocław, Poland
{marcin.jodlowiec,marek.krotkiewicz}@pwr.edu.pl

Abstract. In this paper, the authors introduce a novel approach to data metamodel conceptualization called Conceptual Layer of Metamodels. This conceptualization method gives an common conceptual layer based on Semantics of Business Vocabulary and Rules for expressing data metamodels built using different categories and having other characteristics but representing similar semantics. This paper describes abstraction and concretization dependency and covers the metamodeling layer and core modeling concepts layers.

Keywords: Conceptualization · Data modeling · Metamodeling · SBVR

1 Introduction

Nowadays, information systems are modeled, designed, and implemented using various tools, standards, and languages. This abundance of techniques makes it difficult to compare existing systems since some do not share common metamodels. There are some effort to standardize the software development process (e.g., Model-Driven Architecture – MDA) frameworks. Although the initiative is valuable, in reality still some non-MDA compliant are used and popular. This remark applies in particular to conceptual data modeling, where existing approaches such as Object-Role Modeling (ORM), Entity-Relationship (E-R), and Association-Oriented Modeling (AOM) do not share a metamodel and are built on different assumptions.

This paper's motivation was to introduce Conceptual Layer of Metamodels (CLoM), a common conceptual layer, which abstracts from metamodeling frameworks' specific syntactic rules. The common conceptual layer gives the possibility to argue on their semantic capacity and complexity while setting distinct metamodels next to each other. This metamodel setting has essential consequences: there is no state-of-the-art approach for comparing and expressing semantic capacity and expressiveness of data metamodels. Conceptualization being understudy will allow for further development of tools that will characterize data metamodels, and in the next stage, compare them. The other critical need for

© Springer Nature Switzerland AG 2021
H. Fujita et al. (Eds.): IEA/AIE 2021, LNAI 12798, pp. 274–282, 2021.
https://doi.org/10.1007/978-3-030-79457-6_24

such a conceptualization is developing a semantics-aware translation method of models for different metamodels, which is currently being researched [9].

The contribution of this research is the delivery of foundations of an approach to data metamodel conceptualization. Conceptualization is here understood as the expression of the concepts and limitations in defining the syntax and semantics of a given metamodel within the adopted system of concepts (meta-conceptualization) [5]. This action is to get rid of syntactic structures to capture metamodel's semantics to share meaning between different metamodels.

This paper is constructed as follows. In the next section, we give a short review of currently known conceptualizations of information systems. In the Sect. 2 we present the conceptual system. The description is divided into three parts. The first one presents the basic conceptualization of the metamodeling layer, then the description of abstraction layers is described, followed by the presentation of the system's core concepts. The last section contains a summary and conclusions.

2   Related Works

There are some well-known approaches to conceptualization specification. Some of them could be used for the conceptualization of data modeling and the metamodeling domain. One of such approaches is the Bunge-Wand-Weber (BWW) metamodel [13], which is based on Bunge's ontology [1]. However, despite being used in the metamodeling domain (see, e.g., [11]), it lacks some features that could make it usable the modeling and metamodeling domain. The original Bunge's ontology is concordant to the material world and not a conceptual one, in which existing information systems' modeling and metamodeling. Bunge distinguished two types of objects: concrete objects and constructs (which he referred to as *substantial individuals* or formal ideal objects). He intentionally left the latter out of his ontology.

The other important approach in this field is Guizzardi's ontology-driven approach to conceptual modeling [5]. Guizzardi settled relations between modeling language, reference ontology and proposed a foundational ontology for conceptual modeling. This research initiated a significant current of conceptual modeling: UFO. UFO is an ontology used to integrate conceptual reference models across multiple domains, including i.a.: software engineering [6], agent-based modeling [7]. UFO is, in a sense, an extension of the Wand and Weber approach and covers such modeling issues as object types, taxonomic relations, associations and relationships between associations, roles, properties, and data types.

3   Conceptual Layer of Metamodels

The following chapter presents the approach to the construction of CLoM and its selected areas. The CLoM covers the subset of interrelated concepts from the data modeling domain. Each of the data metamodels has a particular set of concepts in which it operates. The concept system should abstract from a specific metamodel. The system has the feature of generalizing specific features while maintaining a proper abstraction level. For example, in CLoM there exist the **association** concept that can be represented in a different way in various metamodels: as association (AOM [12], UML [3]), as relationship type (Entity-Relationship approach [4]), as fact type (Object-Role Modeling [8]).

The authors' approach is to define sets of constraints for each element of the framework set of modeling concepts very precisely. Basic concepts in the field of metamodel reasoning were also defined, which are a loose reference to the approach presented in [10]. It should also be added that the approach to the conceptualization of relationships proposed in this paper focuses solely on structural relationships. Therefore, some types of relationships were not included in information modeling (such as *materialization, point of view, generation*, see e.g. [2]). In the CLoM we have proposed a number of subsystems which define a particular areas of data modeling which exist in the domain of data metamodeling: *metamodeling, patterns, core, classifiers, features, categorization, associations*. In this research we present *metamodeling* and *core* at length. The first one specifies basic concepts in the proposed meta-metamodeling framework. The other defines a common, abstract platform, which defines other areas by specialization.

3.1   Metamodeling Concepts

The adopted approach to metamodeling in CLoM is based on an idea presented in [10]. This idea defines that a metamodel consists of abstract syntax and semantics. The abstract syntax of a metamodel can be represented in the form of a rooted graph. The nodes are its categories, which constitute its building blocks. The relationships between them are the edges of the graph. For example, the Association-Oriented Metamodel's graph consist of such nodes as i.a.: *Db, Assoc, Coll*. The fact, that *Db* contains a list of *Coll*s and *Assoc*s is represented by a node. The metamodel categories have a level within the graph of the abstract metamodel syntax. The category representing the model's instance is the root of the graph and has a class level of 0 (in the case when such a category does not exist in the metamodel, the concept of zero-class category reflects the very fact that the model is instantiated).

For instance, the zero-level metamodel category for AOM is *Db* – the database instantiation is required to create its model. Only in case of having an instance of *Db* it is possible to create specific instances of *Assoc* and *Coll*, which constitute first-class categories. Similarly, *Attr* and *Role* are second-class categories. Consequently, there is a strictly defined sequence in terms of the instantiation of the metamodel's elements. In particular, in the example of *Attr*, it cannot exist in isolation from the previously instantiated *Coll*, which it is part of. In this context, it should be noted that, for example, the concept of association in some metamodels may be a first-class category, such as in AOM. In others, for example, E-R, the concept of *relationship* specifying association is a second-class category. The list of definitions of vocabulary used in this part of conceptual system is as follows.

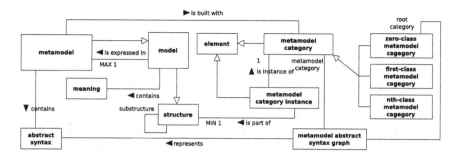

Fig. 1. SBVR concept diagram of CLoM *metamodeling* concepts

element

Definition: component part of a whole

model

Definition: a simplified image of a fragment of a certain reality

model *contains* meaning

metamodel

Definition: model that *contains* abstract syntax and provides a framework for description of models
Example: EER
Example: natural language

model *is expressed in* metamodel

Necessity: each model *is expressed in* exactly one metamodel

abstract syntax

Definition: structure describing metamodel taking no account of representation

metamodel *contains* abstract syntax

metamodel *contains* meaning

structure

Definition: nonempty set of metamodel category instances

substructure

Definition: structure that *is part of* a given structure

metamodel category instance *is part of* structure

Necessity: each metamodel category instance *is part of* at least one structure

metamodel abstract syntax graph

Definition: rooted graph consisting of nodes representing metamodel categories and edges representing relationships between metamodel categories

metamodel category

Definition: element *of* metamodel abstract syntax graph that is its node

metamodel *is built with* metamodel category

zero-class metamodel category

Definition: arbitrarily designated metamodel category that constitutes a root of metamodel abstract syntax graph

first-class metamodel category

Definition: metamodel category that has distance from zero-class metamodel category in metamodel abstract syntax graph equals 1

n^{th}-class metamodel category

Definition: metamodel category that has distance from zero-class metamodel category in metamodel abstract syntax graph equals n

metamodel category instance

Definition: element *of* structure and *being instance of* metamodel category

metamodel category instance *is instance of* metamodel category

3.2   Modeling Layers

Conceptualization within the modeling and metamodeling domain requires referring to different layers of the *instanceOf* relationship. In classical modeling, one distinguishes four layers: (M3) to express meta-metamodeling concepts (e.g. MOF's Class), (M2) to express metamodeling concepts (e.g. UML's Class), (M1) to express model's concept (a concrete class, e.g. Person), (M0) to refer to a specific data described by model (instance level).

In Conceptual Layer of Metamodels, due to the need for unambiguity, the concepts are generative. Consequently, new concepts can be introduced in terms of *instanceOf* relationship, constituting a lower abstraction layer. To distinguish between such understood layers, we have introduced the abstraction/concretization relationship between concepts. The concepts which are *instances* in terms of *instanceOf* relationship of some modeling category m will be called as concrete m. Similarly, while the opposite relationship occurs, the concept can be referred to as abstract m. This naming convention has been adopted in order to avoid terminological convergence with meta-conceptualization defined in SBVR, which defines instance as: thing that *is in* an extension of a concept.

This means that extension of abstract concepts having the semantics of modeling concepts consists of metamodel categories which have the characteristics and constrains defined by a given modeling concept. For example, the extension of association concept consist of UML's *Association* category, ORM's fact type and AOM's *Assoc*. Moreover, each of these categories constitute an instance of individual concept: **association (UML)**, **fact type (ORM)**, and **Assoc (AOM)** respectively. The *concretizations* of those concepts refer to instances of modeling categories which are parts of structures. Naturally, the concretization relationship is on each contact of modeling layers, i.e. M0-M1, M1-M2, M2-M3. When the contact M1-M2 is concerned, for the association concept one should consider the concrete association concept which is defined as: modeling concept that *is concretization of* association.

The extension of concrete association consist of each associations, which in any possible world could ever be modeled. For example, on the contact of M2-M1 in association-oriented modeling paradigm, the *abstraction* and *concretization* of modeling concept have been designated in the Table 1.

3.3 Core Concepts

In the Fig. 2 the *core concepts* of the CLoM has been presented. These concepts constitute a common, abstract platform on which the entire concept system was based. The purpose of the CLoM is to reason about different data metamodels. The adopted concept system assumes a specific modeling concept space, which reflects the multitude of categories of various metamodels. It allows these modeling categories to be assigned the role of individual elements of the concept system (modeling concept specializations). This applies to both the intensional categories, which concretize the concepts used to build data models, and the intensional categories that implement the instance level.

Table 1. Dependencies between abstract and concrete concepts and their extensions

	general concept	individual concept	general concept extension	individual concept extension
abstract	association	Assoc (AOM)	totality of all modeling categories in all data metamodels that have the semantics of the named relationship between other categories	the association category defined in terms of AOM
concrete	some specific concrete association defined as modeling concept that is concretization of association	concrete association (in terms of Association-Oriented Metamodel) defined as modeling concept that is concretization of Assoc (AOM)	all instances of modeling categories created by IT system designers that have the semantics of the named relationship between specific categories	some specific association defined in some particular data model

Due to the diversity of data metamodels and the need to ensure a high degree of generality, mapping concept system categories into meta-model categories is many-to-many, and specific metamodel categories, in particular, can represent many elements of the concept system. Modeling concepts are based on a constraint system implemented by modeling concept characteristics. This concept constitutes a categorization basis for individuals, various constraints resulting from the semantic capacity and semantic richness of data metamodels. It should be noted that the proposed system of concepts is open, and along with the emergence or attempt to conceptualize new data metamodels, new constraints may arise that reflect the modeled entities. Additionally, it should be noted that the system does not determine the modeling layer under consideration but allows mapping the roles of individual concepts at the interface between these layers. For this purpose, a mechanism was defined based on the notions *is abstraction of / is concretization of*, defining the relationships between the concepts on different modeling layers, according to the assumptions described in the Sect. 3.2.

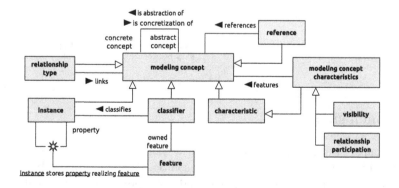

Fig. 2. SBVR concept diagram of CLoM *core* concepts

The list of definitions of vocabulary used in this part of conceptual system is as follows:

modeling concept

Definition: concept used within modeling domain

abstract concept *is abstraction of* **concrete concept**

abstract concept

Definition: modeling concept being in the meta-level towards the totality of modeling concepts that *are* its *concretization*

concrete concept

Definition: modeling concept that has a modeling concept in meta-level *is* its *abstraction*

classifier

Definition: modeling concept having features enabling classification of instances

feature

Definition: modeling concept for describing classifiers and realized by properties in the context of instances

classifier *has* **owned feature**

owned feature

Definition: feature that *is of* a given classifier

instance

Definition: modeling concept *in* extensional modeling layuer *classified by* classifier

classifier *classifies* **instance**

Definition: instance *has* properties that *realize* all features *of* classifier

property

Definition: instance thta *is realization of* feature in *storing* instance

instance *stores* **property** *realizing* **feature**

Definition: property which takes part in description of instance state by realizing feature
Necessity: each feature that *is of* classifier *classifing* given instance must *be realized by* property *stored by* given instance

characteristics

Definition: modeling concept that specifies constraints and mechanisms defined within metamodels

modeling concept characteristics

Definition: visibility or relationship participation

modeling concept characteristics   *features* **modeling concept**

visibility

Definition: modeling concept characteristics that constraints the possibility to refer to given modeling concept due to referring context

relationship participation

Definition: modeling concept characteristics that constraints the possibility to participate in specific roles of relationship type instances

reference

Definition: modeling concept being an indication of a given modeling concept

reference *references* **modeling concept**

relationship type

Definition: modeling concept specifying relationship between modeling concepts

4   Conclusions

In this paper, we have proposed CLoM – a framework to build conceptualization for different data metamodels. This solution is a compromise between the approach of very high semantic capacity and low expressiveness (e.g., natural language) and the opposite – low semantic capacity and high expressiveness (meta-metamodels, such as Meta Object Facility). Because the ground framework has been chosen as SBVR, the solution proposed is featured by semi-formality. Moreover, there is the possibility to define semantics for mutually related concepts.

CLoM constitutes a platform in terms of a method for mapping metamodel semantics. It gives the possibility to maintain a high level of detail due to concept definition, which defines concepts specifying particular features of metamodels. Moreover, a high level of generality features this solution due to adopted abstraction layers. CLoM is also the subject of current and future work on building metrics. These metrics will enable us to compare data metamodels with each other in a multidimensional space of semantic features. There is also research conducted on the methods for specifying semantics alternations of models being translated between different data metamodels.

References

1. Bunge, M.: Treatise on Basic Philosophy: Ontology I: the Furniture of the World, vol. 3. Springer, Cham (1977). https://doi.org/10.1007/978-94-010-9924-0
2. Dahchour, M., Pirotte, A., Zimányi, E.: Generic relationships in information modeling. In: Spaccapietra, S. (ed.) Journal on Data Semantics IV. LNCS, vol. 3730, pp. 1–34. Springer, Heidelberg (2005). https://doi.org/10.1007/11603412_1
3. Falah, B., Akour, M., Arab, I., M'hanna, Y.: An attempt towards a formalizing UML class diagram semantics. In: Proceedings of the New Trends in Information Technology (NTIT-2017), The University of Jordan, Amman, Jordan, pp. 21–27 (2017)
4. Frantiska, J.: Entity-relationship diagrams. In: Visualization Tools for Learning Environment Development. SpringerBriefs in Educational Communications and Technology, pp. 21–30. Springer, Cham (2018). https://doi.org/10.1007/978-3-319-67440-7_4
5. Guizzardi, G.: On ontology, ontologies, conceptualizations, modeling languages, and (meta) models. Front. Artif. Intell. Appl. **155**, 18 (2007)
6. Guizzardi, G., Falbo, R., Guizzardi, R.: Grounding software domain ontologies in the unified foundational ontology (UFO): The case of the ode software process ontology, pp. 127–140 (2008)
7. Guizzardi, G., Wagner, G.: Towards ontological foundations for agent modelling concepts using the unified fundational ontology (UFO). In: Bresciani, P., Giorgini, P., Henderson-Sellers, B., Low, G., Winikoff, M. (eds.) AOIS -2004. LNCS (LNAI), vol. 3508, pp. 110–124. Springer, Heidelberg (2005). https://doi.org/10.1007/11426714_8
8. Halpin, T.A.: Object-role modeling. In: Liu, L., Özsu, M.T. (eds.) Encyclopedia of Database Systems, Second Edition. Springer, Cham (2018). https://doi.org/10.1007/978-1-4614-8265-9_251
9. Jodłowiec, M., Pietranik, M.: Towards the pattern-based transformation of SBVR models to association-oriented models. In: Nguyen, N.T., Chbeir, R., Exposito, E., Aniorté, P., Trawiński, B. (eds.) ICCCI 2019. LNCS (LNAI), vol. 11683, pp. 79–90. Springer, Cham (2019). https://doi.org/10.1007/978-3-030-28377-3_7
10. Karagiannis, D., Kühn, H.: Metamodelling platforms. In: Bauknecht, K., Tjoa, A.M., Quirchmayr, G. (eds.) EC-Web 2002. LNCS, vol. 2455, pp. 182–182. Springer, Heidelberg (2002). https://doi.org/10.1007/3-540-45705-4_19

11. Kiwelekar, A.W., Joshi, R.K.: An object-oriented metamodel for bunge-wand-weber ontology. In: Workshop on Semantic Web for Collaborative Knowledge Acquisition at IJCAI (2010)
12. Krótkiewicz, M.: Formal definition and modeling language of association-oriented database metamodel (AssoBase). Vietnam J. Comput. Sci. **06**(02), 91–145 (2019)
13. Wand, Y., Weber, R.: An ontological model of an information system. IEEE Trans. Softw. Eng. **16**(11), 1282–1292 (1990)

Medical and Health-Related Applications

Birth-Death MCMC Approach
for Multivariate Beta Mixture Models
in Medical Applications

Mahsa Amirkhani$^{(\boxtimes)}$, Narges Manouchehri, and Nizar Bouguila

Concordia Institute for Information Systems Engineering, Concordia University,
Montreal, Quebec, Canada
{mahsa.amirkhani,narges.manouchehri}@mail.concordia.ca,
nizar.bouguila@concordia.ca

Abstract. Lately, data mining tools have received significant attention
because of their capability in modeling and analyzing collected data in
various fields including medical research. With the growing availability
of medical data, it is crucial to develop models that can discover hidden
patterns in data and analyze them. Among various techniques, mixture
models have been widely used for categorization problems in statistical
modeling. In this paper, a Bayesian learning framework is proposed for
multivariate Beta mixture model. Previous works have shown that multivariate Beta distribution can be considered as an alternative to Gaussian
due to the flexibility of its shape and convincing performance. In particular, we use the Birth and Death Markov Chain Monte Carlo (MCMC)
algorithm, which allows simultaneous parameters estimation and model
selection. Experimental results on medical applications demonstrate the
effectiveness of the proposed algorithm.

Keywords: Mixture modeling · Multivariate beta distribution ·
Medical applications · Birth-Death MCMC · Bayesian analysis

1 Introduction

Over the past few decades, with huge growth in the amount of collected data, the
demand for designing effective approaches to analyze and model these data has
increased. Recent development of data mining and machine learning techniques
has made them suitable tools to extract valuable information and meaningful
patterns from data [1]. In medical field, data mining has emerged to assist the
healthcare experts in early detection, diagnosis and prevention of diseases [2,3].
Among various approaches, cluster analysis has been widely adopted for knowledge discovery and finding underlying structure of the data [4]. Clustering is an
unsupervised learning method suitable for partitioning data into different groups
with similar characteristics and finds its way into many applications from different domains, such as computer vision, information retrieval and pattern recognition. Learning appropriate statistical models is a fundamental task of many

© Springer Nature Switzerland AG 2021
H. Fujita et al. (Eds.): IEA/AIE 2021, LNAI 12798, pp. 285–296, 2021.
https://doi.org/10.1007/978-3-030-79457-6_25

clustering approaches. In this context, finite mixture models have demonstrated high capability to model complex data sets assuming that each observation has arisen from one of the different groups or components [5].

An important problem in mixture modeling is the choice of component distributions that can properly describe the data. In particular, Gaussian Mixture Models (GMMs) have received considerable attention and demonstrated satisfactory fitting abilities in different applications [6]. The normality assumption is, however, not realistic under more general conditions and data obtained from real-world applications may have non-Gaussian and asymmetric nature. Several recent works have shown that other distributions such as Dirichlet, inverted Dirichlet, Beta-Liouville could be considered as flexible alternatives [7,8]. In this paper, we propose Multivariate Beta (MB) as a parent distribution for our mixture model. It can be considered as an alternative to Gaussian distribution, where it offers flexibility and various shapes with promising attributes. The results of previous works have confirmed the convincing performance of Multivariate Beta Mixture Model (MBMM) in different applications [9].

There are two other challenging problems in deploying mixture models. The first one is estimating the mixture parameters and the second is selecting the number of mixture components. To tackle the first issue, two main categories of approaches can be considered namely deterministic (e.g., maximum likelihood) and Bayesian techniques [10]. The Expectation Maximization (EM) algorithm as a way of performing maximum likelihood estimation is the most commonly used technique, but it suffers from convergence to local maxima, dependency on initialization and over fitting problems. To overcome these drawbacks, several learning frameworks based on pure Bayesian approximation have been proposed, where they have shown competitive performance [11]. The main idea behind Bayesian methods is to incorporate our prior beliefs about parameters and update them using knowledge extracted from the data to obtain posterior probability [11,12]. These methods have been applied successfully in many practical applications thanks to the development of Markov Chain Monte Carlo (MCMC) methods [13].

To estimate the number of mixture components, several model selection approaches can be employed, such as Bayesian information criterion and Minimum Message Length (MML) [14]. In this paper, we consider a Bayesian algorithm based on the Birth-Death MCMC approach proposed in [15], which simultaneously performs the estimation of parameters and model selection for MB mixture. It is based on generating an ergodic Markov chain with the joint posterior distribution of the parameters and the model as its stationary distribution, where the number of components is considered as unknown.

The rest of this paper is organized as follows: In Sect. 2, the MB mixture model is described. Section 3 is dedicated to the development of our birth-death MCMC algorithm. Section 4 presents the experimental results obtained from two medical applications. Finally, this work is concluded in Sect. 5.

2 MB Mixture Model

Lets assume D-dimensional vector $\vec{X}_i = (x_{i1}, \ldots, x_{id})$ from a set of N independent and identically distributed data observations $\mathcal{X} = \{\vec{X}_1, \ldots, \vec{X}_N\}$ originated from MB distribution with the following probability density function:

$$p(\vec{X}_i \mid \vec{\alpha}_j) = c \frac{\prod_{d=1}^{D} x_{id}^{\alpha_{jd}-1}}{\prod_{d=1}^{D}(1 - x_{id})^{(\alpha_{jd}+1)}} \left[1 + \sum_{d=1}^{D} \frac{x_{id}}{(1 - x_{id})}\right]^{-|\alpha_j|} \tag{1}$$

where

$$c = \frac{\Gamma(\alpha_{j1} + \cdots + \alpha_{jD})}{\Gamma(\alpha_{j1}) \ldots \Gamma(\alpha_{jD})} = \frac{\Gamma(|\alpha_j|)}{\prod_{d=1}^{D} \Gamma(\alpha_{jd})} \tag{2}$$

such that $0 < x_{id} < 1$ and $\Gamma(.)$ denotes the Gamma function. A positive vector $\vec{\alpha}_j = (\alpha_{j1}, \ldots, \alpha_{jD})$ shows the shape parameters of this distribution where $\alpha_{jd} > 0$ for $d = 1, \ldots, D$ and $|\alpha_j| = \sum_{d=1}^{D} \alpha_{jd}$. Examples of MB distribution with different shape parameters is shown in Fig. 1.

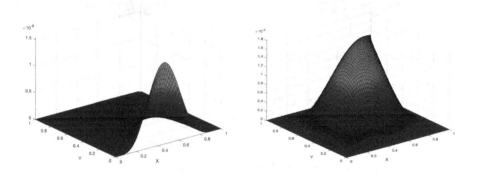

Fig. 1. Two examples of multivariate Beta distribution

Lets consider that an unlabeled data set $\mathcal{X} = \{\vec{X}_1, \ldots, \vec{X}_N\}$ with N observations, is generated from a finite mixture of MB distribution with K components:

$$p(\vec{X}_i \mid \Theta) = \sum_{j=1}^{K} \pi_j p(\vec{X}_i \mid \vec{\alpha}_j) \tag{3}$$

$p(\vec{X}_i \mid \vec{\alpha}_j)$ is MB distribution and π_j represent mixing weights which are constrained to be positive and sum to one. The symbol $\Theta = (\vec{\pi}, \vec{\alpha})$ refers to the entire set of parameters to be estimated, where $\vec{\alpha} = (\alpha_1, \ldots, \alpha_K)$ and $\vec{\pi} = (\pi_1, \ldots, \pi_K)$. Figure 2 displays four examples of MB mixture model with different components. Then the likelihood function of our data set $\mathcal{X}$ is given by:

$$p(\mathcal{X} \mid \Theta) = \prod_{i=1}^{N} \left[\sum_{j=1}^{K} \pi_j p(\mathcal{X} \mid \vec{\alpha}_j)\right] \tag{4}$$

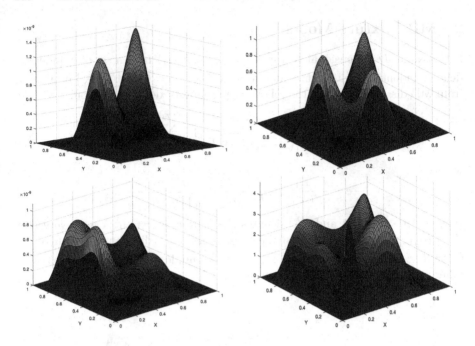

Fig. 2. Examples of Multivariate Beta mixture model with multiple components

In mixture modeling, generally we introduce a K-dimensional latent allocation vector $\vec{Z}_i = (Z_{i1}, \ldots, Z_{iK})$, where each $\vec{Z}_i$ indicates to which component $\vec{X}_i$ belongs, such that:

$$Z_{ij} = \begin{cases} 1 & \text{if } \vec{X}_i \text{ belongs to component } j \\ 0 & \text{otherwise} \end{cases} \tag{5}$$

In other words, if $\vec{X}_i$ has the highest probability of being in cluster j, then $Z_{ij} = 1$ and for other clusters $Z_{ij} = 0$. Thus for data set $\mathcal{X}$, the set of membership (or missing) vectors $\mathcal{Z} = \{\vec{Z}_1, \ldots, \vec{Z}_N\}$ is defined and its elements Z_i are supposed to be drawn independently and identically distributed with following probability mass function:

$$p(Z_i = j) = \pi_j \qquad (i = 1, \ldots, N; \quad j = 1, \ldots, K) \tag{6}$$

Therefore, the conditional distribution of the data set $\mathcal{X}$ given the class labels $\mathcal{Z}$ can be written as:

$$p(\mathcal{X} \mid \mathcal{Z}, \vec{\alpha}) = \prod_{i=1}^{N} \prod_{j=1}^{K} p(\vec{X}_i \mid \vec{\alpha}_j)^{Z_{ij}} \tag{7}$$

3   Bayesian Inference of MB Mixture

In this section, we propose a Bayesian framework for parameters estimation of our mixture model and determining the proper number of mixture components as two major challenges in mixture modeling. Concerning parameters estimation, several studies have shown that Bayesian learning can offer better capabilities for this purpose due to its remarkable characteristics over deterministic ones by introducing prior knowledge in the learning process [16,17]. Indeed, the prior belief about parameters is incorporated with the likelihood of data to determine the final posterior probability. Moreover, thanks to the development of computational tools and simulation techniques such as Markov Chain Monte Carlo (MCMC) methods, the Bayesian estimation has become more feasible [11,18]. With the help of the most commonly used MCMC techniques, namely Gibbs sampling and Metropolis–Hastings algorithm, the posterior distribution of the mixture model can be approximated.

Another challenge in the context of the mixture of distributions is model selection, for which several approaches have been suggested within Bayesian inference such as Bayes factors, Bayesian Information Criterion (BIC), reversible jump MCMC (RJMCMC) and birth and death processes [15,19,20]. For variable dimension problems, a common approach in literature is RJMCMC, where it consists of split/combine and birth/death moves for changing the number of components [21]. However, the extension of this method to multivariate cases is difficult. Therefore, a birth-death MCMC (BDMCMC) algorithm has been introduced in [15] which we will use in this work for learning of MB mixture model. This approach is based on continuous time birth-death events and can be employed for multivariate dimensions [22]. Moreover, the results of several studies based on this algorithm have shown convincing performance in the case of mixture of various distributions such as gamma, Dirichlet and Beta [23–25].

3.1   Priors and Posteriors

In fully Bayesian framework, the unknown number of components K with the other parameters of the model $(\vec{\pi}, \vec{\alpha})$ are regarded as random variables drawn from some prior distributions that we have to determine. The joint distribution of all these variables is:

$$p(K, \vec{\pi}, Z, \vec{\alpha}, \mathcal{X}) = p(K)p(\vec{\pi} \mid K)p(Z \mid \vec{\pi}, K) \qquad (8)$$
$$p(\vec{\alpha} \mid Z, \vec{\pi}, K)p(\mathcal{X} \mid \vec{\alpha}, Z, \vec{\pi}, K)$$

Following [20], by imposing common conditional independencies, the joint distribution can be written as following:

$$p(K, \vec{\pi}, Z, \vec{\alpha}, \mathcal{X}) = p(K)p(\vec{\pi} \mid K)p(Z \mid \vec{\pi}, K)p(\vec{\alpha} \mid K)p(\mathcal{X} \mid \vec{\alpha}, Z) \qquad (9)$$

Then, the main goal of the Bayesian inference is to create realizations from the conditional joint density $p(K, \vec{\pi}, Z, \vec{\alpha} \mid \mathcal{X})$.

One of the important steps in Bayesian learning is the choice of suitable prior distributions for the parameters of mixture model. First for the number of components K, we assume a truncated Poisson prior as below:

$$p(K = k) \propto \frac{\lambda^k}{k!}, \quad (k = 1, \ldots, k_{max}) \tag{10}$$

Assuming that the parameters of the MB are statistically independent, for the shape parameters $\vec{\alpha}$, an appealing choice as a prior is a Gamma distribution denoted by $\mathcal{G}(.)$ that can be written as follows:

$$p(\vec{\alpha}_j) = \mathcal{G}(\vec{\alpha}_j \mid \vec{u}, \vec{v}) = \prod_{d=1}^{D} \frac{v_d^{u_d}}{\Gamma(u_d)} \alpha_{jd}^{u_d-1} e^{-v_d \alpha_{jd}} \tag{11}$$

Here $\{u_{jd}\}$ and $\{v_{jd}\}$ are hyperparameters which have constraint such that $u_{jd} > 0$ and $v_{jd} > 0$. Having this prior in hand, the full conditional posterior distribution for $\vec{\alpha}_j$ is:

$$p(\vec{\alpha}_j \mid \ldots) \propto p(\vec{\alpha}_j \mid \vec{u}, \vec{v}) \prod_{i=1}^{N} p(\vec{X}_i \mid \Theta_{Z_i}) \tag{12}$$

$$\propto \prod_{d=1}^{D} \frac{v_d^{u_d}}{\Gamma(u_d)} \alpha_{jd}^{u_d-1} e^{-v_d \alpha_{jd}}$$

$$\times \left[\frac{\Gamma(\mid \alpha_j \mid)}{\prod_{d=1}^{D} \Gamma(\alpha_{jd})} \right]^{n_j} \prod_{Z_i=j} \left[\frac{\prod_{d=1}^{D} x_{id}^{\alpha_{jd}-1}}{\prod_{d=1}^{D} (1 - x_{id})^{(\alpha_{jd}+1)}} \left(1 + \sum_{d=1}^{D} \frac{x_{id}}{(1 - x_{id})} \right)^{-\mid \alpha_j \mid} \right]$$

where $n_j = \sum_{i=1}^{N} \mathbb{I}_{Z_i=j}$ indicates the number of observations belonging to cluster j and symbol $\mid \ldots$ represent conditioning on all other variables. Moreover, for the mixing weight vector $\vec{\pi}$, we know that it is defined on $(\pi_1, \ldots, \pi_K)$: $\sum_{j=1}^{K-1} \pi_j < 1$, then the typical prior choice is a Dirichlet distribution with parameters $\delta = (\delta_1, \ldots, \delta_M)$ as following:

$$p(\vec{\pi} \mid K, \delta) = \frac{\Gamma(\sum_{j=1}^{K} \delta_j)}{\prod_{j=1}^{K} \Gamma(\delta_j)} \prod_{j=1}^{K} \pi_j^{\delta_j-1} \tag{13}$$

Also, the prior for the latent variable Z is:

$$p(Z \mid \vec{\pi}, K) = \prod_{j=1}^{K} \pi_j^{n_j} \tag{14}$$

Then, using Eqs. (13) and (14) we obtain:

$$p(\vec{\pi} \mid \ldots) \propto p(Z \mid \vec{\pi}, K)p(\vec{\pi} \mid K, \delta) \tag{15}$$

$$\propto \prod_{j=1}^{K} \pi_j^{n_j} \frac{\Gamma(\sum_{j=1}^{K} \delta_j)}{\prod_{j=1}^{K} \Gamma(\delta_j)} \prod_{j=1}^{K} \pi_j^{\delta_j - 1}$$

$$\propto \prod_{j=1}^{K} \pi_j^{n_j + \delta_j - 1}$$

which indicates a Dirichlet distribution with parameters $(\delta_1 + n_1, \ldots, \delta_K + n_K)$. Moreover, using Eq. (6) we can obtain the posterior for the membership variables as follows:

$$p(Z_i = j \mid \ldots) \propto \pi_j p(\vec{X}_i \mid \vec{\alpha}_j) \tag{16}$$

3.2   Birth-Death MCMC Methodology

In this section, we follow the algorithm proposed in [15] for parameter estimation and model selection. The method is designed based on generating a continuous time Markov birth-death process with the proper stationary distribution. In this approach, the model parameters can be considered as observations from a marked point process, where each point represents a component of the mixture [26]. In order to create an ergodic Markov chain, the mixture size, K, can change, where it can allow new components to be born or existing components to die. Therefore, births and deaths may happen in continuous time, where their happening rates could define the stationary distribution of the process [23].

Whenever the birth event occurs, the weight of new component is calculated from a Beta distribution with parameters $(1, K)$ and the number of components is increased. Then, in order to keep the sum of all the weights equal to unity, the old component weights are scaled down proportionally through multiplying each mixing weight by $(1 - \pi^*)$, where π^* is the weight of the new component. On the other hand, after eliminating a component, each mixing weight is divided by $(1 - \pi^*)$, (π^* is the weight of the removed component) [25]. A death event decreases the number of mixture components, where the death rate for each component is computed as a likelihood ratio of the model with and without that component as follows [23]:

$$\Delta_j = \prod_{i=1}^{N} \left(\frac{p(\vec{X}_i \mid \Theta) - \pi_j p(\vec{X}_i \mid \vec{\alpha}_j)}{(1 - \pi_j)p(\vec{X}_i \mid \Theta)} \right), \qquad j = 1, \ldots, K \tag{17}$$

where $p(\vec{X}_i \mid \Theta) = \sum_{j=1}^{K} \pi_j p(\vec{X}_i \mid \vec{\alpha}_j)$. Then, the total death rate of the process at any time is obtained by the sum of the individual death rates, i.e., $\Delta = \sum_j \Delta_j$, for $j = 1, \ldots, K$. Since births and deaths are independent Poisson processes, the time between each birth or death occurrence is exponentially distributed with mean $1/(\Delta + \lambda)$. We assume the constant λ from prior of K in Eq. (10) for birth rate of mixture component.

The complete BDMCMC algorithm can be summarized in Algorithm 1. The first step of this algorithm is the birth-death process, while the rests are standard Gibbs sampling moves. In order to sample from $\vec{\alpha}_j$ posterior, we exploit Metropolis-Hastings method as suggested in [27]. It is used to avoid direct sampling of mixture parameters since the full conditional distribution given by Eq. (12) is complex and does not have a well-known form.

For a specific iteration t, the steps of the M-H algorithm, to sample $\vec{\alpha}_j$, are as follows [28]:

1. Generate $\tilde{\alpha}_{jd} \sim q\left(\vec{\alpha}_j \mid \vec{\alpha}_j^{(t-1)}\right)$ and $u \sim \mathcal{U}_{[0,1]}$

2. Compute $r = \dfrac{p(\tilde{\alpha}_j|\dots)q\left(\vec{\alpha}_j^{(t-1)}|\tilde{\alpha}_j\right)}{p(\vec{\alpha}_j^{(t-1)}|\dots)q\left(\tilde{\alpha}_j|\vec{\alpha}_j^{(t-1)}\right)}$

3. If $r < u$ then $\vec{\alpha}_j^{(t)} = \tilde{\alpha}_j$ else $\vec{\alpha}_j^{(t)} = \vec{\alpha}_j^{(t-1)}$

The main issue related to this algorithm is the choice of proposal distribution. Since all $\tilde{\alpha}_{jd} > 0$, $d = 1, \dots, D$, we assumed a random walk M-H with the following proposal $\tilde{\alpha}_{jd} \sim \mathcal{LN}(\log(\alpha_{jd}^{(t-1)}), \sigma^2)$, where $\mathcal{LN}(\log(\alpha_{jl}^{(t-1)}), \sigma^2)$ is the log-normal distribution with mean $\log(\alpha_{jl}^{(t-1)})$ and variance σ^2.

Algorithm 1. Birth-Death MCMC learning of MBMM

Initialize parameters $k^{(0)}, \vec{\pi}^{(0)}, \vec{\alpha}^{(0)}$

1. Begin the birth-death process for a virtual fixed time t_0 and let the birth rate equivalent to λ.

   (a) Calculate the death rates for each component, Δ_j, and the total death rate, $\Delta = \sum_j \Delta_j$.

   (b) Simulate the time to the next jump from an exponential distribution with mean $1/(\Delta + \lambda)$.

   (c) If the run time is lower than t_0 continue otherwise jump to step 2.

   (d) Simulate the type of jump: birth or death with probabilities: $p(\text{birth}) = \frac{\lambda}{\lambda + \Delta}$, $p(\text{death}) = \frac{\Delta}{\lambda + \Delta}$

   (e) Make the adjustment for mixture components.
   MCMC steps

2. Update the allocation $Z^{(i+1)}$.

3. Update the mixing parameters $\vec{\pi}^{(i+1)}$.

4. Update the parameters $\vec{\alpha}_j^{(i+1)}$

5. Set $i = i + 1$ and iterate

---

4   Experimental Results

In this section, we validate the performance of our proposed BDMCMC algorithm for MB mixture model (BD-MBMM) on real-world medical tasks. We investigate its ability to estimate the mixture parameters and simultaneously select the proper number of components. We compared our proposed models with similar algorithms for GMM (BD-GMM) and present the result in comparison tables. It should be noted that we use min-max normalization in the preprocessing step of our algorithm, since one of the assumptions of MB distribution is that the values of all observations are positive and less than one. For each of the experiment, we ran the algorithm with varying initial hyperparameter values and different numbers of iterations several times and considered $k_{max} = 10$. Furthermore, our experiments are based on clustering with no training step as entire data is given into the algorithm with no prior knowledge about the labels. For this, we first removed the original labels of datasets and with the help of our proposed clustering model, we found the predicted labels of each observation.

The effectiveness of the model is evaluated in terms of the accuracy, precision, recall and F1-score based on confusion matrix which are defined as follows:

$$Accuracy = \frac{TP + TN}{Total\ no\ of\ observations} \qquad Precision = \frac{TP}{TP + FP} \qquad (18)$$

$$Recall = \frac{TP}{TP+FN} \qquad F1\text{-}score = 2 * \frac{precision * recall}{precision + recall}$$

where TP, TN, FP, and FN represent the total number of true positives, true negatives, false positives, and false negatives respectively.

4.1   Heart Failure Detection

Cardiovascular diseases (CVDs) as serious health issues still remain the leading cause of death globally. In particular, heart failure is a condition caused by CVDs in which the pumping power of the heart is not sufficient to move blood and oxygen in the body. The CVDs can be preventable if the underlying main risk factors, such as high blood pressure, level of cholesterol, diabetes and stress be under control. For this purpose, medical records can be considered as useful resources for designing automatic diagnosis systems using data mining tools [29].

In this experiment, we used real-world data set obtained from the UCI Repository[1], which includes medical records of 299 patients having heart failure to evaluate our proposed model. It consists of 13 features derived from multiple medical tests, lifestyle and body information. The data set is comprised of two target classes that imply whether patients with heart failure died or survived. The confusion matrices obtained using the models are given in Table 1. Actual labels and predicted labels are denoted by (ac) and (p), respectively. Table 2 represents the comparison between different results of performance metrics for both models which shows that BD-MBMM outperforms BD-GMM.

---

[1] https://archive.ics.uci.edu/ml/datasets/Heart+failure+clinical+records.

Table 1. Confusion matrices for heart failure

BD-MBMM	Survive(p)	N.Survive(p)
Survive(ac)	188	15
N.Survive(ac)	44	52

BD-GMM	Survive(p)	N.Survive(p)
Survive(ac)	179	24
N.Survive(ac)	61	35

Table 2. Model performance results for heart failure

Model	Accuracy(%)	Precision(%)	Recall(%)	F1-score(%)
BD-MBMM	80.27	77.61	54.16	63.8
BD-GMM	71.57	59.32	36.45	45.15

4.2 Thyroid Disease Detection

Thyroid as a primary gland produces hormones to regulate the metabolism of the body. The most common thyroid disorders can occur when the thyroid hormones are abnormal. Hyperthyroidism and hypothyroidism are the two main diseases of the thyroid that happen either by releasing too much T4 hormone or by releasing less. Most thyroid problems can be treated by early detection and proper diagnosis [30].

In our study, we applied our model on a publicly available data set[2], which includes a sample of 215 patients. The features are the results of the five laboratory tests, namely: RT3U, T4, T3, TSH and DTSH. The data set has three classes which indicate the diagnosis of thyroid operation as Hypo, Normal, and Hyper. The confusion matrices in Table 3 and the results presented in Table 4 illustrate the potential of our proposed model performance in this application.

Table 3. Confusion matrices for Thyroid disease

BD-MBMM	Hyper(p)	Norm(p)	Hypo(p)
Hyper(ac)	22	8	5
Norm(ac)	0	144	6
Hypo(ac)	2	5	23

BD-GMM	Hyper(p)	Norm(p)	Hypo(p)
Hyper(ac)	20	15	0
Norm(ac)	1	132	17
Hypo(ac)	4	7	19

Table 4. Model performance results for Thyroid disease

Model	Accuracy(%)	Precision(%)	Recall(%)	F1-score(%)
BD-MBMM	87.9	83.67	78.5	81.0
BD-GMM	79.53	72.83	69.49	71.12

---

[2] https://archive.ics.uci.edu/ml/datasets/thyroid+disease.

5   Conclusion

In this paper, a fully Bayesian framework has been developed for MB mixture model. The consideration of MB distribution is motivated by its high flexibility for modeling non-Gaussian data. Learning of the proposed model has been accomplished via a birth-death MCMC algorithm which allows automatic and simultaneous estimation of the parameters and model selection by constructing birth and death moves. The effectiveness of the proposed framework was evaluated using real-world medical applications, where the experimental results reveal that the performance of the proposed approach is convincing.

References

1. Kaufman, L., Rousseeuw, P.J.: Finding Groups in Data: An Introduction to Cluster Analysis, vol. 344. John Wiley & Sons, New Jersey (2009)
2. Soni, J., Ansari, U., Sharma, D., Soni, S.: Predictive data mining for medical diagnosis: an overview of heart disease prediction. Int. J. Comput. Appl. **17**(8), 43–48 (2011)
3. Sohail, M.N., Jiadong, R., Uba, M.M., Irshad, M.: A comprehensive looks at data mining techniques contributing to medical data growth: a survey of researcher reviews. In: Patnaik, S., Jain, V. (eds.) Recent Developments in Intelligent Computing, Communication and Devices. AISC, vol. 752, pp. 21–26. Springer, Singapore (2019). https://doi.org/10.1007/978-981-10-8944-2_3
4. Chen, W., Feng, G.: Spectral clustering with discriminant cuts. Knowl.-Based Syst. **28**, 27–37 (2012)
5. McLachlan, G.J., Peel, D.: Finite Mixture Models. John Wiley & Sons, New Jersey (2004)
6. Channoufi, I., Bourouis, S., Bouguila, N., Hamrouni, K.: Image and video denoising by combining unsupervised bounded generalized gaussian mixture modeling and spatial information. Multimedia Tools Appl. **77**(19), 25591–25606 (2018). https://doi.org/10.1007/s11042-018-5808-9
7. Bourouis, S., Al-Osaimi, F.R., Bouguila, N., Sallay, H., Aldosari, F., Al Mashrgy, M.: Bayesian inference by reversible jump MCMC for clustering based on finite generalized inverted dirichlet mixtures. Soft Comput. **23**(14), 5799–5813 (2019)
8. Fan, W., Bouguila, N.: Learning finite beta-liouville mixture models via variational bayes for proportional data clustering. In: Twenty-Third International Joint Conference on Artificial Intelligence (2013)
9. Manouchehri, N., Bouguila, N., Fan, W.: Nonparametric variational learning of multivariate beta mixture models in medical applications. Int. J. Imaging Syst. Technol. **31**(1), 128–140 (2020)
10. McLachlan, G.J., Krishnan, T.: The EM algorithm and extensions, vol. 382. John Wiley & Sons, New Jersey (2007)
11. Robert, C.: The Bayesian Choice: From Decision-theoretic Foundations to Computational Implementation. Springer Science & Business Media, Berlin (2007)
12. Bdiri, T., Bouguila, N.: Bayesian learning of inverted dirichlet mixtures for SVM kernels generation. Neural Comput. Appl. **23**(5), 1443–1458 (2013)
13. Bolstad, W.M., Curran, J.M.: Introduction to Bayesian Statistics. John Wiley & Sons, New Jersey (2016)

14. Bouguila, N., Ziou, D.: Unsupervised selection of a finite dirichlet mixture model: an mml-based approach. IEEE Trans. Knowl. Data Eng. **18**(8), 993–1009 (2006)
15. Stephens, M.: Bayesian analysis of mixture models with an unknown number of components-an alternative to reversible jump methods. Annals of Statistics, pp. 40–74 (2000)
16. Shawe-Taylor, J., Williamson, R.C.: A pac analysis of a bayesian estimator. In: Proceedings of the Tenth Annual Conference on Computational Learning Theory, pp. 2–9 (1997)
17. Elguebaly, T., Bouguila, N.: Bayesian learning of generalized gaussian mixture models on biomedical images. In: Schwenker, F., El. Gayar, N. (eds.) ANNPR 2010. LNCS (LNAI), vol. 5998, pp. 207–218. Springer, Heidelberg (2010). https://doi.org/10.1007/978-3-642-12159-3_19
18. Cappe, O., Robert, C.P.: Markov chain monte carlo: 10 years and still running! J. Am. Stat. Assoc. **95**(452), 1282–1286 (2000)
19. Bouguila, N., Wang, J.H., Hamza, A.B.: Software modules categorization through likelihood and bayesian analysis of finite dirichlet mixtures. J. Appl. Stat. **37**(2), 235–252 (2010)
20. Richardson, S., Green, P.J.: On bayesian analysis of mixtures with an unknown number of components (with discussion). J. R. Stat. Soc. Ser. B (Stat. Methodol.) **59**(4), 731–792 (1997)
21. Bouguila, N., Elguebaly, T.: A fully bayesian model based on reversible jump MCMC and finite beta mixtures for clustering. Expert Syst. Appl. **39**(5), 5946–5959 (2012)
22. Shi, J., Murray-Smith, R., Titterington, D.: Birth-death MCMC methods for mixtures with an unknown number of components. Technical report, Citeseer (2002)
23. Mohammadi, A., Salehi-Rad, M., Wit, E.: Using mixture of gamma distributions for bayesian analysis in an m/g/1 queue with optional second service. Comput. Stat. **28**(2), 683–700 (2013)
24. Elguebaly, T., Bouguila, N.: Medical image classification using birth-and-death MCMC. In: IEEE International Symposium on Circuits and Systems. IEEE 2012, pp. 2075–2078 (2012)
25. Elguebaly, T., Bouguila, N.: A bayesian approach for the classification of mammographic masses. In: 2013 Sixth International Conference on Developments in eSystems Engineering, pp. 99–104. IEEE (2013)
26. Cappé, O., Robert, C.P., Rydén, T.: Reversible jump, birth-and-death and more general continuous time markov chain monte carlo samplers. J. R. Stat. Soc. Ser. B (Stat. Methodol.) **65**(3), 679–700 (2003)
27. Robert, C., Casella, G.: Monte Carlo Statistical Methods. Springer Science & Business Media, Berlin (2013)
28. Bdiri, T., Bouguila, N.: Bayesian learning of inverted dirichlet mixtures for svm kernels generation. Neural Comput. Appl. **23**(5), 1443–1458 (2013)
29. Chicco, D., Jurman, G.: Machine learning can predict survival of patients with heart failure from serum creatinine and ejection fraction alone. BMC Med. Inform. Decis. Making **20**(1), 16 (2020)
30. Tyagi, A., Mehra, R., Saxena, A.: Interactive thyroid disease prediction system using machine learning technique. In: 2018 Fifth International Conference on Parallel, Distributed and Grid Computing (PDGC), pp. 689–693. IEEE (2018)

Intelligent Asthma Self-management System for Personalised Weather-Based Healthcare Using Machine Learning

Radiah Haque[1], Sin-Ban Ho[1](✉) ⓘ, Ian Chai[1], Chin-Wei Teoh[1], Adina Abdullah[2] ⓘ, Chuie-Hong Tan[3], and Khairi Shazwan Dollmat[1]

[1] Faculty of Computing and Informatics, Multimedia University, 63100 Cyberjaya, Malaysia
{sbho,ianchai,shazwan.dollmat}@mmu.edu.my
[2] Faculty of Medicine, University of Malaya, 50603 Kuala Lumpur, Malaysia
adina@ummc.edu.my
[3] Faculty of Management, Multimedia University, 63100 Cyberjaya, Malaysia
chtan@mmu.edu.my

Abstract. Asthma is a common chronic disease that affects people from all age groups around the world. Although asthma cannot be cured, strategies to enhance applications on self-management can be effective to control asthma exacerbations. In recent years, researchers have been developing various mHealth tools and applications for self-management. However, there is a lack of effective personalised self-management solution for asthma that can be adopted widely. Personalisation is important for identifying each patient's demographic characteristics, measuring their asthma severity level, and most importantly, predicting the triggers of asthma attacks. It has been observed that weather attributes (e.g. temperature, humidity, air pressure and thunderstorms) impact on triggering asthma attacks and adversely affect the symptoms of asthmatic patients. Hence, developing an intelligent asthma self-management system for personalised weather-based healthcare using machine learning technique can help predict weather impact on asthma exacerbations for individual patients and provide real-time feedback based on daily weather forecasts. Therefore, this paper explores the impact of weather on asthma exacerbations and examines the effectiveness and limitations of several recent asthma self-management tools and applications. Consequently, based on the uses and gratifications theory, an engineering model for personalised weather-based healthcare is proposed which incorporates major constructs including mHealth application, asthma control test, demographic characteristics, weather attributes, machine learning technique and neural networks.

Keywords: Intelligent system · Machine learning · Personalisation

1 Introduction

Asthma is a common disease that affects people from all age groups around the world. The World Health Organisation (WHO) estimates more than three hundred million people are currently living with asthma. It is considered a major cause of economic burden

H. Fujita et al. (Eds.): IEA/AIE 2021, LNAI 12798, pp. 297–308, 2021.
https://doi.org/10.1007/978-3-030-79457-6_26

among asthmatic patients due to the need for frequent visits to medical centres and health-care providers [1]. Asthma is a chronic acute airway disorder which is accompanied by extreme coughs, chest pains, wheezing and shortness in breathing [2]. Depending on individual patients' asthma severity level, asthma exacerbations (also known as asthma attacks) can occur that vary from manageable discomforts which can be handled with inhalers to extreme situations which need immediate visits to Emergency Rooms (ER) [3]. The frequent occurrences of asthma exacerbations depend on the exposure to trigger-ing factors of asthma, which commonly includes weather attributes such as temperature, humidity, wind and thunderstorms [4].

When the temperature is high, pollutants and exhaust fumes increase, which can cause lung airways to become narrower for some patients, leading to shortness in breath. When the temperature is low, cold and damp air can cause the lung airways to spasm for other patients, leading to extreme coughing. Meanwhile, humidity in the air can cause lung moisture, leading to faster breathing and wheezing. Wind and thunderstorm can cause pollen grains to break into small pieces, which enter the lung, leading to breathing difficulties. Therefore, all these weather attributes are considered to be common triggers of asthma exacerbations [1]. It has to be noted that weather impact on asthma exacerbations is specific to individual patients due to varied lung performances that depend on demographic characteristics of patients, such as age and gender [4]. Although asthma cannot be cured, strategies to enhance applications on self-management can be effective to control asthma exacerbations and decrease their frequency of occurrences. In effect, fewer visits to healthcare providers and ER is needed, thus reducing the economic burden on asthmatic patients.

2   Problem Statement and Motivation

Weather-based healthcare refers to self-management of chronic diseases that are affected by the weather. For asthmatic patients, weather-based healthcare can help them avoid weather triggers that cause asthma exacerbations by changing their lifestyle. However, it is difficult for individual patients to change their lifestyle for asthma self-management based on the weather, because many of them are unaware of which weather triggers they are vulnerable to, which may depend on their demographic characteristics and asthma severity level. Therefore, personalisation is important in weather-based healthcare which can provide personalised feedback based on individual patients' demographic charac-teristics, severity level and weather triggers. Consequently, an asthma self-management system for weather-based healthcare should be able to learn through observing demo-graphic characteristics of patients and monitoring weather attributes in their location, predict weather impact on patients' asthma exacerbations and the severity level of their asthma, and suggest personalised feedback and actions to patients for self-care (see Fig. 1). Such intelligent system can limit asthmatic patients' exposure to weather triggers and reduce asthma exacerbations.

Nevertheless, there is a lack of effective intelligent self-management solutions for asthma that can be adopted widely. This is because, although researchers have identified weather attributes as asthma triggers, the effort to engineer an intelligent asthma self-management system for personalised weather-based healthcare is still lacking. This paper reviews prior work and identifies the limitations that cause them not to be adopted widely. Subsequently, a machine learning approach will be introduced for engineering an intelligent asthma self-management system for personalised weather-based healthcare that can predict weather impact on asthma exacerbations based on individual patient's demographic characteristics and severity level.

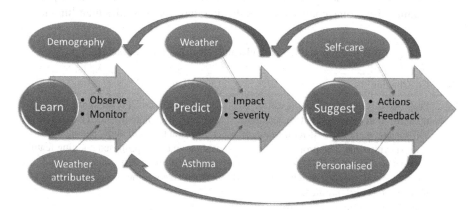

Fig. 1. Effective approach for an intelligent asthma self-management system.

3   Weather Impact on Asthma Exacerbations

Several researchers have supported the association of weather attributes with asthma. For example, Alharbi and Abdullah [1] conducted an experimental study where they developed a decision tree to identify the link between monthly asthma hospitalisations and different weather attributes. Their predictive model confirms that temperature, humidity, precipitations and thunderstorms have an impact on worsening asthma symptoms. Palmu et al. [5] provided evidence via analysing the results of a questionnaire that asthmatic patients are susceptible to cold weather which leads to functional disability and exacerbation of asthma. Shoraka et al. [6] conducted a systematic review of more than twenty papers and articles and concluded that a majority of the findings indicate that extreme weather temperatures (cold or hot) cause exacerbations of asthma.

To explain this further, Charandabi et al. [2] states that weather has an impact on asthma because of the existence of pollen grains, pollutants, and allergens in the air, which increase due to certain weather conditions, such as extreme temperature, humidity and thunderstorms. Inhaling these pollens and allergens causes asthma exacerbations among asthmatic patients. To confirm this, Sharma et al. [7] used a spatiotemporal approach where they tested weather attributes (temperature, humidity and rainfall) against acute attacks of asthma. They found that particulate matters in the air, such as dusts and pollen grains, relatively increase asthma exacerbations. In the same vein, a recent study [8] on the climate and weather changes and their impact on asthma reports that aeroallergens, which exacerbate asthma, correlate with increased temperature and pollen production in the air.

Consequently, these studies indicate that weather has an adverse impact on asthma. Monitoring asthmatic patients and their surrounding weather attributes for self-management can limit their exposure to increased pollens and allergens in the air and hence reducing their asthma exacerbations. In this regard, recently, with the expansion of computer assisted systems in health, much attention is driven on developing Internet of Things (IoT) tools and mobile health (mHealth) applications for self-management. Table 1 summarises some contributions in the literature and identifies their limitations.

Table 1. Proposed IoT and mHealth self-management solutions.

Ref.	Contribution	Limitation
[3]	Proposed mHealth application with nudging strategy for patient engagement, self-management and self-monitoring of asthma symptoms. The proposed application will provide information about weather and air quality which is presented to the user as push notification to avoid exposure in certain weather conditions	The mHealth model is implemented theoretically. There is a need to develop an application that will allow testing and evaluation of the proposed nudging feature and identifying its effectiveness on personalised weather-based healthcare
[9]	Developed an IoT smart sensor that can be attached to inhalers and can record date, time, location and number of puffs. This helps to identify the severity level of asthma and monitor the weather condition when the puff is taken. When the sensor is attached to a laptop or smartphone, a comprehensive report with prediction is produced for asthma self-management	There is no scope for real-time feedback as the sensor needs to be connected manually to another device to access the report, hence there is no guarantee for sustained user engagement. Moreover, installing this sensor to inhalers can be expensive which hinders mass production
[10]	Developed an Android based prototype model, which contains knowledge generation via intelligent learning system to sense the surrounding environment and weather conditions. The model recommends the use of machine learning in the future for predicting the weather triggers, and thus providing feedback to the users	The model does not propose identifying the severity level of asthma. Furthermore, no user testing has been conducted of the prototype. To measure intelligent learning effectiveness, a usable infrastructure needs to be modelled and evaluated
[11]	Built a smartwatch with wireless sensor to be connected with an application for asthma self-management. APIs are used to transfer sensor data to the application which is then stored in the cloud for real-time analysis. Simple graphics are created to illustrate the analysed data via the smartwatch application which contains weather information and pollen levels	The smartwatch application does not provide prediction based on user's demographic characters and asthma triggers. Also, personalised feedback is not provided. Moreover, purchasing the smartwatch can be problematic for many users due to its potential high cost

From reviewing the literature, it can be identified that although a few tools and strategies have been used to predict asthma attacks based on the weather, their performance is limited because relevant information on the demographic characteristics and asthma severity level is often omitted. Fortunately, machine learning can be used to solve this issue [12]. This is because machine learning teaches the computer to solve problems by obtaining relevant weather, asthma severity and demography data, learning from them and then using the learning experience to provide personalised prediction results. However, the effect of machine learning on personalised weather-based healthcare for self-management has not been addressed in the literature thus far. Moreover, application of machine learning techniques to predict asthma exacerbations using personalisation is still in its infancy. Therefore, there is a need to understand how machine learning techniques affect the personalisation of weather-based healthcare.

Multiple machine learning techniques can be used for personalised weather-based healthcare. Firstly, a classification technique can be used to predict the category of a case, such as chances of asthma attacks based on weather triggers. Secondly, a regression technique can be used to predict a continuous value, such as asthma control test scores. Thirdly, a clustering technique can be used to group similar cases, such as finding similar group of patients based on their demographic characteristics. Fourthly, an association technique can be used for finding events that often co-occur, such as identifying weather attributes that are linked to a particular patient's occurrences of asthma attacks. Finally, a recommendation technique can be used to associate patients' activities with their asthma attacks and recommend actions to do in certain weather conditions. Consequently, for this study, the classification technique is considered to predict the chances of asthma attacks (i.e. high or low chance) based on weather triggers.

4 Engineering Model for Weather-Based Healthcare

In this paper, an intelligent self-management model for personalised weather-based healthcare is engineered that can predict asthma exacerbations based on the weather.

4.1 Conceptual Representation

The proposed model is based on the Uses and Gratification Theory (UGT) that considers user demographic characters, personalisation effectiveness, weather attributes and uses machine learning techniques. UGT helps to identify the media and elements that benefit users' social needs, thus ensuring sustained user engagement [13]. This model suggests developing an mHealth android-based application (media) and machine learning classification technique (element) for personalised weather-based healthcare (social need). Figure 2 illustrates the conceptual representation of the proposed model.

4.2 Demographic Characteristics

Demographic characteristics track the specific aspects of asthmatic patients which includes age, gender and the severity level of their asthma. This shapes the underlying learning target for modelling an effective approach for the intelligent asthma self-management model. Demography observation can help to provide personalised prediction and feedback based on each patient's characteristics. Thus, the following hypothesis is formulated: **H1.** Observing user demographic characteristics has positive effects on personalised weather-based healthcare.

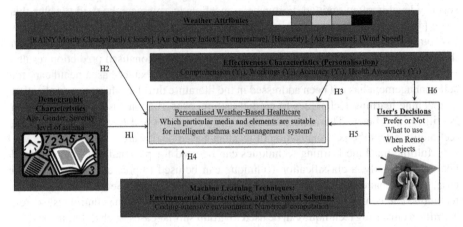

Fig. 2. Conceptual representation of the proposed model.

4.3 Weather Attributes

The weather attributes included in the proposed model are: temperature, humidity, air quality index, air pressure, rain, and wind speed. Monitoring the daily weather forecasts in user's location is vital in the intelligent asthma self-management model for personalised weather-based healthcare. This formulates the following hypothesis: **H2.** Monitoring weather attributes has positive effects on personalised weather-based healthcare.

4.4 Personalisation

Personalisation ensures the effectiveness of the intelligent asthma self-management model for personalised weather-based healthcare. In fact, it was identified that the main reason for the lack of several existing asthma self-management systems' adoption is because they fail to provide personalised feedback to users [10–12]. To achieve person-alisation effectiveness, the machine learning process with analytics approach in Fig. 3 has been constructed. The following hypotheses are also formulated: **H3.** Personalisation has positive effects on asthma self-management; **H4.** Using machine learning techniques has positive effects on personalised weather-based healthcare.

4.5 User's Decisions

Users play the main role in making the mHealth application successful. This is because considering users' decisions on whether to use the application or not, what features to use in the application and when to use the application assists the developer in engineering the intelligent asthma self-management model for personalised weather-based healthcare. Based on this, the following hypotheses are formulated: **H5.** User's decision to use the mHealth application has positive effects on personalised weather-based healthcare. **H6.** Personalisation has positive effects on user's decision to use the mHealth application for asthma self-management.

In order to measure the effect of machine learning on the proposed intelligent asthma self-management model for personalised weather-based healthcare, a machine learning algorithm (neural networks) is applied which will contribute in identifying the classification model that can provide predictions with high accuracy.

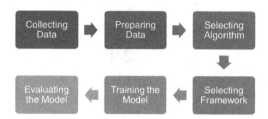

Fig. 3. Proposed machine learning approach.

4.6 Schematic Representation

The schematic representation of the proposed intelligent asthma self-management model for weather-based healthcare is illustrated in Fig. 4. The essential part of the system is the weather monitoring unit which collects and provides weather information to users. Users can then decide to go through the reporting unit to conduct the Asthma Control Test (ACT). The ACT is recommended by medical experts as the standard test to monitor asthma severity [14]. The ACT is used to collect data from users, which helps to identify weather triggers based on each users' ACT result. It is a five-item self-administered

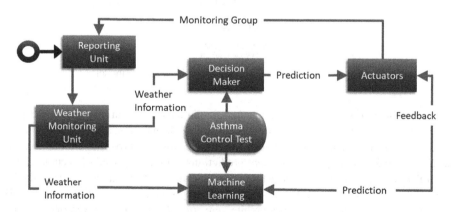

Fig. 4. Schematic representation of the proposed model.

survey which has a scaling index for patients to record the severity of their asthma easily. Consequently, if the ACT score is low, the severity level is high and if the score is high, the severity level is low.

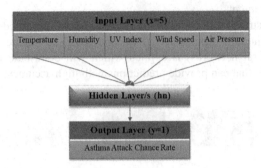

Fig. 5. Personalisation neural network architecture model.

In this regard, a recent analysis finds that an ACT score of below 19 indicates poorly controlled asthma, which means a high chance rate of asthma exacerbation [15]. Subsequently, once users submit their ACT answers, a timestamp is created with the weather forecast information of that day and time in their location. Afterward, two neural networks models are applied as the machine learning algorithm on the collected data from individual users to provide predictions.

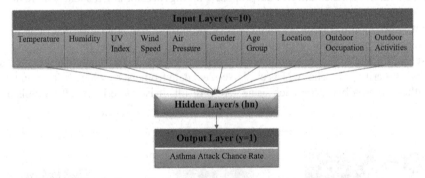

Fig. 6. Generalisation neural network architecture model.

Neural networks are biologically inspired simulations from neurons used for data prediction and pattern recognition. Neural networks have been used in several recent healthcare and self-management applications for chronic diseases [16–19]. This is because neural networks can provide healthcare predictions with a high level of accuracy [20]. Neural networks are proposed due to the nonlinear nature of the weather-based healthcare data. Subsequently, two architecture models are proposed: personalisation and generalisation. Typically, a neural network architecture consists of an input layer, one or more hidden layers, and an output layer. In the personalisation model, there are five input neurons at the input layer and one output neuron at the output layer (see Fig. 5). This indicates that the type of neural networks architecture is "many-to-one", where several inputs are used to create a single output. The personalisation architecture model will contain input data from one user, hence there is no need for the demography data.

In the generalisation model, there are ten input neurons at the input layer and one output neuron at the output layer (see Fig. 6). The generalisation model will contain input data from all users and will include demography and location data of each user.

5 Results and Discussion

The proposed intelligent asthma self-management model for personalised weather-based healthcare is based on an mHealth android application. Recently, with the development of smartphones, mHealth applications have become mainstream tools that assist patients in self-management and self-care [21]. This is because smartphones are used for essential needs such as communication, as well as the ubiquity of internet connected smartphones makes users carry these devices everywhere. Furthermore, there is no need to invest extra money to purchase a smartphone, since the majority of the people around the world already own them [9]. Therefore, providing real-time feedback to users for asthma self-management through the mHealth application is an effective strategy.

Consequently, for this study, an android-based mHealth application was developed that collects demography data of individual users and monitors weather triggers in each users' location. Moreover, the application allows users to conduct the ACT on a regular basis to report their asthma severity [22]. Subsequently, data has been collected over 5 months from 10 asthmatic patients who conducted the ACTs by answering five multiple choice questions. The goal is to predict the chances of asthma attacks using the ACT scores. The experiments of predicting the asthma exacerbations have been deployed using neural networks on Jupyter notebook. As such, both personalisation and generalisation models were implemented on the dataset attained from the mHealth application. Thereafter, the performance of both classification models was measured in order to identify the impact of weather and demographic characteristics on personalisation.

Figure 7 illustrates the prediction loss and accuracy of both personalisation and generalisation models. Both models performed similarly and achieved an accuracy rate of 94%. It has to be mentioned that the dataset of the personalisation model contained data from one user only, whereas the generalisation model contained data from all users. As such, the generalisation model was able to provide similar prediction results because it has personalisation feature due to the inclusion of demography data. Therefore, the personalisation involves identifying an individual asthmatic patient's demographic characteristics, measuring their asthma severity level, and monitoring the weather triggers in their location. Moreover, the generalisation model would be able to provide predictions to new users from different climate regions based on the similarities of the demographic characteristics with existing users in the same climate region.

From the results, the weather attributes (temperature, humidity, air pressure, UV index, and thunderstorms) impact the triggering of asthma attacks and adversely affect the symptoms of asthmatic patients. Hence, developing the asthma self-management system for personalised weather-based healthcare would help identify the impact of

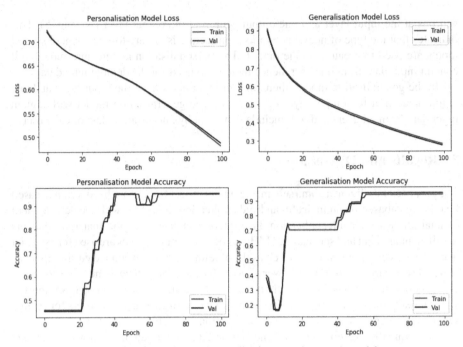

Fig. 7. Personalisation vs. generalisation neural network models.

weather on asthma severity of individual patients, predict their asthma attack chance rate based on their demographic characteristics and weather triggers, and provide real-time feedback based on daily weather forecasts. Consequently, such an intelligent system would enhance asthma self-management by limiting asthmatic patients' exposure to weather triggers and reduce asthma exacerbations. Overall, the results of this study confirmed that personalisation has positive effects on asthma self-management. Moreover, we observed that user demographic characteristics and weather attributes have positive effects on personalised weather-based healthcare.

Meanwhile, prolonged engagement is relevant to identify the effect of users' decision to use the mHealth application on weather-based healthcare. It has to be mentioned that, as of writing this paper, there has been no development of a standard proxy that can be utilised to predict the prolonged use of asthma self-management applications. Having said that, certain strategies have been identified as usable, such as sending reminders through emails or push notifications to users, which can increase patient engagement in self-management applications leading to prolonged use. This is important for asthma as a chronic disease related to weather, which requires frequent monitoring of weather conditions and long-term monitoring of asthma symptoms. Therefore, the mHealth application will apply cohort retention analysis for increasing patient engagement, which subsequently can lead to the wide adoption of the intelligent asthma self-management system for personalised weather-based healthcare.

6 Conclusions

Asthma is a serious health disorder that affects the quality of life adversely and causes economic burden. Unmonitored and uncontrolled asthma leads to frequent occurrences of asthma exacerbations, which forces patients to continuously visit health providers and emergency rooms (ERs), hindering their healthy activities. Self-management of asthma is an effective way to overcome this issue. A typical self-management approach should reduce the exposure to triggers of asthma exacerbations, such as weather attributes. While researchers have identified the impact of weather on asthma exacerbations, the effort to build an intelligent asthma self-management system for personalised weather-based healthcare still lags behind. In fact, many of the recently developed IoT tools and mHealth applications for asthma self-management do not offer personalised algorithms for providing tailored feedback.

This paper demonstrated engineering an intelligent asthma self-management model for personalised weather-based healthcare, which uses a machine learning classification technique for prediction. Neural network has been proposed as the machine learning algorithm in order to solve nonlinear optimisation problems of the weather-based healthcare data. Moreover, an mHealth android-based application has been proposed to collect data from users through the ACT reporting interface for training and evaluating the proposed neural network models. For future work, a deep neural network algorithm will be applied using multiple frameworks to identify the highest prediction accuracy in order to build a comprehensive intelligent asthma self-management system for personalised weather-based healthcare.

Acknowledgments. The authors appreciate the financial support given by the Fundamental Research Grant Scheme, FRGS/1/2019/SS06/MMU/02/4.

References

1. Alharbi, E., Abdullah, M.: Asthma attack prediction based on weather factors. Period. Eng. Nat. Sci. **7**(1), 408–419 (2019)
2. Kaffash-Charandabi, N., Alesheikh, A.A., Sharif, M.: A ubiquitous asthma monitoring framework based on ambient air pollutants and individuals' contexts. Environ. Sci. Pollut. Res. **26**(8), 7525–7539 (2019). https://doi.org/10.1007/s11356-019-04185-3
3. Almutairi, N., Vlahu-Gjorgievska, E., Win, K.: Asthma management application for consumers: nudging as a feature. In: Proceedings of the Seventh International Workshop on Behavior Change Support Systems, Limassol, Cyprus, vol. 2340, pp. 1–10 (2019)
4. Do, Q., Doig, A., Son, T., Chaudri, J.: Predicting lung healthiness risk scores to identify probability of an asthma attack. Procedia Comput. Sci. **160**, 424–431 (2019)
5. Palmu, H., Ikäheimo, T., Laatikainen, T., Jousilahti, P., Jaakkola, M., Jaakkola, J.: Cold weather increases respiratory symptoms and functional disability especially among patients with asthma and allergic rhinitis. Sci. Rep. **8**(1) (2018)
6. Shoraka, H., Soodejani, M., Abobakri, O., Khanjani, N.: The relation between ambient temperature and asthma exacerbation in children: a systematic review. J. Lung Health Dis. **3**(1), 1–9 (2019)

7. Sharma, A., Saini, S., Chhabra, P., Chhabra, S., Ghosh, C., Baliyan, P.: Air pollution and weather as the determinants of acute attacks of asthma: spatiotemporal approach. Indian J. Public Health **64**(2), 124–129 (2020)

8. Poole, J., et al.: Impact of weather and climate change with indoor and outdoor air quality in asthma: a work group report of the AAAAI environmental exposure and respiratory health committee. J. Allergy Clin. Immunol. **143**(5), 1702–1710 (2019)

9. Himes, B., Leszinsky, L., Walsh, R., Hepner, H., Wu, A.: Mobile health and inhaler-based monitoring devices for asthma management. J. Allergy Clin. Immunol. Pract. **7**(8), 2535–2543 (2019)

10. Gaynor, M., et al.: A user-centered, learning asthma smartphone application for patients and providers. Learn. Health Syst. **4**(3), e10217 (2020)

11. Hosseini, A., et al.: Feasibility of a secure wireless sensing smartwatch application for the self-management of pediatric asthma. Sensors **17**(8), 1780 (2017)

12. Tsang, K., Pinnock, H., Wilson, A., Shah, S.: Application of machine learning to support self-management of asthma with mHealth. In: Proceedings of the 42nd Annual International Conference of the IEEE Engineering in Medicine and Biology Society (EMBC), Montreal, QC, Canada, pp. 5673–5677 (2020)

13. Hossain, M.: Effects of uses and gratifications on social media use. PSU Res. Rev. **3**(1), 16–28 (2019)

14. AAFA: Weather can trigger asthma. Asthma and Allergy Foundation of America (2017). https://www.aafa.org/weather-triggers-asthma

15. GINA: Global Initiative for Asthma. 2020 GINA Report, Global Strategy for Asthma Management and Prevention, p. 35 (2020). https://ginasthma.org/gina-reports/

16. Kim, C., Son, Y., Youm, S.: Chronic disease prediction using character-recurrent neural network in the presence of missing information. Appl. Sci. **9**(10), 2170 (2019)

17. Xiang, Y., et al.: Asthma exacerbation prediction and risk factor analysis based on a time-sensitive, attentive neural network: retrospective cohort study. J. Med. Internet Res. **22**(7), e16981 (2020)

18. Uddin, M.: A wearable sensor-based activity prediction system to facilitate edge computing in smart healthcare system. J. Parallel Distrib. Comput. **123**, 46–53 (2019)

19. Pandey, K., Janghel, R.: Recent deep learning techniques, challenges and its applications for medical healthcare system: a review. Neural Process Lett. **50**, 1907–1935 (2019)

20. Phan, D., Yang, N., Kuo, C., Chan, C.: Deep learning approaches for sleep disorder prediction in an asthma cohort. J. Asthma 1–9 (2020)

21. Ernsting, C., et al.: Using smartphones and health apps to change and manage health behaviors: a population-based survey. J. Med. Internet Res. **19**(4), e101 (2017)

22. Ho, S.-B., et al.: Integrating mobile devices with cohort analysis into personalised weather-based healthcare. In: Nguyen, N.T., Hoang, B.H., Huynh, C.P., Hwang, D., Trawiński, B., Vossen, G. (eds.) ICCCI 2020. LNCS (LNAI), vol. 12496, pp. 606–618. Springer, Cham (2020). https://doi.org/10.1007/978-3-030-63007-2_47

Deep Forecasting of COVID-19: Canadian Case Study

Fadoua Khennou$^{(\boxtimes)}$ ⓘ and Moulay A. Akhloufi ⓘ

Perception, Robotics, and Intelligent Machines Research Group (PRIME),
Department of Computer Science, University of Moncton, Moncton, NB, Canada
{fadoua.khennou,moulay.akhloufi}@umoncton.ca

Abstract. COVID-19 is an infectious disease, which is caused by severe acute respiratory syndrome coronavirus 2 (SARS-CoV-2). In this research, we firstly present an overview of the main forecasting models to predict the new cases of COVID-19. In this context, we focus on univariate time series models to analyze the dynamic change of this pandemic through time. We also introduce multivariate time series forecasting using weather and daily tests data, to study the impact of exogenous features on the progression of COVID-19. Finally, we present an ensemble learning model based on LSTM and GRU and evaluate the results using the MAE, RMSE and MAPE. The results show that the ensemble approach performs well in comparison to other models. In addition, this research provides an outcome regarding the dynamic correlation between temperature, humidity and daily test data and its impact on the new reported cases of contamination.

Keywords: Covid-19 · Time series · LSTM · GRU · Ensemble learning

1 Introduction

The COVID-19 pandemic has spread at a phenomenal rate. From December 2019 to December 2020, 82,872,473 cases have been confirmed, 1,826,809 are reported dead and 60,282,421 recovered worldwide.

Research models that have been proposed since the announcement of the first cases of COVID-19 have made it possible to estimate the size of the pandemic and the severity of the disease. Yet, several questions still remain unanswered due to the new and different characteristics of this virus. Therefore, to understand its dynamics, it is necessary to look at the time scale of action of the virus. In this serious situation, many countries report the details of daily infection, hospitalization and mortality indicators. The main goal of this research is to demonstrate the possibility of using myriad modeling strategies to analyze and forecast the future of the COVID-19.

Supported by Atlantic Canada Opportunities Agency (proj. 217148), Natural Sciences and Engineering Research Council of Canada (ALLRP 552039-20), and the New Brunswick Innovation Foundation (COV2020-042).

H. Fujita et al. (Eds.): IEA/AIE 2021, LNAI 12798, pp. 309–315, 2021.
https://doi.org/10.1007/978-3-030-79457-6_27

2   Related Work

Different research projects are actually taking place to forecast the spread of the COVID-19 [5,10]. While we are in the beginning of the vaccination stage, it is still important to analyse the virus data in order to overcome future viruses and global pandemics.

The researchers in [9] presented a SEIR based model. Their prediction was effective for China use case in late February, yet they based their study on the 2003 SARS data. Other researchers [1] proposed a hybrid model for the forecast of new COVID-19 cases, combining ARIMA and wavelet-based forecasting techniques. Their model results emphasized on the deficiencies of the classical ARIMA time series model.

Another research was proposed as an automated real-time forecasting model for COVID-19 transmission using LSTM networks [2]. They used collected data from Johns Hopkins University and Canadian Health authority, provided with the number of confirmed cases until March 31, 2020. In their LSTM model, they trained and tested the network on Canadian dataset; the RMSE error was 34.83 with an accuracy of 93.4% for short term predictions in Canada.

A recent comparative study was conducted by [6]. They implemented ARIMA, LSTM and NARNN on data from Denmark, Belgium, Germany, France, UK, Finland, Switzerland and Turkey. Their LSTM model showed high performances compared to other models. Yet, they base their study on univariate time series without considering external features.

Through the analysis of the aforementioned studies, we sum up that they focused mainly on using univariate time series or classical statistical models. Our goal is to overcome this shortcoming by developing an ensemble model of GRU and LSTM using external features such as weather data and the number of daily tests for the forecast of new cases in Canada.

3   Forecasting COVID-19 Cases

In this paper, we focus on two main steps to train the models. The first concerns univariate time series to estimate the forecast for future cases of COVID-19 based only on time stamps data, while the second concerns multivariate modeling to estimate the forecast based on different features as temperature, precipitations, humidity and the number of daily tests.

Dataset. The collected weather data (temperature, humidity and precipitations) [3] was merged with the database containing the number of confirmed cases, the number of deaths as well as the number of daily tests for each province [4].

Evaluation Metrics. The performance of the proposed approach is evaluated based on three performance measures: MAE, RMSE and MAPE.

The mean absolute error (MAE) represents the difference between the actual and the measured value. Indeed, if we know the measured value and the real one, it is then possible to perform a simple subtraction to find the absolute error. This is obtained using Eq. (1).

$$MAE = \frac{1}{N} \sum_{t=1}^{n} |F_t - O_t| \tag{1}$$

The root mean squared error (RMSE) is a statistical measure, which calculates the average magnitude of errors. In fact, the mean square error gives more weight to large errors than to others when calculating the mean. The RMSE is calculated using Eq. (2).

$$RMSE = \sqrt{\frac{\sum_{t=1}^{n}(F_t - O_t)^2}{N}} \tag{2}$$

The mean absolute percentage error (MAPE) helps to depict the difference between an exact value and an estimated one. It is used generally to compare the fitted values of different time series models. The MAPE is calculated using Eq. (3).

$$MAPE = \frac{1}{N} \sum_{t=1}^{n} |\frac{O_t - F_t}{O_t}| \tag{3}$$

4   Results

In this section we analyze the obtained results for the COVID-19 forecast applied to the Canadian case study, using different methods.

4.1   Forecasting Using Univariate Time Series

In the first phase, we used univariate time series modeling in order to forecast the new cases in Canada without considering any exogenous variable. For that, we developed three models, the first is a statistical auto regressive model, we forecast using a linear combination of past values of the variable. We split the data into 80% of train data and 20% of test sets, then we trained the model using the TSA python library for statistical modeling. In order to fit our model, we tested over 7 and 8 lags representing the p parameter of the auto regressive model. The forecast results are presented in Table 1.

The second is the ARIMA model, we used the same number of training and testing sets for each of the three models. Here we used the auto ARIMA function to obtain the best combination of the (p, d, q) orders. This is schematized in Fig. 1.

The third is a deep learning model based on LSTM and GRU. Our network is composed of a first layer with 100 neurons and a dense node to consolidate the output. Adam was used as optimizer. We used the time series generator class to create batches of temporal data. We selected a validation set to avoid over-fitting and tested over 20 time steps to predict the next data point. We also added the "restore best weights" callback, which saves the best model observed during training after 20 iterations. Table 1 illustrates the results of the forecast.

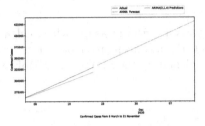

Fig. 1. ARIMA forecasting

Table 1. Evaluation metrics results

Model	RMSE	MAE	MAPE
AR(8)	32429.11	22849.30	7.83%
AR(7)	31099.72	21700.22	7.41%
ARIMA	11045.35	9191.84	2.77%
LSTM	2420.22	2130.80	0.74%
GRU	1131.97	929.83	0.30%

LSTM and GRU achieved better results for the forecast of new cases. With a RMSE of 2420.22 and 1131.97 respectively. As for testing over different AR lags, the AR(7) provided the best results in the autoregressive modeling category. While we notice that statistical models provide promising results for COVID-19 forecast, they have major limitations in regards to model tuning and optimization.

For Stacked, Bi-directional and convolutional LSTM the researchers [8] obtained a MAPE of 4%, 3.33% and 2.17% for INDIA. As for USA, they obtained 10%, 6.66% and 2% respectively. Other researchers [7] compared the results of (ITALY, JAPAN, SPAIN, UK and US) using both LSTM and ARIMA. For ARIMA their MAPE ranges between 1.36% and 21.75% and for LSTM it ranges between 4.39% and 16.67%. In fact, since each country has a glaring difference in the number of cases, it is difficult to compare the results, as they depend mainly on the used data.

4.2 Forecasting Using Multivariate Time Series

We present in Fig. 2 the forecasting models for four Canadian provinces with a high number of confirmed cases. Here, the model performs well as training and validation loss are projecting at a minimal value. After different iterations, we fine tuned the model using a batch size of 4, 20 lag timestamps and final features of (humidity, mean temperature and daily tests).

For Quebec and Ontario (Fig. 2b and 2d), we see that the next 20 days forecast, is reaching more than 140,000 and 120,000 cases respectively. As for Alberta, Fig. 2c shows a highly exponential increase reaching 70,000, while for British Columbia it reaches more than 30,000. Table 2 presents a summary of the forecasting errors for the four models tested on all the provinces.

We note that LSTM did not provide good results in comparison to the GRU model. In fact, GRU presented the best MAPE, RMSE and MAE for Alberta, Nova Scotia, Newfoundland and Labrador and New Brunswick, while LSTM

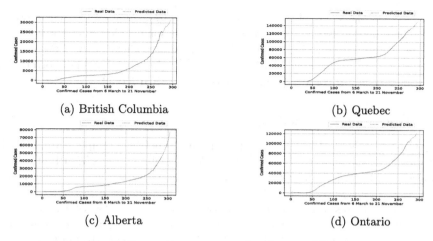

(a) British Columbia

(b) Quebec

(c) Alberta

(d) Ontario

Fig. 2. Forecasting new cases for the next 20 days

Table 2. Evaluation metrics of multivariate time series models

Province	Model	RMSE	MAE	MAPE	Province	Model	RMSE	MAE	MAPE
QC	SARIMAX	467.19	394.70	0.65%	ON	SARIMAX	1312.01	1274.38	1.65%
	LSTM	825.34	723.96	0.62%		LSTM	**1055.87**	**844.42**	**0.92%**
	GRU	465.62	410.14	0.34%		GRU	1706.65	1495.58	1.60%
	LSTM+GRU	**401.11**	**356.71**	**0.30%**		LSTM+GRU	1360.78	1168.58	1.26%
AB	SARIMAX	4902.06	4074.36	10.39%	NB	SARIMAX	7.39	5.60	3.11%
	LSTM	2577.23	2512.41	7.04%		LSTM	3.41	3.01	0.83%
	GRU	**588.86**	**506.76**	**1.47%**		GRU	**2.71**	**2.21**	**0.60%**
	LSTM+GRU	1552.61	1509.59	4.25%		LSTM+GRU	2.99	2.57	0.70%
MB	SARIMAX	262.33	231.51	2.60%	NL	SARIMAX	13.14	13.11	4.91%
	LSTM	96.44	80.39	0.86%		LSTM	2.90	2.42	0.82%
	GRU	100.37	81.12	0.83%		GRU	**2.48**	**2.35**	**0.79%**
	LSTM+GRU	**78.71**	**96.91**	**0.82%**		LSTM+GRU	2.62	2.37	0.80%
BC	SARIMAX	194.11	149.02	3.59%	PE	SARIMAX	2.88	1.76	4.38%
	LSTM	359.48	302.64	1.61%		LSTM	**0.50**	**0.39**	**0.58%**
	GRU	354.48	304.65	1.56%		GRU	1.10	1.08	1.62%
	LSTM+GRU	**303.32**	**267.53**	**1.41%**		LSTM+GRU	0.76	0.72	1.08%
NT	SARIMAX	0.73	0.55	3.70%	NS	SARIMAX	4.51	4.19	0.39%
	LSTM	0.37	0.17	1.32%		LSTM	8.53	6.23	0.55%
	GRU	0.14	0.10	**0.87%**		GRU	**3.87**	**3.39**	**0.30%**
	LSTM+GRU	**0.11**	**0.05**	0.94%		LSTM+GRU	5.69	4.14	0.36%
SK	SARIMAX	96.08	73.71	5.40%	YT	SARIMAX	0.73	0.55	3.70%
	LSTM	**127.71**	**118.11**	**2.79%**		LSTM	0.45	0.27	1.08%
	GRU	146.22	139.37	3.23 %		GRU	0.29	0.26	1.11%
	LSTM+GRU	135.22	128.29	3.00%		LSTM+GRU	**0.27**	**0.18**	**0.75%**

delivered good performance for Saskatchewan, Ontario and Prince Edward Island. The ensemble of GRU and LSTM provided the best results for the rest of the provinces. In fact, it is proven that LSTM works best when having more data, while GRU is less parametric and boosted the results for the ensemble model.

The SARIMAX model achieved very low results compared to other models. This is mainly affected by the absence of clear seasonality in the majority of the provinces. In addition, after altering between different exogenous features, the number of daily tests proved to be the only variable that has high correlation with the number of confirmed cases for this statistical model.

4.3 Discussion and Analysis

The Quebec forecast demonstrates the correlation between temperature, humidity and the actual number of cases, with a RMSE of 401.11 and a MAPE of 0.30%. Alberta and Ontario also captured the association between the above mentioned features with a RMSE of 588.86, 1055.87 and a MAPE of 1.47%, 0.92% respectively. Overall, this study presented a contribution in the COVID-19 research by providing a comparison between univariate and multivariate time series. This research highlights the potential of ensemble modelling and GRU in forecasting new cases. Firstly, implementing the models on all Canadian provinces data gave us the ability to understand how the models perform on varied portion of data. Secondly, the use of deep learning models add relevant value in optimizing the performance of the models compared to statistical ones. As such an approach based upon ensembling LSTM and GRU, the model is well suited to extension via the inclusion of additional new data for the COVID-19 or for other countries.

5 Conclusion

We proposed an ensemble learning model based on LSTM and GRU to predict new cases using Canadian datasets. The results depicted apparent correlation between humidity, temperature and the number of confirmed cases in provinces with high cases such as Quebec, Alberta and Ontario. The performance for each model has been verified using RMSE, MAE and MAPE. Further studies need to be conducted in our future work to study new features that may have a direct impact on the forecast.

References

1. Chakraborty, T., Ghosh, I.: Real-time forecasts and risk assessment of novel coronavirus (COVID-19) cases: a data-driven analysis. Chaos Solitons Fractals **135**, 109850 (2020)
2. Chimmula, V.K.R., Zhang, L.: Time series forecasting of COVID-19 transmission in Canada using LSTM networks. Chaos Solitons Fractals **135**, 109864 (2020)
3. ClimateData.ca: Canadian Centre for Climate Services (CCCS) (2020). https://climatedata.ca/. Accessed 19 Aug 2020
4. Dong, E., Du, H., Gardner, L.: An interactive web-based dashboard to track COVID-19 in real time. Lancet Infect. Dis. **20**(5), 533–534 (2020)
5. Khennou, F., Akhloufi, M.: Forecasting Covid-19 spread using LSTM. In: 42nd Annual International Conferences of the IEEE Engineering in Medicine and Biology Society. EMBS Academy, Canada (2020)

6. Kirbaş, I., Sozen, A., Tuncer, A.D., Kazancıoglu, F.S.: Comparative analysis and forecasting of COVID-19 cases in various European countries with ARIMA, NARNN and LSTM approaches. Chaos Solitons Fractals **138**, 110015 (2020)

7. Kumar, M., et al.: Spreading of Covid-19 in India, Italy, Japan, Spain, UK, US: a prediction using ARIMA and LSTM model. Digit. Gov. Res. Pract. **1**(4), 1–9 (2020)

8. Shastri, S., et al.: Time series forecasting of Covid-19 using deep learning models: India-USA comparative case study. Chaos Solitons Fractals **140**, 110227 (2020)

9. Yang, Z., et al.: Modified SEIR and AI prediction of the epidemics trend of COVID-19 in China under public health interventions. J. Thorac. Dis. **12**(3), 165–174 (2020)

10. Zeroual, A., Harrou, F., Dairi, A., Sun, Y.: Deep learning methods for forecasting COVID-19 time-Series data: a Comparative study. Chaos Solitons Fractals **140**, 110121 (2020)

COVID-19 Genome Analysis Using Alignment-Free Methods

M. Saqib Nawaz[1], Philippe Fournier-Viger[1(✉)], Xinzheng Niu[2], Youxi Wu[3], and Jerry Chun-Wei Lin[4]

[1] School of Humanities and Social Sciences, Harbin Institute of Technology, Shenzhen, China
msaqibnawaz@hit.edu.cn, philfv8@yahoo.com
[2] School of Computer Science and Engineering, University of Electronic Science and Technology of China, Chengdu, China
[3] Department of Computer Science and Engineering, Hebei University of Technology, Tianjin, China
[4] Department of Computing, Mathematics and Physics, Western Norway University of Applied Sciences (HVL), Bergen, Norway
jerrylin@ieee.org

Abstract. Examining the genome sequences of the novel coronavirus (COVID-19) strains is critical to properly understand this disease and its functionalities. In bioinformatics, alignment-free (AF) sequence analysis methods offer a natural framework to investigate and understand the patterns and inherent properties of biological sequences. Thus, AF methods are used in this paper for the analysis and comparison of COVID-19 genome sequences. First, frequent patterns of nucleotide base(s) in COVID-19 genome sequences are extracted. Second, the similarity/dissimilarity between COVID-19 genome sequences are measured with different AF methods. This allows to compare sequences and evaluate the performance of various distance measures employed in AF methods. Lastly, the phylogeny for the COVID-19 genome sequences are constructed with various AF methods as well as the consensus tree that shows the level of support (agreement) among phylogenetic trees built by various AF methods. Obtained results show that AF methods can be used efficiently for the analysis of COVID-19 genome sequences.

Keywords: COVID-19 · Genome sequence · Nucleotide bases · Alignment-free methods

1 Introduction

The novel coronavirus disease (COVID-19), caused by the Severe Acute Respiratory Syndrome Coronavirus 2 (SARS-CoV-2) virus, was first identified in Wuhan, China in December 2019 [1]. The World Health Organization (WHO) declared COVID-19 a pandemic on March 11, 2020 [2]. Till now, more than 132 million people have been infected by the COVID-19, with more than 2.5 million

© Springer Nature Switzerland AG 2021
H. Fujita et al. (Eds.): IEA/AIE 2021, LNAI 12798, pp. 316–328, 2021.
https://doi.org/10.1007/978-3-030-79457-6_28

deaths worldwide. The mortality rate of SARS-CoV-2 is 3.4%, much lower than that of SARS-CoV-1 (9.6%) and the Middle East Respiratory Syndrome Coronavirus (MERS-CoV (35%)) [3]. However, this disease infection rate is much greater than those of SARS-CoV-1 and MERS-CoV.

The COVID-19 genome sequence is made from single-stranded sequence of nucleotides called RNA. Identifying the sequence of neucleotides in a genome is called genome sequencing. The genome of SARS-CoV-2 has been sequenced by different groups around the world which revealed multiple strains of the virus and showed that its genome is 79% similar to the SARS-CoV-1 and 50% to the MERS-CoV, respectively [4]. COVID-19 genome sequencing and its analysis are critical to understand its behavior, its origin, how fast it mutates, and for the development of effective therapeutics or vaccines that produce long-term immunity. Thus, our focus in this paper is on the analysis and comparison of COVID-19 genome sequences with sequence alignment methods.

Sequence alignment in bioinformatics is the process of comparing and finding similarities/dissimilarities between biological sequences. The most prominent tools for sequence analysis are based on alignment-based methods (either global or local, pairwise or multiple sequence alignment (MSA). Alignment-based approaches are very popular and are generally considered the references for sequence analysis and comparison. However, they are inappropriate in some situations. For example, (1) these methods cannot obtain qualified and reliable alignment for divergent sequences. (2) These approaches are memory and time-consuming when aligning very large datasets that contain hundreds or thousands of sequences. (3) These methods are not suitable for scenarios of low sequence identity. (4) Obtained results with these methods depend on various a priori assumptions (about sequence evolution) and parameters (substitution matrices, gap opening and extension penalties, etc.) [5–8]. To overcome these limitations, various alignment-free (AF) methods [9] have been proposed.

AF methods have emerged as a natural framework in understanding the patterns and properties of biological sequences. AF methods are based on mapping symbolic sequences (that describe DNA/RNA and proteins) into vectors spaces. The main purpose of converting sequences to vectors is to apply techniques for filtering, normalization, similarity/dissimilarity calculation and clustering more efficiently. Some main advantages of using AF methods are: (1) computational inexpensiveness. (2) effortlessly dealing with whole genomes. (3) robustness to shuffling and recombination events. (4) applicability on low sequence conservation that cannot be handled by alignment. (5) no dependence on assumptions about the evolutionary trajectories of sequence changes [7,9,10]. AF methods are now applied to problems that range from the study of phylogenetic and regulatory elements to protein classification and sequence assembly.

In recent years, various new AF methods have been proposed. The applicability and potential of these methods for COVID-19 genome sequence analysis is an important research topic. We believe that the information that AF methods provide can not only support computational investigations of COVID-19 genome sequences but also can facilitate the clinical research. In this paper, the goal is to analyse and compare COVID-19 genome sequences with AF methods. More specifically, various AF methods are used on COVID-19 genome sequences to:

1. Find frequent patterns of nucleotides in COVID-19 genome sequences.
2. To find similarity/dissimilarity between COVID-19 genome sequences by using different distance measures. Moreover, the performance of different distance measures are compared.
3. Investigate various AF methods for the construction of the phylogenetic tree of COVID-19 genome sequences as well as the consensus tree.

The remainder of this paper is organized as follows. Section 2 provides a background on SARS-CoV-2. Moreover, the details for AF methods and the Alfree tool that is used for COVID-19 genome analysis and comparison is also provided. Obtained results by applying AF methods on COVID-19 genome sequences are discussed in Sect. 3, followed by the conclusion in Sect. 4.

2   Analyzing COVID-19 Genome Sequences with Alignment-Free Methods

This section provides an overview of SARS-CoV-2 and AF methods that can be used for the analysis of COVID-19 genome sequences.

2.1   SARS-CoV-2

SARS-CoV-2 is a betacoronavirus with enveloped, single-stranded (positive-sense) RNA genomes of zoonotic origin [11]. The SARS-CoV-2 contains four structural proteins: (1) Spike (S), (2) Envelope (E), (3) Membrane (M) and (4) Nucleocapsid (N) (shown in Fig. 1). The S, M, and E proteins make the envelope of this virus. The E protein also plays a role in the production and maturation of SARS-CoV-2. The S and M proteins are also involved in the process of virus attachment during replication. N proteins remain associated with the RNA to form a nucleocapsid inside the envelope.

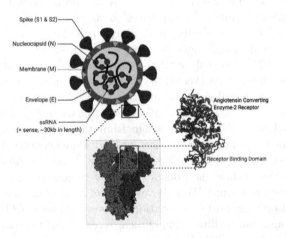

Fig. 1. SARS-CoV-2 structure [12]

SARS-CoV-2 can be contracted from animals such as bats and humans. The virus can enter the human body through its receptors, ACE2. The process of CoV entering into the host cell begins when the S protein, that comprises S1 and S2 sub-units, binds itself to the ACE2 receptor in the host cells [13]. After binding, the viral envelope fuses with the cell membrane and releases the viral genome into the target cell. The genomic material released by this virus is mRNA. In its genome range, this virus is complemented by about six to twelve open reading frames (ORFs). The genome size of the SARS-CoV-2 varies from 29.8 kb to approximately 30 kb and its genome structure follows the specific gene characteristics of known CoVs. At the 5'UTR (terminal region), more than two-thirds of the genome comprises ORF1ab that encodes ORF1ab polyproteins. Whereas at the 3'UTR, one third consists of genes that encode structural proteins (S, E, M and N), SARS-CoV-2 also contains six accessory proteins that are encoded by ORF3a, ORF6, ORF7a, ORF7b, ORF8 and ORF10 genes [14].

A SARS-CoV-2 genome sequence is an ordered list of nucleotides bases (Adenine-A, Guanine-G, Cytosine-C and Thymine-T). For example, Table 1 shows a sample of SARS-CoV-2 genome sequences. Note that a codon in the genome sequence represents a sequence of three nucleotide bases. There are $4^3 = 64$ different codons, in which 61 represent different amino acids that make up proteins. The remaining three codons represent the stop signals. As there are only 20 different amino acids and 61 possible codons, most amino acids are encoded by more than one codon. The genetic code defines a mapping between codons and amino acids; such that every three nucleotide bases (codon) encodes one amino acid [15]. On the other hand, k-mers are unique subsequences of a genome sequence of length k. For example, for $k = 1$, there are four k-mers: A, C, G and T. The sequence $ATCCG$ contains four $2 - mers$ (AT, TC, CC and CG) and three 3-mer (ATC, TCC and CCG).

Table 1. A sample of nucleotides in SARS-CoV-2 genome sequences

ID	Sequence
1	⟨....$AAT\,AACT\,CT\,ATT\,GCC\,AT\,ACCC\,AC\,AAATT$.....⟩
2	⟨....$TGC\,AGC\,AAT\,CTTTT\,GTT\,GC\,AAT\,AT\,GGC$.....⟩
3	⟨....$C\,AGGT\,GCT\,GC\,ATT\,AC\,AAAT\,ACC\,ATTT\,G$.....⟩
4	⟨....$CCCT\,AAT\,GT\,GT\,AAAATT\,AATTTT\,AGT\,A$.....⟩

2.2   Alignment-Free Methods

There are two main categories of AF sequence analysis methods:

1. Word-based Methods: These methods are based on the frequencies of subsequences of a defined length, and

2. Information Theory-based Methods: These methods evaluate the informational content between full-length sequences.

Other methods, that cannot be classified in the aforementioned two groups, are based on the length of common substrings, sequence representation based on chaos theory, iterated maps, the moments of the positions of the nucleotides, micro-alignments and Fourier transformation, etc. Interested readers can find more details on AF methods for sequence comparison in [7–10, 16–18]. Mathematically, all AF approaches are well founded in the fields of information theory, linear algebra, statistics and probability, and calculate pairwise measures of dissimilarity or distance between sequences.

Word/k-mer-Based AF Methods. The word/k-mer-based AF methods provide dissimilarity measures by comparing genome sequences based upon the occurrences of all *k-mers* (sequences of length k). These methods share the same working principle: similar sequences share similar words/*k-mers*, and applying mathematical operations on the occurrences of *k-mers* provide a relatively good measure for computing sequence dissimilarity. Three main steps involved in this process (shown in Fig. 2(a)) are [7]:

1. Sequences division with *k-mers*: The sequences under consideration are divided into unique words of a given length (*k-mer*). Let two sequences be $x = ATGTGTG$ and $y = CATGTG$. For the word size of 3 nucleotides (*3-mer*), x and y are sliced up into: $W_3^x = \{ATG, TGT, GTG, TGT, GTG\}$ and $W_3^y = \{CAT, ATG, TGT, GTG\}$. Note that W_3^x contains three unique words (ATG, TGT, GTG). Sets of words in W_3^x and W_3^y are joined together (the union) to create a full set of words $W^3 = \{CAT, ATG, TGT, GTG\}$. The words in W^3 belong to either W_3^x or W_3^y.

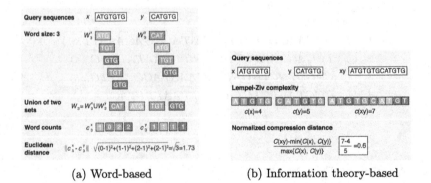

(a) Word-based   (b) Information theory-based

Fig. 2. AF calculations of word-based and information theory-based distances between two sequences [7]

2. Sequences Transformation to Vectors: After splicing, the sequences are transformed into vectors. For example, for the sequence x, its respective vector contains the number of times each particular $k\text{-}mer$ (from W^3) appeared in x. Hence for x and y, the two generated vectors are: $c_3^x = (1, 0, 2, 2)$ and $c_3^y = (1, 1, 1, 1)$.

3. Finding dissimilarity by applying distance functions: The dissimilarity between sequences is found by applying a distance function on the sequence-representing vectors c_3^x and c_3^y. For example Euclidean distance can be used to compute this difference [6]:

$$Eu(x, y) = \sqrt{\sum_{w \in A^k} (f_w^{(x)} - f_w^{(y)})^2}$$

where A^k represents the $k\text{-}mers$ present in both sequences and $f_w^{(x)}$ and $f_w^{(y)}$ represent the frequency of the $k\text{-}mer$ in x and y, respectively.

A high dissimilarity value indicates that sequences are more distant. Mapping of sequences into vectors allows one to use more than forty distance functions (such as Euclidean distance, Minkowski distance, Jaccard index, Manhattan distance, Hamming distance and Google distance) to compute the dissimilarity.

Information Theory-Based AF Methods. Information theory has provided successful methods for AF sequence analysis. These methods recognize and compute the amount of information shared between two sequences. As sequences made from nucleotides and amino acids are strings of symbols, so their digital organization is naturally interpretable with information theory metrics such as complexity and entropy.

For genome sequences, the Kolmogorov complexity of a sequence can be measured by the length of its shortest description. Intuitively, sequences with longer descriptions indicate a higher complexity and Kolmogorov complexity fails to find the shortest description for a given string of characters. To overcome this issue, the complexity is most commonly approximated with general compression algorithms where the length of a compressed sequence gives an estimate of its complexity. This means that a more complex string will be less compressible. The process of calculating the distance between sequences using complexity (also known as compression) consists of three main steps: (shown in Fig. 2(b)).

In the first step, the sequences being compared ($x = ATGTGTG$ and $y = CATGTG$) are joined to create a long sequence ($xy = ATGTGTGCATGTG$). The second step is to calculate the complexity. If x and y are exactly the same, then the complexity of xy will be very close to that of x or y. However, if x and y are dissimilar, then the complexity of xy will be close to the cumulative complexities of x and y. In the literature, many different information-based distance functions are found. For example, the Lempel–Ziv complexity [19] calculates the number of different subsequences encountered when viewing a sequence from beginning to end, as shown in Fig. 2(b). In the third step, the difference between sequences is calculated by using the compressed distance measures such as normalized compression distance (NCD) [20]:

$$NCD(x, y) = \frac{C(xy) - min\{C(x), C(y)\}}{max\{C(x), C(y)\}}$$

where C is a compressor (for example gzip, bzip2 or PPMZ).

Another information measurement is entropy-based measures such as Kullback–Leibler divergence to compare two biological sequences. The procedure involves the calculation of the frequencies of symbols or words in a sequence and the summation of their entropies in the compared sequences. Another measure known as Base-base correlation (BBC), a novel sequence feature, reflects genome information structure. BBC has been applied to distinguish various functional regions of genomes. A genome sequence is converted into a unique numeric vector (16-dimensional) with the following equation [17]:

$$T_{ij}(K) = \sum_{n=1}^{K} P_{ij}(n).log_2\left(\frac{P_{ij}(n)}{P_i P_j}\right)$$

where P_i and P_j are probabilities of bases i and j, $P_{ij}(n)$ is the probability of i and j at distance n in the genome and K is the maximum distance between i and j. More details on compression algorithms in AF can be found in [21].

Alfree [7][1] is a pairwise and multiple AF sequence comparison tool with a web support. Methods in Alfree calculate distances between sequences by discovering various patterns and properties in unaligned sequences. It implements 38 popular AF methods to calculate distances among given nucleotide or protein sequences, tree construction and creating consensus trees. The consensus phylogenetic tree provides an estimate for the level of support (agreement) between various individual methods' trees. This allow examining the reliability of given phylogenetic relationships among different methods. Table 2 lists the word-based and information theory-based AF methods implemented in Alfree. Besides these methods, Alfree provides implementation for some graphical representation-based methods, such as d^{2DSV}, d^{2DMV} and d^{2DNV}. In such methods, features from the graphical representation of DNA sequences are used to find the essence of the base composition and distribution of sequences in a quantitative manner.

---

[1] www.combio.pl/alfree.

Table 2. AF methods in Alfree

Method name	Distance
Word-based methods	
Euclidean distance	d^S, d^E, d^{Eseq1}, d^{Eseq2}
Minkowski distance	$d^{Minkowski}$
Absolute-based metrics	d^{abs_mean}, d^{abs_mult}, $d^{Manhattan}$, $d^{Canberra}$
Absolute-based metrics	d^{abs_mult1}, d^{abs_mult2}, $d^{Bray-Curtis}$, $d^{Chebyshev}$
Angle metrics	d^{EVOL1}, d^{EVOL2}
Composition distance	d^{CV}
Feature Frequency Profiles	d^{FFP}
Normalized Google Distance	d^{Google}
Linear Correlation Coefficient	d^{LCC}
Return Time Distribution	d^{RTD}
Boolean vectors	$d^{Jaccard}$, $d^{Hamming}$, $d^{Sorensen-Dice}$
Frequency Chaos Game Repr	d^{FCGR}
Information theory-based methods	
Lempel-Ziv complexity	d^{LZ}, d_*^{LZ}, d_1^{LZ}, d_{*1}^{LZ}, d_{**1}^{LZ}
NCD	d^{NCD}
Base-Base Correlation	d^{BBC}
DNA graphical representation-based methods	
2D Graph DNA Representation	d^{2DSV}, d^{2DMV}, d^{2DNV}

3 Experiments and Results

This section presents results obtained by applying the AF methods discussed in the previous section on the COVID-19 genome sequences. The online genome sequence database GenBank [22] was used to acquire sequencing data for strains of SARS-CoV-2. It is maintained by the National Center for Biotechnology Information (NCBI) and is built primarily by submissions from individual laboratories and large-scale sequencing centers. Statistics about the collected genome sequences are presented in Table 3, where ID is the accession number of the genome sequence. The NCBI GenBank offers to download each sequence in the form of nucleotide, coding region or protein. We downloaded the genome sequences in nucleotide form. The first genome sequence for COVID-19 (NC_045512) in Table 3 is the RefSeq in NCBI, as this was the first genome sequence released by Shanghai Public Health Clinical Center & School of Public Health [1].

We first run Alfree to extract frequent words (nucleotide sets) from the corpus that contains sequences listed in Table 3. Obtained results are shown in Table 4, that lists the extracted frequent words in one genome sequences (NC_045512) and also in all the sequences. The first four extracted patterns (of length 1)

Table 3. Characteristics of COVID-19 genome taken from NCBI

ID	Release date	Length	Location	Collection date
NC_045512	2020-01-13	29903	China	2019-12
MW052550	2020-11-03	719	South Korea	2020-07-07
MW192918	2020-10-31	654	Gabon	2020-03-14
MW173089	2020-10-26	3819	USA	2020-04-25
MW165491	2020-10-24	3822	Iran	2020-04
MW161041	2020-10-23	4043	Russia	2020-06-04
MW092768	2020-10-12	2383	Sweden	2020-02-25
MW040503	2020-09-26	1009	Venezuela	2020-05-22
MT843234	2020-08-28	287	Italy	2019-12-18
MT750057	2020-07-13	29782	USA	2020-06-17
MT750058	2020-07-13	29782	USA	2020-06-09
MT291827	2020-04-06	29858	China	2019-12-30
MT291828	2020-04-06	29858	China	2019-12-30

show the total occurrence of nucleotides in genome sequences. For NC_045512, two nulceotides A and T make up for 62% of the sequence (approximately 30% for A and 32% for T). Moreover, C and G makes up the remaining 38% of the sequence (approximately 19.6% for G and 18.4% for C). For all genome sequences in the corpus, the content of A and T is 61.3% (approximately 29.9% for A and 32.2% for T), and 37.9% for C and G (approximately 19.5% for G and 18.4% for C). The extracted frequent codons (sequences of 3 nucleotides) and frequent pattern of length six (two codons) are also listed in Table 4. Interestingly, the extracted frequent words in one genome and all genome sequences are almost the same.

Next, the pairwise dissimilarities among the COVID-19 genome sequences is calculated through various distance measure methods in Alfree. The K is set to 3 for all word-based distance measures. Figure 3 shows the heatmap for the normalized compression distance (d^{NCD}) and standard Euclidean (d^E) distance measures. We found that the two methods produced two different heatmaps as d^E is a word-based method and d^{NCD} is based on information theory. Due to the space limitation, heatmaps for other methods are not presented here.

Table 5 compares the performance of various word-based and information theory-based AF methods for two sequences (MT750057 and MT750058). The calculated dissimilarity by two Euclidean distance-based measures (d^S and d^E) was very different, whereas d^{Eseq1} and d^{Eseq2} yield the same results. $d^{Minkowski}$ and d^S indicated same similarity and the same is observed for Angle metrics measures (d^{EVOL1} and d^{EVOL2}). The performance of absolute-based metrics measures (d^{abs_mult}, d^{abs_mult1} and d^{abs_mult2}) was same. Whereas $d^{Manhattan}$ performed differently than other absolute-based metrics-based measures. On the

Table 4. Extracted frequent words of nucleotides

Patterns	Occurrence	Patterns	Occurrence
NC_045512		All sequences	
T	9594	T	53442
A	8954	A	49532
G	5863	G	32358
C	5492	C	30587
TTT	1004	TTT	5701
AAA	923	AAA	5009
TTA	876	TTA	4846
TGT	858	TGT	4734
TTG	817	TTG	4586
ACA	809	ACA	4509
TTGTTA	42	TTGTTA	231
TGTTAA	41	TGTTAA	223
GGTGTT	35	GGTGTT	210
TTTTAA	35	TTGGTG	206
TGTTGT	34	TTTTAA	202
TGTTGT	34	CTTTTG	196

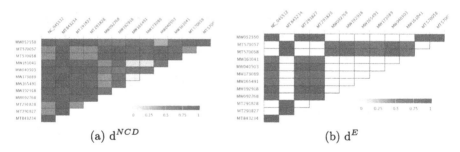

(a) d^{NCD} (b) d^{E}

Fig. 3. Distance between genome sequences calculated using d^{NCD} and d^{E}

other hand, the performance of three Boolean vectors-based measures ($d^{Jaccard}$, $d^{Sorenson\_dice}$ and $d^{Hamming}$) was same. The D^{KL} is the Kullback–Leibler divergence measure that uses entropy-based measure for genome sequences comparison. Overall, it was observed that one can easily and efficiently compare the performance of different AF methods on COVID-19 genome sequences in Alfree to get useful insights about this virus.

Lastly, the phylogenetic tree for COVID19 genome sequences are shown in Fig. 4. A phylogenetic or evolutionary tree (also known as phylogeny) diagrammatically describes the evolutionary history and relationship of an organism or

Table 5. Distance measure values for two sequences

Measures	AD*	ND**	Measure	AD	ND
MT570057, MT570058					
d^E	68	0	d^S	8.246	0.002
d^{Eseq1}	0.0022	0.000	d^{Eseq2}	0.0022	0.000
$d^{Minkowski}$	8.246	0.002	d^{abs_mean}	0.625	0.001
d^{abs_mult}	1.219	0.003	d^{abs_mult1}	1.097	0.003
d^{abs_mult2}	1.219	0.003	$d^{Manhattan}$	40	0.001
d^{Bray_Curtis}	0.0006	0.001	$d^{Canberra}$	0.0564	0.001
d^{EVOL1}	9.798	0.000	d^{EVOL2}	9.798	0.000
d^{FFP}	6.486	0.000	d^{Google}	0.0006	0.001
d^{LCC}	0.000	0.000	d^{FCGR}	8.246	0.002
d^{KL}	2.890	0.000	$d^{Sorenson\_Dice}$	0	0.000
$d^{Jaccard}$	0.00	0.000	$d^{Hamming}$	0.000	0.000
d^{RTD}	0.001	0.002	d^{CV}	0.0001	0.000
d^{NCD}	0.438	0.443	d^{BBC}	0.001	0.003
d^{2DSV}	2.159	0.000	d^{2DMV}	2.195	0.000
d^{2DNV}	1.944	0.000	$d^{Chebyshev}$	4	0.001

*AD = Actual distance, **ND = Normalized distance

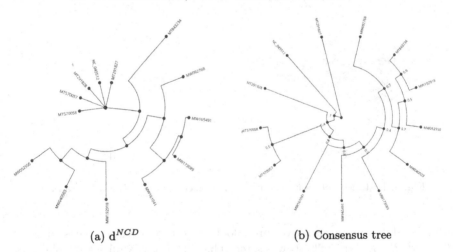

(a) d^{NCD} (b) Consensus tree

Fig. 4. Phylogeny for COVID-19 strains

group of organisms. Phylogenetic relationships provide valuable information on shared ancestry but not necessarily on how organisms are similar or different. Figure 4(a) shows the pyhlogenetic tree for d^{NCD} as a phylogram and the phylogram in Fig. 4(b) represents a majority-rule consensus tree that summarizes the agreement among various AF methods. This tree is constructed for 27 AF methods (22 word-based methods, 2 information theory-based methods and 3 DNA graphical representation-based methods). For every node in the consensus tree, the support values is represented in the range [0, 1]. These trees describe how different strains are connected with other and how they have evolved over time. A recent study [23] used an AF method, called the Natural Vector method, to analyze the phylogeny of SARS-CoV-2 with human coronaviruses. In this paper, we observe that AF methods can also analyse and compare genome sequences efficiently. Moreover, Alfree also provides the features for extracting frequent patterns for nucleotides as well as the consensus phylogenetic tree.

4   Conclusion

The genome sequences for COVID-19 strains, taken from NCBI's GenBank, are compared and analyzed with AF methods for: (1) extracting frequent patterns of nucleotides in COVID-19 genome sequences, (2) finding the similarity/dissimilarity between COVID-19 genome sequences by using different distance measures and their performance comparison and (3) Phylogeny construction with various AF methods for COVID-19 genome sequences. Our experiments and obtained results show that AF methods provide an efficient framework for the analysis of COVID-19 genome sequences to get useful insights about this virus. As discussed in [24], including more COVID-19 data and applying more algorithms will allow researchers to obtain results that may guide the clinical research for this pandemic.

In the future, we plan to analyse protein sequences for COVID-19 strains with AF methods. Another direction is to use other AF similar tools like CAFE [6] for more analysis and comparison. This will also enable us to compare the aforementioned tools with each other. We are also interested in analyzing public reactions to the COVID-19 pandemic [25].

References

1. Wu, F., et al.: New coronavirus associated with human respiratory disease in China. Nature **579**, 265–269 (2020)
2. Cucinotta, D., Vanelli, M.: WHO declares COVID-19 a pandemic. Acta Biomed. **91**(1), 157–160 (2020)
3. Perlman, S.: Another decade, another coronavirus. N. Engl. J. Med. **382**(8), 760–762 (2020)
4. Lu, R., et al.: Genomic characterisation and epidemiology of 2019 novel coronavirus: Implications for virus origins and receptor binding. The Lancet **395**(10224), 565–574 (2020)
5. Kang, Y., et al.: PVTree: a sequential pattern mining method for alignment independent phylogeny reconstruction. Genes **10**(2), 73 (2019)
6. Lu, Y.Y., et al.: CAFE: a C celerated A lignment-FrEe sequence analysis. Nucleic Acids Res. **45**(Web Server issue), W554–W559 (2017)

7. Zielezinski, A., et al.: Alignment-free sequence comparison: benefits, applications, and tools. Genome Biol. **18**, 186 (2017)

8. Vinga, S.: Information theory applications for biological sequence analysis. Brief. Bioninform. **15**(3), 376–389 (2014)

9. Vinga, S., Almeida, J.: Alignment-free sequence comparison–a review. Bioinformatics **19**, 513–523 (2003)

10. Zielezinski, A., et al.: Benchmarking of alignment-free sequence comparison methods. Genome Biol. **20**, 144 (2019)

11. Nawaz, M.S., Fournier-Viger, P., Shojaee, A., Fujita, H.: Using artificial intelligence techniques for COVID-19 genome analysis. Appl. Intell. **51**(5), 3086–3103 (2021). https://doi.org/10.1007/s10489-021-02193-w

12. Cascella, M., et al.: Features, evaluation, and treatment of coronavirus. In: StatPearls [Internet], NBK554776. https://www.ncbi.nlm.nih.gov/books/NBK554776/

13. Xu, H., et al.: High expression of ACE2 receptor of 2019-nCoV on the epithelial cells of oral mucosa. Int. J. Oral Res. **12**(8), 1–5 (2019)

14. Khailany, R.A., Safdar, M., Ozaslanc, M.: Genomic characterization of a novel SARS-CoV-2. Gene Rep. **19**, 100682 (2020)

15. Shu, J.-J.: A new integrated symmetrical table for genetic codes. Biosystems **151**, 21–26 (2017)

16. Ren, J., et al.: Alignment free sequence analysis and applications. Ann. Rev. Biomed. Data Sci. **1**, 93–114 (2018)

17. Bonham-Carter, O., et al.: Alignment-free genetic sequence comparisons: a review of recent approaches by word analysis. Brief. Bioinform. **15**(6), 890–905 (2014)

18. Song, J., et al.: New developments of alignment-free sequence comparison: measures, statistics and next-generation sequencing. Brief. Bioinform. **15**(3), 343–353 (2014)

19. Otu, H.H., Sayood, K.A.: A new sequence distance measure for phylogenetic tree construction. Bioinformatics **19**(1), 2122–2130 (2003)

20. Li, M., et al.: The similarity metric. IEEE Trans. Inf. Theory **50**(12), 3250–64 (2004)

21. Giancarlo, R., Rombo, S.E., Utro, F.: Compressive biological sequence analysis and archival in the era of high-throughput sequencing technologies. Brief. Bioinform. **15**(3), 390–406 (2014)

22. Sayers, E.W., et al.: Genbank. Nucleic Acids Res. **48**(D1), D84–D86 (2019)

23. Dong, R., et al.: Analysis of the hosts and transmission paths of SARS-CoV-2 in the COVID-19 outbreak. Genes **11**(6), 637 (2020)

24. Ahsan, M.A., et al.: Bioinformatics resources facilitate understanding and harnessing clinical research of SARS-CoV-2. Briefings Bioinform. bbaa416 (2020)

25. Noor, S., et al.: Analysis of public reaction to the novel coronavirus (COVID-19) outbreak on Twitter. Kybernetes (2020). https://doi.org/10.1108/K-05-2020-0258

Deep Efficient Neural Networks for Explainable COVID-19 Detection on CXR Images

Mohamed Chetoui[ID] and Moulay A. Akhloufi[(✉)][ID]

Perception, Robotics, and Intelligent Machines Research Group (PRIME),
Department of Computer Science, Université de Moncton,
Moncton, NB E1A 3E9, Canada
{emc7409,moulay.akhloufi}@umoncton.ca

Abstract. With the spread of COVID-19 pandemic worldwide, medical imaging modalities and deep learning can play an important role in the fight against this disease. Recent years have seen the impressive results obtained using deep neural networks in different fields. Radiology is among the medical fields that can benefit from this recent progress and improve disease's diagnosis, monitoring and prognosis. In this work, we propose the use of a deep efficient neural network based on EfficientNet B7 to detect COVID-19 in Chest X-rays (CXR). The obtained results on a large dataset are promising and show the high performance of the proposed model, with in average an accuracy of 95%, an AUC of 95%, a specificity of 90% and a sensitivity of 97%. In addition, an explainability model was developed and shows the high performance and high generalization degree of the proposed model in detecting and highlighting the signs of the disease.

Keywords: Coronavirus · COVID-19 · SARS-CoV-2 · Convolutional neural networks · Chest X-ray · EfficientNet

1 Introduction

The 2019 coronavirus disease (COVID-19), caused by severe coronavirus (SARS-CoV-2) acute respiratory syndrome, spread and caused a new pandemic. Up to January 16, 2021, 93.8 million cases of COVID-19 have been reported in over 200 countries and territories, resulting in approximately 2.01 million deaths [39]. As the World Health Organization (WHO) considered the epidemic to be a globally critical public health emergency, on January 30, 2020, this triggered substantial

This work was supported by Atlantic Canada Opportunities Agency (ACOA), Regional Economic Growth through Innovation - Business Scale-Up and Productivity (Project 217148), Natural Sciences and Engineering Research Council of Canada (NSERC), Alliance Grants (ALLRP 552039-20), New Brunswick Innovation Foundation (NBIF), COVID-19 Research Fund (COV2020-042), and the Microsoft AI For Health program.

© Springer Nature Switzerland AG 2021
H. Fujita et al. (Eds.): IEA/AIE 2021, LNAI 12798, pp. 329–340, 2021.
https://doi.org/10.1007/978-3-030-79457-6_29

public health concern in the international community and identified it as a pandemic on March 11, 2020 [40,41], Fig. 1 show an example of this infection. For patients reported with COVID-19, the reverse transcription polymerase chain reaction (RT-PCR) test serves as the gold standard. However, in many areas that were seriously affected, particularly during the early outbreak of this illness, the RT-PCR tests were limited. The laboratory test, as stated in Fang *et al.* [10], also suffers sensitivity in some cases (71%). This is due to several variables, such as sample preparation and quality control [19].

Medical imaging [7] is also a method for studying and predicting the impacts of COVID-19 on the human body. In this, normal individuals and COVID-19 infected patients can be studied in parallel with the aid of CT [9] and CXR images. The fight against COVID-19 [32] and other diseases [4,5] has successfully led to the increasing use of AI in medical imaging technology. AI allows for more efficient, accurate and effective imaging solutions compared to the conventional imaging workflow that relies heavily on human labor. For COVID-19 detection, numerous research studies are already available. For the most part, deep learning approaches are used on CXR images to classify infected patients, and the results have been shown to be very good in accuracy AUC, sensitivity and specificity terms. Apostolopoulos *et al.* [1] evaluated the performance of five pre-trained CNN networks for COVID-19 detection using CXR images. Their algorithm was trained and tested using 224 COVID-19 CXR images, 700 for other pneumonias and 504 normal images. The results showed that VGG19 [34] and MobileNetv2 [29] networks achieved an accuracy of 93.48% and 92.85% respectively. Sethy and Behera *et al.* [31] combined CNN and SVM for COVID-19 detection, the authors used CNN for feature extraction and SVM for classification, the model achieved a 95.38% accuracy using ResNet50 [12] on a test of 50 images. Wang *et al.* [37] used a deep CNN called COVID-Net for COVID-19 detection using CXR images. The network design is consisting of two stages, a human-machine collaborative design strategy and a machine-driven design exploration stage. The architecture utilizes a lightweight residual projection-expansion-projection-extension (PEPX) design pattern. In addition, an explainability is performed for the disease signs visualization. The results showed a sensitivity of 91.0%, a precision of 96.4% and an accuracy of 93.3%. Farooq *et al.* [11] presented CNN for COVID-19 detection. They utilized a three-step technique to fine-tune ResNet-50 [12] in order to improve the performance of the model. Progressive resizing of input images 128x128x3, 224x224x3, 229x229x3 and fine-tuning of the network at each stage was used. The authors achieved an accuracy of 96.23%. The study of Hemdan *et al.* [13] used a system based on seven CNN called COVIDX-Net with in order to classify COVID-19 disease from CXR images. The best performance achieved for the VGG19 [34] and DenseNet201 [15] with an accuracy of 90%.

In this work, we fine-tuned a CNN called EfficientNet-7 [36] to detect COVID-19 using CXR images, multiple datasets were used during training and testing. Several performance measures were used to validate the performance of our proposed model in terms of accuracy, specificity, sensitivity and AUC.

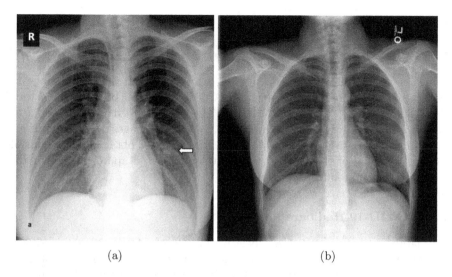

(a)   (b)

Fig. 1. Examples of CXR images. (a) patient with COVID-19 (The arrows indicated the lesion of COVID-19); (b) normal.

2 Proposed Approach

For COVID-19 detection, we used several datasets: BIMCV COVID19+ [2], RSNA [25], NIH [20], Covid-19 image data collection [8], Chest X-Ray Images (Pneumonia) [17], COVID-19 Radiography [26] and Montfort [22] datasets. The latter is a proprietary dataset, the remaining datasets are public. A robust CNN named EfficientNet-B7 was fine-tuned for the detection of the COVID-19 infection. Figure 2 gives a overview of our approach. The details of each dataset is presented in the following subsections.

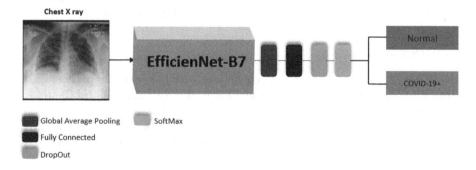

Fig. 2. Proposed deep CNN architecture for COVID-19 and normal detection

3 Datasets

3.1 Covid-19 Image Data Collection

Cohen *et al.* [8] released an open dataset of CXR and CT scan images of patients which are positive or suspected of COVID-19 and of other viral/bacterial pneumonia (MERS, SARS and ARDS). The data were mainly scraped from online medical websites collecting released COVID-19 images from hospitals and physicians. The dataset contains 654 COVID-19 images obtained from multiple sources. The goal of this dataset is to develop AI-based approaches to predict and understand the infection.

3.2 COVID-19 Radiography

The database contains 219 CXR positive images of COVID-19 obtained from Kaggle [26] and developed by a team of researchers from the University of Qatar (Doha, Qatar), the University of Dhaka (Bangladesh) and their Pakistani and Malaysian collaborators with the aid of various medical doctors who have created a CXR image database for positive cases of COVID-19.

3.3 BIMCV COVID19+

BIMCV COVID19+ [2] dataset is a broad dataset of COVID-19 patients' CXR and computed tomography (CT) images together with their radiographic observations, pathologies, polymerase chain reaction (PCR) test results, diagnostic antibody tests for immunoglobulin G (IgG) and immunoglobulin M (IgM) and radiographic records from the Medical Imaging Databank in Valencia Area Medical Imaging Bank (BIMCV). The images were collected by a team of specialist radiologists in high resolution and annotated. In addition, comprehensive information is given, including demographic information of the patient, projection type (PA-AP) and criteria of acquisition for imaging analysis, among others. 1,380 CX, 885 DX and 163 CT images are included in the database.

3.4 RSNA

The RSNA [25] dataset is a CXR image dataset with metadata for patients. This dataset was provided by the US National Institutes of Health Clinical Center for a challenge in Kaggle and is available on the competition website for Kaggle [33]. It comprises 26,684 unique patient CXR images and each image is labelled with one of three distinct groups from the associated radiology reports: 'Normal', 'No Lung Opacity/Not Normal', 'Lung Opacity'.

3.5   Chest X-Ray Images (Pneumonia)

Chest X-ray (Anterior-posterior) [17] was chosen from the Guangzhou Women and Children's Medical Center retrospective cohorts of pediatric patients aged one to five years (Guangzhou, China). Both CXR imaging was conducted as part of the routine clinical treatment of the patients. All CXRs were initially screened by eliminating all low-quality images for quality control. Two specialized physicians then graded the diagnoses for the images before being cleared for the AI system training. The dataset is split into 3 training, testing and validation folders and includes subfolders for each group of images (Pneumonia or Normal). 5,863 CXR images and 2 Pneumonia and Regular classes are included in the dataset.

3.6   National Institute of Health (NIH)

There are 112,120 CXR images with disease labels from 30,805 unique patients in the NIH [20] Chest X-ray dataset. This dataset was collected by the National Health Institute (USA). The dataset comprises 15 grades (14 diseases, and one for "No findings"). Images may be labeled as "No findings" or one or more classes of disease: Atelectasis, Consolidation, Infiltration, Pneumothorax, Emphysema, Edema, Fibrosis, Effusion, Pneumonia, Pleural_thickening, Cardiomegaly, Nodule, Mass, and Hernia. The images were graded by expert physicians.

3.7   Montfort Dataset

This dataset was collected by health professionals from Montfort Hospital (Ontario, Canada) in addition to the above datasets and developed the Montfort [22] dataset. This dataset contains 236 CXR images, including 150 COVID-19, 29 pneumonia (other than COVID-19) and 57 normal cases, which are proprietary. Radiology reports and RT-PCR tests are used to labeling the CXR images.

3.8   Deep Learning Model

In order to detect COVID-19 using CXR images, we fine-tuned the CNN named EfficientNet-B7, based on the architecture suggested by Tan *et al.* [36]. The authors suggested all dimensions of the network should be balanced: width, resolution and depth. As compared to conventional CNN scaling approaches using one dimension scaling, EfficientNet was the first to empirically calculate the interaction of all three dimensions.

The authors use the network MnasNet [35] to build their basic architecture. They use a multi-objective for neural architecture which optimizes accuracy and FLOPS. Due to the larger FLOPS goal, they generate a robust network called EfficientNet-B0 similar to MnasNet [35], but much larger. The architecture incorporates the mobile inverted bottleneck block MBConv [28] and the squeeze and excitation optimization [14].

The authors use a compound scaling approach based on EfficientNet-B0 to scale the network width, resolution, and depth using the compound coefficient ϕ using the following equation:

$$
\begin{aligned}
depth &: d = \alpha^{\phi} \\
width &: w = \beta^{\phi} \\
resolution &: r = \gamma^{\phi} \\
\alpha &\geq 1, \beta \geq 1, \gamma \geq 1
\end{aligned}
\tag{1}
$$

Where α, β, γ are constants that a limited grid search can be used to evaluate. ϕ is a user-defined coefficient that regulates the amount of additional resources necessary for model scaling, while α, β, γ specify how these additional resources can be allocated to network width, resolution, and depth, respectively.

EfficientNet-B0 can be configured as constants by setting α, β, γ and extending the base network with different α to achieve an EfficientNet family (B1, B2, B3 to B7). With a 97.1% top-5 accuracy on ImageNet, EfficientNet-B7 achieves state-of-the-art results, while being 8.4x smaller and 6.1x faster on inference than other known ConvNets, such as SENet [14] and Gpipe [16].

The proposed model is based on EfficientNet-B7. We customized the last convolution layer of the network by adding a Global Average Pooling (GAP) to improve the accuracy and reduce overfitting. After (GAP), we added a Dense layers of size 1024 and used a 50% Dropout after Dense layers. Finally, a Softmax layer is added to give the probability prediction scores for detecting COVID-19 and normal on CXR images.

4   Experimental Results

To train the model to detect COVID-19, we used RSNA dataset with 4,000 normal CXR images, and 873 COVID-19 obtained from Covid-19 image data collection and COVID-19 Radiography. In the test set, we took a normal samples from NIH, RSNA and Chest X-Ray Images (Pneumonia) datasets in order to create the normal class. BIMCV COVID19+ and Montfort are reserved for COVID-19 class. We obtained a total of 3,189 CXR images as a test set, including 2,385 of COVID-19.

Keras Library [6] was used to develop the proposed model and training was carried out in 8 Nvidia RTX 2080 Ti [23], other test we are also done on Microsoft Azure servers by using Nvidia K80 [24]. SGD [18] was used as optimizer, Batch size is fixed to 32 for the proposed model with 200 epochs. All CXR images were resized to 512x512. The model was trained with swish activation, self-gated activation function proposed by researchers at Google. According to their paper [27], it works better than ReLU With a comparable computational efficiency standard. In experiments on ImageNet, the new function achieved top 1 classification accuracy 0.6–0.9% higher. For the unbalanced classes, we used the class-weight technique. The technique takes directly into account the asymmetry of cost errors during the model training. Hyperparameter optimization was conducted on the validation set and the best results were kept for testing. All measures are calculated on the basis of sensitivity (SE), specificity (SP), area under curve (AUC) and accuracy (ACC). In relation to 2 groups (COVID-19 Vs. normal), the SE and SP illustrate the effectiveness of the proposed solution. AUC measured using the ROC curve is a performance metric generally used for issues of medical classification.

For COVID-19 detection, the proposed fine-tuned EfficientNet-B7 gives interesting results. The model achieved a SP of 90%, a SN of 97%, and an AUC of 0.950 using the 3,189 CXR images in the test set. Figure 3 shows the ROC curve for the COVID-19 detection. We can see the high performance achieved by our model. The confusion matrix is given in Fig. 4, only 74 CXR images from 2,385 and 85 from 804 are misclassified, this shows the performance of our model in the detection of COVID-19 cases.

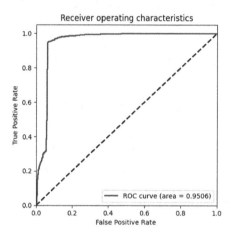

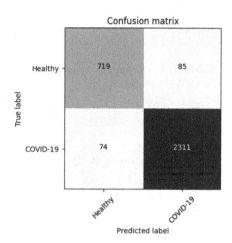

Fig. 3. ROC curve (Detection of COVI-19 and normal).

Fig. 4. Confusion matrix for our model predictions.

To understand how the model learned to detect the pathology signs of COVID-19 signs, we integrate an explainability algorithm named Grad-CAM, it is based on the use of Gradient-weighted Class Activation Mapping [30]. This method was used for providing a visual overview of the findings of our proposed CNN model. Grad-CAM uses the gradients of any target to produce a coarse localization map that highlights significant regions in the predictive picture, flowing into the final convolutional layer. This methodology applies to our existing CNN model, without any architectural or retraining changes. To create a high-resolution class-discriminative visualization, the proposed methodology combines Grad-CAM with fine-grained visualizations. Figure 5 demonstrates positive COVID-19 cases. We can see that around the most significant symptoms, the heatmap is precisely located. The dense homogeneous opacity regions identified as the most important for COVID-19 were identified in our model.

A comparison with recent COVID-19 detection methods is provided in the Table 1. We can see that for COVID-19 detection using CXR images, our model outperforms most of the recently published work. Moreover, relative to other studies, the number of COVID-19 images used in this analysis is higher, supporting the degree of generalization of the proposed model for COVID-19 detection. The proposed model enhances our previous model [3], which was created using a limited amount of positive COVID-19 CXR images (192 images). Our previous model was based on ResNet50 and obtained an AUC of 0.973, a specificity of 0.966 and a sensitivity of 0.951. This shows that the new proposed model is robust and able to detect COVID-19 with a high sensitivity (97%). Furthermore, our explainability (EXP) model shows a very detailed localization of the signs of COVID-19 and can be used as a CAD tool to further assist doctors in their diagnosis.

Table 1. Performance comparison with state-of-the-art methods using CXR images for COVID-19 detection

Ref.	#COVID-19 images	ACC (%)	AUC	SN (%)	SP (%)	EXP
Apostolopoulos *et al.* [1]	224	93.48	–	98.66	96.46	No
Sethy *et al.* [31]	25	95.38	–	97.29	93.47	No
Chetoui *et al.* [3]	192	–	0.973	95.10	96.60	Yes
Wang *et al.* [37]	226	93.30	–	91	–	Yes
Hemdan *et al.* [13]	25	90	–	1	83	No
Wehbe [38]	4,253	83	0.900	71	92	Yes
Minaee *et al.* [21]	203	–	0.986	98	90	Yes
Our	**2,385**	**95.01**	**0.950**	**97**	**90**	**Yes**

5   Conclusion

In this work, we developed a deep convolutional neural network (CNN) model. The model was fine-tuned and trained to use CXR images based on EfficienNet-B7 for COVID-19 detection. The obtained results show that our proposed model outperforms several recent deep learning approaches for COVID-19 detection. On a test set of 3,189 CXR images, including 2,385 of COVID-19, we obtained high AUC scores with 0.950 and an accuracy of 95.01% to classify the CXR images as COVID-19 or healthy. Previously published work used a small number of data in their research. This demonstrates the robustness of our proposed model

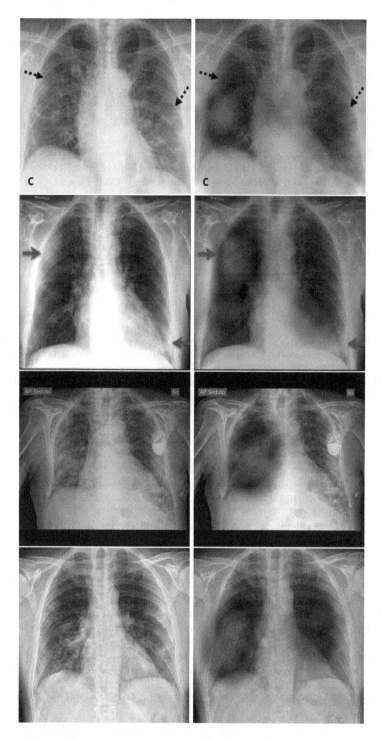

Fig. 5. Positive cases COVID-19 disease. The heatmap coloured areas in the CXR images show the signs detected by our deep learning model for predicting COVID-19 disease on CXR images.

to detect COVID-19 on a large number of images. An explainability algorithm was also developed and showed that the most significant pathology regions can be effectively identified by our proposed model. The proposed technique is an interesting contribution to the development of a diagnostic device capable of detecting COVID-19 cases on CXR images. Future work includes working with CT images as well as changing the model to recognize other health problems with other type of pneumonia images.

Acknowledgments. The authors would like to acknowledge El Mostafa Bouattane and Joseph Abdulnour (Institut du Savoir Montfort, Hôpital Montfort) for their assistance with organizing and sharing Montfort anonymized CXR images.

Disclosures. The authors declare no conflict of interest.

Ethical Conduct of Research. The research ethics board at Université de Moncton waived ethics approval since our study does not involve direct work with humans, but only with anonymized images as described in the dataset section.

References

1. Apostolopoulos, I.D., Mpesiana, T.A.: COVID-19: automatic detection from x-ray images utilizing transfer learning with convolutional neural networks. Phys. Eng. Sci. Med. **43**(2), 635–640 (2020)
2. BIMCV Valencia Region, Pertusa, A., de la Iglesia Vaya, M.: BIMCV-COVID19+ (2020). https://doi.org/10.17605/OSF.IO/NH7G8. https://osf.io/nh7g8/
3. Chetoui, M., Abadarahmane, T., Akhloufi, M.A.: Deep learning for COVID-19 detection on chest x-ray and CT scan. In: 2020 42nd Annual International Conference of the IEEE Engineering in Medicine & Biology Society (EMBC). IEEE (2020, poster)
4. Chetoui, M., Akhloufi, M.A.: Deep retinal diseases detection and explainability using OCT images. In: Campilho, A., Karray, F., Wang, Z. (eds.) ICIAR 2020. LNCS, vol. 12132, pp. 358–366. Springer, Cham (2020). https://doi.org/10.1007/978-3-030-50516-5_31
5. Chetoui, M., Akhloufi, M.A.: Explainable diabetic retinopathy using efficient-net. In: 2020 42nd Annual International Conference of the IEEE Engineering in Medicine & Biology Society (EMBC), pp. 1966–1969. IEEE (2020)
6. Chollet, F., et al.: Keras (2015). https://keras.io
7. Chung, A.C.S., Gee, J.C., Yushkevich, P.A., Bao, S.: Information processing in medical imaging. In: Information Processing in Medical Imaging (2019)
8. Cohen, J.P., Morrison, P., Dao, L., Roth, K., Duong, T.Q., Ghassemi, M.: COVID-19 image data collection: prospective predictions are the future. arXiv 2006.11988 (2020). https://github.com/ieee8023/covid-chestxray-dataset
9. Domingues, I., Pereira, G., Martins, P., Duarte, H., Santos, J., Abreu, P.H.: Using deep learning techniques in medical imaging: a systematic review of applications on CT and pet. Artif. Intell. Rev. **53**(6), 4093–4160 (2020)
10. Fang, Y., et al.: Sensitivity of chest CT for COVID-19: comparison to RT-PCR. Radiology 200432 (2020)
11. Farooq, M., Hafeez, A.: COVID-ResNet: a deep learning framework for screening of COVID19 from radiographs. arXiv preprint arXiv:2003.14395 (2020)

12. He, K., Zhang, X., Ren, S., Sun, J.: Deep residual learning for image recognition. In: Proceedings of the IEEE Conference on Computer Vision and Pattern Recognition, pp. 770–778 (2016)
13. Hemdan, E.E.D., Shouman, M.A., Karar, M.E.: COVIDX-Net: a framework of deep learning classifiers to diagnose COVID-19 in x-ray images. arXiv preprint arXiv:2003.11055 (2020)
14. Hu, J., Shen, L., Sun, G.: Squeeze-and-excitation networks. In: Proceedings of the IEEE Conference on Computer Vision and Pattern Recognition, pp. 7132–7141 (2018)
15. Huang, G., Liu, Z., Van Der Maaten, L., Weinberger, K.Q.: Densely connected convolutional networks. In: Proceedings of the IEEE Conference on Computer Vision and Pattern Recognition, pp. 4700–4708 (2017)
16. Huang, Y., et al.: GPipe: efficient training of giant neural networks using pipeline parallelism. In: Advances in Neural Information Processing Systems, pp. 103–112 (2019)
17. Kermany, D.S., et al.: Identifying medical diagnoses and treatable diseases by image-based deep learning. Cell **172**(5), 1122–1131.e9 (2018). https://doi.org/10.1016/j.cell.2018.02.010
18. Kingma, D.P., Ba, J.: Adam: a method for stochastic optimization. arXiv preprint arXiv:1412.6980 (2014)
19. Liang, T., et al.: Handbook of COVID-19 prevention and treatment. The First Affiliated Hospital, Zhejiang University School of Medicine. Compiled According to Clinical Experience, vol. 68 (2020)
20. Malhotra, A., et al.: Multi-task driven explainable diagnosis of COVID-19 using chest x-ray images. arXiv preprint arXiv:2008.03205 (2020)
21. Minaee, S., Kafieh, R., Sonka, M., Yazdani, S., Soufi, G.J.: Deep-COVID: predicting COVID-19 from chest x-ray images using deep transfer learning. arXiv preprint arXiv:2004.09363 (2020)
22. Montfort, H.: Hopital Montfort (2020). https://hopitalmontfort.com/
23. NVIDIA: 2080 Ti. https://www.nvidia.com/en-us/geforce/graphics-cards/rtx-2080. Accessed Jan 2021
24. NVIDIA: K80. https://www.nvidia.com/fr-fr/data-center/tesla-k80/. Accessed Jan 2021
25. Pan, I., Cadrin-Chênevert, A., Cheng, P.M.: Tackling the radiological society of North America pneumonia detection challenge. Am. J. Roentgenol. **213**(3), 568–574 (2019)
26. Rahman, T.: COVID-19 radiography database (2020). https://www.kaggle.com/tawsifurrahman/covid19-radiography-database
27. Ramachandran, P., Zoph, B., Le, Q.V.: Searching for activation functions. arXiv preprint arXiv:1710.05941 (2017)
28. Sandler, M., Howard, A., Zhu, M., Zhmoginov, A., Chen, L.C.: Mobilenetv 2: inverted residuals and linear bottlenecks. In: Proceedings of the IEEE Conference on Computer Vision and Pattern Recognition, pp. 4510–4520 (2018)
29. Sandler, M., Howard, A.G., Zhu, M., Zhmoginov, A., Chen, L.: Inverted residuals and linear bottlenecks: mobile networks for classification, detection and segmentation. CoRR abs/1801.04381 (2018). http://arxiv.org/abs/1801.04381
30. Selvaraju, R.R., Cogswell, M., Das, A., Vedantam, R., Parikh, D., Batra, D.: Gradcam: visual explanations from deep networks via gradient-based localization. In: Proceedings of the IEEE International Conference on Computer Vision, pp. 618–626 (2017)

31. Sethy, P.K., Behera, S.K.: Detection of coronavirus disease (COVID-19) based on deep features. Preprints **2020030300**, 2020 (2020)
32. Shi, F., et al.: Review of artificial intelligence techniques in imaging data acquisition, segmentation and diagnosis for COVID-19. IEEE Rev. Biomed. Eng. (2020)
33. Shih, G., et al.: Augmenting the national institutes of health chest radiograph dataset with expert annotations of possible pneumonia. Radiol. Artif. Intell. **1**(1), e180041 (2019)
34. Simonyan, K., Zisserman, A.: Very deep convolutional networks for large-scale image recognition. arxiv 2014. arXiv preprint arXiv:1409.1556 1409 (2014)
35. Tan, M., et al.: Mnasnet: platform-aware neural architecture search for mobile. In: Proceedings of the IEEE Conference on Computer Vision and Pattern Recognition, pp. 2820–2828 (2019)
36. Tan, M., Le, Q.V.: Efficientnet: rethinking model scaling for convolutional neural networks. CoRR abs/1905.11946 (2019). http://arxiv.org/abs/1905.11946
37. Wang, L., Lin, Z.Q., Wong, A.: COVID-Net: a tailored deep convolutional neural network design for detection of COVID-19 cases from chest x-ray images. Sci. Rep. **10**(1), 1–12 (2020)
38. Wehbe, R.M., et al.: DeepCOVID-XR: an artificial intelligence algorithm to detect COVID-19 on chest radiographs trained and tested on a large US clinical dataset. Radiology 203511 (2020)
39. WHO: Coronavirus disease 2020 (2020). https://www.who.int/emergencies/ diseases/novel-coronavirus-2019/situation-reports
40. WHO: Statement on the second meeting of the international health regulations (2005) emergency committee regarding the outbreak of novel coronavirus (2019-ncov) (2020). https://www.who.int/
41. WHO: WHO director-general's opening remarks at the media briefing on COVID-19 (2020). https://www.who.int

Predicting Psychological Distress from Ecological Factors: A Machine Learning Approach

Ben Sutter[1], Raymond Chiong[1(✉)], Gregorius Satia Budhi[1,2],
and Sandeep Dhakal[1]

[1] School of Electrical Engineering and Computing, The University of Newcastle,
Callaghan, NSW 2308, Australia
`Raymond.Chiong@newcastle.edu.au`
[2] Informatics Department, Petra Christian University, Surabaya 60236, Indonesia

Abstract. Over 300 million people worldwide were suffering from
depression in 2017. Australia alone invests more than \$9.1 billion each
year on mental health related services. Traditional intervention methods require patients to first present with symptoms before diagnosis,
leading to a reactive approach. A more proactive approach to this problem is highly desirable, and despite ongoing work using approaches such
as machine learning, further work is required. This paper aims to provide a foundation by building a machine learning model across multiple
techniques to predict psychological distress from ecological factors alone.
Eight different classification techniques were implemented on a sample
dataset, with the best results achieved through Logistic Regression, providing an accuracy of 0.811. The preliminary results suggest that, with
future improvements to implementation and analysis, an accurate and
reliable model is possible. This study, with the proposed base model, can
potentially lead to the development of a proactive solution to the global
mental health crisis.

1 Introduction

The World Health Organisation (WHO), in 2017, reported that more than 300
million people worldwide – ≈4.4% of the global population – were suffering from
depression [34,37]. Similarly, according to the Australian Institute of Health
and Welfare, \$9.1 billion was spent on mental health-related services in 2016-17,
and 2.5 million people (≈10% of the Australian population) received Medicare-
subsidised mental health-specific services in 2017–18 [1]. These statistics highlight the severity and the widespread nature of mental health issues, and with
the growing awareness of the problem, there has been a significant increase in
research and funding for the detection and prediction of mental health issues.

Leightley et al. [21], while focusing on the identification of post-traumatic
stress disorder (PTSD) in a United Kingdom military cohort, also assessed the
impact of mental health on the day-to-day duties of serving and ex-serving sol-
diers, specifically on their retention and productivity. Similarly, Walsh et al. [36]

© Springer Nature Switzerland AG 2021
H. Fujita et al. (Eds.): IEA/AIE 2021, LNAI 12798, pp. 341–352, 2021.
https://doi.org/10.1007/978-3-030-79457-6_30

outlined the significance of psychological distress in adolescents, with suicide being the second leading cause of death in adolescents. For each suicide in the United States, there are 100–200 non-fatal attempts [36]. Mental health and psychological distress is a global issue, which costs our health care systems billions of dollars each year, and it is clearly non-discriminatory.

The application of machine learning (ML) approaches towards mental health and psychological distress problems is an ongoing research endeavour. Several studies have successfully built prediction models for psychological distress using ML techniques such as the Support Vector Machine (SVM), Artificial Neural Network (ANN), Logistic Regression (LR), Naive Bayes (NB), K-Nearest Neighbour (KNN), Decision Tree (DT) and Random Forest (RF) [13, 23, 28, 29, 34, 36]. Despite the growing body of research on improving mental health and psychological distress diagnosis with ML, the reoccurring theme, however, is the use of historical records or user reported surveys to train the ML models. Although different ML classification techniques can be used to accurately predict psychological distress, a vast majority of them rely on people self-presenting for assessment, or self-identifying their condition before the key features are available for analysis [20, 34]. There is, thus, a void with regards to generalised prediction from ecological factors alone [16]. We propose that the use of ecological factors would provide a proactive approach to generalised prediction. The few studies that have been conducted using ecological factors (e.g., see [25]) are based only on formulated questionnaire responses rather than scrutinised psychological assessment and screening tools. Therefore, this study aims to bridge this gap in the literature and supplement existing modelling research by providing a strategy to predict psychological distress based on ecological factors.

More specifically, the primary objective here is to bridge the gap between real-time ecological factors and existing psychological distress research. For this to be successful, the ML model should accurately and reliably categorise a specific person's psychological distress based solely on their ecological factors. All measurements, such as the accuracy, precision, recall, F-measure (F1), and area under the curve (AUC), should be comparable to or outperform similar ML techniques in the referenced literature. It should be noted that, in the context of this study, recall must give high scores. Failure to predict positive cases of psychological distress would be a major disadvantage. If successful, the developed model could be complemented by other ML classification techniques, or used independently in real-time software to predict and report psychological distress, providing a proactive rather than reactive approach to mental health. Ultimately, a proactive approach could then be used to offer alternate content, or even to alert a third party to provide more intense intervention methods, before the person reaches the state of potential self-harm or suicide.

Trotzek et al. [34] conducted an exhaustive literature review to identify the ecological risk factors for PTSD. They used this information to develop a questionnaire, which was then used to generate the dataset for their study. Once ecological risk factors and psychometric properties of a questionnaire are established, further research is generally required to validate the questionnaire and verify its performance against existing questionnaire screening tools. Considering the limited time frame of our study, rather than devising a new screening tool, an ML model was developed to predict screening results based on existing and real-time ecological risk factors.

The K10 and K6 are two screening scales commonly utilised for assessing psychological distress [20], and both contain the psychometric properties required to quickly and efficiently categorise a person's psychological distress. Although other screening tools exist in the literature, such as the General Health Questionnaire (GHQ-12), research has shown that the K10 and K6 surveys perform better and are more informative in recognising or ruling out target disorders [9,15]. Considering that the K6 survey is a reduced version of the K10 survey (using six of the ten questions), this study uses only the K10 screening scale. The aim here is to propose an ML-based model to efficiently predict a K10 score, or psychological distress classification based on ecological factors. This base model can potentially be extended to incorporate other ML aspects, such as facial recognition [28] and text analysis [34], to further enhance its efficiency and effectiveness as a real-time, proactive prediction tool. It can also be easily included as part of a real-time tool or mobile application for predicting psychological distress.

The rest of this paper is organised as follows. In Sect. 2, we first discuss the relevant literature and how existing research has contributed to the psychological prediction space. The research methodology used in this study is then described in Sect. 3, and the results of the study are presented in Sect. 4. Finally, we draw our conclusion in Sect. 5, along with proposed future work.

2   Related Work

Mor et al. [25] conducted a study in 2018 to evaluate an ML approach for identifying individuals at risk of PTSD using ecological risk factors. Initially, they generated a list of ecological risk factors, which resulted in a 37-question survey. The questionnaire was distributed to 1,290 residents of southern Israel who had been exposed to terror attacks. An ML model was then trained – using 10-fold cross-validation – on the provided ecological risk factors with a value indicating whether or not the study participants had previously reported a PTSD diagnosis. Their model yielded the best results of AUC = 0.91 and F1 score = 0.83. This study was one of the few that included ecological factors. Even though the study does use ecological factors for assessment, it must be noted that these factors were assessed in the context of the study itself, and then used to assess a population of the same specific demographic. Although good results were achieved, the model could have been validated in a general manner by utilising commonly scrutinised psychological assessment tools and applying over a more generalised demographic.

A similar study in 2019 screened a total of 470 seafarers for anxiety and depression using ML [33]. This study also used a range of ecological factors such as age, educational qualifications, marital status and income as feature inputs to target a known Hamilton Anxiety and Depression rating. Results of 5 classification techniques produced high accuracy (>0.75) and AUC scores (>0.8, except for the SVM with 0.759) [33]. With accurate predictions, this study successfully predicted anxiety and/or depression from ecological factors. Results could have been further validated by including a control set of people from the general population, outside of the same occupation and demographic to that of the seafarers.

Kessler et al. [20] tested ML algorithms to predict the persistence and severity of major depressive disorder. This study consisted of an initial survey of 5,877 participants, and then a re-survey of 5,001 of those participants 10–12 years later. The study used ensemble regression trees and 10-fold cross-validated penalised regression to generate a model, which was then compared against the self-reported results 10–12 years after the baseline. The study resulted in 34.6–38.1% of respondents with high persistence and 40.8–55.8% with severity indicators being in the top 20% of the baseline ML predicted distribution. Interestingly, the ML model also showed that 20% of respondents with lowest predicted risk account for only 0.9% of all hospitalisations, resulting in a prediction model useful for both high risk prediction and ruling out low risks. This study successfully outlined the benefits of using ML algorithms in psychological prediction. Re-assessing after 10–12 years allowed the ML model to be validated against real-world data, instead of just data subsets. The disadvantage of this approach, however, is the requirement of self-assessment for reporting; because, with self-assessment, there is no way of validating whether a respondent is reporting based on prior diagnosis, reporting false diagnosis or failing to report positive diagnosis.

In 2020, Priya et al. [29] applied ML algorithms to predict anxiety, depression and stress in modern life. They focused on these mental health factors by collecting results of the Depression, Anxiety and Stress Scale questionnaire (DASS 21) of 348 participants of varying age, gender and demographic. The questionnaire results were then classified using the DT, RF, NB, SVM and KNN models, with results ultimately measured by F1. The dataset was divided 70:30 into training and testing subsets. NB classification resulted in the best overall accuracy, with anxiety, depression and stress ranging between 0.73-0.85. RF classification, however, produced the best F1 scores (0.47–0.76). Similar to the work of Kessler et al. [20], all classification models also produced good results for negative cases. However, this study focused specifically on the self-reported DASS 21 questionnaire – although accurate models can be trained, comparing results against generalised ecologically inspired models is difficult in practice.

Trotzek et al. [34] addressed the early detection of depression using ML models based on messages published on the social platform, Reddit. The study compiled a range of 10 to 2,000 messages collected from a total of 135 depressed users and a random control group of 752 users [34]. The 135 depressed users were identified as depressed by posting language such as "I was diagnosed with depression". As with other studies based on self-reporting or self-diagnosis, such identification puts the validity of these messages into question. Without any context of the message, or some form of sentiment analysis (e.g., see [7]), it is possible that people in the depressed category were posting negligently, or people in the control group who may actually be depressed simply did not use depressive language in their comments.

A 2018 study by Walsh et al. [36] aimed to use ML to predict suicide attempts in adolescents. This retrospective study used data from 974 adolescents with non-fatal suicide attempts, 496 adolescents with other self-injury, 7,059 adolescents with depressive symptoms, and 25,081 adolescent general hospital controls [36]. Using a range of ML classification techniques, some accurate predictive models were found. Although ecological factors were not prioritised, this study still outlined the significance of medical history in prediction analysis, and suggested that a generalised model should utilise a holistic approach.

Studies have also been conducted in psychological distress prediction by analysing MRI images [23], relating whole-brain activity patterns to facial expressions [28], and further analysis of text-based comments on social platforms [13]. All these contribute to the research space; however, they fail to fill the void in research around proactive prediction without relying on historical data. Understandably, supervised ML requires historical data to train models, so it will always play a role in this field of research. The gap in the literature, and one that this study aims to address, is to use these known classification techniques to create a generalised prediction model based on ecological factors entirely.

Numerous studies on psychological distress prediction have also been done outside the ML domain. For example, Brooks et al. [3] conducted a study on self-reported psychological distress following a concussion incident among children and adolescents. Participants were assessed 4 and 12 weeks post-concussion using multiple psychological categorisation scales, and logistic regressions were used for prediction. Loula and Monteiro adopted a game theory-based model for predicting depression due to frustration in competitive environments [22]. This study introduced a game, relating investment in formal education to professional success, and proposed that an individual becomes depressed when the difference in their earnings and those of their neighbours in the game is above a threshold. Despite the research outside the ML domain, we have chosen ML in this study because of the motivating examples and existing work in the ML field, as well as the potential for future work in using a trained model in real time applications.

3 Methods

This work was initially broken into three phases: (1) Dataset and Targets, (2) Model Creation, and (3) Classification Analysis.

3.1 Dataset and Targets

In order to test the performance of the model proposed in this study, we used a public dataset by Every-Palmer et al. [12], which consists of 2 numeric and 15 categorical features, as shown in Table 1. This dataset was chosen because it

Table 1. Normalised dataset dictionary

Type	Variable	Variable detail
Categorical	gender_fct3	Gender
Categorical	eth_fct4	Prioritised Ethnicity
Categorical	r3.2_livealone_fct2	Participant lives alone
Categorical	r3.4_fct2	Happiness with bubble
Categorical	r3.6_fct4	Easy to maintain contact with friends and family
Categorical	r3.9	Family relationships
Categorical	r3.10_fct2	Poor relationships with other occupants (of house)
Categorical	r3.11_fct3	Loneliness
Categorical	r4.1_fct6	Employment status
Categorical	r4.5_fct3	Type of work (essential, non-essential worker)
Categorical	r5.2_fct2	Self-rated health
Categorical	r5.3_incpreg_fct3	Health vulnerabilities for COVID (including pregnancy)
Categorical	r8.17_fct2	Prior mental health diagnosis
Categorical	r11.2_anyfamilyharm_fct2	Any reported family harm in lockdown
Categorical	r11.3_fct3	Witnessed any reported family harm in lockdown
Numeric	age_num	Age (in years)
Numeric	r6.4_num	Alcohol intake (pre lockdown)
Target	r8.6_k10_num	K-10 score (numeric)

contains quantifiable ecological factors as well as a K10 score, and is therefore highly suited for the purpose of our study.

A number of metrics from the dataset were dropped from our study, such as internal identifiers and duplicate groupings – a numeric age metric was used instead of the categorical age range grouping. Given that we used only the K10 score in this study, the remaining psychological distress scales were also dropped, including the WHO-5 and GAD-7 scores. Specific COVID-19 metrics, such as infection and test results, were also dropped, since we wanted to generalise our study outside of the COVID-19 context. Even though the proposed model would have trained successfully with the data, the aim of this work is to create a generalised psychological prediction model. Scaling was used on the age and alcohol consumption numeric metrics. One-hot encoding was used to normalise the remaining categorical metrics, which mostly consist of 3 or 4 pre-determined string formatted answers. Before normalisation, any missing data in a categorical column was replaced with the string "no value" to prevent exception. Following this, any rows with missing data were dropped entirely.

3.2   Model Creation

The 'r8.6_k10_fct2' variable in the dataset is a two-level variable based on the K10 score, where the range 0–11 represents none/low/moderate and the range 12–40 represents high/very high [12]. Based on these K10 levels, we created binary targets: Low Distress (0–11) and High Distress (12–40). In this study, five single ML classifiers – the LR, SVM, ANN, NB and DT – and three ensembles – the RF, Adaptive Boosting (AD) and Gradient Boosting (GB) – were used for modelling and prediction analysis. The LR, SVM, ANN, NB, DT and RF were selected based on their demonstrated success in related studies [6,13,25,29, 34,35], whereas AB and GB were selected because they performed well in our previous work [4].

The LR classifier [24] is a generalised linear model [17,26]. Generalised linear models overcome limitations of linear models – including the use of dependent variables that are continuous and normally distributed, which are not always desirable – by using non-normal dependent variables [10,11]. In LR, the dependent variables can either be unordered or ordered polytomous, while the independent predictor variables can either be interval/ratio or dummy variables [24].

The SVM is a supervised learning model that learns from training data and performs classification on new data. It separates different classes by a hyperplane, and then maximises the separation distance as much as possible. Larger the margin, lower the error generated by the classifier [5].

The ANN is a feedforward neural network that uses supervised learning. This algorithm continually computes and updates all the weights in its network to minimise error. It consists of two phases: a feedforward phase where the training data is forwarded to the output layer; and the second phase, where the difference between this output and the desired target (the error) is backpropagated to update the weights of the network [32].

The DT classifier is based on Hunt's algorithm [18], and was developed by Quinlan [30]. It builds a tree-like decision model for classification and prediction, and is a useful explanatory tool for expressing the cause and effect chain [31]. It is typically used as a base classifier for ensemble models (e.g., RF, and AB).

NB is the simplest form of Bayesian network classifiers given the independence of each feature. Nevertheless, many applications have successfully implemented NB, and it is included among the top 10 data mining algorithms [19].

The RF is an ensemble of DT predictors where each tree is independently trained using a random vector. Error generalisation of RF depends on the strength of each individual tree and the correlation between them. This ensemble model is relatively robust to outliers and noise [2].

The AB ensemble algorithm iteratively combines multiple weak classifiers over several rounds. It starts with equal weights for all training data. When the training data points are misclassified, the weights of these data points are boosted, then a new classifier is created using the new unequal weights. This process is repeated for a set of classifiers [38].

GB is an ensemble of gradient boosted regression trees for the classification of dirty data, which produces a robust, competitive and interpretable algorithm for classification and regression. However, it uses only a single regression tree for binary classification [14].

As the dataset used in this study is relatively small (n = 2,010, and 1,985 after normalisation), the 10-fold cross-validation technique was applied. 10-fold cross-validation requires the dataset to be randomly partitioned into 10 equal subsets. 10 model building and test runs were then completed, each time utilising a different arrangement of 9 subsets for training and 1 subset for testing [25]. The

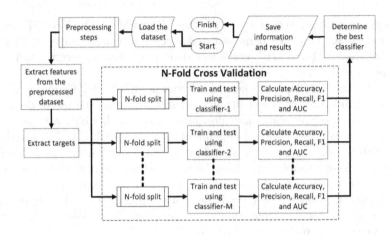

Fig. 1. An overview of the experiment workflow

entire experiment workflow is described in Fig. 1. All the code for the experiments was written and run on Google Colaboratory using Scikit Learn [27].

Five metrics, namely the accuracy, precision, recall, AUC, and F1 score (weighted average of precision and recall), were used for analysing the results of the proposed model, as well as for comparing them with the results obtained using other models from the literature. Accuracy was calculated by taking the number of correct predictions on the test set. Precision was calculated using Eq. 1, where tp is the number of true positives, and fp is the number of false positives [27]. Recall was calculated using Eq. 2, where fn is the number of false negatives [27]. Equation 3 is then used with precision and recall values to give the F1 score.

$$tp/(tp + fp) \tag{1}$$

$$tp/(tp + fn) \tag{2}$$

$$2 * (precision * recall)/(precision + recall) \tag{3}$$

3.3 Classification Analysis

Model validation is critical in ML training in order to prevent the over-fitting of a specific trained model. Hence, during the final phase of this study, the results of each classification model were compared to each other. As in the model creation phase, precision, recall, AUC and F1 scores were used as primary metrics to measure the performance of each classifier.

4 Experiments and Results

All experiments were run using the 10-fold validation technique and averages were taken over 10 runs. Hyperparameters remained constant based on their default implementations.

Table 2 shows the average accuracy, precision, recall, F1 and AUC scores of each classifier. The results indicate that the LR model provided the best results. Its AUC score of 0.730 indicates that it made more correct than incorrect predictions. Similarly, with a recall score of 0.918, the LR model accurately predicted those positive cases. Therefore, despite the potential for improvement, we can conclude that our model can accurately predict psychological distress using ecological factors alone. Among other single classifiers, the ANN also performed well (accuracy of 0.807, better precision but a lower recall value than LR). The NB classifier had the best precision but lower accuracy – meaning that it made more similar mistakes than other classifiers. The DT and SVM, while still providing accuracies above 70%, seem less suitable for psychological distress prediction than the other models.

The ensemble models tested in our study (AB, GB, and RF) also generally performed well, with the RF providing slightly worse results than the others. Given that the GB ensemble uses a regression tree as its base classifier, the good results are both expected and obvious. As discussed above, LR, which is based on regression analysis, was the best classifier; however, the DT, which is the base classifier of AB and RF, performed only moderately. In other words, the ensemble models performed well despite their base classifiers performing only moderately. This means that better results can be achieved if we boost the weak classifiers continuously (as in AB) or bind some weak single classifiers (e.g., DT) in the RF.

Table 2. Results obtained with different classification methods

Classifier	Accuracy	Precision	Recall	F1	AUC
LR	0.811	0.835	0.918	0.875	0.730
AB	0.810	0.835	0.916	0.874	0.729
GB	0.810	0.837	0.912	0.873	0.732
ANN	0.807	0.840	0.904	0.871	0.734
RF	0.795	0.836	0.888	0.861	0.723
NB	0.778	0.856	0.830	0.843	0.739
DT	0.736	0.820	0.809	0.814	0.681
SVM	0.736	0.835	0.815	0.825	0.678

As the input dataset was mapped 1:1 to the feature layout of the model, it is possible that further manipulation could enhance the performance of the model. Such manipulation may involve adjusting weights based on bias, removing non-dominant features or implementing feature crosses that would provide a better depiction of the data in the given context. Additionally, the performance of the model could also be enhanced through tuning of the hyperparameters.

Our experiments utilised the MLPClassifier class (i.e., multilayer perceptron) of the Scikit Learn library to implement an ANN [27]. Related studies have shown neural networks can successfully predict in areas of psychological distress [34]. Therefore, results may be further improved by re-implementing an ANN model, or implementing additional neural network models using specialised neural network frameworks such as TensorFlow Keras [8].

Further work on the actual ecological metrics included in the dataset would also be necessary to optimise the models. Removing metrics with little impact on K-10 scores, and adding further metrics with known positive impacts on K-10 scores would likely improve the model's scores. It is also important to note that the data sample used in this study was generated in the context of the COVID-19 pandemic, for the purpose of a study in that context. Therefore, we believe that a different data sample within the context of a more holistic, generalised view may also be beneficial.

5   Conclusion

In this paper, we proposed an ML-based model for psychological distress prediction using only ecological factors. Implementing eight classifiers using Scikit Learn [27], our LR classifier produced the best results, presenting an AUC of 0.73. Although below the 0.8 target, its accuracy of 0.811, precision of 0.835 and recall of 0.918 suggested that the model can accurately predict positive cases of psychological distress. Our results indicated that, although it is possible to create an ML model to predict psychological distress, the challenge lies in finding suitable ML model parameters and ecological features. Future work in this area would be to further analyse and tweak parameters to enhance the current models. Accuracy may also be improved by implementing alternative ecological factors as metrics in order to provide a greater holistic view.

Once an accurate model has been built, it can be used to bridge the gap in existing research in the literature, and also incorporated into real world software or mobile applications. This could include the integration with brain activity data [28], text sequence classification [34], or possibly with wearable devices to provide sleep, activity and heart rate information. With an enhanced model using metrics from multiple areas, some in real time, it will then be possible to provide the proactive approach required to effectively deal with this mental health crisis.

Acknowledgement. The first author would like to acknowledge financial support from a Research and Innovation Summer Research Internship Program scholarship awarded by the University of Newcastle, Australia.

References

1. Australian Institute of Health and Welfare: Mental health services in Australia: in brief 2019. AIHW (2019). https://doi.org/10.25816/5ec5bac5ed175
2. Breiman, L.: Random forests. Mach. Learn. **45**(1), 5–32 (2001)
3. Brooks, B.L., et al.: Predicting psychological distress after pediatric concussion. J. Neurotrauma **36**(5), 679–685 (2019)

4. Budhi, G.S., Chiong, R., Pranata, I., Hu, Z.: Using machine learning to predict the sentiment of online reviews: a new framework for comparative analysis. Arch. Comput. Methods Eng. **28**, 2543–2566 (2021). https://doi.org/10.1007/s11831-020-09464-8
5. Campbell, C., Ying, Y.: Learning with Support Vector Machines. Morgan & Claypool (2011)
6. Chiong, R., Fan, Z., Hu, Z., Chiong, F.: Using an improved relative error support vector machine for body fat prediction. Comput. Methods Programs Biomed. **198**, 105749 (2021)
7. Chiong, R., Satia Budhi, G., Dhakal, S.: Combining sentiment lexicons and content-based features for depression detection. IEEE Intell. Syst. **36**(6) (2021)
8. Chollet, F., et al.: Keras (2015). https://keras.io
9. Cornelius, B.L.R., Groothoff, J.W., van der Klink, J.J.L., Brouwer, S.: The performance of the K10, K6 and GHQ-12 to screen for present state DSM-IV disorders among disability claimants. BMC Public Health **13**(1), 1–8 (2013)
10. Dobson, A., Barnett, A.: An Introduction to Generalized Linear Models, 3rd edn. CRC Press, Boca Raton (2008)
11. Dunteman, G., Ho, M.: Generalized linear models. In: An Introduction to Generalized Linear Models, pp. 2–6. SAGE Publications, Inc. (2011)
12. Every-Palmer, S., et al.: Psychological distress, anxiety, family violence, suicidality, and wellbeing in New Zealand during the COVID-19 lockdown: a cross-sectional study. PLOS ONE **15**(11), e0241658 (2020)
13. Fatima, I., Mukhtar, H., Ahmad, H.F., Rajpoot, K.: Analysis of user-generated content from online social communities to characterise and predict depression degree. J. Inf. Sci. **44**(5), 683–695 (2018)
14. Friedman, J.: Greedy function approximation: a gradient boosting machine. Ann. Stat. **29**(5), 1189–1232 (2001)
15. Furukawa, T.A., Kessler, R.C., Slade, T., Andrews, G.: The performance of the K6 and K10 screening scales for psychological distress in the Australian national survey of mental health and well-being. Psychol. Med. **33**(2), 357–362 (2003)
16. Galatzer-Levy, I.R., Karstoft, K.I., Statnikov, A., Shalev, A.Y.: Quantitative forecasting of PTSD from early trauma responses: a machine learning application. J. Psychiatr. Res. **59**, 68–76 (2014)
17. Hastie, T., Tibshirani, R.: Generalized Additive Models. Chapman and Hall/CRC, UK (1990)
18. Hunt, E., Marin, J., Stone, P.: Experiments in Induction. Academic Press, New York (1966)
19. Jiang, L., Li, C., Wang, S., Zhang, L.: Deep feature weighting for Naïve Bayes and its application to text classification. Eng. Appl. Artif. Intell. **52**, 26–39 (2016)
20. Kessler, R.C., et al.: Testing a machine-learning algorithm to predict the persistence and severity of major depressive disorder from baseline self-reports. Mol. Psychiatry **21**(10), 1366–1371 (2016)
21. Leightley, D., Williamson, V., Darby, J., Fear, N.T.: Identifying probable post-traumatic stress disorder: applying supervised machine learning to data from a UK military cohort. J. Ment. Health **28**(1), 34–41 (2019)
22. Loula, R., Monteiro, L.H.A.: A game theory-based model for predicting depression due to frustration in competitive environments. Comput. Math. Methods Med. **2020**, 3573267 (2020)
23. Patel, M.J., Khalaf, A., Aizenstein, H.J.: Studying depression using imaging and machine learning methods. NeuroImage Clin. **10**(C), 115–123 (2016)

24. Menard, S.: Logistic Regression: From Introductory to Advanced Concepts and Applications. SAGE, Los Angeles (2010)
25. Mor, N.S., Dardeck, K.L.: Quantitative forecasting of risk for PTSD using ecological factors: a deep learning application. J. Soc. Behav. Health Sci. **12**(1), 61–73 (2018)
26. Nelder, J.A., Wedderburn, R.W.: Generalized linear models. J. R. Stat. Soc. Ser. A (General) **135**(3), 370–384 (1972)
27. Pedregosa, F., et al.: Scikit-learn: machine learning in python. J. Mach. Learn. Res. **12**, 2825–2830 (2011)
28. Portugal, L.C., et al.: Predicting anxiety from whole brain activity patterns to emotional faces in young adults: a machine learning approach. NeuroImage Clin. **23**, 101813 (2019)
29. Priya, A., Garg, S., Tigga, N.P.: Predicting anxiety, depression and stress in modern life using machine learning algorithms. Procedia Comput. Sci. **167**, 1258–1267 (2020)
30. Quinlan, J.: Induction of decision trees. Mach. Learn. **1**(1), 81–106 (1986)
31. Rokach, L., Maimon, O.: Data Mining with Decision Trees: Theory and Applications. World Scientific Publishing, Singapore (2007)
32. Rumelhart, D.E., Hinton, G.E., Williams, R.J.: Learning internal representations by error propagation. Technical report, California Univ San Diego La Jolla Inst for Cognitive Science (1985)
33. Sau, A., Bhakta, I.: Screening of anxiety and depression among the seafarers using machine learning technology. Inform. Med. Unlocked **16**, 100149 (2019)
34. Trotzek, M., Koitka, S., Friedrich, C.M.: Utilizing neural networks and linguistic metadata for early detection of depression indications in text sequences. IEEE Trans. Knowl. Data Eng. **32**(3), 588–601 (2020)
35. Walsh, C.G., Ribeiro, J.D., Franklin, J.C.: Predicting risk of suicide attempts over time through machine learning. Clin. Psychol. Sci. **5**(3), 457–469 (2017)
36. Walsh, C.G., Ribeiro, J.D., Franklin, J.C.: Predicting suicide attempts in adolescents with longitudinal clinical data and machine learning. J. Child Psychol. Psychiatry **59**(12), 1261–1270 (2018)
37. World Health Organization: Other common mental disorders: Global health estimates. Geneva: World Health Organization, pp. 1–24 (2017)
38. Zhu, J., Zou, H., Rosset, S., Hastie, T.: Multi-class adaboost. Stat. Interface **2**, 349–360 (2009)

Graphic and Social Network Analysis

Configuration Model of Employee Competences in a Social Media Team

Jarosław Wikarek[ID] and Paweł Sitek[(✉)][ID]

Kielce University of Technology, Kielce, Poland
{j.wikarek,sitek}@tu.kielce.pl

Abstract. In the age of economics and knowledge-based economy, the competences of enterprises and organizations focus on the competences of their employees. It is especially visible in enterprises using advanced IT technologies and
modern communication channels, such as social media. In recent years, social
media has become an indispensable and very common channel of the business
information flow, e.g., in the terms of advertising and marketing, payment processing, placing orders and tracking progress in their implementation. Thus, to
support all these functionalities, usually in addition to specialized software and
hardware, one needs highly qualified specialists, conventionally called the 'social
media team'. This paper proposes a competency configuration model for the social
media team. The presented model is the basis for supporting decisions in the selection, configuration, and optimization of the social media team in the context of
the execution of a certain set of tasks. The implementation of the model using
mathematical programming methods and a genetic algorithm with the original
coding system for the modelled problem has also been proposed.

Keywords: Social media team · Resource allocation · Decision support ·
Mathematical programming · Genetic algorithm · Constraint Logic Programming

1 Introduction

The knowledge-based economy is characterized by a high level of use of IT technologies,
AI methods as well as modern forms and techniques of communication, including those
applying social media. Nowadays, social media is one of the most powerful tools for
reaching target audiences (customers, potential customers, associates, subcontractors,
etc.) and engaging them in issues related to the company's activity. The presence in
social networks and the introduction of modern IT is a tool for company development
by increasing its competitiveness and raising the level of competences.

Despite—or perhaps even thanks to this fact—the competence of the entire company or organization is still to a large extent based on the competences of its employees.
Bearing in mind the high degree of automation and digitization of modern enterprises,
and the saturation of IT, it is the aspect of employee competences that becomes crucial
for them. It is all the more an important and vital aspect of the functioning of modern companies, because recruiting employees with high and specialist qualifications is

© Springer Nature Switzerland AG 2021
H. Fujita et al. (Eds.): IEA/AIE 2021, LNAI 12798, pp. 355–368, 2021.
https://doi.org/10.1007/978-3-030-79457-6_31

extremely difficult. Also, an employee turnover risk and a risk related to absenteeism, e.g., due to illness, quarantine, etc. occurs. The main contribution of this paper is to present the problem of configuring employee competences for the social media team [1] and proposing a model of the problem along with its implementation. The proposed model is the basis for supporting decisions in the selection and configuration of the social media team and allows for finding answers to key operational questions such as: *Does our social media team have the appropriate number and competence to complete a specific set of tasks? What competences and what team members are missing to perform a specific set of tasks?* etc. The proposed model enables supporting decisions both in the active—i.e., both above questions etc.—and proactive mode, i.e., finding answers to questions such as *Is our social team able to complete the set of tasks in the absence of any employee?*, etc. The paper also presents numerous computational experiments aimed at verifying the correctness of the model and assessing the effectiveness of the applied methods of implementation.

2 Literature Review

The problem of configuring employee competences should be classified as a certain variant of the problem of resource allocation [2], which is usually considered along with the problem of scheduling tasks [3], and in our case with its variant called 'timetabling problem' [4]. Timetabling problems can be classified as complex problems with scheduling that usually includes the narrowness of resources. As a rule, these are NP-difficult problems, which have practical application in drawing up lesson plans at schools and universities (UCTTP-university course timetabling problem) [4], defining the work schedule of production employees, in transport, etc. The studied issue of employee competence configuration can be considered with other variants of scheduling problems, such as nurse scheduling problem (NSP) [5], crew scheduling problem (CSP), etc.

In case of all known resource allocation problems, resources are typically included in a quantitative dimension with an assigned usage cost. In some resource allocation problems, different types of resources are considered. This is quite common in Resource Constrained Project Scheduling Problems (RCPSP) [6]. The paper presents a discussion on resources that are characterized by many features/properties, which can additionally be properly configured (i.e. supplemented, or changed, etc.). This is a new type of resource that can be described as a multi-dimensional resource. In the discussed problem, the members of the social media team stand for multidimensional resources, and the dimensions are their competences.

3 Problem Statement and Illustrative Example

The spread of the Internet, the emergence of mobile technologies and, finally, the ubiquity of social media have changed the way of running businesses. New areas of economic activity and new specializations have emerged. New forms of communication have been appreciated, which has resulted in the formation of social media teams in many companies, just the same way as the development of IT departments many years ago. Highly qualified specialists from various areas with professional experience are needed in order to build an effective social media team. It is also required that the recruited employees—apart from their basic specialization—have such additional competences that will allow them to handle tasks that go beyond this specialization. The departure from narrow specialists, who are single-discipline experts, is the resultant of two reasons. Firstly, it is the development of advanced IT tools supporting the operational activities of individual members of the social media team. Secondly, during a pandemic, more often than before, we deal with the increased unavailability of employees, reduction of their productivity and remote work. Hence, each social media team should have such a composition and a set of competences that will ensure efficient handling of the assigned tasks within a given period and, as a collective, will be resistant to the absence of individual team members, or will be able to carry out additional tasks. To achieve this, the members of the social media team must be competent to perform basic functions within the team, such as [7]: social media manager, content creator, community manager, social media analyst, social media advertiser as well as complementary functions such as live video creator or influencer, etc. What is more, each member of the social media team should have more than one of the above-mentioned competences in order to ensure the team's resistance to absenteeism. Of course, the question of how many members such a team should be composed of, and what competencies they should have (what should be the configuration of competences in the team) in the context of the set of tasks entrusted to them to be carried out within a specified period remains opened. To better understand the problem described, let us consider the illustrative example EXP_ST01.

Illustrative Example: EXP_ST01
A set of tasks to be performed from the social media area is provided (such as accurate information, creation of both micro and macro content, sharing and publishing the content on social media platforms, engaging in conversations on social media platforms, providing reports, defining audience, setting a target audience, planning campaigns, etc.) in the form of a weekly schedule (Fig. 1), the implementation of which is the responsibility of the social media team consisting of eight members. A member of the social media team with specific competences should be assigned to implement a single task (Table 1). The description of the particular competences is presented in Table 2. Each team member has a specific work time limit (5 days a week) and a specific labor cost. The block in the diagram specifies the engagement time of the team member. It can be a whole day or half a day.

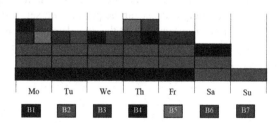

Fig. 1. Weekly schedule for the illustrative example EXP_ST01

Table 1. Competences (B) of members (F) of the social media team

	B1	B2	B3	B4	B5	B6	B7	Labour cost
F1	+	−	−	+	−	−	−	100
F2	−	+	+	−	−	−	−	80
F3	−	+	+	−	−	+	+	80
F4	+	+	−	−	+	−	−	100
F5	−	+	+	+	−	+	+	100
F6	−	+	+	−	−	−	−	80
F7	−	+	−	−	−	−	−	75
F8	−	+	−	−	+	−	−	75

(+) the member Bi has a given competence Fi; (−) the member Bi has not a given competence Fi

Table 2. Competences of the social team

B	Name
B1	Social media manager
B2	Content creator
B3	Community manager
B4	Social media analyst
B5	Social media advertiser
B6	Live video creator or
B7	Influencer

Most generally, the problem of configuring competences in the social media team can be formulated using a general question:

Does the given social media team have the appropriate composition and appropriate set of competences to perform a given set of tasks in accordance with a given schedule?

This is the main and key question in the presented problem. Depending on the answer obtained, further detailed questions can be posed. The set of questions related to the problem of competency configuration in the social media team is presented in Table 3. Finding answers to these questions largely supports decision-making in the team management process.

Table 3. Set of questions of the presented problem

Q	Description
Q-1	Does the given social media team F have the appropriate composition and has the appropriate set of competences to perform a given set of tasks in accordance with a given weekly schedule?
Q-2	How many members of the social media team ($f \in F$) and what competences ($b \in B$) are missing to complete a set of tasks according to a given weekly schedule?
Q-3	What is the minimum cost of completing a set of tasks by the social media team F data in accordance with a given weekly schedule?
Q-4	Will a given social media team perform a set of tasks according to a given weekly schedule in the absence of a fx team member?
Q-5	What configuration of the social media team (composition and competences) guarantees completion the set of tasks with a given weekly schedule in the absence of any member of social team?

4 Mathematical Model of the Problem of Competency Configuration in the Social Media Team

The model was formulated as CSP (Constraint Satisfaction Problem) [8] with the set of questions Q-1...Q-5. Depending on the question under consideration, the model may be BIP (Binary Integer Programming) [9], or stay in the form CSP.

The following assumptions were made when building the model:

- A social media team F, which consists of members $f \in F$ is provided. Each team member is described by three parameters (minimum working time, maximum working time, labor cost per unit of time).
- Team member $f \in F$ has specific competences $b \in B$. By B we denote a set of all competences that the members of the social media team F may have.
- Each task r ($r \in R$) is characterized by the coefficient determining how many team members with competency b should be allocated and the time needed to complete it.
- There is a specific set of tasks to be performed by R.
- Unavailability of a team member $f \in F$ is modelled by the unavailability state $w \in W$ defined at the data instance level. The unavailable state determines which persons are unavailable during the schedule execution. Examples a team member availability conditions are as follows: $w1 = \{f1, f5\}$, $w2 = \{f3\}$, $w3 = \{f1, f2, f5\}$, etc.

The description of the model parameters and model decision variables is presented in Table 5. The model has numerous constraints regarding the method of assigning team members, working time, costs of implementing tasks, etc. The description of the set of model constraints (1)...(12) is presented in Table 4. The proposed model has a very interesting feature. The method of selecting decision variables and their function is such that when implementing the model, we always find a solution. There will never be an NFSF (No Feasible Solution Found) situation that adds little to the decision-making process. The applied problem modelling method is favorable in terms of the decision support process and for answering questions Q-1…Q-5. This is due to the fact that the decision variables in the solution will always assume specific values that will be easy to interpret, and the information obtained will be used in the decision-making process.

Table 4. Constraints of the presented problem

Constraint	Description
(1)	If a specific competence is required to perform a task, only the team member who has it will be assigned to the task
(2)	If a team member has been assigned to a task owing to the required competency, s/he must have it or obtain/supplement it
(3)	The cost of completing the tasks
(4)	A team member only works within the allowed time frame
(5)	A team member completes a task using only one of his/her competencies
(6)	Determination of the number of uncompleted tasks
(7, 8)	Relationship between the variables $X_{w, f, r, b}$ and $Z_{w, f, r}$
(9)	A team member only works the allowed number of days a week
(10)	A team member only works when he is available
(11, 12)	Binarity constraint of decision variables (12)

$$\sum_{f \in F} X_{w,f,r,b} = (1 - Cr_{w,r,b}) \cdot ga_{r,b} \quad \forall r \in R, b \in B, w \in W \tag{1}$$

$$X_{w,f,r,b} \leq ag_{f,b} \quad \forall w \in W, f \in F, r \in R, b \in B \tag{2}$$

$$Cost\_1 = \sum_{w \in W} \sum_{f \in F} \sum_{r \in R} \sum_{b \in B} tw_{r,b} \cdot ur_f \cdot X_{w,f,r,b} \tag{3}$$

$$ub_f \leq \sum_{r \in R} \sum_{b \in B} (tw_{r,b} \cdot Z_{w,f,r}) \leq uc_f \quad \forall w \in W, f \in F \tag{4}$$

$$\sum_{b \in B} X_{w,f,r,b} \leq 1 \quad \forall w \in W, f \in F, r \in R \tag{5}$$

$$Count\_1 = \sum_{w \in W} \sum_{r \in R} \sum_{b \in B} Cr_{w,r,b} \tag{6}$$

$$\sum_{b \in B} X_{w,f,r,b} \leq con \cdot Z_{w,f,r} \quad \forall w \in W, f \in F, r \in R \tag{7}$$

$$\sum_{b \in B} X_{w,f,r,b} \geq Z_{w,f,r} \quad \forall w \in W, f \in F, r \in R \tag{8}$$

Table 5. Indices, parameters, and decision variables

Symbol	Description
Indices	
F	Social media team
R	A set of tasks
B	A set of competences
W	A set of unavailability states of team members
F	Team member index ($f \in F$)
R	Job index ($r \in R$)
B	Competency index ($b \in B$)
W	Unavailability state index ($w \in W$)
Parameters	
$ga_{r,b}$	The $ga_{r,b}$ coefficient stands for the number of team members with competencies b that should be allocated to the task r. If the coefficient $ga_{r,b} = 0$ *it* means that in order to perform the task r, no team member with competencies b ($f \in F$, $b \in B$)*is needed*
$ag_{f,b}$	If the coefficient $ag_{f,b} = 1$, it means that the team member f has competence b. If $ag_{f,b} = 0$, it means that the group member f does not have the feature b
$tw_{r,b}$	Time of task completion r using competence b
ur_f	Labour cost of the team member f per unit of time
ub_f	Minimum time the team member f should work
uc_f	Maximum time the team member f can work
$ra_{w,f}$	Is team member f available in the absence state w
Lw_f	A team member only works the allowed number of days a week ($f \in F$)
con	Arbitrarily large constant
Decision variables	
$X_{w,f,r,b}$	If, in the absence state of w, the team member f using competence b performs the task r $X_{w,f,b,r} = 1$ otherwise $X_{w,f,b,r} = 0$
$Z_{w,f,r}$	If, in the absence state w the team member f performs task r
$Cost\_1$	The cost of completing the tasks
$Count\_1$	How many tasks cannot be performed/completed
$Cr_{w,r,b}$	If the task r cannot be performed due to the impossibility of obtaining competency b in the absence state w $Cr_{w,r,b} = 0$ (decision variable introduced only to achieve a solution in each case—so that the NFSF state does not appear) otherwise $Cr_{w,r,b} = 1$

$$\sum_{r \in R} Y_{w,f,r} \leq lw_f \quad \forall w \in W, f \in F \tag{9}$$

$$X_{w,f,r,b} = 0 \,\forall w \in W, f \in F, r \in R, b \in B \wedge ra_{f,b} = 0 \tag{10}$$

$$X_{w,f,r,b} \in \{0, 1\} \,\forall w \in W, f \in F, r \in R, b \in B \tag{11}$$

$$Z_{w,f,r} \in \{0, 1\} \,\forall w \in W, f \in F, r \in R \tag{12}$$

5 Implementation Methods

The implementation of the proposed model was conducted in two ways. The first method (A) involved the use of the AMPL modeling language (A Mathematical Programming Language) [10] and the Gurobi [11] mathematical programming environment. The second method (B) is an original approach, which uses the CLP (Constraint Logic Programming) environment [8] to presolve the model using available data instances [12, 13] and the genetic algorithm along with the original representation of the modeled problem. Schematically, both of the implementation methods are shown in Fig. 2. In practice, the first implementation method consisted in the implementation of the mathematical model of the problem using the AMPL language and solving it with the Gurobi Solver. The second method was slightly more complicated. In the first phase, the model was implemented using the Eclipse CLP tool [14].

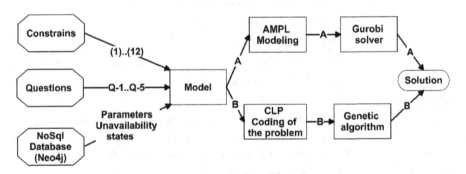

Fig. 2. Implementation methods for modeled problem

This implementation is aimed at using a certain feature of the CLP environment, i.e. the ability to propagate constraints. In our model, it allowed to narrow down the domains of decision variables and, consequently, to reduce the size of the modeled problem. In practice, partial solutions were also obtained during presolving. It was related to situations where, for example, due to the necessity to carry out many tasks requiring competences, e.g. *B1*, it was vital so that the selected employee—despite the fact that s/he has other competences, and *B1* is not his/her leading competence—worked on tasks that require it. The second case presented a situation, referred to the limit of working time and competences, which resulted that a given team member had to perform a specific task. Then, the results obtained during the presolving phase were the entry into the genetic algorithm. In genetic algorithm we applied standard selection methods, crossing, mutation, [15] etc., while the way of coding the problem was unique. Schematically, the coding of the modeled problem is presented in Fig. 3. The proposed coding method means that the following might not be met: constraint (4) employees work too much or too little, constraint (5) one employee has two tasks during the day (s/he would be working in two specialties on one day) and constraint (9) employee is working more than the number of days allowed.

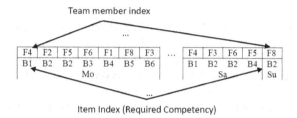

Fig. 3. Schematically, the coding of the presented problem

Nevertheless, the remaining constraints are satisfied. The correction of the chromosome to make it acceptable consists in agreeing on a list of tasks assigned to the employee, and their execution results in failure to meet the constraints for the selected employee. Next, for these tasks, a list of alternative methods of their implementation by other employees is built, for whom this additional task will be acceptable and the constraints will be met. For each day, it is determined which employee (f_i) uses which competence (B_j). The competences are coded by a specific position in the chromosome, e.g. the first position in the chromosome stands for the competency that is needed for the first task on the first day, and the value of the gene with this index is the team member number.

6   Computational Experiments

A series of computational experiments were carried out in order to verify the correctness of the proposed model and to test the effectiveness of the proposed method of its implementation. The experiments were conducted in two stages. The first stage concerned experiments with small data instances of an illustrative example (Tables 1 and 2), which were to confirm the correctness of the model. For the above data, answers to selected questions from the Table 3 were found. Thus, similarly to the manual allocation performed by the operator (Fig. 4), the answer to question *Q-1*, using the model, was YES (Fig. 5) (i.e. it is possible to carry out a set of tasks according to a given schedule (Fig. 1) through the social media team).

The difference consisted in the speed of obtaining the answer in this case, calculated in seconds, not in minutes, and in a different allocation of tasks to the team members,

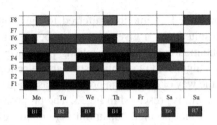

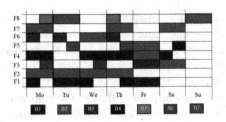

Fig. 4. Allocation of team members to implement the schedule from Fig. 1—manual allocation—cost 17,715 (Q-1)

Fig. 5. Allocation of team members to implement the schedule from Fig. 1—allocation using proposed model—cost 17,235 (Q-1)

which resulted in the objective function $Fc = 17,235$ (previously 17,715). Question Q-2 was not considered as irrelevant in the case of a positive answer to question Q-1. In the subsequent step, the answer to the question Q-3 was obtained, which determines the optimal allocation of the team members to tasks according to a given schedule (Fig. 6). The value of the objective function (the cheapest way to perform tasks) was $Fc = 16,740$). The Q-4 question was formulated in several versions, which defined the situations of absence of selected team members. The details of the particular variants of the Q-4 question and the results obtained are presented in Table 6.

Table 6. Answer for Q-4

Variant of Q-4	Team member absent	Answer	Variant of Q-4	Team member absent	Answer
Q-4A	F1	NO	Q-4A	F5	YES
Q-4B	F2	YES (Fig. 7)	Q-4B	F6	YES
Q-4C	F3	YES	Q-4C	F7	YES
Q-4D	F4	NO	Q-4D	F8	YES

The answer to the last Q-5 question specifies what competencies should be supplemented so that the tasks can always be completed in accordance with the prearranged schedule in the case of absence of any team member. For the illustrative example data, the response to Q-5 was as follows: any team member competences, except $F1$ and $F4$, must be supplemented with $B1$! After such supplement, the competences and composition of the social media team considered in the illustrative example will guarantee the performance of tasks according to the schedule in the absence of any of the team members. As you can see, the proposed model in the form of a set of constraints (1)…(11), and a set of questions Q-1…Q-5, enables to support the decisions related to the structure and competences of the social media team. This applies both to decisions made in a reactive—on occurring events, i.e. answers to questions Q-1, Q-2, Q-3—and proactive mode: answer to question Q-5, specifying the configuration and composition of the team that will be resistant to certain events. Depending on the time of the considered question *Q-4*, it may be in a proactive mode/before starting the implementation of tasks/or reactive mode/if absences appear already during the implementation of tasks/.

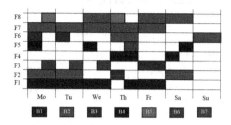 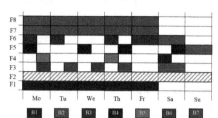

Fig. 6. Optimal allocation of team members to implement the schedule from Fig. 1—allocation using proposed model—cost 16,600 (*Q-3*)

Fig. 7. Allocation of team members to implement the schedule from Fig. 1—allocation using proposed model (absent *F2*)—cost 16,640 (*Q4-B*)

In the second stage of the experiments, the effectiveness of the proposed implementations was checked. Particular data instances differed in the number of employees, the number of days covered by the schedule and the number of competencies for question *Q-3*, as well as in additionally introduced numerous employee absences for question *Q-5*. For the question *Q-3* (optimization), the application of the proprietary method B resulted in a reduction of the computation time up to 5 times compared to the use of method A (Table 7). For the question *Q-5* (proactive search for a configuration resistant to a single absenteeism of a team member), the calculation time was also accelerated up to six times using the B method in relation to the use of method B. Moreover, for

Table 7. Results obtained for different data instances of Q-3

No	nD	nF	nB	Method (A)			Method (B)	
				V	T [min]	Fc	T [min]	Fc
1	7	10	6	560	3	4500	5	4500
2	21	10	6	1680	8	14,500	6	14,500
3	7	15	8	1050	6	5,400	5	5400
4	30	15	8	4500	14	21,300	8	21,300
5	7	20	10	1680	9	6700	10	6700
6	14	20	10	3360	11	13400	11	13400
7	30	20	10	7200	19	32500	11	32,500
8	7	40	12	3920	12	9500	14	9500
9	14	40	12	7840	21	21,400	14	21,400
10	30	40	12	16,800	84	45,500	17	45,500

nD - number of days, nF number of employees, nB - number of competences, V - number of decision variables, Fc - value of the objective function (Q-3), — no solution in time 90 min, NO(nF,nB) - missing number of nF employees and missing number of nB competencies larger instances, method A proved ineffective and after 90 min the calculations were interrupted without a solution (Table 8).

Table 8. Results obtained for different data instances of Q-5

No	nD	nF	nB	Method (A)			Method (B)	
				V	T [min]	Fc	T [min]	Fc
1	7	10	6	1680	10	YES	6	YES
2	21	10	6	5040	22	YES	8	YES
3	7	15	8	5250	24	YES	8	YES
4	30	15	8	22,500	90^*	NO(1,2)	12	NO(1,2)
5	7	20	10	11,760	54	YES	8	YES
6	14	20	10	23,520	90^*	NO(2,1)	9	YES
7	30	20	10	50,400	90^*	—	20	NO(1,3)
8	7	40	12	35,280	90^*	—	12	YES
9	14	40	12	70,560	90^*	—	22	NO(1,1)
10	30	40	12	151,200	90^*	—	28	NO(1,1)

nD - number of days, nF number of employees, nB - number of competences, V - number of decision variables, Fc - value of the objective function (Q-3), — no solution in time 90 min, NO(nF,nB) - missing number of nF employees and missing number of nB competencies, * - calculations were stopped after 90 minutes

7 Conclusions

The proposed model of the employee competency configuration (Chapter 4) for the social media team enables a wide range of decision support, in particular in the field of: (a) selection of the team composition and set of competences for the social media team to perform a specific set of tasks according to a given schedule; (b) optimal (cheapest) allocation of employees to tasks in accordance with a given schedule; (c) determining the configuration of competences for the social media team resistant to the absence of a selected or any team member, etc. What is more, the proposed model can be used both in a reactive (decisions related to the occurrence of unexpected situations such as the absence of an employee, the appearance of additional tasks, etc.) and proactive mode (determining the configuration resistant to the absence of a selected or any employee, two employees, etc.). The proposed set of questions in the presented version of the Q-1...Q-5 model is quite representative, nonetheless in the future it can be extended with questions on the possibility of implementing an additional set of tasks by the social media team without changing the base schedule, temporary unavailability of individual employees, e.g. during the day etc. In future research, it might also be possible to extend the set of model constraints with logical constraints, e.g. excluding the work of two selected employees at the same time on a given day, holding two selected competences by a given employee, etc. The presented original method of the model implementation (B), which applies the CLP and GA methodology, turned out to be extremely effective in relation to the implementation of the model by means of mathematical programming methods (A). Firstly, the calculation time was shortened several times (5 or 6 times, depending on the question). The achieved efficiency resulted from the use of model presolving in the CLP environment and the application of GA with an original method of coding the modeled problem. There are plans to use other AI methods to implement the model, such as Artificial Neural Networks [16], Fuzzy Logic [17, 18], etc. It is also planned to integrate the proposed model with our supply chain management models [13, 19].

References

1. How to Build the Perfect Social Media Team—From Roles to Goals & Tools. https://planable. io/blog/social-media-team/. Accessed 5 Jan 2021
2. Panik, M.: Linear Programming and Resource Allocation Modeling. Wiley, Hoboken (2018). ISBN-13: 9781119509448
3. Kuster, J., et al.: Project Management Handbook. Springer-Verlag, Berlin (2015). https://doi. org/10.1007/978-3-662-45373-5
4. Babaeia, H., Karimpourb, J., Hadidic, A.: A survey of approaches for university course timetabling problem. Comput. Ind. Eng. **86**, 43–59 (2015). https://doi.org/10.1016/j.cie.2014. 11.010
5. Duka, E.: Nurse Scheduling Problem: A Case Study in a Hospital. LAP LAMBERT Academic Publishing (2016). ISBN-13: 978-3659828225
6. Artigues, C., Demassey, S., Néron, E. (eds.): Resource-Constrained Project Scheduling: Models, Algorithms, Extensions and Applications. ISTE Ltd., London (2008). ISBN: 9780470611227, https://doi.org/10.1002/9780470611227
7. The Essential Roles and Responsibilities of Your Social Media Team. https://flypchart.co/soc ial-media-team/. Accessed 5 Jan 2021
8. Rossi, F., Van Beek, P., Walsh, T.: Handbook of constraint programming. In: Foundations of Artificial Intelligence. Elsevier Science Inc., New York (2006)
9. Conforti, M., Cornuéjols, G., Zambelli, G.: Integer Programming. Springer International Publishing, Cham (2014). https://doi.org/10.1007/978-3-319-11008-0
10. Home AMPL. https://ampl.com/. Accessed 5 Jan 2021
11. Gurobi. http://www.gurobi.com/. Accessed 5 Jan 2021
12. Sitek, P., Wikarek, J.: A multi-level approach to ubiquitous modeling and solving constraints in combinatorial optimization problems in production and distribution. Appl. Intell. **48**(5), 1344–1367 (2017). https://doi.org/10.1007/s10489-017-1107-9
13. Sitek, P., Wikarek, J., Nielsen, P.: A constraint-driven approach to food supply chain management. Ind. Manag. Data Syst. **117**(9), 2115–2138 (2017). https://doi.org/10.1108/IMDS-10-2016-0465
14. Eclipse: The Eclipse Foundation open source community website. www.eclipse.org. Accessed 5 Jan 2021
15. Sivanandam, S.N., Deepa, S.N.: Introduction to Genetic Algorithms. Springer-Verlag, Berlin (2008). S.N.: 9783642092244, https://doi.org/10.1007/978-3-540-73190-0
16. Relich, M., Pawlewski, P.: A fuzzy weighted average approach for selecting portfolio of new product development projects. Neurocomputing **231**, 19–27 (2017). https://doi.org/10.1016/ j.neucom.2016.05.104

17. Bocewicz, G., Nielsen, I.E., Banaszak, Z.: Production flows scheduling subject to fuzzy processing time constraints. Int. J. Comput. Integr. Manuf. **29**(10), 1105–1127 (2016). https://doi.org/10.1080/0951192X.2016.1145739

18. Ramya, R., Anandanatarajan, R., Priya, R., Arul Selvan, G.: Applications of fuzzy logic and artificial neural network for solving real world problem. In: Proceedings of the IEEE-International Conference on Advances in Engineering, Science and Management (ICAESM-2012), Nagapattinam, Tamil Nadu, 2012, pp. 443–448 (2012)

19. Sitek, P., Wikarek, J., Bzdyra, K.: A hybrid method for modeling and solving supply chain optimization problems with soft and logical constraints. Math. Probl. Eng. **2016**, 1532420 (2016). https://doi.org/10.1155/2016/1532420

The Extended Graph Generalization as a Representation of the Metamodels' Extensional Layer

Marcin Jodłowiec[(✉)] [ID], Marek Krótkiewicz[ID], and Piotr Zabawa[ID]

Department of Applied Informatics, Wrocław University of Science and Technology,
Wybrzeże Stanisława Wyspiańskiego 27, 50-370 Wrocław, Poland
{marcin.jodlowiec,marek.krotkiewicz,piotr.zabawa}@pwr.edu.pl

Abstract. The paper is related to modeling and metamodeling disciplines, which are applicable in the software engineering domain. It is focused on the subject of finding the way leading to the selection of the right metamodel for a particular modeling problem. The approach introduced in the paper is based on a specific application of the *Extended Graph Generalization*, which is used to identify features of known metamodels in relation to the extensions and generalizations introduced by the *Extended Graph Generalization* definition. The discussion is related to an illustrative case-study. The paper introduces the *Extended Graph Generalization* definitions in Association-Oriented Metamodel, the *Extended Graph Generalization* symbolic notation, which are used when comparing features of different metamodels in relation to the *Extended Graph Generalization* features.

Keywords: Graph · Hypergraph · Data modeling · Metamodeling · Extended graph generalization

1 Introduction

Data structures like graphs and hypergraphs play important role in the software engineering domain. They are used to define metamodel structures for modeling languages as well as the structures of models, which are created in these languages. One example of such a language is the Unified Modeling Language (UML) [2]. It has the graph metamodel structure and allows to construct models the structures of which are even more complex. The graphs are relatively general structures, but sometimes they are not sufficient for correct modeling a complex reality. In the consequence some simplifications are introduced, which deform the reality (see e.g. the problem of reifying n-ary relationships [3]). The application of just graphs results of a lack of competences in applicating contemporary modeling languages as well as from the limits of these languages. The especially troublesome is, such motivated, unavailability of hypergraph [11] and/or ultragraphs (a.k.a. ubergraphs) [7,12], which admittedly are known from the graph theory generalizations but are rarely met when modeling. The redundance of the

© Springer Nature Switzerland AG 2021
H. Fujita et al. (Eds.): IEA/AIE 2021, LNAI 12798, pp. 369–382, 2021.
https://doi.org/10.1007/978-3-030-79457-6_32

available modeling language constructs resulting from more complex metamodels may also give a chance for an optimization.

In [5] some extensions and generalization of graph structures, named *Extended Graph Generalization* (EGG) were proposed. The EGG notion helps to define and describe complex graph-like structures with data associated with these structures in a uniform way. Paradoxically, modeling languages are used to order reality but the metamodels themselves are not subject of such an ordering efforts even if they are so complex as e.g. the UML is. This observation led to introducing the EGG concept.

The goal of the paper is to propose EGG as a platform for mapping data models expressed in particular data metamodels: Extensible Markup Language (XML), Relational Database Metamodel (RDBM), UML, Association-Oriented Metamodel (AOM) just to EGG models. The presented research results are connected to the problem of choosing the EGG configuration (the right extensions and generalizations) in the way leading to the most accurate expressing the extensional data structures, which are originally created in particular metamodels in EGG.

In Sect. 2 the EGG is defined with the help of the association-oriented model in two concrete syntaxes - symbolic and graphical ones and the EGG abstract syntax in the UML is recalled. Moreover, the symbolic concrete syntax for EGG is introduced. A case-study, which plays the reference role for the disscussion in the paper is introduced in Sect. 3. Section 4 presents mapping between the elements of models created in different metamodels and the elements of the EGG metamodel. In Sect. 5, which is the main part of the paper the case-study example is modeled with the help of the graphical concrete EGG syntax, which in turn expresses a possible way of modeling the example with the help of particular metamodels. The Sect. 6 presents the conclusions from the presented research.

2   Extended Graph Generalization

The concept of the EGG was introduced in the paper [5]. The EGG constitutes the generalization and extension of all contemporary known data structures and thus it can be used to define these structures in a unified way. The EGG definition together with the EGG abstract syntax can be also applied when both the well known and unknown data structures are defined in terms of the EGG. The cited paper shows how the EGG can be used for the purpose of defining hypergraphs, graphs, trees and chains. Each element of the definition of the mentioned structures can be easily mapped to the EGG notions. The EGG formal definition has been presented in [5].

The formal definition, which is based on classic mathematical notions and traditional mathematical symbolic notation is not unambiguous enough in the context of defining this kind of data structures, which are characteristic for modeling and metamodeling purposes. That is why the proposed structures are defined in the form of the association-oriented models (Eq. 1–6).

$$\diamond Edge \left\{ [*] \xrightarrow{\substack{+connection \cdots Navigation}} [*] \diamond Element^{\varnothing} \atop [1..*] \xrightarrow{\substack{+Element::data}} [*] \Box Data \right\}; \tag{1}$$

$$\diamond EGG \left\{ [*] \xrightarrow{\substack{+element}} [*] \diamond Element^{\varnothing} \atop [1..*] \xrightarrow{\substack{+Element::data}} [*] \Box Data \right\}; \tag{2}$$

$$\diamond Element [1..*] \xrightarrow{\substack{+data}} [*] \Box Data \tag{3}$$

$$\diamond Vertex [1..*] \xrightarrow{\substack{+Element::data(\Box Data)}} [*] \Box Data \tag{4}$$

$$\left\{ \begin{matrix} \diamond Edge \\ \diamond EGG \\ \diamond Vertex \end{matrix} \right\} \xrightarrow{rf^v} \diamond Element^{\varnothing} \tag{5}$$

$$\Box Data \langle \rangle; \quad \Box Navigation \langle +navigation : ascii \rangle; \tag{6}$$

Moreover, some additional constraints (Eq. 7) should be put on the minimal number of *Vertex* and *Edge* participations in the *element* role of the EGG association.

$$\diamond EGG [1..*] \left\{ \xrightarrow{\substack{+element::Vertex}} [*] \diamond Vertex :: Element^{\varnothing} \atop \xrightarrow{\substack{+element::Edge}} [*] \diamond Edge :: Element^{\varnothing} \right\}; \tag{7}$$

Also the EGG abstract syntax, which was introduced in the paper [5] is shown in the Fig. 2 with some slight corrections (Fig. 1).

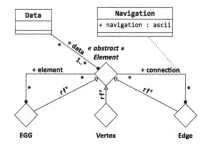

Fig. 1. EGG implementation in AOM

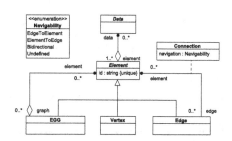

Fig. 2. EGG abstract syntax expressed in UML 2.5.1 and OCL 2.4 [5]

The UML diagram from Fig. 2 should be completed by constraints to be correct. The constraints are specified in natural language and are expressed in the form of the OCL expressions as follows:

372   M. Jodłowiec et al.

- each Vertex must be contained in at least one EGG
          context Vertex inv: self.graph->size() > 0
- each Edge must be contained in at least one EGG
          context Edge inv: self.graph->size() > 0

It is worth noticing that, in the Fig. 2:

- the EGG is a data structure, which may aggregate some elements (Element),
- a special case of the aggregated Element is the EGG itself that is an EGG is a self-contained data structure,
- each element of the EGG is just the EGG or plays the role of a vertex (Vertex) or an edge (Edge) of the structure,
- the EGG does not play the role of a Vertex nor an Edge,
- the EGG structures, their vertices (Vertex) and edges (Edge) can be interconnected by many-to-many connections (*connection*), which may be navigable,
- each Element may be related to data (Data) elements through the shared aggregation relationship,
- it is intentionally not specified what is the form of Data.

2.1 *Extended Graph Generalization* Symbolic Concrete Syntax

Egg symbol: ▲*id* or *id* : *EGG*, graphical symbol: $\boxed{\text{Id}}$
The EGG is a data structure, which may aggregate other eggs, vertices and edges:
▲*egg*⟨▲*eggs*, ●*vertices*, ◆*edges*, ■*data*⟩. Each element is optional.
Example: ▲g_1⟨▲g_2, ●v_1, ◆e_1, ■d_1⟩; ▲g_2⟨◆e_2, ■d_2⟩.

Vertex symbol: ●*id* or *id* : *Vertex*, graphical symbol: $\bigcirc$
The Vertex may be related to data elements through the shared aggregation relationship: ●*vertex*⟨■*data*⟩. Data element is optional.
Example: ▲v_1⟨■d_1⟩.

Edge symbol: ◆*id* or *id* : *Edge*, graphical symbol: $\diamondsuit$ 
The Edge may be connected (by a *connection*) to other edges, eggs or vertices and may be related through the shared aggregation relationship to data:
edge ⟨ *connection*▲*eggs*, *connection*●*vertices*, *connection*◆*edges*, ■*data* ⟩. Each element is optional.
Example: ◆e_2⟨↔▲g_1, ↔●v_2, ■d_3⟩; ◆e_3⟨↔▲g_2, ↔●v_2, ■d_3⟩.

Connection symbol: ⟵ – undefined navigability, ↦ – from edge, �leftarrow – to edge, ↔ – bidirectional.
Data symbol: ■*id* or *id* : *Data*, graphical symbol: $\boxed{\text{d}_1}$
The Data can not exist independently. It may be related through the shared aggregation relationship with the first-order elements: eggs, edges or vertices.
Example: ▲g_2⟨▲g_1, ■d_3⟩.

id is an identifier which is unique in the scope of the category.

$\langle\cdot\rangle$ is a list of shared aggretated elements like eggs, edges or vertices, and related data, separated by comma symbol.

$\{\cdot\}$ are brackets grouping elements of the same type, for example, expression $\bullet\{v_1, v_2\}$ is equivalent to $\bullet v_1, \bullet v_2$. This kind of braces can be also used for grouping elements connected by the same type of *connection*, so expression $\rightarrowtail\{\bullet v_1, \blacklozenge e_4\}$ is equivalent to $\rightarrowtail\bullet v_1, \rightarrowtail\blacklozenge e_4$.

3   Case Study: Training Group Social Group Structure

Taking into consideration the specificity of various domains, in order to incorporate EGG-based structural modeling let us introduce a model of social training group structure based on the EGG concepts. This structure holds the semantics of the following facts. In the domain TD there is a group TG of people $p_1, \ldots, p_n$ who train with each other, they are represented as EGG vertices. Let the fact, that specific people train with each other be represented with tw edge connecting subsequent vertices. Information about people's age is associated with the vertices using data blocks prefixed with $a:$. Some people might be the supervisors; they are introduced inside a shared sub-EGG S. Let the fact, that a specific supervisor set is responsible for a specific supervision be represented as the sup edge, which connects this set to a specific tw edge. Some people might *tutor* other people (or themselves), this fact is represented as a binary, directed edge. Moreover, this edge is attributed with data containing temporal information about this tutoring, prefixed with $y:$.

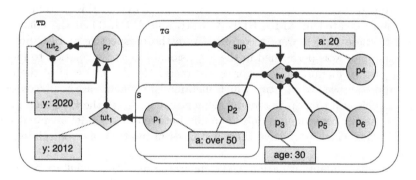

Fig. 3. An example of EGG_{FDN}^{HUMS} modeling domain of a social training group

$$\begin{array}{cccc}
\bullet p_1\langle\blacksquare a:over\ 50\rangle & \bullet p_3\langle\blacksquare a:\ 30\rangle & \bullet p_5\langle\langle\rangle\rangle & \bullet p_7\langle\rangle \\
\bullet p_2\langle\blacksquare a:over\ 50\rangle & \bullet p_4\langle\blacksquare a:\ 20\rangle & \bullet p_6\langle\langle\rangle\rangle &
\end{array} \quad (8)$$

$$\blacktriangle TD\left\langle\begin{array}{l}\blacktriangle\{TG, S\}, \\ \blacklozenge\{tut_1, tut_2\}, \\ \bullet p_7\end{array}\right\rangle \quad \blacktriangle TG\left\langle\begin{array}{l}\bullet\left\{\begin{array}{l}p_1, p_2, p_3, \\ p_4, p_5, p_6\end{array}\right\}, \\ \blacklozenge\{sup, tr\}\end{array}\right\rangle \quad \blacktriangle S\langle\bullet\{Mark_1, p_2\}\rangle \quad (9)$$

$$\blacklozenge sup \left\langle \; \leftarrow \blacktriangle S, \leftrightarrow \blacklozenge tr \; \right\rangle \qquad \blacklozenge tut_1 \left\langle \; \leftarrow \bullet p_1, \leftrightarrow \bullet p_7, \blacksquare y : 2012 \; \right\rangle$$
$$\blacklozenge tr \left\langle \; \leftarrow \bullet \{p_2, p_3, p_6, p_5, p_4\} \; \right\rangle \quad \blacklozenge tut_2 \left\langle \; \leftarrow \bullet p_7, \leftrightarrow \bullet p_7, \blacksquare y : 2020 \; \right\rangle \qquad (10)$$

The model in the Fig. 3 has been invented especially to express all possible extensions and generalizations which can be defined within the EGG structures. It means that these structures hold the properties of a EGG_{FDN}^{HUMS} and the proposed EGG is generalized by the features: HYPER, ULTRA, MULTI, SHARED AGGREGATION as well as is extended by the features: FIRST CLASS, DATA, and NAVIGABILITY. Detailed description of these features has been presented in the paper [5]. The presented example will constitue a reference for expressing the similar semantics with the help of extensional structures of the particular data metamodels across the paper.

4 Mapping Selected Metamodels to the EGG

This section contains a proposal of one possible set of mapping schemes. Some alternative mappings may be introduced as well, however the one faithfully reflects the characteristic features of each basic metamodels category. The following metamodels are discussed in this section: XML, RDBM, UML and AOM. It must be underlined that the metamodels must be considered not only in the metamodel categories and its syntax context but the constraints defined in the metamodel must be taken into account as well.

In order to infer the mappings, which are presented in this section several models were created in XML, RDBM, UML and AOM. Then the constructs applied in these models were recognized from the perspective of EGG notions. So, the mapping was performed in the extensional aspect (in relation to models and not just on metamodel categories abstraction level). The goal of the mentioned approach was to identify which metamodel elements are really required by the models and to map the model element categories to the EGG metamodel elements. As the consequence only mapping between metamodel terminal symbols (the ones which may have their instances in models) may be related this way.

The results of mapping each model element to the EGG element are presented in the Tables 1, 2, 3 and 4 of the succeeding subsections. The first column of each table contains the elements of a particular metamodel while the second one - the elements of the EGG metamodel.

4.1 Extensible Markup Language

The XML is a markup language, which is dedicated to store data in the textual and structural form [10]. It is interesting from the perspective of data modeling and due to its relationships to the more general and novel EGG concept. The XML metamodel elements are inferred from the possible XML files (models) in isolation from any general definition of possible structures of the considered

Table 1. XML to EGG mapping schemas

XML model element	EGG model element
Node with children	Parent is nesting **EGG**
Node without children with identifier	Vertex
Nodes' attributes	Data
XML IDREFS (referential attributes)	Attribute is mapped to **Edge**, subsequent references are mapped to directed **Connection** with Direction EdgeToElement; parent-attribute relationship is mapped to **Connection** with Direction ElementToEdge

XML files, e.g. XML Schema. The results of the identified mapping between model elements of XML and **EGG** are presented in the Table 1.

It can be seen in the Table 1 that the **EGG** element is applied with some limits, more specifically - it cannot be shared and the **Edge** is also applied with some limits.

4.2 Relational Database Model

RDBM has been introduced as a formal approach to represent databases. It is based upon the mathematical notions of *relation* and *tuple*. It has been defined by Codd [1] in terms of the set theory. The mapping between data contained in the relational databases (models) and the elements of the **EGG** model elements is contained in the Table 2.

Table 2. RDBM to EGG mapping schemas

RDBM element	EGG model element
Relation	EGG
Tuple	Vertex
Value	Data
Referential integrity constraint	vertices connected by edges

It is clear from the Table 2 that there are limits connected to the way the **Edge** is applied in RDBM.

4.3 Unified Modeling Language

The UML [2] is a modeling language defined by Object Management Group (OMG), which is dedicated to model both structure and behaviour of software-intensive systems. It is also a subject of standardization since many years. This language was chosen due to its very rich semantic capacity. The results of the analysis of the EGG constructs which can be met in the UML models and mapping the identified constructs to the EGG model elements are presented in the Table 3.

According to the Table 3, the UML model elements cannot be mapped to the EGG metamodel element. Nevertheless, the mapping to the remaining elements is clear and there are no limits for these elements.

4.4   Association-Oriented Metamodel

The AOM is a data metamodel, which can be characterized by the following features: implementability, semantic unambiguity, high semantic capacity and high expressiveness. It is based on the notion of *association*, which is a first-class element in the AOM [8,9]. The Table 4 contains the identified mapping between AOM model elements and the EGG model elements.

Table 3. UML to EGG mapping schemas

UML model element	EGG model element
InstanceSpecification with classifier of type Class (object)	Vertex
Slot with ValueSpecification	Data
InstanceSpecification with classifier of type Association (link)	Edge
Slot with InstanceValue owned by link	Connection

It is clear from the Table 4 that the AOM metamodel contains good decomposition of the responsibilities of metamodel elements. As the result they can be mapped to all EGG notions and the mapping is very clear. In contrast to the UML the AOM model elements map to all EGG metamodel elements.

Table 4. AOM to EGG mapping schemas

AOM model element	EGG model element
Object	Vertex
Association Object	Edge
Role Object	Connection
Value	Data
Collection (extensional aspect)	EGG
Association (extensional aspect)	EGG

5   Evaluation of Data Complexity in Data Metamodels

In this section we will deliberate upon the cohesion of the individual approaches do data modeling into EGG based structures. Taking into consideration the fact, that EGG structures are graph-like at the same time being more general and more extensive, we have taken the methodology as follows. We have examined the example presented in Fig. 3, which is a small and comprehensive EGG, and we have tried to express the most adequate semantics using the individual data metamodels. It is important to see, that this process has not been a simple mapping, but a trial to translation of a domain-specific domain. The constructed artifacts consisted of extensional data structures. For strongly typed metamodels, the models has been also created as a side effect. Using mappings described in Sect. 4, the EGG structures have been generated. These EGG structures hold EGG-specific semantics which stems from the approach, but also metamodel-specific form, which uses only EGG expressions having reasonable understanding in the individual data metamodel. For example, for data metamodels with reference-based relationships, the edges might be binary and navigated in a strictly defined manner. We have followed all the EGG features and tried to find metamodel-specific constructs for a specific EGG generalization or extension. If a proper such construct existed either in or beyond mapping, then a feature has been marked as a present in a metamodel.

5.1   Extensible Markup Language

Mapping the domain structure of a training group into XML was made in the form, which makes it possible to reflect the tree-like document representation. The whole document represents EGG, which contains attributed nodes each modeling a person. The edges were represented as nodes and the connections were represented via mechanism of references known from XML schemas. If the direction of edges must be taken into account, then specific attributes pointing to the appropriate nodes are applied. The resulting EGG is shown in the Eq. 11–13.

XML makes it possible to represent HYPER generalizations thanks to the *XMLREFS* ability. One consequence is that one connection representation may refer to many elements. It is also possible to model the MULTI generalization as there is no limit on the multiple referencing an element from one connection representation. All possible EGG extensions can be modeled in XML. XML is capable to be featured by FIRST CLASS due to the fact that the XML nodes are represented as EGGs which can be connected by edges. The attributes make it possible to map from a DATA. The NAVIGABILITY feature is strictly defined as the result of the uni-directional nature of the XML references. However, there are no bidirectional references.

$$\blacktriangle TD \left(\begin{array}{l} \blacktriangle TG, \\ \bullet \{tut_1, tut_2, p_7\}, \\ \blacklozenge \{i_{tut_1}, o_{tut_1}, i_{tut_2}, o_{tut_2},\} \end{array} \right)$$

$$\blacktriangle TG \left(\begin{array}{l} \bullet \{p_3, p_4, p_5, p_6, sup, tr\}, \\ \blacklozenge \{i_{sup}, o_{sup}, ppl\} \blacktriangle S \end{array} \right)$$

$$\blacktriangle S \langle \bullet \{p_1, p_2\} \rangle \tag{11}$$

$$\blacklozenge ppl \left(\begin{array}{l} \longleftarrow \blacklozenge tr, \\ \dashrightarrow \bullet \{p_3, p_4, p_6, p_5\} \end{array} \right)$$

$$\blacklozenge i_{sup} \left(\begin{array}{l} \longleftarrow \bullet sup, \\ \dashrightarrow \bullet \{p_1, p_2\} \end{array} \right)$$

$$\blacklozenge o_{sup} \langle \longleftarrow \bullet sup, \dashrightarrow \bullet tr \rangle \tag{12}$$

$$\blacklozenge i_{tut_1} \langle \longleftarrow \bullet tut_1, \dashrightarrow \bullet p_1 \rangle$$

$$\blacklozenge o_{tut_1} \langle \longleftarrow \bullet tut_1, \dashrightarrow \bullet p_7 \rangle$$

$$\blacklozenge i_{tut_2} \langle \longleftarrow \bullet tut_2, \dashrightarrow \bullet p_7 \rangle$$

$$\blacklozenge o_{tut_2} \langle \longleftarrow \bullet tut_2, \dashrightarrow \bullet p_7 \rangle$$

$$
\begin{array}{lll}
\bullet p_1 \langle \blacksquare a : over\ 50 \rangle & \bullet p_4 \langle \blacksquare a : 20 \rangle & \bullet p_7 \langle\ \rangle \\
\bullet p_2 \langle \blacksquare a : over\ 50 \rangle & \bullet p_5 \langle\ \rangle & \bullet sup \langle\ \rangle \quad \bullet tut_1 \langle \blacksquare y : 2012 \rangle \\
\bullet p_3 \langle \blacksquare a : 30 \rangle & \bullet p_6 \langle\ \rangle & \bullet tr \langle\ \rangle \quad \bullet tut_2 \langle \blacksquare y : 2020 \rangle
\end{array} \tag{13}
$$

5.2 Relational Database Model

Relational implementation of a domain structure is based on the representation of both nodes and edges as tuples. Data is represented as the attributes of the tuples. In order to preserve the strong structural nature and common set of attributes of each tuple the data blocks with $NULL$ values were generated. The relational representation of the domain model expressed in EGG which is compliant to the mapping is shown in the Eq. 14-16.

In order to express EGG in the form of relational data only two following generalizations may be taken into account: MULTI and SHARED AGGREGATION. MULTI is possible as the result of the possible creation of extensional references that is a self-pointing ability of a tuple. In the consequence of theoretical nature of the SHARED AGGREGATION in relational model it must be underlined that a particular relation constitutes a finite set of tuples. It results from the set notion features that there are no reasons not to share elements of a particular set with other sets. Therefore, purely theoretically, RDBM allows to share tuples between different relations. This however, conflicts with an intuitive approach to the issue of sharing tuples and, especially with the RDBM implementations that is Relational Database Management Systems (RDBMS). Also the following two extensions are possible: DATA and NAVIGABILITY. In the case of NAVIGABILITY it should be noted that the connections navigability is strictly determined by reference direction. That is, each reference has exactly one referring and exactly one referred element.

$$\blacktriangle TD \langle \blacktriangle \{Ppl, S, Sup, Tr, SupTr, Tut\} \rangle \quad \blacktriangle Ppl \langle \bullet \{p_1, p_2, p_3, p_4, p_6, p_5, p_7\} \rangle$$

$$\blacktriangle Tr \langle \bullet tr, \blacklozenge \{tr_1, tr_2, tr_3, tr_4, tr_5\} \rangle \qquad \blacktriangle S \langle \bullet \{p_1, p_2\} \rangle$$

$$\blacktriangle Tut \left(\begin{array}{l} \bullet \{tut_1, tut_2\}, \\ \blacklozenge \{tut_{11}, tut_{12}, tut_{21}, tut_{22}\} \end{array} \right) \quad \blacktriangle SupTr \left(\begin{array}{l} \bullet supTr, \\ \blacklozenge \{supTr_1, supTr_2\} \end{array} \right) \tag{14}$$

$$\blacktriangle Sup \langle \bullet sup, \blacklozenge \{sup_1, sup_2\} \rangle$$

$$\bullet p_2\langle\blacksquare a : over\ 50\rangle \quad \bullet p_7\langle\blacksquare a : NULL\rangle \quad \bullet tr\langle\ \rangle \quad \bullet p_3\langle\blacksquare a : 30\rangle$$
$$\bullet p_6\langle\blacksquare a : over\ 50\rangle \quad \bullet p_5\langle\blacksquare a : NULL\rangle \quad \bullet sup\langle\ \rangle \quad \bullet tut_1\langle\blacksquare y : 2012\rangle \quad (15)$$
$$\bullet p_4\langle\blacksquare a : 20\rangle \quad \bullet p_1\langle\blacksquare a : NULL\rangle \quad \bullet supTr\langle\ \rangle \quad \bullet tut_2\langle\blacksquare y : 2020\rangle$$

$$\blacklozenge tr_1\langle\leftarrow\!\bullet tr, \rightarrow\!\bullet p_6\rangle \quad \blacklozenge tr_2\langle\leftarrow\!\bullet tr, \rightarrow\!\bullet p_3\rangle \quad \blacklozenge tr_3\langle\leftarrow\!\bullet tr, \rightarrow\!\bullet p_5\rangle$$
$$\blacklozenge tr_4\langle\leftarrow\!\bullet tr, \rightarrow\!\bullet p_4\rangle \quad \blacklozenge tr_5\langle\leftarrow\!\bullet tr, \rightarrow\!\bullet p_2\rangle \quad \blacklozenge sup_1\langle\leftarrow\!\bullet sup, \rightarrow\!\bullet p_1\rangle$$
$$\blacklozenge sup_2\langle\leftarrow\!\bullet sup, \rightarrow\!\bullet p_2\rangle \quad \blacklozenge supTr_1\left\langle\begin{matrix}\leftarrow\!\bullet supTr, \\ \rightarrow\!\bullet sup\end{matrix}\right\rangle \quad \blacklozenge supTr_2\left\langle\begin{matrix}\leftarrow\!\bullet supTr, \\ \rightarrow\!\bullet sup\end{matrix}\right\rangle \quad (16)$$
$$\blacklozenge tut_{11}\langle\leftarrow\!\bullet tut_1, \rightarrow\!\bullet p_1\rangle \ \blacklozenge tut_{12}\langle\leftarrow\!\bullet tut_1, \rightarrow\!\bullet p_7\rangle \ \blacklozenge tut_{21}\langle\leftarrow\!\bullet tut_2, \rightarrow\!\bullet p_7\rangle$$
$$\blacklozenge tut_{22}\langle\leftarrow\!\bullet tut_2, \rightarrow\!\bullet p_7\rangle$$

5.3 Unified Modeling Language

Implementation of the example domain structure in the UML consists in elaborating an object diagram, which contains some InstanceSpecifications compliant to the model, which is defined in the form of the class diagram. It was assumed that the EGG nodes, which are associated with persons are related to the instances of a class the attributes of which represent data. The fact of distinguishing a nodes subset is represented by subclassing. The edges adorned by data are modeled by the association class instances. It was assumed in mapping that there is no a counterpart for the EGG on the object diagram (Eq. 17–19).

Representing the EGG in the form of a UML object diagram makes possible to accomplish two generalizations: HYPER and ULTRA. HYPER is a consequence of the existing *many* multiplicity in the Slots which are owned by an InstanceSpecification, which is a link representation. ULTRA is a consequence of the lack of a limit in the standard on the participation in Slots of such the InstanceValue elements that refer other connections. The UML makes possible to map two EGG extensions: Data and Navigability. The first one is based on a possible specification of the slots, which accomplish attributes while the second one is a map of navigability, which is based on the association instance. It is worth noticing that, according to the rules defined by the UML, it is not possible to accomplish navigability EdgeToElement as the navigability is defined on the border Association-Property and as the result a particular Property is, in the context of this association either navigable or not navigable. The navigability in the opposite direction always exists.

$$\blacktriangle TD\langle \bullet\{p_1, p_2, p_3, p_4, p_5, p_6, p_7\}, \blacklozenge\{sup, tw, tut_1, tut_2\}\ \rangle \quad (17)$$

$$\bullet p_1\langle\blacksquare a : over\ 50\rangle \quad \bullet p_5\langle\ \rangle \quad \bullet p_3\langle\blacksquare a : 30\rangle \quad \bullet p_7\langle\ \rangle$$
$$\bullet p_2\langle\blacksquare a : over\ 50\rangle \quad \bullet p_6\langle\ \rangle \quad \bullet p_4\langle\blacksquare a : 20\rangle \qquad (18)$$

$$\blacklozenge sup\langle\leftarrow\!\bullet\{p_1, p_2\}, \leftarrow\!\blacklozenge tr\rangle \quad \blacklozenge tut_1\langle\leftarrow\!\bullet p_1, \leftarrow\bullet p_7, \blacksquare y : 2012\rangle$$
$$\blacklozenge tr\ \langle \leftarrow\bullet\{p_2, p_3, p_6, p_5, p_4\}\ \rangle \quad \blacklozenge tut_2\langle\leftarrow\!\bullet p_7, \leftarrow\bullet p_7, \blacksquare y : 2020\rangle \quad (19)$$

5.4 Association-Oriented Metamodel

The extensional domain model was expressed in the associative way taking into account constraints occuring in the intensional layer of the associative model. The nodes were mapped to the objects while the edges as the association objects. Connection has been mapped to the role object and Data – to the attribute realizations of values. The edges, which require data annotations are mapped to the instances of the associative *Bicompositive Tandem Association-Collection* (BACT) structural modeling pattern (see [4]). Additionally, it is worthy of notice that due to the same reason they were also mapped in the resulting EGG (Eq. 20–22).

The extensional associative structures allow to express all EGG generalizations and extensions except of FIRST CLASS and SHARED AGGREGATION. They assume respectively the participation of the EGG representation in relationships and possible sharing of the grouped elements. It is impossible to express these features of the extensional structures in the AOM directly.

$$
\begin{aligned}
&\blacktriangle TD\big\langle\blacktriangle\{Ppl, Sup, Tr, Tut_\square, Tut_\diamond\}\big\rangle \quad \blacktriangle Sup\big\langle\blacklozenge sup_1\big\rangle \\
&\blacktriangle Tr\big\langle\blacklozenge tr_1\big\rangle \qquad\qquad\qquad\qquad \blacktriangle Tut_\square\big\langle\bullet\{tut_{\diamond 1}, tut_{\diamond 2}\}\big\rangle \\
&\blacktriangle Tut_\diamond\big\langle\blacklozenge\{tut_{\square 1}, tut_{\square 2}\}\big\rangle \quad \blacktriangle Ppl\big\langle\bullet\{p_3, p_6, p_5, p_4, p_7\}, \blacktriangle S\big\rangle \\
&\blacktriangle S\big\langle\bullet\{p_1, p_2\}\big\rangle
\end{aligned} \tag{20}
$$

$$
\begin{aligned}
&\blacklozenge sup_1\big\langle\leftarrow\bullet\{p_1, p_2\}, \longmapsto\blacklozenge tr_1\big\rangle \quad \blacklozenge tut_{\diamond 1}\big\langle\leftarrow\bullet tut_{\square 1}, \longmapsto\bullet p_7, \leftarrow\bullet p_1\big\rangle \\
&\blacklozenge tr_1\big\langle\leftarrow\bullet\{p_2, p_3, p_6, p_5, p_4\}\big\rangle \quad \blacklozenge tut_{\diamond 2}\big\langle\leftarrow\bullet tut_{\square 2}, \longmapsto\bullet p_7, \leftarrow\bullet p_7\big\rangle
\end{aligned} \tag{21}
$$

$$
\begin{aligned}
&\bullet tut_{\square 1}\big\langle\blacksquare y:2012\big\rangle \bullet p_1\big\langle\blacksquare a:over\ 50\big\rangle \bullet p_3\big\langle\blacksquare a:30\big\rangle \bullet p_5\big\langle\blacksquare a:0\big\rangle \bullet p_7\big\langle\blacksquare a:0\big\rangle \\
&\bullet tut_{\square 2}\big\langle\blacksquare y:2020\big\rangle \bullet p_2\big\langle\blacksquare a:over\ 50\big\rangle \bullet p_4\big\langle\blacksquare a:20\big\rangle \bullet p_6\big\langle\blacksquare a:0\big\rangle
\end{aligned} \tag{22}
$$

5.5 Summary

The Table 5 presents the summary of the EGG features in terms of considered data metamodels. The black circle denotes the presence of a specific feature in the extensional layer of a metamodel, while the dash - its absence therein. White circle indicates that a specific EGG feature exists in a metamodel however its syntactical constraints enforce some limitations. EGG can be used as a reference data metamodel in order to evaluate expressiveness and semantic capacity [6] of a metamodel. Such the analysis helps select a right metamodel for a specific modeling issue better as long as the complexity of the EGG structure representation of the domain problem is taken into account.

Table 5. EGG features configuration

EGG features		XML	RDBM	UML	AOM
Generalizations	Hyper	•	–	•	•
	Ultra	–	–	•	•
	Multi	•	•	–	•
	Shared Aggregation	–	$\circ^a$	–	–
Extenstions	First Class	•	–	–	–
	Data	•	•	•	•
	Navigability	$\circ^b$	$\circ^b$	$\circ^c$	$\circ^d$
EGG configuration symbol		EGG_{FDN}^{HM}	EGG_{DN}^{MS}	EGG_{DN}^{HU}	EGG_{DN}^{HUM}

^{a} – it is only possible formally, ^{b} – without Bidirectional, ^{c} – without `EdgeToElement`,
^{d} – `ElementToEdge`

6   Conclusions

The EGG notion, which constitutes a generalization and extension of graph is referred in the paper. It is specified and enriched as follows. The EGG notion has been defined in terms of the AOM that is in the form well suited to the modeling and metamodeling disciplines. Also, the symbolic notation for the EGG concrete syntax has been introduced.

Moreover, the way of the application of the EGG notion to investigating models complexity and, indirectly - metamodels expressiveness is shown in the paper. It was achieved through illustrating mappings particular models to the EGG and evaluating the complexity of several metamodels in the data layer in terms of the generalizations and the extensions of the graph notion defined in the EGG notion.

The research results presented in the paper are one stage for further work dedicated to application of the EGG notion to the modeling and metamodeling disciplines. They constitute an important starting point for investigating problems of evaluating semantic capacity and expressive power of particular metamodels. However, the mentioned subjects will be discussed in future research.

References

1. Codd, E.F.: A relational model of data for large shared data banks. Commun. ACM **26**(1), 64–69 (1983)
2. Cook, S., et al.: Unified modeling language (UML) version 2.5.1. Standard, Object Management Group (OMG), December 2017. https://www.omg.org/spec/UML/2.5.1
3. Dahchour, M., Pirotte, A.: The semantics of reifying n-ary relationships as classes. In: ICEIS, vol. 2, pp. 580–586 (2002)
4. Jodłowiec, M., Krótkiewicz, M., Wojtkiewicz, K.: Defining semantic networks using association-oriented metamodel. J. Intell. Fuzzy Syst. **37**(6), 7453–7464 (2019)

5. Jodłowiec, M., Krótkiewicz, M., Zabawa, P.: Fundamentals of generalized and extended graph-based structural modeling. In: Nguyen, N.T., Hoang, B.H., Huynh, C.P., Hwang, D., Trawiński, B., Vossen, G. (eds.) ICCCI 2020. LNCS (LNAI), vol. 12496, pp. 27–41. Springer, Cham (2020). https://doi.org/10.1007/978-3-030-63007-2_3

6. Jodłowiec, M., Pietranik, M.: Towards the pattern-based transformation of SBVR models to association-oriented models. In: Nguyen, N.T., Chbeir, R., Exposito, E., Aniorté, P., Trawiński, B. (eds.) ICCCI 2019. LNCS (LNAI), vol. 11683, pp. 79–90. Springer, Cham (2019). https://doi.org/10.1007/978-3-030-28377-3_7

7. Joslyn, C.A., Aksoy, S., Arendt, D., Firoz, J., Jenkins, L., Praggastis, B., Purvine, E., Zalewski, M.: Hypergraph analytics of domain name system relationships. In: Kamiński, B., Prałat, P., Szufel, P. (eds.) WAW 2020. LNCS, vol. 12091, pp. 1–15. Springer, Cham (2020). https://doi.org/10.1007/978-3-030-48478-1_1

8. Krótkiewicz, M.: A novel inheritance mechanism for modeling knowledge representation systems. Comput. Sci. Inf. Syst. **15**(1), 51–78 (2018)

9. Krótkiewicz, M.: Cyclic value ranges model for specifying flowing resources in unified process metamodel. Enterp. Inf. Syst. **13**(7–8), 1046–1068 (2019)

10. Singh, P., Sachdeva, S.: A landscape of XML data from analytics perspective. Procedia Comput. Sci. **173**, 392–402 (2020)

11. Smarandache, F.: Extension of hypergraph to n-superhypergraph and to plithogenic n-superhypergraph, and extension of hyperalgebra to n-ary (classical-/neutro-/anti-)hyperalgebra. Neutrosophic Sets Syst. **33**, 18 (2020)

12. Yadati, N.: Neural message passing for multi-relational ordered and recursive hypergraphs. In: Advances in Neural Information Processing Systems, vol. 33 (2020)

WawPart: Workload-Aware Partitioning of Knowledge Graphs

Amitabh Priyadarshi[(⊠)] and Krzysztof J. Kochut[(⊠)]

University of Georgia, Athens, GA 30602, USA
{amitabh.priyadarshi,kkochut}@uga.edu

Abstract. Large-scale datasets in the form of knowledge graphs are often used in numerous domains, today. A knowledge graph's size often exceeds the capacity of a single computer system, especially if the graph must be stored in main memory. To overcome this, knowledge graphs can be partitioned into multiple sub-graphs and distributed as shards among many computing nodes. However, performance of many common tasks performed on graphs, such as querying, suffers, as a result. This is due to distributed joins mandated by graph edges crossing (cutting) the partitions. In this paper, we propose a method of knowledge graph partitioning that takes into account a set of queries (workload). The resulting partitioning aims to reduces the number of distributed joins and improve the workload performance. Critical features identified in the query workload and the knowledge graph are used to cluster the queries and then partition the graph. Queries are rewritten to account for the graph partitioning. Our evaluation results demonstrate the performance improvement in workload processing time.

Keywords: Knowledge graph · Graph partitioning · Query workload

1 Introduction

In today's world, the data or information is interconnected and form large knowledge graphs or information networks. Such knowledge graphs are often used to represent data in social networking systems, shopping and movie preferences, bioinformatics, and in other real-world systems. The availability of large-scale data, represented as knowledge graphs composed of millions or even billions of vertices and edges, requires large-scale graph processing systems. Such data is often too large to be stored at one place in a centralized data store and needs to be partitioned into multiple sub-graphs, often called shards, and transferred to multiple computing nodes in a distributed system. However, with the overall knowledge graph split into distributed shards, many typical graph-base tasks, such as query processing, suffer from network latency and other problems related to the original graph being partitioned. One of the techniques to improve query processing performance in such a system is to reduce the inter-node communication between graph processing systems. The graph partitioning can be an effective pre-processing technique to balance the runtime performance.

© Springer Nature Switzerland AG 2021
H. Fujita et al. (Eds.): IEA/AIE 2021, LNAI 12798, pp. 383–395, 2021.
https://doi.org/10.1007/978-3-030-79457-6_33

In this paper, we will assume that a knowledge graph is a dataset represented using the Resource Description Framework (RDF) [1]. An RDF knowledge graph is a set of RDF triples in a form of (s, p, o), where s is the subject, p predicate, and o the object. A predicate represents a semantic relationship connecting a subject and an object. Consequently, an RDF dataset is a directed graph, where nodes (vertices) and edges have types, often described using the Resource Description Framework Schema (RDFS) [2]. In many recent publications, a knowledge graph has often been defined as a Heterogeneous Information Network (HIN) [3], a form of a directed graph, where nodes and edges have heterogeneous types. HINs are a bit more restrictive than RDF/RDFS in that if two edges are labeled by the same relationship type, their starting and ending nodes must have the same object types, respectively. RDF/RDFS does not have this restriction. Recently, graph databases, such as Neo4j [4], have also been used to represent and store knowledge graphs.

Knowledge graphs have been used for many different tasks, such as data mining, link (edge) prediction, and data classification, to mention a few. Query processing, intended to retrieve some data of interest, is one of the most common tasks. The SPARQL query language is the query language for RDF/RDFS datasets [5], while Cypher is an example graph query language used with the popular Neo4j graph database [4]. A critical part of a SPARQL query is a graph pattern composed of *triple patterns* involving variables. Without going into details here, a query processor matches the query pattern against the knowledge graph and reports matches as query solutions.

Typically, graph tasks become computationally intensive, when considering graphs with millions, even billions of vertices. A large knowledge graph can easily overload the memory and processing capacity even on relatively large servers, especially for in-memory knowledge graph systems. Partitioning a knowledge graph into smaller components (sub-graphs) and distributing the partitions, called shards, across a cluster of servers may enable handling of very large graphs and potentially offer performance improvements in executing different tasks.

Given a graph $G = (V, E)$, where V is a set of vertices and E is a set of edges and a number $k > 1$, a *graph partitioning of G* is a subdivision of vertices of G into *subsets* of vertices $V_1, ..., V_k$ that partition the set V. A *balance constraint* requires that all partition blocks are equal, or close, in size. In addition, a common objective function is to minimize the *total number of cuts*, i.e., edges crossing (cutting) partition boundaries.

This paper is outlined as follows. Section 2 provides an overview of related work. Section 3 discuss about the partitioning method. Section 4 is about the Architecture the experiments, and Sect. 5 concludes the paper.

2 Related Work

It is generally expected that partitioning a large-scale graph decreases query processing efficiency. However, this decrease can be moderated if the partitioning is sensitive to a query workload used on a daily basis and optimized to minimize the inter-partition communication needed by the workload. In this section, we discuss research results related to graph partitioning and their impact on querying.

The graph partitioning is an NP-complete [9] problem. To alleviate this problem, many practical solutions have been developed, including spectral partitioning methods

[10] and geometric partitioning methods [11]. The multilevel method was introduced to the graph partitioning by Barnard and Simon [6] and then improved by Hendrickson and Leland [7]. The multilevel method consists of three main phases: coarsening, initial partitioning, and uncoarsening. A partitioning approach of Karypis et al. [8] uses recursive multilevel bisection method for bisection of a graph to obtain a k-partition on the coarsest level.

ParMETIS [12] and LogGP [13] are state-of-the-art parallel graph processing systems. Also, LogGP is a graph partitioning system that records, analyzes, and reuses the historical statistical information to generate a hyper-graph and uses a novel hyper-graph streaming partitioning approach to generate a better initial streaming graph partition. Pregel [14] is used for graphs with billions of vertices and is built upon MapReduce [15], and its open-source Apache Giraph [16], PEGASUS [17] and GraphLab [18] used as a default partitioner of vertices. Sedge [19] implements a similar technique as Pregel, which is also a vertex-centric processing model for SPARQL query execution implemented on top of this model. These methods, however, do not take into account a set of queries, called a workload, executed against the partitioned graph. This requires distributed query processing which penalizes workload processing performance.

DREAM [20], WARP [21], PARTOUT [22], AdPart [23], and WISE [24] are workload-aware, distributed RDF systems. DREAM [20] partitions only SPARQL queries into subgraph patterns and not the RDF dataset. The RDF dataset is replicated among nodes. It follows a master-slave architecture, where each node uses RDF-3X [25] on its assigned data for statistical estimation and query evaluation. WARP [21] uses the underlying METIS system to assign each vertex of the RDF graph to a partition. Triples are then assigned to partitions, which are stored at dedicated hosts in a triple store (RDF-3X). WARP determines a query's center node and radius based on an n-hop distance. If the query is within n-hops, WARP sends the query to all partitions to be executed in parallel. A complex query is decomposed into several sub-queries and executed in parallel and then the results are combined. PARTOUT [22] extracts representative triple patterns from a query workload by applying normalization and anonymization by replacing infrequent URIs and literals with variables. Frequent URIs (above a frequency threshold) are normalized. PARTOUT uses an adapted version of RDF-3X as a triple store for their n hosts. AdPart [23] is an in-memory RDF system that re-partitions the RDF data incrementally. It uses hash partitioning that avoids the cost associated with initial partitioning of the dataset. Each worker stores its local set of triples in an in-memory data structure. AdPart provides an ability to monitor and index workloads in the form of hierarchical heat maps. It introduces Incremental ReDistribution (IRD) technique for data portions that are accessed by hot patterns. IRD is a combination of hash-partitioning and k-hop replication, guided by a query workload. WISE [24] is a runtime-adaptive workload-aware partitioning framework for large scale knowledge graphs. A partitioning can be incrementally adjusted by exchanging triples, based on changes in the workload. SPARQL queries are stored in a Query Span structure with their frequencies. To reduce communication overhead, the system redistributes frequent query patterns among workers. A cost model which maximizes the migration the gain while preserving the balanced partition is used for migration of triples.

Our query workload-aware knowledge graph partitioning method, called WawPart, which extracts critical features from the query workload as well as from the dataset. These features are used to establish distance among queries in a form of distance matrix and then cluster similar queries together using hierarchical agglomerative clustering. Subgraphs (partitions) associated with these features are then created from the knowledge graph data and distributed as shards in a computing cluster.

The five closely related systems discussed in the previous paragraph rely on specialized RDF/SPARQL processing systems. In contrast, these systems, ours does not rely on a specialized data store implementation and uses an *off-the-shelf* knowledge graph storage and query processing system (Virtuoso [28]) and relies on standard SPARQL queries for distributed processing. We believe that it is an important advantage.

3 Workload-Aware Knowledge Graph Partitioning

Knowledge graph partitioning created by WawPart attempts to optimize query workload processing time. Critical features of both the workload queries and the knowledge graph are extracted and analyzed. Subsequently, the queries are clustered based on their similarity and the knowledge graph is then partitioned based on the clustering. Original queries are re-written into federated SPARQL queries, since partitions are distributed among computing nodes. Typically, query processing times are increased, due to the distributed joins, as connected triples may be stored in partitions distributed to different nodes (such distributed partitions are usually called *shards*.) In this paper we focus on the effects of workload-aware knowledge graph partitioning, given a query workload. Here, we do not consider the changes in the workload and necessary modifications to the partitioning.

3.1 Query and Knowledge Graph Feature Extraction

Searching for similarities among query graph patterns is computationally expensive, as finding overlaps among query graph patterns is similar to finding isomorphic subgraphs. To help with these problems, we identify and extract critical features of graph patterns in a workload. Similarly, we identify critical features in the knowledge graph (later, we refer to it as the dataset, as well). These features are used to analyze the similarity among triples in queries. We identify the following features in the workload query graph patterns and in the knowledge graph:

- *Predicate (P)* feature represents all triples that share a given predicate (edge label).
- *Predicate-Object (PO)* represents all triples that share a given predicate *and* an object value. This feature is useful in analyzing similarity of some queries.

Other features may be useful in query analysis, as well. These include:

- *Subject-Subject (SS)* feature represents triples that share the same subject, i.e., edges sharing the same source vertex. This feature is used for analyzing queries involving multiple predicates/edges with the same subject (often called star shape patterns).

- *Object-Subject (OS)* represents triples where one triple's object (destination vertex) is another triple's subject (source vertex). Such data representation is beneficial when a query includes pairs of triples with connection based on object - subject (sometimes called an elbow join).
- *Object-Object (OO)* feature represents triples that share the same object (target).

Triples identified by the SS, OS, and OO features represent joins on connecting vertices, which are shared entities (RDF resources) in the knowledge graph. Typically, query patterns also involve joins based on variables shared between triple patterns. All features extracted from the workload queries and from the knowledge graph are stored as metadata. We use them to drive the knowledge graph partitioning. To extract the features from these queries, we use a query analyzer, which analyzes the entire workload. Our query analyzer has been tailored for SPARQL queries, but it can be easily modified for other graph pattern-based query languages and knowledge graph representations, such as the Cypher language used in the Neo4j graph database [4].

In order to speed up handling of the features in the knowledge graph, we created indices on all triples in the knowledge graph, based on their subjects, predicates and objects. We used Apache Lucene API [26] to create the indices and to quickly materialize the necessary features in the knowledge graph. For example, it is possible to materialize the *Predicate (P)* feature and find all triples using a given predicate or materialize the *Predicate-Object (PO)* and find triples sharing a given predicate *and* object. Selected triples can then be easily assigned to their intended partitions, as needed.

3.2 Query Workload Clustering and Knowledge Graph Partitioning

We measure similarity between queries based on their features, as explained above. A distance matrix is often used as the basis for many data mining tasks, such as multi-dimensional scaling, hierarchical clustering, and others. We use Jaccard similarity to construct the distance matrix for the graph patterns in the workload queries. The Jaccard similarity of sets A and B is the ratio of the intersection of set A and B to the union of set A and B, or $J_{sim}(A, B) = |A \cap B|/|A \cup B|$, while the Jaccard distance between sets A and B is given by $1 - J_{sim}(A, B)$. Intuitively, if graph patterns in two queries are nearly identical, based on their features, the distance between them is zero or close to zero. We use a similarity matrix to represent the similarity of queries in the workload and use the matrix to split the workload queries into subsets of similar queries. The details of the computation are skipped here. As an example, consider 2 queries in Fig. 1. Query 7 has 4 features: (2 *PO* features: *rdf:type* → *ub:Student, rdf:type* → *ub:Course* and 2 *P* features: *ub:takesCourse, ub:teacherOf*) while query 9 has 6 features (3 *PO* features: *rdf:type* → *ub:Student, rdf:type* → *ub:Course, rdf:type* → *ub:Faculty* and 3 *P* features: *ub:takesCourse, ub:teacherOf, ub:advisor*). Consequently, the distance between these queries is $(1 - J_{sim}) = 1 - |Q7 \cap Q9|/|Q7 \cup Q9| = 0.33$.

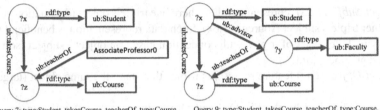

Query 7: type:Student, takesCourse, teacherOf, type:Course   Query 9: type:Student, takesCourse, teacherOf, type:Course,
                                                                 advisor, type:Faculty

Fig. 1. Distance between Q.7 and Q.9 is $1 - J_{sim} = 1 - |Q7 \cap Q9|/|Q7 \cup Q9| = (1 - 4/6) = 0.33$.

For cluster analysis of the features in queries, we used the hierarchical agglomerative clustering (HAC), which is a method of creating a hierarchy of clusters in a bottom-up fashion (Algorithm 1). The decision as to which features should be kept together is established by HAC based on the measure of similarity between queries and selection of a linkage method. The cluster grouping is done according to the shortest distance among all pairwise distances between queries. Once the two most similar queries are grouped together, the distance matrix is recalculated. The first similarity measure is provided by the initial distance matrix. Recalculation of the distance matrix is based on the choice of the linkage from single, complete, or average. Figure 2 shows linkages in which a single linkage is the proximity between two nearest neighbors where a complete linkage is the proximity between the farthest neighbor. These steps are repeated until there is only a single cluster left. We ran HAC using a single linkage against queries to obtain a dendrogram which is then used to partition the dataset. This method of partitioning reduces the inter-partition communication and reduces distributed joins in federated queries.

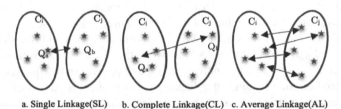

a. Single Linkage(SL)   b. Complete Linkage(CL)   c. Average Linkage(AL)

Fig. 2. Linkages a) $SL(C_i, C_j) = \min(D(Q_a, Q_b))$, b) $CL(C_i, C_j) = \max(D(Q_a, Q_b))$ and c) $AL(C_i, C_j) = \frac{1}{n_{C_i} n_{C_j}} \sum_{a=1}^{n_{C_i}} \sum_{b=1}^{n_{C_j}} D(Q_a, Q_b)$

Algorithm 1. Hierarchical Agglomerative Clustering of Query Workload	
Input	Feature Distance Matrix D of workload Query.
Output	HAC Dendrogram I
1	Assign for each D[n][n] into C[m] where C = c_1, c_2, ..., c_m
2	**while** C.size > 1 **do**
3	**for** i = 1 **to** C.size **do**
4	**if** (c_a,c_b) = *min* d(c_a,c_b) in C **then** // *distance function d(c_1,c_2)*
5	delete c_a and c_b from C
6	add *min* d(c_a,c_b) in C
7	assign **I** = (old, $c_a c_b$,, *min* d(c_a,c_b)) ///(oldGroup, newGroup, distance)
8	recalculate proximity matrix using (SL/CL/AL) **P = modifyD(** c_a ,c_b ,*min* d(c_a,c_b)**)** ///(oldGroup, newGroup, distance)
9	for each P , c_m = P[i][j]
10	Update C = c_1, c_2, ..., c_m
11	Output **I**

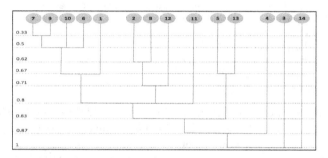

Fig. 3. HAC Dendrogram of LUBM's 14 queries

The partitioning algorithm (Algorithm 2) takes a dendrogram created for a given workload and outputs a partitioning optimized for the workload. For example, we used HAC with a single linkage on the LUBM queries to produce a dendrogram shown in Fig. 3. A statistics module of the algorithm calculates the score for each replicated feature in every partition. These scores are based on 1) features which move together or are tightly connected with a replicated feature, 2) the size of the replicated feature and its peers, 3) dependencies of other queries on these features (replicated and their peer features) and 4) the number of distributed joins, when involved replicated features is on another partition. This score helps the algorithm to determine where to place the replicated features. The balancing module of the algorithm uses these features and also features that are not involved in any workload but present in the dataset to balance the partitions.

Algorithm 2. Knowledge Graph Partitioning Algorithm	
Input	HAC Dendrogram **I**, Features F_G
Output	Partition metadata **P**
1	Create Feature set **g** based on **I** at similarity distance **d**
2	**Statistics(g, F_Q)** //All Features F_G = (Queries features F_Q+ Unused features F_X)
3	Find F_R replicated features in **g**.
4	Find Query distributed joins of replicated features D_{QR}
5	Find stats $S_R \forall F_R$
6	Find p, q and c for C and T.
7	$S_R = \sum (p_c w_1 + q_c w_2 + s_c w_3) + (p_t w_4 + q_t w_5 + s_t w_6)$
	//p(Peer Features), q(Features in query) and s(Feature data size), w(weights), C(shards) and T(dataset).
8	**score** for each $F_R = (D_{QR} * w_7)+ S_R$
9	**Balance_Partition(score, g , F_G)**
10	Remove all F_R from sets of **g** with lower **scores** for each F_R
11	Assign **data** associated to features set **g** into **P**
12	**Proximity_Query()**
13	Find proximity F_{prox} = proximity of $F_{Unclustered}$ with $F_{Clustered}$. // $F_Q = F_U + F_C$.
14	Assign max(F_{prox}) in cluster P_i where its neighbor features are.
15	Assign $F_X = F_X$ + remaining F_U
16	**while** F_X not empty **do**
17	P_{min} = Find min(P_i) by size of shard
18	F_{max} = Find max(F in F_X) by size/count of triples
19	Assign F_{max} into P_{min}
20	Output **P**

Queries are rewritten as federated SPARQL queries [27] to accommodate the distributed shards. The overall objective is to limit the number of distributed joins in federated queries. The query rewriter computes a cost-effective query execution plan by analyzing the metadata, converts the query into a federated SPARQL query and sends it to the most suitable processing node, where the query is executed. The SERVICE keyword followed by a SPARQL endpoint directs a part of the query for processing by SPARQL endpoint on remote shard. Table 1 shows an example of an original and a rewritten, (federated) query. If all data needed for a query is present in the same shard, the query is not rewritten. If the needed triples are in different shards, we need a federated query to obtain the required data from different shards, in order to produce the final result.

Table 1. Original and Federated query of LUBM 2nd query.

Original Query	**Federated Query**

SELECT ?X ?Y ?Z FROM <lubm>
WHERE
{
  ?X rdf:type ub:GraduateStudent .
  ?Y rdf:type ub:University .
  ?Z rdf:type ub:Department .
  ?X ub:memberOf ?Z .
  ?Z ub:subOrganizationOf ?Y .
  ?X ub:undergraduateDegreeFrom ?Y
}
	SELECT ?X ?Y ?Z FROM <lubm>
	WHERE
	{
	  ?X rdf:type ub:GraduateStudent .
	  ?Y rdf:type ub:University .
	  ?Z rdf:type ub:Department .
	  SERVICE <http://172.19.48.185:8890/sparql> {?X ub:memberOf ?Z .}
	  SERVICE <http://172.19.48.185:8890/sparql> {?Z ub:subOrganizationOf ?Y .}
	  SERVICE <http://172.19.48.183:8890/sparql> {?X ub:undergraduateDegreeFrom ?Y}
	}

4 Experiments and Evaluation

We have implemented a prototype system which stores an RDF knowledge graph by partitioning it into shards and distributing them among computing nodes. Our system is deployed on cluster with a Master node and separate triple stores (Virtuoso [28]) are on shared-nothing nodes. The master node is responsible for querying and getting results along with tracking execution time. Each node with a triple store is called a Processing Node, as shown in the Fig. 4. In the context of distributed RDF stores, the triples of the knowledge graph are partitioned into shards and assigned to different processing nodes with the help of the Partition Manager. The Query Rewriter/Processor (QRP) rewrites the incoming query into a federated query, according to the current location of features. The new federated query is executed on the specific shard (partition) with a maximum number of features to minimize the need for distributed joins. The shard where the query is executed is called Primary Processing Node (PPN) for that specific federated query. The system returns the results of that query to the user.

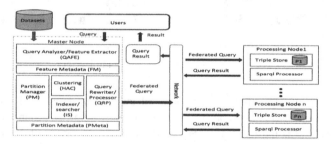

Fig. 4. System architecture

In order to evaluate our knowledge graph partitioning method based on a query workload we used two synthetic datasets and associated data generation: Lehigh University Benchmark (LUBM) [29] and Berlin SPARQL Benchmark (BSBM) [30]. Both datasets were created for the purpose of testing and benchmarking Semantic Web triple store systems and their SPARQL query processing. LUBM includes a data generator, which creates synthetic OWL datasets with basic data about universities, and a set of 14 SPARQL queries for evaluation purposes. BSBM represents data about e-commerce, in which vendors offer products to customers and customers review those products. BSBM provides a dataset generator and a set of 12 SPARQL queries.

We used a cluster of Intel i5 based systems running Linux Ubuntu 18.04.4 LTS 64-bit operating system. We used relatively small machines to observe the effects of partitioning on manageable sizes of datasets. Each computer node had an instance of Virtuoso Open Source 7.2, which we used as a triple store and query processor for the triple shards. The knowledge graph partitioning systems and the experiments were coded in the Java programming language with the use of Apache Jena framework [31].

4.1 Results and Evaluation

Experiment shows the improvements of our workload-aware partitioning method over random partitions (complete sets of all triples with the same predicate were randomly assigned to partitions). For this experiment we have chosen LUBM dataset of 10 universities with 1,563,927 triples and BSBM dataset of 1000 products with 374,911 triples. The experiment shows the workload-aware partitioning has a significant improvement in the query processing time over a random partition.

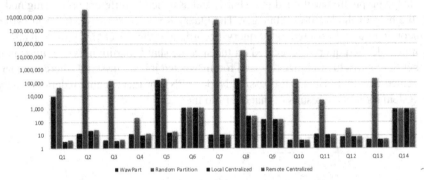

Fig. 5. LUBM 14 queries runtime in milliseconds.

Our partitioning algorithm created shards of the LUBM dataset, which were then distributed among the nodes in our test cluster. As an example of balancing the shard sizes, WawPart splits the LUBM's 1,564k triples into three shards of 481k, 481k and 600k triples, which is within −8% to +15% of the exact average shard size. Random Partition has shards with 521k triples each. This experiment uses two distributed and two centralized datasets and demonstrates the improvement of query workload runtime performance on a distributed system. It also shows the comparison against the baseline query workload runtime. For distributed triple datasets, we used WawPart's and randomly partitioned datasets, marked as *Random Partition*. To compute network latency, we used difference in runtime between centralized datasets, one marked as *Local Centralized* and another marked as *Remote Centralized*. Figure 5 shows the runtime of all 14 LUBM queries in milliseconds. For 12 twelve queries (out of 14), performance of WawPart exceeded the *Random Partition* For two queries, 6 and 14, performance was the same because both queries include only a single triple pattern. In fact, performance of all queries in WawPart is very close to *Local Centralized*, which is a centralized dataset. Figure 7 shows the average runtime of all queries and it demonstrates a dramatic improvement of WawPart's (26 s versus roughly 38 days *on Random Partition*). The average runtime for centralized datasets 0.2 s. For the BSBM dataset, Fig. 6 shows the query runtime for all 12 queries. Figure 8 shows the average runtime of all 12 queries, where we can see the improvement of WawPart against the *Random Partition*. The distributed random partition average runtime is 1 h 49 min and WawPart average runtime is only 16.7 ms. The base average runtime is around 12.9 ms for *Local All* in the centralized dataset. Performance of WawPart (distributed) is almost always very close to the centralized *Local All* partitioning.

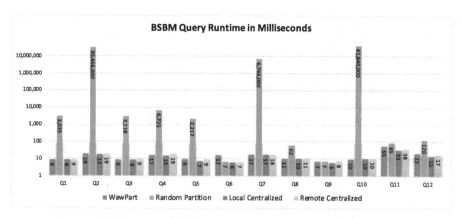

Fig. 6. BSBM 12 queries runtime in milliseconds.

Our experiments demonstrate that partitioning the dataset without workload aware-ness significantly decreases the query workload performance since distributed joins are expensive. Partitioning the knowledge graph takin into account a given query workload leads to significant performance gains. In contrast these systems, ours does not rely on a specialized data.

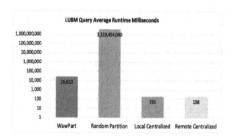

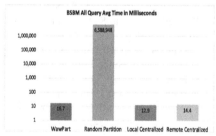

Fig. 7. LUBM 14 queries average runtime   **Fig. 8.** BSBM 12 queries average runtime

5   Conclusions and Future Work

In this paper, we have proposed a WawPart system, which is a knowledge graph parti-tioning and query processing system. It partitions the RDF dataset based on the query workload and aims to reduce the number of distributed joins during query execution, to improve the workload run-time. WawPart requires no replication of the data. For the evaluation of the system, we used LUBM and BSBM, two synthetic RDF/SPARQL benchmarks. Our experiments investigated the effect of workload-aware knowledge graph partitioning. The results showed a significant increase in the performance for the workload queries in comparison to a non-workload aware partitioning.

WawPart can easily be modified to function with other forms of knowledge graph representation such as graph databases, for example, Neo4j. In the near future, we plan to test WawPart on a different knowledge graph system and investigate the impact of workload-aware partitioning on different types of knowledge graphs.

Furthermore, we are planning to extend WawPart to adaptive re-partitioning due the changes in the workload. We plan to investigate the adaptability of partitioning due to (1) the changes in the frequency of queries in the workload (currently, we assume that all queries are executed with the same frequency) and (2) the changes in the composition of the workload (queries may be eliminated and new queries may be added to the workload).

References

1. https://www.w3.org/RDF/
2. https://www.w3.org/2001/sw/wiki/RDFS
3. Sun, Y., Han, J.: Mining heterogeneous information networks: a structural analysis approach. ACM SIGKDD Explor. Newsl. **14**, 20–28 (2013)
4. http://www.neo4j.org
5. https://www.w3.org/TR/rdf-sparql-query/
6. Barnard, S., Simon, H.: Fast multilevel implementation of recursive spectral bisection for partitioning unstructured problems. Concurr. Pract. Experience **6**(2), 101–117 (1994). https://doi.org/10.1002/cpe.4330060203
7. Hendrickson, B., Leland, R.: A multi-level algorithm for partitioning graphs (1995)
8. Karypis, G., Kumar, V.: A fast and high quality multilevel scheme for partitioning irregular graphs. SIAM J. Sci. Comput. **20**, 359–392 (1998)
9. Garey, M.R., Johnson, D.S., Stockmeyer, L.: Some simplified NP-complete problems. In: Proceedings of the Sixth Annual ACM Symposium on Theory of Computing, pp. 47–63. ACM (1974)
10. Donath, W., Hoffman, A.: Algorithms for partitioning of graphs and computer logic based on eigenvectors of connections matrices. IBM Tech. Discl. Bull. **15**, 938–944 (1972)
11. Gilbert, J.R., Miller, G.L., Teng, S.-H.: Geometric mesh partitioning: implementation and experiments. SIAM J. Sci. Comput. **19**, 2091–2110 (1998)
12. Karypis, G., et al.: METIS and ParMETIS. In: Padua, D. (ed.) Encyclopedia of Parallel Computing, pp. 1117–1124. Springer, Boston (2011). https://doi.org/10.1007/978-0-387-09766-4_500
13. Xu, N., Chen, L., Cui, B.: LogGP: a log-based dynamic graph partitioning method. Proc. VLDB Endow. **7**, 1917–1928 (2014)
14. Malewicz, G., et al.: Pregel: a system for large-scale graph processing. In: Proceedings of the 2010 ACM SIGMOD International Conference on Management of Data, pp. 135–146. ACM (2010)
15. Gonzalez, J.E., Low, Y., Gu, H., Bickson, D., Guestrin, C.: Powergraph: distributed graph-parallel computation on natural graphs. In: OSDI, p. 2 (2012)
16. Apache Giraph. https://github.com/apache/giraph/
17. Kang, U., Tsourakakis, C.E., Faloutsos, C.: Pegasus: a peta-scale graph mining system implementation and observations. In: Ninth IEEE International Conference on Data Mining 2009, ICDM 2009, pp. 229–238. IEEE (2009)
18. Low, Y., Gonzalez, J.E., Kyrola, A., Bickson, D., Guestrin, C.E., Hellerstein, J.: GraphLab: a new framework for parallel machine learning. arXiv preprint arXiv:1408.2041 (2014)
19. Yang, S., Yan, X., Zong, B., Khan, A.: Towards effective partition management for large graphs. In: Proceedings of the 2012 ACM SIGMOD International Conference on Management of Data, pp. 517–528. ACM (2012)

20. Hammoud, M., Rabbou, D.A., Nouri, R., Beheshti, S.-M.-R., Sakr, S.: DREAM: distributed RDF engine with adaptive query planner and minimal communication. Proc. VLDB Endow. **8**, 654–665 (2015)
21. Hose, K., Schenkel, R.: WARP: workload-aware replication and partitioning for RDF. In: 2013 IEEE 29th International Conference on Data Engineering Workshops (ICDEW), pp. 1–6. IEEE (2013)
22. Galárraga, L., Hose, K., Schenkel, R.: Partout: a distributed engine for efficient RDF processing. In: Proceedings of the 23rd International Conference on World Wide Web, pp. 267–268. ACM (2014)
23. Harbi, R., Abdelaziz, I., Kalnis, P., Mamoulis, N., Ebrahim, Y., Sahli, M.: Accelerating SPARQL queries by exploiting hash-based locality and adaptive partitioning. VLDB J. **25**(3), 355–380 (2016). https://doi.org/10.1007/s00778-016-0420-y
24. Guo, X., Gao, H., Zou, Z.: WISE: workload-aware partitioning for RDF systems. Big Data Res. **22**, 100161 (2020)
25. Neumann, T., Weikum, G.: RDF-3X: a RISC-style engine for RDF. Proc. VLDB Endow. **1**, 647–659 (2008)
26. Lucene, A.: Apache Lucene-Overview (2010). http://lucene.apache.org/iava/docs/. Accessed 15 Jan 2009
27. https://www.w3.org/TR/sparql11-federated-query/
28. https://virtuoso.openlinksw.com/
29. Guo, Y., Pan, Z., Heflin, J.: LUBM: a benchmark for OWL knowledge base systems. J. Web Semant. **3**, 158–182 (2005)
30. Bizer, C., Schultz, A.: Berlin SPARQL benchmark (BSBM) specification-v2.0 (2008)
31. McBride, B.: Jena: a semantic web toolkit. IEEE Internet Comput. **6**, 55–59 (2002)

Analysis of Sentimental Behaviour over Social Data Using Machine Learning Algorithms

Abdul Razaque[1], Fathi Amsaad[2], Dipal Halder[2], Mohamed Baza[3(✉)],
Abobakr Aboshgifa[4], and Sajal Bhatia[5]

[1] International IT University, Almaty, Kazakhstan
a.razaque@iitu.kz
[2] Eastern Michigan University, Ypsilanti, MI, USA
{famsaad,dhalder}@emich.edu
[3] Department of Computer Science, College of Charleston, Charleston, SC, USA
mxb117@shsu.edu
[4] The Higher Technical Center for Training and Production, Tripoli, Libya
Aboshgifa@tpc.ly
[5] Computer Science and Engineering, The Sacred Heart University,
West Campus East Building WCE*E-1137, Fairfield, USA
Bhatias@sacredheart.edu

Abstract. A person's sentiment is rigorously influenced by his emotional feelings which is evoked from every single incident, occurring every day in his surroundings. In this case, the decision that he makes is greatly affected by his sentiment rather than facts. Sentimental behavior can be applied to many applications in health, business, education, etc. This paper proposes and develops a sentimental behavior based on machine learning algorithms for pre-processing feature selection, and classification that helps identify, extract, quantify the feelings to twitter social dataset. Based on the Sentimental behavior, an analytical prediction has been developed that can be used to understand the behavior of the customers or users. Conducting the testing process for three state-of-the-art algorithms, the unique methodology is devised based on these proposed algorithms (support vector machine (SVM), logistic regression (LR), and XGboost), our extensive experiments show that our approach has high accuracy. Based on the testing results, the accurate sentimental behavior detection algorithm is identified and recommended to be used for textual data in the future.

Keywords: Machine learning · Opinion mining · Logistic regression · Support vector machine · Sentimental behavior detection

1 Introduction

Sentimental Behavior is one of the smart detection mechanisms for opinion or text mining. Fundamentally, SB is a procedure of enumerating expressive assessment in a series of words and text. Also, SB can be applied in other fields such

H. Fujita et al. (Eds.): IEA/AIE 2021, LNAI 12798, pp. 396–412, 2021.
https://doi.org/10.1007/978-3-030-79457-6_34

as hotels, banking, e-commerce, social media. Many Companies and/or organizations can gain insight from consumers about their services by employing sentimental behavior or text mining. Recently, sentimental behavior attracts more attention since social data can be available over the internet privately or publicly in many forms. Understanding such data is important to extract valuable information and get public opinions about different topics i.e. products, services, brands, politics, or any other topic that people may express their opinions about. Most of these data are unstructured and needs a lot of work before it can be usefully used (structured data). Sentimental behavior systems can help to transform unstructured data into structured data. Structured data is beneficial in many areas such as public relations, product feedback, marketing analysis, and customer service [1].

The sentiment analysis is one of the major tools that can be used to extract a ton of information from raw data. Sentiment analysis refers to applying Natural Language Processing and Text Analysis techniques to identify and obtain subjective info from a text. People's feelings or opinions are subjective, not facts; this means it extremely difficult to accurately analyze a person's opinions or feelings from a text. Through sentiment analysis from a text analytic opinion, we are looking to get an understanding of the attitude of a writer with respect to a topic in a given text and its polarity, whether it is positive or negative [5].

A sentimental behavior or widely known as text mining framework, typically includes following sub-tasks: acquiring text data, data cleaning and preprocessing, data normalization, conversion of text to machine-readable vectors, features selection, and finally, applying Natural Language Processing (NLP) and machine learning algorithms [2]. NLP is designed to provide the best generalization of the sentence, the final target is to use machine learning algorithms to create the best model for classification. Data normalization is the technique to adjust the scales of the features required for the machine learning without distorting differences in the ranges of values. It is important to get rid of from duplicate data and redundancy as well as to group data together logically. In the data preprocessing, data gets transformed for implementing it easily in machine learning algorithm. This paper aims to analyze the significance of three algorithms to determine which algorithm produces better performance in term of quality and reliability of data collected by IoT devise. Additionally, these algorithms are used as a tool for better understanding as well as to judge different opinions of many users that use social media with the help of connected smart IoT devices. Three unique algorithms which are SVM, LR and XGboost are used for pre-processing, feature selection, and classification to identify, extract, and quantify the feelings from a twitter dataset.

The sentimental behavior could improve the environment in social networks by reducing negative comments and banning angry and provocative users. Moreover, it could prevent suicides by analyzing the tone and meaning of posts. Furthermore, by combining several machine learning algorithms, companies will be able to predict crimes or even organized terrorist attacks. After our research in order to get the full view of the problem and its solutions, we decided to compare three different methods that apply to sentimental analysis: Logistic Regression, Support Vector Machine and XGboost.

The rest of the paper is organized as follows: Sect. 2, the problem identification. The related work is explained in Sect. 3. The proposed methodology is presented in Sect. 4. Section 5 shows the implementation and experimental results. Section 5 discusses the significance of the result and limitations, including suggestions for improvement. Section 6 concludes the entire paper.

2   Problem Identification

Nowadays, the internet plays a significant role in human lives. 2.5 quintillion bytes data is generated every single day according to IBM [3], it is estimated that 80% of generated data is unstructured. Some innovative companies try to enhance their value proposition and increase customer satisfaction using this data [4]. Such as, Apple has used the data to present to consumers products and services that might be relevant to them though it has vastly different business models [5]. However, it is difficult to understand and find meaning in unstructured data. They have a hard time processing unstructured data. Through sentiment analysis from a text analytic opinion, we are looking to get an understanding of the attitude of a writer with respect to a topic in a given text and its polarity, whether it is positive or negative [6].

The problem of identifying a ton of the text is handled by using powerful and effective machine learning algorithms in the question of processing a massive pile of data. Using these technologies for sentiment analysis systems helps many companies to understand an enormous collection of unstructured data by automating business processes, getting actionable insights, saving hours of manual data processing. In other words, sentiment analysis helps to handle it efficiently.

3   Related Works

Interdependent Latent Dirichlet Allocation (ILDA) was introduced in 2011. ILDA is considered each review as a combination of aspects and ratings. Presumably, aspects and their ratings can be represented by multinomial distributions and attempt to cluster head in aspects and sentiments in ratings. ILDA is based on the concept of Latent Dirichlet Allocation (LDA). ILDA shows much higher accuracy than standard LDA models. The basic idea is that each item of a collection is modeled as a finite mixture over an underlying set of latent variables [7]. It measures and reports the general mood of a review by rating.

Another method presented for semantically classifying sentiment for customer reviews, it works in three parts [8,9]. First, the review sentences are divided into sentences. Second, the polarity of a sentence is determined based on the contextual information and structure of the sentence. Third, Sentences are classified into an objective or subjective using a rule-based module. For evaluating the three types of online customer review data sets were collected by the authors to verify the performance of the system (hotel reviews, airline, and movie). The data sets have an average of 2,600 hotel reviews, 1,000 airline reviews, and 1,000 movie reviews. The performance has been assessed with an accuracy of 91% at the review level and 86% at the sentence level [10].

In [11], a the multi-classification approach for classifying the mobile app traffic has been proposed. It improves the performance of mobile app traffic classification using a multi-classification approach that combines the outputs offered for classifying mobile and encrypted traffic data. The paper compares four classes of different combiners. These classes differ in acceptance of the results of soft or hard classifiers, learning requirements, and learning philosophy. The multi-classification approach has a modularity property that makes it easy to connect and disconnect any classifiers to improve performance. Based on user activity data, the results show that classification performance can be enhanced according to all the metrics considered. Moreover, the proposed system is capitalized to validate new preprocessing of traffic traces and assess performance sensitivity to object segmentation of traffic before actual classification.

[12] consider anonymity services such as Tor, I2P, and JonDonym. It uses five machine learning classifiers to examine the extent to which a particular anonymity tool and the traffic it hides can be identified, compared to the traffic of other anonymity tools under consideration. Flow-based Traffic Classification (TC) is considered, and the influence of the importance of features and associated temporal characteristics on the network is investigated. Moreover, the role of fine-grained features, such as a joint histogram of packet lengths with the time of their receipt, is determined. The results show that the considered anonymities of the network (Tor, I2, JonDonym) can be distinguished with an accuracy of 99.87% in the case of flow-based TC, and 99.80% in the early-TC.

[13] discuss the hierarchical traffic classification of anonymity tools. Based on an in-depth analysis of TC and comparison of the proposed hierarchical approach with a flat analog, a structure is proposed, which is investigated both in the usual TC setup and in its "early" version. The results of the study show an overall improvement over the flat approach in terms of all classification metrics and further performance improvements by adjusting thresholds to ensure progressive censorship. An in-depth performance study allows us to demonstrate less severity of errors caused by a hierarchical approach (as opposed to a flat case) and highlight the poorly classified services and applications of each anonymity tool, collecting user feedback on their privacy level.

4   Proposed Methodology

The sentimental behavior model is developed based on machine learning algorithms for processing unstructured data. Figure 1 illustrates the proposed model. After completing the pre-processing data phase, the most important features should be identified and selected; In this phase, the less essential features can be removed then, consequently, the computational time can be significantly improved. While in the classification phase, various classifiers can be used to create the model such as SVM, NN, and DT.

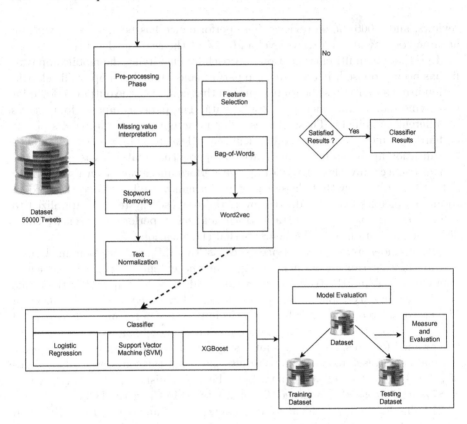

Fig. 1. The proposed machine leaning model for the analysis of sentimental social network behaviour.

Nevertheless, this research only focused on how to use LR, SVM, XGBoost to classify documents. Based on the characteristic of Logistic Regression, SVM, each training document is represented into a vector by a trained classifier. Finally, evaluate the classifier based on testing data. In order to test the model's ability to classify documents, several evaluation metrics are used, such as precision, recall, and F-measure, to conclude Logistic Regression and SVM are suited to use as the classifier, its testing result will be compared with other classifiers results as well.

4.1   Preprocessing

Preprocessing is performed to provide significant information for the models. Of the many preprocessing processes, there are two main ones: data cleaning process and feature Selection. The data cleaning stage involves removing special characters, hashtags, meaningless words. Feature Selection allows choosing only the most essential predictors for the model, which critically improve accuracy. For these processes below are shown the algorithms.

Algorithm 1 describes the data cleaning process. In step 1, the initialization of variables is given. Steps 2–3 show the input and output processes respectively. In step 4, the database is set to obtain the data set. In steps 5–6, the data set cleaning process is performed. Steps 7–8 shows the checking process of data cleaning whether the data set is cleaned or not. If a data set is cleaned, then we used data because it is cleaned. Steps 9–10, In case the data is not cleaned then further processing process will be conducted.

Algorithm 1: Data cleaning process

---

1 Initialization: D_s: Data set; D_b: Database; D_c: Data set Clean;
2 Input: D_s;
3 Output: D_c;
4 Set:D_b;
5 Obtain: $D_s \rightarrow D_b$;
6 Clean: D_s;
7 **if** $D_s = D_c$ **then**
8 | Return D_s;
9 **else**
10 | Do process;
11 **end**

4.2 Feature Selection

Feature selection takes essential pre-processing steps in data mining. This is an efficient method reduction technique for extracting noise items. The main idea of the feature selection is to searches overall probable combinations of the item in the dataset to find which subset of features makes the best performance in prediction. Therefore, the number of features can be reduced by keeping the most significant features and remove irrelevant or redundant features. In this research, all the data sets in the training data are sorted in four categories based on how frequently a term occurred in such categories. Like this, some features can be removed if they are irrelevant.

As this is described in [14], Cfs Subset evaluator which evaluates the worth of a subset of features by considering the individual predictive ability of each feature along with the degree of redundancy between them is the best way to get the feature set; While random search or rank search is recommended for a good feature set. Therefore, in this research rank search and Cfs subset evaluator are used as feature selection method [15]. Algorithm 2 describes the feature selection initial process. In step 1, the initialization of variables is given. Steps 2–3 show the input and output processes respectively. In step 4, the process of writing

---

Algorithm 2: Feature selection process

---

1 Initialization: D_c: Data set Clean; W: Words; V_o: Vocabulary; V_e: Vector; B_{ow}: Bag of Words ;
2 Input: D_s;
3 Output: B_{ow};
4 In: B_{ow} Do process;
5 Get: W from D_c;
6 Set:$W \rightarrow V_o$;
7 Get: $V_e \rightarrow V_o$;
8 Set: $V_o \rightarrow B_{ow}$;
9 End ;
10 Return: B_{ow};

---

data into Bag of Words. In steps 5, the word extracting process is performed. Steps 6 shows the vocabulary filling with words from the data set. Steps 7 get from vocabulary vectors. In steps 8, putting vectors into Bag of Words. Step 9–10 is the end of the process and getting final results as Bag of Words vectors.

4.3   Building Models for Classification

Once the feature selection process is completed, the number of features will be reduced, and the selected features are explicit for building the classification model. LR is used as the classifier for its simplicity and excellent performance in handling text classification [16]. LR is classified output in terms of input based on the concept of probability. The output is based on a probability score between 0 and 1 to decide which terms go to each class based on its number of occurrences within that particular documents. Through the training, Logistic regression can recognize the pattern of the test set documents, therefore compare the terms within the class feature by creating a list of these terms with the number of their appearances by using this list to classify new documents to the right class according to their probability score. Logistic regression evaluates the relation between class instances by using a logistic function to estimate probabilities, which is also called the sigmoid function. In this approach, the class feature is categorical so either class A or class B which is a binary regression it can be also multinomial regression by a range of finite classes A, B, C or D. Binary logistic regression is a well-known type of logistic regression that can make only two classification classes. Although the outcomes are constrained, the possibilities are not. Binary logistic regression can be used to study everything: from baseball statistics to a landslide inclination and handwriting analysis.

The LR algorithm uses a logistic function to compress the output of a linear equation between 0 and 1. The logistic function is defined as

$$log(x) = \frac{1}{1 + exp(x)} \tag{1}$$

Algorithm 3: Getting sentimental type of the sentence using the logistic regression model

---

1 Initialization: M_{log}: Logistic Regression model, S_q: Query string, S_r: Response string, D_b: Database ;
2 Input: S_q;
3 Output: S_r;
4 Set: D_b;
5 Training: $M_{log} \rightarrow D_b$;
6 Apply: $M_{log} \rightarrow S_q$;
7 **if** $M_{log} \rightarrow S_q = 0$ **then**
8 | Return S_r = positive;
9 **else**
10 | Return S_r = negative;
11 **end**

For classification, we must get probabilities between 0 and 1, so we need to transform of the linear regression into the logistic function. This forces the output to assume only values between 0 and 1 [17].

$$P(y^i) = \frac{1}{1 + exp(\beta_0 + \beta_1 x_1^i + \cdots + \beta_p x_p)} \qquad (2)$$

By taking the logarithm, we can get equation for logistic regression:

$$log(\frac{p(X)}{1 - p(X)}) = \beta_0 + \beta_1 X \qquad (3)$$

In a logistic regression, growing X by one block changes the log odds by β_1, or equivalently it multiplies the odds by β_1. It because the relationship between $p(X)$ and X in is not a line $beta_1$ does not match to the change in $p(X)$ associated with a one-unit increase in X. The amount that $p(X)$ changes due to a one block change in X will depend on the current value of X. But regardless of the value of X, if β_1 is positive then growing X will be associated with growing $p(X)$, and if β_1 is negative then growing X will be related with decreasing $p(X)$. Algorithm 3 describes the steps of sentimental type of the sentence using the logistic regression model. In step-1, initialization of variables is given. Steps 2–3 shows the input string and output string respectively. In step 4–5, the process of training model logistic regression on data set. In steps 6, conducting training model on input string. In steps 7–8, if the model predicted a label equal to 0 for the input string, then the string is classified as positive tweet. Steps 9,10 If the model predicted a label equal to 1 for the input string, then the string is classified as negative tweet and output string will be assigned as negative. Support vector machines (SVM) were lately developed algorithm witch successfully used in a number of applications, from time series prediction to face recognition, to processing biological data for medical diagnostics.

The support vector machine (SVM) is one of the well-known machine leaning-based classifier method. It constructed for creating a solution boundary between

---

Algorithm 4: Pre-processing feature selection building models for the classification SVM model

1 Initialization: M_{SVM}: Support vector machine model, S_q: Query string, S_r: Response string, D_b: Database ;
2 Input: S_q;
3 Output:S_r;
4 Set: D_b;
5 Training: $M_{SVM} \rightarrow D_b$;
6 Apply: $M_{SVM} \rightarrow S_q$;
7 **if** $M_{SVM} \rightarrow S_q = 0$ **then**
8 $\quad$| $\quad$ Return S_r= positive;
9 **else**
10 $\quad$| $\quad$ Return S_r= negative;
11 **end**

Algorithm 5: Description of the XGboost Algorithm

1 Initialization: $M_{XGboost}$: XGboost model, S_q: Query string, S_r: Response string, D_b: Database ;
2 Input: S_q;
3 Output: S_r;
4 Set: D_b;
5 Training: $M_{XGboost} \rightarrow D_b$;
6 Apply: $M_{XGboost} \rightarrow S_q$;
7 **if** $M_{M_X Gboost} \rightarrow S_q = 0$ **then**
8 $\quad$| $\quad$ Return S_r= positive;
9 **else**
10 $\quad$| $\quad$ Return S_r= negative;
11 **end**

---

two classes, that allows predict class from one or several feature vectors. This method, known as hyper-plane, is oriented so that it is as far as possible from the nearest data points for each class. the nearest points are the support vectors.

The optimal hyper-plane can then be defined as:

$$wx^T + b = 0 \tag{4}$$

where, w is the weight vector
x is the input feature vector
b is the bias

The w and b most fulfill the following constrain for all elements of the training set:

$$wx_i^T + b \geq +1 \; \text{ if } y_i = 1$$

The main reason of training an SVM algorithm is to find the weight and bias so that the hyperplane separates the data and maximizes the margin $1/\|w\|^2$ Vectors x_i for which $|y_i| (wx_i^T + b = 1)$ will be termed support vector. An alternative use of SVM is the kernel method, which allows us to model non-linear models with high dimensional. In a non-linear problem, an extra dimension is added to the raw data by using the kernel function, to make it a linear problem higher dimensional space [18]. The kernel function can help perform certain calculations more quickly, which would require calculations in higher dimensional space. It is defined as:

$$K(x, y) = \ <f(x), f(y)> \tag{5}$$

where,

K is the function of the kernel

x, y are extensional inputs

f is function which return input data from n-dimensional to m-dimensional space

$<x, y>$ define the dot product

By using the kernel functions, to compute the scalar product between two data points in a higher dimension space without clear computing the mapping from the input space to the higher dimension space. It is easy to compute the kernel, in going to higher dimensional space it is difficult to compute the production of two feature vectors. The feature vector even for simple kernels can increase rabidly in size, especially kernels like the Radial Basis Function (RBF) kernel can have infinite dimensional for feature vector. The choice the function type can significantly affect the performance of an SVM model. Nevertheless, there is no a specific way to choose which kernel could fit a specific problem. The only way to choose the best kernel is to use trial and error method. It can be started with a simple SVM, and then "standard" kernel functions. based on the nature of the problem, it is always possible that one kernel is suited better than the other kernels.

The optimal kernel function can be selected from a set of kernels in a statistically rigorous way using cross-validation.

Algorithm 4 describes the pre-processing feature selection building models for the classification support vector machine model. In step-1, the initialization of variables is given. Steps 2–3 shows the input string and output string respectively. In step 4–5, the process of training model Support vector machine on data set. In steps 6, conducting training model on the input string. In steps 7 and 8, If the model predicted a label equal to 0 for the input string, then the string is classified as a positive tweet. In steps, 9 and 10 if the model predicted a label equal to 1 for the input string, then the string is classified as a negative tweet and output string will be assigned as negative.

The last model for the classification of tweets was selected XGboost model. XGBoost is one of the most efficient implementations of the Gradient Boosted Trees algorithm, a supervised process, based on function approximation by optimizing certain loss functions as well as applying several regularization techniques. XGBoost uses ensemble learning techniques to improve overall performance. Ensemble learning provides a collective solution to several machine learning models. These models could be from the same learning algorithm or various learning algorithms. Although it can be applied with any type, it is easier to use the

id	label	tweet
0	1	0	@user when a father is dysfunctional and is s...
1	2	0	@user @user thanks for #lyft credit i can't us...
2	3	0	bihday your majesty
3	4	0	#model i love u take with u all the time in ...
4	5	0	factsguide: society now #motivation
5	6	0	[2/2] huge fan fare and big talking before the...
6	7	0	@user camping tomorrow @user @user @user @use...
7	8	0	the next school year is the year for exams.ᵟ❑❑...
8	9	0	we won!!! love the land!!! #allin #cavs #champ...
9	10	0	@user @user welcome here ! i'm it's so #gr...

(a)

id	label	tweet
13	14	1	@user #cnn calls #michigan middle school 'buil...
14	15	1	no comment! in #australia #opkillingbay #se...
17	18	1	retweet if you agree!
23	24	1	@user @user lumpy says i am a prove it lumpy.
34	35	1	it's unbelievable that in the 21st century we'...
56	57	1	@user lets fight against #love #peace
68	69	1	ᵟ❑❑the white establishment can't have blk fol...
77	78	1	@user hey, white people: you can call people '...
82	83	1	how the #altright uses & insecurity to lu...
111	112	1	@user i'm not interested in a #linguistics tha...

(b)

Fig. 2. (a) Data set with positive tweets; (b) Data set with negative tweets.

id	label	tweet	tidy_tweet
0	1	0.0	@user when a father is dysfunctional and is s...	when a father is dysfunctional and is so sel...
1	2	0.0	@user @user thanks for #lyft credit i can't us...	thanks for #lyft credit i can t use cause th...
2	3	0.0	bihday your majesty	bihday your majesty
3	4	0.0	#model i love u take with u all the time in ...	#model i love u take with u all the time in ...
4	5	0.0	factsguide: society now #motivation	factsguide society now #motivation
5	6	0.0	[2/2] huge fan fare and big talking before the...	huge fan fare and big talking before the...
6	7	0.0	@user camping tomorrow @user @user @use...	camping tomorrow danny
7	8	0.0	the next school year is the year for exams.ᵟ❑❑...	the next school year is the year for exams ...
8	9	0.0	we won!!! love the land!!! #allin #cavs #champ...	we won love the land #allin #cavs #champ...
9	10	0.0	@user @user welcome here ! i'm it's so #gr...	welcome here i m it s so #gr

(a)

	id	label	tweet	tidy_tweet
0	1	0.0	@user when a father is dysfunctional and is so selfish he drags his kids into his dysfunction. #run	when father dysfunctional selfish drags kids into dysfunction #run
1	2	0.0	@user @user thanks for #lyft credit i can't use cause they don't offer wheelchair vans in pdx. #disapointed #getthanked	thanks #lyft credit cause they offer wheelchair vans #disapointed #getthanked
2	3	0.0	bihday your majesty	bihday your majesty
3	4	0.0	#model i love u take with u all the time in urᵟ❑❑±!!! ᵟ❑❑❑ᵟ❑❑❑ᵟᵟ❑❑ᵟ❑❑❑ᵟᵟ❑❑¡ᵟᵟᵟ❑❑ᵟ¡	#model love take with time
4	5	0.0	factsguide: society now #motivation	factsguide society #motivation

(b)

Fig. 3. The cleaned Twitted data set.

decision tree algorithm, they exhibit very different behavior. Aggregation helps reduce dispersion in any waylearners for training. The final fore-cast is the average result of all learners. Trees are constructed sequentially to boost the classifier and to reduce the error from the prior tree. Every tree learns from its previous tree. Therefore, the tree will grow subsequently from the updated version of the residuals.

The base learners several decision trees, which are generated in parallel, form the basis for studying packaging techniques. Replacement data is transferred to these not powerful enough wherein the bias is high in boosting, and the accuracy

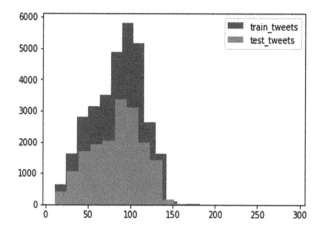

Fig. 4. The distribution of the social tweets length

Table 1. Tools used for conducting the experiments

Tools	Description
CPU	Intel Core i7 4702MQ
GPU	Nvidia Geforce 750 m
RAM	Micron PC3L 8 GB
SSD	Kingston SUV500480G
Operating System	Windows 10
Platform	Jupyter Notebook, Google Colab Notebook
Programming language	Python
Additional libraries	Pandas, Numpy, Seaborn, Matplotlib, Sklearn, TfidfVectorizer, CountVectorizer

performance is slightly better than guessing. Each of these non-powerful learners provides some information to the final prediction, empowering the boosting process to generate strong learner by successfully combining these non-powerful learners. The final strong learner brings down both the bias and the variance. Unlike the Random Forest technique, where trees are grown to their highest, boosting takes advantage of trees with fewer splits. Such small trees that are not very deep are interpreted. Parameters such as iterations or the number of trees, the depth of the tree and the gradient boosting learns rate, can be selected using verification methods similar to k-fold.

There are three steps consider for applying boosting technique:

- initial the model F_0 to predict the variable y, so this will be correlated with a residual (yF_0).
- A new model called h_1 is fit into the residuals from the prior step
- The F_0 and h_1 are merged together to create F_1, the boosted model of F_0.

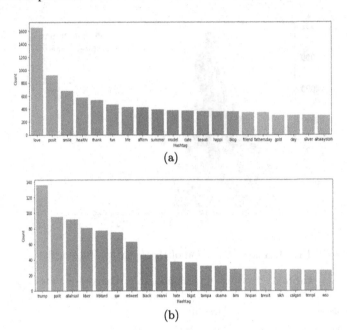

(a)

(b)

Fig. 5. The cleaned twitted data set.

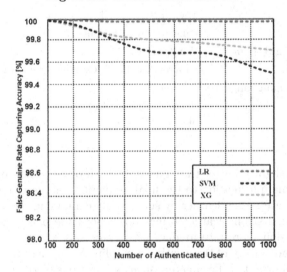

Fig. 6. False genuine rate accuracy verses the authenticated user

$$F_1(x) \leftarrow F_0(x) + h_1(x) \tag{6}$$

To improve F1 accuracy performance, a new model of F2 is created after the residuals of F1 [19]:

$$F_2(x) \leftarrow F_1(x) + h_2(x) \qquad (7)$$

It can be applied for "m" iterations, so the residuals reach the minimum as possible:

$$F_m(x) \leftarrow F_{m-1}(x) + h_m(x) \qquad (8)$$

The collective learners do not affect the functions that have been created in the previous steps, they impart some information of their own to minimize the errors [20]. The addition learners do not interfere with the methods created in the previous phases. However, they transfer data of their own to bring down the errors. In addition, XGboost model has unique features:

- Quantile weighted sketch: Tree based algorithms are not equipped to handle weighted data. XGBoost has a distributed weighted quantile design algorithm for efficiently processing weighted data.
- Regularization: It has the ability to define complex models by regularizing L1 and L2. Regularization helps to handle over-fitting
- Sparse data processing: XGBoost includes a sparse search separation algorithm for processing various types of sparsity patterns in data.

Algorithm 5 describes the algorithm of the XGboost model. In step-1, initialization of variables is given. Steps 2–3 shows the input string and output string respectively. In step 4–5, the process of training model XGboost on data set. In steps 6, conducting training model on input string. Steps 7, 8 If the model predicted a label equal to 0 for the input string, then the string is classified as positive tweet. Steps 9, 10 If the model predicted a label equal to 1 for the input string, then the string is classified as negative tweet and output string will be assigned as negative.

5   Implementation and Results

The purpose of this article is to recognize the reaction of users through their feedback. Therefore, it is necessary to define positive or negative feedback from users. Considering the training sample of tweets and tags, where the "0" label indicates a positive tweet, and the "1" label means a negative tweet as shown in Figs. 2(a)–(b). The finished model should be capable to predict positive or negative feedback from users. The train set has 31,962 tweets and the test set has 17,197 tweets. First consider data set with positive, negative tweets. Positive tweets will be represented in the first ten lines with label 0. Next, consider negative tweets with label 1. In the training data set 2,242 (7%) tweets labeled as negative, and 29,720 (93%) tweets labeled as positive. Before building a model, it is necessary to clean the data [21]. Since the data set consists of tweets, it needs to be removed punctuation, numbers, and special characters as shown in Fig. 3(a). It is also necessary to clear data sets from unnecessary meaningless words, for example, "he", "a". Figure 3(b) shows the clean Dataset with stop words.

Figure 4 shows the distribution of the tweets length. The tweet-length distribution is more or less the same in both train and test data. Graphical word is normally created to see how well the mood data is distributed across the train data set. A word cloud is a visualization in which the most common words appear large, and less frequent words appear in smaller ones. The most common words in a data set have a positive meaning. Words like love, great, thank, life are the most frequent ones.

For conducting sentiment analysis, the tweets are required to be tested on the various software and hardware tools. These tools are presented in Table 1.

For the presentation of textual information for training the model, three different methods have been used: *Bag-of-words*, TF-IDF and Word embedding. A bag-of-words illustrate the occurrence of words inside a document. This includes the vocabulary of words and the measure of the presence of words. The model determines if the words occur in a document or not and does not concerned about where is located in the document. The term *Frequency Inverse Document Frequency (TF-IDF)* is used with statistical weight to evaluate the importance of a word for a document in a collection or package. Importance increases in proportion to how many times a word appears in a document but shifts to the frequency of the word in the corpus. Word2vec is a two-layer neural network that processes text. Its input is a text corpus, and the output is a set of vectors. Although Word2vec is not a deep neural network, but it turns text into a numerical form that machine learning algorithms can understand. Depending on the method, the accuracy of the model can be different.

For a better understanding of the data, the most common hashtags for positive and negative tweets were found. The distribution graphs are presented in Figs. 5 and 6. Most conditions are negative or positive, as well as several neutral conditions. These values should be kept for better prediction. Three unique algorithms are proposed for pre-processing, feature selection and classification to support the LR, SVM, XGboost.

The false genuine accuracy is detected in Fig. 6. The results in the figure clearly proves that proposed approach performs better as compared to other existing approaches. As seen in Fig. 6, the highest accuracy is achieved when using the Word2vec method while Bag-of-words and TF-IDF show worse results. The SVM model has the lowest accuracy of all three models, which may indicate non-linear data distribution. On the other hand, LR and XGboost produce better accuracy as compared to SVM/ As, LR and XGboost use the nonlinear regularities. Although LR is simply designed, it has the highest prediction accuracy. The confusion matrix is used for a detailed review of the results. The left diagonal of the confusion matrix shows erroneous predictions, and the right diagonal shows the correct ones. Thus, it has been observed that 8646 are correctly classified as negative, 417 are correctly classified as positive tweets. And also 259 are mistakenly classified as positive, and 267 are mistakenly classified as negative. As a result, it can be observed that out of 9589 test predictions, 9063 are classified correctly and 526 found incorrect. The results prove that LR produces better accuracy.

6   Conclusion

Sentimental behavior detection has been presented using machine learning algorithms. This paper aims to use textual data to determine the negative or positive behavior of the users. Three machine learning algorithms (e.g. Logistic Regression, Support Vector Machine, XGboost) have been tested. As Conducting the testing process, the unique methodology is devised supported with three algorithms, which perform the pre-processing, feature selection and classification. The algorithms also help in identifying, extracting, quantifying the feelings of the user from the data set obtained from twitter. The testing process consists of three steps. In the first step, the data is cleared from the useless characters and words. After this, an exploratory data analysis is performed to visualize the data. In the second step, the text is represented for model training such as Bag-of-words, TF-IDF and Word Embedding. The final step is the construction and training of models and the calculation of the accuracy of their predictions on tested data. The highest accuracy of 66.1% was shown by the Logistic Regression model using the Word2vec method. For a more detailed examination of the results, a confusion matrix is built, which shows that out of 9589 test predictions, 9063 are classified correctly and 526 found incorrect.

References

1. Sahayak, V., Shete, V., Pathan, A.: Sentiment analysis on twitter data. (IJIRAE) ISSN: 2349–2163, January 2015
2. Bouazizi, M., Ohtsuki, T.: Sentiment analysis: from binary to multi-class classification. In: IEEE ICC 2016 SAC Social Networking, ISBN 978-1-4799-6664-6 (2016)
3. Balas, V.E., et al. (eds.): Internet of Things and Big Data Analytics for Smart Generation, vol. 154, p. 3. Springer, Heidelberg (2019). https://doi.org/10.1007/978-3-030-04203-5
4. Mamgain, N., Mehta, E., Mittal, A., Bhatt, G.: Sentiment analysis of top colleges in India using Twitter data, ISBN -978-1-5090-0082-1. IEEE (2016)
5. https://businessmodelsinc.medium.com/exploring-big-data-business-models-the-winning-value-propositions-behind-them-f7b182458d98
6. Halima Banu, S., Chitrakala, S.: Trending topic analysis using novel sub topic detection model, ISBN- 978-1-4673-9745-2. IEEE (2016)
7. Moghaddam, S., Ester, M.: ILDA: interdependent LDA model for learning latent aspects and their ratings from online product reviews. In: Proceedings of the 34th International ACM SIGIR Conference on Research and Development in Information Retrieval (2011)
8. Khan, A., Baharudin, B., Khan, K.: Sentiment classification from online customer reviews using lexical contextual sentence structure. In: Mohamad Zain, J., Wan Mohd, W.M., El-Qawasmeh, E. (eds.) ICSECS 2011. CCIS, vol. 179, pp. 317–331. Springer, Heidelberg (2011). https://doi.org/10.1007/978-3-642-22170-5_28. ISBN 978-3-642-22170-5
9. Dietmar, G., Markus, Z., Günther, F., Matthias, F.: Classification of customer reviews based on sentiment analysis. In: Fuchs, M., Ricci, F., Cantoni, L. (eds.) Information and Communication Technologies in Tourism, pp. 460–470. Springer, Vienna (2012). https://doi.org/10.1007/978-3-7091-1142-0_40. ISBN 978-3-7091-1142-0

10. Bermingham, A., Smeaton, A.F.: Classifying sentiment in microblogs: is brevity an advantage is brevity an advantage? (2010)
11. Aceto, G., Ciuonzo, D., Montieri, A., Pescapé, A.: Multi-classification approaches for classifying mobile app traffic. J. Netw. Comput. Appl. **103**, 131–145 (2018)
12. Montieri, A., Ciuonzo, D., Aceto, G., Pescape, A.: Anonymity services Tor, I2P, JonDonym: classifying in the dark (web). IEEE Trans. Dependable Secure Comput. **17**, 662–675 (2018)
13. Montieri, A., Ciuonzo, D., Bovenzi, G., Persico, V., Pescapé, A.: A dive into the dark web: hierarchical traffic classification of anonymity tools. IEEE Trans. Netw. Sci. Eng. **7**, 1043–1054 (2019)
14. Devi, M.I., Rajaram, R., Selvakuberan, K.: Generating best features for web page classification. Webology, **5**(1), Article 52 (2008)
15. Gamon, M.: Sentiment classification on customer feedback data: noisy data, large feature vectors, and the role of linguistic analysis (2014)
16. Go, A., Bhayani, R., Huang, L.: Twitter sentiment classification using distant supervision. Technical report, Stanford (2009)
17. Blei, D., Lafferty, J.: Topic models. In: Text Mining: Classification, Clustering, and Applications, p. 10 (2015)
18. Pouliquen, B., Steinberger, R., Best, C.: Automatic detection of quotations in multilingual news (2017)
19. Uddin, M.F., Rizvi, S., Razaque, A.: Proposing logical table constructs for enhanced machine learning process. IEEE Access **6**, 47751–47769 (2018)
20. Almi'ani, M., Ghazleh, A.A., Al-Rahayfeh, A., Razaque, A.: Intelligent intrusion detection system using clustered self organized map. In: 2018 Fifth International Conference on Software Defined Systems (SDS), pp. 138–144. IEEE (2018)
21. Kolk, R., Razaque, A.: Scalable and energy efficient computer vision for text translation. In: 2016 IEEE Long Island Systems, Applications and Technology Conference (LISAT), pp. 1–6. IEEE (2016)

Signal and Bioinformatic Processing

A Large-Scale Dataset for Hate Speech Detection on Vietnamese Social Media Texts

Son T. Luu[1,2(✉)], Kiet Van Nguyen[1,2], and Ngan Luu-Thuy Nguyen[1,2]

[1] University of Information Technology, Ho Chi Minh City, Vietnam
{sonlt,kietnv,ngannlt}@uit.edu.vn
[2] Vietnam National University, Ho Chi Minh City, Vietnam

Abstract. In recent years, Vietnam witnesses the mass development of social network users on different social platforms such as Facebook, Youtube, Instagram, and Tiktok. On social media, hate speech has become a critical problem for social network users. To solve this problem, we introduce the ViHSD - a human-annotated dataset for automatically detecting hate speech on the social network. This dataset contains over 30,000 comments, each comment in the dataset has one of three labels: CLEAN, OFFENSIVE, or HATE. Besides, we introduce the data creation process for annotating and evaluating the quality of the dataset. Finally, we evaluate the dataset by deep learning and transformer models.

Keywords: Hate speech detection · Social media texts · Machine learning · Text classification

1 Introduction

There are approximately 70 million Internet users in Vietnam, and most of them are familiar with Facebook and Youtube. Nearly 70% of total Vietnamese people use Facebook, and spend an average of 2.5 h per day on it [24]. On social network, hate easily appears and spread. According to Kang and Hall [21], hate-speech does not reveal itself as hatred. It is just a mechanism to protect an individual's identity and realm from the others. Hate leads to the destruction of humanity, isolating people, and debilitating society. Within the development of social network sites, the hate appears on social media as hate-speech comments, hate-speech posts, or messages, and it spreads too fast. The existence of hate speech makes the social networking spaces toxic, threatens social network users, and bewilders the community.

The automated hate speech detection task is categorized as the supervised learning task, specifically closed to the sentiment analysis task[26]. There are several state-of-the-art approaches such as deep learning and transformer models for sentiment analysis. However, to be able to make experiment on hate speech

© Springer Nature Switzerland AG 2021
H. Fujita et al. (Eds.): IEA/AIE 2021, LNAI 12798, pp. 415–426, 2021.
https://doi.org/10.1007/978-3-030-79457-6_35

detection task, the datasets, especially large-scale datasets, play an important role. To handle this, we introduce ViHSD - a large-scale dataset used for automatically hate speech detection on Vietnamese social media texts to overcome the hate-speech problem on social networks. Then, we present the annotation process for our dataset and the method to ensure the quality of annotators. Finally, we evaluate our dataset on SOTA models and analyze the obtained empirical results to explore the advantages and disadvantages of the models on the dataset.

The content of the paper is structured as follows. Section 2 takes an overview on current researching for hate-speech detection. Section 3 shows statistical figures about our dataset as well as our annotation procedure. Section 4 presents the classification models applied for our dataset to solve the hate-speech detection problem. Section 5 describes our experiments on the dataset and the analytical results. Finally, Sect. 6 concludes and proposes future works.

2   Related Works

In English as well as other languages, there are many datasets constructed for hate speech detection. We divided them into two categories: flat labels and hierarchical labels. According to Cerri et al. [7], flat labels are treated as no relation between different labels. In contrast, hierarchical labels has a hierarchical structure which one or more labels can have sub-labels, or being grouped in super-labels. Besides, Hatebase [27] and Hurtlex [6] are two abusive words sets used for lexicon-based approaching for the hate speech detection problem.

For flat labels, we introduce two typical and large-scale datasets in English. The first dataset is provided by Waesem and Hovy [30], which contains 17,000 tweets from Twitter and has three labels: racism, sexism, and none. The second dataset is provided by Davidson et al. [12], which contains 25,000 tweets from Twitter and also has three labels including: hate, offensive, and neither. Apart from English, there are other datasets in other languages such as: Arabic [2], and Indonesian [3].

For hierarchical labels datasets, Zampieri et al. [32] provide a multi-labelled dataset for predicting offensive posts on social media in English. This dataset serves two tasks: group-directed attacking and person-directed attacking, in which each task has binary labels. Another similar multi-labelled dataset in English are provided by Basile et al. [5] in SemEval Task 5 (2019). Other multi-labelled datasets in other non-English languages are also constructed and available such as: Portuguese [17], Spanish [16], and Indonesian [19]. Besides, multi-lingual hate speech corpora are also constructed such as hatEval with English and Spanish [5] and CONAN with English, French, and Italian [9].

The VLSP-HSD dataset provided by Vu et al. [29] is a dataset used for the VLSP 2019 shared task about Hate speech detection on Vietnamese language[1]. However, the authors did not mention the annotation process and the method for evaluating the quality of the dataset. Besides, on the hate speech detection problem, many state-of-the-art models give optimistic results such as deep

---

[1] https://www.aivivn.com/contests/8.

learning models [4] and transformer language models [20]. Those models require large-scale annotated datasets, which is a challenge for low-resource languages like Vietnamese. Moreover, current researches about hate speech detection do not focus on analyzing about the sentiment aspect of Vietnamese hate speech language. Those ones are our motivation to create a new dataset called ViHSD for Vietnamese with strict annotation guidelines and evaluation process to measure inter-annotator agreement between annotators.

3 Dataset Creation

3.1 Data Preparation

We collect users' comments about entertainment, celebrities, social issues, and politics from different Vietnamese Facebook pages and YouTube videos. We select Facebook pages and YouTube channels that have a high-interactive rate, and do not restrict comments. After collected data, we remove the name entities from the comments in order to maintain the anonymity.

3.2 Annotation Guidelines

The ViHSD dataset contains three labels: HATE, OFFENSIVE, and CLEAN. Each annotator assigns one label for each comment in the dataset. In the ViHSD dataset, we have two labels denoting for hate speech comments, and one label denoting for normal comments. The detailed meanings about three labels and examples for each label are described in Table 1.

Practically, many comments in the dataset are written in informal form. Comments often contain abbreviation such as *M.n* (English: Everyone), *mik* (English: us) in **Comment 1** and *Dm* (English: f*ck) in **Comment 2**, and slangs such as *chịch* (English: f*ck), *cái lol* (English: p*ssy) in **Comment 2**. Besides, comments has the figurative meaning instead of explicit meaning. For example, the word: *lũ quan ngại* (English: dummy pessimists) in **Comment 3** is usually used by many Vietnamese Facebook users on social media platform to mention a group of people who always think pessimistically and posting negative contents.

3.3 Data Creation Process

Our annotation process contains two main phases as described in Fig. 1. The first one is the training phase, which annotators are given a detailed guidelines, and annotate for a sample of data after reading carefully. Then we compute the inter-annotator agreement by Cohen Kappa index (κ) [10]. If the inter-annotators agreement not good enough, we will re-train the annotator, and re-update the annotation guidelines if necessary. After all annotators are well-trained, we go to annotation phase. Our annotation phase is inspired from the IEEE peer review process of articles [15]. Two annotators annotate the entire dataset. If there are any different labels between two annotators, we let the third annotators annotate

Table 1. Annotation guidelines for annotating Vietnamese comments in the Hate Speech Detection task.

Label	Description	Example
CLEAN	The comments have no harassment at all.	**Comment 1**: M.n ơi cho mik hỏi mik theo dõi cô mà mik hk pít cô là con gái thiệt hả m.n (*English*: Hey everyone! Is she a truly girl?) (This comment is thoroughly clean, in which there are no bad words or profane language, and does not attack anyone)
OFFENSIVE	The comments contain harassment contents, even profanity words, but do not attack any specific object.	**Comment 2**: Đồ khùng (*English*: Madness) (This comment has offensive word *"khùng"*. Nevertheless, it does not contain any word that aims to a person or a group. In addition, *"khùng"* is also a slang, which means mad)
HATE	The comments have harassment and abusive contents and directly aim at an individual or a group of people based on their characteristics, religion, and nationality. Some exceptional cases happened with the HATE label: **Case 1**: The comments have offensive words and attack a specific object such as an individual, a community, a nation, or a religion. This case is easy to identify hate speech. **Case 2**: The comments have racism, harassment, and hateful meaning, however, does not contain explicit words. **Case 3**: The comments have racism, harassment, and hateful meaning, but showed as figurative meaning. To identify this comment, users need to have particular knowledge about social.	**Comment 3**: Dành cho lũ quan ngại (*English: This is for those dummy pessimists*) (This comment contains a phrase, which is underlined, mentions to a group of people with bad meaning) **Comment 4**: Dm Có a mới không ổn. Mày rình mày chịch riết ổn cái lol (*English: F*ck you. I am not fine. You are fine why you're making sex ?*) (This comments contained many of profanities, which are underlined. Besides, it contains personal pronoun "Mày", which aims to a specific person) **Comment 3**: Ở đấy ngột ngạt quá thì đưa nó qua <LOC> cho nó thoáng mát (*English: If this place is so stifling and not suitable for bitch like you, why don't you choose <LOC>? *) (This comment has the phrase <LOC> mentioned to a specific location, which has racism meaning. However, this comment does not has any bad words at all)

those labels. The fourth annotators annotate if all three annotators are disagreed. The final label are defined by Major voting. By this way, we guaranteed that each comment is annotated by one label and the objectivity for each comment. Therefore, the total time spent on annotating is less than four annotators doing with the same time.

3.4   Dataset Evalutation and Discussion

We randomly take 202 comments from the dataset and give them to four different annotators, denoted as A1, A2, A3 and A4, for annotating. Table 2 shows the inter-annotator agreement between each pair of annotators. Then, we compute

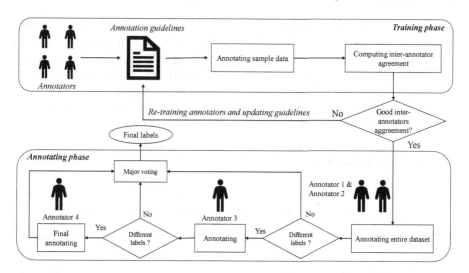

Fig. 1. Data annotation process for the ViHSD dataset. According to Eugenio [14], $\kappa > 0.5$ is acceptable.

the average inter-annotator agreement. The final inter-annotator agreement for the dataset is $\kappa = 0.52$.

Table 2. The confusion matrix between annotators in a set of 202 comments computed by Cohen Kappa index (κ).

	A1	A2	A3	A4
A1	–	0.46	0.51	0.65
A2	–	–	0.47	0.53
A3	–	–	–	0.55
A4	–	–	–	–

The ViHSD dataset was crawled from the social network so they had many abbreviations, informal words, slangs, and figurative meaning. Therefore, it confuses annotators. For example, the **Comment 1** contains the phrase: *mik*, which mean mình (English: I), and the **Comment 4** in Table 1 has the profane word *Dm* (English: m*ther f**ker). Assume that two annotators assign label for **Comment 4**, and it contains the word *Dm* written in abbreviation form. The first annotator knew about this word before, thus he/she annotates this comment as hate. The second annotator instead, annotates this comment as clean because he/she do not understand that word. The next example is the phrase *lũ quan ngại* (English: dummy pessimists) in the **Comment 3** in Table 1. Two annotators assign label for **Comment 3**. The first annotator does not understand the real meaning of that phase, thus he/she marks this comment as clean. In contrast, the second annotator knows what is the real meaning of this word (See Sect. 3.2 for the meaning of that phase) so he/she knows the abusive meaning of **Comment 3** and annotates it as hate. Although the guidelines have clearly definition about the CLEAN, OFFENSIVE, and HATE labels, the annotation process is mostly impacted by the knowledge and subjective of annotators. Thus, it is necessary to re-train annotators and improve the guidelines continuously to increase the quality of annotators and the inter-annotator agreement.

3.5 Dataset Overview

Table 3. Several examples extracted from the ViHSD dataset.

#	Comments	Label
1	Nhanh thực sự (*English: It is really fast*)	clean
2	Đm chứ biết làm gì (*English: How f*ck damn to do that!*)	offensive
3	Nó học cách của thằng anh nó đó, hèn, khốn nạn (*English: He is coward and bastard likes his brother*)	hate
4	<person name> người ư? sinh vật hạ đẳng chứ ngươi ai lam thế (*English: <person name> person ? It is a inferior animal. Human don't do that*)	hate
5	Đm vcl (*English: God damn it!!*)	offensive

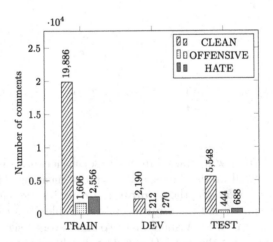

Fig. 2. The distributions of three labels on the train, dev, and test sets.

The ViHSD contains 33,400 comments. Each one was labelled as CLEAN (0), OFFENSIVE (1), and HATE (2). Table 3 displays some examples from the ViHSD dataset. Then we divided our dataset into training (train), development (dev), and test sets, respectively, with proportion: 7-1-2. Figure 2 describes the distribution of data on three labels on those sets. According to Fig. 2, the distribution of data labels on the training, development, and test sets are the same, and the data are skewed to the CLEAN label.

4   Baseline Models

The problem of text classification is defined according to Aggarwal and Zhai [1] as given a set of training texts as training data $D = \{X_1, X_2, ..., X_n\}$, in which each $X_i \in D$ has one of the label in the label set $\{1..k\}$. The training data is used to build the classification model. Then, for unlabeled data coming, the classification model predicts the label for it. In this section, we introduce two approaches for constructing prediction models on the ViHSD dataset.

4.1   Deep Neural Network Models (DNN Models)

Convolutional Neural Network (CNN) uses particular layers called the CONV layer for extracting local features in the image [23]. However, although invented for computer vision, CNN can also be applied to Natural Language Processing (NLP), in which a filter W relevant to a window of h words [22]. Besides, the pre-trained word vectors also influence the performance of the CNN model [22]. Besides, Gated Recurrent Unit (GRU) is a variant of the RNN network. It contains two recurrent networks: encoding sequences of texts into a fixed-length word vector representation, and another for decoding word vector representation back to raw input [8].

We implement the Text-CNN and the GRU models, and evaluate them on the ViHSD dataset with the *fasttext*[2] pre-trained word embedding of 157 different languages provided by Grave et al. [18]. This embedding transforms a word into a 300 dimension vector.

4.2   Transformer Models

The transformer model [28] is a deep neural network architecture based entirely on the attention mechanism, replaced the recurrent layers in auto encoder-decoder architectures with special called multi-head self-attention layers. Yang et al. [31] found that the transformer blocks improved the performance of the classification model. In this paper, we implement BERT[13] - the SOTA transformer model with multilingual pre-training[3] such as bert-base-multilingual-uncased (m-BERT uncased) and bert-base-multilingual-cased (m-BERT cased), Distil-BERT [25] - a lighter but faster variant of BERT model with multilingual cased pre-trained model[4], and XLM-R[11] - a cross-lingual language model with xlm-roberta-base pre-trained[5]. Those multilingual pre-trained models are trained on various of languages including Vietnamese.

---

[2] https://fasttext.cc/docs/en/crawl-vectors.html.

[3] https://github.com/google-research/bert/blob/master/multilingual.md.

[4] https://huggingface.co/distilbert-base-multilingual-cased.

[5] https://huggingface.co/xlm-roberta-base.

5   Experiment

5.1   Experiment Settings

First of all, we pre-process our dataset as belows: (1) Word-segmentation texts into words by the pyvi tool[6], (2) Removing stopwords[7], (3) Changing all texts into lower cases[8], and (4) Removing special characters such as hashtags, urls, and mention tags.

Next, we run the Text-CNN model with 50 epochs, batch size equal to 256, sequence length equal to 100, and the dropout ratio is 0.5. Our model uses 2D Convolution Layer with 32 filters and size 2, 3, 5, respectively. Then, we run the GRU model with 50 epochs, sequence length equal to 100, the dropout ratio is 0.5, and the bidirectional GRU layer. We use the Adam optimizer for both Text-CNN and GRU. Finally, we implement transformer models includes BERT, XLM-R, and DistilBERT with the batch size equal to 16 for both training and evaluation, 4 epochs, sequence length equal to 100, and manual seed equal to 4.

5.2   Experiment Results

Table 4 illustrates the results of deep neural models and transformer models on the ViHSD dataset. The results are measured by Accuracy and macro-averaged F1-score. According to Table 4, Text-CNN achieves 86.69% in accuracy and 61.11% in F1-score, which is better than GRU. Transformer models such as BERT, XLM-R, and DistilBERT give better results than deep neural models in F1-score. The BERT with bert-base-multilingual-cased model (m-bert cased) obtained best result in both Accuracy and F1-score with 86.88% and 62.69% respectively on the ViHSD dataset.

Table 4. Empirical results of baseline models on the test set

	Model	Pre-trained model	Accuracy (%)	F1-macro (%)
DNN models	Text CNN	fastText	86.69	61.11
	GRU	fastText	85.41	60.47
Transformer models	BERT	bert-base-multilingual-uncased	86.60	62.38
		bert-base-multilingual-cased	**86.88**	**62.69**
	XLM-R	xlm-roberta-based	86.12	61.28
	DistilBERT	distilbert-base-multilingual-cased	86.22	62.42

Overall, the performance of transformer models are better than deep neural models, indicating the power of BERT and its variants on text classification task, especially on hate speech detection even if they were trained on various languages. Additionally, there is a large gap between the accuracy score and the F1-score, which caused by the imbalance in the dataset, as described in Sect. 3.

---

[6] https://pypi.org/project/pyvi/.

[7] List Vienamese stopwords https://github.com/stopwords/vietnamese-stopwords.

[8] We do not lower case texts with cased pre-trained transformer models.

5.3 Error Analysis

Figure 3 shows the confusion matrix of the m-BERT cased model. Most of the offensive comments in the dataset are predicted as clean comments. Besides, Table 5 shows incorrect predictions by the m-BERT cased model. The comments number 1, 2, and 3 had many special words, which are only used on the social network such as: *"dell"*, *"coin card"*, and *"éo"*. These special words make those comments had wrong predicting labels, misclassified from offensive labels to clean labels. Moreover, the comments number 4 and 5 have profane words and are written in abbreviation form and teen codes such as *"cc"*, *"lol"*. Specifically, for the fifth comments, in which *"3"* represents for *"father"* in English, combined which other bad words such as: *"Cc"* - profane word and *"m"* - represents for *"you"* in English. Generally, the fifth comment has bad meaning (see Table 5 for the English meaning) thus it is the hate speech comment. However, the classification model predicts that comment as an offensive label because it cannot identify the target objects and the profane words written in irregular form.

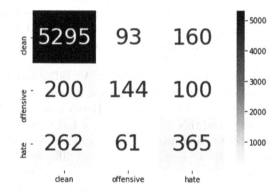

Fig. 3. Confusion matrix of the m-BERT cased model on the ViHSD dataset

In general, the wrong prediction samples and most of the ViHSD dataset comments are written with irregular words, abbreviations, slangs, and teencodes. Therefore, in the pre-processing process, we need to handle those characteristic to enhance the performance of classification models. For abbreviations and slangs, we can build a Vietnamese slangs dictionary for slangs replacement and a Vietnamese abbreviation dictionary to replace the abbreviations in the comments. Besides, for words that are not found in mainstream media, we can try to normalize them to the regular words. For example, words like *gìiiiii*, *ừmmmm* should be normalized to *gì* (what) and *ừ* (ok). In addition, the emoji icons are also a polarity feature to define whether a comment is negative or positive, which can support for detecting the hate and offensive content in the comments.

Table 5. Wrong prediction samples in the ViHSD dataset

#	Comments	True	Predict
1	coin card :3 (*English: F*ck d*ck*)	1	0
2	\<person name\> dell hiểu kiểu gì :)) (*English: I do not f*cking understand why*)	1	0
3	Éo thích thì biến đi thọc con mắt chóng cái tai lên xem làm ghì (*English: Get out, damn! Prick your eyes if you don't care.*)	1	0
4	\<person name\>chửi cc (*English: f*ck you*)	2	1
5	Cc 3 m (*English: Like your dad's d*ck*)	2	1

6 Conclusion

We constructed a large-scale dataset called the ViHSD dataset for hate speech detection on Vietnamese social media texts. The dataset contains 33,400 comments annotated by humans and achieves 62.69% by the Macro F1-score with the BERT model. We also proposed an annotation process to save time for data annotating.

The current inter-annotator agreement of the ViHSD dataset is just in moderate level. Therefore, our next studies focus on improving the quality of the dataset based on the data annotation process. Besides, the best baseline model on the dataset is 62.69%, and this is a challenge for future researches to improve the performance of classification models for Vietnamese hate-speech detection task. From the error analysis, we found that it is difficult to detect the hate speech on Vietnamese social media texts due to their characteristics. Hence, we will improve the pre-processing technique for social media texts such as lexicon-based approach for teen codes and normalizing acronyms on next studies to increase the performance of this task.

References

1. Aggarwal, C.C., Zhai, C.: A survey of text classification algorithms. In: Aggarwal, C., Zhai, C. (eds.) Mining Text Data, pp. 163–222. Springer, Boston (2012). https://doi.org/10.1007/978-1-4614-3223-4_6
2. Albadi, N., Kurdi, M., Mishra, S.: Are they our brothers? Analysis and detection of religious hate speech in the Arabic Twittersphere. In: IEEE/ACM International Conference on Advances in Social Networks Analysis and Mining (ASONAM), pp. 69–76 (2018)
3. Alfina, I., Mulia, R., Fanany, M.I., Ekanata, Y.: Hate speech detection in the Indonesian language: a dataset and preliminary study. In: 2017 International Conference on Advanced Computer Science and Information Systems (ICACSIS), pp. 233–238 (2017)

4. Badjatiya, P., Gupta, S., Gupta, M., Varma, V.: Deep learning for hate speech detection in tweets. In: WWW 2017 Companion, International World Wide Web Conferences Steering Committee, Republic and Canton of Geneva, CHE, pp. 759–760 (2017)
5. Basile, V., et al.: SemEval-2019 task 5: multilingual detection of hate speech against immigrants and women in twitter. In: Proceedings of the 13th International Workshop on Semantic Evaluation. Association for Computational Linguistics, Minneapolis (2019)
6. Bassignana, E., Basile, V., Patti, V.: Hurtlex: a multilingual lexicon of words to hurt. In: CLiC-it (2018)
7. Cerri, R., Barros, R.C., de Carvalho, A.C.: Hierarchical multi-label classification using local neural networks. J. Comput. Syst. Sci. **80**(1), 39–56 (2014)
8. Cho, K., et al.: Learning phrase representations using RNN encoder-decoder for statistical machine translation. In: Proceedings of the 2014 Conference on Empirical Methods in Natural Language Processing (EMNLP), pp. 1724–1734. Association for Computational Linguistics, Doha (2014)
9. Chung, Y.L., Kuzmenko, E., Tekiroglu, S.S., Guerini, M.: CONAN - COunter NArratives through nichesourcing: a multilingual dataset of responses to fight online hate speech. In: Proceedings of the 57th Annual Meeting of the Association for Computational Linguistics. Association for Computational Linguistics, Florence (2019)
10. Cohen, J.: A coefficient of agreement for nominal scales. Educ. Psychol. Measur. **20**(1), 37–46 (1960)
11. Conneau, A., et al.: Unsupervised cross-lingual representation learning at scale. In: Proceedings of the 58th Annual Meeting of the Association for Computational Linguistics, pp. 8440–8451. Association for Computational Linguistics, Online (2020)
12. Davidson, T., Warmsley, D., Macy, M., Weber, I.: Automated hate speech detection and the problem of offensive language (2017)
13. Devlin, J., Chang, M.W., Lee, K., Toutanova, K.: BERT: pre-training of deep bidirectional transformers for language understanding. In: Proceedings of the 2019 Conference of the North American Chapter of the Association for Computational Linguistics: Human Language Technologies, vol. 1 (Long and Short Papers). Association for Computational Linguistics, Minneapolis (2019)
14. Di Eugenio, B.: On the usage of kappa to evaluate agreement on coding tasks. In: Proceedings of the Second International Conference on Language Resources and Evaluation (LREC 2000). European Language Resources Association (ELRA), Athens (2000)
15. El-Hawary, M.E.: What happens after i submit an article? [Editorial]. IEEE Syst. Man Cybern. Mag. **3**(2), 3–42 (2017)
16. Fersini, E., Rosso, P., Anzovino, M.: Overview of the task on automatic misogyny identification at ibereval 2018. In: IberEval@ SEPLN 2150, pp. 214–228 (2018)
17. Fortuna, P., Rocha da Silva, J., Soler-Company, J., Wanner, L., Nunes, S.: A hierarchically-labeled Portuguese hate speech dataset. In: Proceedings of the Third Workshop on Abusive Language Online, pp. 94–104. Association for Computational Linguistics, Florence (2019)
18. Grave, E., Bojanowski, P., Gupta, P., Joulin, A., Mikolov, T.: Learning word vectors for 157 languages. In: Proceedings of the Eleventh International Conference on Language Resources and Evaluation (LREC 2018). European Language Resources Association (ELRA), Miyazaki (2018)

19. Ibrohim, M.O., Budi, I.: Multi-label hate speech and abusive language detection in Indonesian Twitter. In: Proceedings of the Third Workshop on Abusive Language Online. Association for Computational Linguistics, Florence (2019)

20. Isaksen, V., Gambäck, B.: Using transfer-based language models to detect hateful and offensive language online. In: Proceedings of the Fourth Workshop on Online Abuse and Harms. Association for Computational Linguistics, Online (2020)

21. Kang, M., Hall, P.: Hate Speech in Asia and Europe: Beyond Hate and Fear. Taylor & Francis Group, Routledge Contemporary Asia (2020)

22. Kim, Y.: Convolutional neural networks for sentence classification. In: Proceedings of the 2014 Conference on Empirical Methods in Natural Language Processing (EMNLP). Association for Computational Linguistics, Doha (2014)

23. Lecun, Y., Bottou, L., Bengio, Y., Haffner, P.: Gradient-based learning applied to document recognition. Proc. IEEE **86**(11), 2278–2324 (1998)

24. Nguyen, T.N., McDonald, M., Nguyen, T.H.T., McCauley, B.: Gender relations and social media: a grounded theory inquiry of young Vietnamese women's self-presentations on Facebook. Gender Technol. Dev. **24**, 1–20 (2020)

25. Sanh, V., Debut, L., Chaumond, J., Wolf, T.: DistilBERT, a distilled version of BERT: smaller, faster, cheaper and lighter (2020)

26. Schmidt, A., Wiegand, M.: A survey on hate speech detection using natural language processing. In: Proceedings of the Fifth International Workshop on Natural Language Processing for Social Media, pp. 1–10 (2017)

27. Tuckwood, C.: Hatebase: online database of hate speech. The Sentinal Project (2017). https://www.hatebase.org

28. Vaswani, A., et al.: Attention is all you need. In: Advances in Neural Information Processing Systems, pp. 5998–6008 (2017)

29. Vu, X.S., Vu, T., Tran, M.V., Le-Cong, T., Nguyen, H.T.M.: HSD shared task in VLSP campaign 2019: hate speech detection for social good. In: Proceedings of VLSP 2019 (2019)

30. Waseem, Z., Hovy, D.: Hateful symbols or hateful people? Predictive features for hate speech detection on Twitter. In: Proceedings of the NAACL Student Research Workshop, pp. 88–93. Association for Computational Linguistics, San Diego (2016)

31. Yang, X., Yang, L., Bi, R., Lin, H.: A comprehensive verification of transformer in text classification. In: Sun, M., Huang, X., Ji, H., Liu, Z., Liu, Y. (eds.) CCL 2019. LNCS (LNAI), vol. 11856, pp. 207–218. Springer, Cham (2019). https://doi.org/10.1007/978-3-030-32381-3_17

32. Zampieri, M., Malmasi, S., Nakov, P., Rosenthal, S., Farra, N., Kumar, R.: Predicting the type and target of offensive posts in social media. In: Proceedings of the 2019 Conference of the North American Chapter of the Association for Computational Linguistics: Human Language Technologies, vol. 1 (Long and Short Papers), Minneapolis, Minnesota (2019)

Determining 2-Optimality Consensus for DNA Structure

Dai Tho Dang[1,3]($\boxtimes$) (iD), Huyen Trang Phan[1] (iD), Ngoc Thanh Nguyen[2] (iD), and Dosam Hwang[1] (iD)

[1] Department of Computer Engineering, Yeungnam University, Gyeongsan 38541, Republic of Korea
daithodang@ynu.ac.kr, huyentrangtin@gmail.com, dshwang@yu.ac.kr
[2] Department of Applied Informatics, Faculty of Computer Science and Management, Wrocław University of Science and Technology, 50-370 Wrocław, Poland
Ngoc-Thanh.Nguyen@pwr.edu.pl
[3] Vietnam - Korea University of Information and Communication Technology, The University of Danang, Danang, Vietnam
ddtho@vku.udn.vn

Abstract. Strings are widely used to describe and store information in bioinformatics, such as DNA and proteins. The determination of a consensus for a string profile plays an important role in bioinformatics. There are several postulates to determine consensus, among which postulate 1-Optimality is the most popular. A consensus that satisfies this postulate is the best representative of the profile. Another essential postulate is 2-Optimality. A consensus satisfying postulate 2-Optimality is the best representative, and the distances between it and the profile members are more uniform than those satisfying the postulate 1-Optimality. However, the determination of the 2-Optimality consensus has not been examined in bioinformatics because of its complexity. It is meaningful to investigate this type of consensus. Thus, this study focuses on formulating and proposing algorithms to determine the 2-Optimality consensus for DNA motif profiles.

Keywords: Algorithm · Consensus · DNA · Optimization

1 Introduction

DNA contains the instructions required for organisms to develop, grow, survive, and reproduce. The identification of motifs is becoming crucial because of their biological functions. Motifs are short and constant in size and frequently repeat in DNA sequences [1]. The motifs are never the same as the conserved sequences because several sequence variabilities are present for a single motif. The determination of a DNA motif often includes founding a set of motif candidates and determining their consensus [2]. For example, the Rox1 transcription factor binds at least eight sites in three genes in the Saccharomyces cerevisiae genome [3]. The motifs and consensus of the eight motifs are shown in Fig. 1. Another example is the five motifs of sequences from the E. coli 10 promoter region [4]. These motifs and their consensus are shown in Fig. 2.

© Springer Nature Switzerland AG 2021
H. Fujita et al. (Eds.): IEA/AIE 2021, LNAI 12798, pp. 427–438, 2021.
https://doi.org/10.1007/978-3-030-79457-6_36

In general, a string is understood as a sequence of characters from a finite alphabet Σ, and it is applied to describe and store information in bioinformatics. A DNA sequence is described as a string of characters from $\Sigma = \{A, C, T, G\}$. Each letter represents a standard amino acid [2, 5]. Several postulates have been proposed to determine a consensus. Among them, Postulates 1-Optimality and 2-Optimality play important roles [6]. The postulate 1-Optimality is widely used, and it demands the representative string to be as close as possible to the strings of the set. The 2-Optimality consensus is the best representative of the string profile [7].

	ATTGTT		
	CTGGTT		TATTAT
	ATTGTT		TACTTT
Motifs:	ATTGTT	Motifs:	CACAGT
	ATTGTT		TAGTCT
	ATTGTT		TAACTT
	ATTGTT		TACTTT
	ATTGTT		
Consensus:	ATTGTT	Consensus:	TACTTT

Fig. 1. Motifs and consensus of the ROX1 binding sites.

Fig. 2. Motifs and the consensus from the E.coli 10.

In the Consensus theory [6, 8], the author introduced the postulate 2-Optimality for determining a consensus. This postulate asserts that the sum of the squared distances between the consensus and the profile members is minimal. The consensus fulfilling the postulate 2-Optimality is the best representative of the profile, and the distances between it and profile elements are more uniform than those fulfilling the postulate 1-Optimality [9]. The following is an example illustrating the difference between the 1-Optimality consensus and 2-Optimality consensus of a string profile.

Consider a DNA motif profile $S = \{s_1, s_2, s_3\}$, where $s_1 = $ "ACCAACC", $s_2 = $ "ATCAGAG", and $s_3 = $ "ACCATGA". If the consensus is generated by the postulate 1-Optimality postulate, then $s = $ "ACCAACC" can be determined. The distances from s to s_1, s_2, and s_3 are 0, 4, and 3, respectively. If the consensus is generated by the postulate 2-Optimality, then $s = $ "ACCAGCA" can be determined. The distances from s to s_1, s_2, and s_3 are 2, 3, and 2, respectively. Notably, the 2-Optimality consensus is neither too far from profile elements nor "harmful" to any of them because the distances to the 2-Optimality consensus are more uniform than those to 1-Optimality consensus [6]. The sum of the squared distances of the 1-Optimality consensus and 2-Optimality consensus are 25 and 17, respectively.

However, the 2-Optimality consensus has not been investigated for a DNA motif profile. This study focuses on investigating the use of the postulate 2-Optimality consensus for a DNA motif profile. The main contributions of this study are as follows:

- We introduce a formal description for determining the 2-Optimality consensus for a DNA motif profile.
- We propose three algorithms for determining the 2-Optimality consensus for a DNA motif profile: the BLDC, ELDC, and HDC algorithms. The consensus quality of these algorithms was high.

The determination of a DNA motif often includes (1) founding a set of motif candidates and (2) determining their consensus [2]. This study focuses on (2). This study can support some needful bioinformatics tasks, such as string selection, motif determination, and comparison problems [5].

The remainder of this paper is organized as follows. Section 2 introduces the related studies. The problem formation and the proposed algorithms are described in Sect. 3. In Sect. 4, the experimental results and their evaluation are presented. The conclusions are presented in Sect. 5.

2 Related Works

Consensus problems have been of interest in several fields, including economics, computer science, and bioinformatics [2, 10]. Postulates have been proposed for consensus choice functions: Unanimity, consistency, Condorcet consistency, simplification, general consistency, proportion, reliability, quasi-unanimity, 1-Optimality, and 2-Optimality [6]. No consensus choice function meets all these axioms. If one consensus satisfies the postulates 1-Optimality or 2-Optimality, it satisfies most postulates [6].

In bioinformatics, consensus problems have been investigated for a long time. Different problems regarding the determination of a consensus for a string profile have been proposed, such as minimizing the sum of distances from profile elements to the consensus and minimizing the longest distance (or radius) from profile elements to the consensus [11]. The determination of a DNA motif often includes determining a set of motif candidates and their consensus [2]. There are three methods for determining motifs in DNA: enumeration, probabilistic, and evolutionary approaches [12].

The YMF algorithm is based on the enumeration approach. It identifies short motifs with a small number of degenerate positions in yeast genomes using consensus representation. The YMF algorithm lists all motifs in the search space and calculates the z-score to produce motifs with the greatest z-scores [13, 14]. The CisFinder algorithm uses the word clustering method to detect motifs. First, it estimates position frequency Position Frequency Matrices directly from the counts of n-mer words, with and without gaps. Second, the Position Frequency Matrices are extended over gaps and flanking regions and clustered to generate the non-redundant sets of motifs [15].

The GA-DPAF algorithm is the evolutionary approach. It applies a multi-objective fitness function, mutation operations, and a two-point crossover. The mutation operator is applied using a Position Frequency Matrix to reserve completely conserved positions. The solutions required for the population pool were optimized by the Gibbs sampling method [16]. In [17], the authors presented a motif finding algorithm based on ant colony optimization called MFACO. This algorithm uses a consensus score to determine motifs and information content to locate their appearances (binding sites) in each DNA sequence.

The EM algorithm is based on the deterministic approach. The algorithm includes two main stages. The first stage is "Expectation" step, and the second stage is "Maximization" step. The expectation step evaluates the values of certain sets of unknowns based on a set of parameters. The maximization step uses the evaluated values to refine the parameters over various iterations [18]. Many algorithms have been developed based on the EM algorithm, such as the MEME algorithm [12]. The MEME is a popular algorithm for recognizing motifs. First, the MEME algorithm determines the initial motif. Second, it utilizes expectation and maximization steps to improve the motif until the Position-specific Weight Matrices values do not improve, or the pre-selected number of iterations is reached. The MEME algorithm begins from a single site, that is, k-mer (specified or random) and estimates the motif model (position-specific weight matrices) [12, 18].

The postulate 1-Optimality is used in three approaches for determining the consensus [5, 12–20], but the postulate 2-Optimality has not been investigated.

Local search algorithms and genetic algorithms are often used to solve NP-hard optimization problems [21, 22]. Local search can be used for problems that can be formulated as determining a solution that minimizes a criterion among several candidate solutions. It proceeds from one solution to another in the search space by applying local changes until a deemed optimal solution is found, or a time-bound is elapsed [23].

The genetic algorithm is inspired by natural selection. It is a population-based search algorithm that utilizes the concept of survival of the fittest [24, 25]. The new populations are produced by the iterative use of genetic operators on individuals present in the population. The individual, selection, crossover, mutation, and fitness function are the key elements of this algorithm [27]. The classical genetic algorithm has been modified to improve its performance and adapt to particular problems [26]. Hybrid algorithms based on genetics have been developed to solve NP-hard problems [27].

3 Problem Formation and Our Proposed Solution

3.1 Problem Formation

There are four different types of nucleotides in DNA: adenine (A), guanine (G), cytosine (C), and thymine (T). The length of the motifs is a short constant, from 10 to 25 [1]. We used integers 0, 1, 2, and 3 to encode four nucleotide bases. The mapping from nucleotide bases to the integer is represented as A-0, C-1, G-2, and T-3.

Let $\Sigma = \{0, 1, 2, 3\}$ and U denote a finite set of all vectors over Σ with length m where $10 \leq m \leq 25$. Thus, the set U contains 4^m elements. For example, if $m = 5$, then $card(U) = 4^{15} = 1073741824$.

Definition 1. *Let s_1, $s_2 \in U$, distance between vector s_1 and vector s_2 is defined as*

$$\mu(s_1, s_2) = \sum_{j=1}^{m} \theta\left(s_1^j, s_2^j\right)$$

where s_1^j and s_2^j denote the value at position j in vectors s_1 and s_2, and

$$\theta(s_1^j, s_2^j) = \begin{cases} 1 & \text{if } s_1^j \neq s_2^j \\ 0 & \text{if } s_1^j = s_2^j \end{cases}$$

Definition 2. *Let s_1, $s_2 \in U$, the squared distance between s_1 and s_2 is defined as*

$$\mu^2(s_1, s_2) = \left(\sum_{j=1}^{m} \theta\left(s_1^j, s_2^j\right)\right)^2$$

Definition 3. *A DNA motif profile* $S \in \Pi(U)$ *is defined as*

$$S = \{s_1, s_2, \ldots, s_n\}$$

where each s_i $(i = 1, 2, \ldots, n)$ is a vector over Σ with the length m.

Definition 4. *For a DNA motif profile* $X \in \Pi(U)$, *the consensus of S is determined by the postulate 2-Optimality iff*

$$\mu^2(s, \ S) = \min_{y \in U} \mu^2(y, \ S)$$

where s is a 2-Optimality consensus of the DNA motif profile S.

Denote $f(s) = \mu^2(s, S)$. Determining the 2-Optimality consensus for a DNA motif profile S is a discrete optimization problem. The size of the search space is 4^m. The objective function is $f(s)$. We need to find a vector $s \in U$ that minimizes $f(s)$.

3.2 Problem Solution

The brute-force algorithm determines the optimal consensus. In this algorithm, first, a current consensus or current solution cur_C is randomly generated, and $\mu^2(cur\_C, S)$ is calculated. The algorithm then repeats the following tasks:

- For each member in the search space, the algorithm calculates the sum of the squared distances from it to profile S members.
- If this sum is smaller than $\mu^2(cur\_C, S)$, this member is considered as the current consensus cur_C.

The algorithm completes when all the members in the search space are considered. However, the brute-force algorithm is not practical because of its computational complexity.

We propose three algorithms to determine a 2-Optimality consensus for a DNA profile. First, a local search algorithm called BLDC is developed. Because the BLDC can get stuck in local optima, in the second algorithm, called the ELDC algorithm, we keep track of several initial candidates to overcome the local optima. Finally, the HDC algorithm is developed based on the genetic algorithm and the local search algorithm.

3.2.1 BLDC Algorithm

This section introduces a basic local search algorithm to determine the 2-Optimality consensus for a DNA profile. Local search is a widely used method for solving combinatorial optimization problems. The BLDC algorithm starts from a candidate solution and then iteratively moves to a neighbour solution.

First, this algorithm generates an initial solution (or an initial consensus) that is considered as the current consensus cur_C. In the next steps, the algorithm attempts to improve the current consensus. The algorithm sequentially determines the value of the components from the 1st component to the mth component of the consensus.

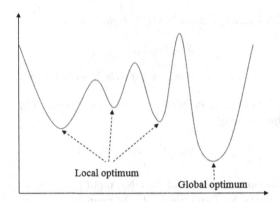

Fig. 3. Limitation of the BLDC algorithm.

For each component, its value is determined by changing the current value to three other values. For example, if the current value is 2, the component is changed to 0, 1, and 3. Subsequently, the values μ^2 of the current solution and the three new solutions are computed. The solution with the lowest value of μ^2 is chosen.

Finally, all components of the consensus are determined. The algorithm is presented as follows:

Algorithm1. BLDC

      Input: DNA profile $S = \{s_1, s_2, ..., s_n\}$
      Output: 2-Optimality consensus
    BEGIN
    1.   Creating an initial consensus cur_C randomly;
    2.   **for** i=1 **to** m **do**
    3.   **begin**
    4.   Creating three new consensuses by changing the value of the ith
             component of cur_C from its current value to three other values;
    5.   Computing μ^2 of three new candidates and cur_C;
    6.   Choosing the best one and it is considered as cur_C;
    7.   **end**
    END

The complexity of the BLDC algorithm $O(m^2 n)$. The result of this algorithm depends on one initial solution and might converge to a local optimum, instead of a global optimum. This problem is shown in Fig. 3.

3.2.2 ELDC Algorithm

The BLDC algorithm may become stuck at a local minimum. One efficient approach to improve the consensus quality is to restart the search from several initial consensuses and choose the best of the local optimum obtained from them. In other words, the proposed algorithm keeps track of p initial consensuses to avoid local optima.

For each initial consensus, the algorithm generates a final consensus. Finally, a set of p final consensuses was created. The consensus of profile S was the best solution

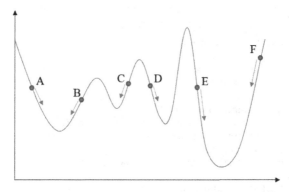

Fig. 4. Avoiding local optimum.

among p final consensuses. For example, in Fig. 4, if the initial consensus is set {A, B, C, E}, the algorithm can reach the global optimum. The ELDC algorithm is represented as follows:

Algorithm2. ELDC

    Input: DNA profile $S = \{s_1, s_2, ..., s_n\}$
    Output: 2-Optimality consensus
BEGIN
1. C={} ;
2. **for** i=1 **to** p **do**
3.   **begin**
4.   Creating an initial consensus cur_C randomly;
5.   **for** i=1 to m **do**
6.   **begin**
7.   Creating three new consensuses by changing the value of the ith
8.   component of cur_C from its current value to three other values;
9.   Computing μ^2 of them;
10.   Choosing the best one and it is considered as cur_C;
11.   **end**
12.   C=C U {cur_C};
13. **end**
14. Choosing the best one in C;
END

The computational complexity of the ELDC algorithm is $O(pm^2n)$.

3.2.3 HDC Algorithm

The HDC algorithm is developed by combining a genetic algorithm and a local search algorithm to find the 2-Optimality consensus for the DNA. This algorithm is presented as follows:

Algorithm3. HDC

Input: DNA profile S = $\{s_1, s_2, ..., s_n\}$
Output: 2-Optimality consensus
BEGIN
1. Initial population generation;
2. **while** (condition) **do**
3.   **begin;**
4.   Fitness computation: $\mu^2(x, S)$;
5.   Selection: tournament selection with a size of 3;
6.   Crossover: two-point crossover;
7.   Mutation: triple-value;
8.   Survivor selection: parents and children;
9.   **end**
10.   call BLDC (best individual);
END

- *Initial population:*

A set of individuals called a population is randomly generated. Each individual is a solution to the problem. Each individual is a vector over $\Sigma = \{0, 1, 2, 3\}$, and the length of each vector is m.

- *Fitness computation:*
Fitness function is defined as

$$f(s) = \min_{s \in U} \mu^2(s, S)$$

where $\mu^2(s, S)$ denotes the sum of the squared distances from an individual s to the members of S.

- *Selection:*
Selection pairs of individuals models for reproduction is selected based on their fitness values. Individuals with high fitness have more chances to survive and reproduce, whereas those with lower fitness are less likely to be selected. This study uses tournament selection with a size of three to choose the individuals in the reproduction process. Tournament selection is the most popular selection technique because of its efficiency. This method ensures the diversity of the population, as individuals have equal chances.

- *Crossover:*
Crossover creates the exchange of information between paired parents, thereby generating new pairs of offsprings. The crossover aims to produce offsprings for the next generation to explore a much broader region of the solution space. This study uses a two-point crossover operator, in which two points are randomly chosen on the parent chromosomes. Then, two offsprings are generated by the swap of genes between the two points.

- *Mutation:*
The mutation occurs after crossover is performed; it randomly changes a part of the offspring. The mutation is exploitative; it creates random small diversions, thereby staying near (in the area of) the parent. The mutation operator maintains the population

diversity to prevent the genetic algorithm from converging to the local optima. In this study, we a mutation operator called triple-value that randomly selects an individual and altering one individual gene with one of the other three bases. For example, 1 can be replaced by 0, 2, or 3 (Fig. 5).

The individual

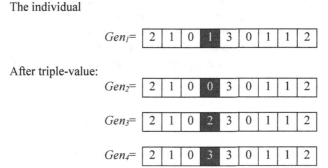

$Gen_1=$ | 2 | 1 | 0 | 1 | 3 | 0 | 1 | 1 | 2 |

After triple-value:

$Gen_2=$ | 2 | 1 | 0 | 0 | 3 | 0 | 1 | 1 | 2 |

$Gen_3=$ | 2 | 1 | 0 | 2 | 3 | 0 | 1 | 1 | 2 |

$Gen_4=$ | 2 | 1 | 0 | 3 | 3 | 0 | 1 | 1 | 2 |

Fig. 5. Triple-value operator.

Gen2, Gen3, and *Gen4* are created using the triple-value operator from *Gen1*. All are chosen to generate the next generation to maintain the diversity of the population.
– *Survivor selection:*
Survivor selection determines which individuals are to be kicked out and which are to be kept in the next generation. Different from the traditional genetic algorithm, the population is formed by mixing the parents and children. Then, it chooses the best chromosomes for the next generation.
– *Local search algorithm:*
The BLDC algorithm finds the best solution in the neighbours of the best individual in the final population. The best solution is also the consensus generated by the HDC algorithm.

The computational complexity of the HDC algorithm is $O(gm^2n)$, where g denotes the number of generations, n denotes the population size, and n denotes the length of individuals or vectors.

4   Experiments and Evaluation

In this section, the consensus qualities of the proposed algorithms are investigated. The dataset was created from https://www.bioinformatics.org. The length of the elements was 15, and the size of the DNA profile was 200. The significance level was set to 0.05 ($\alpha = 0.05$).
The optimal consensus was generated using the brute-force algorithm. The quality of the consensus generated by the heuristic algorithm was determined based on the optimal consensus. This is calculated as follows:

$$Q_u = 1 - \frac{\left|\mu^2(s_*, S) - \mu^2(s_{opt}, S)\right|}{\mu^2(s_{opt}, S)} \tag{1}$$

where s_{opt} denotes the optimal consensus and s_* denotes the consensus of the proposed algorithm.

In the ELDC algorithm, the number of initial consensuses was set to 20.

In the HDC algorithm, the population size of the initial population was 20. The number of generations was 15. The number of selecting paired parents was 20, and the number of offspring was 40. After the mutation step, 120 individuals were generated. In the survivor selection step, the algorithm determined 20 individuals from 180 individuals to be kept in the next generation (parents, offsprings, and mutated offsprings).

We ran the BLDC, ELDC, and HDC algorithms on the dataset 20 times. Each time a consensus was generated, and its quality was computed using (1). The results are presented in Table 1.

Table 1. Consensus quality of the BLDC, ELDC, and HDC algorithms.

ORD	BLDC algorithm	ELDC algorithm	HDC algorithm
1	0.975	0.993	1.000
2	0.982	0.993	1.000
3	0.993	1.000	0.998
4	0.981	0.993	1.000
5	0.977	0.993	1.000
6	0.983	0.993	1.000
7	0.979	1.000	1.000
8	0.985	0.998	1.000
9	0.984	0.993	1.000
10	1.000	0.998	1.000
11	0.971	0.998	1.000
12	0.982	1.000	1.000
13	0.981	1.000	1.000
14	0.998	0.998	1.000
15	0.983	0.998	1.000
16	1.000	1.000	1.000
17	0.982	1.000	1.000
18	0.975	0.993	1.000
19	0.987	0.998	1.000
20	0.978	0.993	1.000

First, we used the Shapiro-Wilk test to determine the distribution of the three consensus quality samples. The *p-values* of these samples were smaller than the significance level (p-value was 0.03838, 0.0002, and 0.000000003 for the sample of the BLDC,

ELDC, and HDC algorithms, respectively). It implied that these samples did not come from a normal distribution.

The hypotheses to compare the consensus quality of these algorithms were presented as follows:

- Hypothesis H_0: The difference in the consensus quality of the BLDC, ELDC, and HDC algorithms is not significant.
- Hypothesis H_1: The difference in the consensus quality of the BLDC, ELDC, and HDC algorithms is significant.

Since consensus quality samples did not come from a normal distribution, we used the Kruskal-Wallis test for comparison. We obtained *p-value* of 0.001; thus, the hypothesis H_0 was rejected. In other words, the difference in the consensus quality of the BLDC, ELDC, and HDC algorithms is significant.

The medians of the consensus quality samples were compared in pairs. The consensus quality of HDC was 0.2% higher than that of ELDC and 1.8% higher than that of BLDC algorithm. The consensus quality of the ELDC was 1% higher than that of the BLDC algorithm.

5 Conclusion

In this study, we introduced a formal description of the problem of determining the 2-Optimality consensus for a DNA profile. Based on this formulation, we proposed three algorithms for the 2-Optimality consensus for a DNA profile. The consensus quality of the algorithms was high.

In the future, we will investigate this result for string selection, motif search, and comparison problems in bioinformatics. In addition, the 2-Optimality consensus of other structures of string profiles, such as proteins, will be examined.

References

1. Pradhan, M. : Motif Discovery in Biological Sequences. San Jose State University, San Jose, CA, USA (2008)
2. Compeau, P., Pevzner, P.: Bioinformatics algorithms: an active learning approach. United States of America (2015)
3. D'haeseleer, P.: What are DNA sequence motifs? Nat. Biotechnol. **24**(4), 423–425 (2006)
4. Gribskov, M.: Identification of sequence patterns, motifs and domains. Encycl. Bioinforma. Comput. Biol. ABC Bioinforma. **1–3**, 332–340 (2018)
5. Blum, C., Festa, P.: Metaheuristics for String Problems in Bio-informatics, vol. 6. Wiley, Hoboken (2016)
6. Nguyen, N.T.: Advanced Methods for Inconsistent Knowledge Management. Springer, London (2008). https://doi.org/10.1007/978-1-84628-889-0
7. Nguyen, N.T.: Inconsistency of knowledge and collective intelligence. Cybern. Syst. **39**(6), 542–562 (2008)
8. Nguyen, N.T.: Using distance functions to solve representation choice problems. Fundam. Inf. **48**, 295–314 (2001)

9. Nguyen, N.T.: Processing inconsistency of knowledge in determining knowledge of a collective. Cybern. Syst. **40**(8), 670–688 (2009)

10. Dang, D.T., Nguyen, N.T., Hwang, D.: Multi-step consensus: an effective approach for determining consensus in large collectives. Cybern. Syst. **50**(2), 208–229 (2019)

11. Amir, A., Landau, G.M., Na, J.C., Park, H., Park, K., Sim, J.S.: Efficient algorithms for consensus string problems minimizing both distance sum and radius. Theor. Comput. Sci. **412**(39), 5239–5246 (2011)

12. Hashim, F.A., Mabrouk, M.S., Al-Atabany, W.: Review of different sequence motif finding algorithms. Avicenna J. Med. Biotechnol. **11**(2), 130–148 (2019)

13. Sinha, S.: YMF: a program for discovery of novel transcription factor binding sites by statistical overrepresentation. Nucleic Acids Res. **31**(13), 3586–3588 (2003)

14. Sinha, S.: Discovery of novel transcription factor binding sites by statistical overrepresentation. Nucleic Acids Res. **30**(24), 5549–5560 (2002)

15. Sharov, A.A., Ko, M.S.H.: Exhaustive search for over-represented DNA sequence motifs with cisfinder. DNA Res. **16**(5), 261–273 (2009)

16. Zare-Mirakabad, F., Ahrabian, H., Sadeghi, M., Hashemifar, S., Nowzari-Dalini, A., Goliaei, B.: Genetic algorithm for dyad pattern finding in DNA sequences. Genes Genet. Syst. **84**(1), 81–93 (2009)

17. Bouamama, S., Boukerram, A., Al-Badarneh, A.F.: Motif finding using ant colony optimization. In: Dorigo, M., et al. (eds.) ANTS 2010. LNCS, vol. 6234, pp. 464–471. Springer, Heidelberg (2010). https://doi.org/10.1007/978-3-642-15461-4_45

18. Bailey, T.L., Williams, N., Misleh, C., Li, W.W.: MEME: discovering and analyzing DNA and protein sequence motifs. Nucleic Acids Res. **34**, 369–373 (2006)

19. Das, M.K., Dai, H.K.: A survey of DNA motif finding algorithms. BMC Bioinf. **8**, 1–13 (2007)

20. Amir, A., Landau, G.M., Na, J.C., Park, H., Park, K., Sim, J.S.: Consensus optimizing both distance sum and radius. In: Karlgren, J., Tarhio, J., Hyyrö, H. (eds.) SPIRE 2009. LNCS, vol. 5721, pp. 234–242. Springer, Heidelberg (2009). https://doi.org/10.1007/978-3-642-03784-9_23

21. Lin, F.-T., Kao, C.-Y., Hsu, C.-C.: Applying the genetic approach to simulated annealing in solving some NP-hard problems. IEEE Trans. Syst. Man. Cybern. **23**(6), 1752–1767 (1993)

22. Dang, D.T., Nguyen, N.T., Hwang, D.: A quick algorithm to determine 2-optimality consensus for collectives. IEEE Access **8**, 221794–221807 (2020)

23. Michiels, W., Aarts, E.H.L., Korst, J.: Theory of local search. In: Martí, R., Pardalos, P., Resende, M. (eds.) Handbook of Heuristics, vol. 1–2, pp. 299–339. Springer, Cham (2018). https://doi.org/10.1007/978-3-319-07124-4_6

24. Benito-Parejo, M., Merayo, M.G., Nunez, M. : An evolutionary technique for supporting the consensus process of group decision making. In: 2020 IEEE International Conference on Systems, Man, and Cybernetics (SMC), pp. 2201–2206 (2020)

25. Katoch, S., Chauhan, S.S., Kumar, V.: A review on genetic algorithm: past, present, and future. Multimed. Tools Appl. **80**(5), 8091–8126 (2020). https://doi.org/10.1007/s11042-020-10139-6

26. Dang, D.C., et al.: Escaping local optima using crossover with emergent diversity. IEEE Trans. Evol. Comput. **22**(3), 484–497 (2018)

27. Schnecke, V., Vornberger, O., Schnecke, V.: Hybrid genetic algorithms for constrained placement problems. IEEE Trans. Evol. Comput. **1**(4), 266–271 (1997)

Evolutionary Computation

Utilizing Center-Based Sampling Theory to Enhance Particle Swarm Classification of Textual Data

Anwar Ali Yahya[1,2]([✉]), Yousef Asiri[2], and Ahmed Abdu Alattab[1,2]

[1] Thamar University, Thamar, Yemen
{aaesmail,aaalttab}@nu.edu.sa
[2] Najran University, Najran, Saudi Arabia
yasiri@nu.edu.sa

Abstract. The curse of dimensionality is a well-known problem in data classification. In this paper, the Center-Based Sampling (CBS) theory is utilized to develop a new variant of Particle Swarm Optimization (PSO), dubbed CBS-PSO, capable of dealing with the curse of dimensionality problem in text classification. More specifically, the CBS is exploited to equip PSO with two specialized mechanisms to attract the search toward the center region of the search space. The first mechanism estimates the coordinates of the center point of the search space using Rocchio Algorithm (RA), whereas the second mechanism uses the RA-based estimation to generate informed particles, located at the center region, and incorporate them in the swarm to gradually attract the search for the optimal classifiers toward this promising region. The performance of the CBS-PSO is evaluated against three Machine Learning (ML) approaches on three classification tasks of textual datasets from UC Irvine ML repository. The results indicate that the CBS-PSO can be regarded as a very competitive and promising text classifier with much space for improvement.

Keywords: Particle swarm optimization · Center-based sampling theory · Rocchio algorithm · Text classification

1 Introduction

In swarm intelligence field, Particle Swarm Optimization (PSO) is a population-based algorithm proposed by Kennedy and Eberhart [1], who took its inspiration from cooperation and communication behavior of birds swarm. Thanks to its simplicity, fast convergence, and fewer parameters it demands, PSO has been successfully applied to solve optimization problems in various domains [2]. A recent domain of PSO applications is data mining [3], in which PSO has been applied to tackle many problems such as clustering, classification, feature selection, and outlier detection. As for data classification, PSO has been widely applied as rule-based PSO classifiers [4, 5] or neighbor-based PSO classifiers [6, 7], where it was found suitable and competitive in many demanding domains, especially when accurate, yet comprehensible classifiers, fit for dynamic

© Springer Nature Switzerland AG 2021
H. Fujita et al. (Eds.): IEA/AIE 2021, LNAI 12798, pp. 441–446, 2021.
https://doi.org/10.1007/978-3-030-79457-6_37

distributed environments, are required [3]. Recently a major concern has been raised regarding PSO performance when applied to classify data in high dimensional domains [7].

In continuation of the forgoing research efforts, this paper proposes a center-based sampling theory method to enhance the PSO performance on a textual data classification. The center-based sampling theory [8, 9], states that in the search space of a given problem, the center region contains points with higher chance to be closer to the solution and this chance increases directly with the dimensionality of the search space. On this basis, it is hypothesized that if the PSO evolution is attracted toward the center region of the search space, the probability that the PSO evolution converges to global optimum becomes higher.

The remaining sections of this paper review the related works, present the proposed CBS-PSO, demonstrate how the proposed CBS-PSO is applied for text classification, present the results of validation experiments, and lastly conclude the work.

2 Related Works

In the literature, the seminal application of PSO to data classification is dated back to 2004 [10]. Since then PSO has been widely applied [6, 7]. A major concern of data classification in high-dimensional domain, such as text classification, is the curse of dimensionality. In such domains, the PSO performance deteriorates drastically, because the particles become highly sparse and achieving a uniform coverage of the search space is almost meaningless. This concern was initially addressed in [11], where PSO is applied to classify nine UCI datasets, and the conclusion is that PSO performance tends to decrease with increasing values of classes, and with increasing values of the product of data set size and dimension as well. In [12], these conclusions are questioned by investigating PSO on a more complex dataset and positive results are obtained, when using a confinement mechanism. A more investigation is carried out in [6] with more datasets and the conclusion is that PSO with wind dispersion and confinement mechanisms has good potential as a classification tool even for high dimensioned problems with large number of instances and multiple classes.

In an influential work to enhance the performance of population-based algorithms, Rahnamayan and Wang [8] proposed the center-based sampling theory, which states that the center region of the search space is very useful for population-based algorithms, because the points located in the center region have higher chance to be closer to the solution of a given problem. They also measured the closeness of points in a search space from an unknown solution using the Euclidean distances. They observed that as the points got closer to the center of the search space, the probability of closeness to the unknown solution rose drastically. They also investigated the validity of the center-based sampling theory for high-dimensional problems; and interestingly found that with the increase of the problem dimensionality, the probability of the closeness to the solution increases on the center of the search space, as well.

In the literature, the center-based sampling theory has been utilized to enhance the performance of population-based algorithms through the development of new mechanisms for initializing the population [9, 13, 14], or guiding the evolution of the population towards the center region of the search space [15].

3 The Proposed CBS-PSO

CBS-PSO is a PSO variant developed specifically for data classification tasks. It utilizes a center-based sampling theory to deal with curse of dimensionality problem by developing a mechanism to identify the center point of the search space and a mechanism to guide the PSO search toward it. In doing so, the CBS-PSO uses Rocchio algorithm [16] as a centroid-based classifier to generate for each class c a prototype vector, which is the average vector overall training set vectors that belong to the class c and uses it to classify a new data instance by calculating the similarity between the vector of the new data instance and each of prototype vectors and assigns it to the class with maximum similarity. Moreover, in CBS-PSO, RA is used to generate estimation of the center point to generate informed particles and incorporate them in the swarm to attract the PSO evolution toward the center region of the search space.

Formally speaking, for a given class c whose data instances, represented as vector space models $<x_1, ..., x_j, ..., x_N>$, in the dataset is denoted D_c, the CBS-PSO first applies RA to estimate the center of the search space of the class c by computing the vector average or center of mass of its members in the data set as follows:

$$\vec{\mu}^c = \frac{1}{|D_c|} \sum_{x \in D_c} \vec{x} \tag{1}$$

Then the RA-based estimation of the center point is used to generate informed particles located at the center region of the search space as follows

$$\vec{p}_i^c = \vec{\mu}^c + \vec{\alpha}_i \tag{2}$$

where $\vec{\mu}^c$ is a vector of mean values $<\mu_1, ..., \mu_j, ..., \mu_N>$, such that μ_j is the mean value of dimension j over all data instances x_j of in D_c and $\vec{\alpha}_i$ is a random vector $<\alpha_1, ..., \alpha_j, ..., \alpha_N>$, such that α_j is a small random value generated independently for dimension j in the interval $[-R, R]$, such that the dimension j of the generated particle $\vec{p}_i^C$ falls in the range $[\mu_j - R, \mu_j + R]$ centered at μ_j. After the generation of the informed particles, they are incorporated into the swarm gradually, such that one informed particle replaced a randomly selected particle at every PSO iteration. During the PSO evolution, it is highly probable that the incorporated informed particle is selected as the global best particle, which attract other particles toward the center region of the search space.

4 CBS-PSO Application to Text Classification

The methodology of applying CBS-PSO to a text classification task begins with a preprocessing step, which typically involves:

- *Tokenization:* reducing text to lower case characters and generating terms set.
- *Un-useful Term Removal:* removing the stop words, Punctuation marks, Numbers, and less frequent terms.
- *Stemming:* reducing the inflected words to their roots using porter stemmer.

- *Term Selection:* selecting the most representative terms from the original terms using term frequency metric.
- *Term Weighting:* assigning a non-binary weight in the form of term frequency inverse document frequency.
- *Vector Space Representation:* each document d_j is represented as a vector of term weights $<w_{1j}, ..., w_{Tj}>$, where $0 \leq w_{kj} \leq 1$ is the weight of term t_k in d_j.

After the preprocessing steps, the processed data is divided into training set for classifiers induction and testing set for classifiers evaluation. In classifiers induction, *CBS-PSO* is applied to induce a classifier for each class from the training set. It starts with a swarm of random particles, where each particle represents potential centroids of the C and $\overline{C}$, then iteratively generates RA-based informed particle, incorporates it in the swarm, and updates the velocity and position of all particles until the maximum number of iterations is reached. During the search, each particle i is evaluated to assess its suitability using a fitness function f computed over training set as follows.

$$f(i) = \frac{1}{D_C} \sum_{j=1}^{D_c} d\left(\vec{x}_j, \vec{p}_i^C\right) + \frac{1}{D_{\overline{c}}} \sum_{j=1}^{D_{\overline{c}}} d\left(\vec{x}_j, \vec{p}_i^C\right) \tag{3}$$

where $\vec{x}_j$, $\vec{p}_i^C$, and $\vec{p}_i^{\overline{C}}$ represent a data instance, centroid of C, and centroid of $\overline{C}$ respectively, D_C and $D_{\overline{c}}$ are training sets of C and $\overline{C}$, and d is the Euclidean distance.

In the evaluation step, the performance of the *CBS-PSO* classifiers is evaluated using the following common measures, which are based on True Positive (*TP*), False Positive (*FP*), False Negative (*FN*) of the contingency table.

- Precision (*P*): probability that if a random question is classified under C, then this classification is correct, that is,

$$P = \frac{TP}{TP + FP} \tag{4}$$

- Recall (*R*): probability that if a random question ought to be classified under a given C, then this classification is done, that is.

$$R = \frac{TP}{TP + FN} \tag{5}$$

Normally, the P and R measures are combined into a single F_β measure (harmonic mean), which is defined for $\beta = 1.0$, as follows

$$F_{1.0} = \frac{2RP}{R + P} \tag{6}$$

The performance across a set of Cs' classifiers is measured by Macro-Average F_1 (unweight mean across all classes).

5 Validation Experiments

The proposed CBS-PSO and the three ML approaches, ML approaches are k-Nearest Neighbor (kNN), Naïve Bayes (NB), Support Vector Machine (SVM) are experimented on three UCI datasets. Table 1 shows the specification of the datasets.

Table 1. Specifications of the three UCI datasets

Dataset name	Language	# of classes	# of instances	# of attributes
DBWorld e-mails	English	2	64	4702
Opinion Corpus for Lebanese Arabic Reviews (OCLAR)	Arabic	2	3916	7095
Benchmark dataset for Turkish text categorization	Turkish	6	3600	4814

The parameters of the three ML approaches are set with the default values of Weka [17], while the CBS-PSO are set as described in [6, 7]. The obtained results are summarized in Table 2 in terms of the best macro-average F_1.

Table 2. CBS-PSO vs. ML Approaches (Macro-Average F_1)

Dataset	kNN	NB	SVM	CBS-PSO
DBWorld e-mails	0.533	0.833	0.840	0.857
Arabic Reviews (OCLAR) Dataset	0.777	0804	0.846	0.839
Benchmark dataset for Turkish text categorization	0.471	0.756	0.844	0.851

In summary, the comparison between CBS-PSO and ML approaches show the competitiveness of the CBS-PSO. As discussed in [18], the low uniformity of the search space affects the performance of PSO significantly, however with the center-based sampling theory, the PSO is competitive to the best ML approaches.

6 Conclusion

This paper proposes a new variant of PSO, dubbed CBS-PSO, which utilizes the center-based sampling theory to tackle the curse of dimensionality problem, and ultimately improve the performance of PSO for text classification. The comparison of the experimental results of CBS-PS with three ML approaches on three text classification tasks confirm the competitiveness of the proposed CBS-PSO.

References

1. Kennedy, J., Eberhart, R.: Particle swarm optimization. In: IEEE International Conference on Neural Networks (1995)
2. del Valle, Y., Venayagamoorthy, G.K., Mohagheghi, S., Hernandez, J.C., Harley, R.G.: Particle swarm optimization: basic concepts, variants and applications in power systems. IEEE Trans. Evol. Comput. **12**(2), 171–195 (2008)
3. Abraham, A., Grosan, C., Ramos, V.: Swarm intelligence in data mining. Stud. Comput. Intell. **34**, 1–20 (2006)
4. Punitha, S., Jeyakarthic, M.: Particle swarm optimization based classification algorithm for expert prediction systems. In: The International Conference on Inventive Computation Technologies (ICICT), Coimbatore, India (2020)
5. Santana, P.J., Lanzarini, L., Barivier, A.F.: Variations of particle swarm optimization for obtaining classification rules applied to credit risk in financial institutions of Ecuador. Risks **8**(1), 1 (2019)
6. Nouaouria, N., Boukadoum, M.: Particle swarm classification for high dimensional data sets. In: 22th International IEEE Conference on Tools with Artificial Intelligence (2010)
7. Nouaouria, N., Boukadoum, M., Proulx, R.: Particle swarm classification: a survey and positioning. Pattern Recogn. **46**(7), 2028–2044 (2013)
8. Rahnamayan, S., Wang, G.G.: Center-based sampling for population-based algorithms. In: 2009 IEEE Congress on Evolutionary Computation, Trondheim, Norway (2009)
9. Esmailzadeh, A., Rahnamayan, S.: Enhanced differential evolution using center-based sampling. In: IEEE Congress on Evolutionary Computation (2011)
10. Sousa, T., Silva, A., Neves, A.: Particle swarm based data mining algorithms for classification tasks. Parallel Comput. **30**(5–6), 767–783 (2004)
11. De Falco, I., Della Cioppa, A., Tarantino, E.: Evaluation of particle swarm optimization effectiveness in classification. In: Bloch, I., Petrosino, A., Tettamanzi, A.G.B. (eds.) WILF 2005. LNCS (LNAI), vol. 3849, pp. 164–171. Springer, Heidelberg (2006). https://doi.org/10.1007/11676935_20
12. Nouaouria, N., Boukadoum, M.: A particle swarm optimization approach for substance identification. In: GECCO 2009 (2009)
13. Mahdavi, S., Rahnamayan, S., Deb, K.: Center-based initialization of cooperative co-evolutionary algorithm for large-scale optimization. In: IEEE Congress on Evolutionary Computation (CEC), 25–29 July 2016, Vancouver, Canada (2016)
14. Yahya, A.A., Osman, A., El-Bashir, M.S.: Rocchio algorithm-based particle initialization mechanism for effective PSO classification of high dimensional data. Swarm Evol. Comput. **34**, 18–32 (2018)
15. Liu, Y., Qin, Z., Shi, Z.W., Lu, J.: Center particle swarm optimization. Neurocomputing **70**(4–6), 672–679 (2007)
16. Rocchio, J.J.: Relevance feedback in information retrieval. SMART Retrieval System: Exp. Autom. Doc. Process. 313–323 (1971)
17. Hall, M., Frank, E., Holmes, G., Pfahringer, B.R.: The WEKA data mining software: an update. ACM SIGKDD Explor. Newsl. **19**(2), 10–18 (2009)
18. Kazimipour, B., Qin, A.K.: Why advanced population initialization techniques perform poorly in high dimension? In: Dick, G., et al. (eds.) SEAL 2014. LNCS, vol. 8886, pp. 479–490. Springer, Heidelberg (2014). https://doi.org/10.1007/978-3-319-13563-2_41

Conditional Preference Networks
Refining Solution Orderings Beyond Pareto Dominance

Nahla Ben Amor[1]([✉]), Didier Dubois[2]([✉]), Henri Prade[2]([✉]),
and Syrine Saidi[2]([✉])

[1] LARODEC Laboratory, ISG de Tunis, 41 rue de la Liberté, 2000 Le Bardo, Tunisia
nahla.benamor@gmx.fr
[2] IRIT - CNRS, 118, route de Narbonne, 31062 Toulouse Cedex 09, France
{dubois,prade,syrine.saidi}@irit.fr

Abstract. When handling preferences, the inclusion-based partial order (called here Pareto dominance) is a natural basis for comparing solutions: one is then preferred to another as soon as the set of preferences violated by the former is a subset of the preferences violated by the latter. In order to obtain refinements of this partial order, various general principles can be used, such as Ceteris Paribus, or optimistic (resp. pessimistic) principles stating that what is not explicitly said to be satisfactory according to the preferences should be regarded as satisfactory (resp. disregarded). Algorithms taking advantage of the two last principles are presented and discussed. They enable us to refine the Pareto ordering of solutions.

Keywords: Preference modeling · Possibilistic network · Default reasoning · Pareto ordering

1 Introduction

Conditional preference networks are a natural format for specifying context-dependent local preferences. Still, this specification does not provide a direct way of comparing any two solutions or configurations corresponding to complete instantiations of the choice variables. To this end, some general principle is needed.

In the popular CP-nets approach [1], a "Ceteris Paribus" principle is applied, which amounts to completing two partial configurations corresponding to a preference specification with the same instantiations of the remaining variables. This principle seems natural and leads to a computational method for comparing any two configurations and obtaining a partial order. However, it has been discovered later that this principle has undesirable side effects that cannot be repaired [2]. More recently, it has been proved [3], in the case of Boolean variables, that the CP-net-induced partial order always agrees with a weaker, inclusion-based principle that seems desirable and indisputable: a configuration is preferred to another one as soon as the set of preferences violated by the former is a subset of the preferences violated by the latter (inclusion principle). The inclusion-based

© Springer Nature Switzerland AG 2021
H. Fujita et al. (Eds.): IEA/AIE 2021, LNAI 12798, pp. 447–459, 2021.
https://doi.org/10.1007/978-3-030-79457-6_38

partial order is also referred to here as Pareto dominance, for reasons made clear later. There is another approach to the handling of conditional preference networks, which has been proposed some years ago, based on so-called "π-pref nets" [4]. This approach is based on a possibility theory-based reading of the network. Each conditional preference statement is modelled by a conditional possibility distribution, with symbolic possibility values. In the absence of additional constraints, the π-pref net approach exactly coincides with the application of the inclusion principle [5]. If additional constraints are stated between symbolic possibility values, more comparisons can be obtained. In the particular case where the violation of the preferences associated with a node is modelled by the same symbol whatever the instantiation of the parent(s), the partial order obtained corresponds to an ordering reflecting the number of constraints violated. Besides, in the setting of possibility theory, there are two information principles: minimum, and maximum specificity [6]. When dealing with preference modeling, the application of the minimum specificity principle amounts to saying that a solution is considered satisfactory unless preference statements say otherwise. In contrast with this optimistic view, the maximum specificity principle amounts to saying that a solution is considered unsatisfactory unless preference statements say otherwise. These principles lead to a "default-like" reading of conditional preferences [7] yielding complete pre-orders of the configurations. However, the pre-orders so obtained may partially disagree with the inclusion principle.

In this paper, we consider that the inclusion principle should be always respected, and that the controlled application of different principles (Ceteris Paribus, minimum specificity, maximum specificity, cardinality) may be used for obtaining more discriminating partial orders or even complete pre-orders of solutions. The paper is organized as follows. Section 2 provides a background on CP-nets, π-pref nets, and the default-like approach to preference handling. A proposition showing the agreement between the two latter approaches is also established. Section 3 discusses different algorithms for obtaining refinements of the ordering corresponding to the inclusion-based principle.

2   Graphical Preference Networks

A Conditional Preference network [8] (CP-net for short) is a graphical preference representation composed of two components: a graph and a set of preference statements.

Definition 1. *A CP-net consists of a directed acyclic graph (DAG) $\mathcal{G} = (\mathcal{X}, E)$ composed of a set of Boolean decision variables $\mathcal{X} = \{X_1, \ldots, X_N\}$ each associated with a conditional preference table $CPT(X_i)$ where $i \in \{1, \ldots, N\}$. Edges E represent preference dependencies between the variables. Let $\mathcal{U}_i$ be the set of parents of X_i. A conditional preference table $CPT(X_i)$ encodes a strict total order $\succ_{\mathcal{U}_i}$ over the domain $\mathcal{D}_{X_i}$ of X_i in the context of each instance u_i of its parents $\mathcal{U}_i$. A conditional preference statement is of the form $u_i : x_i \succ x_i'$.*

2.1   Ceteris Paribus Networks

The term "CP-net" not only refers to Conditional Preference networks, but also to preferential independence assumption called *Ceteris Paribus* [1]. It stipulates that given a preference between two partial configurations, this preference can be extended to complete configurations obtained by assigning the same values to the remaining variables.

Definition 2. *Ceteris Paribus Let $\mathcal{Y}_i = \{\mathcal{X} \setminus \mathcal{U}_i \cup \{X_i\}\}$. Let $u_i : x_i \succ x_i'$, be a preference statement; the Ceteris Paribus assumption states that the configuration $\omega = u_i x_i y_i$ is preferred to $\omega' = u_i x_i' y_i$. ω' is obtained from ω via a worsening flip.*

Let $\Omega = \{\omega_0, \ldots, \omega_{2^N-1}\}$ be the set of all possible configurations of the N variables in $\mathcal{X}$. The most widely used queries in this model are the *Optimization* and the *Dominance* queries. Finding the optimal solution is done by sweeping through conditional preferences from top to bottom while assigning to each variable its preferred instantiation in the context of its parents. The *Dominance* query consists of determining if $\omega_i \succ \omega_j$ for a pair of configurations. A worsening flip chain needs to be constructed based on the Ceteris Paribus property, starting from an alternative ω_i, and repetitively swapping one variable instantiation to its less preferred value until ω_j is obtained. A directed acyclic graph of configurations, called an *induced worsening flip graph* can thus be constructed. The top configuration corresponds to the best outcome, the latter represents the worst.

2.2   Possibilistic Preference Networks

Possibilistic preference networks [4] (π-pref nets) are inspired from possibilistic nets and based on a *Markovian* independence property. They share the same DAG structure as CP-nets, but conditional preference statements receive a possibilistic reading:

Definition 3. *A π-pref net is a DAG $\mathcal{G} = \{\mathcal{X}, E\}$ where $\mathcal{X} = \{X_1, \ldots, X_N\}$ are decision variables. To each preference statement $u_i : x_i \succ x_i'$ we associate a local conditional possibility distribution $\pi(x_i \mid u_i)$ using symbolic weights expressing an ordering between the values of X_i. The symbolic weights are unspecified degrees in the real interval $(0, 1)$.[1] In each context u_i, there must exist a preferred instantiation of X_i with degree equal to 1.*

In this approach, each variable X_i is independent from other variables in $\mathcal{Y}_i = \{\mathcal{X} \setminus \mathcal{U}_i \cup \{X_i\}\}$ in the context of its parents $(\mathcal{U}_i)$ (Markovian assumption). Consider a variable X_i s.t. $\mathcal{D}_{X_i} = \{x_i, \bar{x}_i\}$, the possibility degree $\pi(x_i \mid u_i)$ evaluates the satisfaction degree of decision x_i in context u_i. $\pi(x_i \mid u_i) = 1$ if x_i is preferred, and it is a symbol $\alpha < 1$ otherwise. We use one symbolic weight for each variable X_i and each context u_i. In order to rank configurations, the degree

---

[1] Constraints between symbolic weights may be added (this option is not used in this paper).

of satisfaction of each $\omega_i \in \Omega$ can be calculated by means of the product-based chain rule formally expressed by:

$$\pi(X_i, ..., X_N) = \prod_{i=1}^{N} \pi(X_i|\mathcal{U}_i) . \tag{1}$$

Then, ω_i is considered preferred to ω_j iff its satisfaction degree $\pi(\omega_i)$ is higher than $\pi(\omega_j)$. Note that configurations ω_j of a π-pref net can also be represented by vectors of weights $\overrightarrow{\omega_i} = (\rho_1, \ldots, \rho_N)$, where $\rho_i = \pi(x_i|u_i)$. A pair of configurations can thus be compared using the Pareto ordering which is defined as follows:

Definition 4. $\forall \omega_j \neq \omega_k \in \Omega$ associated to distinct vectors $\overrightarrow{\omega_j} = (\rho_1, \ldots, \rho_N)$ and $\overrightarrow{\omega_k} = (\lambda_1, \ldots, \lambda_N)$, $\omega_j \succ_{Pareto} \omega_k$ iff $\forall i = \{1, \ldots, N\}, \rho_i \geq \lambda_i$ and for some $\ell, \rho_\ell = 1 > \lambda_\ell$.

Under the assumption of one symbolic weight per variable and parent context, the Pareto ordering is probably equivalent to the chain rule ordering [4]. It corresponds to comparing the sets of preference statements satisfied by configurations using inclusion. If there is only one symbolic weight per variable regardless of the context, the comparison of configurations comes down to comparing the sets of variables having their best values using inclusion.

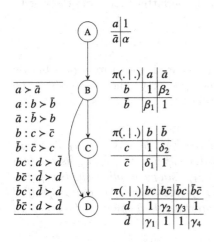

Fig. 1. Example of a π-pref net with normalized possibility distribution tables

Table 1. Vectors and weights associated to the configurations of the π-pref net in Fig. 1. In the last two columns the symbolic weights associated to the violation of a preference are the same in all contexts

Ω	$\overrightarrow{\omega}$	$\pi(\omega)$	$\overrightarrow{\omega}$	$\pi(\omega)$
ω_0 abcd	$(1,1,1,1)$	1	$(1,1,1,1)$	1
ω_1 abcd	$(1,1,1,\gamma_1)$	γ_1	$(1,1,1,\gamma)$	γ
ω_2 abcd	$(1,1,\delta_1,\gamma_2)$	$\delta_1\gamma_2$	$(1,1,\delta,\gamma)$	$\delta\gamma$
ω_3 abc̄d	$(1,1,\delta_1,1)$	δ_1	$(1,1,\delta,1)$	δ
ω_4 abc̄d	$(1,\beta_1,\delta_2,\gamma_3)$	$\beta_1\delta_2\gamma_3$	$(1,\beta,\delta,\gamma)$	$\beta\delta\gamma$
ω_5 abc̄d	$(1,\beta_1,\delta_2,1)$	$\beta_1\delta_2$	$(1,\beta,\delta,1)$	$\beta\delta$
ω_6 ab̄c̄d	$(1,\beta_1,1,1)$	β_1	$(1,\beta,1,1)$	β
ω_7 ab̄c̄d	$(1,\beta_1,1,\gamma_4)$	$\beta_1\gamma_4$	$(1,\beta,1,\gamma)$	$\beta\gamma$
ω_8 ābcd	$(\alpha,\beta_2,1,1)$	$\alpha\beta_2$	$(\alpha,\beta,1,1)$	$\alpha\beta$
ω_9 ābcd	$(\alpha,\beta_2,1,\gamma_1)$	$\alpha\beta_2\gamma_1$	$(\alpha,\beta,1,\gamma)$	$\alpha\beta\gamma$
ω_{10} āb̄cd	$(\alpha,\beta_2,\delta_1,\gamma_2)$	$\alpha\beta_2\delta_1\gamma_2$	$(\alpha,\beta,\delta,\gamma)$	$\alpha\beta\delta\gamma$
ω_{11} āb̄cd	$(\alpha,\beta_2,\delta_1,1)$	$\alpha\beta_2\delta_1$	$(\alpha,\beta,\delta,1)$	$\alpha\beta\delta1$
ω_{12} ābcd	$(\alpha,1,\delta_2,\gamma_3)$	$\alpha\delta_2\gamma_3$	$(\alpha,1,\delta,\gamma)$	$\alpha\delta\gamma$
ω_{13} ābcd	$(\alpha,1,\delta_2,1)$	$\alpha\delta_2$ ·	$(\alpha,1,\delta,1)$	$\alpha\delta$
ω_{14} ābcd	$(\alpha,1,1,1)$	α	$(\alpha,1,1,1)$	α
ω_{15} ābcd	$(\alpha,1,1,\gamma_4)$	$\alpha\gamma_4$	$(\alpha,1,1,\gamma)$	$\alpha\gamma$

The figure content (preference statements, nodes and conditional possibility tables):

$a > \bar{a}$
$a : b > \bar{b}$
$\bar{a} : \bar{b} > b$
$b : c > \bar{c}$
$\bar{b} : \bar{c} > c$
$bc : d > \bar{d}$
$b\bar{c} : \bar{d} > d$
$\bar{b}c : \bar{d} > d$
$\bar{b}\bar{c} : d > \bar{d}$

Node A:
a	1
$\bar{a}$	α

Node B:
$\pi(.|.)$	a	$\bar{a}$
b	1	β_2
$\bar{b}$	β_1	1

Node C:
$\pi(.|.)$	b	$\bar{b}$
c	1	δ_2
$\bar{c}$	δ_1	1

Node D:
$\pi(.|.)$	bc	$b\bar{c}$	$\bar{b}c$	$\bar{b}\bar{c}$
d	1	γ_2	γ_3	1
$\bar{d}$	γ_1	1	1	γ_4

Example 1. *Figure 1 provides an example of a π-pref net expressing the preferences of an agent in terms of 4 binary variables (with no additional constraints). $\pi(d \mid \bar{b}c) = \gamma_3$ encodes the preference statement $\bar{b}c : \bar{d} \succ d$. The vector representation of the satisfaction of the preferences by each configuration is given in Table 1. In column 2, there is one weight per variable and parent configuration, in column 4 there is one weight per variable. For each node the weight corresponding to the violation of the preferred value depends on the context of parent values, while in column 4 the symbolic weight is attached to the variable, but not to a particular violation context. The preference degrees of configurations are given in column 3 and 5 of Table 1. The optimal configuration is ω_0*

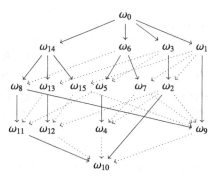

Fig. 2. Pareto graph of Example 1 going from best to worst configurations. Solid (resp. dotted) arrows represent comparisons for different symbolic weights per variable (resp. assuming one weight per variable)

since it corresponds to the highest degree (=1). Figure 2 exhibits the Pareto orderings of the vectors associated to configurations (an arc $\omega_i \rightarrow \omega_j$ means that $\omega_i \succ_{Pareto} \omega_j$), both in the case of weights depending on contexts and in the case of equal weights for a given variable. In the latter case, more comparisons can take place, and there is a unique worst configuration, $\bar{a}\bar{b}\bar{c}\bar{d}$ with $\pi(\omega_{10}) = \alpha\beta\delta\gamma$ (ω_{10} violates the preferred choice for the 4 decision variables), while otherwise $\pi(\omega_{10}) = \alpha\beta_2\delta_1\gamma_2$ and there are other non comparable worst cases due to distinct symbols expressing violation of all constraints.

2.3   Default Rules for Preferences Based on Possibilistic Approaches

A default rule "If u is true then generally x is true" is represented in possibility theory by a constraint stating that having u and x true is strictly more possible than having u and not x true [9]. When adapted to preference representation, this rule becomes the conditional preference statement "x is preferred to $\bar{x}$ in the context of u" namely, $ux \succ u\bar{x}$ (ux is more satisfactory than $u\bar{x}$). This can be expressed by the constraint $\Pi(u_i \wedge x_i) > \Pi(u_i \wedge \bar{x}_i)$ where Π is a possibility measure associated with a possibility distribution π and is defined by $\Pi(A) = \max_{\omega \in A} \pi(\omega)$. Thus, the conditional preference $u : x \succ \bar{x}$ is understood as "the best case in which $u \wedge x$ is true is preferred to the best case in which $u \wedge \bar{x}$ is true". Given a set $\mathcal{C}$ of conditionals, one obtains the set of constraints

$$\mathcal{C}_\Pi = \{\Pi(u_i \wedge x_i) > \Pi(u_i \wedge \bar{x}_i) \text{ s.t. } u_i : x_i \succ \bar{x}_i \in \mathcal{C}\}. \tag{2}$$

Thus the set $\mathcal{C}_\Pi$ is implicitly associated with a set of possibility distributions compatible with (2). It can be shown that any possibility distribution that is in agreement with (2) obeys the conditional preference statements associated with the conditional preference graph. This directly follows from the definition of the conditional possibility: $\pi(x_i \mid u_i) = 1 > \pi(\bar{x}_i \mid u_i)$ (where $\Pi(u_i \wedge X_i) = \pi(X_i \mid u_i) \cdot \Pi(u_i)$) iff $\Pi(u_i \wedge x_i) > \Pi(u_i \wedge \bar{x}_i)$.

The following proposition establishes the agreement of the Pareto ordering with the constraints in $\mathcal{C}_\Pi$ expressing the preference statements.

Proposition 1. *Given a π-pref net, the associated possibility distribution obtained by the chain rule and the corresponding Pareto ordering between configurations agree with the constraints in $\mathcal{C}_\Pi$ expressing the preference statements of the π-pref net.*

Proof. Let ω and ω' be two configurations associated with their satisfaction vectors $\vec{\omega}$ and $\vec{\omega}'$. $\pi(\omega) > \pi(\omega')$ is known to be equivalent to $\vec{\omega} \succ_{Pareto} \vec{\omega}'$ [5] assuming one weight per preference statement. It means that for each vector component (corresponding to a variable) either the two vectors are equal with the same satisfaction degree, or the component of $\vec{\omega}$ is 1 and the same component for $\vec{\omega}'$ is equal to some symbolic weight, say ρ, assuming $\vec{\omega} \succ_{Pareto} \vec{\omega}'$. Each inequality $1 > \rho$, corresponds to an inequality of the form $\pi(x_i \mid u_i) = 1 > \pi(\bar{x}_i \mid u_i')$. If $u_i = u_i'$ this refers to a preference statement in a conditional table $\pi(x_i \mid u_i) = 1 > \pi(\bar{x}_i \mid u_i)$ equivalent as already said to the constraint $\Pi(u_i \wedge x_i) > \Pi(u_i \wedge \bar{x}_i)$. If $u_i \neq u_i'$, this violates no preference statement. It means that the comparison of 1 with ρ refers to different contexts and no preference statement is involved. Besides, the vector components where $\vec{\omega}$ and $\vec{\omega}'$ are equal cannot correspond to a violation of a preference statement.

One can observe in the example that the case $u_i \neq u_i'$ mentioned in the proof does take place, e.g., with $\vec{\omega_0}$ and $\vec{\omega_7}$ on the fourth component where the value 1 for $\vec{\omega_0}$ is associated with context bc and the value γ_4 for $\vec{\omega_7}$ is associated with context $\bar{b}\bar{c}$.

Thus the π-pref net approach and the constraints of the "default rule" approach are in full agreement. However, once we are going to apply a minimal specificity principle to these constraints, as explained now, some violation of the Pareto ordering may appear. The problem will be then to take advantage of the complete ordering thus obtained for refining the Pareto ordering without violating it.

Given the set of constraints $\mathcal{C}_\Pi$, a natural way to select a possibility distribution satisfying the constraints is to maximize the preference degrees of the configurations in agreement with the constraints (optimistic assumption). If some configurations are not constrained they will be associated to the highest possible preference degree, namely $\pi(\omega_i) = 1$. This maximisation principle is known as the minimum specificity principle [6], and means for preferences that a configuration is considered satisfactory unless preference statements say otherwise.

Another reading of the conditional preference $u_i : x_i \succ \bar{x}_i$ is in terms of worst case: "the worst case in which $u \wedge x$ is true is preferred to the worst case in which $u \wedge \bar{x}$ is true". This is formally expressed by the inequality $\Delta(x_i \wedge u_i) > \Delta(\bar{x}_i \wedge u_i)$ where Δ is a guaranteed possibility measure [6] defined by $\Delta(A) = \min_{\omega \in A} \pi(\omega)$.

In this case, preference degrees should be minimized as much as possible (pessimistic assumption). If some configurations are not involved in the constraints, they are associated to degrees equal to 0. This is the maximal specificity principle [6]. In terms of preference, this means that a configuration is considered unsatisfactory unless preference statements say otherwise. We denote by $\mathcal{C}_\Delta$ the set of such constraints associated with a conditional preference network:

$$\mathcal{C}_\Delta = \{\Delta(x_i \wedge u_i) > \Delta(\bar{x}_i \wedge u_i) \text{ s.t. } u_i : x_i \succ \bar{x}_i \in \mathcal{C}\}. \tag{3}$$

Example 2. *Let f be the minimum or the maximum function depending on whether the assumption is optimistic or pessimistic. The possibilistic default constraints relative to preference specifications of Fig. 1 are:*

$c_0 : a \succ \bar{a}$	$f(\pi(\omega_0), \ldots, \pi(\omega_7)) > f(\pi(\omega_8), \ldots, \pi(\omega_{15}))$
$c_1 : a : b \succ \bar{b}$	$f(\pi(\omega_0), \ldots, \pi(\omega_3)) > f(\pi(\omega_4), \ldots, \pi(\omega_7))$
$c_2 : \bar{a} : \bar{b} \succ b$	$f(\pi(\omega_{12}), \ldots, \pi(\omega_{15})) > f(\pi(\omega_8), \ldots, \pi(\omega_{11}))$
$c_3 : b : c \succ \bar{c}$	$f(\pi(\omega_0), \pi(\omega_1), \pi(\omega_8), \pi(\omega_9)) > f(\pi(\omega_2), \pi(\omega_3), \pi(\omega_{10}), \pi(\omega_{11}))$
$c_4 : \bar{b} : \bar{c} \succ c$	$f(\pi(\omega_6), \pi(\omega_7), \pi(\omega_{14}), \pi(\omega_{15})) > f(\pi(\omega_4), \pi(\omega_5), \pi(\omega_{12}), \pi(\omega_{13}))$
$c_5 : bc : d \succ \bar{d}$	$f(\pi(\omega_0), \pi(\omega_8)) > f(\pi(\omega_1), \pi(\omega_9))$
$c_6 : b\bar{c} : \bar{d} \succ d$	$f(\pi(\omega_3), \pi(\omega_{11})) > f(\pi(\omega_2), \pi(\omega_{10}))$
$c_7 : \bar{b}c : \bar{d} \succ d$	$f(\pi(\omega_5), \pi(\omega_{13})) > f(\pi(\omega_4), \pi(\omega_{12}))$
$c_8 : \bar{b}\bar{c} : d \succ \bar{d}$	$f(\pi(\omega_6), \pi(\omega_{14})) > f(\pi(\omega_7), \pi(\omega_{15}))$

A well-ordered partition E that classifies all possible configurations of Ω can be derived by satisfying constraints in $\mathcal{C}_\Pi$. This reasoning was first introduced by Benferhat et al. [9] to order models derived from pieces of knowledge encoded by default rules using an optimistic approach (such optimistic order is denoted by E_Π. The first layer of the partition is composed of configurations that do not appear on the right-hand side ($RC(c_i)$) of any constraint $c_i \in \mathcal{C}_\Pi$, which means that they are never dominated and are thus assigned maximal possibility. A number of constraints is then satisfied. This process is repeated until all constraints are satisfied. The last step consists of assigning the least possibility degree to all remaining configurations of Ω. The same procedure can be adapted to the pessimistic case and the *minimum* operator in order to rank configurations from the worst to the best, this cautious ranking is denoted by E_Δ. Partition layers are now constructed by iteratively considering configurations that are not dominating, i.e., those that do not appear on the left-hand side ($LC(c_i)$) of any formula of $\mathcal{C}_\Delta$. From a representation point of view the well ordered partition E_Π (resp. E_Δ) of k layers, can be considered as a table of k sets of configurations i.e. $E_\Pi[l]$ ($l = 0..k-1$) contains the configurations of layer l and $\forall l = 0..k-2, \forall \omega \in E_\Pi[l], \forall \omega' \in E_\Pi[l+1], \omega \succ \omega'$ (resp. $\omega \prec \omega'$).

Example 3. *Consider the set C_Π of possibilistic constraints of Example 2 ($f = max$). The configuration that does not appear in the right-hand side of any constraint is ω_0, it then forms the highest partition layer $E_\Pi[0]$. Constraints c_0, c_1, c_3 and c_5 are thus satisfied and deleted from C_Π. The second partition layer $E_\Pi[1]$ is composed of configurations $\omega_1, \omega_3, \omega_6$ and ω_{14}. Constraints c_2, c_4, c_6 and*

c_8 are subsequently removed from C_Π. C_Π holds now a single constraint: c_7. Satisfying this constraint consists of assigning all unclassified configurations of Ω to $E_\Pi[2]$ except for ω_4 and ω_{12} that form the lowest partition set i.e. $E_\Pi[3]$. A similar procedure (starting with the lowest ranks) applies to derive the cautious ordering). See Table 2.

Note that both optimistic and cautious orders contradict the Pareto order with equal variable weights (Fig. 2) In fact, $\omega_{10} \succ_\Pi \omega_4$ and $\omega_{10} \succ_\Pi \omega_{12}$ in E_Π while $\omega_4 \succ_{Pareto} \omega_{10}$ and $\omega_{12} \succ_{Pareto} \omega_{10}$. Moreover, E_Δ states that $\omega_6 \succ_\Delta \omega_0$ and $\omega_{14} \succ_\Delta \omega_0$ while $\omega_0 \succ_{Pareto} \omega_6$ and $\omega_0 \succ_{Pareto} \omega_{14}$. If we consider the other weaker Pareto order of Fig. 2 for the case of different symbolic weights per variable, E_Π is in coherence with Pareto while E_Δ leads to the same contradictions. This is due to the convention used to encode conditional preferences by possibility degrees (1 for preferred values and Greek letter symbols such as α for non-preferred). The Pareto preference graph adapted to the cautious ordering should rely on another convention (α for preferred values and 0 for non-preferred ones).

Table 2. Well-ordered partitions

Optimistic ordering E_Π	Cautious ordering E_Δ
$\{\omega_0\}$	$\{\omega_6, \omega_{14}\}$
$\{\omega_1, \omega_3, \omega_6, \omega_{14}\}$	$\{\omega_0, \omega_1, \omega_2, \omega_3, \omega_5, \omega_7, \omega_8, \omega_{13}, \omega_{15}\}$
$\{\omega_2, \omega_5, \omega_7, \omega_8, \omega_9, \omega_{10}, \omega_{11}, \omega_{13}, \omega_{15}\}$	$\{\omega_4, \omega_9, \omega_{11}, \omega_{12}\}$
$\{\omega_4, \omega_{12}\}$	$\{\omega_{10}\}$

2.4 Improving Possibilistic Default Rules Ordering

The ordering generated by means of default rules in addition to some informational principles not only leads to a sparsely discriminant ranking (often composed of 3 layers [7]) but can also lead to contradictions with the Pareto semantic that can easily be detected if symbolic weights of variables in the context of parents are equal. In fact, at some step of the ranking algorithm, some configurations might no longer appear in any of the remaining constraints but yet are still being assigned to a set in the partition, highest or lowest possible, depending on whether we adopt an optimistic or pessimistic assumption [7]. For instance, in the above example, ω_1 no longer appears in the set of constraints remaining after removing the ones satisfied thanks to ω_0.

In order to overcome this problem, we propose Algorithm 1 which is a new version of *Benferhat et al.* algorithm [9] that considers the same sets of inputs but checks at each iteration if there exists configurations that do not appear in any remaining constraint. These configurations are assigned to a set E_Π' (respectively E_Δ') and are considered just not better than previously ranked configurations. $Config(C_\Pi)$ (respectively $Config(C_\Delta)$) returns all configurations in C_Π (respectively C_Δ). This improved version results in a partial order over configurations that is in full accordance with the Pareto semantic.

Algorithm 1: ORDERING Ω USING AN OPTIMISTIC APPROACH (IMPROVED VERSION)

Input: Ω , $\mathcal{C}_\Pi$
Output: E_Π, E'_Π
begin
   $i \leftarrow 0$
   while $\mathcal{C}_\Pi \neq \emptyset$ **do**
      foreach $\omega \in \Omega$ **do**
           if $\omega \notin Config(\mathcal{C}_\Pi)$ **then** $E'_\Pi[i] \leftarrow E'_\Pi[i] \cup \{\omega\}$; $\Omega \leftarrow \Omega \setminus \{\omega\}$
      foreach $\omega \in \Omega$ **do**
           foreach $c \in \mathcal{C}_\Pi$ **do if** $\omega \notin RC(c)$ **then** $E_\Pi[i] \leftarrow E_\Pi[i] \cup \{\omega\}$; $\Omega \leftarrow \Omega \setminus \{\omega\}$
   foreach $\omega \in E_\Pi[j]$ **do**
       foreach $c \in \mathcal{C}_\Pi$ **do** **if** $\omega \in LC(c)$ **then** $\mathcal{C}_\Pi \leftarrow \mathcal{C}_\Pi \setminus \{c\}$
   $i \leftarrow i + 1$
   if $\Omega \neq \emptyset$ **then** **foreach** $\omega \in \Omega$ **do** $E_\Pi[i] \leftarrow E_\Pi[i] \cup \{\omega\}$
   Return E_Π, E'_Π

Example 4. *Let us consider constraints C_Π of Table 2. After constructing the second partition set $E_\Pi[1]$ we note that the remaining constraints c_2, c_4, c_6, c_7 and c_8 impose no restriction on ω_1. Therefore this configuration is assigned to $E'_\Pi[1]$. After the second iteration of the Algorithm 1, constraints c_2, c_4 and c_6 are satisfied. The last remaining formula is c_7 and covers only $\omega_4, \omega_5, \omega_{13}$ and ω_{12}. All other unclassified configurations are added to $E'_\Pi[2] = \{\omega_2, \omega_7, \omega_8, \omega_9, \omega_{10}, \omega_{11}, \omega_{15}\}$ and are all considered worse than configurations in $E_\Pi[1]$. Figure 3 gives a graphical representation of results of Algorithm 1 for the optimistic (a) and cautious (b) orders. Configurations in E_Π and E_Δ are equivalent. No preference information over configurations in clusters E'_Π and E'_Δ is provided by C_Π or C_Δ. They remain incomparable to one another.*

3 Refining Pareto Order with Default Rules

For symbolic π-pref nets, with one symbol per preference statement it has been shown that given a symbolic framework and no additional constraints, the product based ordering on configurations coincides with the Pareto ordering. If additional constraints over symbolic weights are considered, the product based ordering turns out to be more refined than the latter [5]. Recent research on the compatibility of CP-nets ordering with the Pareto ordering [3] have proved that the CP-net ordering refines the Pareto ordering adding the *Ceteris Paribus* assumption to it. The former can be recovered adding constraints between products of symbolic weights to the latter. In this section, we propose to refine the Pareto ordering by chiefly considering it as the basic order to which we add information. We will in particular consider refining it by optimistic and cautious possibilistic orders.

To represent any order, we use a $2^N \times 2^N$ incidence matrix M such that if $\omega_i \succ \omega_j$ (resp. $\omega_i \simeq \omega_j$) then $M[i,j] = 1$ and $M[j,i] = 0$ (resp. $M[i,j] = M[j,i] = 1$). Algorithm 3 outlines the refining process. The function $pref(M,i,j)$ returns 1 (resp. 2, 0, -1) if $\omega_i \succ \omega_j$ (resp. $\omega_i \prec \omega_j, \omega_i \simeq \omega_j$, ω_i and ω_j are incomparable) in M. The Warshall function computes the transitive closure after each refinement.

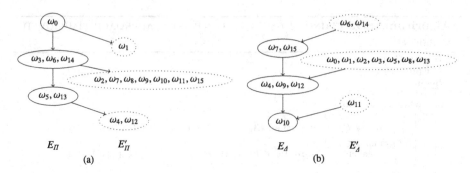

Fig. 3. (a) Improved optimistic order (b) Improved cautious order. Configurations in nodes with straight (resp. dotted) lines are equivalent (resp. incomparable)

Algorithm 2 has as input the Pareto incidence matrix P and a total order O (e.g., the incidence matrix relative to E_Π or E_Δ), thus it checks for each couple of incomparable configurations (ω, ω') in P if O gives more dominance information (i.e., $\omega \succ \omega'$ or $\omega \prec \omega'$). If it is the case, P is refined and this modification is propagated through the Warshall function. Let $m = 2^N$, the time complexity of Warshall is $O(m^3)$, thus the complexity of Algorithm 2 is $O(m^2 * m^3) = O(m^5)$ since it performs m^2 comparisons with at most a call to Warshall function each time. i.e., $O(2^{N^5}) = O(2^N)$.

Example 5. *Returning to Example 1, we can check that the number of incompatibilities in the Pareto matrix P relative to equal symbolic weights (comparisons with dotted arrows in Fig. 2) is equal to 84 and that this number decreases to 38 if we refine it by E_Π and to 34 if we refine it by E_Δ. Moreover, if we refine P by improved optimistic order (comparisons with straight arrows in Fig. 2) we obtain 63 incompatibilities while if we refine it by improved cautious order (Fig. 3(b)), we obtain 62 incompatibilities. We can also check that the Pareto order relative to different symbolic weights (comparisons with straight arrows in Fig.2) we have 55 incompatibilities. This number decreases to 29 if we refine it by E_Π*

Algorithm 2: REFINING PARETO ORDERING

Input: P, O
Output: P^O
$RP \leftarrow P$
for $i \in range(0, len(P^O))$ **do**
    for $j \in range(i+1, len(P^O))$ **do**
        $p \leftarrow pref(P^O, i, j)$; $o \leftarrow pref(O, i, j)$
        if $((p = -1)$ *and* $(o = 1))$ *or* $((p = -1)$ *and* $(o = 2))$ **then**
            $P^O[i, j] \leftarrow O[i, j]$; $P^O[j, i] \leftarrow O[j, i]$
            $P^O \leftarrow warshall(P^O)$
Return P^O

---

or E_Δ, to 48 if we refine it by improved optimistic order and to 41 if we refine it by improved cautious order.

4   Refining Default Rules Order by Pareto

Let us consider the refinement problem dual to the one studied in the previous section, namely *given a well-ordered partition E (optimistic E_Π or cautious E_Δ), how can we possibly refine it by the Pareto order?* By definition, the partition E is a set of k ordered layers, thus the refinement can be performed in two steps; the first is an intra-layer refinement (i.e., a pairwise comparison within all configurations in a given layer $l = 0 \ldots k-1$) and the second is an inter-layer refinement (i.e. a pairwise comparison within configurations in a given layer l and those of lower layers $l+1 \ldots k-1$). In the intra-layer refinement, for each pair of configurations (ω, ω'), we check whether P gives additional dominance information (i.e. $\omega \succ \omega'$ or $\omega \prec \omega'$) in this case the less preferred configuration will be removed to a new less preferred intermediary layer (between l and $l+1$). The same principle is applied in the inter-layer refinement where we check that any configuration in a layer of level l is preferred to all configurations at lower levels according to P, otherwise it will be moved down. Obviously, if P says nothing about ω and ω' and E stipulates that $\omega \succ \omega'$ or $\omega \prec \omega'$, then this preference is saved. Algorithm 3 outlines this iterative process. Function $extend(S, i)$ adds intermediary layers from level i down, i.e., an extra layer after each level following i. Function $move(S, \omega, i, j)$ displaces ω from $S[i]$ to $S[j]$. Function $pref(M, \omega, \omega')$ returns 1 (resp. 2, 0, -1) if $\omega \succ \omega'$ (resp. $\omega \prec \omega'$, $\omega \simeq \omega'$, ω and ω' are incomparable) in M.

Table 3. Refined well-ordered partitions based on Algorithm 4

Refined optimistic ordering E_Π		Refined cautious ordering E_Δ	
Pareto $\neq$	Pareto $=$	Pareto $\neq$	Pareto $=$
$\{\omega_0\}$	$\{\omega_0\}$	$\{\omega_0\}$	$\{\omega_0\}$
$\{\omega_1, \omega_3, \omega_6, \omega_{14}\}$	$\{\omega_1, \omega_3, \omega_6, \omega_{14}\}$	$\{\omega_6, \omega_{14}\}$	$\{\omega_6, \omega_{14}\}$
$\{\omega_2, \omega_5, \omega_7, \omega_8, \omega_{13}, \omega_{15}\}$	$\{\omega_2, \omega_5, \omega_7, \omega_8, \omega_{13}, \omega_{15}\}$	$\{\omega_1, \omega_3, \omega_5, \omega_7, \omega_8, \omega_{13}, \omega_{15}\}$	$\{\omega_1\}$
$\{\omega_9, \omega_{11}\}$	$\{\omega_9, \omega_{11}\}$	$\{\omega_2\}$	$\{\omega_3, \omega_7, \omega_8, \omega_{15}\}$
$\{\omega_{10}\}$	$\{\omega_4, \omega_{12}\}$	$\{\omega_4, \omega_9, \omega_{11}\omega_{12}\}$	$\{\omega_2, \omega_5, \omega_{13}\}$
$\{\omega_4, \omega_{12}\}$	$\{\omega_{10}\}$	$\{\omega_{10}\}$	$\{\omega_4, \omega_9, \omega_{11}\omega_{12}\}$
$-$	$-$	$-$	$\{\omega_{10}\}$

Algorithm 3 has as input the Pareto incidence matrix P and a well-ordered partition E such that its layers are sorted from best to worst ones. The worst case corresponds to E containing all configurations i.e. $m = 2^N$ in a unique layer and that we should create one layer by configuration at the end. At the first iteration (resp. 2, 3, $\ldots$, m) we have m^2 (resp. $(m-1)^2$, $(m-2)^2$, $\ldots$, 1) pairwise comparisons. Thus the total number of comparisons is $\sum_{i=1}^{m} i^2 = \frac{m(m+1)(2m+1)}{|E|}$, which means that the time complexity of Algorithm 3 is $O(m^3) = O(2^{N^3}) = O(2^N)$.

Algorithm 3: REFINING SPECIFICITY PARTITION BY PARETO

Input: P, E
Output: S
begin
    $S \leftarrow E; i \leftarrow 0$
    while $i < len(S)$ **do**
        $S \leftarrow extend(S, i)$
        `// intra-layer refinement`
        foreach $\omega \in S[i]$ **do**
            foreach $\omega' \in S[i]$ s.t. $\omega' \neq \omega$ **do**
                `// i+1 is the intermediary intra-layer of i`
                if $pref(P, \omega, \omega') = 1$ **then** $S \leftarrow move(S, \omega', i, i+1)$ **else if**
                $pref(P, \omega, \omega') = 2$ **then** $S \leftarrow move(S, \omega, i, i+1)$

        foreach $\omega \in S[i]$ **do**
            $j \leftarrow i + 2$ `// escape the intermediary intra-layer`
            `// inter-layer refinement`
            while $j < len(S)$ **do**
                foreach $\omega' \in S[j]$ **do**
                    if $pref(P, \omega, \omega') = 2$ **then** $S \leftarrow move(S, \omega, i, j+1)$ **else if**
                    $pref(P, \omega, \omega') = 0$ **then** $S \leftarrow move(S, \omega, i, j)$ **else if**
                    $pref(P, \omega, \omega') = -1$ **then**
                      if $pref(E, \omega, \omega') = 2$ **then** $S \leftarrow move(S, \omega, i, j+1)$ **else if**
                      $pref(E, \omega, \omega') = 0$ **then** $S \leftarrow move(S, \omega, i, j)$

                $j \leftarrow j + 2$ `// escape the intermediary inter-layers`

        $S \leftarrow clean(S, i)$ `// deletes empty layers in S from i`
        $i \leftarrow i + 1$
    $S \leftarrow clean(S, 0)$ `// deletes all empty layers in S`
    Return S

Example 6. *The refined well-ordered partition of Table 2 by the Pareto order considering one symbolic weight per preference statement (Pareto $\neq$) and one weight per variable (Pareto $=$) are given in Table 3. Note that the refined E_{Π} contains 6 layers in the two cases instead of 4 and that the refined E_{Δ} contains 6 (resp. 7) layers instead of 4 if refined by the Pareto order with several (resp. one) symbolic weight(s) per variable.*

5 Conclusion

When comparing two potential solutions with respect to a set of conditional preferences, the Pareto partial order acknowledging that the set of preferences violated by one is a subset of the preferences violated by the other, is a natural basis for ordering solutions. In this paper, we show that it is possible to enrich the Pareto ordering. To this end, we take advantage of two approaches, one in terms of possibilistic network and one in terms of default-like possibilistic constraints, which are proved here to be compatible. The constraints-based approach can lead to a complete preorder once an optimistic or a pessimistic principle is applied, but at the price of some violations of the Pareto order. The paper proposes two algorithms for mending this situation, one that leads to enrich the partial

Pareto preorder, and the other that yields a complete preorder without Pareto violations. The next step would be to extend the proposed approach to the case where constraints between symbolic weights are added for expressing the relative importance of decision variables. This line of thought brings us closer to methods based on a lexicographic handling of preferences (e.g., [10]), which calls for detailed comparison with the π-pref net approach.

References

1. Boutilier, C., Brafman, R.I., Domshlak, C., Hoos, H.H., Poole, D.: CP-nets: a tool for representing and reasoning with conditional ceteris paribus preference statements. J. Artif. Intell. Res. (JAIR) **21**, 135–191 (2004). https://doi.org/10.1613/jair.1234

2. Dubois, D., Hadjali, A., Prade, H., Touazi, F.: Erratum to: database preference queries - a possibilistic logic approach with symbolic priorities. Ann. Math. Artif. Intell. **73**(3–4), 359–363 (2015). https://doi.org/10.1007/s10472-014-9446-2

3. Wilson, N., Dubois, D., Prade, H.: CP-Nets, π-pref nets, and pareto dominance. In: Ben Amor, N., Quost, B., Theobald, M. (eds.) SUM 2019. LNCS (LNAI), vol. 11940, pp. 169–183. Springer, Cham (2019). https://doi.org/10.1007/978-3-030-35514-2_13

4. Ben, A.N., Dubois, D., Gouider, H., Prade, H.: Possibilistic preference networks. Inf. Sci. **460–461**, 401–415 (2018). https://doi.org/10.1016/j.ins.2017.08.002

5. Ben Amor N., Dubois D., Gouider H., Prade H. Preference modeling with possibilistic networks and symbolic weights: a theoretical study. In: Proceedings of 22nd European Conference on Artificial Intelligence (ECAI 2016), The Hague, pp. 1203–1211 (2016). https://doi.org/10.3233/978-1-61499-672-9-1203

6. Dubois, D., Prade, H.: Possibility theory and its applications: where do we stand? In: Kacprzyk, J., Pedrycz, W. (eds.) Springer Handbook of Computational Intelligence, pp. 31–60. Springer, Heidelberg (2015). https://doi.org/10.1007/978-3-662-43505-2_3

7. Ben Amor, N., Dubois, D., Prade, H., Saidi, S.: Revisiting conditional preferences: from defaults to graphical representations. In: Kern-Isberner, G., Ognjanović, Z. (eds.) ECSQARU 2019. LNCS (LNAI), vol. 11726, pp. 187–198. Springer, Cham (2019). https://doi.org/10.1007/978-3-030-29765-7_16

8. Boutilier C., Brafman R.I., Hoos H.H., Poole D.: Reasoning with conditional Ceteris Paribus preference statements. In: Proceedings of 15th Conference on Uncertainty in AI (UAI 1999), Stockholm, pp. 71–80 (1999)

9. Benferhat S., Dubois D., Prade H.: Representing default rules in possibilistic logic. In: Proceedings of 3rd International Conference Principles of Knowledge Representation and Reasoning (KR 1992), Cambridge, pp. 673–684 (1992)

10. Lang, J., Mengin, J., Xia, L.: Aggregating conditionally lexicographic preferences on multi-issue domains. In: Milano, M. (ed.) CP 2012. LNCS, pp. 973–987. Springer, Heidelberg (2012). https://doi.org/10.1007/978-3-642-33558-7_69

Enhancing Multi-objective Evolutionary Neural Architecture Search with Surrogate Models and Potential Point-Guided Local Searches

Quan Minh Phan[1,2] and Ngoc Hoang Luong[1,2(✉)]

[1] University of Information Technology, Ho Chi Minh City, Vietnam
17520941@gm.uit.edu.vn, hoangln@uit.edu.vn
[2] Vietnam National University, Ho Chi Minh City, Vietnam

Abstract. In this paper, we investigate two methods to enhance the efficiency of multi-objective evolutionary algorithms (MOEAs) when solving Neural Architecture Search (NAS) problems. The first method is to use a surrogate model to predict the accuracy of candidate architectures. Only promising architectures with high predicted accuracy values would then be truly trained and evaluated while the ones with low predicted accuracy would be discarded. The second method is to perform local search for potential solutions on the non-dominated front after each MOEA generation. To demonstrate the effectiveness of the proposed methods, we conduct experiments on benchmark datasets of both macro-level (MacroNAS) and micro-level (NAS-Bench-101, NAS-Bench-201) NAS problems. Experimental results exhibit that the proposed methods achieve improvements on the convergence speed of MOEAs toward Pareto-optimal fronts, especially for macro-level NAS problems.

Keywords: Evolutionary computation · Memetic algorithm · Neural architecture search · Multi-objective optimization

1 Introduction

Deep neural networks (DNNs) play a crucial role in state-of-the-art machine learning-based Artificial Intelligence (AI) technologies and applications. However, designing high-performance DNN architectures often involves a lengthy manual trial-and-error process and requires non-trivial experiences from domain experts. Neural Architecture Search (NAS), attempting to automate the design process of DNN architectures that are suitable for a given dataset, is thus a central challenge in the automated machine learning (AutoML) paradigm.

Most studies on NAS aim is to find DNN architectures of the highest accuracy values. Nowadays, DNNs are deployed not only on computer workstations, but also on a wide range of other platforms, such as smartphones, self-driving cars, or drones [9]. The characteristics (e.g., memory capacity, processing speed, power

© Springer Nature Switzerland AG 2021
H. Fujita et al. (Eds.): IEA/AIE 2021, LNAI 12798, pp. 460–472, 2021.
https://doi.org/10.1007/978-3-030-79457-6_39

consumption) of devices on each platform can be very dissimilar. For the effective application of DNNs on these devices, NAS needs to consider not only the accuracy performance but also other computational efficiency aspects such as the inference latency, the number of network parameters, etc. In recent years, NAS is often formulated as multi-objective optimization problems. The first objective to optimize is usually the accuracy performance achieved by the architectures, and the other objectives are often efficiency metrics (e.g., the cost of computational resources, the number of network parameters, the inference latency) [12,13]. When a preference among the objectives is known *a priori* (e.g., accuracy is more important than computational cost), the objectives can be weighted by their corresponding importances and then aggregated into a single objective to be optimized. However, it is typically difficult to determine such a concrete set of weights properly before running the optimization, and different decision-makers could even have different preferences among the objectives. Because NAS is an inherent multi-objective optimization problem, NAS should be solved by a true multi-objective optimization approach, i.e., the conflicting objectives should be kept separately rather than being aggregated. Multi-Objective Evolutionary Algorithms (MOEAs [5]) have been shown to be the appropriate methodology to address (multi-objective) NAS problems [8,10,13,15]. NSGA-Net [13] uses Non-dominated Sorting Genetic Algorithm II (NSGA-II [6]) to minimize the classification error and computational complexity. The found networks are significantly better than handcrafted networks on both objectives. Efficiency of MOEAs on NAS can also be enhanced with the Lamarckian mechanism [8], where each time an offspring network architecture is created, its weights are inherited from its parents and are then further fine-tuned instead of being trained from scratch. In this paper, we present two efficiency enhancement methods to improve the performance of multi-objective evolutionary NAS (MOENAS). First, a surrogate model is used to predict the accuracy of each candidate architecture. Only promising architectures are then truly evaluated to obtain their exact accuracy values. Costly computational resources are thus saved from being wasted on evaluating unpromising architectures. Second, we consider certain solutions on the *non-dominated front* (see definition in Sect. 2.2) of the current population to be *potential* solutions. We argue that *extreme* solutions and *knee* solutions are the solutions which could be further improved by local search techniques, thus potentially enhancing the search efficiency of MOENAS rather than performing local search on the entire non-dominated front.

The remainder of this paper is organized as follows. The details of our proposed methods are introduced in Sect. 2. Section 3 shows benchmark problems, their characteristics, and experimental setup. Experimental results are presented and discussed in Sect. 4. Finally, the paper is concluded in Sect. 5.

2 Our Proposed Methods

2.1 Using Surrogate Model

Performance prediction is a method to predict the accuracy of neural network architectures on a specific dataset instead of actually training and evaluating them. The benefit of the performance prediction method is to reduce computational costs while still obtaining acceptable results. Different studies have made use of surrogate models for estimating the performance of architectures in order to enhance the efficiency of NAS runs [3,4,11,12]. OnceForAll [3] and Cham-Net [4] use surrogate models that are trained offline based on datasets of sample architectures collected prior to the NAS runs. On the other hand, similar to [12], our surrogate model is trained online while the search process is running, and the data to fit the model is sampled from the found architectures.

The advantage of using a surrogate model is the reduction in the cost of computational resources. This only happens if a high correlation between the predicted accuracy and true accuracy can be established. To this end, we often need a large number of sample architectures to simulate the entire search space for training surrogate models. However, training and evaluating these architectures prior to the actual NAS run would incur a very large overhead. Such a drawback of using surrogate models can be circumvented as follows. First, we do not entirely rely on accuracy values predicted by surrogate models, but only use them as a *filter*. In [12], a candidate architecture will be truly trained if it is predicted to be near the current non-dominated front. In this paper, when the predicted accuracy of an architecture is greater than a threshold α, we will truly train and evaluate that architecture to obtain its true accuracy. The value of α is equal to the average accuracy of truly trained architectures. Second, instead of keeping the surrogate model parameters unchanged from the initialization to the end of the search, we update its parameters after every t generations to ensure that the predicted accuracy approximates the true accuracy. In [12], surrogate models are updated based on only architectures that are near the current non-dominated front. Here, the dataset for surrogate model updating is sampled from the set of found architectures. We update the model after every t generations, but before updating, we compute the average squared difference between the predicted values and the actual values. If this value is relatively small (e.g., $<1e{-}3$), no model updating is performed for the rest of the search.

2.2   Improving Potential Solutions

At the end of every generation, the *non-dominated front* $\mathcal{S}$ of the current population is made out of a set of solutions that are not Pareto dominated by any other population individuals. We firstly find potential solutions out of $\mathcal{S}$ and store them in the potential set $\mathcal{K}$. We then perform quality improvement for every solution in $\mathcal{K}$. This efficiency enhancement method has two major phases: **identifying** and **improving** potential solutions.

The first phase is to identify potential solutions. First, we define what a potential solution is. Branke et al. [2] propose a definition of *knee* solutions on the non-dominated front, i.e., a knee solution is a solution where a small improvement in one objective would lead to a large deterioration in at least one other objective. In the situation where no *a priori* preference is defined, knee solutions are more likely to be chosen by the decision-maker than other solutions on the non-dominated front. Beside knee solutions, so-called *extreme* solutions are also important in multi-objective optimization. An extreme solution can be defined as the one that optimizes a single objective, i.e., the best solution for that specific objective on the current non-domination front. Even though decision makers are unlikely to choose such a solution (because while one objective is optimized, other objectives are considerably compromised), extreme solutions together represent the range of a Pareto front. Optimization performance could potentially be improved if these extreme solutions are specially handled during the search. We here consider knee solutions and extreme solutions on the non-dominated front of each MOEA generation as the *potential* solutions that should be further improved by local searches, thereby enhancing the efficiency of MOEAs.

The identifying procedure is as follows. We first create an empty set $\mathcal{K}$ to store potential solutions. Given the non-dominated front $\mathcal{S}$ and the objective values of solutions on it, we can easily pick the extreme solutions and put them into $\mathcal{K}$. We then check the remaining solutions whether they are knee solutions by employing the same method as in [2]. For each solution, we calculate the angle measure $\measuredangle$ created by itself and two closest neighboring solutions. Note that these neighbors must be on both sides (i.e., left and right) of the solution. We set a threshold $\gamma \in [0, 360]$ for selecting the knees. If a solution has an angle measure $\measuredangle$ larger than γ, we consider it as a knee solution and put it into $\mathcal{K}$.

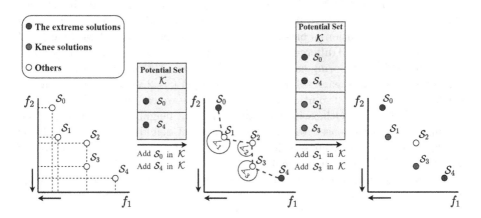

Fig. 1. An example of identifying potential solutions.

Figure 1 illustrates an example of the identifying procedure. The front $\mathcal{S}$ has five non-dominated solutions: $\mathcal{S}_0$, $\mathcal{S}_1$, $\mathcal{S}_2$, $\mathcal{S}_3$, and $\mathcal{S}_4$. It can be seen that $\mathcal{S}_0$ is the best solution for objective f_1 and $\mathcal{S}_4$ is the best solutions for objective f_2. Thus, they are put into $\mathcal{K}$. For three remaining solutions $\mathcal{S}_1$, $\mathcal{S}_2$, and $\mathcal{S}_3$, we calculate the angles $\measuredangle_1$, $\measuredangle_2$, and $\measuredangle_3$ respectively. Because $\measuredangle_1$ and $\measuredangle_3$ are larger than γ, $\mathcal{S}_1$ and $\mathcal{S}_3$ are considered knee solutions and are then added into $\mathcal{K}$. The final $\mathcal{K}$ contains 4 solutions: $\mathcal{S}_0$, $\mathcal{S}_1$, $\mathcal{S}_3$, and $\mathcal{S}_4$.

In the second phase, we improve the solutions in $\mathcal{K}$. The improvement of a solution is made by replacing it with a better neighboring solution. We use a variant of k-opt local search to implement the improving procedure as follows.

Algorithm 1. IMPROVING($\mathcal{K}$, C, k)

```
 1: m ← l
 2: for x ∈ K do
 3:     L ← [ ]
 4:     n ← 0
 5:     while n < m do
 6:         x' ← x
 7:         I ← RANDOMINRANGE(0, |x'|− 1, k)
 8:         for i ∈ I do
 9:             C' ← C \ {x'ᵢ}
10:             x'ᵢ ← RANDOM(C')
11:         if x' ∉ L and x' ∉ P then
12:             L ← ADD(L, x')
13:             f(x') ← EVALUATE(x')
14:             b ← THEBETTERONE((x, f(x)), (x', f(x')))
15:             if b == x' then
16:                 x ← x' ;   f(x) ← f(x')
17:             n ← n + 1
```

For each solution in $\mathcal{K}$, checking all neighboring solutions would incur a lot of costly computational resources. For example, in the MacroNAS-C10 problem (see Sect. 3.1), a solution is presented as a string of length $l = 14$ variables, and each variable has $n = 3$ different choices. If we perform a search on $k = 1$ variable, we will have 28 neighboring solutions (i.e., $\binom{l}{k} * (n-1)^k$) for each solution, and this number is 364 for each solution if we search on $k = 2$ variables. Checking all neighbors of a potential solution is beneficial only if we can find a better solution in its neighborhood. Otherwise, checking all of its neighbors is too costly and meaningless. We thus need to limit the number of neighbors m that would be checked for each potential solution. We here assign $m = l$, i.e., equal to the solution length l, to ensure a local search of linear growth.

The improving procedure is presented as follows. For every solution $x \in \mathcal{K}$, we search for m neighboring solutions. To figure out a new neighboring solution x', we first pick randomly k variables of x. For each selected variable, its value is changed to a new value, which must belong to the available set C and is not the same as the old one. To avoid a new neighbor solution x' that has been found earlier, we check if it is a member of $\mathcal{L}$, where $\mathcal{L}$ is the set used to memorize the searched neighbors of x. We also check whether x' is in the current population $\mathcal{P}$ to avoid duplication. If x' has these above properties, we dismiss it and search for a new neighbor. In contrast, we add x' into $\mathcal{L}$ and calculate the objective function values $f(x')$. After that, we compare the objective values of the neighbor $f(x')$ with the objective values of the current solution $f(x)$ to find out which one is the better solution b. There are two cases that may occur. If x is an extreme solution, we only use the objective value which x is the best at to compare. In this case, b is the solution has the lesser (for minimization) or the greater (for maximization) objective value. Otherwise, if x is a knee solution, we use all objective values for comparison. In this case, we use the definition of Pareto dominance [5] to find out b, i.e., solution x' is said to dominate solution x if and only if x' is not worse than x in any objective and x' is strictly better than x in at least one objective. After comparing, x is replaced by b. Pseudo-code of improving process is given in Algorithm 1.

3 Experimental Settings

3.1 Benchmark Problems

MacroNAS [15] is a benchmark built for macro-level NAS. This dataset contains $4,782,969$ encodings, that map to $208,538$ unique architectures, and their corresponding performance on the CIFAR-10 and CIFAR-100 datasets. The performance metrics of each architecture are: the testing accuracy, the validation accuracy, the number of trainable model parameters, and the Mega Multiply-ACcumulation (MMACs). For the MacroNAS dataset, we consider two problems MacroNAS-C10 (for CIFAR-10) and MacroNAS-C100 (for CIFAR-100) created in [15]. For each problem, the validation error (i.e., 1.0 - the validation accuracy) and MMACs are chosen as the minimization objectives.

NAS-Bench-101 [16] is the benchmark built for micro-level NAS. It consists of about 423k unique architectures and their performance on the CIFAR-10 dataset. The performance metrics of each architecture are: the training accuracy, the validation accuracy, the testing accuracy, the training time in seconds, and the number of trainable model parameters. For the NAS-Bench-101 dataset, we create the NAS-101 problem. The goal of this problem is to minimize the validation error and the number of trainable model parameters.

NAS-Bench-201 [7] is also a benchmark built for micro-level NAS, consisting of $15,625$ architectures and their performance on the CIFAR-10, CIFAR-100 and ImageNet16-120 dataset. The performance metrics of the architectures are: the validation accuracy, the testing accuracy, the number of trainable model parameters, the latency of model, and the floating point operations per second (FLOPS). For the NAS-Bench-201 benchmark, three problems are built: NAS-201-1 (for CIFAR-10 dataset), NAS-201-2 (for CIFAR-100 dataset), and NAS-201-3 (for ImageNet16-120 dataset). The goal of all problems is to minimize the validation error (i.e., 1.0 - the validation accuracy) and FLOPS.

3.2 Experimental Setup

We use an *elitist archive* $\mathcal{A}$ (which is similar to an external secondary population) to store non-dominated solutions obtained so far during the search [14]. Each time a new solution is generated, we verify if it is not dominated by any solutions in $\mathcal{A}$, and it can then be inserted into $\mathcal{A}$. Solutions existed in $\mathcal{A}$ but are dominated by the newly-added solution would be removed from $\mathcal{A}$. The elitist archive thus forms the *non-dominated front* obtained so far during the search. At the end of the run, the elitist archive forms the *approximation front*, which can be considered as the optimization results achieved by the algorithm. Besides, we also use a set to store dominated solutions $\mathcal{D}$. If the solution is already in $\mathcal{D}$, we disregard it and search for a new solution. Using $\mathcal{D}$ helps avoid evaluating a dominated solution. The update of $\mathcal{D}$ is performed in parallel with the update of $\mathcal{A}$. While $\mathcal{A}$ is updating, if a solution is dominated, it is added into $\mathcal{D}$. In this paper, we do not limit the size of $\mathcal{A}$ and $\mathcal{D}$. This is still a realistic implementation regarding that the total number of evaluations is relatively small and the architecture evaluation time dominates the entire NAS run in practice.

We employ a standard NSGA-II variant (2-point crossover with probability 0.9 and bit-string mutation with probability $1/l$) as the baseline MOEA. We then choose the Multi-Layer Perceptron (MLP) as the surrogate model to predict the accuracy of candidate architectures during an NSGA-II run solving NAS. The hyper-parameters of MLP are set following [12]. We update the model parameters after every $t = 10$ generations for every problem. We set $\gamma = 210$ as the threshold to choose knee solutions. We consider two k−opt local search variants: $k = 1$ and $k = 2$, where the neighborhood of a solution involves changing 1 and 2 variables at a time, respectively. As a result, we perform six variants for each benchmark: baseline NSGA-II, NSGA-II with a surrogate model, NSGA-II with improving potential solution $k = 1$, NSGA-II with improving potential solution $k = 2$, NSGA-II with a surrogate model and improving potential solution $k = 1$, NSGA-II with a surrogate model and improving potential solution $k = 2$. For each variant, we perform 21 independent runs for each problem. For problems created on MacroNAS and NAS-Bench-101 dataset, we set the population size and the maximum number of evaluations to be 100 and 30,000, respectively. For problems created on NAS-Bench-201 dataset, we set the population size and the maximum number of evaluations are 20 and 3,000, respectively.

We use the non-dominated fronts $\mathcal{S}$ over generations of each algorithm variant to compare their performance. To measure the quality of $\mathcal{S}$, we employ two performance indicators: the Inverted Generational Distance [1] (IGD) and the hypervolume [5]. The IGD performance indicator can be computed as follows

$$IGD(\mathcal{S}, \mathcal{P}_F) = \frac{1}{|\mathcal{P}_F|} \sum_{f^0 \in \mathcal{P}_F} \min_{x \in \mathcal{S}} \{d(f(x), f^0)\} \tag{1}$$

where $\mathcal{P}_F$ is the Pareto-optimal front (or a reference front), $\mathcal{S}$ is a approximation front (i.e., a non-dominated front obtained by a multi-objective algorithm), and $d(\cdot, \cdot)$ computes the Euclidean distance (in the objective space). IGD indicates the proximity (i.e., how close $\mathcal{S}$ is to the Pareto-optimal front $\mathcal{P}_F$) and diversity (i.e., how well-spread $\mathcal{S}$ is along $\mathcal{P}_F$) of the approximation front $\mathcal{S}$ [1]. When using IGD to make a comparison of the performance of two MOEAs, the algorithm that achieves the smaller value is the better one. Note that $IGD(\mathcal{S}, \mathcal{P}_F) = 0$ if and only if $\mathcal{S} = \mathcal{P}_F$, i.e., the entire Pareto-optimal front $\mathcal{P}_F$ is found.

The Pareto-optimal fronts $\mathcal{P}_F$ (or reference fronts) are required to compute IGD values. In this paper, because the objective values of all architectures in the benchmarks have already been evaluated, the Pareto-optimal front for each benchmark can be straightforwardly made by selecting non-dominated architec-

Table 1. Means and standard deviations (in brackets) of the IGD and the hypervolume of algorithms on 21 runs on MacroNAS-C100. The bold results indicate the better algorithm between the original algorithm and the algorithms integrating our proposed methods (99% confidence level)

IGD

#Eval	NSGA-II	With SM	With LS $k=1$	With SM + LS $k=1$	With LS $k=2$	With SM + LS $k=2$
1000	0.024396 (0.005962)	**0.016862 (0.005584)**	**0.008888 (0.003663)**	**0.007606 (0.003416)**	0.017454 (0.004836)	**0.014283 (0.004913)**
2000	0.012723 (0.003333)	0.011514 (0.002511)	0.005205 (0.001287)	**0.005306 (0.002758)**	0.009205 (0.003677)	**0.008798 (0.003556)**
5000	0.002127 (0.001434)	0.002317 (0.001419)	0.001697 (0.000829)	0.002161 (0.001024)	0.002324 (0.000802)	0.002517 (0.001153)
10000	0.000818 (0.000404)	0.000863 (0.000356)	0.00079 (0.000335)	0.000818 (0.000379)	0.00082 (0.000341)	0.000863 (0.000346)
30000	0.000314 (0.000125)	0.000279 (0.000146)	0.000371 (8.5e−05)	0.000312 (0.000143)	0.00031 (0.000111)	0.000288 (0.000154)

Hypervolume

#Eval	NSGA-II	With SM	With LS $k=1$	With SM + LS $k=1$	With LS $k=2$	With SM + LS $k=2$
1000	0.373877 (0.00925)	**0.386463 (0.00974)**	**0.399686 (0.005047)**	**0.403843 (0.001884)**	0.386821 (0.008644)	**0.392714 (0.0082)**
2000	0.395612 (0.005882)	0.395542 (0.004881)	0.406057 (0.001326)	**0.40632 (0.001012)**	0.400273 (0.00678)	**0.401496 (0.005853)**
5000	0.408259 (0.000457)	0.408311 (0.000336)	0.40836 (0.000309)	0.40833 (0.00039)	0.408195 (0.000534)	0.40806 (0.000346)
10000	0.408737 (0.00015)	0.408777 (9.8e−05)	0.408788 (7.4e−05)	0.408804 (6.9e−05)	0.408774 (0.000122)	0.40878 (0.000119)
30000	0.408895 (8e−06)	0.408899 (8e−06)	0.408893 (6e−06)	0.408896 (9e−06)	0.408896 (7e−06)	0.408897 (8e−06)

Table 2. Means and standard deviations (in brackets) of the IGD and the hypervolume of algorithms on 21 runs on NAS-201-3. The bold results indicate the better algorithm between the original algorithm and the algorithms integrating our proposed methods (99% confidence level)

IGD

#Eval	NSGA-II	With SM	With LS $k=1$	With SM + LS $k=1$	With LS $k=2$	With SM + LS $k=2$
100	0.036213 (0.01181)	0.037466 (0.014055)	0.037642 (0.014051)	0.032575 (0.009012)	0.034283 (0.013407)	0.038555 (0.016343)
200	0.024911 (0.012629)	0.030012 (0.014307)	0.030344 (0.011354)	0.02516 (0.010705)	0.029305 (0.015393)	0.030604 (0.016669)
500	0.016546 (0.010482)	0.01478 (0.008897)	0.013861 (0.009892)	0.018952 (0.009725)	0.014584 (0.009398)	0.02256 (0.013566)
1000	0.009963 (0.010435)	0.012057 (0.011143)	**0.003158 (0.001294)**	0.006425 (0.008199)	0.009294 (0.009608)	0.011459 (0.01079)
3000	0.000841 (0.000654)	0.000855 (0.000754)	0.000539 (0.000372)	0.000928 (0.000599)	0.000503 (0.000394)	0.000785 (0.000482)

Hypervolume

#Eval	NSGA-II	With SM	With LS $k=1$	With SM + LS $k=1$	With LS $k=2$	With SM + LS $k=2$
100	0.423089 (0.006537)	0.425559 (0.006778)	0.425817 (0.005113)	**0.429186 (0.004475)**	0.425876 (0.004926)	0.427601 (0.005158)
200	0.431768 (0.004405)	0.432487 (0.004947)	0.433817 (0.004273)	**0.435755 (0.004124)**	0.433065 (0.004507)	0.434772 (0.003446)
500	0.440033 (0.002903)	0.440006 (0.002995)	0.440196 (0.00334)	0.440608 (0.002995)	0.439689 (0.002759)	0.43978 (0.002651)
1000	0.443823 (0.001392)	0.44397 (0.000989)	0.444434 (0.000974)	0.444159 (0.00127)	0.443662 (0.00133)	0.443848 (0.001125)
3000	0.445539 (0.000458)	0.445604 (0.000415)	0.445739 (0.000102)	0.445604 (0.000304)	0.445765 (7.2e−05)	0.445716 (8e−05)

tures from the corresponding dataset. In many real-world problems, however, it is impossible to have access to such Pareto-optimal fronts. The hypervolume is an alternative performance indicator to evaluate the performance of MOEAs if we do not have a reference front. Hypervolume [5] can be computed as the volume enclosed by the non-dominated front S and a reference point (which is often defined in relation to the nadir point, i.e., its coordinates are the worst possible objective values). When using hypervolume to compare the fronts obtained by different MOEAs, the one that yields the larger hypervolume value is the better one. We here consider employing both IGD and hypervolume as the performance indicators for all MOEA variants.

4   Results and Discussions

4.1   Macro-level NAS

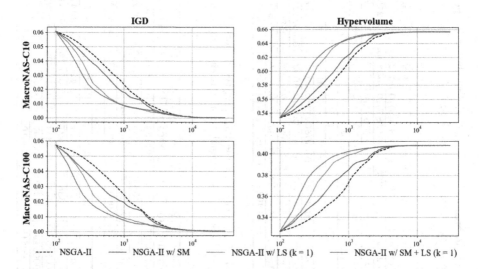

Fig. 2. Average performance of algorithms on macro-level NAS problems. Horizontal axis: the number of evaluations (logarithm).

Figure 2 exhibits that all algorithms perform effectively on both macro-level problems MacroNAS-C10 and MacroNAS-C100. All algorithms find out almost all of the entire Pareto-optimal fronts (i.e., the final IGD values are nearly 0) even though the budget of architecture evaluations is much smaller compared to the search space size ($30,000 \ll 4,782,969$). Figure 2 and Table 1 show that the performance of the baseline NSGA-II is significantly enhanced on both IGD and hypervolume metrics in early generations of the searches by integrating with the proposed enhancement techniques. Such improvements offer great practicalities for NAS because, in real-world situations, we do not have much computational resource for training and evaluating a large number of architectures. Either surrogate model or local search alone is sufficient to accelerate NSGA-II in converging toward the Pareto-optimal fronts and the accelerations are found to be statistically significant (see Table 1). The best efficiency enhancements are yielded when both surrogate model and local search are incorporated with NSGA-II.

The k value influences the performance of our proposed k-opt local search. We conduct additional experiments with $k \geq 2$ (only the results of $k = 1, 2$ are reported in Tables 1 and 2). We observe that the higher k value is, the lower performance enhancement can be achieved. Increasing the k value enlarges the neighborhood of each potential solution exponentially. Our local search, which is linear in terms of the solution length l, does not explore this neighborhood enough. A more thorough local search, however, would incur the cost of each local search run exponentially. We conclude that k-opt local search with $k = 1$ is suitable for the macro-level NAS problems considered in this paper.

4.2 Micro-level NAS

For micro-level NAS problems, the algorithms are also able to obtain almost the entire (reference) Pareto-optimal fronts. Similar to the results on macro-level NAS, the results in Fig. 3 show that our efficiency enhancement techniques also improve the performance of NSGA-II solving micro-level NAS problems in early generations. Table 2 shows that, at the 99% confidence level, significant improvements are achieved for the hypervolume indicator, but not for the IGD indicator. During local searches, we observe that there are few better solutions can be found in the neighborhoods of potential solutions. This issue relates to the representation mechanisms that are used to encode candidate architectures. For NAS problems on the micro level, the characteristics of each architecture involve the operators and the connections of its layers. The neighborhood of our k-opt local search is defined directly on such representations, in which k indicates the number of components can vary at a time. We argue that just a few micro-level changes (i.e., k-opt with small values of k) would yield little impact on the overall performance of a deep neural network. On the other hand, local searches that thoroughly explore too large neighborhoods (i.e., k-opt with big values of k) would be prohibitively expensive, especially for NAS problems. Besides, the effectiveness of surrogate models also depends on the neural architecture representation, which is the input of our MLP in this paper. This suggests that a more dedicated design is required for surrogate models to function well with micro-level architecture encoding schemes.

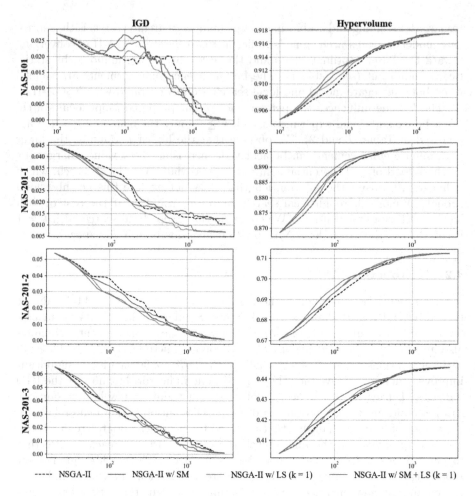

Fig. 3. Average performance of algorithms on micro level NAS problems. Horizontal axis: number of evaluations (logarithm).

5   Conclusions

We investigated two methods to enhance the efficiency of evolutionary algorithms when tackling multi-objective NAS problems. First, a surrogate model, an MLP in particular, was used to predict the performance of candidate architectures so that only architectures deemed promising should be accurately evaluated. Second, we suggested that local search could be performed for certain potential solutions, which were defined as the extreme and knee solutions on the non-dominated front. To verify the effectiveness of these two techniques, we performed experiments on both macro-level and micro-level NAS benchmark datasets. The obtained results showed that our proposed methods brought about significant enhancements over the baseline algorithm for NAS problems on the macro level. For micro-level NAS, more sophisticated local search techniques and more dedicated surrogate models would be required and are left for future work.

Acknowledgements. This research is funded by University of Information Technology - Vietnam National University HoChiMinh City under grant number D1-2021-09.

References

1. Bosman, P.A.N., Thierens, D.: The balance between proximity and diversity in multiobjective evolutionary algorithms. IEEE Trans. Evol. Comput. **7**(2), 174–188 (2003)
2. Branke, J., Deb, K., Dierolf, H., Osswald, M.: Finding knees in multi-objective optimization. In: Yao, X., et al. (eds.) PPSN 2004. LNCS, vol. 3242, pp. 722–731. Springer, Heidelberg (2004). https://doi.org/10.1007/978-3-540-30217-9_73
3. Cai, H., Gan, C., Wang, T., Zhang, Z., Han, S.: Once-for-all: train one network and specialize it for efficient deployment. In: Proceedings of the International Conference on Learning Representations (ICLR) (2020)
4. Dai, X., et al.: ChamNet: towards efficient network design through platform-aware model adaptation. In: Proceedings of the IEEE Conference on Computer Vision and Pattern Recognition (CVPR) (2019)
5. Deb, K.: Multi-objective Optimization Using Evolutionary Algorithms. Wiley-Interscience Series in Systems and Optimization. Wiley, Hoboken (2001)
6. Deb, K., Agrawal, S., Pratap, A., Meyarivan, T.: A fast and elitist multiobjective genetic algorithm: NSGA-II. IEEE Trans. Evol. Comput. **6**(2), 182–197 (2002)
7. Dong, X., Yang, Y.: NAS-Bench-201: Extending the scope of reproducible neural architecture search. In: Proceedings of the International Conference on Learning Representations (ICLR) (2020)
8. Elsken, T., Metzen, J.H., Hutter, F.: Efficient multi-objective neural architecture search via Lamarckian evolution. In: Proceedings of the International Conference on Learning Representations (ICLR) (2019)
9. Howard, A.G., et al.: MobileNets: efficient convolutional neural networks for mobile vision applications. arXiv preprint arXiv:1704.04861 (2017)
10. Kim, Y.H., Reddy, B., Yun, S., Seo, C.: NEMO: neuro-evolution with multiobjective optimization of deep neural network for speed and accuracy. In: ICML 2017 AutoML Workshop (2017)
11. Liu, C., et al.: Progressive neural architecture search. In: Ferrari, V., Hebert, M., Sminchisescu, C., Weiss, Y. (eds.) ECCV 2018. LNCS, vol. 11205, pp. 19–35. Springer, Cham (2018). https://doi.org/10.1007/978-3-030-01246-5_2
12. Lu, Z., Deb, K., Goodman, E., Banzhaf, W., Boddeti, V.N.: NSGANetV2: evolutionary multi-objective surrogate-assisted neural architecture search. In: Vedaldi, A., Bischof, H., Brox, T., Frahm, J.-M. (eds.) ECCV 2020. LNCS, vol. 12346, pp. 35–51. Springer, Cham (2020). https://doi.org/10.1007/978-3-030-58452-8_3
13. Lu, Z., et al.: NSGA-Net: neural architecture search using multi-objective genetic algorithm. In: Proceedings of the Genetic and Evolutionary Computation Conference (GECCO) (2019)
14. Luong, H.N., Bosman, P.A.N.: Elitist archiving for multi-objective evolutionary algorithms: to adapt or not to adapt. In: Coello, C.A.C., Cutello, V., Deb, K., Forrest, S., Nicosia, G., Pavone, M. (eds.) PPSN 2012. LNCS, vol. 7492, pp. 72–81. Springer, Heidelberg (2012). https://doi.org/10.1007/978-3-642-32964-7_8

15. Ottelander, T.D., Dushatskiy, A., Virgolin, M., Bosman, P.A.N.: Local search is a remarkably strong baseline for neural architecture search. In: Proceedings of the International Conference on Evolutionary Multi-Criterion Optimization (EMO) (2021)
16. Ying, C., Klein, A., Christiansen, E., Real, E., Murphy, K., Hutter, F.: Nas-bench-101: towards reproducible neural architecture search. In: International Conference on Machine Learning. pp. 7105–7114 (2019)

Insightful and Practical Multi-objective Convolutional Neural Network Architecture Search with Evolutionary Algorithms

Tu Do[1,2] and Ngoc Hoang Luong[1,2(✉)]

[1] University of Information Technology, Ho Chi Minh City, Vietnam
18521578@gm.uit.edu.vn, hoangln@uit.edu.vn
[2] Vietnam National University, Ho Chi Minh City, Vietnam

Abstract. This paper investigates a comprehensive convolutional neural network (CNN) representation that encodes both layer connections, and computational block attributes for neural architecture search (NAS). We formulate NAS as a bi-objective optimization problem, where two competing objectives, i.e., the validation accuracy and the model complexity, need to be considered simultaneously. We employ the well-known multi-objective evolutionary algorithm (MOEA) nondominated sorting genetic algorithm II (NSGA-II) to perform multi-objective NAS experiments on the CIFAR-10 dataset. Our NAS runs obtain trade-off fronts of architectures of much wider ranges and better quality compared to NAS runs with less comprehensive representations. We also transfer promising architectures to other datasets, i.e., CIFAR-100, Street View House Numbers, and Intel Image Classification, to verify their applicability. Experimental results indicate that the architectures on the trade-off front obtained at the end of our NAS runs can be straightforwardly employed out of the box without any further modification.

Keywords: Multi-objective optimization · Deep learning · Neural architecture search · Evolutionary algorithms

1 Introduction

Neural Architecture Search (NAS [7]) aims to automate the cumbersome process of finding proper deep neural network architectures for a given machine learning task. NAS problems often involve competing objectives that need to be considered at the same time. On the one hand, we would like to find architectures that achieve high accuracy, but on the other hand, we prefer compact networks with small numbers of trainable parameters or fewer floating-point operations (FLOPs). We wish to obtain a so-called Pareto *front* of architectures that exhibit the best possible *trade-offs* between the objectives. Practitioners can straightforwardly compare all these architectures, investigate their trade-offs, and select the

© Springer Nature Switzerland AG 2021
H. Fujita et al. (Eds.): IEA/AIE 2021, LNAI 12798, pp. 473–479, 2021.
https://doi.org/10.1007/978-3-030-79457-6_40

suitable one for the given task/dataset to implement. Such Pareto front-based decision-making is much more insightful than solving a single-objective NAS problem and obtaining a single solution that only optimizes a single aspect.

In NSGA-Net [7], the widely-used multi-objective evolutionary algorithm (MOEA) nondominated sorting genetic algorithm II (NSGA-II [1]) is employed to obtain the trade-off front for the multi-objective NAS problem with regard to a classification task on the CIFAR-10 dataset. However, the architecture selected from the final result trade-off front (i.e., the one with the lowest error rate) is then further fine-tuned by altering the number of filters of each layer in each computational block in order to achieve the desired performance. We argue that such modifications and other architecture re-configurations should be automated by NAS algorithms such that the obtained architectures could be straightforwardly used out of the box. To this end, we introduce a more comprehensive CNN architecture representation that includes decision variables associated with not only connections in convolutional blocks but also other details such as block types, numbers of channels, kernel sizes, and pool sizes.

2   CNN Architecture Representation Mechanism

Many state-of-the-art CNN-based architectures can be described as a series of computational *blocks* (which are also referred to as *phases*). Each computational block is followed by a spatial pooling operation to reduce the resolution. Each phase consists of multiple operations, which are represented as nodes in a graph. Nodes in the same phase share certain attributes.

2.1   Connection Encoding

We encode the node connections in the same phase following the approaches of Lu et al. [7] and Xie et al. [9]. An architecture is denoted as an ordered set $\mathcal{P} = (p_1, p_2, \ldots, p_N)$ where N is the number of phases. Each p_x in the set is a directed acyclic graph consisting of an ordered sequence of M nodes $(n_1, n_2, ..., n_M)$. A CNN architecture can thus be thought of as a chain-shaped architecture. Each node is a basic computation unit such as convolution, batch normalization, non-linear activation function, or a sequence of operations. All of which form a respective feature map. Note that only connections from lower-indexed to higher-indexed nodes are encoded. During a phase, the cubic dimensionality (C × H × W) of a tensor remains unchanged. After passing through the nodes' operations, the data will be concatenated by the depth and then fed into the last convolutional layer, which adjusts the number of channels specified in that phase. Following each phase is a scheme of reducing resolution through the spatial pooling operation. In the final phase, the global average pooling (GAP) is used to reduce overfitting [5]. The pooling layer, as well as the fully-connected part, are excluded from the encoding. Figure 1 illustrates the connection encoding.

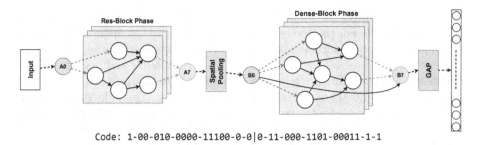

Code: 1-00-010-0000-11100-0-0|0-11-000-1101-00011-1-1

Fig. 1. Dashed arrows represent connections that are not encoded. The last bit in each phase represents the phase-type (Dense phase: 0 or Residual phase: 1).

2.2 Node's Attributes Encoding

Inspired by the study of Wang et al. [8], we choose to encode the following four attributes: the kernel size, the pool size, the number of channels, and the phase-type. The phase-type defines some state-of-the-art layer-wise computation (e.g., Dense Phase [3], Residual Phase [2], etc.). For example, with a residual phase, each node (layer) will include a convolution, followed by batch normalization and a ReLU function. Note that the pooling operation at the last phase, which is the global average pooling (GAP), is excluded in the encoding space. The range of each attribute is described in Table 1.

Table 1. Range of values for operations for each phase

Parameter	Values	# of bits
Kernel size	[3, 5, 7, 9]	2
Pool size	[1, 2]	1
# of channels	[16, 32, 64, 128]	2
Phase types	[Dense, Residual, Preact-Residual]	2

2.3 NAS Experiment Setup

During a NAS run, we consider two conflicting objectives: minimizing the *error rate* and minimizing the *model complexity*. We use CIFAR-10 [4] to evaluate candidate architectures. Each candidate architecture is trained from scratch for 25 epochs on the training set as in [7]. The trained model (obtained at the last epoch) is then validated on the test set, and this test set error is used as the error rate objective value. The number of floating-point operations (FLOPs) is used as the evaluation metric that indicates the architecture's complexity [7].

Our NAS runs are performed on a Ubuntu 18.04 workstation equipped with an NVIDIA GTX 1070 8 GB GPU. We perform two NAS runs with two different random seeds (to verify the stability of EAs solving NAS problems as in [9]). In both runs, we limited the number of phase N to 3, with the number of nodes in each phase $M = 6$. For the node's attribute encoding, we use the same number of attributes mentioned in Table 1, which results in 68 bits representing one specific architecture. This means there exist $2^{68} \approx 3 \times 10^{20}$ possible architectures in our search space. In each run, the population contains 40 individuals and is run for 25 generations, i.e., 1,000 architecture evaluations in total. The individual's encoding genotype is decoded into the corresponding network architecture phenotype for evaluation, where it is trained on the CIFAR-10 training set for 25 epochs. The SGD optimizer is used with the cosine learning rate decay, initial learning rate of 0.025, momentum = 0.9, and L2 regularization of 3e−4. The batch size is set to 64. We employ the same data preprocessing procedures, i.e., image normalization, random flipping, and random cropping, as in [7]. The crossover and mutation probabilities of NSGA-II are set as 0.9 and 0.02, respectively.

2.4 NAS Results and Discussions

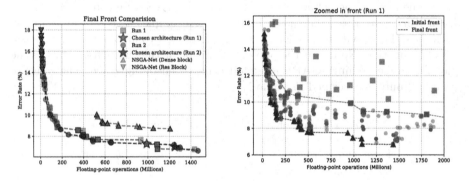

Fig. 2. Left: NAS trade-off fronts obtained by our approach and NSGA-Net when dense blocks or residual blocks are used. Right: zoomed-in NAS trade-off front.

Figure 2 (left) shows no considerable difference between the trade-off fronts obtained at the end of our two NAS runs. Similar to when the genetic algorithm is used to solve the single-objective NAS problem in Genetic-CNN [9], the result here indicates the reliability of using NSGA-II to solve the multi-objective NAS with our neural architecture representation mechanism. We also re-run NSGA-II with NSGA-Net's encoding scheme. Because NSGA-Net only encodes node connections, the phase-type must be determined *a priori* and fixed during NAS. It can be seen in Fig. 2 that NAS, where only Dense blocks or Residual blocks are used, would yield just a very small part of the possible trade-off fronts. Our encoding scheme allows the phase-type of each phase to vary (i.e., dense, residual, or preact-residual block) and is thus able to result in trade-off fronts of much wider ranges. Both of our result fronts completely dominate the trade-off fronts of dense block-based NSGA-Net.

Figure 2 (right) shows the evolutionary progress of the NSGA-II population from the first generation, which is randomly initialized, to the final generation. Clear shifts are observed between the first-generation and the last-generation trade-off fronts in both runs. In the early phase of a NAS run, the complexity of random architectures could be more than 10,000 MFLOPS while the error rate objective could still be improved. The population gradually evolves through generations and obtains neural architectures that are better in both objectives.

2.5   Architecture Validation

We select from the result trade-off fronts two architectures (marked as the red star dot in Run 1 and the blue star dot in Run 2 in Fig. 2). To validate their quality, we re-train them on different datasets from scratch using an SGD optimizer (momentum 0.9) with extended numbers of epochs: CIFAR-10, CIFAR-100, and Street View House Numbers SVHN (600 epochs, batch size 96), and Intel Image Classification (350 epochs, batch size 16).

Table 2 provides a summary comparing our obtained architectures with NSGA-Net on the CIFAR-10, CIFAR-100, and SVHN datasets. The error rate result of NSGA-Net (trained in 600 epochs) is taken from [7]. Because Liu et al. [6] showed that training on the CIFAR-10 and CIFAR-100 datasets might result in high variation, we perform 10 evaluation runs for our two selected architectures with 10 different random seeds. The average error rates with the standard deviation are reported in Table 2. It can be seen that after being trained for 600 epochs, the architecture selected from the result front of NSGA-Net and our chosen architectures have similar performance on CIFAR-10. The results on the SVHN and CIFAR-100 datasets suggest a potential drawback of our representation mechanism. While our encoding is more comprehensive, and the obtained architectures can thus be straightforwardly employed, they might be overfitted to the specific dataset used in the NAS run. When being transferred to other datasets, their performance might not be as good as architectures found by NSGA-Net with a less comprehensive representation.

Table 2. Architecture validation on CIFAR-10, CIFAR-100, and SVHN datasets

Architectures	#Params (M)	CIFAR-10 error rate (%)	CIFAR-100 error rate (%)	SVHN error rate (%)	FLOPS (M)
NSGA-Net [7]	3.3	3.85	20.74	2.6 ± 0.06	1290
Run 1	2.89	3.93 ± 0.078	20.96 ± 0.23	3.092 ± 0.127	988
Run 2	4.4	3.81 ± 0.11	20.88 ± 0.35	3.15 ± 0.05	1250

For the Intel Image Classification (IIC) dataset, we perform 3 evaluation runs for each architecture in this experiment. Contrary to the results on the SVHN dataset, Table 3 shows that our selected architectures achieve superior performance compared to the selected NSGA-Net architecture on the IIC dataset regarding both accuracy and model complexity. This suggests a potential solution to the overfitting problem mentioned above for our encoding scheme: multiple datasets could be used to evaluate candidate architectures during NAS runs.

Table 3. Architecture validation on Intel Image Classification (IIC) dataset

Architectures	#Params (M)	Error rate (%)			FLOPS (M)
NSGA-Net	3.3	8.14	8.267	8.14	31816
Run 1	2.89	7	7.13	7.17	21677
Run 2	4.4	7.16	7.16	7.267	27346

3   Conclusion

This paper investigated a comprehensive CNN architecture encoding mechanism and an adapted crossover operator of NSGA-II for representing and solving multi-objective NAS problems. Our representation allows a large search space of many competent architectures with important operations and implementation details (i.e., block type, the number of channels, kernel size, and pool size) to be encoded. The achieved trade-off fronts provided insights into possible trade-offs between the two conflicting objectives: error rate and model complexity, which decision-makers could investigate and choose the architecture that exhibits their preferred trade-off. Furthermore, CNN architectures obtained with NAS using our encoding mechanism do not need to be further modified and could be straightforwardly employed. Future works need to investigate more robust architecture evaluation methods to better address the overfitting problem when running NAS with a comprehensive network representation.

Acknowledgements. This research is funded by Vietnam National University HoChiMinh City (VNU-HCM) under grant number DSC2021-26-06.

References

1. Deb, K., Agrawal, S., Pratap, A., Meyarivan, T.: A fast and elitist multiobjective genetic algorithm: NSGA-II. IEEE Trans. Evol. Comput. **6**(2), 182–197 (2002)
2. He, K., Zhang, X., Ren, S., Sun, J.: Deep residual learning for image recognition. In: Proceedings of the IEEE/CVF Conference on Computer Vision and Pattern Recognition (CVPR) (2016)
3. Huang, G., Liu, Z., van der Maaten, L., Weinberger, K.Q.: Densely connected convolutional networks. In: Proceedings of the IEEE/CVF Conference on Computer Vision and Pattern Recognition (CVPR) (2017)
4. Krizhevsky, A.: Learning multiple layers of features from tiny images. Technical report TR-2009, University of Toronto (2009)

5. Lin, M., Chen, Q., Yan, S.: Network in network. In: International Conference on Learning Representations (ICLR) (2014)
6. Liu, H., Simonyan, K., Vinyals, O., Fernando, C., Kavukcuoglu, K.: Hierarchical representations for efficient architecture search. In: International Conference on Learning Representations (ICLR) (2018)
7. Lu, Z., et al.: NSGA-Net: neural architecture search using multi-objective genetic algorithm. In: Genetic and Evolutionary Computation Conference (GECCO) (2019)
8. Wang, B., Sun, Y., Xue, B., Zhang, M.: A hybrid differential evolution approach to designing deep convolutional neural networks for image classification. In: Mitrovic, T., Xue, B., Li, X. (eds.) AI 2018. LNCS (LNAI), vol. 11320, pp. 237–250. Springer, Cham (2018). https://doi.org/10.1007/978-3-030-03991-2_24
9. Xie, L., Yuille, A.L.: Genetic CNN. In: Proceeding of the IEEE/CVF International Conference on Computer Vision (ICCV) (2017)

Method for Automatic Furniture Placement Based on Simulated Annealing and Genetic Algorithm

Eliška Svobodová[1] and Ladislava Smítková Janků[2]([envelope])

[1] Faculty of Information Technology, Czech Technical University in Prague,
Prague, Czech Republic
`svoboel5@fit.cvut.cz`
[2] Faculty of Information Technology, Department of Applied Mathematics,
Czech Technical University in Prague, Prague, Czech Republic
`ladislava.smitkova@fit.cvut.cz`
`https://fit.cvut.cz`

Abstract. This paper deals with a method for the automatic furniture placement, which combines simulated annealing and genetic algorithm. The system proceeds similarly to a human interior designer when designing a furniture layout. First, functional zones are designed and distributed using simulated annealing, then the genetic algorithm is used to distribute the furniture in a specific functional zone. Unlike previous work that uses genetic algorithms to solve a similar problem, our method uses a combination of functional zone design and the genetic algorithm is used to optimize the placement of furniture in a given zone. The algorithm is designed in a way not to be limited to simple rectangular room floor planes, but rather to be able furnish rooms with more complicated floor plans. Experimental results generated for the differently shaped rooms are presented.

Keywords: Artificial intelligence · Automatic furniture placement · Genetic algorithm

1 Introduction

Interior design is a highly creative task. It depends on the artistic feeling and experience of the designer. However, there are some guidelines that professional designers follow and techniques that they use. In our work, we propose a system, which realizes a part of interior design process, particularly room space dividing in the functional zones, and its automatic furnishing using artificial intelligence methods. We were inspired by the interior design method where the designer first sketches, what functions will parts of the room have, before arranging the furniture itself. This helps the designer to divide the space into smaller areas and plan a flow (how will the client move through the room). The proposed system can serve not only as a support for interior designers, but also as a support

© Springer Nature Switzerland AG 2021
H. Fujita et al. (Eds.): IEA/AIE 2021, LNAI 12798, pp. 480–491, 2021.
https://doi.org/10.1007/978-3-030-79457-6_41

for architects in the design of buildings. The automatic design of the furniture layout can be used to assess the possibilities of furnishing the room with furniture and with regard to its layout. This makes it possible to analyze the shape and dimensions of rooms during the design of buildings and, if necessary, to optimize their dimensions so that these rooms can be easily, efficiently and ergonomically equipped with furniture in the future.

2   Related Work

Requirements for the development of algorithms for the automatic generation of indoor furniture placement arose primarily in the field of computer games and virtual reality, where designers of large-scale gaming environments needed tools for automatic generation of gaming environments taking place in large urban areas. Thus, the works were published mainly in the field of computer graphics and algorithms for the creation of cyberspace.

Yu et al. [2] proposed an algorithm for automatic furniture generation for the cyberspace environments. They presented system, which extracted relationships among furniture objects from the furnished rooms examples, encoded them and used them in the form of a cost function whose optimization yields realistic furniture arrangements. They proposed the cost function optimization by simulated annealing using a Metropolis-Hastings state search step.

Akase et al. [3] proposed automatic optimization method by using interactive evolutionary computation. Furniture placement is optimized through the use of prior information stored in a semantic database and the user preference. Kan et al. [4] proposed application of genetic algorithm with combination of furniture generation for virtual environments.

Yeang et al. [5] proposed automatic layout method combining both the room division into functional zones using conditional generative adversarial networks (CGAN) and furniture placement into specific functional zone using a learning-based furniture filling algorithm, based on training of a fully connected network model for different kinds of functional zone. Similarly, Chen et al. [8] explores GAN in automatic furniture placement.

3   Method Description

The main goal of our work was to design a module for automatic furniture placement, which is part of a larger system called Artificial Intelligence Interior Designer. We proposed a method based on combination of simulated annealing and genetic algorithm. Our approach utilizes functional zones. Functional zones are widely used by human interior designers in order to divide the space to be furnished into smaller, functionally compact areas. Functional zones are areas of a room with a specific purpose. Each functional zone is equipped with furniture that is specific to the purpose of the zone. The input data contain information on room and requirements for the design (aisle width, room functions, etc.) and information on furniture, e.g. which furniture belongs to which zone or description of the relationships between objects. The proposed method has three steps: The first step is the automatic placement of functional zones in the room. The shapes and positions of functional zones are optimized using simulated annealing. The second step includes an application of a genetic algorithm to the furniture placement in each functional zone found in the room. The third step is to reject system-generated solutions that meet the basic conditions for furniture placement (eg placing a piece of furniture just in front of a door).

3.1 Zone Placement Optimization

This subsection describes a method used for automatic functional zone proposal and placement. As was said above, each functional zone is equipped with furniture that is specific to the purpose of the zone. We differ between storage functional zones and the rest. That is because storage areas (like bookshelves or wardrobes) are often positioned independently on each other and other pieces of furniture. Also, storage furniture is always placed by a wall with its back which we must take into account in generating solutions.

Representation. The solution, that we are trying to optimize, is composed of representations of all zones. Every zone has a shape which is a polygon (mostly rectangle) in the coordinate space. Storage zones have fixed size (size of the storage object that they represent) and are positioned along walls. Other activity zones can be placed anywhere in the room and have a variable size (provided that their area is larger than the total area of furniture that is supposed to be arranged within it).

Initialization of the Algorithm. One of the hyper-parameters of simulated annealing is initial temperature. Our cost function is very spiky and even a small change in the solution can cause a significant drop or increase in its cost. So, we generate *num_trials* (we used 200) random solutions and their random neighbours and calculate the largest difference between their costs *max_diff*. For initial temperature we take $T = max\_diff * 1.2$

At the beginning of the algorithm, solutions are allowed to make bigger steps towards their neighbors. We started at *room_min_dimension/2*, which mean that solutions can move/resize their zones up to half of the lesser dimension of the room. This step decreases after every completion of iterations for the current temperature. For an initial solution, we generate a random solution.

Simulated Annealing. We used the simulated annealing algorithm with 100 iterations per cycle (so that the search has enough time to explore), 0.9 temperature decrease ratio, and 0.95 max step decrease ratio. Neighboring solutions are generated by moving or resizing a random number of its zones. The stopping condition is met when the solution doesn't improve by more than 0.1 points.

$solution \leftarrow$ generate_init_solution()
while $temp\_diff > 0.1$ **or** $temp\_diff < 0$ **do**
  $init\_cost \leftarrow solution.cost$
  for i in range($iter\_per\_temp$) **do**
    $neighbour \leftarrow solution.get\_neighbour(max\_step)$
    if $neighbour.cost < solution.cost$ **then**
      $solution \leftarrow neighbour$ math.exp($cost/self.temperature$)
    else if random()$< e^{(solution.cost-neighbour.cost)/T}$ **then**
      $solution \leftarrow neighbour$
    end if
  end for
  $T \leftarrow T * cool\_down\_ratio$
  $max\_step \leftarrow$min($max\_step * step\_decrease\_ratio, min\_step$)
  $temp\_diff \leftarrow init\_cost - solution.cost$
end while

After the simulated annealing, we further improve the solution with gradient descent. We generate all direct neighbors (solutions that have only one zone 1 step away) and choose the best one. We repeat this process until we find the local optimum.

Cost Function. Solutions are evaluated based on the following criteria:

- **Overlapping and flow.** Zones shouldn't overlap each other and should leave enough space between each other for the user to walk through. For each zone, we calculate the overlapping area with other "extended" zones and penalize it:

$$\sqrt{\sum_{allzones} overlapping\_area}$$

Extension of the zone means, that its shape is expanded in each direction by aisle width (specified by the user). We are calculating the cost for the green zone (see Fig. 1a). It overlaps with two other zones that are extended by aisle width - illustrated by red rectangles around blue ones (actual zones). We take the square root of the overlapping area. Figure 1b shows the room that will receive 0 penalty, green areas are free spaces left around zones.

- **Free space.** We want to use all the space in the room that we have, so we penalize area that is not covered by extended zones. We do that by first subtracting shapes of all extended zones from the shape of the room - an area of this shape is *area_diff*. Then, we subtract this area from the total area of the room *total_area*. Penalty is:

$$\sqrt{total\_area - area\_diff}$$

Overlapping and Free space criteria operate against each other to create functional and efficiently used space.

- **Zone shape.** To avoid awkwardly long zones, we get the min and max dimension of the zone and if the larger dimension is more than three times bigger than the smaller one, we add penalty:

$$\sum_{allzones} (max\_dim_i - 3 * min\_dim_i)/4$$

- **Space ratio.** Every zone contains a different number of furniture pieces with different areas. We want the zone with the largest furniture area to be the biggest one. So, we calculate the perfect ratio of zone areas from the sum of areas of all their furniture and compare it with the ratio of the actual area (calculated from the zone's shape). We penalize the difference between them.

$$\sum_{allzones} abs(\frac{furniture\_area}{sum\_all\_furniture\_areas} - \frac{area}{sum\_all\_areas})$$

- **By wall.** Zones are mostly by walls and in corners. For every zone, we calculate distances between the corners of the zone i and the wall and take the smallest 3 ($d_{i1} \leq d_{i2} \leq d_{i3}$). Cost:

$$\sum_{allzones} d_{i1} + d_{i2} + \frac{d_{i3}}{2}$$

- **By window.** Some zones are more likely to be by a window than others (because they need more light or a view). This is represented by a probability *window_prob*. Penalty is given by:

$$\sum_{allzones} window\_prob_i * zone\_wall\_distance_i * 2$$

- **Door space.** There has to be free space right in front of the door. We add a penalty for any area overlapping with zones.

$$\sqrt{\sum_{allzones} overlap\_space\_area}$$

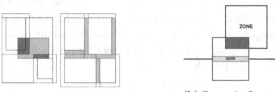

(a) Overlapping and flow penalty   (b) Space in front of the door

Fig. 1. Overlapping and door space demonstration

Note on How Our Method Calculates Overlapping and Flow Penalty. We first tried to ensure reachability of all zones by converting the room into a grid maze with the length of tile equal to the width of an aisle. Then we started BFS that searched through the grid and tried to find all zones and other doors. We added a penalty for every zone and door not reached. However, this method was very slow gives poor results: zones and doors were often unreachable. Our method with extended zones is much more successful, especially in rectangular rooms.

3.2   Furniture Placement Optimization

This section describes an application of genetic algorithms to the furniture placement problem. In comparison to [3,4], where a genetic algorithm was applied, but no functional zones were taken into account, we applied a genetic algorithm to take into account the affiliation of the furniture to individual functional zones. Placing furniture belonging to a specific functional zone outside this functional zone is penalized. In our work, we have developed two approaches. The first approach involved the optimization based primary on the crossover of the individuals, where the mutations were random and did not reflect any relationships among objects. The second approach was inspired by the method described in [4]; the optimization was based on more advanced mutations which were applied to 50% of the population. When solving the problem of furniture placement, the second method was more successful than the first one.

Representation. Every furniture object was represented by an object type (desk, bed, sofa, etc.), shape (the size and position in the coordinate space), orientation (north, east, south, west), and constraints. Constraints contain required free space around the object, probability of standing by a wall, and relationships with the other objects (next to, opposite to, around, etc.) An individual is defined as a list of objects. Every individual in a specific population has the same amount of objects. Each population represents one zone and is optimized separately. So, we have as many populations as we have non-storage zones. Storage zones are optimized separately during the zone optimization phase.

Cost Function

- **Overhanging room.** We penalize any furniture area that is outside of the room.
- **Overhanging zone.** If the object isn't inside its zone we add the its overlapping area and distance to the zone to the penalty.
- **Overlapping.** Objects or the areas around them that they required empty shouldn't overlap.
- **By wall.** Some objects are more likely to be placed by a wall. Every object has a probability of standing by a wall by_wall_prob and if this probability is greater than zero, it also has sides that should touch the wall. As a penalty,

we take the minimal distance between corners of this side and the nearest wall.
- **Object relationships.** Solution gets bigger cost if its object doesn't follow their relationships. Each relationship has different cost function which quantifies how differently is objects placed from where it is supposed to be.

Relationships Between Objects. Most relationships are defined on the child's side and have specified parent's type (desk, coffee table, etc.). When calculating the cost or satisfying the relationship, the closest object with the required type is taken as a parent. Object that is **Next to** its parent should have the same orientation, should be aligned with the *center* or a *side* and its distance to the parent should be between *min_distance* and *max_distance* (Fig. 2).

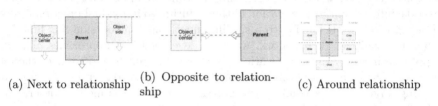

(a) Next to relationship   (b) Opposite to relationship   (c) Around relationship

Fig. 2. Furniture object relationships

Object that is **Opposite to** its parent should have the opposite orientation to its parent, their centers should be aligned and its distance to the parent should be between *min_distance* and *max_distance*. Last relationship is around, this relationship has to be defined on "both sides" - child object must have the **Around** relationship with specified type of the parent object and parent object has to have **AroundCenter** relationship defined. Around relationship is satisfied when the distance to the parent object is between *min_distance* and *max_distance*. Cost of AroundCenter relationship is calculated as the minimum difference between the areas of children objects in opposite sectors:

$$diff\_up\_down = abs((sector1 + sector2) - (sector3 + sector4))$$

$$diff\_left\_right = abs((sector1 + sector4) - (sector2 + sector3))$$

$$\sqrt{min(diff\_up\_down, diff\_left\_right)}$$

As children objects, we take objects that are close enough and have defined the Around relationship with a parent object of the same type. When we use a mutation that should satisfy the AroundCenter relationship, the function divides children into 4 groups (one group for each side of the center object). Groups that will be on the longer sides of the center object have a higher chance to receive more objects. Opposite groups try to have the same sum of object's areas. Then are objects in the group regularly positioned on their side.

Genetic Algorithm. In both approaches, the selection by stochastic universal sampling was applied. Crossover was implemented by switching random objects between parent objects. Relationships between objects are mostly realized as parent-child and are defined on the "child-side".

Genetic Algorithm 1. We tried using a genetic algorithm that in each generation selects an intermediate population and creates a new population by a crossover from it. Then mutation is applied to 1% of the new population. Mutation types: (1) Move a random piece of furniture in a random direction. (2) Randomly change the orientation of a random object. (3) Move a random object to its nearest wall. (4) Move a random object to the object that is nearest to it. (5) Pick a random object and align it with another random object. Randomly choose whether to align their centers or one of its sides.

Genetic Algorithm 2. In this approach, we generate a new population differently. First, we perform elitism and move the best 70% of the old population to the new. The remaining 30% we generate using the crossover. Then we apply mutation to 50% of this new population. In our approach, we reduced the number of mutations to 6, in comparison to [4], where 10 types of mutation were used. Mutation types explored in our work include (1) Move a random piece of furniture in a random direction. If the object has a parent, move parent with the object. (2) Randomly change the orientation of a random object. If the object has a parent, rotate them together. (3) Move a random object to its nearest wall. (4) Move a random object to the object that is nearest to it. (5) Pick a random object and align it with another random object. Randomly choose whether to align their centers or one of its sides. (6) Every relationship (so far we have defined opposite to, next to, and around) has a cost function and a function that can move the child object to the position where the spatial relationship is satisfied.

4   Experimental Results

In total, we performed 4 different experiments, each of them on the set of different room floor plans and with differently defined sets of furniture. The aim of the first experiment was to compare two proposed approaches using two different modifications of the genetic algorithm. Both approaches use simulated annealing to deploy functional zones. They differ only in the genetic algorithm used. The aim of the second experiment was to verify the applicability of the second method to a set of different simple rectangular floor plans with differently defined windows and doors and with differently defined sets of furniture. The aim of the third experiment was to verify the applicability of the second method to the set of different l-shaped floor plans with differently defined windows and doors and with differently defined sets of furniture. The aim of the fourth experiment was to verify the applicability of the second method to the set of different irregular room floor plans (e.g. other floor plans than simple rectangular and L-shaped room floor plans) with differently defined windows and doors and with differently defined sets of furniture. Floor plan data sets include: 10 rectangular room floor plans, 10 L-shape room floor plans, 7 irregular room floor plans. For each plan, the set of furniture for placement in the particular room was defined. In the first experiment, we randomly selected 5 rectangular room floor plans with defined set of furniture and 5 room floor plans with defined set of furniture. All the selected floor plans were used as input data for both the compared methods. The first approach based on combination of simulated annealing and genetic algorithm 1 didn't perform very well. The first algorithm was not able to find a solution in which furniture object's relationships were satisfied and furniture objects mostly weren't aligned with each other or the wall (which is important for aesthetics). The second experiment was performed on the complete set of 10 rectangular room floor planes. For each room floor plan, a set of 7 different solutions proposed by the system was randomly selected. Solutions that do not significantly meet some of the criteria for furniture placement (e.g. designs containing doors built into a piece of furniture) were excluded. Other solutions can be used. The solution evaluated as the most aesthetic by the human assessor was chosen as the best solution for the placement of the furniture (Figs. 3, 4, 5 and 6).

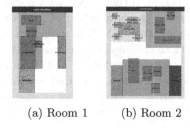

(a) Room 1   (b) Room 2

Fig. 3. Furniture placement optimized with SA + GA1

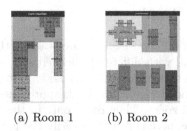

(a) Room 1   (b) Room 2

Fig. 4. Furniture placement optimized with SA + GA2

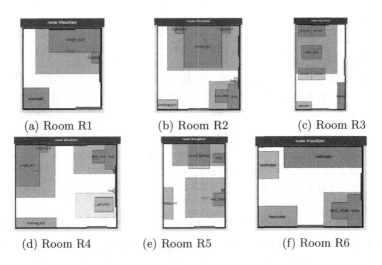

(a) Room R1   (b) Room R2   (c) Room R3

(d) Room R4   (e) Room R5   (f) Room R6

Fig. 5. Furniture placement optimized with GA2 for different rectangular rooms

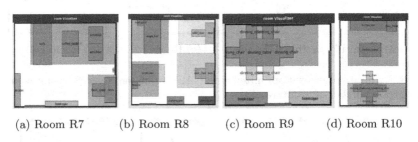

(a) Room R7   (b) Room R8   (c) Room R9   (d) Room R10

Fig. 6. Furniture placement optimized with GA2 for different rectangular rooms equipped with higher number of furniture pieces

The third experiment was performed on the complete set of 10 L-shape room floor planes. For each room floor plan, a set of 7 different solutions proposed by the system was randomly selected. Similarly to the second experiment, the solutions that do not significantly meet some of the criteria for furniture placement were excluded. Other solutions can be used. The solution evaluated as the most aesthetic by the human assessor was chosen as the best solution for the placement of the furniture. The fourth experiment was performed on the complete set of 7 irregular room floor planes. For each room floor plan, a set containing 7 different solutions proposed by the system was randomly selected. The solutions that do not significantly meet some of the criteria for furniture placement were excluded. Other solutions were accepted. The solution evaluated as the most aesthetic by the human assessor was chosen as the best solution for the placement of the furniture (Figs. 7, 8 and 9).

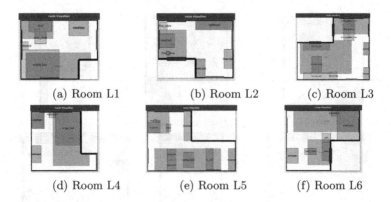

(a) Room L1   (b) Room L2   (c) Room L3

(d) Room L4   (e) Room L5   (f) Room L6

Fig. 7. Furniture placement optimized with GA2 for different L-shape rooms

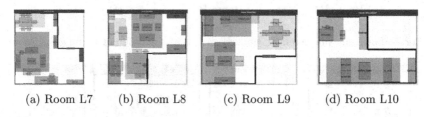

(a) Room L7   (b) Room L8   (c) Room L9   (d) Room L10

Fig. 8. Furniture placement optimized with GA2 for different L-shape rooms equipped with higher number of furniture pieces

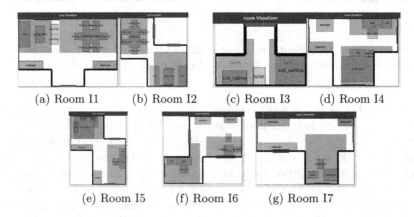

(a) Room I1   (b) Room I2   (c) Room I3   (d) Room I4

(e) Room I5   (f) Room I6   (g) Room I7

Fig. 9. Furniture placement optimized with GA2 for different irregular floor plan rooms

5   Conclusions

We presented a new method for the automatic furniture placement, which combines simulated annealing and genetic algorithm. The system proceeds similarly to a human interior designer when designing a furniture layout. First, functional zones are designed and distributed using simulated annealing, then genetic algorithm is used to distribute the furniture in a specific functional zone. Unlike previous work that uses genetic algorithms to solve a similar problem, our method uses a combination of functional zone design and the genetic algorithm is used to optimize the placement of furniture in a given zone. The algorithm is designed to be able to furnish rooms with more complicated floor plans. Experimental results generated for the differently shaped rooms are presented. In the last step, the solutions generated by the system were evaluated. The solutions that do not significantly meet some of the criteria for furniture placement were excluded. Other solutions were accepted. Approximately ninety percent of the solutions proposed by the system for each scenario were accepted ant ten percent of the solutions were rejected.

Acknowledgments. This work was supported by the Student Summer Research Program 2020 of FIT CTU in Prague.

References

1. Yang, B., Li, L., Song, C., Jiang, Z.: Automatic interior layout with user-specified furniture. Comput. Graph. **94**, 124–131 (2021)
2. Yu, L.F., Yeung, S.K., Tang, C.K., Demetri, T., Chan, F., Osher, S.J.: Make it home: automatic optimization of furniture arrangement. ACM Trans. Graph. **30**(4), 1–12 (2011)
3. Akase, R., Okada, Y.: Automatic 3D furniture layout based on interactive evolutionary computation. In: 2013 Seventh International Conference on Complex, Intelligent, and Software Intensive Systems, Taichung, pp. 726–731 (2013)
4. Kan, P., Kaufmann, H.: Automated interior design using a genetic algorithm. In: Proceedings of the 23rd ACM Symposium on Virtual Reality Software and Technology. Association for Computing Machinery, New York (2017)
5. Yang, B., Li, L., Song, C., Jiang, Z., Ling, Y.: Automatic furniture layout based on functional area division. In: 2019 International Conference on Cyberworlds (CW), Kyoto, Japan, pp. 109–116 (2019)
6. Kán, P., Kaufmann, H.: Automatic furniture arrangement using greedy cost minimization. In: 2018 IEEE Conference on Virtual Reality and 3D User Interfaces (VR), Reutlingen, pp. 491–498 (2018)
7. Merrell, P., Schkufza, E., Koltun, V.: Computer-generated residential building layouts. ACM Trans. Graph. **29**(6), 1 (2010)
8. Chen, Y., Li, B.: A household design method based on improved generative adversarial networks. In: Proceedings of the 4th International Conference on Computer Science and Application Engineering (CSAE 2020), Article 19, pp. 1–6. Association for Computing Machinery, New York (2020)

Attack and Security

Recent Research on Phishing Detection Through Machine Learning Algorithm

Do Nguyet Quang[1(✉)], Ali Selamat[1,2,3], and Ondrej Krejcar[3]

[1] Malaysia-Japan International Institute of Technology (MJIIT), Universiti Teknologi Malaysia,
Kuala Lumpur, Malaysia
aselamat@utm.my
[2] School of Computing, Faculty of Engineering, Universiti Teknologi Malaysia, Johor Bahru,
Malaysia and Media and Games Center of Excellence (MagicX), Universiti Teknologi Malaysia,
Johor Bahru, Malaysia
[3] Center for Basic and Applied Research, Faculty of Informatics and Management, University
of Hradec Kralove, Rokitanskeho 62, 500 03 Hradec Kralove, Czech Republic
ondrej.krejcar@uhk.cz

Abstract. The rapid growth of emerging technologies, smart devices, 5G communication, etc. have contributed to the accumulation of data, hence introducing the big data era. Big data imposes a variety of challenges associated with machine learning, especially in phishing detection. Therefore, this paper aims to provide an analysis and summary of current research in phishing detection through machine learning for big data. To achieve this goal, this study adopted a systematic literature review (SLR) technique and critically analyzed a total of 30 papers from various journals and conference proceedings. These papers were selected from previous studies in five different databases on content published between 2018 and January 2021. The results obtained from this study reveal a limited number of research works that comprehensively reviewed the feasibility of applying both machine learning and big data technologies in the context of phishing detection.

Keywords: Cybersecurity · Phishing detection · Machine learning (ML) · Big data

1 Introduction

With the advancement in information technology, cybersecurity has become a top priority in the global interest [1]. Among many types of cyber threats, it is believed that malware is the crucial weapon to attack in cyberspace. There are several mediums to spread malware, including spam, phishing and web download. Amongst them, phishing is the most commonly used medium for cyber-attacks [2]. The rapid increase in the number of phishing attacks due to the COVID-19 pandemic catches more attention among researchers in the phishing detection domain. As the demand for Internet usage and the volume of data circulating on the web is rising exponentially, we are now living in the big data era. As a result, having a comprehensive solution to detect phishing attacks

© Springer Nature Switzerland AG 2021
H. Fujita et al. (Eds.): IEA/AIE 2021, LNAI 12798, pp. 495–508, 2021.
https://doi.org/10.1007/978-3-030-79457-6_42

is extremely important. Machine learning has emerged as a promising algorithm for phishing detection in big data in the past few years.

This paper is aimed to examine the trends or patterns in the current research works related to machine learning for phishing detection in the context of big data. The expected outcome is the identified research gaps and future research directions. Through the data analysis and synthesis collected from 30 reviewed papers, the key contributions of this study are as below:

- Proposing a taxonomy to classify the existing literature into several categories, depending on research area, research type and research contribution
- Employing the mapping technique to demonstrate the correlation among various parameters from the collected data
- Identifying the potential research gaps for phishing detection through machine learning in big data.

2 Research Methodology

2.1 Research Questions

This paper aims to identify the patterns of publications related to phishing detection in big data through the use of machine learning, the classification techniques used for phishing detection, and issues that are most discussed in phishing detection for big data. To achieve this goal, the SLR was conducted following the guidelines provided by Kitchenham [3]. To start with, the research questions and their corresponding objectives are listed in Table 1.

Table 1. Research questions and their objectives.

Code	Research question	Objective
RQ1	What are the trends in publications related to phishing detection using machine learning algorithms in big data?	To classify the existing literature in the relevant area and provide a taxonomy of the related topics
RQ2	What are the popular classification techniques used for phishing detection in big data?	To search for the most frequently used classification techniques for phishing detection in big data
RQ3	What are the most discussed issues and challenges in phishing detection for big data?	To identify the open issues and research gaps in the related area

2.2 Search Procedure

A search string was used with Boolean operators' help to find the most relevant information related to the research topic. The search term is described as follows: "phishing detection AND machine learning AND big data". In this study, five database resources were utilized to extract data based on the formulated search string. The literature review data include Scopus, Web of Science (WoS), IEEEXplore, Springer Link, and Science Direct. Two types of search procedures were used in this SLR, namely automated and manual protocol, to ensure that as many relevant papers were identified and selected as possible.

2.3 Paper Selection

Study Scrutiny. To be selected for this SLR, the published papers must address at least one of the research questions mentioned in Sect. 2.1. Only papers written in English and published between 2018 and 2021 were included in this study. Moreover, they should focus on phishing detection, machine learning or big data, and discuss various classification techniques for phishing detection. Figure 1 demonstrates the paper selection process based on PRISMA guidelines [4]. The process consists of four phases: identification, screening, eligibility and inclusion. These four phases are further divided into six stages. The first stage used an automatic search method and a total of 376 papers were retrieved. After going through the next three stages, 44 papers have remained. These papers were read in full-text and passed through a quality assessment stage for further analysis.

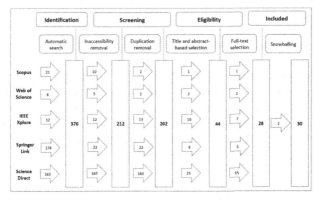

Fig. 1. Paper selection process

Quality Assessment. Quality assessment (QA) is a step in the paper selection process that aims to evaluate the selected papers' quality. Five QA questions were used in this SLR to obtain the most relevant papers. A weighting or scoring technique used by Kitchenham [3] was also adopted in this study to assess the relevance of the selected papers. At the end of this process, 28 articles were chosen for further review. After a snowballing method introduced by Wohlin [5] was applied, 2 papers were added, bringing the final total to 30 papers for this SLR.

2.4 Threats to Validity

As suggested by [6], many threats to validity (TTVs) need to be considered to support the SLR. The four common types of TTVs involve constructing validity, internal validity, external validity and conclusion validity. First of all, construct validity was ensured through paper scrutiny and quality assessment, in addition to the existing research questions, inclusion and exclusion criteria. Second, to ensure that the paper selection process was unbiased, a manual and automated search approach was incorporated to identify the studies related to the topics of interest exhaustively. Third, the external validity was minimized by searching for papers published between 2018 and January 2021 to generalize the study's findings. Last but not least, the conclusion validity was managed by employing the methods and techniques used in this study following the guidelines provided by several authors [3, 7, 8]. Therefore, it is possible for each procedure in this SLR to be repeated with the same results being produced.

2.5 Data Extraction and Data Synthesis

In this study, data were extracted from 30 selected papers using Nvivo, a qualitative data analysis software. After being collected, all 30 papers went through a process call data synthesis. The primary purpose of data synthesis is to present the extracted data in order to answer the research questions in Table 1 using visualization tools such as tables, figures, and charts.

3 Results and Discussion

This section presents the results obtained from data collection, data extraction, data analysis and data synthesis in order to answer the research questions in Sect. 2.1. Figure 2 is a three-dimensional mapping of the selected papers in each year from 2018 to 2021, together with the related journals and their impact factor. Most of the studies were from the year 2019 and 2020. Besides, 60% of the selected papers were published in top-ranking journals (Q1, Q2 and Q3) with high impact factor, while 40% of them were published in non-indexed (NI) journals and conference proceedings (CP). Out of 30 papers, 25 of them were articles (research, review, journal, etc.), whereas only 5 were conference papers. The SLR in this study was carried out based on high-quality reviewed papers.

Furthermore, the keywords used in the articles were analyzed and presented in Fig. 3. Using VOSviewer software to evaluate the recurring term, the publications related to the research topic were categorized according to different disciplines and represented in different clusters. From the figure, there are three clusters with three different colors. A bubble represents each keyword and the size of the bubble indicates the frequency of appearance of a term. Two bubbles are placed nearer to each other if the terms co-appeared more often.

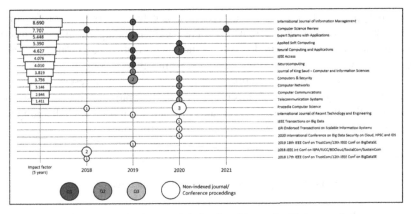

Fig. 2. The publications and their related journal with impact factor

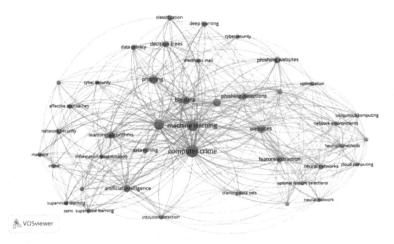

Fig. 3. Frequency of keywords in the publications

3.1 Research Question 1 (RQ1)

To answer RQ1, we looked into each papers' objective, methodology and contribution to categorize them according to their application domain, research type and research contribution.

Application Domain. The 30 included papers were categorized into three groups based on their application domain, namely website phishing, email phishing and unspecified. Website phishing and email phishing are two forms of phishing attacks that normally take place in cyberspace. The majority of the selected papers belong to the former group (18 papers), followed by the latter category (7 papers). The unspecified group consists of 5 papers that do not belong to either of the two aforementioned categories since they are case studies which discussed general topics without focusing on either website or email phishing.

Research Type. Another way to categorize the selected papers is according to their research type. There are four different types of research, including exploratory, empirical, descriptive and comparative. Table 2 shows the categorization based on these research types. Some papers belong to a single category, while others belong to two categories or three categories. Generally, the comparative is the most common research type among the four, followed by an empirical and descriptive study. Exploratory has the least number of papers, with only 2 out of 30. These figures indicate that it is more challenging to find a new research area than improve or enhance the existing ones.

Table 2. Categorization of papers based on research type.

Reference	Research type				Frequency
	Exploratory	Empirical	Descriptive	Comparative	
[9]			x		1
[10]		x	x	x	1
[11, 12]	x			x	2
[13]–[15]			x	x	3
[16]–[19]		x		x	4
[20]–[38]				x	19

Research Contribution. To answer RQ1, the 30 reviewed papers can also be categorized according to their research contribution, which is further divided into contribution type and contribution area.

Contribution Type. There are six different research types depending on their size, ranging from tool, technique, method, model, and framework to the case study. Table 3 summarizes the number of papers based on their contribution type. It is clear that model and technique have the highest number of papers, followed by case study, framework, method and tool, meaning that there are still rooms for research in terms of designing a new framework, applying a new method, or developing a new tool in the area related to phishing detection, machine learning and big data.

Contribution Area. An in-depth analysis of 30 selected papers reveals that the contribution made by each study fell into either one of the following areas: data pre-processing, feature extraction and classification, which are the three phases in a typical phishing detection model. Most of the papers' contributions were made in these three phases. Table 4 displays the categorization of papers based on contribution area. These findings show that future research novelty can be made by having one or more contributions at different phases in the phishing detection model, conducting a review study to provide a taxonomy of interest topics, or integrating various solutions in a hybrid approach.

Table 3. Categorization of papers based on contribution type.

Contribution type	Frequency	Reference
Tool	1	[27]
Technique	10	[17]–[19, 23, 28, 30, 31, 33, 34, 38]
Method	1	[20]
Model	12	[11, 12, 16, 21, 24]–[26, 29, 32, 35]–[37]
Framework	1	[22]
Case study	5	[9, 10, 13]–[15]

Besides, to study the current trends related to phishing detection using machine learning, we also look into the selected features and the datasets used for training and testing the ML models. The distribution of the extracted features and evaluation datasets used in the reviewed articles is illustrated in Fig. 4. Thirty features are commonly used for extraction and selection in several reviewed papers [11, 18, 21, 22, 30, 31, 33]. As for evaluation datasets, PhishTank is the most common dataset used in most experiments, followed by UCI machine learning repository and Alexa. Phishing URLs, websites or emails are generally collected from PhishTank, Phishing Corpus, OpenPhish, SpamAssassin, etc. [12, 23, 31], whereas legitimate ones are selected from Alexa, Common Crawl, Ham, etc. [16, 24, 28, 31, 35].

Table 4. Categorization of papers based on contribution area.

Contribution	Reference	Contribution area				Total
		Data pre-processing	Feature extraction	Classification	Other	
Dual	[11]	x	x			7
	[16, 17, 21, 25, 35, 36]		x	x		
Single	[32–34]	x				21
	[12, 19, 20, 24, 28, 31, 37]		x			
	[18, 23, 29, 30]			x		
	[9, 10, 13–15, 22, 26]				x	
Limited	[27, 38]				x	2
Total		4	14	10	9	30

3.2 Research Question 2 (RQ2)

To answer RQ2, an in-depth analysis was carried out to identify the classification techniques used for phishing detection in each paper. Figure 5 shows the frequency of numerous classification techniques used as a primary classifier in the phishing detection model

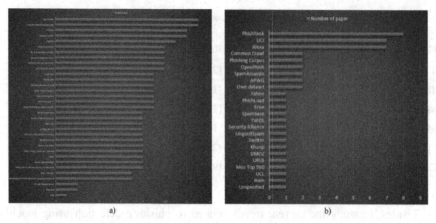

Fig. 4. Distribution of a) Selected features and b) Evaluation datasets for phishing detection [9–38]

or as baseline classifiers for evaluation and benchmarking purposes. From the mapping of the classification techniques, it is clear that Support Vector Machine (SVM) and Random Forest (RF) are the two most common algorithms. Hybrid approaches were also utilized in 4 papers by incorporating two machine learning algorithms to achieve better performance accuracy. Additionally, a two-dimensional mapping method (Fig. 6) was also used to demonstrate the correlation between the classification techniques and the research types and contributions presented in Sect. 3.1.

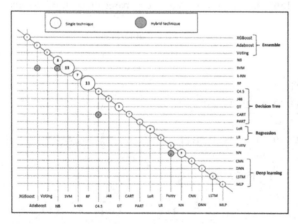

Fig. 5. Frequency of various classification techniques

Based on the analysis of 30 selected papers, machine learning classification techniques can be divided into three categories: past trends, current trends, and future trends, as depicted in Fig. 7. As deep learning (DL) algorithms have not yet been widely employed in the reviewed papers, it is believed that applying these techniques for phishing detection in big data might become one of the future research directions.

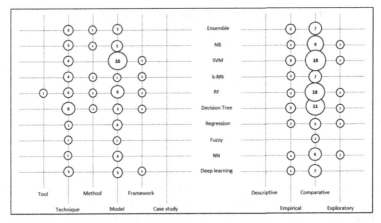

Fig. 6. Two-dimensional mapping of classification techniques, research types and contribution types

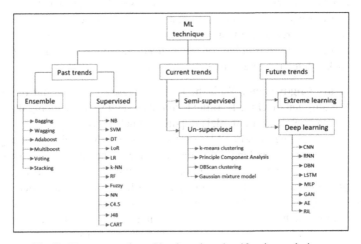

Fig. 7. Taxonomy of machine learning classification techniques

3.3 Research Question 3 (RQ3)

In this study, the 30 selected papers were also categorized according to three different research domains: phishing detection, machine learning and big data, as shown in Table 5. It is clear from the table that most of the existing literature focused on phishing detection and machine learning. The authors in [10] and [13] discussed both machine learning and big data technologies but in different application domains, such as the Internet of Things (IoT) and anomaly detection. There were four studies that discussed all three domains [20, 32, 34, 37].

Imbalanced Learning. To answer RQ3, one of the significant issues that big data is facing in the phishing detection domain is imbalanced learning. Imbalanced learning is a classification problem where the distribution of samples is biased. With the enormous

Table 5. Categorization of papers based on research domain.

Reference	Research domain		
	Phishing detection	Machine learning	Big data
[9, 11, 12, 14–19, 21–31, 33, 35, 36, 38]	x	x	
[10, 13]		x	x
[20, 32, 34, 37]	x	x	x

amount of data generated, traditional approaches used to handle imbalance learning problems become insufficient. Moreover, there is a trade-off between false positives and false negatives, especially in highly imbalanced data where the class distribution is biased. Problems will arise when such classification techniques are applied to massive imbalance datasets. As a result, the authors in [34] proposed a method, called MILES, that can detect phishing attacks with high accuracy and address the issue of multiclass ensemble imbalanced learning in big data. In the proposed approach, parallel processing was used in a big data environment to generate and rebalance training sets, and the training time can be reduced by increasing the cluster size. In general, the authors suggested that solving the problem of imbalanced learning can significantly enhance phishing attacks' detection rate in massive datasets.

Manual Feature Engineering. With the rapid increase in the amount of data in the big data era, traditional machine learning techniques cannot deal with big datasets [39]. Conventional machine learning models require manual feature engineering which fails to cope with multi-dimensional and large-scale data [40]. Manual feature engineering will become even more challenging as dataset' size is increasing enormously in the big data environment. One possible solution to deal with this problem is applying deep learning algorithms because of their ability to handle massive data. When the dataset grows bigger, deep learning techniques start providing better results and higher phishing detection accuracy than traditional machine learning classifiers. Due to deep learning's benefits, the authors in [32] implemented LSTM algorithm to detect phishing attacks for big email data and solve the problem faced by classical ML methods. By using LSTM, features were extracted automatically which eliminated the need for manual feature selection. The authors claimed that their proposed method based on deep learning architecture improved accuracy, reduced false-negative rate and false positive rate, hence allowed to detect phishing emails on big email data efficiently.

Computational Constraints. Another challenge for big data in the context of phishing detection is computational constraints. Deep learning techniques can manage and analyze big data, yet they require longer training time and higher computational cost. Hence, to increase the training speed of deep learning algorithms, the authors in [41] incorporated the management and computing technologies of big data with a deep learning algorithm to enhance the performance of an intrusion detection system (IDS). DNN was implemented for classification using Keras library and Apache Spark's built-in machine learning library. The study claimed that the training and prediction time of the DNN classifiers was significantly improved with the help of Apache Spark techniques compared to other conventional ML algorithms. Moreover, Apache Spark and the Keras library have increased the deep learning's capabilities to perform more efficiently and quickly. Nevertheless, the integration of deep learning and big data technologies was applied to IDS and not for phishing detection.

4 Research Gaps and Future Directions

Table 6 summarizes research gaps and future research directions based on the findings obtained from in-depth analysis of 30 reviewed papers. The findings and research gaps are identified from the data synthesis process. Meanwhile, future research directions are drawn from the identified research gaps in this SLR. Through the analysis of 30 selected papers, this study has identified the current trends in the recent research works and highlighted the research gaps related to phishing detection using machine learning for big data.

Table 6. Summary of research gaps and future research directions

Ref	Findings	Research gaps	Future directions
[9] to [38]	None of the reviewed papers discussed the applicability of employing ML and big data technologies for phishing detection	Phishing detection, machine learning and big data	Incorporate phishing detection, machine learning and big data to investigate the relationship among them
[34]	Traditional approaches are insufficient in handling imbalanced learning in big data	Multiclass ensemble imbalanced learning	Use parallel processing to generate and rebalance training sets by applying parallel k-means clustering
[32]	Traditional ML techniques rely on manual feature engineering	Handcrafted feature selection	Apply deep learning algorithms to extract the features automatically from raw data
[41]	DL techniques require longer training time and high computational resources	Computational constraint	Integrate deep learning and big data technologies to reduce the training time and computational resources

5 Conclusion and Future Work

In the big data era, phishing attacks have become more complicated, creating more challenges for phishing detection. A practical classification algorithm can help mitigate phishing attacks, and it is believed that machine learning is the solution. In this paper, a SLR was conducted based on 30 papers to analyze the current trends related to phishing detection using machine learning for big data. Three research questions have been answered through a data synthesis process, which eventually enabled us to make the three corresponding key contributions. As for future work, we plan to conduct an in-depth analysis of three leading-edge domains, namely phishing detection, deep learning, and big data technologies, to investigate the relationship among them and search for possible solutions to fill in the research gaps identified in this study.

Acknowledgement. This work was supported/funded by the Ministry of Higher Education under the Fundamental Research Grant Scheme (FRGS/1/2018/ICT04/UTM/01/1). The authors sincerely thank Universiti Teknologi Malaysia (UTM) under Research University Grant Vot-20H04, Malaysia Research University Network (MRUN) Vot 4L876, for the completion of the research.

References

1. von Solms, R., van Niekerk, J.: From information security to cyber security. Comput. Secur. **38**, 97–102 (2013). https://doi.org/10.1016/j.cose.2013.04.004
2. Jang-Jaccard, J., Nepal, S.: A survey of emerging threats in cybersecurity. J. Comput. Syst. Sci. **80**(5), 973–993 (2014). https://doi.org/10.1016/j.jcss.2014.02.005
3. Kitchenham, O.B., Brereton, P., Budgen, D., Turner, M., Bailey, J., Linkman, S.: Systematic literature reviews in software engineering – a systematic literature review. Inf. Softw. Technol. **51**(1), 7–15 (2009). https://doi.org/10.1016/j.infsof.2008.09.009
4. Moher, D., Liberati, A., Tetzlaff, J., Altman, D.G., Group, T.P.: Preferred reporting items for systematic reviews and meta-analyses: the PRISMA statement PLOS Med. 6(7), e1000097 (2009). https://doi.org/10.1371/journal.pmed.1000097
5. Wohlin, C.: Guidelines for snowballing in systematic literature studies and a replication in software engineering. In: Proceedings of the 18th International Conference on Evaluation and Assessment in Software Engineering - EASE 2014, London, England, United Kingdom, pp. 1–10 (2014). https://doi.org/10.1145/2601248.2601268
6. Zhou, X., Jin, Y., Zhang, H., Li, S., Huang, X.: A map of threats to validity of systematic literature reviews in software engineering. In: 2016 23rd Asia-Pacific Software Engineering Conference (APSEC), pp. 153–160, December 2016. https://doi.org/10.1109/APSEC.2016.031
7. Orabi, M., Mouheb, D., Al Aghbari, Z., Kamel, I.: Detection of bots in social media: a systematic review. Inf. Proc. Manage. 57(4), p. 102250 (2020). https://doi.org/10.1016/j.ipm.2020.102250
8. Lim, K.C., Selamat, A., Alias, R.A., Krejcar, O., Fujita, H.: Usability measures in mobile-based augmented reality learning applications: a systematic review. Appl. Sci. 9(13), Art. no. 13, (2019). https://doi.org/10.3390/app9132718
9. Qabajeh, I., Thabtah, F., Chiclana, F.: A recent review of conventional vs. automated cybersecurity anti-phishing techniques. Comput. Sci. Rev. **29**, 44–55 (2018). https://doi.org/10.1016/j.cosrev.2018.05.003
10. Amanullah, M.A., et al.: Deep learning and big data technologies for IoT security. Comput. Commun. **151**, 495–517 (2020). https://doi.org/10.1016/j.comcom.2020.01.016
11. Zhu, E., Ju, Y., Chen, Z., Liu, F., Fang, X.: DTOF-ANN: an artificial neural network phishing detection model based on decision tree and optimal features. Appl. Soft Comput. **95**, 106505 (2020). https://doi.org/10.1016/j.asoc.2020.106505

12. Tan, C.L., Chiew, K.L., Yong, K.S.C., Sze, S.N., Abdullah, J., Sebastian, Y.: A graph-theoretic approach for the detection of phishing webpages. Comput. Secur. **95**, 101793 (2020). https://doi.org/10.1016/j.cose.2020.101793

13. Habeeb, R.A.A., Nasaruddin, F., Gani, A., Hashem, I.A.T., Ahmed, E., Imran, M.: Real-time big data processing for anomaly detection: A Survey. Int. J. Inf. Manage. **45**, 289–307 (2019). https://doi.org/10.1016/j.ijinfomgt.2018.08.006

14. Dixit, P., Silakari, S.: Deep learning algorithms for cybersecurity applications: a technological and status review. Comput. Sci. Rev. **39**, 100317 (2021). https://doi.org/10.1016/j.cosrev.2020.100317

15. Mahdavifar, S., Ghorbani, A.A.: Application of deep learning to cybersecurity: a survey. Neurocomputing **347**, 149–176 (2019). https://doi.org/10.1016/j.neucom.2019.02.056

16. Rao, R.S., Pais, A.R.: Detection of phishing websites using an efficient feature-based machine learning framework. Neural Comput. Appl. **31**(8), 3851–3873 (2018). https://doi.org/10.1007/s00521-017-3305-0

17. Hota, H.S., Shrivas, A.K., Hota, R.: An Ensemble model for detecting phishing attack with proposed remove-replace feature selection technique. Procedia Comput. Sci. **132**, 900–907 (2018). https://doi.org/10.1016/j.procs.2018.05.103

18. Subasi, A., Kremic, E.: Comparison of adaboost with multiboosting for phishing website detection. Procedia Comput. Sci. **168**, 272–278 (2020). https://doi.org/10.1016/j.procs.2020.02.251

19. Janjua, F., Masood, A., Abbas, H., Rashid, I.: Handling Insider Threat Through Supervised Machine Learning Techniques. Procedia Computer Science **177**, 64–71 (2020). https://doi.org/10.1016/j.procs.2020.10.012

20. Sahingoz, O.K., Buber, E., Demir, O., Diri, B.: Machine learning based phishing detection from URLs. Expert Syst. Appl. **117**, 345–357 (2019). https://doi.org/10.1016/j.eswa.2018.09.029

21. Adebowale, M.A., Lwin, K.T., Sánchez, E., Hossain, M.A.: Intelligent web-phishing detection and protection scheme using integrated features of Images, frames and text. Expert Syst. Appl. **115**, 300–313 (2019). https://doi.org/10.1016/j.eswa.2018.07.067

22. Mahdavifar, S., Ghorbani, A.A.: DeNNeS: deep embedded neural network expert system for detecting cyber attacks. Neural Comput. Appl. **32**(18), 14753–14780 (2020). https://doi.org/10.1007/s00521-020-04830-w

23. Zhu, H.: Online meta-learning firewall to prevent phishing attacks. Neural Comput. Appl. **32**(23), 17137–17147 (2020). https://doi.org/10.1007/s00521-020-05041-z

24. Zhu, E., Chen, Y., Ye, C., Li, X., Liu, F.: OFS-NN: an effective phishing websites detection model based on optimal feature selection and neural network. IEEE Access **7**, 73271–73284 (2019). https://doi.org/10.1109/ACCESS.2019.2920655

25. Orunsolu, A.A., Sodiya, A.S., Akinwale, A.T.: A predictive model for phishing detection. J. King Saud Univ. – Comput. Inf. Sci. (2019). https://doi.org/10.1016/j.jksuci.2019.12.005

26. Ding, Y., Luktarhan, N., Li, K., Slamu, W.: A keyword-based combination approach for detecting phishing webpages. Comput. Secur. **84**, 256–275 (2019). https://doi.org/10.1016/j.cose.2019.03.018

27. Liew, S.W., Sani, N.F.M., Abdullah, M.T., Yaakob, R., Sharum, M.Y.: An effective security alert mechanism for real-time phishing tweet detection on Twitter. Comput. Secur. **83**, 201–207 (2019). https://doi.org/10.1016/j.cose.2019.02.004

28. Wei, W., Ke, Q., Nowak, J., Korytkowski, M., Scherer, R., Woźniak, M.: Accurate and fast URL phishing detector: a convolutional neural network approach. Comput. Netw. **178**, 107275 (2020). https://doi.org/10.1016/j.comnet.2020.107275

29. Anupam, S., Kar, A.K.: Phishing website detection using support vector machines and nature-inspired optimization algorithms. Telecommun. Syst. **76**(1), 17–32 (2020). https://doi.org/10.1007/s11235-020-00739-w

30. Moorthy, R.S., Pabitha, P.: Optimal detection of phising attack using SCA based K-NN. Procedia Comput. Sci. **171**, 1716–1725 (2020). https://doi.org/10.1016/j.procs.2020.04.184

31. Deep Learning Based-Phishing Attack Detection. IJRTE, **8**(3), 8428–8432 (2019). https://doi.org/10.35940/ijrte.C6527.098319

32. Li, Q., Cheng, M., Wang, J., Sun, B.: LSTM based phishing detection for big email data. IEEE Trans. Big Data, 1 (2020). https://doi.org/10.1109/TBDATA.2020.2978915

33. Suryan, A., Kumar, C., Mehta, M., Juneja, R., Sinha, A.: Learning model for phishing website detection. EAI Endorsed Trans. Scalable Inf. Syst. **7**(27), Art. no. 27 (2020). https://doi.org/10.4108/eai.13-7-2018.163804

34. Azari, A., Namayanja, J.M., Kaur, N., Misal, V., Shukla, S.: Imbalanced Learning in Massive Phishing Datasets. In: 2020 IEEE 6th Intl Conference on Big Data Security on Cloud (Big-DataSecurity), IEEE Intl Conference on High Performance and Smart Computing, (HPSC) and IEEE Intl Conference on Intelligent Data and Security (IDS). May 2020, pp. 127–132 (2020). https://doi.org/10.1109/BigDataSecurity-HPSC-IDS49724.2020.00032

35. Huang, Y., Yang, Q., Qin, J., Wen, W.: Phishing URL detection via CNN and attention-based hierarchical RNN. In: 2019 18th IEEE International Conference on Trust, Security and Privacy in Computing and Communications/13th IEEE International Conference on Big Data Science And Engineering (TrustCom/BigDataSE), Aug. 2019, pp. 112–119 (2019). https://doi.org/10.1109/TrustCom/BigDataSE.2019.00024

36. Zhu, E., Ye, C., Liu, D., Liu, F., Wang, F., Li, X.: An effective neural network phishing detection model based on optimal feature selection. In: 2018 IEEE Intl Conf on Parallel Distributed Processing with Applications, Ubiquitous Computing Communications, Big Data Cloud Computing, Social Computing Networking, Sustainable Computing Communications (ISPA/IUCC/BDCloud/SocialCom/SustainCom), December 2018, pp. 781–787 (2018). https://doi.org/10.1109/BDCloud.2018.00117

37. Yuan, H., Yang, Z., Chen, X., Li, Y., Liu, W.: URL2Vec: URL modeling with character embeddings for fast and accurate phishing website detection. In: 2018 IEEE Intl Conf on Parallel Distributed Processing with Applications, Ubiquitous Computing Communications, Big Data Cloud Computing, Social Computing Networking, Sustainable Computing Communications (ISPA/IUCC/BDCloud/SocialCom/SustainCom), December 2018, pp. 265–272 (2018). https://doi.org/10.1109/BDCloud.2018.00050

38. Chawathe, S.: Improving email security with fuzzy rules. In: 2018 17th IEEE International Conference on Trust, Security and Privacy in Computing and Communications/ 12th IEEE International Conference on Big Data Science and Engineering (TrustCom/BigDataSE), August 2018, pp. 1864–1869 (2018). https://doi.org/10.1109/TrustCom/BigDataSE.2018.00282

39. Qamar, A., Karim, A., Chang, V.: Mobile malware attacks: review, taxonomy and future directions. Futur. Gener. Comput. Syst. **97**, 887–909 (2019). https://doi.org/10.1016/j.future.2019.03.007

40. Aldweesh, A., Derhab, A., Emam, A.Z.: Deep learning approaches for anomaly-based intrusion detection systems: a survey, taxonomy, and open issues. Knowl.-Based Syst. **189**, 105124 (2020). https://doi.org/10.1016/j.knosys.2019.105124

41. Faker, O., Dogdu, E.: Intrusion detection using big data and deep learning techniques. In: Proceedings of the 2019 ACM Southeast Conference, New York, April 2019, pp. 86–93 (2019). https://doi.org/10.1145/3299815.3314439

A Transaction Classification Model of Federated Learning

Usman Ahmed[1], Jerry Chun-Wei Lin[1(✉)], Gautam Srivastava[2,3], and Philippe Fournier-Viger[4]

[1] Department of Computer Science, Electrical Engineering and Mathematical Science, Western Norway University of Applied Sciences, Bergen, Norway
usman.Ahmed@hvl.no, jerrylin@ieee.org
[2] Department of Mathematics and Computer Science, Brandon University, Brandon, Canada
[3] Research Center for Interneural Computing, China Medical University, Taichung, Taiwan
SRIVASTAVAG@brandonu.ca
[4] School of Humanities and Social Sciences, Harbin Institute of Technology (Shenzhen), Shenzhen, China

Abstract. In this paper, we first propose a federated learning-based embedding model for transaction classification. The model takes the transaction data as a set of frequent item-sets. After that model is able to learn low dimensional continuous vector by preserving the frequent item-sets contextual relationship. Results then indicated that the designed model can help and improve the decision boundary by reducing the global loss function.

Keywords: Federated learning · Classification · Data mining · Embedding

1 Introduction

Currently, pattern mining techniques have dramatically increased in recent decades to discover varied knowledge such as frequent pattern mining (FPM) [9, 11], association rule mining (ARM) [1], frequent episode mining (FEM) [19], and sequential pattern mining (SPM) [8]. Mining information from them is a non-trivial process which requires contemplation of various essential constraints. Most of the existing state-of-the-art algorithms in pattern mining focus on handling binary databases because it has comparatively less complicated structure than other types of databases [14].

A common solution in data mining is the usage of the frequency of the items as features. The threshold values are being used as the criteria to for pattern extraction. The bitmap representation is used to represent items. However, this approach results in the curse of high dimensionality issues and data sparsity problems. Although Chen et al. [4] solve the dimensionality and data sparsity problems by using the measures, it still fails into some limitations. First, they

© Springer Nature Switzerland AG 2021
H. Fujita et al. (Eds.): IEA/AIE 2021, LNAI 12798, pp. 509–518, 2021.
https://doi.org/10.1007/978-3-030-79457-6_43

consider representation of transactional data for particular tasks, i.e., transaction classification. As a result, they cannot transfer the patterns or learning mechanism to other different tasks. Second, the methods required the number of instances structured in the database. However, the real world applications are often dynamic, and some domain application, for example, stream scenario, does not allow re-scanning of the databases. Third, the model does not tackle the problem of extracting patterns without using the actual data. The databases often collaborate in the centralized structure. This structuring often results in overhead as it requires time consuming approvals because of data privacy and ethical concerns associated with data sharing of personal records. Even when the challenges being addressed, data sets are valuable for the organization, so they prefer not to share the full data sets [3].

To overcome the weakness of the static FIM-based model, we summarize the contributions in this paper as follows:

1. We propose attention-based transaction embedding model for transactional data to learn low dimensional continuous representation.
2. We prove that the federated learning helps to improve the performance of learnt embedding without raw data sharing.
3. We demonstrate that the developed embedding model helps in transaction classification tasks on several benchmark datasets.

2   Related Work

2.1   Deep Neural Networks

Different machine learning and different deep learning architectures are proposed over the past two decades [5,23,29]. The difference in the neural architecture is in terms of hidden layers, layers type, layer shapes and connection between layers [28]. To learn higher dimension features from tabular data, Wainberg *et al.* used fully connected networks [30]. The convolutional neural networks (CNN) learn features embedding from the image pixels. The translation invariant pixel data brings the benefits to the architecture and increases learning compatibility. Many studies were respectively presented for solving distinct problems related to wildlife [13], X-ray scans [25] and autonomous driving [27]. For sequential data, recurrent neural network (RNN) architecture was proposed and used in the domain of natural language process including Neural Machine Translation, language generation, and time series analysis [6].

Typically, RNN is an encoder and decoder framework where encoder takes the sequence of input and decode into the fixed length of the vector. The model uses different gates to process the input features based on the loss function. However, while compression, the model loss relevant information [5]. Another issue with the RNN encoder and decoder model is the alignment of input and output vector. The sequence is influenced by neighbors' features values. The decoder lacks a selective focus on input features. Another variant for RNN is an attention-based sequence they proposed to sequence model [5]. The idea behind the attention is to allow the usage of the complete input sequence and then apply attention based weights on the selective input sequence to prioritize the importance and position of relevant information. After that decoder uses the position, context vector and corresponding weights for the higher feature representation. They then feed the learnt weights to RNN model for further usage [5]. The attention model takes the multiple inputs, and joint learnt the attention weights [16]. The soft attention model was proposed [2]. The model used the weighted average of the hidden states and then built the context vector. The method helps the neural network to efficient learns the hidden pattern and reduce the loss function. The hard attention model was proposed by Xu *et al.* [31] that computes the context vector from sampling the hidden states in the input vectors. The hard computation reduces the computation cost; however, the convergence of the architecture is difficult to achieve. Luong *et al.* [18] propose local and global attention method. The global attention architecture is like soft attention, and global attention is intermediate between soft and hard attention. The model is to pick the attention point or position of input features for each round. This creates a local attention model. The attention position is learned by the predictive function. The global attention takes advantage of soft and hard attention by remaining computational efficient and differentiability within the attention windows.

2.2 Federated Learning

Federated learning [15] was proposed to prevent data leakage and build machine learning model based on the distributed dataset. The framework only shares the model weights to the network nodes, and the model trains locally without sharing the actual datasets [21,24]. The above works focused on handling issues related to data distribution, unbalance data, and device ability for optimization. Federated learning can be classified as two types of learning model, i.e., horizontal and vertical [32]. In horizontal federated learning, feature space is the same, but the data distribution is different [32]. The method has overlapping characteristic with privacy preservation machine learning as it considers the privacy of data in decentralized collaborative learning [32]. In vertical federated learning, the dataset feature space is different, and data distribution is overlapping [32]. The federated learning mechanism is proposed by Shokri *et al.* [26] to train the multiple deep learning models on joint inputs. The trusted model sharing mechanism was proposed by Hayes and Ohrimenko [12]. Fredrikson *et al.* proposed a federated model by utilizing the output of the machine learning algorithm [10]. Mohassel and Rindal [20] proposed the aggregation function that uses the approximation of fixed-point multiplication protocols.

3 Developed Attention-Based Federated Learning Model

Given a dataset D shown in Table 1 and the set of FIs discovered from D, $\mathcal{F}(\mathcal{D}) = \{X_1, X_2, \ldots, X_F\}$, as mentioned in Table 2, the feature vector of a transaction T is defined as $f(T) = [x_1, x_2, \ldots, x_F]$, where $x_i = 1$ if $X_i \subseteq T$ otherwise $x_i = 0$. as describe in Table 3.

Table 1. Transaction database

Trans	Items
T_1	a, b, c
t_2	b, c, d
t_3	a, d
t_4	b, c, d, e
t_5	a, c, d

Table 2. FIs from the transaction data under min support of 0.6

FI	Items	Sup
X_1	a	0.6
X_2	b	0.6
X_3	c	0.8
X_4	d	0.8
X_5	b, c	0.6
X_6	c, d	0.6

Table 3. Transaction represented as set of FIs and used as input features.

Trans	FIs
T_1	$\{X_1, X_2, X_3, X_5\}$
T_2	$\{X_2, X_3, X_4, X_5, X_6\}$
T_3	$\{X_1, X_4\}$
T_4	$\{X_2, X_3, X_4, X_5, X_6\}$
T_5	$\{X_1, X_3, X_4, X_6\}$

Problem statement: Consider Table 1 as an example that will be used by the proposed algorithm shown in Algorithm 1. There are five transactions in the table $(T_1, T_2, T_3, T_4, T_5)$. Given items $\mathcal{I} = \{i_1, i_2, \ldots, i_M\}$ and a transaction dataset $\mathcal{D} = \{T_1, T_2, \ldots, T_N\}$. Our goal is to map the transaction data by learning a function $f : \mathcal{D} \to \mathbb{R}^d$ such that every transaction $T_i \in \mathcal{D}$ is mapped to a d-dimensional continuous vector. The learning requires to have the similarity among the transactions in a way that correlated item sets should have similar embedding. The embedding $\mathbf{X} = [f(T_1), f(T_2), \ldots, f(T_N)]$ can be used by any machine learning classifier for the data mining as well as classification task.

3.1 Client-Server-Based Federated Learning

The proposed framework uses multi-client data mentioned in Fig. 1. For experimentation purpose, we split the data among six clients, and each client is with equal distribution. In addition, each client data exhibits with non-overlapping data, local model and database. The data distribution is varied among clients randomly. Given these differences, framework typically exhibits real-world datasets, where a store's multiple branches are placed in the city and connected in the server for the supply and demands analysis. The setting also exhibits that environment is non-independent and identically distributed. The federated learning algorithm uses a server-client environment. The client data is locally stored for each model. The local data is used to train the initialized model. For each iteration, we require the client to transfer the locally trained weights or their gradient towards the server *(Algorithm 1 - lines 3 to 9)*. The server receives and aggregates the weights *(Algorithm 1 - lines 5 to 6)*. The purpose is to share training of the client model without sharing the actual data and using the weights. The global model then uses the aggregate weights to update the global model *(Algorithm 1 - lines 8 to 9)*. After aggregation, the next round of local client models starts with the global weights. After a certain number of federated learning iterations, the convergence point for the client reaches. For experimental purpose, we used the early termination method to check the convergence point. During the empirical analysis, we set the early stopping patient value to ten. After that, the client may select the best model for each iteration based on hold out data. The client monitors the validation loss on the local test set. The client can select from the global aggregated model or from the best local iteration model. We used the federated averaging method as its converges early and reduce over-fitting of the model [15]. However, in our empirical analysis, embedding size is required to be set higher number for optimal performance. The reason is that decoder model is able to have bigger vector space to map the positional attention. The federated averaging is to reduce the global loss function L which is resulted from the weighted combination of K losses $\{\mathcal{L}_k\}_{k=1}^{K}$ (client losses) of the distributed aggregated function. The model could learn the embedding by using the parameter ϕ that minimizes the L on local data X_k where X combination of local data sets and representation of the embedding. Equation 1 represents the loss function.

$$\min_{\phi} \mathcal{L}(X; \phi) \quad \text{with} \quad \mathcal{L}(X; \phi) = \sum_{k=1}^{K} w_k \mathcal{L}_k (X_k; \phi) \tag{1}$$

The coefficient $w_K > 0$ denotes the weights of client K model. The model K is trained on local data, and only weights are distributed among the server. The weight is aggregated by summing the number of client in the network.

3.2   Attention Network

In our approach, we use the transnational data and represented as set frequent itemsets as contextual information described in Table 1. The frequency to purchase the likely items is always highly relevant. Thus, the item frequency in transnational data is considered as the contextual data points in the developed

---

Algorithm 1. Attention-based federated averaging method.

INPUT: T transaction data, R are the number of rounds, n_K are the local training
  epochs to minimize loss $\mathcal{L}_k\left(X_k; \phi^{(t-1)}\right)$ for client K

OUTPUT: Optimize weights

 1: $Weights \leftarrow \phi^{random}$

 2:                   ▷ Initialize weights randomly

 3: **for** $all\ r \in R$ **do**

 4: **for** $all\ client \in K$ **do**

 5:   $Send\ \phi^{r-1}$

 6:   $Receive\left(\Delta\phi_k^{(r)}, n_k\right)$

 7: **end for**

 8: $\phi_k^{(r)} \leftarrow \phi^{(r-1)} + \Delta\phi_k^{(r)}$

 9: $\phi^{(r)} \leftarrow \frac{1}{\sum_k n_k}\sum_k\left(n_k \cdot \phi_k^{(r)}\right)$ ▷ Aggregate( )

10: **end for**

11: **Return** $\phi^{(r)}$

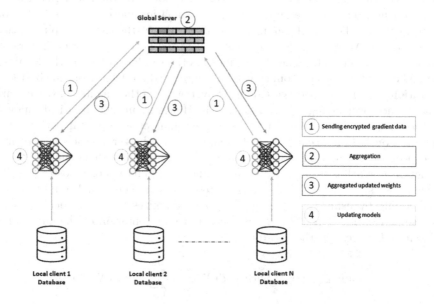

Fig. 1. The framework of the designed attention based federated learning for transaction embedding.

model. After that, we use the attention mechanism to exploit the contextual relevance of similar items to create embedding and then used it to predict output class. For comparison, we use the Table 4 for configuration.

We first transfer the items features through the dense 100 Relu units. We then pass the developed model through Luong attention method that uses the decoder hidden state [17]. The attention score is calculated and concatenated with the hidden state of the decoder. We then pass the obtained output sequence through the 100 and 350 Relu units. The last layer was Softmax, and we use Adam optimizer for the learning rate. We mask the input data for padding and train the network for 10 epochs per iteration. The number of iterations is set to 100. The input features are padded and fixed length vector is passed to the models.

4   Experimental Evaluation

For experimental analysis, we used two benchmark datasets from the SPMF library [7]. We mention the characteristic summary of the dataset in Table 4. Snippets dataset is from the web search transaction, and each item represents the keywords. Cancer is the dataset of patient admission based on diagnoses symptoms.

4.1   Baseline

In Bag-of-Words (BOW) and Term Frequency-Inverse Document Frequency (TF-IDF) methods, each transaction is treated as document and items as a word. By using the mechanism, we can apply the natural language processing based models on transaction data. For comparison, we used the bag of word model, term frequency inverse document frequency and Trans2vec model [22] as the baselines compared with the proposed model. Moreover, we used the elbow method for the selection of the support threshold of the frequent item-sets as used by the Nguyen *et al.* [22]. The vector representation of attention embedding was used for the classification task. This is done by using the Softmax layer. The loss function is used to evaluate the classification task. The model is measured in terms of accuracy and F-measure.

Table 4. Characteristic of the dataset.

Dataset	# trans	# train	# test	# items	Avg. length
Snippets	12,340	10,060	2,280	23,686	13.00
Cancer	15,000	12,000	3,000	3,234	6.00

4.2   Results Discussion

In Table 5, the proposed attention-based embedding model is able to perform better compared with traditional and embedding-based model. The proposed model is able to achieve 2–13% percentage improvement over TF-IDF. Against to word embedding, the developed model is able to perform 0.2 to 1% improvement for Snippets ans Cancer datasets that we can observe in Table 5. The federated environment helps to learn the embedding without sharing the actual

Table 5. Experimental results.

	Snippets		Cancer	
Methods	AC	F1	AC	F1
TF-IDF	70.26	69.52	49.43	49.43
Proposed	81.02	80.01	57.03	57.01
Support threshold	0.2		0.2	

data and results demonstrate that learning of transaction information for frequent itemsets and then applying on the classification can be enhanced with some hyper tuning. The attention network is able to extract the meaningful relation among transaction data.

To obtain the robustness results, it requires proposed model to be run for more extended epochs. This helps to increase the weights per instances. However, it is also observed that the correlated features set decreases the performance with the increasing of the training time. All methods are well-performed for the classification task by using the transaction as set of frequent itemsets. We also observe that we should increase the feature set for the method. Other features, i.e., support, weight or occupancy of itemset should be combined to get a suitable learning method, which can be future explored for subsequent developments.

5   Conclusion

In this paper, we use the attention-based mechanism for transaction embedding and then used the embedding to classify transaction data by using the transaction data. The developed model can achieve high accuracy. The federated averaging learning-based method significantly reduces the global loss of the shared weights. From the experimental results, it can be seen that the federated learning can obtain the practical benefits over traditional supervised learning methods. The model could perform better locally without shared and distributing the raw data across the network.

References

1. Agrawal, R., Srikant, R., et al.: Fast algorithms for mining association rules. Int. Conf. Very Large Data Bases **1215**, 487–499 (1994)
2. Bahdanau, D., Cho, K., Bengio, Y.: Neural machine translation by jointly learning to align and translate. In: Bengio, Y., LeCun, Y. (eds.) International Conference on Learning Representations (2015)
3. Chang, K., et al.: Distributed deep learning networks among institutions for medical imaging. J. Am. Med. Inform. Assoc. **25**(8), 945–954 (2018)
4. Cheng, H., Yan, X., Han, J., Hsu, C.: Discriminative frequent pattern analysis for effective classification. In: The International Conference on Data Engineering, pp. 716–725 (2007)

5. Cho, K., et al.: Learning phrase representations using RNN encoder-decoder for statistical machine translation. In: The Conference on Empirical Methods in Natural Language Processing, pp. 1724–1734 (2014)
6. Fawaz, H.I.: Deep learning for time series classification. CoRR abs/2010.00567 (2020)
7. Fournier-Viger, P., et al.: The spmf open-source data mining library version 2. In: Joint European Conference on Machine Learning and Knowledge Discovery in Databases, pp. 36–40 (2016)
8. Fournier-Viger, P., Lin, J.C.W., Kiran, R.U., Koh, Y.S., Thomas, R.: A survey of sequential pattern mining. Data Sci. Pattern Recognit. 1(1), 54–77 (2017)
9. Fournier-Viger, P., Lin, J.C.W., Vo, B., Chi, T.T., Zhang, J., Le, H.B.: A survey of itemset mining. Wiley Interdisc. Rev.: Data Mining Knowl. Discov. 7(4), e1207 (2017)
10. Fredrikson, M., Jha, S., Ristenpart, T.: Model inversion attacks that exploit confidence information and basic countermeasures. In: ACM SIGSAC Conference on Computer and Communications Security, pp. 1322–1333 (2015)
11. Han, J., Pei, J., Yin, Y., Mao, R.: Mining frequent patterns without candidate generation: a frequent-pattern tree approach. Data Min. Knowl. Disc. 8(1), 53–87 (2004)
12. Hayes, J., Ohrimenko, O.: Contamination attacks and mitigation in multi-party machine learning. CoRR abs/1901.02402 (2019)
13. Horn, G.V., et al.: The inaturalist species classification and detection dataset. In: IEEE Conference on Computer Vision and Pattern Recognition, pp. 8769–8778 (2018)
14. Kalra, M., Lal, N., Qamar, S.: K-mean clustering algorithm approach for data mining of heterogeneous data. In: Information and Communication Technology for Sustainable Development, pp. 61–70 (2018)
15. Konecný, J., McMahan, H.B., Ramage, D., Richtárik, P.: Federated optimization: distributed machine learning for on-device intelligence. CoRR abs/1610.02527 (2016)
16. Lu, J., Yang, J., Batra, D., Parikh, D.: Hierarchical question-image co-attention for visual question answering. In: Advances in Neural Information Processing Systems, pp. 289–297 (2016)
17. Luong, M.T., Pham, H., Manning, C.D.: Effective approaches to attention-based neural machine translation. arXiv preprint arXiv:1508.04025 (2015)
18. Luong, T., Pham, H., Manning, C.D.: Effective approaches to attention-based neural machine translation. In: The Conference on Empirical Methods in Natural Language Processing, pp. 1412–1421 (2015)
19. Mannila, H., Toivonen, H., Verkamo, A.I.: Discovery of frequent episodes in event sequences. Data Min. Knowl. Disc. 1(3), 259–289 (1997)
20. Mohassel, P., Rindal, P.: Aby[3]: A mixed protocol framework for machine learning. In: Lie, D., Mannan, M., Backes, M., Wang, X. (eds.) ACM SIGSAC Conference on Computer and Communications Security, pp. 35–52 (2018)
21. Mothukuri, V., Parizi, R.M., Pouriyeh, S., Huang, Y., Dehghantanha, A., Srivastava, G.: A survey on security and privacy of federated learning. Future Gener. Comput. Syst. (2020)
22. Nguyen, D., Nguyen, T.D., Luo, W., Venkatesh, S.: Trans2Vec: learning transaction embedding via items and frequent itemsets. In: Phung, D., Tseng, V.S., Webb, G.I., Ho, B., Ganji, M., Rashidi, L. (eds.) PAKDD 2018. LNCS (LNAI), vol. 10939, pp. 361–372. Springer, Cham (2018). https://doi.org/10.1007/978-3-319-93040-4_29

23. Nguyen, G., Dlugolinsky, S., Bobák, M., Tran, V.D., García, Á.L., Heredia, I., Malík, P., Hluchý, L.: Machine learning and deep learning frameworks and libraries for large-scale data mining: a survey. Artif. Intell. Rev. **52**(1), 77–124 (2019)

24. Połap, D., Srivastava, G., Jolfaei, A., Parizi, R.M.: Blockchain technology and neural networks for the internet of medical things. In: IEEE Conference on Computer Communications Workshops, pp. 508–513 (2020)

25. Rajpurkar, P., et al.: Chexnet: Radiologist-level pneumonia detection on chest x-rays with deep learning. CoRR abs/1711.05225 (2017)

26. Shokri, R., Shmatikov, V.: Privacy-preserving deep learning. In: Proceedings of the ACM SIGSAC conference on Computer and Communications Security, pp. 1310–1321 (2015)

27. Siam, M., Elkerdawy, S., Jägersand, M., Yogamani, S.K.: Deep semantic segmentation for automated driving: Taxonomy, roadmap and challenges. In: IEEE International Conference on Intelligent Transportation Systems, pp. 1–8 (2017)

28. Sze, V., Chen, Y., Yang, T., Emer, J.S.: Efficient processing of deep neural networks: a tutorial and survey. Proc. IEEE **105**(12), 2295–2329 (2017). https://doi.org/10.1109/JPROC.2017.2761740

29. Vinayakumar, R., Soman, K.P., Poornachandran, P.: Applying convolutional neural network for network intrusion detection. In: International Conference on Advances in Computing, Communications and Informatics, pp. 1222–1228 (2017)

30. Wainberg, M., Merico, D., Delong, A., Frey, B.J.: Deep learning in biomedicine. Nat. Biotechnol. **36**(9), 829–838 (2018)

31. Xu, K., et al.: Show, attend and tell: neural image caption generation with visual attention. Int. Conf. Mach. Learn. **37**, 2048–2057 (2015)

32. Yang, Q., Liu, Y., Chen, T., Tong, Y.: Federated machine learning: concept and applications. ACM Trans. Intell. Syst. Technol. **10**(2), 1–19 (2019)

On the Assessment of Robustness of Telemedicine Applications against Adversarial Machine Learning Attacks

Ibrahim Yilmaz[1], Mohamed Baza[2(✉)], Ramy Amer[3], Amar Rasheed[4],
Fathi Amsaad[5], and Rasha Morsi[6]

[1] Department of Computer Science, Tennessee Technological University,
Cookeville, TN, USA
[2] Department of Computer Science, College of Charleston, Charleston, SC, USA
mibaza42@tntech.edu
[3] CONNECT, The Centre for Future Networks and Communication Trinity College
Dublin, Dublin, Ireland
[4] Department of Computer Science, Sam Houston State University,
Huntsville, TX, USA
[5] School of Information Security and Applied Computing (SISAC),
Eastern Michigan University (EMU), Ypsilanti, MI 48197, USA
[6] Department of Computer Science at Norfolk State University, Norfolk, VA, USA

Abstract. Telemedicine applications have been recently evolved to allow patients in underdeveloped areas to receive medical services. Meanwhile, machine learning (ML) techniques have been widely adopted in such telemedicine applications to help in disease diagnosis. The performance of these ML techniques, however, are limited by the fact that attackers can manipulate clean data to fool the model classifier and break the truthfulness and robustness of these models. For instance, due to attacks, a benign sample can be treated as a malicious one by the classifier and vice versa. Motivated by this, this paper aims at exploring this issue for telemedicine applications. Particularly, this paper studies the impact of adversarial attacks on mammographic image classifier. First, mamographic images are used to train and evaluate the accuracy of our proposed model. The original dataset is then poisoned to generate adversarial samples that can mislead the model. For this, structural similarity index is used to determine similarity between clean images and adversarial images. Results show that adversarial attacks can severely fool the ML model.

Keywords: Telemedicine applications · Machine learning · Convolutional neural network · Structural similarity index

1 Introduction

The requirement of medical resources increases dramatically driven by the increase of population and the unprecedented spreed of disease such as COVID-19. Moreover, patients in underdeveloped areas lack of adequate transportation

© Springer Nature Switzerland AG 2021
H. Fujita et al. (Eds.): IEA/AIE 2021, LNAI 12798, pp. 519–529, 2021.
https://doi.org/10.1007/978-3-030-79457-6_44

systems, especially if they are disabled or old. In this regard, telemedicine sys-temd have recently been adopted to close this gap [10]. This system takes advan-tage of telecommunication and technology to supply remote healthcare services so as to overcome the distance barriers and improve the medical services in rural communities.

Recently, the research community increasingly incorporated machine learn-ing algorithms in the telemedicine applications [15]. The primary goal of these algorithms is to develop models usable by physicians to predict health status and help prevent future diseases. As an example, Google developed a machine learn-ing algorithm to identify cancerous tumours on mammograms [3]. In addition, Google's DeepMind Health project [4] aimed to create the best treatment plans for cancer patients by rapidly analyzing their medical test results and instantly referring them to the right specialist.

Despite the benefits provided by these ML models, their *robustness* needs to be investigated. For example, attackers can manipulate clean data fooling the ML classifiers and, as a result, the reputation of these models can be put in doubt. This indeed can yield many financial losses, serious injuries, or even deaths. As a first step in this direction, this paper explores this issue with the aim to raise awareness and obtain useful insights. In particular, we consider identifying can-cerous cells on mammographic images breast cancer as a case study. Recently, there have been much successful research to diagnose and classify breast cancer using deep neural network (DNNs). Due to their high performance and effec-tive computation, DNNs are commonly used for classification of mammographic images. More specifically, convolutional neural networks (CNNs) can effectively classify malicious and benign samples on mammogram images [17].

In this paper, we aim to show if *there are adversarial attacks that can fool mammographic image classifiers*. Based on our study, it is found that mammo-graphic image classifiers might misclassify the input images if they are poisoned by adversarial attacks. As a result, the robustness of the breast cancer classifier model will be impacted. We address issue by showing different case studies and analyze a potential solution for this problem. This paper contains the follow-ing constructive contributions to highlight this security weakness and heighten awareness of physicians when giving a diagnosis of cancer.

- We highlight and assess the security vulnerability of CNN, which are widely used in the diagnosis of breast cancer.
- We implement an efficient adversarial attack on mammographic images in order to fool the mammographic image classifier.
- We analyze the comparison between original and crafted mamograpgic images using structural similarity index (SSIM) and investigate how original image changes based on different perturbation coefficient.

The rest of this paper is organized as follows. In Sect. 2, we discuss some preliminaries used in this research. We present the proposed attack strategy on mammographic image in Sect. 3 and implement of attack on CNN models in Sect. 4. The evaluation results of our adversarial attack are presented in Sect. 5. In Sect. 6, we discuss the related works. In Sect. 7, we conclude our paper.

2 Background

In this section, we briefly go through learning process of DNNs along with a deep learning approach using CNN on the mammographic image. We also give an overview about structural similarity Index (SSIM).

2.1 Learning Process

DNNs like humans, have learning process with experience. Available data is the experience of DNNs. DNNs try to capture distribution of training data which helps to determine boundary decisions between the normal and the cancerous images. Built model then predicts whether the unlabelled image is cancerous or normal.

DNN is supervised learning process meaning that a paired training data X and Y is given. Here X represents the mammographic image and Y represents the ground-truth label as cancer or normal. The aim of the model is to find a function f(X) that fits the map perfectly from X to Y. Model takes each mammographic image and their corresponding label data and learns the behaviour of model by minimizing error.

2.2 Convolutional Neural Network (CNN)

CNN is a special type of deep neural network which is widely used for image classification. As DNN, CNN comprises of input, output and hidden layers. However, in CNN, the hidden layer is comprised of different parts knowns as convolution, pooling and fully connected. An example of CNN architecture with two phase is illustrated in Fig. 1.

Convolutional layer and pooling layer is used for feature selection of the image, and these feature are connected with each other in the fully connected layer.

Convolutional layer: In this layer, filter matrix which is special matrix and its size depend on architecture model is applied over mammographic image. Convolution operation is a linear operation, so to make it non-linear, activation function is applied following convolution operation. This is because mostly complex problems are nonlinear and can be solved by nonlinear functions.

Pooling Layer: Pooling layer is a subsampling process. It is mostly used following convolutional process and there is no learning part in this layer. There are different types of pooling layers such as max pooling, mean pooling, sum pooling etc. Most often, max pooling is used because of its high performance. In the maximum pooling, the maximum pooling function takes group of pixel values as input and chooses the biggest one of this group as output.

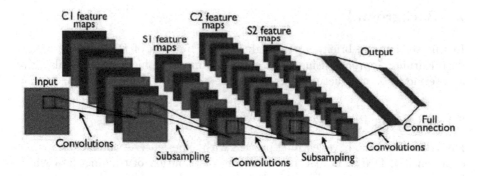

Fig. 1. CNN architecture with two phase.

Fully connected layer: CNN is completed with this layer. In this layer, all nodes are connected and are used with softmax or sigmoid function in order to predict probabilities of each output through learning process.

2.3   Structural Similarity Index (SSIM)

Structural similarity Index is used to compare different images in terms of similarity. Prior to the SSIM, mean square error was preferred by researchers, yet because of its limited functionality, a new image quality assessment was needed. Wang et al. in [20] brought a new solution to evaluate image quality assessment in terms of *luminance, contrast,* and *structure*.

Luminance is a measure that indicates how much light passes through, along with what is reflected or spread from a certain region at a certain time [5]. However, the simple definition of contrast is differences between lowest and highest pixel density in a image [1]. In addition, structure is another metric used to distinguish images from each other. It is used to tell objects apart. If a image is considered, then it assesses in terms of edges, corners, sub-regions etc. of the image. Multiplicative function of these three features give a structural similarity index value. If the SSIM value is high, it means that these two images are very similar. If it is low when two images are compared, it is interpreted as different images.

3   Attack Model

In this section, we introduce our attack model based on CNN which is inspired in [9] in order to generate adversarial mammographic image samples that fool the mamograpgic image classifier.

ML models are data driven approach and aim to minimize cost function using the gradient descent algorithm. The idea behind this attack is to find a adversarial direction and all pxel values change based on that direction in an attempt to lead to a misclassification. Adding imperceptibly small computed noise on the same direction of cost function is able to maximize cost function instead of minimize it. To put it simply, attackers use gradient cost function with respect to input data and add small amount of perturbation to maximize the cost. By doing this way, attackers craft adversarial samples which are assigned to the incorrect labels. We can explain the mathematical definition of our algorithm below.

Let M be our mammograpgic image classifier model. x is a real mammographic image and y is the corresponding ground-truth output label (cancer or normal) of given the image. C(M, x, y) is the cost function used to train model, ϵ is the penetration coefficient, $\hat{x}$ is the adversarial mammographic image is crafted by the adversarial and $\hat{y}$ is the prediction of the model given a adversarial image $(\hat{x})$ as an input.

$$objective \quad max\, c(M, \hat{x}, y) \tag{1}$$

$$subject\, to \quad \hat{x} = x + \delta x \tag{2}$$

$$|x|_d \quad \leq \quad \epsilon * |x| \tag{3}$$

in (3) represents dimensionality of mammographic image data is allowed to be altered. We set d is infnity as proposed in [9]. It means that it is allowed to add perturbation on any dimension of the original mammograpgic images.

In addition, δx in (2) denotes perturbation added to the original mamographic images. The magnitude of this perturbation should be equal or less than ϵ as constrained in (3) where ϵ controls perturbation amount. The aim is to maximize error in (1).

δx is computed as follows:

$$\delta x = \epsilon * \, sign(\nabla x \, c(M, x, y)) \tag{4}$$

where $sign$ $(\nabla x\ c(M, x, y)))$ is the direction of minimizing cost function of the model and ϵ controls the penetration magnitude in (3).

Therefore, cost function of adversarial mammographic images is $c(M, \hat{x}, y)$ and $y \neq \hat{y}$ must be true if this attack is succeed.

To visualize, we draw our attack scenario in Fig. 2 with triangulars representing cancer cells and circles representing normal cells. A normal cell which is close to the boundary decision is predicted truly by the CNN model. After adding subtle perturbation on test phase, the same model predicts the cancer cell incorrectly. Because of the limited feature precision, small changes of pixel value are not able to be realized by human eyes. However, these changes may cause the activation function to grow exponentially and fool the breast cancer classifier.

Range of the ϵ value is between 0 and 1. Rising ϵ value increases the probability of $\hat{x}$ being misclassified by the model M. On the other hand, increasing ϵ value leads to adversarial samples to be detected by human eyes. There is a trade-off between increasing the probablity an attack will be successful and being

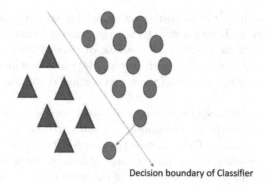

Fig. 2. Adversarial attack visualization.

recognizable by human. In Evaluation Section, we also evaluate the how much the original images are modified through adversarial attacks using a structural similarity index.

4 Material and Method

4.1 Data Processing

The University of South Florid provides mammographic image dataset in order for researchers to develop new techniques for early diagnosis of breast cancer [2]. The database includes roughly 2500 samples. However, we could use 100 od them for our work because of limitations. Each sample has ground-truth label as normal or cancer.

Collection of data from dataset is challenging since the dataset has different files, each file includes different studies, and the image format is 'GIF'. After data has been collected from different files, each image has been converted 'JPG' format manually. Furthermore, each image size is different. Prior to images have been used as input of our model, with the dimensions of the images being set up 256 × 256.

4.2 Implementation of Model

We encode our implementation in Python using Tensorflow [6] in ourder build our model based on a CNN. Number of convolution layers, pooling layers, fully connected layers and iterations mainly depends on the CNN's architecture and the dataset itself to find optimum parameters. Therefore, we try different archi-tectures until we reach an optimum solution. We train our model with optimum accuracy performance including 2 different convolution layers, each with a 5 × 5 kernel size, two different max pool layers and two different fully connected layers, with 180 × 50 and 50 × 2 sizes respectively.

Afterwards, we apply FGSM attacks to our trained model with different ϵ values. We produce adversarial samples for each ϵ value so as to deceive victim model and we monitor how its accuracy changes based on different ϵ values. We set ϵ value to 0 as well because it represents the model performance on the original test set. In addition, we monitor how original image changes with different ϵ values using SSIM technique and try to figure out which epsilon value can be more successful without being recognizable by people.

5 Evaluation

We use 100 mammographic images taken from 'Digital Database for Screening Mammography' (DDSM) database released by the University of South Florida. 70 of the images are obtained from a healthy person and rest of them are taken from cancerous patient. We divide our database in two parts. 90 images are used to train our model and the 10 remaining images are used to test accuracy of our model.

Fig. 3. Cancer images.   **Fig. 4.** Normal images.

There are some samples of cancer images in Fig. 3 and normal images in Fig. 4. We evaluate our attack success by observing decreasing accuracy of the CNN model. Adversarial samples which we generate mislead the model into making incorrect decision.

Using FGSM attack algorithm, we craft attack samples for both cancer and normal images. Some are depicted in Fig. 5 and in Fig. 6 based on different epsilon values.

We sometimes set epsilon values high intentionally to demonstrate maximum damage to victim model and to show how the penetrated image is easily detected by observer with high epsilon values. We modify epsilon values with small values and monitor how much adversarial samples impair performance of our model without being recognizable. Adversarial samples are produced with small epsilon values In Fig. 7 and in Fig. 8.

When we train our model, the model's accuracy reach to 70 with clean image. The reason of the higher performance value is not found is because being trained with a small dataset. It is believed that this number would be higher if the model was trained with a bigger dataset. In this study, we emphasize how a CNN classifier is vulnerable against adversarial attack rather than enhance the model's

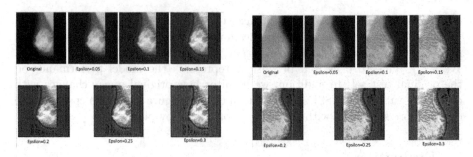

Fig. 5. Adversarial samples for cancer images with high epsilon values.

Fig. 6. Adversarial samples for normal images with high epsilon values.

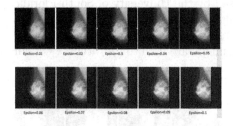

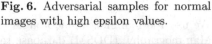

Fig. 7. Adversarial samples for cancer images with small epsilon values.

Fig. 8. Adversarial samples for normal images with small epsilon values.

performance. Graphics show how the model's performance is compromised with different penetration coeficients in Fig. 9 and in Fig. 10.

Also, we observe how penetrated images are degenerated by different epsilon values using SSIM. Graphics illustrate these differences in Fig. 11 and in Fig. 12.

6   Related Work

Adversarial attacks against DNN classifiers were discussed previously by different researchers. in this research, we carry out a FGSM attack against a mammographic image classifier based on CNN to compromise its performance first time. Szegedy et al. [19] showed various of intriguing attributes of neural networks and relevant models. Malicious samples which they produced were very close to original examples that the human eye perceives as identical. They performed on ImageNet dataset and their adversarial examples were misclassified by several classifiers with different architectures. Goodfellow et al. [9] introduced FGSM attack for the first time. They applied their attack on MNIST dataset [8] including handwritten digits from 0 to 9 and achieved to mislead classifiers. They attempted to maximize error by adding optimum noise.

Papernot et al. [14] address an issue as well and applied Jacobian-based Saliency Map Attack (JSMA). They attempted to find most important pixel features which lead to significant changes to the output by modifying in a way that

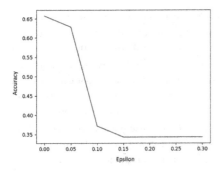

Fig. 9. Accuracy vs. penetration coefficient with high epsilon values.

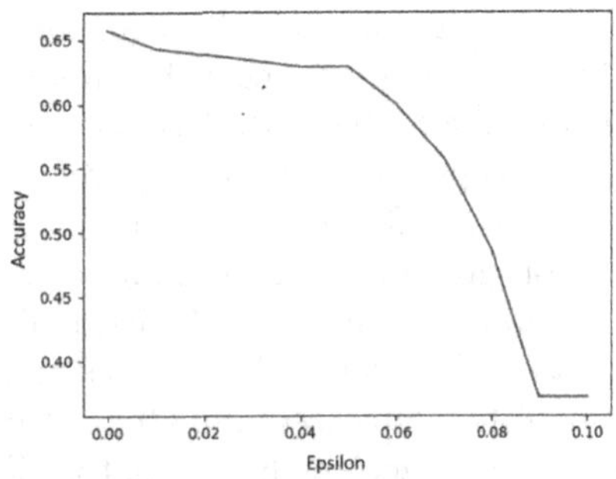

Fig. 10. Accuracy vs. penetration coefficient with small epsilon values.

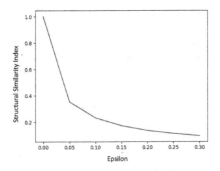

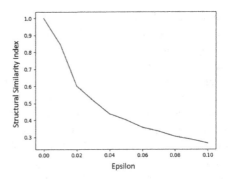

Fig. 11. Structural similarity index vs. penetration coefficient with high epsilon values.

Fig. 12. Structural similarity index vs. penetration coefficient with small epsilon values.

is imperceptible. Moosavi-Dezfooli et al. [12] also discussed adversarial attack . They identified the decision boundary of deep learning classifier based on inputs and tried to find closest distance to the decision boundary pixels of the original input which were manipulated to misguide the model. They implemented adversarial attacks against only deep learning classifiers. Therefore, they called it a deepfool attack. Then, they improved their deepfool adversarial attack and they formulated to find universal penetration vector in [11].

Nguyen et al. [13] designed a different adversarial attack using evolutionary algorithms (EAs) in which they managed to fabricate images to misclassify a high confidence classifier in an optimum way. Carlini and Wagner [7] created a novel adversarial attack called a cws attack as the initial letter of their names . They claimed that their attack type could evade all existing adversarial detection defenses at this time when they published their works.

Su et al. [18] aproached adversarial attacks from a different point of view and managed to produce adversarial samples by altering one pixel value of original image. Rozsa et al. [16] generated great numbers of adversarial attack samples from one original image by transformation or rotation of that image. Zhao et al. [21] generated adversarial samples synthetically using generative adversarial network (GAN) instead of transformation or rotation of an original image. In GAN concept, there are two different classifiers named discriminator and generator. Generator first creates a random noise and tries to capture data distribution of the original image. Discriminator takes original images and images fabricated by generator as input and distinguishes between them and give feedback to generator. Generator always tries to fabricate better images which can not be distinguishable by discriminator. At one point generator's synthetic images can not be recognized by discriminator. Thus, new samples can be created.

7   Conclusion

NN is used a lot for breast cancer detection and classification with high accuracy. In this research, we discuss the security and vulnerability of CNNs. We present an attack algorithm to exploit the security gap of CNNs in breast cancer classification and raise awareness of radiologists and doctors. The adversarial strategy is viable without changing the architecture of the algorithm, however, in order to solely modify input data. We evaluate our adversarial attack with different penetration coefficients and show these changes in a mathematical way using structural similarity index. Hopefully, our work will promote further research to increase the robustness of CNN in breast cancer classification. Although there have been much research regarding defense strategy against adversarial attacks, countermeasures for detection of malicious samples have not been well-studied and are still a significant problem. Currently, we are working to find adapted threshold value to differentiate real image from fake one. In this way, intrusion samples can be detected automatically.

References

1. Contrast. https://en.wikipedia.org/wiki/Contrast
2. Database. http://marathon.csee.usf.edu/Mammography/Database.html
3. Google machine learning project. https://www.mercurynews.com/2017/03/03/google-computers-trained-to-detect-cancer/
4. Google's deepmind. https://deepmind.com/applied/deepmind-health/
5. Luminance. https://en.wikipedia.org/wiki/Luminance
6. Abadi, M., et al.: Tensorflow: a system for large-scale machine learning. In: 12th {USENIX} Symposium on Operating Systems Design and Implementation ({OSDI} 16), pp. 265–283 (2016)
7. Carlini, N., Wagner, D.: Adversarial examples are not easily detected: bypassing ten detection methods. In: Proceedings of the 10th ACM Workshop on Artificial Intelligence and Security, pp. 3–14 (2017)
8. Deng, L.: The mnist database of handwritten digit images for machine learning research [best of the web]. IEEE Sign. Process. Mag. **29**(6), 141–142 (2012)
9. Goodfellow, I.J., Shlens, J., Szegedy, C.: Explaining and harnessing adversarial examples. arXiv preprint arXiv:1412.6572 (2014)

10. Guo, R., Shi, H., Zheng, D., Jing, C., Zhuang, C., Wang, Z.: Flexible and efficient blockchain-based abe scheme with multi-authority for medical on demand in telemedicine system. IEEE Access **7**, 88012–88025 (2019)
11. Moosavi-Dezfooli, S.M., Fawzi, A., Fawzi, O., Frossard, P., Soatto, S.: Analysis of universal adversarial perturbations. arXiv preprint arXiv:1705.09554 (2017)
12. Moosavi-Dezfooli, S.M., Fawzi, A., Frossard, P.: Deepfool: a simple and accurate method to fool deep neural networks. In: Proceedings of the IEEE Conference on Computer Vision and Pattern Recognition, pp. 2574–2582 (2016)
13. Nguyen, A., Yosinski, J., Clune, J.: Deep neural networks are easily fooled: high confidence predictions for unrecognizable images. In: Proceedings of the IEEE Conference on Computer Vision and Pattern Recognition, pp. 427–436 (2015)
14. Papernot, N., McDaniel, P., Jha, S., Fredrikson, M., Celik, Z.B., Swami, A.: The limitations of deep learning in adversarial settings. In: 2016 IEEE European Symposium on Security and Privacy (EuroS&P), pp. 372–387. IEEE (2016)
15. Rajkomar, A., et al.: Scalable and accurate deep learning with electronic health records. NPJ Digit. Med. **1**(1), 18 (2018)
16. Rozsa, A., Rudd, E.M., Boult, T.E.: Adversarial diversity and hard positive generation. In: Proceedings of the IEEE Conference on Computer Vision and Pattern Recognition Workshops, pp. 25–32 (2016)
17. Sahiner, B., et al.: Classification of mass and normal breast tissue: a convolution neural network classifier with spatial domain and texture images. IEEE Trans. Med. Imaging **15**(5), 598–610 (1996)
18. Su, J., Vargas, D.V., Sakurai, K.: One pixel attack for fooling deep neural networks. IEEE Trans. Evol. Comput. **23**(5), 828–841 (2019)
19. Szegedy, C., et al.: Going deeper with convolutions. In: Proceedings of the IEEE conference on computer vision and pattern recognition, pp. 1–9 (2015)
20. Wang, Z., Bovik, A.C.: A universal image quality index. IEEE Sign. Process. Lett. **9**(3), 81–84 (2002)
21. Zhao, Z., Dua, D., Singh, S.: Generating natural adversarial examples. arXiv preprint arXiv:1710.11342 (2017)

A 1D-CNN Based Deep Learning for Detecting VSI-DDoS Attacks in IoT Applications

Enkhtur Tsogbaatar[1]([✉]), Monowar H. Bhuyan[2], Doudou Fall[1], Yuzo Taenaka[1], Khishigjargal Gonchigsumlaa[3], Erik Elmroth[2], and Youki Kadobayashi[1]

[1] Laboratory for Cyber Resilience, NAIST, Nara 630 0192, Japan
{tsogbaatar.enkhtur.ta4,doudou-f,yuzo,youki-k}@is.naist.jp
[2] Department of Computing Science, Umeå University, 901 87 Umeå, Sweden
{monowar,elmroth}@cs.umu.se
[3] SICT, MUST, Ulaanbaatar 133 43, Mongolia
khishigjargal@must.edu.mn

Abstract. The proliferation of the Internet of Things (IoT) applications and devices make human life more comfortable by employing automation in daily operations. These applications are typically deployed in the cloud to offer diverse and healthy services to the users. Due to the inherent demand for low response time, applications need to be secure and closer to the users. However, there is a lack of solutions for assessing and protecting IoT applications against Very Short Intermittent Distributed Denial of Service (VSI-DDoS) attacks. Such attacks send intermittent bursts (in tens of milliseconds) of legitimate HTTP requests to the target services for degrading providers Quality of Service (QoS). Because of the stealthy nature of VSI-DDoS, it is challenging to pinpoint the root-cause when the system resource usage remains at a moderate level. We propose a 1D-CNN-based deep learning method for detecting VSI-DDoS attacks in IoT applications to ensure secure services towards users. The experimental evaluation on both testbed and benchmark datasets proves that our method achieves better detection accuracy, 0.07%–33.15%, than baseline approaches.

Keywords: IoT applications · VSI-DDoS attacks · Quality of Service (QoS) · Deep learning · Convolutional Neural Network (CNN)

1 Introduction

The rise of the Internet of Things (IoT) increases the daily use of devices and applications for making life more comfortable. IoT has already transformed several domains by offering a wide range of services, e.g., creating an intelligent smart grid, developing smart car parking, and personal health monitoring. IoT devices and cloud-deployed applications are crucial to achieving particular objectives, such as healthcare monitoring. These broad-spectrum uses of IoT devices

© Springer Nature Switzerland AG 2021
H. Fujita et al. (Eds.): IEA/AIE 2021, LNAI 12798, pp. 530–543, 2021.
https://doi.org/10.1007/978-3-030-79457-6_45

and applications open up multiple security issues that hinder the deployment of legitimate services to the users. The existing IoT applications cannot reach on-demand services with expected Quality of Service (QoS) because of the lack of secure IoT eco-systems. One of the critical challenges facing IoT applications is the degradation of the Quality of Service (QoS) as a result of multiscale distributed denial of service (DDoS) attacks. The DDoS attacks have been increasing despite numerous DDoS defense mechanisms deployed at different levels in the IoT eco-systems. For instance, Kaspersky Lab's "DDoS attacks in Q1 2020" reports that the number of DDoS attacks doubled against the previous reporting period, and by 80% against Q1 2019 [1]. One of the primary reasons for the growing number of DDoS attacks is the ever-evolving new types of DDoS attacks that can bypass state-of-the-art defense mechanisms. For instance, one of the most significant DDoS attack trends Radware observed in 2017 was an increase in short-burst attacks, becoming more complex, frequent, and persistent. In addition, 42% of organizations in Radware's investigation experienced this type of DDoS attack in 2017 [2].

Moreover, Huasong et al. [3] present a new burst of low-rate DDoS attacks which is known as very short intermittent (VSI) DDoS attacks. This attack is difficult to detect by existing security defense systems since it mimics the legitimate users' behaviour. Despite being low-rate, VSI-DDoS significantly degrades the QoS for users. To evaluate the impact of VSI-DDoS attacks on the QoS of users, they carry out experiments using the RUBBoS[1] benchmark web application. Furthermore, they find that the proposed VSI-DDoS attacks can successfully cause the benchmark website's long-tail latency problem while bypassing the DDoS defense systems. Hence, efficient early detection and prevention of VSI-DDoS attacks remain still a challenge to address. We are the first to come up with a deep learning-based solution for detecting VSI-DDoS attacks in IoT applications, to the best of our knowledge. However, there are deep learning methods to detect and prevent classical DDoS attacks [4–7] for IoT eco-systems. Also, existing studies insufficiently evaluate VSI-DDoS attacks' impact on QoS implications in IoT applications. Hence, we propose a 1D-CNN deep learning approach to detect VSI-DDoS attacks in IoT applications. Our proposed 1D-CNN model combines feature extraction and learning with a cheaper computational cost that result in high detection accuracy. The main contributions of this paper are as follows:

- We prepare a new VSI-DDoS IoT applications dataset with diverse attack scenarios and make it available for public use to fill the research gap.
- We propose a 1D-CNN deep learning approach to detect VSI-DDoS attacks early for IoT applications.
- The experimental evaluation illustrates the performance of the proposed approach using testbed datasets. We carry out experiments on benchmark datasets as well to compare with baseline models.

The remainder of the paper is organized as follows. Section 2 describes our proposed deep learning approach. Section 3 presents the experimental results and

---

[1] https://github.com/michaelmior/RUBBoS.

the analysis of our proposed deep and machine learning models on the testbed and benchmark datasets. Finally, we summarize our findings and suggest possible directions for future work in Sect. 4.

2   System Model

In this section, we first introduce the problem we aim to study, then we elaborate the proposed 1D CNN-based deep learning for detecting VSI-DDoS attacks in IoT applications to combat QoS degradation of users' services. A system architecture of 1D CNN-based VSI-DDoS detection is shown in Fig. 1.

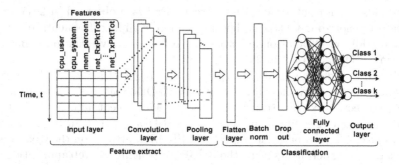

Fig. 1. A system architecture for 1D CNN-based VSI-DDoS detection.

2.1   Problem Statement

Given the data of nth different time-series with length T, i.e., $x = (x_1, x_2, x_3, \cdots, x_n)^T$, and collected data from multiple IoT applications in the presence and absence of VSI-DDoS attacks. We aim to achieve the following three goals:

- **VSI-DDoS datasets**, i.e., generating a VSI-DDoS IoT applications dataset with diverse attack scenarios and make it public.
- **VSI-DDoS detection**, i.e., detecting VSI-DDoS attacks in IoT applications to alleviate QoS interruption.
- **Experimental analysis**, i.e., carry out exhaustive experimental analysis using both testbed and benchmark datasets with diverse attack scenarios.

2.2   VSI-DDoS Attacks

Goal and Operation. The VSI-DDoS attack is a new form of application-layer short-burst low-rate DDoS attack with as aim to degrade the users QoS. Specifically, IoT applications are mostly latency-sensitive where even a little degradation of performance at the user is not acceptable either for the short or long run. Many service providers such as Google and Amazon have put a lot of effort to lessen the tail latency that creates inconvenience to users. If a user experiences such weariness of service from a service provider then they immediately switches to another provider for preventing the target services from being used. Unlike the classical DDoS attacks that aim to exhaust servers' resources, VSI-DDoS attacks cause transient saturation of resources and increase tail latency of legitimate requests. Because the number of requests is made in a short period of time, like within a millisecond, and it exceeds the server's queue capacity. As a result, the transmission of a legitimate user's request is delayed significantly and the delay is materialized in the TCP retransmission. These repeated retransmissions aggravate the user's experience because of serious packet drops. To alleviate the impact of VSI-DDoS attacks, we generated VSI-DDoS attacks towards IoT applications deployed in edge cloud as reported in Fig. 5.

Detection Adversity. Requests in VSI-DDoS attacks are similar to legitimate users' requests, but they exhaust a server's queues in milliseconds. Hence, adverse effects happen to the detection systems when they use second-level monitoring systems such as sar[2], vmstat[3], and top[4]. VSI-DDoS attacks can easily bypass the state-of-art detection systems and make significant impact on the QoS of the legitimate users of the target services in IoT applications with tail latency. Therefore, we propose a deep learning-based approach to detect VSI-DDoS attacks in IoT applications.

2.3 Proposed CNN-Based Detection Model

Convolutional Neural Network (CNN), inspired by the visual cortex of animals, is widely used for object recognition tasks [8]. As a deep learning architecture, CNN is proposed to minimize the data preprocessing requirements. The most powerful part of CNN is the learning feature hierarchies from large amount of unlabeled data. Thus, CNN are quite promising for applications in network attack detection [9]. The basic structure of CNN is composed of input and output layers and multiple hidden layers which include convolution layer, pooling layer, and fully-connected layer [10].

Convolution Layer. The convolution layers are the core of the CNN and useful for extracting dominant features which are rotational and positional invariants, thus maintaining the process of effectively training the model. The preprocessing required in a CNN is much lower as compared to other classification algorithms where convolution and pooling layers of the CNN perform a role as feature extraction. Typically, the previous layers of convolution layers map features are convolved with multiple convolutional filters. The output of the convolution operators are added by a bias and put through the activation function to form the

---

[2] https://en.wikipedia.org/wiki/Sar_(Unix).

[3] https://linux.die.net/man/8/vmstat.

[4] https://en.wikipedia.org/wiki/Top_(software).

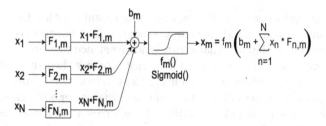

Fig. 2. Typical architecture of a 1D-CNN unit cell.

feature map for the next layer. The convolution is a linear operation and thus limits the ability to learn complex nonlinear behavior of the input. In order to introduce nonlinearity, the intermediate feature maps of a convolution layer are put through an activation function to form the formal feature maps [11]. The basic cell of a 1D-CNN layer is given in Fig. 2. A hidden layer output vector $\bar{x}$ of a 1D-CNN cell consists of M hidden units x_m.

$$\bar{x} = [x_1, x_2, x_m, ... x_M]^T \tag{1}$$

where an independent unit is an outcome of a nonlinear transformation applied on a transformation of the N differently filtered input features x. f_m represents the activation function that performs the nonlinear transformation, $F_{n,m}$ are the coefficients of the N filters and b_m is the bias.

$$x_m^l = f_m \left(b_m^l + \sum_{n=1}^{N} x_n^{l-1} * F_{n,m}^l \right) \tag{2}$$

where x_m^l is the output in layer l, b_m^l is the bias in layer l, x_n^{l-1} is the input of the filter n in layer $l-1$, $F_{n,m}^l$ is the mth neuron of the filter n in layer l. The output size of the feature maps is calculated as:

$$O = \frac{I - F + P_{start} + P_{end}}{S} + 1 \tag{3}$$

where I is the length of the input, F is the length of the filter, P is the amount zero padding, S is the stride, and O is the output size of the feature map. For instance, for the testbed dataset of this study, the $I = 9$, the input layer convolved with a 3 filter with stride 1, $O = 7$. Each filter contains its own weight with the defined kernel size, considering the length of the input matrix [12]. In the convolution layer of the 1D-CNN, we use 3 filters to extract 7 handy different features for the testbed dataset and we use a sigmoid activation function for the testbed dataset and a relu activation function for the benchmark dataset. The sigmoid and relu activation functions are defined as in Eq. (4) and Eq. (5), respectively.

$$f_m = \frac{1}{1 + e^{-\hat{x}_n}} \tag{4}$$

and

$$f_m = max(0, \hat{x}_n) \tag{5}$$

where e is Euler's number, $\hat{x}_n$ is expressed as:

$$\hat{x}_n = b_m^l + \sum_{n=1}^{N} x_n^{l-1} * F_{n,m}^l \tag{6}$$

Pooling. The pooling layer aims to decrease the computational power required to process the data through dimensionality reduction [13]. This layer is useful for extracting dominant features which are rotational and positional invariants and effective for model training. There are two types of pooling operations: max pooling [14] and average pooling [15].

$$x_m^l = x_m^{l-1} * P^l \tag{7}$$

where x_m^{l-1} is the convolved features in layer $l - 1$, P^l is the pooling operator in layer l. The output size of the feature maps in a pooling layer is estimated as in Eq. (8).

$$O_{pool} = \frac{O - P_{pool}}{S_{pool}} + 1 \tag{8}$$

where P_{pool} is the length of the pooling operator, S_{pool} is the stride and O is the size of the feature maps of the previous convolution layer. In the pooling layer, we use 1D max pooling with pooling size 2 and stride size 1. The 1D max pooling returns the maximum value that estimates from the portion under filter. A simple example of pooling operation is depicted in Fig. 3. After the pooling layer, we use a dropout to avoid the overfitting of 1D-CNN [16].

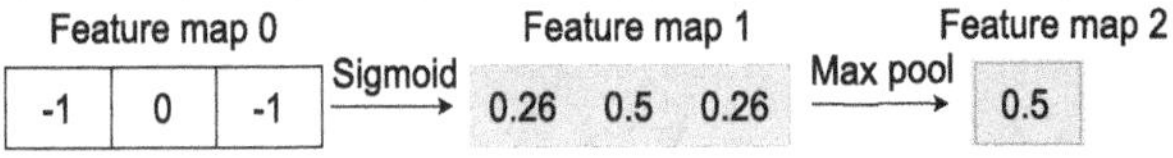

Fig. 3. Sigmoid and max pool operation - an example.

Detection Module. The detection module consists of two layers: the fully connected layers and the softmax layer. We embed two fully connected layers to perform the classification at the end. In the fully connected layer, neurons from the previous layer are reshaped as 1D layers in regular networks, and have full connection to all activation in the previous layer estimated as in Eq. (9).

$$x_j^l = f \left(\sum_{m=1}^{M} x_m^{l-1} W^l + b_j^l \right) \tag{9}$$

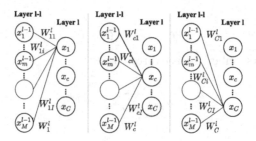

Fig. 4. Demonstration of neurons and weights assignment in the detection module.

where x_j^l is the j-th neuron in fully connected layer and M is the layer size. x_m^{l-1} is a neuron in the previous feature map $l - 1$ (whether the feature map is the output of convolution or a pooling operation). W^l is the corresponding weight with x_m^{l-1} between layer $l - 1$ and layer l, b_j^l is the bias in the input of x_j^l and $f(.)$ denotes an activation function. We have chosen *relu* activation function for our experiments. A demonstration of neurons and weights location in detection module is shown in Fig. 4. Next, the high-level features vectors from the full connection layer are fed into the softmax layer, which is defined as in Eq. (10).

$$y_c = [P(prediction = c|x^{l-1}; W_c^l)] = \frac{e^{W_c^l x^{l-1}}}{\sum\limits_{m=1}^{C} e^{W_m^l x^{l-1}}}$$

$$x^{l-1} = [x_1^{l-1}, \cdots x_m^{l-1}, \cdots x_M^{l-1}]^T$$
$$W_c^l = [W_{c1}^l, \cdots W_{ci}^l, \cdots W_{cI}^l], W_l = [W_1^l, \cdots W_c^l, \cdots W_C^l]^T$$

(10)

Let's assume that l is the softmax layer, y_c is the output probability for a particular class c, and C is the number of classes. Hence, the total probability is given by Eq. (11).

$$\sum_{c=1}^{C} y_c = 1$$

(11)

x_{l-1} is the feature vector of size $M \times 1$, W_c^l is the c-th row weight vector of size $1 \times M$. The detection accuracy of the networks is evaluated by measuring the error between the discrete probability distributions of real classes and predicted classes. The cross-entropy is applied as the objective function to optimize the learning rate and the overall detection accuracy.

3   Performance Evaluation

This section reports and explains the intensive experimental results obtained from a testbed and benchmark datasets. We begin with datasets description and proceed with experimental results.

3.1 Datasets

We evaluate our proposed 1D-CNN deep learning approach using two datasets: (i) testbed data, and (ii) benchmark data. The testbed data is generated by emulating VSI-DDoS attacks when deploying IoT applications in edge cloud.

Testbed Data: We use Time Series Benchmark Suite (TSBS)[5], which simulates data streaming from a set of trucks belonging to a fictional trucking company in IoT applications. As shown in Fig. 5, our system consists of the IoT applications for a fictional trucking company, an IoT applications database server, bots, and legitimate users.

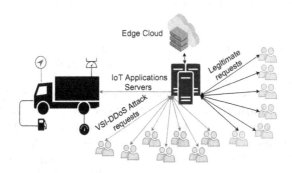

Fig. 5. Experimental testbed setup and topology

IoT Applications Server. We have created multiple IoT applications servers with the specification of a 1.8 GHz two core virtual CPU and a 2 GB of Random Access Memory (RAM) for each. This setup was used to generate, collect and process data for our learning models for the detection of VSI-DDoS attacks.

Legitimate Users. The behavior of a total of 1000 legitimate users is imitated using the query "last-loc" to get the real-time location of each truck of the TSBS setup. The legitimate users continuously send requests to the IoT applications servers for real-time location information of the trucks.

Bot for VSI-DDoS Attacks. First, we create 100 queries to retrieve real-time locations from 1000 trucks using the *tsbs_generate_queries* command of the TSBS setup. The execution time of the 100 queries is 50 ms. Second, every 2 s, we send the created queries to the IoT application servers using the *watch* command. Finally, we increase the number of bots from 2 to 24 as a requirement for generating sets of VSI-DDoS attacks. We observed that most responses for the IoT application's requests are quickly returned to the users within 100 ms in absence of VSI-DDoS attacks. However, some of the responses are delayed for more than 1 s due to VSI-DDoS attacks and we observe more delayed responses based on cumulative distribution function (cdf) analysis when the number of botnets increases from 2 to 24 as shown in Fig. 6.

---

[5] https://github.com/timescale/tsbs#appendix-i-query-types.

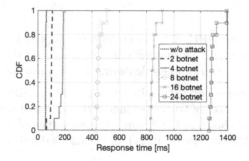

Fig. 6. Cumulative distribution analysis of response time.

Benchmark Data: Since there is a non-availability of benchmark datasets for VSI-DDoS attacks, we use the N-BaIoT [6] dataset for initial empirical validation of our proposed method. This dataset was prepared by using two attack generation tools, i.e., Mirai (scan, ACK flooding, SYN flooding, UDP flooding, UDP-plain attacks) and Bashlite (scan, junk, UDP flooding, TCP flooding, COMBO attacks), with 9 commercial IoT devices such as Provision-PT-838 Security Camera, Ecobee thermostat, and Danmini doorbell. There are 5 Bashlite, 5 Mirai, and 1 legitimate datasets, having 115 features in each of them. As baseline models validation, we employ 1% of the imbalanced multiple attacks data of Provision-PT-838 Security Camera to detect DDoS attacks. This experiment uses seven classes, including benign, Mirai (scan, SYN flooding, ACK flooding) and Bashlite (TCP flooding, junk, UDP flooding). The detailed dataset statistics for both benchmark and testbed are given in Table 1.

Table 1. Dataset statistics - testbed and benchmark.

Dataset	Number of features	Number of legitimate instances	Number of anomalous instances
Testbed	9	276868	90503
Benchmark	115	99494	918

3.2   Results

In this section, we start with the characterization of data and report experimental results.

Characterization of Data. To observe the behaviour of both testbed and benchmark datasets, we estimate the cumulative distribution function for legitimate and attack instances shown in Fig. 7. In the benchmark dataset, the distribution of legitimate instances differs from the distribution of the attack instances as clearly illustrated in Fig. 7 (b). However, in the testbed dataset, we can observe from the Fig. 7 (a) that the distributions of legitimate instances and attack instances are almost the same due to the stealthy behavior of the VSI-DDoS attacks.

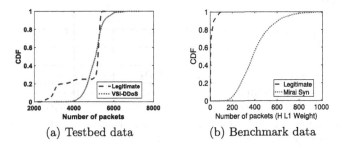

(a) Testbed data   (b) Benchmark data

Fig. 7. Data characterization - cdf for legitimate vs. attack instances over features set.

Hyper-parameters Tuning. The hyper-parameters of the CNN and LSTM models are tuned based on the data for configuring optimal parameters. Batch sizes, numbers of layers, learning rates, and types of loss functions are some of the hyper-parameters tuned by employing a grid search algorithm (GSA) to improve the performance of the model. The proposed 1D-CNN-based deep learning model was modified based on these optimal hyper-parameters and the GSA was run again to find a suitable optimizer.

(a) Experiments with Different Batch Sizes and Number of Layers: The batch size impacts how quickly a model learns and the stability of the learning process. As it plays a vital role in deep learning model performance, we tuned the parameters with respect to our problem [17]. We start with tuning the number of layers and batch sizes at the same time. For the testbed dataset, Fig. 8 illustrates our empirical evaluation results with optimal batch sizes of 32 for the 1D-CNN and 128 for the LSTM, while the optimal number of layers is 1 for the 1D-CNN and 2 for the LSTM. Besides, the benchmark experiment results is obtained as shown in Fig. 8 by choosing optimal batch size 256 for both the 1D-CNN and LSTM, while the optimal number of layers is 2 for the 1D-CNN and 1 for the LSTM. As shown in Fig. 8, we observe that the detection of the VSI-DDoS attacks is a more difficult task than the detection of the classical DDoS attacks in IoT.

(b) Experiments with Different Learning Rates: As the learning rate controls how quickly a model adapts to the problem, it is the most important hyperparameter [18]. Therefore, we perform experiments on 1D-CNN and LSTM models with

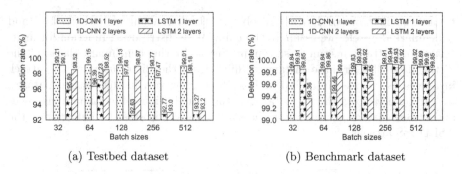

(a) Testbed dataset   (b) Benchmark dataset

Fig. 8. Choosing and analysing optimal batch size and number of layers using GSA.

varied learning rates including 0.5, 0.1, 0.01, 0.001, and 0.0001 for obtaining optimal values. Figure 9 illustrates the experimental results based on the different learning rates. According to the results, we found that 0.01 learning rate gives the best detection rate in the testbed and benchmark datasets, respectively. Hence, we run all trails of experiments with the 0.01 learning rate till 100 epochs.

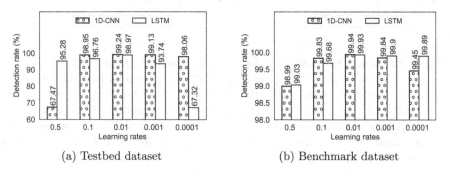

(a) Testbed dataset   (b) Benchmark dataset

Fig. 9. Choosing and analysing of optimal learning rate for the testbed and benchmark datasets.

(c) Experiments with Different Loss Functions: As our problem is classification centric, we investigated three binary classification loss functions, *binary_crossentropy*, *hinge*, and *squared_hinge* for the testbed dataset. In addition, we investigated three multi-class classification loss functions, *categorical_crossentropy*, *sparse_categorical_crossentropy* and *kullback_leibler_divergence* for the benchmark dataset. Figure 10 shows that *binary_crossentropy* loss function performs best for both CNN and LSTM for the testbed dataset, while the *categorical_crossentropy* loss function performs best for both CNN and LSTM for the benchmark dataset.

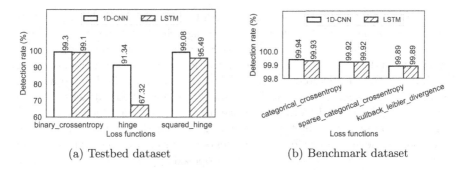

(a) Testbed dataset   (b) Benchmark dataset

Fig. 10. Experimental results - 1 layer 1D-CNN and 2 layers LSTM with different loss functions on the testbed and benchmark datasets.

3.3 Comparison with Competing Methods

We use LSTM [19], Support Vector Machines (SVM) [4], and Naive Bayes (NB) [20] as our baselines. In this study, we consider the classification problem, thus we chose classification-based deep and machine learning methods as our baseline methods. We use classification accuracy to show the performance compared with baselines. Figure 11 shows the accuracy of each model. As results of the hyper-parameters tuning for the benchmark dataset, 1 layer 1D-CNN provides the highest detection accuracy of 100%, with 256 batch size, relu activation function, categorical_crossentropy loss function and the Adam optimizer with a learning rate of 0.01. The experiment results show that our 1D-CNN model has the highest accuracy compared with LSTM and the other baseline machine learning methods.

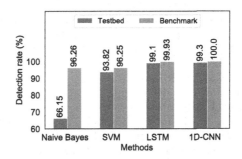

Fig. 11. Comparison of the proposed method with baseline models

4   Conclusion and Future Work

In this paper, we propose a 1D-CNN deep learning method for VSI-DDoS attacks detection with a vector of time series data. Because 1D-CNN lends benefits for extracting fine-grained features together with learning model with low-cost computation but achieves high accuracy in detecting VSI-DDoS attacks. In addition, we design a new IoT application VSI-DDoS attacks dataset and give a detailed description of designing the testbed configuration and emulated IoT application. We evaluate the impact and detect VSI-DDoS attacks on the IoT application. Using concrete experimental results we show that VSI-DDoS attacks are effective and stealthy towards a target service because they cause QoS issues of the target IoT application while the average usage rate of all the system resources is at a moderate level. We perform experiments on our created testbed and benchmark datasets. The results show that our proposed approach achieved maximum detection rate in contrast to LSTM and other machine learning approaches. We comprehensively investigate the hyper-parameters, and we chose the optimal hyperparameter values to obtain maximum detection accuracy. As results of intensive experiments, for the testbed dataset, 1D-CNN able to achieve 99.30% accuracy with cost-and-time.

We are underway to extend this work for detecting VSI-DDoS attacks in IoT devices with synchronization of IoT applications.

Acknowledgment. Part of this study was funded by the ICS-CoE Core Human Resources Development Program. Additional support was provided by the Wallenberg AI, Autonomous Systems and Software Program (WASP) funded by Knut and Alice Wallenberg Foundation, Sweden.

References

1. Kaspersky. DDoS attacks in Q1 2020. https://securelist.com/ddos-attacks-in-q1-2020/96837/. Accessed 10 October 2020
2. Cisco: Cisco 2018 Annual Cybersecurity Report. https://www.cisco.com/c/dam/m/hu_hu/campaigns/security-hub/pdf/acr-2018.pdf. Accessed 13 October 2020
3. Shan, H., Wang, Q., Yan, Q.: Very short intermittent DDoS attacks in an unsaturated system. In: Lin, X., Ghorbani, A., Ren, K., Zhu, S., Zhang, A. (eds.) SecureComm 2017. LNICST, vol. 238, pp. 45–66. Springer, Cham (2018). https://doi.org/10.1007/978-3-319-78813-5_3
4. Susilo, B., Sari, R.: Intrusion detection in IoT networks using deep learning algorithm. Information **11**, 279 (2020)
5. Nickolaos, K., Nour, M., Elena, S., Benjamin, T.: Towards the development of realistic botnet dataset in the Internet of Things for network forensic analytics: Bot-IoT dataset. Future Gener. Comput. Syst. **100**, 779–796 (2019)
6. Yair, M., et al.: N-BaIoT:Network-based detection of IoT botnet attacks using deep autoencoders. IEEE Pervasive Comput. **17**(3), 12–22 (2018)
7. Tsogbaatar, E., et al.: SDN-enabled IoT anomaly detection using ensemble learning. In: Maglogiannis, I., Iliadis, L., Pimenidis, E. (eds.) AIAI 2020. IAICT, vol. 584, pp. 268–280. Springer, Cham (2020). https://doi.org/10.1007/978-3-030-49186-4_23
8. Jinyin, C., Yang, Y., Hu, K., Zheng, H., Wang, Z.: DAD-MCNN: DDoS attack detection via multi-channel CNN. In: Proceedings of 11th International Conference on Machine Learning and Computing, pp. 484–488 (2019)

9. Xin, Y., et al.: Machine learning and deep learning methods for cybersecurity. IEEE Access **6**, 35365–35381 (2018)
10. Wu, Y., Wei, D., Feng, J.: Network attacks detection methods based on deep learning techniques: a survey. Secur. Commun. Netw. **1–17**(08), 2020 (2020)
11. Tang, Z., Chen, Z., Bao, Y., Li, H.: Convolutional neural network-based data anomaly detection method using multiple information for structural health monitoring. Struct. Control Health Monit. **26**(1), e2296 (2019)
12. Azizjon, M., Jumabek, A., Kim, W.: 1D CNN based network intrusion detection with normalization on imbalanced data. In: Proceedings of International Conference on Artificial Intelligence in Information and Communication, pp. 218–224, February 2020
13. Jiuxiang, G., et al.: Recent advances in convolutional neural networks. Pattern Recogn. **77**, 354–377 (2018)
14. Yang, J.B., Nguyen, M.N., San, P.P., Li, X.L., Krishnaswamy, S.: Deep convolutional neural networks on multichannel time series for human activity recognition. In: Proceedings of 24th IJCAI, pp. 3995–4001. AAAI Press (2015)
15. Wang, T., Wu, D.J., Coates, A., Ng, A.Y.: End-to-end text recognition with convolutional neural networks. In: Proceedings of 21st ICPR, pp. 3304–3308 (2012)
16. Srivastava, N., Hinton, G., Krizhevsky, A., Sutskever, I., Salakhutdinov, R.: Dropout: a simple way to prevent neural networks from overfitting. J. Mach. Learn. Res. **15**(1), 1929–1958 (2014)
17. Masters, D., Luschi, C.: Revisiting small batch training for deep neural networks. arxiv:1804.07612 (2018)
18. Ian, G., Yoshua, B., Aaron, C.: Deep Learning, pp. 493–495. MIT Press, Cambridge (2017)
19. Hochreiter, S., Schmidhuber, J.: Long short-term memory. Neural Comput. **9**(8), 1735–1780 (1997)
20. Sharma, R.K., Kalita, H.K., Borah, P.: Analysis of machine learning techniques based intrusion detection systems. In: Nagar, A., Mohapatra, D.P., Chaki, N. (eds.) Proceedings of 3rd International Conference on Advanced Computing, Networking and Informatics. SIST, vol. 44, pp. 485–493. Springer, New Delhi (2016). https://doi.org/10.1007/978-81-322-2529-4_51

Natural Language and Text Processing

Hierarchical Transformer Encoders for Vietnamese Spelling Correction

Hieu Tran[1,2], Cuong V. Dinh[1], Long Phan[1], and Son T. Nguyen[1,2,3(✉)]

[1] Zalo Group - VNG Corporation, Ho Chi Minh City, Vietnam
`hieutt9@vng.com.vn`
[2] University of Science, Ho Chi Minh City, Vietnam
`ntson@fit.hcmus.edu.vn`
[3] Vietnam National University, Ho Chi Minh City, Vietnam

Abstract. In this paper, we propose a Hierarchical Transformer model for Vietnamese spelling correction problem. The model consists of multiple Transformer encoders and utilizes both character-level and word-level to detect errors and make corrections. In addition, to facilitate future work in Vietnamese spelling correction tasks, we propose a realistic dataset collected from real-life texts for the problem. We compare our method with other methods and publicly available systems. The proposed method outperforms all of the contemporary methods in terms of recall, precision, and f1-score. A demo version (https://nlp.laban.vn/wiki/spelling_checker/) is publicly available.

Keywords: Vietnamese · Spelling correction · Transformer

1 Introduction

Spelling correction has always been a practical problem with many real-world applications. Popular word processor applications such as Microsoft Word, Google Docs, LibreOffice Writer, specialized applications such as Grammarly, or other text-support platforms often integrate spelling correction systems to improve their users' productivity in typing and editing documents. Meanwhile, most spoken languages such as English or Chinese are thoroughly researched in the problem, there are only a few studies on Vietnamese language. This leads to a very poor user experience for the people. Therefore, as the aim of this paper, we would like to develop a method to detect and correct spelling mistakes for Vietnamese. This method is integrated into our products to help our news authors and messenger users to check their writings.

With the improvement in computational power, recent studies [7,8,13] prefer machine learning methods over rule-based methods in the spelling correction problem, especially the introduction of Transformer architecture [10] and BERT [1] have boosted not only this problem but a lot of other problems in natural language processing. Not out of the mainstream, specifically for Vietnamese, we design a novel hierarchical neural network model that inspired by contemporary

© Springer Nature Switzerland AG 2021
H. Fujita et al. (Eds.): IEA/AIE 2021, LNAI 12798, pp. 547–556, 2021.
https://doi.org/10.1007/978-3-030-79457-6_46

methods in the field. Our model consists of multiple Transformer encoders that encode the input text in both character-level and word-level simultaneously to detect errors and make corrections.

Furthermore, to the best of our knowledge, currently, there are no common, realistic test sets for Vietnamese that research community can compare their works. Studies in Vietnamese [9] (and some other languages) often artificially generate their test sets based on their own analysis of common mistakes. Although this approach is inexpensive and convenient in research environment, we highly doubt its practicality while using industrial products. Therefore, we propose a test set that highly reflects reality. The data are manually collected by examining Vietnamese Wikipedia drafts, which are usually submitted without much spelling revision and so represent the behaviors in the Vietnamese spelling problem.

In total, this paper offers the following contributions:

- A novel method that applies a hierarchical Transformer model with character-level and word-level encoders for Vietnamese spelling detection and correction;
- We propose a Vietnamese spelling correction test set for comparison with future studies;
- Experimental results with various methods show that the quality of Vietnamese detecting and error correction is promising and usable in industry.

2   Related Work

There have been many studies on the spelling correction problem. In [13], the authors propose a deep model called Soft-Masked BERT for Chinese Spelling error correction. The model is composed of two neural networks, detector, and corrector. The detector network based on bidirectional GRUs is to predict the probability of each token being an error. The correction network is fine-tuned from a pre-trained bidirectional Transformer - BERT [1] to predict the best alternative for the detected token. In the network, the error embeddings are softly masked by summing its original word embeddings and the [MASK] token embedding with the detector's output probabilities as weights. The two networks are jointly trained to minimize their objectives. The model is proved to outperform other architectures in our setting.

In [7], the authors propose a variation of the conventional Transformer that composed of three encoders and a decoder for syntactic spell correction. The three encoders first extract contextual features at character level using unigram, bigram, and trigram, correspondingly, then the decoder processes information from encoders to generate the correct text. All of the encoders have the same architecture as [10], but the decoder is modified a bit by replacing the one encoder-decoder multi-head attention layer in [10] with three encoder-decoder ones, each one takes outputs from an encoder as input. The entire network is trained to generate the sequence of corrected tokens.

Similarly, [8] investigates Korean spelling error correction as a machine translation problem in which an error text is translated to its corrected form. The authors employ common neural machine translation models such as LSTM-Attention, Convolution to Convolution, and the Transformer model. All the models capture context by reading the entire error text through an encoder and translate it by a decoder.

Recent studies that focus on Vietnamese spelling issue tend to focus on diacritic restoration. There has been an attempt in utilizing phrase-based machine translation and recurrent neural networks in diacritic restoration [9]. The phrase-based machine method tries to maximize the probability from source sentence to target sentence by segmented input into a number of phrases (consecutive words) before being analyzed and decoded; the later method employing a neural network model with the encoder-decoder design, trying to maximize the conditional probability of the target/output sentence. The authors claimed both systems had achieved state-of-the-art for the respective tasks on a data set, in which neural network approach performs at 96.15% accuracy compared to 97.32% of the phrase-based one.

In [6], this work deals with the Vietnamese spelling problem by the detecting phase and the correcting phase. The authors combine a syllable Bi-gram and a Part-of-speech (POS) Bi-gram with some characteristic Vietnamese rules for finding errors. In the correcting phase, Minimum Edit Distance and SoundEx algorithms are applied as a weight function to evaluate heuristic generated suggestions. The significant strength of using the weight function is avoiding evaluating suggestions by specific criteria that can not be suitable for all types of documents and errors.

In earliest work [5], instead of focusing on mistyped errors, this study directly cope with the consonant misspelled errors using deep learning approach. The bidirectional stacked LSTM is used to capture the context of the whole sentence, error positions are identified and corrected based on that.

3   Data

In this section, we present our method in generating training data and the process of collecting test set for the Vietnamese spelling correction problem.

3.1   Training Data

The cost of building a big and high-quality training set would be prohibitive. Fortunately, training data for the spelling correction problem can easily be generated through mistake-free texts which are available online and simple analysis of common spelling mistakes. For a mistake-free corpus, we collect news texts published from 2014 to date from various Vietnamese news sources. Those texts were thoroughly revised and spelling checked by the publishers, so they only have a reasonable amount of spelling mistakes. We also include Vietnamese Wikipedia[1]

---

[1] https://vi.wikipedia.org/wiki/Wikipedia.

articles in the data. In addition, we consider oral texts by collecting high-quality movie subtitles, which only contains spoken language. In total, there are up to 2 GB of news/Wikipedia text data and 1 GB of oral text data.

Vietnamese spelling mistakes can be easily encountered in everyday life. We classify the most common mistakes into three categories:

- Typos: this type of mistakes is generated while people are typing texts. It includes letter insertions, letter omissions, letter substitutions, transportation, compounding errors, or diacritic errors. Most people type Vietnamese in two styles: VNI and Telex, which use either numbers or distinctive characters to type tones or special characters. For example, "hà nội" (English: Hanoi, the capital city) is often mistyped as "haf nooij" when one forgot to turn on Vietnamese mode or was typing too fast.
- Spelling errors: this type of mistakes is due to official conventions or regional dialects in Vietnam. For example, people who live in the north of Vietnam typically have trouble differentiating d/r/gi, tr/ch, s/x, n/l sounds. They often mispronounce or misspell the word "hà nội" to "hà lội" (English: no meaning). This type includes both letter or diacritic errors.
- Non-diacritic: although this sometimes is intentional we take the diacritic restoration problem into account. Non-diacritic Vietnamese texts are much faster to type and fairly understandable under specific circumstances and contexts. However, these texts sometimes cause misunderstanding and are very informal. Therefore we would like to offer diacritic restoration to improve further the functionality of the model.

During the training data generation, we try to employ a random rule-based generator that covers all above types of spelling errors in diversity over the corpus. At the end, a generated sentence can have a lot of spelling errors or no errors at all. This ensures the model not only learn the core orthography of Vietnamese but also capture the surrounding context to make accurate spelling detection and correction.

3.2 Wiki Spelling Test Set

For the most realistic performance measurement of the Vietnamese spelling correction problem, we would like to build up a test set that characterizes general behaviors of spelling mistakes while people are typing. We find out that drafts of Vietnamese Wikipedia articles are often submitted without much spelling revision. Therefore, we collect Wikipedia drafts from varied domains. We select ones that have a substantial number of spelling errors and then manually detect the errors and suggest reasonable substitute words. In total, we revised more than 100 articles with about 1,500 spelling errors and 14,000 sentences (approximately 1,300 sentences with errors). A typical sample in the data set can be found in Table 1.

The dataset is available at GitHub repository[2] under the Attribution 4.0 International (CC BY 4.0) license. The dataset is stored in JSON lines and each

---

[2] https://github.com/heraclex12/Viwiki-spelling.

document contains the ids, text contents, current revision ids, previous revision ids, Wikipedia page ids, and mistakes.

Table 1. Some short paragraphs in Wikipedia Spelling Test set

No.	Content	
1	...TA-50 không đơn thuần là một ~~chuếc~~/**chiếc** máy bay huấn luyện mà nó còn được đánh giá như một chiến đấu cơ đích thực. Loại chiến đấu cơ này đạt tốc độ ~~tới~~/**tối** đa lên đến gấp rưỡi vận tốc âm thanh...	...TA-50 is not only a trainer aircraft but also a fighter aircraft. This type of fighter can reach a maximum speed at 1.5 times the speed of sound...
2	...Hà Nội là thành phố trực thuộc trung ~~uowng~~/**ương** có diện tích lớn nhất cả nước từ khi tỉnh Hà Tây ~~xáp~~/**sáp** nhập vào, đồng thời cũng là địa ~~phuong~~/**phương** đứng thứ nhì về dân số với hơn 8 triệu người, tuy nhiên...	..Hanoi has been the largest central city by area in the country since the merging with Ha Tay province; it is also a second most populated city with more than 8 millions people, yet...

4   Neural Network Architecture

In this section, we will describe our proposed neural network architectures deliberately designed to detect and correct Vietnamese spelling errors. The network is inspired by the encoder component of the original Transformer [10] in a hierarchical fashion. The model is depicted in Fig. 1.

4.1   Tokenization

First of all, the inputted piece of text is broken down into tokens, or says, words based on white-space characters. These tokens are further broken down into characters, and then both these tokens and their characters will be passed on to our model as inputs. Normally, WordPiece [11] is a popular Byte Pair Encoding (BPE) sub-word tokenization [2], which would be used to reduce the exceedingly large amount of vocabulary. However, we do not go for sub-word options for the following reasons. Firstly, Vietnamese is a monosyllabic language whose tokens consist of only one syllable, and that sub-words only stand for phonetic features rather than the meaning. Secondly, Vietnamese has a fairly small amount of tokens. In fact, there are only 7184 unique syllables actually used, and they cover more than 94% of the content[3]. Lastly, in the spelling error problem, there are a lot of unexpected tokens that may appear due to typos or foreign languages. If sub-word tokenization is applied, resulting out-of-vocab sub-tokens

---

[3] http://www.hieuthi.com/blog/2017/04/03/vietnamese-syllables-usage.html.

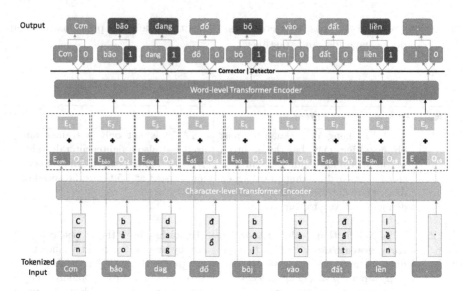

Fig. 1. Proposed neural network architecture (example: the storm is hitting the mainland)

may lead to unknown tokens which either causes loss of character information or redundant computation to deal with too many sub-words. Therefore, we decide to use whitespace tokenization with an additional character-level layer to keep character information. Moreover, we use a special token called UNK to mask out-of-vocab words that are likely to be incorrectly spelled.

4.2 Transformer

For the neural network architecture, at both character and word levels, we adopt Transformer encoder architectures to encode information. The character-level encoder is composed of 4 self-attention layers of hidden size 256 while the word-level one is bigger, with 12 self-attention layers of hidden size 786, which is the same size as conventional BASE-size BERT. Tokenized inputs to the components are vectorized through two embedding tables (i.e. word embedding as E_{string} and character embedding tables as O) and are summed with learned positional embeddings E_n where $n \in [1, 2, ...192]$. In addition, the word embeddings are also concatenated with the corresponding character-level output vectors.

The context and character-aware representations of each word generated by the word-level encoder are used to classify if the token is a mistake and also to predict a substitute in case the token is an actual mistake. The outputting representations are then forwarded to two classifiers, one for detection and the other for correction. Each of two classifiers is composed of two fully-connected layers with the softmax activation function on the last layer. Besides, the correction classifier shares the same weights as the word embedding of the embedding layer.

After going through the detection classifier, each token of the sequence of tokens is predicted to be incorrect or not. If a token is incorrect, the correction classifier will suggest a suitable replacement.

The objective function for the learning process is the sum of two cross-entropy losses of the two classifiers. As accurate tokens do not need to be corrected, we remove those tokens out of the correction loss function. More clearly, given a sequence of words x as input, the loss function formulated as follows, where V is the vocabulary size; N is the length of sequence of words; E ($E <= N$) is the number of true spelling mistakes; y_{ij}, p_{ij} denote the ground-truth labels and the probability of predictions, respectively.

$$\mathcal{L} = \mathcal{L}_{detector} + \mathcal{L}_{corrector}$$

$$\mathcal{L} = -\frac{1}{N + 1e^{-5}} \sum_{i=0}^{N-1} \sum_{j \in \{0;1\}} y_{ij} \log p_{ij} - \frac{1}{E + 1e^{-5}} \sum_{i=0}^{N-1} k_i \sum_{j=0}^{V-1} y_{ij} \log p_{ij}$$

$$\text{where} \quad k_i = \begin{cases} 1 & \text{if } i\text{-th token is a spelling mistake} \\ 0 & \text{otherwise} \end{cases}$$

5 Experiments

In this section, we briefly introduce our metrics for the detection module and the correction module in the Vietnamese spelling correction problem and then present the experiment settings along with results.

In addition to the Wiki spelling test set, we also evaluate our proposed models on informal corpus which are obtained from open-source movie subtitles and we did some text pre-processing to filter out bad/inappropriate words before removed all of the diacritics for evaluation. This test corpus consists of 15,000 informal sentences.

5.1 Experimental Setting

The experiment of our model was implemented based on ALBERT [4] Transformer Encoders. We use LAMB [12] optimizer with learning rate of 1.76e-3 and the power of poly decay is 1.0. The model is trained for 500,000 steps with batch size equal to 512. Word and character vocabulary size are 60,000 and 400 respectively, which include the most common words and characters in the training data. In order to verify performance of our model, we trained three models, one is traditional word-level Bi-LSTM (Bidirectional long short-term memory) approach, one is Bi-LSTM with the combination of word and character, and another is word-level Transformer Encoder to see the effectiveness of our hierarchical model. Bi-LSTM is a special kind of recurrent neural network, which are made of a set of forward LSTM and backward LSTM. LSTM first introduced in [3] alleviates the vanishing gradient problem when captures long-term dependencies by having a set of memory blocks, each of the memory blocks has three different gates including input gate, forget gate, and output gate. Moreover, we also compare our proposed model with an external tool which is obtained from Viettel Group's NLP[4].

Our experiments were evaluated using recall, precision and f1-score of the positive label (is-error label) for error detector. In order to measure correction performance, we computed accuracy score in two aspects:

- Correction accuracy in the detected errors is formed by the ratio of exact correction and total correction.

$$Accuracy_{in \% \ detected} = \frac{n_{exact \ correction}}{n_{exact \ correction} + n_{wrong \ correction}}$$

- Correction accuracy in total errors is counted by exact correction divided by the sum of total correction and wrong detection.

$$Accuracy_{in \ total} = \frac{n_{exact \ correction}}{n_{exact \ correction} + n_{wrong \ correction} + n_{wrong \ detection}}$$

5.2   Results

The results of evaluating on the Wiki corpus are shown in Table 2. First, we observe that the hierarchical Transformer model themselves are quite useful (based on f-1 Score, correction accuracy on total and detected errors) to detect and suggest corrections for spelling errors. It achieves better scores in those metrics than both Bi-LSTM and external tool. Meanwhile, The Transformer model with multiple encoder layers (character and word) achieves higher scores on f1-score and correction accuracy on total errors than the Transformer model with encoders at word level but fails in correction accuracy on detected errors. To further clarify this, a higher detected recall score means the model predicts more errors than actual errors, which can lead to a low precision; therefore, we can observe that the Transformer model with char-word level encoders achieves a higher f-1 score. However, word level Transformer model is worse than char-word level Bi-LSTM model. The main reason is that the mistakes are not part of the vocabulary, and they will be split into sub-words and characters and use the shared embedding, meanwhile, combining character embedding and word embedding utilize more characteristics. Of those errors detected, both Transformer models suggest a high accuracy for spelling error corrections with 0.35% higher for the model with encoders at word level. This difference is insignificant, since it is less than 1%. Moreover, when weighting accuracy on total actual errors, Transformer model with multiple encoder layers at char-word levels achieves a significantly higher score than both Transformer model with encoders at word level and Bi-LSTM model with char-word layers (64.29% compare to 33.28% and 36.62% respectively). The hierarchical Transformer model utilizes both character and word level encoders to detect Vietnamese spelling errors and make corrections outperformed related contemporary models (Transformer and Bi-LSTM) and the external tools available for the task.

---

[4] https://viettelgroup.ai/en/service/nlp.

In the subtitle corpus, the hierarchical Transformer with multiple encoders also proved to be efficacious in restore missing diacritics in short conversation text with 98.50% in correction accuracy in the detected errors and 99.75% in detector f1-score. Proving that our model is also practical for informal text. The results show in Table 3.

Table 2. Evaluation results in Vietnamese spelling corrections on wiki dataset

Model	Level	Detector			Corrector	
		Precision	Recall	F1	in total	in % detected
Transformer Encoder (Ours)	Char-Word	**66.96**	**70.92**	**68.88**	**64.29**	96.01
Transformer Encoder	Word	34.53	68.75	45.97	33.28	**96.36**
Bi-LSTM	Char-Word	39.12	68.76	49.87	36.62	93.59
Bi-LSTM	Word	19.45	65.26	29.97	18.25	93.85
External Tool		22.07	63.68	32.77	18.21	82.54

Notes: The best scores are in bold; second best scores are underlined.

Table 3. Evaluation results for the subtitle diacritics restoration

Model	Level	Detector			Corrector	
		Precision	Recall	F1	in total	in % detected
Transformer Encoder (Ours)	Char-Word	**99.83**	**99.67**	**99.75**	**98.17**	98.50
Transformer Encoder	Word	99.70	99.41	99.56	98.09	**98.51**
Bi-LSTM	Char-Word	99.17	99.33	99.25	94.22	95.14
Bi-LSTM	Word	98.92	97.51	98.21	95.25	96.72

Notes: The best scores are in bold; second best scores are underlined.

6   Discussion and Future Work

In this paper, we have proposed a hierarchical Transformer model for Vietnamese spelling error detection and correction. The model takes advantage of both character and context information in a hierarchical way to make predictions for each token of the input sequence. The model is trained over an extensive training set randomly generated from a corpus of high-quality news, Wiki, and subtitles. Through experiments, we have proved that our proposed model outperforms other architectures with significant margin. The evaluation is conducted under the Wiki spelling test set that we built. We have also employed the models into our products to support the users to write messages, news, and many other types of texts.

Although working well with user expectations, the model does not generally solve the spelling problem due to token-to-token mechanism. As we model the correction as classification problem and make only one prediction per token, the vocabulary of output for a single token is fixed. That means, for use-cases such as joined consecutive words (caused by white-space omission) or abbreviations, we could only set a limited number of phrases in the output vocabulary. In order to solve this use-case, we tested with machine translation model as in [10] but the inference speed is dramatically slower and not worth the response time.

For future work, we plan to expand the Wikipedia spelling test further and build a similar set for typical Vietnamese news and verbal messages. We also want to design more robust and powerful architectures that allow us to offer a more satisfying experience to users.

References

1. Devlin, J., Chang, M.W., Lee, K., Toutanova, K.: Bert: pre-training of deep bidirectional transformers for language understanding. In: NAACL-HLT (2019)
2. Gage, P.: A new algorithm for data compression. C Users J. **12**(2), 23–38 (1994)
3. Hochreiter, S., Schmidhuber, J.: Long short-term memory. Neural Comput. **9**(8), 1735–1780 (1997). https://doi.org/10.1162/neco.1997.9.8.1735
4. Lan, Z., Chen, M., Goodman, S., Gimpel, K., Sharma, P., Soricut, R.: Albert: A lite BERT for self-supervised learning of language representations (2020)
5. Nguyen, H.T., Dang, T.B., Nguyen, L.M.: Deep learning approach for Vietnamese consonant misspell correction. In: Nguyen, L.-M., Phan, X.-H., Hasida, K., Tojo, S. (eds.) PACLING 2019. CCIS, vol. 1215, pp. 497–504. Springer, Singapore (2020). https://doi.org/10.1007/978-981-15-6168-9_40
6. Nguyen, P.H., Ngo, T.D., Phan, D.A., Dinh, T.P.T., Huynh, T.Q.: Vietnamese spelling detection and correction using bi-gram, minimum edit distance, soundex algorithms with some additional heuristics. In: 2008 IEEE International Conference on Research, Innovation and Vision for the Future in Computing and Communication Technologies, pp. 96–102 (2008)
7. Niranjan, A., Shaik, M.A.B., Verma, K.: Hierarchical attention transformer architecture for syntactic spell correction. ArXiv abs/2005.04876 (2020)
8. Park, C., Kim, K., Yang, Y., Kang, M., Lim, H.: Neural spelling correction: translating incorrect sentences to correct sentences for multimedia. Multimed. Tools Appl. (2020). https://doi.org/10.1007/s11042-020-09148-2
9. Pham, T., Pham, X., Le-Hong, P.: On the use of machine translation-based approaches for Vietnamese diacritic restoration. CoRR abs/1709.07104 (2017). http://arxiv.org/abs/1709.07104
10. Vaswani, A., et al.: Attention is all you need. ArXiv abs/1706.03762 (2017)
11. Wu, Y., et al.: Google's neural machine translation system: bridging the gap between human and machine translation (2016)
12. You, Y., et al.: Large batch optimization for deep learning: training BERT in 76 minutes (2020)
13. Zhang, S., Huang, H., Liu, J., Li, H.: Spelling error correction with soft-masked BERT. In: ACL (2020)

Fast and Memory-Efficient TFIDF Calculation for Text Analysis of Large Datasets

Samah Senbel[(✉)]

School of Computer Science and Engineering, Sacred Heart University,
Fairfield, CT 06825, USA
senbels@sacredheart.edu

Abstract. Term frequency – Inverse Document Frequency (TFIDF) is a vital first step in text analytics for information retrieval and machine learning applications. It is a memory-intensive and complex task due to the need to create and process a large sparse matrix of term frequencies, with the documents as rows and the term as columns and populate it with the term frequency of each word in each document.

The standard method of storing the sparse array is the "Compressed Sparse Row" (CSR), which stores the sparse array as three one-dimensional arrays for the row id, column id, and term frequencies. We propose an alternate representation to the CSR: a list of lists (LIL) where each document is represented as its own list of tuples and each tuple storing the column id and the term frequency value. We implemented both techniques to compare their memory efficiency and speed. The new LIL representation increase the memory capacity by 52% and is only 12% slower in processing time. This enables researchers with limited processing power to be able to work on bigger text analysis datasets.

Keywords: Text analysis · Information retrieval · TFIDF · Term frequency · Data structures · Memory allocation

1 Introduction

Information retrieval (IR) is an important part of computing, it is the process of obtaining information that are relevant to an information need from a collection of resources. IR searches can be based on text or other content-based indexing, and the search could be for information in a document, searching for documents themselves, and also searching for the metadata that describes data for data mining applications.

Text Analysis is one of the major application fields for machine learning algorithms used in IR. Natural language data is generated by humans through books, articles, reviews, and social media posts among other sources. However the raw natural language data cannot be fed directly to the machine learning or other text analysis algorithms because most are based on numerical feature vectors rather than the raw text with variable length. In order to solve this problem, researchers designed techniques to extract numerical features from text content. And then, the corpus of text content can be represented by a matrix.

© Springer Nature Switzerland AG 2021
H. Fujita et al. (Eds.): IEA/AIE 2021, LNAI 12798, pp. 557–563, 2021.
https://doi.org/10.1007/978-3-030-79457-6_47

In information retrieval, the "term frequency – inverse document frequency" (also called TFIDF), is a well know method to evaluate how important is a word in a document. TFIDF comes up a lot in research work because it's both a corpus exploration method and a pre-processing step for many other text-mining measures and models.

Research on the TFIDF is mostly concentrated on improving its performance and tailoring it to specific applications. Yamout et al. [8] devised and compared the performance of three new weighting techniques to improve the TFIDF weighting technique. Zhao et al. [10] used a modified TFIDF method to do topic modeling on healthcare related publications. TFIDF is also used in several text mining applications such as research paper classification [2], hate speech on social media detection [3], grading and review systems [5], Spam email detection [7] and sentiment analysis [9].

In this paper, we present a new method for representing and calculating the TFIDF and compare its performance with the traditional method. This paper is organized as follows: In Sect. 2, we describe how to calculate the TFIDF and the review the different methods to represent the data structure needed. We also describe our new algorithm for calculating the TFIDF. Section 3 presents our implementation results, and Sect. 4 concludes our work.

2   TFIDF Calculation

Given a corpus of documents with N documents, our goal is to calculate the TFIDF of all words in the corpus. There are several variations on how to calculate it [6]. The term frequency (TF) used in this paper is defined as

$$TF_{i,j} = \frac{n_{i,j}}{\sum\limits_{K} n_{k,j}} \tag{1}$$

where, $n_{i,j}$ represents the number of occurrences of word t_i in row d_j and $\sum\limits_{K} n_{k,j}$ represents the total number of occurrences of words in row d_j. K and D are the number of keywords and documents (rows), respectively. The document frequency (DF) is how many times each keyword appears in the collection of documents. It is calculated by dividing the number of documents that contain a specific keyword by the total number of documents (Eq. 2).

$$DF_{i,j} = \frac{\left| d_j \in D : t_j \in d_j \right|}{|D|} \tag{2}$$

Keywords with a high DF value cannot have high importance because they commonly appear in the most documents. Accordingly, the IDF that is an inverse of the DF is used to measure an importance of keywords in the collection of documents. The IDF is defined as:

$$IDF_{i,j} = \log \frac{|D|}{|d_j \in D : t_j \in d_j|} \tag{3}$$

Using Eqs. (1) and (3), the TF-IDF is defined as

$$TFIDF = TF \times IDF \tag{4}$$

In order to compute the TFIDF, we start by separating the words in each document into a list of individual words. Calculating the TF is straightforward as it only requires one document at a time: number of repetitions of each word is calculated and divided by the number of words in the document. Calculating the IDF is much harder: To get the IDF, we need four data structures:

- A list of all keywords in the corpus (K). This list is initially empty and grows as documents are read and processed.
- A one-dimensional list of all words in a certain document (W). This structure is used for storing the words of a document as it is being processed.
- The two-dimensional sparse array (TF) for storing the TF: the number of rows is the number of documents, and the columns represent the set of all words used in the corpus.
- A one dimensional list of document frequencies (DF), which is a parallel list of K and has the same size, it has the count of how many document contain that word.

The TF array is typically extremely large and sparse. It is extremely memory intensive and makes calculating the TFIDF impossible for a large dataset. It also slows down the calculation of the DF, as all cells have to added up, those with values and those with zeros. Therefore, it is typical to store it as a sparse matrix and do the calculation directly on it, and that also speeds up the calculations as well. There are several well-known techniques to compress a sparse matrix, Fig. 1 shows an example of a sparse matrix generated from a set of similar documents (tweets in this case) and three possible sparse matrix representations:

a) **Compressed sparse row (CSR or Yale format)**
   The compressed sparse row (CSR) or Yale format represents a sparse matrix by three one-dimensional arrays that respectively contain nonzero values of the count of occurrences of words in a document, the document index, and the word id index in K [1]. This is the default representation used to generate the TFIDF in the R and the Python programming languages.
b) **Coordinate list (COO)**
   COO stores a list of (row, column, value) tuples representing the document number, word index in K and number of occurrences in that document, respectively. The entries are sorted first by row index and then by column index, to improve access times.

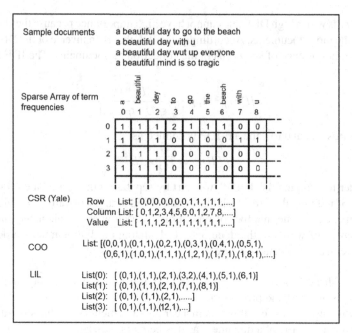

Fig. 1. Sparse matrix storage techniques

c) **List of lists (LIL)**

LIL stores the data as group of lists arranged as an array: one list per document, with each entry containing the column index which references the word id in the word set array (K), and the number of times that word is found in this document. Typically, these entries are kept sorted by column index for faster lookup. This is the most compact representation, as the document number is not stored for each word.

The CSR is the typical representation used in TFIDF calculations. In this work, we implement and test the three representations for the calculation of the TFIDF to compare the performance in time and space. The LIL representation takes the least amount of space as there is no need to add the row number to each data point, providing a saving of about 30% over the CSR & COO and enabling the processing of larger datasets. Algorithm 1 shows our proposed algorithm to get the TFIDF based on the LIL data structure. The code opens the text file containing the documents, one per line, loads them into the data structures, and then calculates the TFIDF for all words in the corpus.

Algorithm 1: Proposed TFIDF calculation using the LIL representation

```
1        Initiate lists: K, W, TF and DF
2        // First: read data from input file and get the term frequencies
3        r = 0  // data row counter
4        while fileinput != EOL
5            Initiate list W
6            Read one line of data and save it in W
7            for ( i=0; i<W.size();i++)
8                Read one word w from row r
9                if  w not in K
10                   Add w to list K
11               if w not in W
12                   Add w to list W
12                   Create tuple (K.get[w], 1) and insert into row r of TF
14               else
15                   Go back in TR until you find the column with that keyword
16                   Add one to its value
17           r++
18       // Next: get DF and calculate TFIDF for all terms
19       for (int i=0 ; i<r ;  i++)
20           for (int j= 0; j < TR[i].size() ; j++)
21               DF[TR[i].get(j).value]++;
22       for (int i=0; i<r ; i++)
23           for (int j= 0; j < TR[i].size() ; j++)
24               TFIDF = (TF[ii].get(j).count )* log( DF.size()/ (DF[TR[i].get(j).value]);
25               // Print it out or save it in TR
```

3   Results

In order to demonstrate the validation and applicability of the proposed technique, we evaluate the performance of the system based on actual social media data. As the experimental data of performance evaluation, we use a large dataset of tweets used for sentiment analysis [4] as our test set. We used the Java programming language to implement four TFIDF calculation techniques: the original two-dimensional representation and the three sparse matrices representation. All were coded and tested using the same i5 laptop with 8G of memory to compare their memory capacity and the time-efficiency. Table 1 shows the dimensions of the data matrix, and the running time for each technique.

The results show two findings: All three sparse matrix representations have a significant decrease in processing time compared to using the original two-dimensional matrix. This is due to the much smaller number of values to be processed. The CSR representation has a slight advantage on speed due to its simple structure of three lists of integers, with no complex tuple structures used.

The second finding is that the LIL data structure can accommodate a bigger dataset in memory for processing. This is due to the fact that there is a significant memory reduction due to the fact that there is no need to store the row number for each word. We were able to process 3,399,946 tweets compared to 2,236,948 using the popular CSR representation or COO.

Table 1. Performance results for the different data structures

Number of tweets (rows)	Number of unique words (Columns)	Number of Cells	Processing time in seconds			
			2D array	CSR	COO	LIL
10,000	14,677	131,760	45	3.15	3.18	3.22
20,000	21,156	249,344	249	6.59	8.34	8.67
100,000	53,551	1,236,186	Fail	38.55	41.16	41.71
500,000	130,015	6,241,033	Fail	242	249	249
1,000,000	202,282	12,431,720	Fail	581	609	685
2,000,000	243,486	26,224,253	Fail	2559	2749	2823
3,000,000	273,866	41,482,271	Fail	Fail	4439	4559
3,200,000	277,921	43,947,980	Fail	Fail	Fail	5036
3,400,000	283,126	46,419,738	Fail	Fail	Fail	5211

4 Conclusion

TFIDF calculation is a starting point in performing text analytics for artificial intelligence and machine learning applications. It provides a challenge in its calculation due to the need to maintain a very large sparse array of the term frequencies. Traditional software libraries use a sparse matrix representation (CSR) that is optimized to reduce time complexity, but has a limit on how many documents can be in the corpus. This is particularly a problem in social media analysis where users tend to use vastly different words and have lots of misspellings that results in a large corpus.

We present a solution to the problem by saving the data into a sparse matrix representation (LIL) that stores the document as a list of lists, where each sub-list represents one document. This resulted in a much larger capacity (52%) more than the traditional representation used (CSR) but the cost is a slight increase in processing time (12%).

References

1. Buluç, A., Fineman, J., Frigo, M., Gilbert, J., Leiserson, C.: Parallel sparse matrix-vector and matrix-transpose-vector multiplication using compressed sparse blocks. In Proceedings of the 21st Annual Symposium on Parallelism in Algorithms and Architectures (SPAA 2009), pp. 233–244. ACM, New York (2009). https://doi.org/10.1145/1583991.1584053
2. Kim, S.-W., Gil, J.-M.: Research paper classification systems based on TF-IDF and LDA schemes. Hum. Cent. Comput. Inf. Sci. 9(1), 1–21 (2019). https://doi.org/10.1186/s13673-019-0192-7
3. Koushik, G., Rajeswari, K., Muthusamy, S.: Automated hate speech detection on Twitter. In: 2019 5th International Conference On Computing, Communication, Control And Automation (ICCUBEA), Pune, India, pp. 1–4 (2019) https://doi.org/10.1109/ICCUBEA47591.2019.9128428
4. Michailidis, M.: Sentiment140 dataset with 1.6 million tweets. http://kaggle.com/kazanova/sentiment140. Accessed 19 Jan 2021

5. Romadon, A., Lhaksmana, K., Kurniawan, I., Richasdy, D.: Analyzing TF-IDF and word embedding for implementing automation in job interview grading. In: 2020 8th International Conference on Information and Communication Technology (ICoICT), Yogyakarta, Indonesia, pp. 1–4 (2020). https://doi.org/10.1109/ICoICT49345.2020.9166364
6. Stoer, J., Bulirsch, R.: Introduction to Numerical Analysis. Springer, New York (2002). https://doi.org/10.1007/978-0-387-21738-3ISBN 978-0-387-95452-3
7. Varol, C., Abdulhadi, H.: Comparision of string matching algorithms on spam email detection. In: 2018 International Congress on Big Data, Deep Learning and Fighting Cyber Terrorism (IBIGDELFT), Ankara, Turkey, pp. 6–11 (2018). https://doi.org/10.1109/IBIGDELFT.2018.8625317
8. Yamout, F., Lakkis, R.: Improved TFIDF weighting techniques in document Retrieval. In: 2018 Thirteenth International Conference on Digital Information Management (ICDIM), Berlin, Germany, pp. 69–73 (2018). https://doi.org/10.1109/ICDIM.2018.8847156
9. Yuan, H., Wang, Y., Feng, X., Sun, S.: Sentiment analysis based on weighted Word2vec and Att-LSTM. In: Proceedings of the 2018 2nd International Conference on Computer Science and Artificial Intelligence (CSAI 2018), pp. 420–424. ACM, New York (2018) https://doi.org/10.1145/3297156.3297228
10. Zhao, G., Liu, Y., Zhang, W., Wang, Y.: TFIDF based feature words extraction and topic modeling for short text. In: Proceedings 2018. TFIDF based Feature Words Extraction and Topic Modeling for Short Text. Proceedings of the 2018 2nd International Conference on Management Engineering, Software Engineering and Service Sciences (ICMSS 2018), pp. 188–191. ACM, New York (2018). https://doi.org/10.1145/3180374.3181354

Collapsed Gibbs Sampling of Beta-Liouville Multinomial for Short Text Clustering

Samar Hannachi[✉], Fatma Najar, Koffi Eddy Ihou, and Nizar Bouguila

Concordia Institute for Information and Systems Engineering (CIISE),
Concordia University, Montreal, QC, Canada

Abstract. With the rise of social media, we have access to more and more text data collected through platforms like Facebook and Twitter. The abundance of these data comes along with short texts challenges. We propose in this paper a collapsed Gibbs Sampling Beta-Liouville Multinomial (CGSBLM) to cope with those challenges. We evaluate the proposed CGSBLM on two datasets extracted from the Google News corpus. Apart from giving a better performance, our approach allows to address the limitations related to short text clustering.

Keywords: Collapsed Gibbs sampling · Short text · Beta-Liouville distribution

1 Introduction

When the social media platforms emerged in the early 2000s, everyone knew that it would have a big impact on the future but on what aspects was still unclear. As of today, we can see how critical those decades were for the whole process of the data collection. From twitter to Facebook posts, servers collect huge amounts of data ready to be managed in different ways for the use of data analytics tasks. Many data scientists are making use of different machine and deep learning techniques to extract patterns and make value out of those large sources of data. While having big amount of data is important for better accuracy results, it becomes essential to use robust techniques aiming at optimizing those information to reduce computational costs and processing time. This is especially right for data like short texts that have many limitations such as data sparsity and high-dimensionality. Latent Dirichlet Allocation (LDA) [1] is one of the well-known approaches used to address the matter. Its architecture allows the expression of the data in the form of topics which relaxes the computational costs and gives a faster processing time. This model still presents some important restrictions making it not suitable for all types of data. Indeed, the Dirichlet distribution has a very restricted covariance structure which assumes that the latent topics are independent from each other. This limitation opened research to many new ideas such as using this concept with some other distributions as priors

© Springer Nature Switzerland AG 2021
H. Fujita et al. (Eds.): IEA/AIE 2021, LNAI 12798, pp. 564–571, 2021.
https://doi.org/10.1007/978-3-030-79457-6_48

which have a more general covariance [2]. Authors in [3] used the Correlated Topic Model (CTM) where a logistic normal distribution is used instead of the Dirichlet distribution which enables a correlated latent topic structure. Authors in [4] improved over the mentioned CTM using Independant Factor Topic Models (IFTM). Others relaxed the limitations of the Dirichlet distribution by replacing it with the generalized Dirichlet distribution which has a more general covariance [5]. In this work, we propose the collapsed Gibbs sampling of Beta-Liouville multinomial distribution for short text clustering. Indeed, previous works already showed how efficient this distribution can be compared to the Dirichlet and generalized Dirichlet distributions [6].

2   Topic Modeling for Short-Text Data

Topic modeling is a statistical set of methods used in natural language processing and data mining to process large amounts of textual data by organizing and understanding them [7]. It helps into extracting the main hidden topics contained into the different documents and annotates them according to the different topics. Common probabilistic models used in topic modeling are mixture models which are representative probabilistic models categorized as unsupervised learning methods [8]. Gibbs sampling Dirichlet Multinomial Mixture (GSDMM) is based on the Markov chain Monte Carlo algorithm proposed for short texts clustering [9]. A very common comparison of the GSDMM algorithm is done with the "Movie Group Approach" analogy [10]. In this scenario, the documents are assimilated to students detaining each a list of movies which are the equivalent of the different words contained in the documents. The students are assigned randomly to K tables from which they will start rotating keeping in mind these two main following rules. When making the choice for a new table, a student should always choose the least empty table gathering students that share the same cinematographic taste. This process is repeated until reaching a certain number of clusters that stays unchanged.

3   Collapsed Gibbs Sampling Beta-Liouville Multinomial Model

The Dirichlet Multinomial mixture model is a very popular model as presented in the previous section. But, due to its many lackings covariance-wise, many researchers turned to a more general distribution as of the generalized Dirichlet. An even more general approach, is the use of the Beta-Liouville distribution which is a generalization of the Dirichlet distribution. Let $\mathcal{X} = (\vec{X}_1, \ldots, \vec{X}_D)$ be a corpus of documents where each $\vec{X}_i$ can be considered as a vector of counts over a set of words $\vec{X} = (X_1, \ldots, X_K)$ with $\vec{P} = (P_1, \ldots, P_K)$ where each P_k is the probability of observing the kth word. It is common to model count vectors by a multinomial distribution giving a probability density function as follows [11]:

$$p(\vec{X}|\vec{\mathbb{P}}) = \frac{N!}{\prod_{k=1}^{K} X_k!} \prod_{k=1}^{K} \mathbb{P}_k^{X_k} \tag{1}$$

As per previous works in [12] and [13], a Beta-Liouville distribution is used as a prior to the multinomial distribution for sampling. The Beta-Liouville distribution is known as the generalization of the Dirichlet distribution and its probability density function is given by [13]:

$$p(\vec{\mathbb{P}}|\theta) = \frac{\Gamma(\sum_{d=1}^{D} \alpha_d)\Gamma(\alpha+\beta)}{\Gamma(\alpha)\Gamma(\beta)}(\sum_{d=1}^{D} \mathbb{P}_d)^{\alpha - \sum_{d=1}^{D} \alpha_d}(1 - \sum_{d=1}^{D} \mathbb{P}_d)^{\beta - 1} \prod_{d=1}^{D} \frac{\mathbb{P}_d^{\alpha_d - 1}}{\Gamma(\alpha_d)} \quad (2)$$

where $\alpha_1, \ldots, \alpha_k$, α and β are the parameters of the Beta-Liouville distribution. The density of the Beta-Liouville Multinomial distribution is obtained by integrating over $\vec{P}$ which will give us the marginal distribution of $\vec{X}$ [13]:

$$p(\vec{X}|\theta) = \int_{\vec{\mathbb{P}}} p(\vec{X}, \vec{\mathbb{P}}|\theta)d\vec{\mathbb{P}}$$

$$= \frac{\Gamma((\sum_{k=1}^{D+1} X_k)+1)}{\prod_{k=1}^{D+1} \Gamma(X_k+1)} \frac{\Gamma(\sum_{k=1}^{D} \alpha_k)\Gamma(\alpha+\beta)\Gamma(\alpha')\Gamma(\beta')\prod_{k=1}^{D} \Gamma(\alpha'_k)}{\Gamma(\sum_{k=1}^{D} \alpha'_k)\Gamma(\alpha'+\beta')\Gamma(\alpha)\Gamma(\beta)\prod_{k=1}^{D} \Gamma(\alpha_k)} \quad (3)$$

where $\alpha_1, \ldots, \alpha_{D+1}$, α and β are the parameters of the Beta-Liouville distribution, where $\alpha'_1, \ldots, \alpha'_{D+1}$, $\alpha' = \alpha + \sum_{k=1}^{D} X_k$ and $\beta' = \beta + X_{D+1}$ are the updated parameters and X_k are the counts of the $D+1$ documents. The main contribution of this work is considering the Beta-Liouville distribution when estimating the parameter of the multinomial distribution that assigns a topic to each word present in a document. The different computations to estimate the different parameters will be done using the collapsed Gibbs sampling algorithm.

Algorithm 1. CGSBLM

1: Set $m_k = 0$, $n_k = 0$ and $n_k^w = \{\}$
2: **for** all the Documents **do**
    Sample $k_d \sim$ Multinomial$(1/K)$
    Increment the variables values by 1, L and N respectively
3: **end for**
4: **for** all the Iterations **do**
    Assign k_d
    Set $m_k = m_k - 1$, $n_k = n_k - L$ and $n_k^w = n_k^w - N$
    Sample $k_d \sim \mathbb{P}(k|k_{\neg d}, \vec{d})$
    Increment the variables values by 1, L and N respectively
5: **end for**

The collapsed Gibbs Sampling Beta-Liouville Multinomial (CGSBLM) is described in the Algorithm 1 where the assignment of each document to a cluster follows two steps. An initial cluster is first randomly assigned to each document as an initialization step. Then, each document is assigned, over a certain number of iterations, a cluster derived from the Dirichlet and Beta-Liouville distribution. The variables present in the algorithm are described as follows: m_k: the number of documents present in the cluster k, n_k: the number of words present in the cluster k, n_k^w: the number of occurrence of word w present in cluster k, L: the legnth of the treated document and N: the number of time a word w is present in the current document. $p(k|k_{\neg d}, \vec{d})$ will give us the latent cluster of a document d by introducing Dirichlet and Beta-Liouville Multinomial distribution. It will allow the estimation of the parameters of the multinomial distributions using the joint probability $p(\vec{d}, k|\alpha_1, \dots, \alpha_k, \alpha, \delta, \beta)$ composed of two probabilities.

$p(\vec{d}|k, \beta)$ is the marginalisation over the product of the probability of the multinomial distribution by the conditional probability of the Dirichlet distribution over its parameter β obtaining after calculations:

$$p(\vec{d}|k, \beta) = \prod_{k=1}^{K} \frac{\Delta(\vec{n}_k + \beta)}{\Delta(\beta)} \qquad (4)$$

where Δ is the function used in [14] and $\vec{n_k} = \{n_k^w\}_{w=1}^{V}$ with n_k^w the number of occurrence of the word w in the cluster k. The contribution of this paper comes in hand with the second probability that marginalizes over the probability of the multinomial with parameter θ and the probability density function of the Beta-Liouville distribution given by:

$$
\begin{aligned}
p(k|\alpha_1, \dots, \alpha_k, \alpha, \delta) &= \int p(k|\theta) p(\theta|\alpha_1, \dots, \alpha_k, \alpha, \delta) d\theta \\
&= \int \prod_{k=1}^{K} \theta_k^{m_k} \frac{\Gamma(\sum_{k=1}^{K} \alpha_k) \Gamma(\alpha + \delta)}{\Gamma(\alpha) \Gamma(\delta)} \prod_{k=1}^{K} \frac{\theta_k^{\alpha_k - 1}}{\Gamma(\alpha_k)} (\sum_{k=1}^{K} \theta_k)^{\alpha - \sum_{k=1}^{K} \alpha_k} \\
&\quad (1 - \sum_{k=1}^{K} \theta_k)^{\delta - 1} d\theta \\
&= \frac{\Gamma(\sum_{k=1}^{K} \alpha_k) \Gamma(\alpha + \delta)}{\Gamma(\alpha) \Gamma(\delta)} \int \prod_{k=1}^{K} \frac{\theta_k^{m_k + \alpha_k - 1}}{\Gamma(\alpha_k)} (\sum_{k=1}^{K} \theta_k)^{\alpha - \sum_{k=1}^{K} \alpha_k} \\
&\quad (1 - \sum_{k=1}^{K} \theta_k)^{\delta - 1} d\theta
\end{aligned}
$$

$$\qquad (5)$$

Marginalizing the probability density function of the Beta-Liouville distribution over the parameter θ with updated parameters corresponding to the remaining integral in the Eq. 6 will allow us to express it in function of a fraction of Gamma functions. Following the work in [13], we will have the updated parameters as follow:

$$
\begin{cases}
\alpha' = \alpha + \sum_{k=1}^{K-1} m_k \\
\alpha'_k = \alpha + m_k \\
\delta' = \delta + m_K
\end{cases}
$$

The Eq. (5) is then equivalent to:

$$
\begin{aligned}
p(k|\alpha_1, \dots, \alpha_k, \alpha, \delta) &= \frac{\Gamma(\sum_{k=1}^{K} \alpha_k) \Gamma(\alpha + \delta)}{\Gamma(\alpha) \Gamma(\delta) \prod_{k=1}^{K} \Gamma(\alpha_k)} \frac{\Gamma(\alpha + \sum_{k=1}^{K-1} m_k) \Gamma(\delta + m_K)}{\Gamma(\sum_{k=1}^{K} (\alpha_k + m_k))} \\
&\quad \frac{\prod_{k=1}^{K} \Gamma(\alpha_k + m_k)}{\Gamma(\alpha + \sum_{k=1}^{K-1} m_k + \delta + m_K)}
\end{aligned}
$$

$$\qquad (6)$$

The conditional distribution that samples a cluster to a document from the Dirichlet and Beta-Liouville distributions will be derived as follows:

$$p(z_d = k | \vec{k}_{\neg d}, \vec{d}) \propto \frac{p(\vec{d}, k | \alpha_1, \ldots, \alpha_K, \alpha, \beta, \delta)}{p(\vec{d}_{\neg d}, k_{\neg d} | \alpha_1, \ldots, \alpha_K, \alpha, \beta, \delta)}$$

$$\propto \frac{\prod_{i=1}^{K-1}(\alpha + \sum_{k=1}^{K-1} m_{k,\neg d} + i - 1)(\delta + m_{K,\neg d})}{\prod_{i=1}^{K}(\sum_{k=1}^{K}(\alpha_k + m_{k,\neg d}) + i - 1)\prod_{i=1}^{N_d}(n_{k,\neg d} + V\beta + i - 1)} \quad (7)$$

$$\frac{\prod_{k=1}^{K}(\alpha_k + m_{k,\neg d}))\prod_{w=1}^{V}(n_{k,\neg d}^{(w)} + \beta)}{\prod_{i=1}^{K}(\alpha + \sum_{k=1}^{K-1} m_{k,\neg d} + \delta + m_{K,\neg d} + i - 1)}$$

where $\alpha_1, \ldots, \alpha_K$, α, δ are the parameters of the Beta-Liouville distribution, β is the parameter of the Dirichlet distribution, $m_{k,\neg d}$ is the number of documents in the cluster k without including the document d, V size of vocabulary, $n_{k,\neg d}^{(w)}$ number of occurence of word w in the cluster k without considering the document d and $n_{k,\neg d}$ number of words in cluster k without considering the cluster of document d.

4   Experimental Results

In this section, we prove the efficiency of our approach compared to the original approach used in [10]. We will do so by using three datasets from [10]. We run the different tests 20 times over each dataset to get the averaged results presented.

4.1   Google News Dataset

Google News homepage contains a very practical setup of short texts on various topics all over the years. These texts usually contain a title and a line of description [15]. For our work, we used the same day of November, 27, 2013 as in [10] with the same crawled titles and snippets from 11,109 articles belonging to 152 clusters. We will work on the two subsets: the Snippet set (SSet) that contains only the snippets of the articles and the TitleSnippet set (TSSet) that contains both the title and snippet of the articles. We followed the same steps when preprocessing our datasets. For the assessment of our work, we used four main metrics which are: Completenss (C), Homogeneity (H), Normalized Mutual Information (NMI) and Adjusted Mutual In-formation (AMI).

4.2   Approaches Comparison

In this subsection, we will compare the results of the GSDMM approach with our approach. For both approaches, we set the initial number of clusters K to 500, the number of iterations to 30 and the value of the parameters to 0.1. Figure 1 shows that our approach improved all the used metrics except for the Completeness where the GSDMM model performed slightly better on the TitleSnippet set. For the Snippet set, Fig. 2 showed some better results than the original approach after 15 iterations.

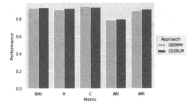

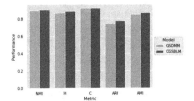

Fig. 1. Comparison of the approaches on the TitleSnippet set

Fig. 2. Comparison of the approaches on the SSet

4.3 Influence of the Initial Number of Clusters

In this part, we will try to assess the impact of the initial number of clusters on the performance of our approach on both datasets. From Fig. 3, we can see that the highest number of clusters equivalent to 500 gave the highest values for the different metrics for the Snippet set. The TitleSnippet set showed its best performance with an initial number of clusters 400 for the metrics AMI, H and NMI. In that sense, we can't conclude on a correlation between the initial number of clusters and the performance of the approach.

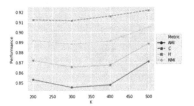

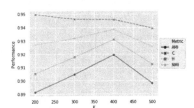

(a) Performance of SSet with different values of K

(b) Performance of TSSet with different values of K

Fig. 3. Impact of K on the performance

4.4 Influence of the Number of Iterations

In this subsection, we will describe the impact of the number of iterations on the number of clusters found by the two approaches on Snippet and TitleSnippet datasets. From Fig. 4, we can see that the number of clusters found drops from 500 to 200 in less than 5 iterations. This corberates the assumption that the most-populated clusters will be chosen first which will lead the less popular clusters to become empty. We can also see that the final number of clusters found for both datasets is very near the original number of clusters of the Google News dataset. This shows how efficient our approach is as it estimates very well the final number of clusters.

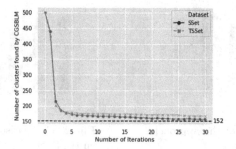

Fig. 4. Number of clusters found by CGSBLM on SSet and TSSet datasets

4.5 Influence of the Parameter α

In this subsection, we will see how the model performs when we change the value of the parameter α. We set the initial number of clusters K to 200 and the number of iterations to 15. We tried different values of α: 0.001,0.01,0.02,0.1,0.2. From Fig. 5, we can see how the value of NMI which is the harmonic mean between the homogeneity and completeness is at its best for $\alpha = 0.01$.

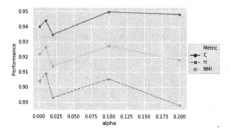

Fig. 5. C, H and NMI for different values of α for TSSet dataset

5   Conclusion

In our paper, we presented a new approach dealing with short texts. We introduced the original approach that uses the Dirichlet distribution and we presented our approach that makes use of the Beta-Liouville distribution. Our approach showed good results compared to the GSDMM approach on one of the datasets. The second dataset needed some twerking to improve its results compared to the original approach. We studied the influence of different parameters and reached some informing conclusions. CGSBLM showed that it can deal with the challenges presented by the short texts. We aim as future work to include some new variations of the Dirichlet distribution.

References

1. Blei, D., Ng, A., Jordan, M.: Latent Dirichlet allocation. Adv. Neural. Inf. Process. Syst. **14**, 601–608 (2001)
2. Bouguila, N.: Clustering of count data using generalized Dirichlet multinomial distributions. IEEE Trans. Knowl. Data Eng. **20**(4), 462–474 (2008)
3. Blei, D.M., Lafferty, J.D., et al.: A correlated topic model of science. Ann. Appl. Stat. **1**(1), 17–35 (2007)
4. Putthividhya, D., Attias, H.T., Nagarajan, S.: Independent factor topic models. In: Proceedings of the 26th Annual International Conference on Machine Learning, pp. 833–840 (2009)
5. Caballero, K.L., Barajas, J., Akella, R.: The generalized Dirichlet distribution in enhanced topic detection. In: Proceedings of the 21st ACM International Conference on Information and Knowledge Management, pp. 773–782 (2012)
6. Bouguila, N.: Hybrid generative/discriminative approaches for proportional data modeling and classification. IEEE Trans. Knowl. Data Eng. **24**(12), 2184–2202 (2011)
7. Albalawi, R., Yeap, T.H., Benyoucef, M.: Using topic modeling methods for short-text data: a comparative analysis. Front. Artif. Intell. **3**, 42 (2020)
8. Kherwa, P., Bansal, P.: Topic modeling: lreview. EAI Endorsed Trans. Scalable Inf. Syst. **7**(24) (2020)
9. Casella, G., George, E.I.: Explaining the Gibbs sampler. Am. Stat. **46**(3), 167–174 (1992)
10. Yin, J., Wang, J.: A Dirichlet multinomial mixture model-based approach for short text clustering. In: Proceedings of the 20th ACM SIGKDD International Conference on Knowledge Discovery and Data Mining, pp. 233–242 (2014)
11. Ratnaparkhi, M.V.: Multinomial distribution: properties and extensions. Wiley StatsRef: Statistics Reference Online (2014)
12. Zamzami, N., Bougila, N.: High-dimensional count data clustering based on an exponential approximation to the multinomial beta-liouville distribution. Inf. Sci. **524**, 116–135 (2020)
13. Bouguila, N.: Count data modeling and classification using finite mixtures of distributions. IEEE Trans. Neural Netw. **22**(2), 186–198 (2010)
14. Heinrich, G.: Parameter estimation for text analysis. Technical report (2005)
15. Banerjee, S., Ramanathan, K., Gupta, A.: Clustering short texts using Wikipedia. In: Proceedings of the 30th Annual International ACM SIGIR Conference on Research and Development in Information Retrieval, pp. 787–788 (2007)

Constructive and Toxic Speech Detection for Open-Domain Social Media Comments in Vietnamese

Luan Thanh Nguyen[1,2], Kiet Van Nguyen[1,2(✉)],
and Ngan Luu-Thuy Nguyen[1,2]

[1] University of Information Technology, Ho Chi Minh City, Vietnam
17520721@gm.uit.edu.vn, {kietnv,ngannlt}@uit.edu.vn
[2] Vietnam National University, Ho Chi Minh City, Vietnam

Abstract. The rise of social media has led to the increasing of comments on online forums. However, there still exists invalid comments which are not informative for users. Moreover, those comments are also quite toxic and harmful to people. In this paper, we create a dataset for constructive and toxic speech detection, named UIT-ViCTSD (**Vi**etnamese **C**onstructive and **T**oxic **S**peech **D**etection dataset) with 10,000 human-annotated comments. For these tasks, we propose a system for constructive and toxic speech detection with the state-of-the-art transfer learning model in Vietnamese NLP as PhoBERT. With this system, we obtain F1-scores of 78.59% and 59.40% for classifying constructive and toxic comments, respectively. Besides, we implement various baseline models as traditional Machine Learning and Deep Neural Network-Based models to evaluate the dataset. With the results, we can solve several tasks on the online discussions and develop the framework for identifying constructiveness and toxicity of Vietnamese social media comments automatically.

Keywords: Constructive speech detection · Toxic speech detection · Machine learning · Deep learning · Transfer learning

1 Introduction

In the era of technology and the Internet, one of the most important factors that need to be concerned about is the quality of online discussions. Focusing on constructive comments and automatically classifying them promotes and contributes to improving online discussion quality and bringing knowledge for users. Besides, toxic comments, which cause the shutting down of user comments completely, are rising dramatically. Hence, filtering toxic comments relied on its level helps improve online conversations.

In this paper, we introduce the UIT-ViCTSD dataset for identifying constructiveness and toxicity of Vietnamese comments on social media. To ensure the quality of the dataset, we build a detailed and clear annotation scheme.

© Springer Nature Switzerland AG 2021
H. Fujita et al. (Eds.): IEA/AIE 2021, LNAI 12798, pp. 572–583, 2021.
https://doi.org/10.1007/978-3-030-79457-6_49

Thereby, annotators can annotate comments correctly. Moreover, our system for detecting constructiveness and toxicity is proposed.

We organize the paper as follows. Section 2 reviews related works that are relevant to our works. Section 3 describes the dataset and defines the meanings of constructiveness and toxicity of comments. Section 4 introduces our proposed system for constructive and toxic speech detection. Section 5 describes experiments, results, and error analysis. Finally, Sect. 6 draws conclusions and future works.

2   Related Work

Constructiveness of comment is an essential element that positively gives users useful information and knowledge and promote online conversations. From these comments, conversations can be extended and more active, provide more information for users. Many Natural Language Processing (NLP) researchers all around the world has concentrated on characteristic. Since 2017, The New York Times has had full-time moderators to evaluate comments of users on their website. They then highlight comments that have constructiveness and label them as NYT Picks [3] manually. In Japan, we can react like or unlike with comments of other users on Yahoo News. So that Yahoo filter their comments of users and rank that one by useful or not. A dataset named The Yahoo News annotated comments dataset was built to find good conversations online [4]. The keyword constructive was focused recently in 2017 by Napoles et al. [11]. They defined a new task for identifying good online conversations, called ERICs, which is used for classifying comments of users and identify good ones.

In 2020, Varada et al. [9] had an in-depth study about the constructiveness of comments, the main element promoting the quality of online conversations. They also built a dataset which is mainly about constructive comments named C3. Furthermore, they discussed the toxicity of comments and demonstrated the relationship between constructiveness and toxicity. They obtained the results of constructive comment detection with 72.59% F1-score by the BiLSTM.

In recent years, NLP is increasing with the rise of high-quality datasets. For Vietnamese, there are several datasets about social media comments such as Vietnamese Social Media Emotion dataset (UIT-VSMEC) [7] with 6,927 labeled comments and achieved a F1-score of 59.74% by CNN model; Vietnamese Students' Feedback dataset (UIT-VSFC) [14] with 16,000 labeled comments and the F1-score they gained by using Maximum Entropy was 84.03%. Moreover, there are still datasets about preventing negative comments or hate speech, like the one presented by Vu et al. [18]. However, Vietnamese is a low-resource language, and there is no dataset about the constructiveness of comments so far. Hence, we aim to build a dataset to develop a framework for automatically identifying the constructiveness and toxicity of Vietnamese comments. With the results, we hope that we can use it to enhance the nature of online conversations, create meaningful and informative content, and make social media more useful.

3   Dataset

3.1   Task Definition

The main task in this paper is **constructive speech detection** of Vietnamese comments. To understand the study, we explain constructive (as label 1) or non-constructive (as label 0) labels and their examples. Following the guidelines, annotators annotate comments with one of the two labels.

- **Constructive:** Comments of users reinforce their point of view for the article. Frequently, those comments provide lots of information and particularized opinions and contribute to promoting the topic.
- **Non-constructive:** Comments of users which have little information. Their contents are only about expressing simple emotions and do not have much meaning.

Furthermore, we also concentrate on another task of **toxic speech detection**. With this characteristic, we annotate comments with one of four different labels consisting of very toxic, toxic, quite toxic, or non-toxic as follows:

- **Very toxic:** Comments which have offensive contents; directly attacking individuals and organizations, showing disrespect to others. Especially using offensive words often causes shutting down conversation rapidly.
- **Toxic:** Comments whose contents are sarcasm and criticism; having a mockery attitude; disagreeing with the opinion but with a lack of delicacy and impolite.
- **Quite toxic:** Comments whose contents might be harmful to people (but not everyone) in specific contexts express disappointment.
- **Non-toxic:** Comments which have non-constructive content only express pure emotions and not make much sense.

Several examples of two tasks in our dataset are shown in Table 1 and Table 2 below.

Table 1. Several examples about constructiveness of comments in our dataset. 1 = Constructive and 0 = Non-constructive.

No.	Comment	Label
1	Nội dung của bài viết là câu trả lời cuối đơn giản cho câu hỏi "Khủng hoảng tài chính là cái gì". Năm 2010,... Cuối cùng một câu trả lời đơn giản được đưa ra: "Bán mà không ai mua !"... cả thế giới đều thế thì khó mà mong đến việc giữ vững tốc độ tăng trưởng kinh tế! *(The content of this article is the right answer for "What is a financial crisis?". Finally, the most suitable answer is: "...")*	1
2	Cầu mong ông sớm khỏe mạnh *I hope you will get well soon*	0
3	Tôi băn khoăn là ... mà không cần chữ kí của người mở thẻ hay sao ạ? Rồi còn phải .... Rồi còn phải làm sao nữa ạ? *I fret about ... without the owner's own signature? Then, ...? What should i do next?*	1

Table 2. Several examples about toxic levels of comments in our dataset.

No.	Comment	Label
1	Đúng là cặn bã ấu dâm! *What a pedophile scum!*	Very toxic
2	Ích kỷ và vô ý thức. *Selfish and unconscious!*	Toxic
3	Xe Việt Nam vẫn quá đắt và đường xá thì quá kém *Vietnamese cars are still too expensive and the quality of roads are too* *poor*	Quite toxic
4	70% cơ thể người là nước mà! *70 percent of the human body is made up of water*	Non-toxic

3.2 Dataset Creation

One of the most challenging issues we have to deal with is differences of Vietnamese language from other high-resource languages as English. A word may have different meanings in different sentences depending on the context. Also, its implications cause difficulties in building the Vietnamese dataset. Therefore, we have to refer to various other researches about the constructiveness of English comments and that definition in Vietnamese to build a high-quality dataset exactly and qualitatively.

Figure 1 shows us the progress of building this dataset with detailed steps. After crawling data, we start to label comments. The comment labeled with the low inter-annotator agreement (IAA) by members is labeled again as the given progression. Besides that, we analyze those cases and then update the annotation scheme again to improve the quality of the dataset.

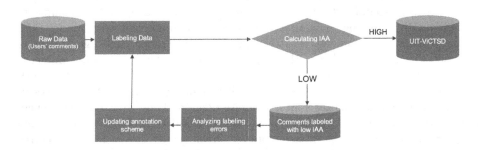

Fig. 1. The process overview of building our annotated dataset.

Before collecting data, we do several surveys about our social media topic, which have many comments relevant to our interests. With the obtained results, we decide to crawl data from comments of users in VnExpress.net[1] because there are huge comments that are useful for our research. Then, we build a tool for

---

[1] https://vnexpress.net/.

crawling data using Python and BeautifulSoup4[2] library useful functions for crawling data. The dataset consists of 10,000 comments and is divided equally into ten domains, including entertainment, education, science, business, cars, law, health, world, sports, and news (1,000 comments each domain)[3].

Three annotators label each comment in our dataset. Before labeling data, we built an annotation scheme with detailed and necessary information, which helps annotators label data quickly and precisely. We describe each task with a detailed definition. Several examples, as well as easily confused comments, are also listed in the annotation scheme. Therefore, annotators can label the data easier and more precisely. We also build a tool for labeling data easily and quickly.

After completing building the dataset, we split it into training, validation, and test sets with a 70:20:10 ratio by train_test_split function of scikit-learn[4].

3.3   Dataset Evaluation

To evaluate the inter-annotator agreement of annotators, we use Fleiss' Kappa [1]. With that result, progress becomes more trustworthy.

$$A_m = \frac{P_e - P_0}{1 - P_0} \qquad (1)$$

Where:

- A_m : The inter-annotator agreement
- P_e : Expected probability of agreement among the annotators
- P_0: Actual probability of agreement among the annotators

To understand the definition of each label, annotators have to be trained strictly and carefully. Hence, we train them with five challenges (200 comments per round). After the challenges, members of the annotation team understand how to annotate comments with their labels. With the first challenge, the inter-annotator agreement is only 21.7% in identifying constructiveness of comments and 30.4% for toxic speech detection. The inter-annotation agreement in both tasks is not as high as expected in the first challenge because of differences in knowledge of each annotator in a separate domain. Thus, after each challenge, we consider conflicting cases, then we edit and update the annotation scheme. After five challenges, the inter-annotator agreement we gained for constructive and toxic speech detection is 59.48% and 58.74% IAA, respectively.

With the task of classifying constructive comments, the final label of a comment is chosen by the above 2/3 annotators. And the final label of comments in toxic speech detection is the average of the results of three annotators.

---

[2] https://pypi.org/project/beautifulsoup4/.
[3] http://nlp.uit.edu.vn/datasets/.
[4] https://scikit-learn.org/.

3.4 Dataset Analysis

Distribution of Constructiveness. To gain an overview of the dataset, we conduct analyses on it. Figure 2 illustrates the distribution of constructive comments. We found that constructive comments are usually long comments and have a huge difference from non-constructive comments.

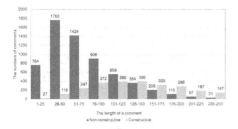

Fig. 2. Distribution of constructive comments in the dataset.

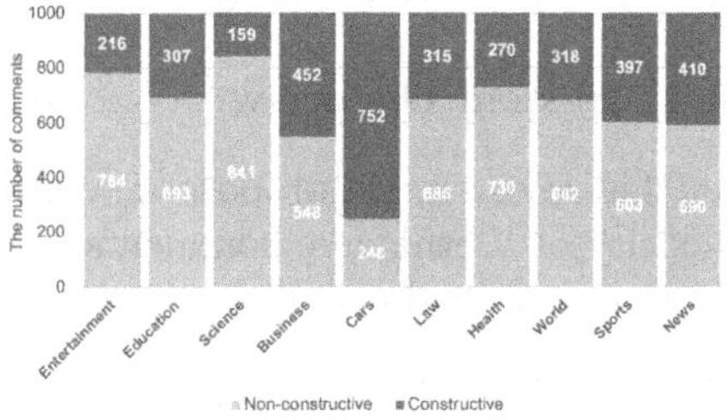

Fig. 3. The number of constructive and non-constructive comments on each domain.

In addition, we analyze the number of constructive and non-constructive labels of comments on each domain to make an overview of the distribution of the dataset. The result is shown in Fig. 3. Nevertheless, there are disadvantages we have to face. That is the imbalance of the dataset. The constructive comments are still less than non-constructive ones. Hence, we plan to balance the dataset in future.

The Relative Between Constructiveness and Toxicity. We analyze the number of constructive comments by their toxic levels to obtain an overview of the relative between them, as shown in Fig. 4. We found that constructive comments also have toxicity. It proves that toxic contents still provide useful information for users.

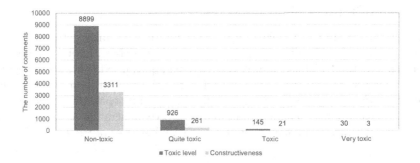

Fig. 4. The number of constructive comments by their toxic levels.

Because the number of non-toxic comments is too large compared to the rest of the comments, we decide to combine the quite toxic, toxic, and very toxic labels into only one label as toxic. Hence, the task about toxic levels of comments becomes a problem with classifying a comment into toxic or non-toxic, a binary text classification task.

4   Proposed System

4.1   System Overview

In this research, we propose a system for identifying the constructiveness and toxicity of Vietnamese comments. Figure 5 shows an overview of our proposed system described as follows.

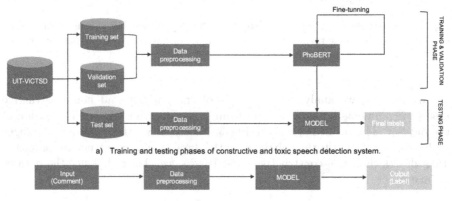

a)   Training and testing phases of constructive and toxic speech detection system.

b)   An overview for constructive and toxic speech detection system.

Fig. 5. The proposed system for identifying constructiveness and toxicity of Vietnamse comments.

4.2   Data Preprocessing

The dataset we built is a collection of texts, and it is an unstructured dataset, which is why it is difficult to be approached with models without applying preprocessing methods. Thus, we use popular techniques in NLP for preprocessing data of dataset. Firstly, we remove HTML tags. Unlike English or other popular languages, the space in Vietnamese is only the sign for separating syllables, not words. Tokenizing texts is important, and it directly affects the result of models. Hence, we tokenize those comments by using ViTokenizer of the library Pivi[5].

---

[5] https://pypi.org/project/pyvi/.

Table 3. Several examples about normalizing Vietnamese abbreviations.

Abbreviations	Normalization
k, kh, hok, hk	không
oke, okay, oki	ok
vn, Vietnam, VN	Việt Nam

In the next step, we normalize texts by building a dictionary for abbreviations. Several examples are mentioned in Table 3.

Within the main model of our system, PhoBERT, which is mentioned in the next subsection, we use VNcoreNLP [17] and FAIRSeq [15] for preprocessing data and tokenizing words before applying to the dataset.

Finally, we eliminate spaces, especially special characters such as capital letters and symbols, before feeding them into training models. But, we still keep numbers because it also has essential information, which promotes constructive features.

4.3 Transfer Learning - PhoBERT

The transfer learning model has attracted increasing attention from NLP researchers around the world for its outstanding performances. One of the SOTA language models as BERT, which stands for Bidirectional Encoder representations from transformers, is published Devlin et al. [2]. It is a bi-directional transformer model for pre-training over lots of text data with no label to understand a language representation. Then, we fine-tune for specific problems.

For Vietnamese, the SOTA method was first released and called PhoBERT by Nguyen et al. [13] for solving Vietnamese NLP problems. PhoBERT is a pre-trained model, which has the same idea as RoBERTa, a replication study of BERT is released by Liu et al. [10], and there are modifications to suit Vietnamese. In our proposed system, we use PhoBERT as the primary method for constructive and toxic speech detection for Vietnamese comments. We set the learning rate of 3e−5 and 24 for batch size.

5   Experiments and Results

5.1   Baseline Systems

Besides our system, we implement various models, including traditional methods as machine learning and neural network-based models.

Machine Learning Models

- **Logistic Regression:** A basic machine learning algorithm for classification, especially binary task.

- **Support Vector Machine (SVM):** This model is widely used for classification, regression and other problems in machine learning.
- **Random Forest:** An ensemble learning method for classification, regression, and other problems. It operates by constructing a multitude of decision trees at the training phase.

Neural Networks Models

- **Long Short-Term Memory (LSTM):** This is a Deep Learning method based on RNN architecture. It is capable of learning long-term dependencies because of its feedback connections [5].
- **Bi-GRU-LSTM-CNN:** A customized ensemble model by Huynh et al. [16]. It is a combination of CNN-1D, Bidirectional LSTM and Bidirectional GRU layers and achieves optimistic results in binary classification task [8].

Unlike machine learning methods, neural network models have different approaches to the dataset. Before the training model, we use the word-embedding for models as below.

- **fastText:** A multilingual pre-trained word vector, including Vietnamese, released by Grave et al. [6].
- **PhoW2V:** PhoW2V is a pre-trained Word2Vec word embedding for Vietnamese, which is published by Nguyen et al. [12]. In this research, we use a PhoW2V word level embedding for preprocessing (300 dims).

5.2   Experimental Settings

For finding suitable parameters of each model, we use the GridSearchCV technique from sklearn. The final parameters we implemented are presented in Table 4.

Table 4. Suitable parameters of each model for constructive and toxic speech detection of Vietnamese comments.

	Parameters	
System	**Constructiveness**	**Toxicity**
Logistic Regression	C = 100	C = 100
SVM	C = 1000, gamma = 0.001, kernel = "rbf"	C = 1000, gamma = 0.001, kernel = "rbf"
Random Forest	n_estimators = 108, max_depth = 400	n_estimators = 108, max_depth = 400
LSTM	units = 128, activation = "sigmoid"	units = 128, activation = "sigmoid"
Bi-GRU-LSTM-CNN	CNN-1D: drop_out = 0.2, Bi-LSTM: units = 128, activation = "sigmoid"	CNN-1D: drop_out = 0.2, Bi-LSTM: units = 128, activation = "sigmoid"

5.3 Experimental Results

Before training models, we vectorize texts from the training set, from which models understand and learn from data. Then, we conduct experiments on our dataset, and the results of each model are shown in the Table 5 below. We use metrics as Accuracy and macro-averaged F1-score (%) for evaluating the performances of models.

Table 5. The experimental results of each model for constructive and toxic speech detection.

System	Constructiveness		Toxicity	
	Accuracy	F1-score	Accuracy	F1-score
Logistic regression	79.91	70.78	90.27	55.35
Random forest	79.10	73.75	90.03	55.30
SVM	78.00	76.10	90.17	59.06
LSTM + fastText	80.00	76.26	88.90	49.63
LSTM + PhoW2V	78.20	77.42	89.00	49.70
Bi-GRU-LSTM-CNN + fastText	79.90	77.53	89.10	48.88
Bi-GRU-LSTM-CNN + PhoW2V	79.50	77.94	88.90	49.62
Our system	79.40	**78.59**	88.42	**59.40**

With the results above, our system achieves the best performance for identifying constructiveness of comments with the F1-score of 78.59% and 59.40% F1-score for toxic speech detection. However, the current results are not the highest ones. In particular, the F1-score result of the toxicity classification task is relatively low on the test set because of the significant imbalance between the toxic label and the non-toxic label, according to Fig. 4. Moreover, it proves that the dataset still has noisy data affecting classifier model performance directly.

5.4 Error Analysis

For analyzing errors of predictions by our system, we calculate a confusion matrix. Figure 6 presents the confusion matrix of our system for constructive and toxic speech detection. We see that in identifying constructiveness, the highest confusing cases are wrong to predict constructive (1) instead of non-constructive (0) with 14% of the incorrect prediction. The confusion matrix of toxic speech detection shows us that the performance of the model for this task is still not high. The reason for that confusion is the imbalance of the dataset. Comments in our dataset are crawled mainly from official online sources, which blocks and prevents toxic contents on their forum. Hence, the number of toxic comments in the dataset are much less than the non-toxic ones, and models cannot be trained well and obtain the highest performances. We plan to improve its quality by adding more toxic comments from other social media platforms in the future.

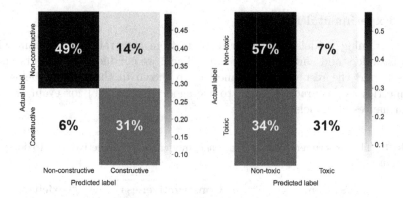

Fig. 6. Confusion matrix of our system for constructive and toxic speech detection.

6   Conclusion and Future Work

This paper presented a new dataset named UIT-ViCTSD, including Vietnamese comments annotated manually with constructiveness and toxic labels. Firstly, we built an annotation scheme for labeling comments. In particular, we achieve the dataset consisting of 10,000 human-annotated comments on ten different domains. Secondly, we proposed a system for constructive and toxic speech detection with the state-of-the-art transfer learning model in Vietnamese NLP as PhoBERT. We achieved 78.59% and 59.40% F1-score for identifying constructive and toxic comments, respectively. Then, we implemented traditional machine learning and neural network models. Finally, we analyzed errors of our system on the dataset.

In future, we plan to evaluate the balanced dataset by removing inappropriately annotated comments and inserting new comments with the appropriate label. Besides, we intend to improve the quality of our dataset and our system in order to obtain the best results on constructive and toxic speech detection for Vietnamese social media comments.

References

1. Bhowmick, P.K., Basu, A., Mitra, P.: An agreement measure for determining inter-annotator reliability of human judgements on affective text. In: Coling 2008: Proceedings of the workshop on Human Judgements in Computational Linguistics, Manchester, UK, August 2008. Coling 2008 Organizing Committee (2008)
2. Devlin, J., Chang, M.W., Lee, K., Toutanova, K.: BERT: pre-training of deep bidirectional transformers for language understanding. In: Proceedings of the 2019 Conference of the North American Chapter of the Association for Computational Linguistics: Human Language Technologies, vol. 1 (Long and Short Papers), Minneapolis, Minnesota (2019)
3. Diakopoulos, N.: Picking the nyt picks: editorial criteria and automation in the curation of online news comments. ISOJ J. **6**(1), 147–166 (2015)

4. Fujita, S., Kobayashi, H., Okumura, M.: Dataset creation for ranking constructive news comments. In: Proceedings of the 57th Annual Meeting of the Association for Computational Linguistics, pp. 2619–2626 (2019)
5. Gers, F.A., Schmidhuber, J., Cummins, F.: Learning to forget: continual prediction with LSTM. (1999)
6. Grave, E., Bojanowski, P., Gupta, P., Joulin, A., Mikolov, T.: Learning word vectors for 157 languages. In: Proceedings of the Eleventh International Conference on Language Resources and Evaluation (LREC 2018), Miyazaki, Japan, May 2018. European Language Resources Association (ELRA)
7. Ho, V.A., et al.: Emotion recognition for Vietnamese social media text. In: Nguyen, L.-M., Phan, X.-H., Hasida, K., Tojo, S. (eds.) PACLING 2019. CCIS, vol. 1215, pp. 319–333. Springer, Singapore (2020). https://doi.org/10.1007/978-981-15-6168-9_27
8. Van Huynh, T., Nguyen, L.T., Luu, S.T.: BANANA at WNUT-2020 task 2: identifying COVID-19 information on Twitter by combining deep learning and transfer learning models. In: Proceedings of the Sixth Workshop on Noisy User-generated Text (W-NUT 2020), pp. 366–370 (2020)
9. Kolhatkar, V., Thain, N., Sorensen, J., Dixon, L., Taboada, M.: Classifying constructive comments. arXiv preprint arXiv:2004.05476 (2020)
10. Liu, Y., et al.: Roberta: a robustly optimized bert pretraining approach. arXiv preprint arXiv:1907.11692 (2019)
11. Napoles, C., Pappu, A., Tetreault, J.: Automatically identifying good conversations online (yes, they do exist!). In: Eleventh International AAAI Conference on Web and Social Media (2017)
12. Nguyen, A.T., Dao, M.H., Nguyen, D.Q.: A pilot study of Text-to-SQL semantic parsing for Vietnamese. In: Findings of the Association for Computational Linguistics: EMNLP 2020, pp. 4079–4085 (2020)
13. Nguyen, D.Q., Nguyen, A.T.: PhoBERT: pre-trained language models for Vietnamese. In: Findings of the Association for Computational Linguistics: EMNLP 2020, pp. 1037–1042, Online, November 2020. Association for Computational Linguistics (2020)
14. Van Nguyen, K., Nguyen, V.D., Nguyen, P.X., Truong, T.T., Nguyen, N.L.T.: UIT-VSFC: vietnamese students' feedback corpus for sentiment analysis. In: 2018 10th International Conference on Knowledge and Systems Engineering (KSE) (2018)
15. Ott, M., et al.: Fairseq: a fast, extensible toolkit for sequence modeling. In: Proceedings of the 2019 Conference of the North American Chapter of the Association for Computational Linguistics (Demonstrations) (2019)
16. Van Huynh, T., Nguyen, V.D., Van Nguyen, K., Nguyen, N.L.T., Nguyen, A.G.T.: Hate speech detection on vietnamese social media text using the bi-gru-lstm-cnn model. arXiv preprint arXiv:1911.03644 (2019)
17. Vu, T., Nguyen, D.Q., Nguyen, D.Q., Dras, M., Johnson, M.: VnCoreNLP: a Vietnamese natural language processing toolkit. In: Proceedings of the: Conference of the North American Chapter of the Association for Computational Linguistics: Demonstrations, p. 2018. Louisiana, June, New Orleans (2018)
18. Vu, X.S., Vu, T., Tran, M.V., Le-Cong, T., Nguyen, H.: Hsd shared task in vlsp campaign 2019: Hate speech detection for social good. arXiv preprint arXiv:2007.06493 (2020)

Fuzzy Inference and Theory

The Behaviour of the Product T-Norm in Combination with Several Implications in Fuzzy PID Controller

Nourelhouda Zerarka$^{(\boxtimes)}$, Saoussen Bel Hadj Kacem, and Moncef Tagina

National School of Computer Sciences, COSMOS Research Laboratory,
University of Manouba, 2010 Manouba, Tunisia
{nourelhouda.zerarka,Saoussen.BelHadjKacem,moncef.tagina}@ensi-uma.tn

Abstract. Fuzzy control is an intelligent software performed to tune a process and make it react in a desirable way. Nowadays, many researchers are interested in the Fuzzy Proportional-Integral-Derivative (FPID) controller because of its performance and simple structure. FPID controller, as fuzzy controller, is based on the Compositional Rule of Inference (CRI) that allows to infer with fuzzy data. As defined by Zadeh, the CRI contains two parameters: t-norm (T) and fuzzy implication (I). Because of the singleton representation of crisp inputs in fuzzy controllers, the t-norm is no longer considered in the CRI, which gives results based only on the fuzzy implication. In this study, we use non-singleton representation of the inputs, and we apply several implications in a fuzzy PID controller combined with the product t-norm. We study the behaviour of the fuzzy PID controller according to each combination (T,I) to evaluate its efficiency in term of quality and time of convergence. We finally compare the obtained results with the theoretical inference results and we find that they are consistent.

Keywords: Fuzzy Logic Controller · FPID controller · Approximate reasoning · Compositional rule of inference · T-norm · Fuzzy Implication

1 Introduction

As human reasoning works with non exact knowledge, it inspired researchers to find a way how to make machines work in this way. For that, fuzzy logic was introduced by Zadeh in 1965 [1], which aims to obtain a result from imprecise inputs. It is an extension of the classical logic. Unlike this last one, fuzzy logic infers with a degree between the full membership and the non membership.

To infer with fuzzy data, approximate reasoning [2] was created to simulate human reasoning. The essential method of approximate reasoning is the Compositional Rule of Inference (CRI) [2]. Its formula has two principal parameters: triangular norm (T) [3], which is a conjunction operation, the second operator is fuzzy implication (I) [4] that aims to evaluate a rule from its premise and conclusion. In practical applications, the CRI is used as the execution phase in the

© Springer Nature Switzerland AG 2021
H. Fujita et al. (Eds.): IEA/AIE 2021, LNAI 12798, pp. 587–597, 2021.
https://doi.org/10.1007/978-3-030-79457-6_50

inference engine of Fuzzy Logic Controller (FLC). We can find in the litterature some works that evaluated the most used implications in FLC [5–8], and that by using crisp inputs.

In the last decades, many industrial control applications use Fuzzy PID (FPID) controller, which is a fusion of FLC and the classical PID Controller. It is used to correct the response of the controlled systems and make it as wanted [9]. FPID controller is a Rule-Based System where rules and fact are fuzzy. Like FLC, it uses the compositional rule of inference in its mechanism of reasoning.

In this paper, we aim to test the CRI parameters (T,I) to find the best couples that give the efficient and best result, and that are suitable to be used in controlling systems. For that, we create a FPID controller where we can put any t-norm and any implication in its CRI. So, using two different representations (singleton/non-singleton) of the inputs in this FPID, the product t-norm and fifteen fuzzy implications are used in the inference engine of this FPID controller. When using fuzzy inputs, our aim is to be able to evaluate the t-norm parameter. After that, the obtained controllers are simulated to see their efficiency, and to see which of them give the best results according to their convergence, time of convergence and overshoot. Finally, the obtained results using crisp and fuzzy inputs are compared with the theoretical study done in [10] which verifies the satisfaction of human intuitions for these combinations.

The paper is organized as follows. In section two, we present the most used vocabulary in this paper, we also show the previous studies of (T,I) combinations in CRI. In section Three, we define our controller and show the obtained results, then, we discuss the results of the simulation. The last section is dedicated to the conclusion and our perspectives.

2   Preliminary Considerations

The inference part in a Fuzzy Logic Controller is covered by approximate reasoning. The latter is based on the Generalized Modus Ponens (GMP), whose aim is to deduce a conclusion using a fuzzy observation and a fuzzy rule:

Ant1: if X is A then Y is B

Ant2: X is A'

Cons: Y is B'

with A, A', B and B' fuzzy sets belonging to the universe of discourses U and V, X and Y are linguistic variables. Using the Compositional Rule of Inference (CRI) [2], we can determine the consequence B' as a composition of the observation A' and the relation between the premise A and the conclusion B of the rule:

$$\forall v \in V \mu_{B'}(v) = \sup_{u \in U} T(\mu_{A'}(u), I(\mu_A(u), \mu_B(v))) \tag{1}$$

where μ_A, $\mu_{A'}$, μ_B and $\mu_{B'}$ are membership functions of the fuzzy sets A, A', B and B' respectively, T is a t-norm, I is a fuzzy implication. A triangular norm

T, or t-norm for short, is a binary operator used in fuzzy logic to extend the classical logic conjunction. A fuzzy implication I represents the extension of the classical logic implication. Tables 1 and 2 specify the most known and used t-norms [11] and implications [12] respectively. Since the first FCLs put in place, the choice of combination (T,I) in the CRI is fixed only on the couple (min, min) due to the simplicity of the execution.

Table 1. Some of the known t-norms.

Name	Notation	Function
Zadeh	$\wedge$	$min(u,v)$
Lukasiewicz	$\odot$	$max(u+v-1,0)$
Goguen	.	$u.v$
Drastic	$\wedge$	$\begin{cases} u & \text{if } v=1 \\ v & \text{if } u=1 \\ 0 & else \end{cases}$

Table 2. List of basic fuzzy implications.

Name	Notation	Function
Zadeh	I_m	max(1-u,min(u,v))
Lukasiewicz	I_a	min(1- u+v, 1)
Mamdani	I_c	min(u,v)
Rescher-Gaines	I_s	$\begin{cases} 1 & \text{if } u \leq v \\ 0 & else \end{cases}$
Brouwer-Gödel	I_g	$\begin{cases} 1 & \text{if } u \leq v \\ v & else \end{cases}$
Kleene-Dienes	I_b	$max(1-u,v)$
Fukami	I_{sg}	$min(I_s(u,v), I_g(1-u,1-v))$
	I_{gg}	$min(I_g(u,v), I_g(1-u,1-v))$
Mizumoto	I_{gs}	$min(I_g(u,v), I_s(1-u,1-v))$
	I_{ss}	$min(I_s(u,v), I_s(1-u,1-v))$
	$I_\triangle$	$\begin{cases} 1 & \text{if } u \leq v \\ \frac{v}{u} & else \end{cases}$
	$I_\blacktriangle$	$\begin{cases} min(1, \frac{v}{u}, \frac{1-u}{1-v}) & \text{if } u > 0 \text{ and } 1-v > 0 \\ 1 & \text{if } u = 0 \text{ or } 1-v = 0 \end{cases}$
	$I_\bigstar$	$1-u+uv$
	$I_\#$	$max(min(u,v), min(1-u,1-v), min(v,1-u))$
	$I_\square$	$\begin{cases} 1 & \text{if } u < 1 \text{ or } v = 1 \\ 0 & \text{if } u = 1 \text{ and } v < 1 \end{cases}$

Many research studied theoretically the CRI with different combinations (T,I) [5–8,10,12–14]. As in [10], authors found that by combining fuzzy implications with the product t-norm, the best couples that imitate the human intuitions are when using: I_{sg}, I_{gg}, I_{gs}, I_{ss}, $I_\triangle$, I_s, and I_g implications. Indeed, the authors proved that these combinations verify the axiomatic of approximate reasoning, which is formed by a set of criteria.

Since their creation, Fuzzy Logic Controllers consider crisp inputs, which means that: $\mu_A(u_0) = 1$ and $\mu_A(u) = 0 \ \forall u \neq u_0$. In this case, the CRI is simplified to be:

$$\forall v \in V \mu_{B'}(v) = \bigvee_{u \neq u_0} T(0, I(\mu_A(u), \mu_B(v))) \vee T(1, I(\mu_A(u_0), \mu_B(v)))$$
$$= T(1, I(\mu_A(u_0), \mu_B(v)))$$
$$= I(\mu_A(u_0), \mu_B(v))$$

Thus, the CRI is influenced only by the fuzzy implication with no impact of a t-norm.

Some works were interested in the practical aspect of the CRI parameters, more precisely in Fuzzy Logic Controller. The authors in [8] evaluated the implications in a fault diagnosis system for which the correct diagnoses were known. They found that in an abnormal scenario, where the operating expense is higher than the normal situation, the implications that give the correct result are: I_g, I_c, $I_\triangle$, $I_\blacktriangle$. Mizumoto [7] also used, in a Fuzzy Logic Controller, various fuzzy implications. Because the premise of the rules contains more than one proposition, the author used two different representations of the "and" between the propositions: min ($\wedge$), and algebraic product ($\cdot$). When simulating the controllers, he found that the best control results are given using I_c implication. In the same context, Kiszka et al. [5,6] have based their studies on the connector "also" used between the rules of a Fuzzy Logic Controller.

3   Fuzzy PID Controller with Various Combinations (T,I)

Our aim is to study the effect of varying the two parameters (T,I) of the CRI on the obtained results. We are interested especially in this work in the product t-norm in combination with the implications of table 2. To do that, we evaluate the performance of a Fuzzy PID controller for these combinations.

3.1   Definition of the Controller

We perform a FPID Controller to simulate various combinations (T,I) in its CRI. As Fig. 1 shows, our Fuzzy PID controller is composed of:

– Reference input signal $r(t)$, which is the value we desire to arrive at, at instant t.
– Fuzzy controller, which detects the error and adjusts it.

– The process or the part that is required to be controlled. Here we choose a simple first order system $(G = \frac{1}{s+1})$.

The objective of this controller is to regulate and apply the correction u to the obtained value from the process y to correspond to the set point r. This will allow minimizing the error e over time.

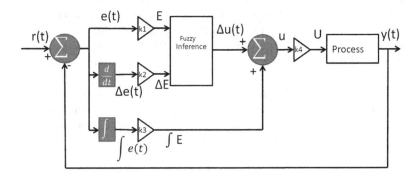

Fig. 1. Block diagram of the used fuzzy PID controller in our simulation.

A Fuzzy PID controller contains two inputs which are:

– The error e, which is the difference between the set point r (desirable value) and the obtained value from the process y at instant t:

$$e(t) = r(t) - y(t) \tag{2}$$

– The derivative of error Δe with respect to time or rate of change in error. This one is used to know if the actual output of the plant is moving towards or away from the set point:

$$\Delta e = e(t) - e(t-1) \tag{3}$$

We have one output from the fuzzy controller: "rate of change in action" Δu which is the derivative of the control signal with respect to time.

Another term, which is the integral of error $\int e$, is added to the output of the fuzzy controller Δu to eliminate errors in the steady state.

The three terms and the control signal u are normalized using the scaling factors, which aims to map the input signal into the range of the controller inputs, and to map the output of the controller into the output range as follows [15]:

$$E(t) = k1 \times e = k1(r(t) - y(t)) \tag{4}$$

$$\Delta E(t) = k2 \times \Delta e = k2(e(t) - e(t-1)) \tag{5}$$

$$\int E(t) = k3 \times \int e(t) \tag{6}$$

$$U(t) = k4 \times u(t) = k4 \left(\int E(t) + \Delta u(t) \right) \tag{7}$$

where E, ΔE, $\int E$ and U are the normalized values of e, Δe, $\int e$ and u by the scaling factors $k1$, $k2$, $k3$ and $k4$ respectively, $e(t)$, $e(t-1)$ are the error at instant t and instant $t-1$.

To simulate this Fuzzy PID controller, we use Matlab and Simulink. Instead of using the FLC of Fuzzy Toolbox that exists in Matlab, we create our fuzzy controller because the FLC of Fuzzy Toolbox only considers crisp inputs. However, in this study, we consider the inputs as fuzzy numbers (triangular membership functions) so that the t-norm is used in the CRI. For that, we developed the controller in Matlab so that it can accept this type of inputs and any t-norm and implication.

In our controller, the inputs e and Δe are represented by two fuzzy sets: *negative* and *positive* in the universe of discourse $[-1\ 1]$. The output Δu is represented by three fuzzy sets: *negative*, *null* and *positive* in the universe of discourse $[-1\ 1]$. Figure 2 shows these fuzzy sets.

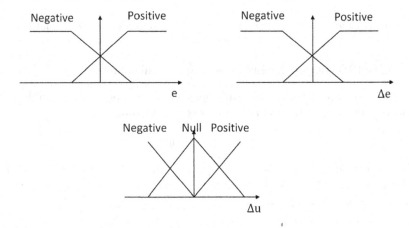

Fig. 2. Partitions of the inputs and the output used in the controller.

The Rule Base of the fuzzy controller contains four rules which are [16]:

1 If e is *negative* and Δe is *negative* Then Δu is *negative*.
2 If e is *negative* and Δe is *positive* Then Δu is *null*.
3 If e is *positive* and Δe is *negative* Then Δu is *null*.
4 If e is *positive* and Δe is *positive* Then Δu is *positive*.

We should mention that the connector "and" in the rule premise is modeled by "min" ($\wedge$). Furthermore, we link the rules using the connector "also", which is defined by "max" when the combination is with I_c implication, and by "min" for the rest of the treated combinations.

3.2   Simulation Results

We expand on this part how the fuzzy controller works by CRI with the product t-norm and the different implications of table 2. For that, we see which of the combinations converge in a desirable manner. The analysis of the results is based on three criteria: convergence, time of convergence and overshoot. We mean by convergence whether it arrives at the steady state or not. And by the time of convergence, we mean the time that it takes to converge, is it a quick or a slow convergence. For the overshoot, this means analyzing if there is an overshoot or not before the convergence. For the scaling factors, we have: $k1 = 1$, $k2 = 1$, $k3 = 1.5$ and $k4 = 1$.

First of all, as seen in Figs. 3 and 4, we begin with the case of crisp inputs, where the t-norm is not considered in the CRI and the inference is based only on the implication parameter. Note that the implications of Fig. 3 are those which verify the axioms of approximate reasoning, as mentioned in Sect. 2. In the FPID controller, the fifteen implications converge. But, as shown in Fig. 3, I_g, I_{gg} and $I_\triangle$ implications have the largest overshoot and the slowest convergence. $I_\blacktriangle$ implication has the second biggest overshoot. However, it converges at the same time as the implications: I_s, I_{ss}, I_{sg}, I_{gs} and $I_\square$ which have the same overshoot.

Furthermore, Fig. 4 shows that the implications I_m, I_b and $I_\#$ have the fastest convergence with a medium overshoot. For the implications I_a, $I_\bigstar$ and I_c, they take more time to arrive at the steady state with approximately the same overshoot as the implications I_m, I_b and $I_\#$.

For the case of fuzzy inputs, according to the two Figs. 5 and 6, all the combinations converge. As Fig. 5 shows, the combinations with the implications: I_g, I_{gg}, $I_\triangle$, I_s, I_{ss} and $I_\blacktriangle$ converge almost at the same time except those with I_{sg} and I_{gs} that converge slightly before. Moreover, the smallest overshoot is with the implication I_{ss}, which is a minor overshoot that we can neglect. We see also that the combinations with implications I_s, $I_\blacktriangle$ and I_{sg} have overshoots close to that of the combination with I_{ss} implication. For the combinations with implications I_g, I_{gg}, I_{gs}, and $I_\triangle$, they have the same overshoot that is the largest in Fig. 5.

On the other hand, as we can see in Fig. 6, the couple with the implication $I_\square$ has the largest overshoot and the slowest convergence which gives a poor stability. For the combinations with I_m, I_b and $I_\#$ implications, they have the fastest convergence with a medium overshoot. While for the combination with Mamdani implication (I_c), it has the second biggest overshoot, but its convergence is medium. It converges at the same time with the combinations with I_a, and $I_\bigstar$ implications that have a small overshoot but which is bigger than those of Fig. 5.

We conclude that the use of fuzzy inputs in a FPID controller gives, in general, results that have a smaller overshoot than results with crisp inputs. This means that with fuzzy inputs, when inferring using CRI, the t-norm gives a positive effect.

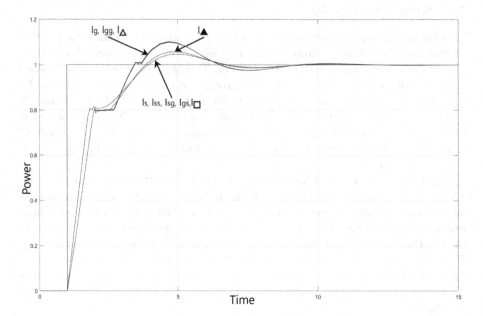

Fig. 3. Step responses using crisp inputs with implications: I_g, I_{gg}, $I_\triangle$, I_s, I_{sg}, I_{gs}, I_{ss}, $I_\blacktriangle$ and $I_\square$.

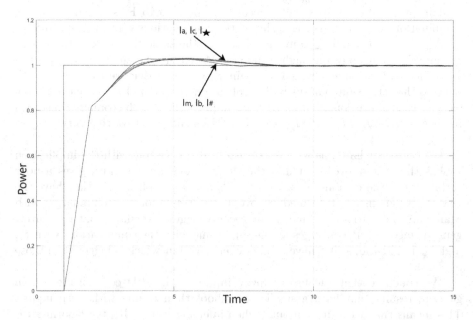

Fig. 4. Step responses using crisp inputs with implications: I_m, I_b, $I_\#$, I_c, I_a and $I_\bigstar$.

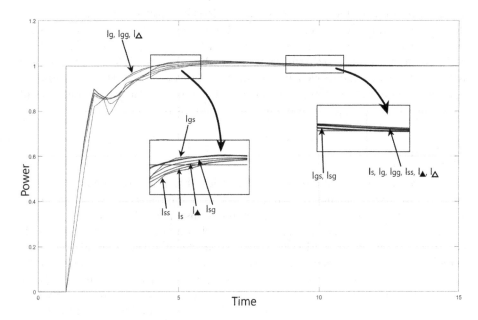

Fig. 5. Step responses using fuzzy inputs from combinations with implications: I_g, I_{gg}, $I_\triangle$, I_s, I_{sg}, I_{gs}, I_{ss} and $I_\blacktriangle$.

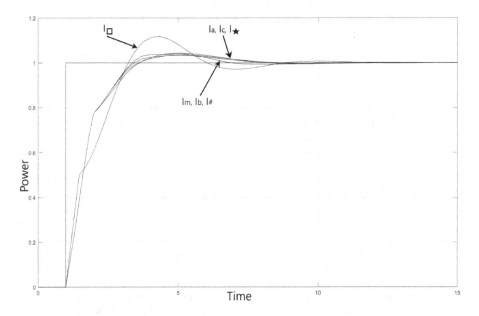

Fig. 6. Step responses using fuzzy inputs from combinations with implications: I_m, I_b, $I_\#$, $I_\square$, I_c, I_a and $I_\bigstar$.

Also, in order to have an efficient Fuzzy PID controller, which is stable and does not consume a lot of energy due to the overshoot, the combinations with the product t-norm and the implications: I_s, I_{sg}, I_{gs}, $I_{\blacktriangle}$, I_g, I_{ss}, I_{gg} and $I_{\triangle}$ are quite good choice. Furthermore, these combinations give the best theoretical results. Indeed, as mentioned in Sect. 2, it is proved in [10] that the product t-norm in combination with these same implications satisfy the axiomatics of approximate reasoning, which model the human intuitions.

4   Conclusion

The compositional rule of inference (CRI) is a method of approximate reasoning that contains two elements: t-norm (T) and fuzzy implication (I). In this paper, we studied the efficiency of various combinations (T,I). To do that, we chose the most used fuzzy controller in the industrial domain, which is the fuzzy PID controller. We used three criteria to see the efficiency of the combinations: convergence, time of convergence and the overshoot. We found that the use of fuzzy inputs affected positively the inference. Particularly, when combining the product t-norm with fifteen fuzzy implications, we got that the combinations which satisfy human intuitions, which are the product t-norm combined with the implications: I_s, I_{sg}, I_{gs}, $I_{\blacktriangle}$, I_g, I_{ss}, I_{gg} and $I_{\triangle}$, gave good results because they had the smallest overshoot. The obtained results can help fuzzy inference system designers in choosing the appropriate parameters. For future work, we aim to use more combinations with different implications and t-norms, and work with different fuzzy controller by using different representations of the fuzzy inputs. We aim also to verify the results using real world scenarios.

References

1. Zadeh, L.A.: Fuzzy sets. Inf. Control **8**(3), 338–353 (1965)
2. Zadeh, L.A.: The concept of a linguistic variable and its application to approximate reasoning-iii. Inf. Sci. **9**(1), 43–80 (1975)
3. Okamoto, K.: Families of triangular norm based kernel function and its application to kernel k-means. In: 2016 Joint 8th International Conference on Soft Computing and Intelligent Systems (SCIS) and 17th International Symposium on Advanced Intelligent Systems (ISIS), pp. 420–425 (2016)
4. Tick, J., Fodor, J.: Fuzzy implications and inference processes. In: IEEE 3rd International Conference on Computational Cybernetics, 2005. ICCC 2005, pp. 105–109 (2005)
5. Kiszka, J.B., Kochańska, M.E., Sliwińska, D.S.: The influence of some fuzzy implication operators on the accuracy of a fuzzy model-part i. Fuzzy sets Syst. **15**(2), 111–128 (1985)
6. Kiszka, J.B., Kochańska, M.E., Sliwińska, D.S.: The influence of some fuzzy implication operators on the accuracy of a fuzzy model-part ii. Fuzzy Sets Syst. **15**(3), 223–240 (1985)
7. Mizumoto, M.: Fuzzy controls under various fuzzy reasoning methods. Inf. Sci. **45**(2), 129–151 (1988)

8. Whalen, T., Schott, B.: Alternative logics for approximate reasoning in expert systems: a comparative study. Int. J. Man-Mach. Stud. **22**(3), 327–346 (1985)
9. Godjevac, J.: Comparison between pid and fuzzy control. Ecole Polytechnique Fédérale de Lausanne, Département d'Informatique, Laboratoire de Microinformatique, Internal Report, vol. 93 (1993)
10. Zerarka, N., Bel Hadj Kacem, S., Tagina, M.: The compositional rule of inference under the composition max-product. In: Endres, D., Alam, M., Şotropa, D. (eds.) ICCS 2019. LNCS (LNAI), vol. 11530, pp. 204–217. Springer, Cham (2019). https://doi.org/10.1007/978-3-030-23182-8_15
11. Gupta, M.M., Qi, J.: Theory of t-norms and fuzzy inference methods. Fuzzy Sets Syst. **40**(3), 431–450 (1991)
12. Masaharu, M.: Fuzzy conditional inference under max-⊙ composition. Inf. Sci. **27**(3), 183–209 (1982)
13. Mizumoto, M.: Fuzzy inference using max-∧ composition in the compositional rule of inference. Approximate Reason. Decis. Anal. 67–76 (1982)
14. Mizumoto, M., Zimmermann, H.-J.: Comparison of fuzzy reasoning methods. Fuzzy sets Syst. **8**(3), 253–283 (1982)
15. Khan, A.A., Rapal, N.: Fuzzy pid controller: design, tuning and comparison with conventional pid controller. In: International Conference on Engineering of Intelligent Systems, pp. 1–6 (2006)
16. Dubois, L.: Utilisation de la logique floue dans la commande des systèmes complexes. Ph.D. thesis, Lille, vol. 1 (1995)

Hub and Spoke Logistics Network Design for Urban Region with Clustering-Based Approach

Quan Duong⑩, Dang Nguyen⑩, and Quoc Nguyen$^{(\boxtimes)}$⑩

GHN Data Science, Ho Chi Minh, Vietnam
{quandb,dangnh1,quocnd}@ghn.vn

Abstract. This study aims to propose effective modeling and approach for designing a logistics network in the urban area in order to offer an efficient flow distribution network as a competitive strategy in the logistics industry where demand is sensitive to both price and time [3]. A multistage approach is introduced to select the number of hubs and allocate spokes to the hubs for flow distribution and hubs' location detection. Specifically, a fuzzy clustering model with the objective function is to minimize the approximate transportation cost is employed, in the next phase is to focus on balancing the demand capacity among the hubs with the help of domain experts, afterward, the facility location vehicle routing problems within the network is introduced. To demonstrate the approach's advantages, an experiment was performed on the designed network and its actual transportation cost for the real operational data in which specific to the Ho Chi Minh city infrastructure conditions. Additionally, we show the flexibility of the designed network in the flow distribution and its computational experiments to develop the managerial insights which contribute to the network design decision-making process.

Keywords: Logistics network design · Hub-and-spoke · Clustering

1 Introduction

The volume of express delivery gets increasing with the rapid development of e-commerce. At the same time, intense competition has forced express delivery service companies to compete in different categories to get ahead in the race. Transportation cost and delivery lead-time are considered to be the most important metrics for success. On the other hand, logistics network design is concerned with the number of locations of stations that allocate for customer's demand points, and the assignment of the stations to the distribution centers within their coverage. The optimal setting must distribute the goods to the customers with the least cost and satisfy the service level agreement. To illustrate these strategies, considering the current configuration of the delivery network of logistics providers in Vietnam, an attempt to design a network that distributes more efficiently and reduces the transportation cost. Thus, the primary goal of

© Springer Nature Switzerland AG 2021
H. Fujita et al. (Eds.): IEA/AIE 2021, LNAI 12798, pp. 598–605, 2021.
https://doi.org/10.1007/978-3-030-79457-6_51

this work is to, firstly, examine the limitation of the single distribution center. Secondly, design a delivery network that optimizes the transportation cost by demonstrating for an urban region. Moreover, we develop an analytical framework that offers multiple distribution scenarios within the designed network and its impact on the operational performance of the firm.

The rest of the paper is organized as follows: In Sect. 2, the relevant studies on logistics network design for the urban region are reviewed. Afterward, Sect. 3 presents our practical approach and framework and establishes the flow distribution scenarios within the network. The experiment results take into account the real operational data from a delivery network with a case study for Ho Chi Minh city will be conducted in Sect. 4. Finally, we conclude the main findings and future research directions in Sect. 5.

2   Literature Review

The logistics network design problem consisting of multiple facilities location problem [6], each facility has a limit of serving demand points contribute the difficulty of problem where need to solve the single facility location problems, but also searching for the optimal number of facilities and assigning the customer demand points for each cluster. Additionally, Cheong et al. [3] explored the benefit of segmenting demand points into different classes, they assumed that each demand point can be divided into two classes of the sensitivity to delivery lead time, the segmentation results in more effective allocation in demand point and reduce the network cost. A typical use of flow distribution, utilizes the distribution centers (DC) to serve the customer's demand points within their coverage. In a single DC scenario, vehicles depart from DC's location and deliver to the customer's demand points, this process makes the logistics resource difficult to be shared in high-density areas. Moreover, the logistics service provider manages to accommodate customer's demanding at time window and price make the operations more challenging. In 2016, Roca-Riu et al. [9] took a further step to evaluate the urban good distribution for several European cities with a single independent DC and proposed continuous models to improve the efficiency of urban distribution with the use of urban consolidation centers (UCC), the quantitative metric indicated that by deploying the UCC can reduce the transportation cost up to 14%. The collaborative and multi-depots in urban areas got a lot of attention in recent years [7,10,12]. Later in 2020, Wang et al. [11] solve collaborative multi-depots vehicle routing problems to deal with the impact of changing time window. In order to group the demand points into a single, weighted K-mean clustering and Fuzzy C-means clustering algorithms stand out for the facility location problem [4–6]. However, Meng et al. [13] figured out that weighted K-mean always traps into local optima and is sensitive to the initial setting, and very limited research incorporate the domain knowledge for the target region with fuzzy c-means clustering capacity.

In this study, the fuzzy c-mean (FCM) clustering algorithm [2] is employed to solve the uncapacitated multi-facility location problem. The FCM allows the data point belongs to multiple clusters with different degrees of membership. Combining the degree of membership features and domain expert for the target region of designing the delivery network, the belonging of demand point to the cluster will be judged by humans in order to balance the capacity among the clustering and other area's characteristics.

3   Methodology

Given all the spokes (know as the demand points that will serve the end customers for a specific area). The methodology aims to find the optimal Hub's Location and spoke to the hub assignment with respect to minimize the transportation cost. The process consisting of three phases: i) Clustering: detecting the group of nearby spokes to a cluster. ii) Hub's location: detect the cluster's center in which serve as the local DC. iii) Vehicle Routing: determine the flow distribution scenario among the Hubs' network, and perform the vehicle routing for good delivery to the spokes.

3.1   Clustering

Formally, a dataset X as a set of N demand points represented as vectors in an 2-dimensional space: $X = \{x_1, x_2, ..., x_N\} \subseteq \Re^2$. A clustering in X is a set of disjoint clusters that partitions X into K groups: $C = \{c_1, c_2, ..., c_k\}$ where $\cup_{c_k \in C} c_k = X, c_k \cap c_l = \emptyset \forall k \neq l$. The Haversine distance between objects x_i and x_j will denote as $d_h(x_i, x_j)$. The approximate transportation cost is calculated as

$$Cost = \sum_{c_k \in C} \left\{ \sum_{c_l \in C \setminus c_k} d_h(\overline{c_k}, \overline{c_l}) + \sum_{x_i \in c_k} d_h(\overline{c_k}, x_i) \right\} \tag{1}$$

$$\overline{c_k} = \frac{\sum_{x_i \in X} w_k(x_i)^m * x_i}{\sum_{x_i \in X} w_k(x_i)^m} \tag{2}$$

where $\overline{c_k}$ is the centroid of a cluster c_k is defined by the FCM, m is the hyperparameter that controls the fuzziness of clustering and $w_k(x)$ is the degree of membership that data point x belong to the cluster k.

Final Cluster Assignment. The degree of membership feature from FCM is utilized for balancing the demand among the cluster together with humans. Specifically, taking into account the domain knowledge of the target designed area, those mixture-membership demand data points will be re-assigned with the domain expert in the loop. Based on the FCM's degree of membership feature, the expert will assign each single demand data point into a target cluster in order to satisfy the capacity balancing requirements. The number of clusters and algorithm parameters is searching by incremental methods with the objective is to minimize the approximate transportation cost in the formula 1. In the Sect. 4.1, the experiment results with specific parameters will be conducted.

3.2   Hub's Location

After allocating of demand data point to cluster, the center of gravity method
[1] is employed to determine the optimal Hub's location. The aims of center of
gravity method is to bring the center of cluster closer to demand points with
higher demand. For all $k \in \{1, 2, ..., K\}$ and $\nu(x)$ is the delivery demand for
demand point x, the center gravity of each cluster k are calculated as:

$$h_k = \sum_{x \in c_k} \beta(x) * x \qquad (3)$$

$$\beta(x) = \frac{\nu(x)}{\sum_{x \in c_k} \nu(x)} \qquad (4)$$

The $\beta(x)$ value serves as the weighted factor within the cluster. The larger
value will pull the hub's location to its side. The real transportation cost corresponding to these locations will be shown in Table 2.

3.3   Flow Distribution and Vehicle Routing

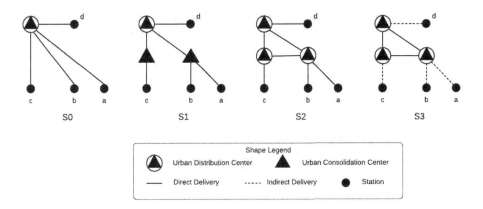

Fig. 1. Flow distribution scenarios

Given a designed network, the authors deliberately prototype three flow distribution scenarios within the network in the Fig. 1, and a default scenario which
is using for daily operation in GHN network as follows: $S0$: Default scenario,
single independent DC. $S1$: Each Hub will serve as Urban Consolidation Center
(UCC). $S2$: Each Hub will serve as Urban Distribution Center (UDC). $S3$: Each
Hub will serve as UDC, and drop the delivery packages at its center for the
nearby demand points. Here, the newly designed network has the ability to offer
three different flow distribution scenarios. Fundamentally, $S1$ only performs the
loading/unloading packages to the designated DC. An upgrade version of $S1$,

$S2$ also has the ability to sort the packages within its coverage and distribute all other packages to other DC/UDC. As an advantage on multi-depot, the DC locate closer to its demand points, $S3$ only need to sort packages, and hand-off the packages at its location, this scenario offers flexibility for the urban area such as reduce the cost for delivering by trucks, restricted during the rush hours.

4   Experiment Result

The numerical results reported in this paper are the real operational data in Ho Chi Minh City, Vietnam. Including, i) 77 active demand data points. ii) All transactions data for the entire December 2020 has been extracted and calculated for two different phases in this paper. First, the average delivery demand for the whole period would be used for representing the demand point's volume that contributes to the Hub's Location inference in Sect. 3.2. Second, transaction data of $22^{nd} December$ has been used to conduct experimental design for pickup and delivery demand in the designed network. Essentially, the actual transportation cost in Sect. 4.2 are computed based on this day.

4.1   Detected Clusters

Regarding to experimental setting, the authors employed the Python's scikit fuzzy package[1] and the configuration ($m = 3$, $error = 0.002$, $maxiter = 1000$, $seed = 12345$, and $c = \{2, 3, 4, 5\}$). The primary parameter is c (the desired number of clusters). The best parameter in determined by the combination of approximate transportation cost in Formula 1, fuzzy partitioning coefficient, and the variation of delivery demand for each cluster.

Table 1. Summary of clustering results

Number of clusters	Approximate transportation cost	Coef
2	527.8	0.568
3	**482.8**	0.424
4	490.3	0.362
5	530.6	0.308

The experimental results of the clustering step shown in Table 1, The transportation cost with *3* and *4* show the better result than the other values. Take a deeper look, we can see that the *3* clusters's cost and *Coef* slightly better than the *4*. Inspiring by these numbers, the exact assignment of data points to the cluster will be adjusted by the domain expert due to the fact that it's mandatory the satisfy the capacity requirements. Figure 2 shows the visual outcome of each

---

[1] https://pythonhosted.org/scikit-fuzzy/.

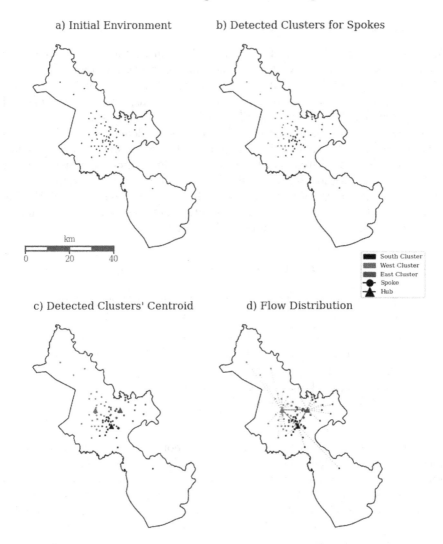

a) Initial Environment

b) Detected Clusters for Spokes

c) Detected Clusters' Centroid

d) Flow Distribution

South Cluster
West Cluster
East Cluster
Spoke
Hub

Fig. 2. The environment and its clusters between the elements in network.

step for the entire process. The initial setting of 77 demand points display as black dots belong to the Ho Chi Minh region in Fig. 2-a, each color in the right next Fig. 2-b represents the 3 detected clusters by virtue of the FCM algorithm and human judgment. A single triangular in Fig. 2-c indicates the Hub's location for each cluster. The right-bottom Fig. 2-d visually shows the flow distribution from Hub to Hub and from Hub to Spokes within sub-network.

4.2   Actual Transportation Cost

Confidentially, with the goal of comparing the transportation cost among the scenarios, also not to disclose the commercial confidentiality information. The values for *number of trucks* and *total cost* for the current operation mode have been changed to v and c respectively. The actual transportation cost specified in the Formula 1. Due to the fact that the actual situation takes into account many important and realistic factors like delivering demand at each demand point, truck capacity, time window requirement, local traffic condition. Thus, we leverage the capacitated vehicle routing with time window solutions. In this regard, the optimization software OR-Tool [8] is used to perform the computational step given the operational constraints and the conditions of Ho Chi Minh city such as travel distance and duration between points, time window requirement, delivery demand, and truck's capacity.

Table 2. Actual transportation cost for scenarios

Scenario	Number of trucks	Total cost	Pickup cost	Delivery cost
S0	v^*	c^{**}	0.7c	0.3c
S1	0.79v	0.75c	0.44c	0.31c
S2	0.8v	0.72c	0.47c	0.25c
S3	0.63v	0.61c	0.46c	0.15c

* Number of trucks need for the *S0* scenario
** The total amount of money take for the *S0* scenario

In the Table 2, we shown the actual transportation cost for all the mentioned scenarios. By introducing the multi-depot in the delivery network, the transportation cost reduces 25%, 28% by adding consolidation and distribution centers respectively. Take a deeper look in the *S2* scenario, we can observe that the delivery cost is cheaper than *S1* scenario 19% by reducing the traveled distance for the delivery trips, *S2* also takes more effort in the pickup trips in order to move the packages to closer DC. On the other side, about 20% of the number of trucks have been reduced for performing delivery with the same demand in the network.

5   Conclusions

This paper analyzes the advantages of collaborative multi-depot settings in the urban area, applied the iterative approaches for the logistics network design problem. By employing the FCM algorithm for clustering and leveraging the degree of membership feature to reassign the demand point to the cluster in order to balance the facility's capacity in each specific sub-network by virtue of domain expert. Based on the real operational data in Ho Chi Minh city, the results indicate that 3 clusters achieve the best solution in approximate transportation cost and reduce the actual transportation cost to 28% and 20% trucks used with 3 distribution centers compared to the original independent DC. Increasing the truckload utilization for the delivery trips between Hubs not only reduces the transportation cost and improves operational efficiency for the firm, but also put an effort into alleviating the traffic congestion, reducing stress for transportation infrastructure. In the future, the studies may focus on two directions. First, calculate the system cost for the designed network including the cost for opening a new facility and operating that facility with a given demand, and perform the experiment for multiple urban regions in Vietnam. Second, schedule the dynamic vehicle routing to deal with the highest demand days and measure its performance. Prospective studies on these directions would contribute to operating more efficiently and resilient on both typical and high demand days, also the promotion of multi-depots setting for the urban regions.

References

1. Ballou, R.H.: Business Logistics Management. Prentice-Hall, Upper Saddle River, New Jersey (1999)
2. Bezdek, J.C., Ehrlich, R., Full, W.: FCM: the fuzzy c-means clustering algorithm. Comput. Geosci. **10**(2–3), 191–203 (1984)
3. Cheong, M.L., Bhatnagar, R., Graves, S.C.: Logistics network design with differentiated delivery lead-time: Benefits and insights (2005)
4. Esnaf, Ş., Küçükdeniz, T.: A fuzzy clustering-based hybrid method for a multi-facility location problem. J. Intell. Manuf. **20**, 259–265 (2009)
5. Hu, W., Dong, J., Hwang, B.G., Ren, R., Chen, Z.: Network planning of urban underground logistics system with hub-and-spoke layout: two phase cluster-based approach. Eng. Constr. Archit. Manag. **27**(8), 2079–2105 (2020)
6. Küçükdeniz, T., Baray, A., Ecerkale, K., Esnaf, Ş.: Integrated use of fuzzy c-means and convex programming for capacitated multi-facility location problem. Expert Syst. Appl. **39**(4), 4306–4314 (2012)
7. Long, Q.: A multi-methodological collaborative simulation for inter-organizational supply chain networks. Knowl. Based Syst. **96**, 84–95 (2016)
8. Perron, L., Furnon, V.: Or-tools. https://developers.google.com/optimization/
9. Roca-Riu, M., Estrada, M., Fernández, E.: An evaluation of urban consolidation centers through continuous analysis with non-equal market share companies. Transp. Res. Procedia **12**, 370–382 (2016)
10. Wang, Y., Ma, X., Liu, M., Gong, K., Liu, Y., Xu, M., Wang, Y.: Cooperation and profit allocation in two-echelon logistics joint distribution network optimization. Appl. Soft Comput. **56**, 143–157 (2017)
11. Wang, Y., et al.: Collaborative multi-depot logistics network design with time window assignment. Expert Syst. Appl. **140**, 112910 (2020)
12. Xu, X.F., Hao, J., Deng, Y.R., Wang, Y.: Design optimization of resource combination for collaborative logistics network under uncertainty. Appl. Soft Comput. **56**, 684–691 (2017)
13. You, M., Xiao, Y., Zhang, S., Yang, P., Zhou, S.: Optimal mathematical programming for the warehouse location problem with euclidean distance linearization. Comput. Ind. Eng. **136**, 70–79 (2019)

Sensor and Communication Networks

Smartphone Sensor-Based Fall Detection Using Machine Learning Algorithms

Mariam Dedabrishvili[1]([✉]), Besik Dundua[1,2], and Natia Mamaiashvili[1]

[1] International Black Sea University, Tbilisi, Georgia
[2] Kutaisi International University, Kutaisi, Georgia

Abstract. Human Activity Recognition and particularly detection of abnormal activities such as falls have become a point of interest to many researchers worldwide since falls are considered to be one of the leading causes of injury and death, especially in the elderly population. The prompt intervention of caregivers in critical situations can significantly improve the autonomy and well-being of individuals living alone and those who require remote monitoring. This paper presents a study of accelerometer and gyroscope data retrieved from smartphone embedded sensors, using iOS-based devices. In the project framework there was developed a mobile application for data collection with the following fall type and fall-like activities: Falling Right, Falling Left, Falling Forward, Falling Backward, Sitting Fast, and Jumping. The collected dataset has passed the preprocessing phase and afterward was classified using different Machine Learning algorithms, namely, by Decision Trees, Random Forest, Logistic Regression, k-Nearest Neighbour, XGBoost, LightGBM, and Pytorch Neural Network. Unlike other similar studies, during the experimental setting, volunteers were asked to have smartphones freely in their pockets without tightening and fixing them on the body. This natural way of keeping a mobile device is quite challenging in terms of noisiness however it is more comfortable to wearers and causes fewer constraints. The obtained results are promising that encourages us to continue working with the aim to reach sufficient accuracy along with building a real-time application for potential users.

Keywords: Fall detection · Data preprocessing · Data classification · Smartphone embedded sensors · Mobile applications

1 Introduction

In Machine Learning (ML) self-learning algorithms can transform data into knowledge without human intervention [17]. The idea behind this is that algorithms analyze data and can produce some output without never knowing input before [13]. This happens mainly focusing on stats and probability and not on some reason and logic. The process of analyzing data, discovering some patterns in large data sets is known as data mining. In data mining data being extracted needs to be transformed and brought in such a form and shape, that it could be

© Springer Nature Switzerland AG 2021
H. Fujita et al. (Eds.): IEA/AIE 2021, LNAI 12798, pp. 609–620, 2021.
https://doi.org/10.1007/978-3-030-79457-6_52

readable and understandable by machines. This ability or technique to build a machine-readable or learning model is known as a data preprocessing technique.

The data preprocessing techniques include a range of methods such as noise removal, missing value imputation, feature extraction, and selection which are interpreted by algorithms as an input for the further process of data classification or predictive modeling to determine which partitioned group belongs to which preprocessed data set, in other words, to predict the class label and produce the training model of the algorithm [1].

ML algorithm usage becomes quite important in human activity recognition (HAR) and in fall detection, too. Falls are dangerous for elderly people from a severely injure perspective, especially for those who live alone and independently. For the purpose of safety, they need some kind of helping gadgets equipped with sensors and detectors. Fall detection sensors help to locate victims and enable prompt supportive intervention. There is a wide range of wearable sensors that can be worn on the different parts of a body, on dominant or non-dominant arms, waist, ankles, wrist, hip, chest, etc. [4]. There are also watches with accelerometers. Nevertheless, as we live in a smart era we can use the advantage of it and allow our daily traveler smartphones to act as the tool for HAR, while device built-in accelerometers and gyroscopes are also capable of collecting data, which can provide informative data for detecting and analyzing human activities.

2   Related Work

Nowadays, vast amount of raw data or real-world data is generated every day for some dedicated purpose and need [7]. In ML, we also need the data, to turn into knowledge using special techniques. But of course, data needs to be understandable for machines. That's why we need to prepare and process it for the system. Naturally, for preparation we need to know which tools and techniques can be applied to data, and how to apply them to bring the benefits promised [16] and that is what data preprocessing represents.

There are several approaches discussed in this work on how to process the data generally in data mining during the ML process and particularly in HAR for Fall Detection.

According to Han and Kamber [9], data preprocessing techniques mainly consists of four steps:

- Data Cleaning - tiding the dirty data, that may have missing values, noisiness, and inconsistencies;
- Data Integration - combining data in one "consistent data store", like warehouses;
- Data Transformation - bringing data in an appropriate shape and form;
- Data Reduction - decreasing volume of dataset, reducing data size;

But these major steps also include sub-techniques that have different solutions depending on the task, time, or approach. Different data preprocessing methods are also reviewed by Alasadi and Bhaya [2]. Garcia et al. [7] in their work consider Data Preprocessing former and latter disciplines:

Former Disciplines:

- Data Transformation
- Data Integration
- Data Cleaning
- Data Normalization

Latter Disciplines:

- Feature Selection
- Instance Selection
- Instance Discretization

However, the picture changes as the techniques and methods are a little bit more different and complex when applied to big data. Primarily, there are five categories:

- Discretization and Normalization
- Feature Indexers and Encoders
- Text Mining/Other Techniques

- Feature Extraction

- Feature Selection

During research other perspectives, [17] work was found, which reviews ML using scikit-learn library and python, it also discusses some tools for data preprocessing techniques. Guan Yuan et al. [19] describe techniques for processing sensor data to detect human activities. According to the work, in the HAR context these important and meaningful steps should be followed in order to achieve better results for the classification process:

- Dealing with Noisy Data and Windowing techniques;
- Feature Engineering and Model Training.

The following authors can be addressed for the detailed information about above mentioned preprocessing methods and their use in special cases [2,7,17,19].

One can observe that methodologies, strategies, tools, and techniques vary from each other. The main intention is to choose the right ones that individually depend on the task and goal. Some methods are faster but less accurate, some are more accurate but requires a longer time, and others are intended for small datasets or large ones.

As described above in the review, data preprocessing is mainly not more than data cleaning, integration, transformation, and reduction. These major steps are important as data that is generated or accumulated during the data collection process, can be noisy, imperfect, it may have inconsistencies, outliers, high volumes, may not in an appropriate form or in a rational data store, etc. In order to eliminate and resolve these negative factors from datasets and to achieve proper results in Data Mining Process (DMP), the right methodologies and techniques need to be elaborated for each particular task.

The present study, with the experimental dataset, will elaborate the appropriate way of data preprocessing strategy based on the above-described approaches. The preprocessed dataset will be used as input to the selected ML algorithms for fall detection analysis. The study tries to optimize the fall detection process's acceptability to users by placing a smartphone in the pocket without any tightening. During the experiments, different kinds of falls and fall-like activities will be recorded using the iOS-based developed application, which makes the work dissimilar to other fall detection approaches, where mostly Android-based systems are involved in the studies. As well, different algorithm performances will be demonstrated and further research steps will be pointed out throughout the study.

3   Preliminaries

Data classification is the process of data analysis after data preprocessing, which deals mostly with categorical or numerical data and constructs a classifier model for class label prediction where these classes are discrete values and ordering of class labels is not essential. Classification is one of two main types of prediction problems: learning when the classification model is constructed and differentiating among classes where this model is used to predict class labels.

The learning process or training phase can be supervised or unsupervised, in other words, during the supervised learning process data class labels are predetermined and are defined as database tuples and their associated class labels, which are in the form of n-dimensional attribute vector $X = \{x_1, x_2, x_3, ...x_n\}$. During unsupervised learning as explained by [9], the class label of each training tuple is not known, and the number or set of classes to be learned may not be known in advance.

As mentioned above, classification consists of two steps; the first training step is like a function, $y = f(X)$, which is the means of a label prediction tool for X tuple. Classification rules, formulas, or decision trees can implement this step.

The second step is the classification based on the constructed model. The most crucial is to define how accurate is the classifier. For this, the given sample is divided into test and training data set. Accuracy check is performed on the test tuples together with their associated class labels, which is measured by the percentage of the test tuples desirably classified by the model. Acceptable value of the accuracy enables classifier usage to classify unknown data tuple labels.

There are various algorithms developed for data classification. In this work, we have employed the following well-known classification algorithms that are well suited to sensor derived numerical data classification cases, see Table 1:

Table 1. List of ML algorithms used in the study

Names of the Algorithms and their abbreviation	
Decision Tree (DT)	XGBoost
Random Forest (RF)	LightGBM
Logistic regression (LR)	Pytorch Neural Network
k-Neatest Neighbor (kNN)	

Decision Tree algorithm at each iteration generates one new feature, based on original and already constructed ones, depending, which one is better. For construction, the greedy search is performed with the help of some predefined operators. The start point of search is an empty dataset from the next point, algorithm adds or deletes attribute-value pair, based on the evaluation of class entropy and model complexity or "the best linear discriminant function and its extension to functional trees" [12].

Random forest, a supervised learning algorithm, is quite a valuable data classification tool. Like, the forest, it is the unity of trees and their abundance defines the strength of it. The algorithm creates decision trees on datasets, performs prediction on each set, and by ranking these solutions where each tree votes, returns the best or most popular class [9].

As a classification algorithm, Logistic Regression is generally, used for binary outputs, when sample feature belongs to one class or not. It is based on the Sigmoid function, which resembles an "S" shaped curve when plotted on a graph. This classifier takes values between 0 and 1 and "squishes" them towards the margins at the top and bottom and denotes them by 0 or 1. The decision about labeling is made by calculating the Sigmoid of the sum of the weighted features [10]. The equation for the Sigmoid function is given in formula 1:

$$y = 1/(1 + e^{-x}) \tag{1}$$

The e denotes the exponential constant, and has a value of approximately 2.71828.

The underlying principle of k-Nearest Neighbour (kNN) Algorithm is the following: the instances within a dataset are classified according to the close proximity to other instances that are having similar properties [8,15]. After an instance is marked with a classification label, then the value of an unclassified instance can be determined by observing the class of its nearest neighbors. The kNN puts the k nearest instances to the query instance and defines their class by detecting the single most frequent class label. Distance measurements between the sample points x and y can be measured, for instance, using Euclidean or Minkowski Distance formulas 2 and 3:

$$d(x, y) = \sqrt{\sum_{i=1}^{n} (x_i - y_i)^2} \tag{2}$$

$$d(x, y) = \left(\sum |x_i - y_i|^p \right)^{1/p} \tag{3}$$

XGBoost, also known as the extreme gradient boosting library involves the gradient boosting decision tree architecture. In the gradient boosting algorithm, new model construction happens by predicting the errors of prior models, and based on the collected information it makes the final prediction. Similar to Gradient Descent framework, Gradient Boosting also minimizes the loss when adds new models [5].

LightGBM is also a gradient boosting approach that implements tree-based learning algorithms. This classifier has high computational speed and that is why it is considered as a fast processing algorithm. To differentiate between LightGBM and other similar tree-structured algorithms, it grows vertically, or leaf-wise way, while others grow horizontally, level-wise. LightGBM selects the leaf with a large loss to grow and gains the ability to lower down more loss compared to level-wise algorithms while growing the same leaf [11].

PyTorch, an open-source ML library is effectively used in the field of deep learning and artificial intelligence, along with computer vision and natural language processing applications. Pytorch can be considered primarily as a research-first library. Neural Networks can be constructed using the torch.nn package and used in fall detection too [14]. A typical neural network (NN) contains many simple, connected processors known as neurons, each generating a sequence of real-valued activations. Input neurons get triggered through sensors observing the environment and other neurons get triggered through weighted connections from formerly active neurons. The learning process or assignment of the credits can be explained by discovering weights that make the NN exhibit anticipated behavior. Contingent upon the problem and how the neurons are related to each other may entail long causal chains of computational stages, where each stage transforms (frequently not in a linear way) the total activation process of the network [6,18].

4   Experimental Study of Sensor Data for Fall Detection

This section is dedicated for building the experimental model of sensor data for fall detection. This experimental study includes data acquisition or data collection, choosing the methodology of data preprocessing based on methods of data cleaning and integration, data transformation and data reduction, data classification and results demonstration. The Fig. 1 illustrates the steps of the experimental model construction by means of preferred algorithms.

4.1   Data Acquisition

In this work, data collection is implemented using mobile embedded sensors, which are considered as the vital sources of the data collection process [3]. Recently, they are used in all kinds of applications as the automatic and virtual tools of data acquisition for further processes of decision-making. Sensor data application is also valuable for health monitoring, location information, activity recognition, and precisely, for fall detection.

4.2   Experimental Setup

In our study, fall detection experiments were conducted by the participation of seven healthy volunteers, whose mean age is 25 and the mean weight equals

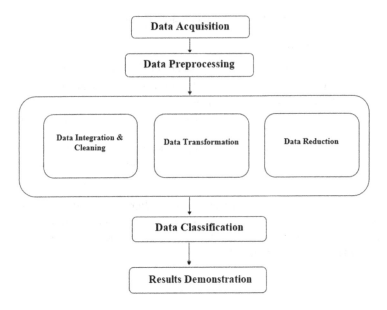

Fig. 1. Steps of experimental model construction

60 kg. During data collection, each subject was asked to perform falls and fall-like activities with their iPhone located in the right front pocket of pants without any restrictions and tightening. This way, in the natural living environment, they were falling intentionally onto a 15 cm thick cushion/mat. Each activity was timed for a maximum of 10 s from start to end. Data was sampled 20 Hz. The falls and fall-like activities together with their descriptions are given in Table 2, while Table 3 represents the list of engineered features.

Table 2. List of fall activities

Fall activity reference	Fall description
F1	Fall forward
F2	Fall backward
F3	Fall towards left
F4	Fall towards right
F5	Sitting fast
F6	Jumping

Table 3. List of engineered features

Feature description	
1. x, y, z coordinates	5. Angles of the derivative values
2. x, y, z angles	6. Avg of x, y, z and angle values
3. Magnitude of the vector	7. x/y, y/x, x/z, z/x etc.
4. Magnitude of the derivative	8. Deviation from avg x, y, z and avg angles
	9. 1st order derivative in time axis for x, y, z values, angles and magnitude

The Fig. 2 visually represents the data, where axes labels represent the parameter name. The color of the scatter points represent each six class labels. There is a number assigned to label for y and z values' axes. These numbers indicate rotational angle of the plot.

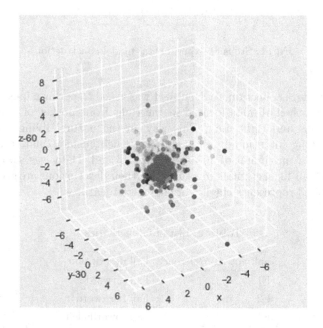

Fig. 2. Obtained data representation for six activities on the scatter plot

The application consists of drop-down menus and buttons, which can be described as follows:

- User first selects activity type from the drop-down menu, where six above mentioned activities are listed;
- "Select user" drop-down menu enables the user to choose a subject number, user1, user2, etc.;

– Start Recording button should be activated in order to activate sensors;
– And consequently, stopped the button when action is recorded after several seconds;
– "Cancel the last experiment" deletes permanently last recorded activity (for example recorded by mistake);
– "Remove all local data" deletes permanently all locally recorded activities;
– The "Share" button enables the user to transmit recorded files to other devices for further processing.

Some of the screenshots from the developed mobile application are presented below in Fig. 3 as visual representation.

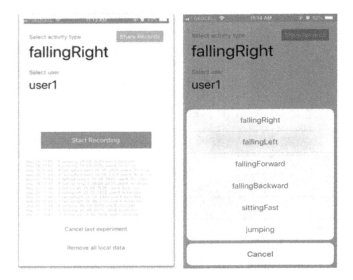

Fig. 3. Application screens: start recording process and choosing activities

4.3   Results of Data Preprocessing and Classification

In this study, Python programming language was preferred for data preprocessing and classification, as this language is one of the most popular in data science. It is open-source and contains many libraries useful for scientific computing, like scikit-learn, which is also very well known and free to use. During data preparation and model construction, this library was chosen along with Pandas and Matplotlib for better data manipulation and data visualization, respectively. During experiments, accelerometer and gyroscope data files were generated as separate .csv format files, for each activity and each user. Later, within data integration, all data files were merged in one "combined.csv" file. The data cleaning process was carried out using the strategy of Missing Value Imputation by a mean value and Outlier Detection Algorithms, as for noise filtering IsolationForest was selected. During feature engineering angles and magnitudes were generated. As

shown in the Fig. 4, the angles have different distribution for each classes. Each
subplot holds additional information like correlation between the features if its
a scatter plot, or mean and std values if its a distribution plot. ML algorithms
performances are given in Fig. 5. For data validation train/test split method was
used with the different ratios: 0.1, 0.15, 0.2 from the sklearn library, where 0.2
turned out to be the optimal ratio. As for the evaluation, the LGBM classifier
was selected with the highest performance, which is represented in Fig. 6.

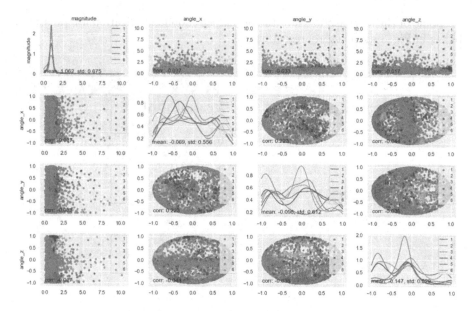

Fig. 4. Distribution of the classes based on the generated features

	0	1	2	3	4	5	Average
knn_Train_set	0.9510	0.9362	0.9009	0.9324	0.8951	0.9101	0.9209
knn_Test_set	0.8656	0.8661	0.9067	0.8683	0.8092	0.8590	0.8625
DT_Train_set	0.9446	0.9818	0.9599	0.8902	0.9525	0.9555	0.9474
DT_Test_set	0.8875	0.8671	0.8728	0.8399	0.8505	0.8767	0.8657
xgb_Train_set	10000	10000	10000	10000	10000	10000	10000
xgb_Test_set	0.8622	0.9159	0.9254	0.8214	0.8732	0.9319	0.8883
lgbm_Train_set	10000	10000	10000	10000	10000	10000	10000
lgbm_Test_set	0.8730	0.9030	0.9548	0.8023	0.8777	0.9461	0.8928
rfc_Train_set	10000	10000	10000	10000	10000	10000	10000
rfc_Test_set	0.8429	0.8925	0.9286	0.7694	0.8578	0.9188	0.8684
LR_Train_set	0.7858	0.8288	0.8042	0.7918	0.7163	0.7769	0.7840
LR_Test_set	0.7476	0.7087	0.6731	0.6671	0.7002	0.7448	0.7069
pytorch_Train_set	0.7948	0.8375	0.7503	0.7712	0.8191	0.7861	0.7932
pytorch_Test_set	0.7413	0.7680	0.6985	0.7319	0.7745	0.7319	0.7410

Fig. 5. ML algorithm performances on the experimental data, test ratio = 0.2

Classes	0	1	2	3	4	5	Average
precision	0.8869	0.8509	0.8744	0.9023	0.9110	0.9210	0.8911
recall	0.8869	0.9238	0.8628	0.8889	0.8776	0.9147	0.8924
specificity	0.9799	0.9729	0.9774	0.9782	0.9828	0.9804	0.9786
f1_score	0.8869	0.8858	0.8686	0.8955	0.8940	0.9178	0.8914
accuracy							0.8928

Fig. 6. Performance evaluation: score matrix for TestSet from $LGBM$

5   Conclusion and Possible Directions for Further Study

This work describes the process of machine learning model construction and preparation for fall detection based on sensor stream data analysis, which consists of data acquisition, data preprocessing and data classification. Firstly, machine learning and its importance in daily life are described, then it is followed by a literature review, describing different kinds of data preprocessing tools employed by several researchers, in order to prepare row data for classification. This comprehensive study reviews data preprocessing steps such as data cleaning techniques to deal with missing values and noisy data; data integration and strategies to bring data in one common store; data transformation methods for data normalization, and data reduction approach for decreasing the complexity of model through dimensionality reduction. Some Classification algorithms, namely, Decision Tree (DT), Random Forest (RF), Logistic regression (LR), k-Neatest Neighbor (kNN), XGBoost, LightGBM, and Pytorch Neural Network that are used in the study are also discussed in terms of their characteristics. Finally, mobile sensor stream data is retrieved and analyzed. During the experiment, accelerometer and gyroscope sensor data are collected with the iOS-based mobile application, developed within the Project framework. Four fall activities and two fall-like activities are investigated in terms of preprocessing and classification procedures. For data cleaning purposes, Mean Value Imputation, Outlier Detection Algorithms, and RobustScaler are used. As for data reduction, Principal Component Analysis (PCA) and Linear Discriminant Analysis (LDA) are tried, from where LDA was selected due to its better performance on our dataset. As for the feature engineering, magnitude and angle features are chosen for data observation. After the above-mentioned classification algorithms application, promising results are achieved and demonstrated, from where LightGBM showed the best performance among other applied algorithms.

This empirical study can be further developed in the following directions:

- Experiments can be continued and different combination of data preprocessing and data classification algorithms can be used for potential higher accuracies;
- Experiments can be done on a larger group of individuals of different age to test model accuracy while keeping smartphones freely placed in the pockets;
- Falls and fall like activities can be studied along with various Activities of Daily Livings (ADLs);

- Real-time mobile application can be developed for fall detection purposes;
- On-device processing technique can be elaborated, where the data preprocessing model, implemented in the smartphone application will able to detect
  falls locally, without sending data for further processing.

Acknowledgments. This work was supported by Shota Rustaveli National Science
Foundation of Georgia (SRNSFG) under the grant YS-19-1633.

References

1. Aggarwal, C.C.: Data classification. Data Mining, pp. 285–344. Springer, Cham
   (2015). https://doi.org/10.1007/978-3-319-14142-8_10
2. Alasadi, S.A., Bhaya, W.S.: Review of data preprocessing techniques in data mining. Eng. Appl. Sci. **12**(16), 4102–4107 (2017)
3. Ali, S., Khusro, S., Rauf, A., Mahfooz, S.: Sensors and mobile phones: evolution
   and state-of-the-art. Pak. J. Sci. **66**(4), 386–400 (2014)
4. Attal, F., Mohammed, S., Dedabrishvili, M., Chamroukhi, F., Oukhellou, L., Ami-
   rat, Y.: Physical human activity recognition using wearable sensors. Sensors (Basel
   Switz.) **15**, 31314–31338 (2015)
5. Chen, T., Guestrin, C.: Xgboost: a scalable tree boosting system. In: Proceedings
   of the 22nd ACM SIGKDD International Conference on Knowledge Discovery and
   Data Mining, pp. 785–794 (2016)
6. Dedabrishvili, M.: Effective ways to overcome classification limitations for activities
   of daily livings (ADLS). In: 2020 IEEE 2nd International Conference on System
   Analysis and Intelligent Computing (SAIC), pp. 1–7 (2020)
7. García, S., Ramírez-Gallego, S., Luengo, J., Benítez, J.M., Herrera, F.: Big data
   preprocessing: methods and prospects. Big Data Anal. **1**(1), 9 (2016)
8. Gent, I.P., et al.: Learning when to use lazy learning in constraint solving. In:
   ECAI, pp. 873–878 (2010)
9. Han, J., Pei, J., Kamber, M.: Data Mining: Concepts and Techniques. Elsevier
   (2011)
10. Kambria: Logistic Regression For Machine Learning and Classification (2019).
    https://kambria.io/blog/logistic-regression-for-machine-learning/. Accessed 28
    December 2020
11. Ke, G., et al.: Lightgbm: a highly efficient gradient boosting decision tree. In: NIPS
    (2017)
12. Motoda, H., Liu, H.: Feature selection extraction and construction. Commun. IICM
    Inst. Inf. Comput. Mach. **5**(2), 67–72 (2002)
13. Müller, A.C., Guido, S. et al.: Introduction to Machine Learning with Python: a
    Guide for Data Scientists. O'Reilly Media, Inc. (2016)
14. Paszke, A., et al.:. Automatic differentiation in pytorch. In: NIPS-W (2017)
15. Phyu,T.N.: Survey of classification techniques in data mining. In: Proceedings of
    the International MultiConference of Engineers and Computer Scientists Vol I
    IMECS 2009, Hong Kong (2009)
16. Pyle, D.: Data Preparation for Data Mining. Morgan Kaufmann (1999)
17. Raschka, S., Mirjalili, V.: Python machine learning: machine learning and deep
    learning with python. In: scikit-learn, and TensorFlow. Packt Publishing (2019)
18. Schmidhuber, J.: Deep learning in neural networks: an overview. Neural Netw. **61**,
    85–117 (2015)
19. Yuan, G., Wang, Z., Meng, F., Yan, Q., Xia, S.: An overview of human activity
    recognition based on smartphone. Sensor Rev. **39**(2), 288–306 (2019)

IPR-SN: Intelligent Packet Routing in Satellite Networks Based on Distributed Deep Reinforcement Learning

Tao Huang[1,2]([✉]), Lixiang Liu[2], and Shuaijun Liu[2]

[1] University of Chinese Academy of Sciences, Beijing, China
[2] Institute of Software Chinese Academy of Sciences, Beijing, China
huangtao18@mails.ucas.ac.cn

Abstract. In terms of avoiding congestion, due to the rapid change of satellite network topology and network traffic, traditional satellite network routing algorithms have problems in computational efficiency and scalability. The rapid expansion of deep reinforcement learning urges a lot of research work to combine DRL with network routing. We propose a novel fully distributed DRL packet routing framework named Intelligent Packet Routing in Satellite Networks (IPR-SN). The fully distributed framework is designed to avoid problems caused by centralized training or centralized execution in IPR-SN. Because DRL is endowed with powerful experience learning ability and feature learning ability, agent learns the hidden features of the model by virtue of the deep structure of neural networks. It avoids choosing the path that aggravates congestion in packet path selection and formulates a better satellite network routing strategy. Through experimental analysis and comparison with other algorithms, the results show that this algorithm can effectively reduce average packet delivery time.

Keywords: Packet routing · Satellite networks · Distributed deep reinforcement learning

1 Introduction

In a satellite communication network, satellites move at a high velocity relative to the ground, which leads to a rapid change inter-satellite range. Compared to the stability of network topology on the ground, there are dynamic characteristics of inter-satellite links (ISLs) in satellite networks. Due to the shorter propagation delay of ISLs in high latitude areas and the characteristics of satellite orbit distribution, the data flow is not averagely distributed and centralized to satellites in high latitude areas [15]. There are different loads on satellites above inland densely populated areas and satellites above the ocean. With the fast movement of satellites, the load of its coverage also changes fast. In addition, a satellite network is more complicated than a ground network because it is limited by the latency of ISLs, lower performance, and insufficient computing

© Springer Nature Switzerland AG 2021
H. Fujita et al. (Eds.): IEA/AIE 2021, LNAI 12798, pp. 621–632, 2021.
https://doi.org/10.1007/978-3-030-79457-6_53

resources [1]. Therefore traditional routing techniques for terrestrial networks cannot be applied directly in a satellite communication system.

Reinforcement learning is a machine learning method, and it obtains rewards through the interaction between agents and environment. With maximum reward as its purpose, it guides the actions of agents [19]. With the rapid development of deep neural networks (DNN) in recent years, deep learning algorithm shows a better performance than the traditional algorithm in the areas such as computer vision, natural language processing, and automatic speech recognition [8]. Many intelligent routing algorithms came out in the computer networks and were widely utilized in routing optimization [18,23], traffic forecast [2], and intrusion detection [16].

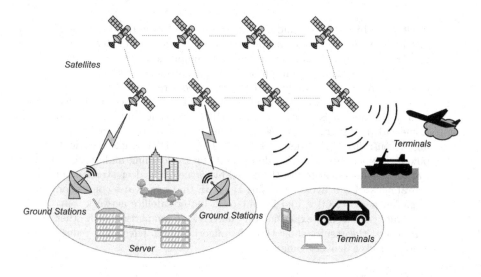

Fig. 1. A satellite communication system

With the development of satellite communication systems (see Fig. 1), there are more and more satellites in a satellite communication system, and the number will reach approximately one thousand in the future. There is an urgent need to develop satellite routing technology to adapt to more complex satellite networks and ISLs. Tu et al. [21] proposed a Machine Learning-based Space-ground Integration Networking (ML-SSGIN) framework which provided a centralized satellite routing strategy based on deep deterministic policy gradient (DDPG) [11]. It needs to obtain real-time global network traffic information and uniformly send routing decisions to satellites through ground servers. However, the effectiveness of centralized control cannot be ensured, more data transmission burden will be brought, and it is difficult to use because of the long ISL and high latency of the satellite system. Based on multi-agent deep deterministic policy gradient (MADDPG) [12], Qin et al. [17] proposed a distributed satellite routing optimizing approach with centralized training but decentralized execution to prevent centralized control problems. But it is difficult to achieve a good result for centralized training, and the difficulty of model convergence is increasing with the rising of satellite numbers.

With the above challenges to satellite networks, we propose a novel fully distributed deep reinforcement learning packet routing framework named Intelligent Packet Routing in Satellite Networks (IPR-SN). Inspired by Deep Recurrent Q-Network (DRQN) [9] and Deep Q-routing with Communication (DQRC) [23], there is a DNN in each agent in IPR-SN, with asynchronous independent training and execution. A fully distributed framework was designed to avoid the problems brought by centralized training or centralized execution[22]. With the help of software defined network (SDN) which decouples control plane and data plane, we put forward a constructed SDN-enabled satellite network. It can realize the deployment for IPR-SN algorithm in the application plane with the help of programmability of SDN architecture. Furthermore, the superiority of IPR-SN was shown through a contrast experiment.

The remaining sections of this paper: Sect. 2 introduces the background of SDN and DRL; Sect. 3 presents the system model and algorithm design; Sect. 4 conducts experiments on algorithms and assesses IPR-SN superiority; Sect. 5 gives a summary of this paper.

2   Background

This section briefly introduces some backgrounds related to IPR-SN, comprising DRL and SDN, traditional satellite network routing algorithm.

2.1   Routing in Satellite Network

In satellite communication system, satellite routing algorithm is a challenging problem and has been widely concerned. To balance the traffic of satellite network, Mohorcic et al. [14] proposed alternate link routing to calculate the optimal and sub-optimal paths respectively, adopting a mixture of optimal and suboptimal next hop. However, in the experiment, the load on the satellite was still biased towards the satellite link at high latitudes. To avoid the congestion of ISLs, Tarik et al. [20] put forward explicit load balancing. When the satellite network is congested, the signal is sent to the neighboring satellites to update the routing table and avoid forwarding data to the congested satellite, which reduces the delay of the satellite network. However, in this case, the additional exchange of information increases the load on ISLs. Chen et al. [4] proposed a geographic backpressure algorithm (GBP) based on the backpressure-type algorithm [7] in satellite networks. Different from the traditional backpressure, GBP takes the distance factor as a cost into the backlog differential calculation. It can deliver packets in time well as satellite network load varies and improve the end-to-end performance.

2.2   Software Defined Network

SDN is a new kind of network architecture. It creates a more flexible and efficient management mechanism for the network through decoupling the data plane and the control plane. Bao et al. [3] proposed a software-defined satellite network architecture named OpenSAN. OpenSAN defined the routing rules of control plane on geostationary earth orbit (GEO) through the application plane on the ground. Then, flow tables were issued to the data plane through GEO satellites. Thus OpenSAN is programmable and flexible. With the approaching of 5G networking, satellite communication is becoming increasingly important. SDN will also bring significant challenges and opportunities to satellite networks [5].

2.3   Reinforcement Learning and Partially Observable Markov Decision Process

Reinforcement learning is a way of learning by interaction between agent and environment. The purpose is to interact with environment and optimize policies based on rewards. Then, actions are carried out according to policies to gain more and better rewards [19].

If the agent of the model does not directly observe the state, it can only make decisions through partially obtained information [9]. Issues like this are modeled as Partially Observable Markov Decision Process (POMDP). Packet routing can be defined as POMDP [21]. It can be effectively resolved by DRQN that a long short-term memory (LSTM) [10] is added based on deep Q-network (DQN) [13]. LSTM establishes connections among inputs through three well-designed gates, thus resolving the issue of long-term dependencies. In addition, deep distributed recurrent Q-networks (DDRQN) [6] provided a multi-agent way of mutual communication. The action information from the previous moment is added to the input of every agent, and network parameters are shared among multiple agents. Meanwhile, the problem of cooperation and exchange among the agents is resolved as well.

3   Algorithm

This section introduces the system model and algorithm framework of IPR-SN.

3.1   System Model

Combined with SDN, we make full use of its data plane and control plane decoupling. By virtue of the programmability of SDN, the algorithm proposed in this paper can play a full role in satellite network model. The information of the data plane is collected by control plane, which is used as the input of routing algorithm. Through the calculation of the algorithm, packet path selection is output. Thus the whole network routing is optimized. Moreover, it acts on the data plane directly through the southbound interface of SDN to realize the combination of algorithm and network.

Considering the high latency of data transmission between ground stations and GEO satellites, and of distributing flow tables from GEO satellites to low earth orbit (LEO) satellites, to make effective use of LEO ISLs, we give priority to the single-layer LEO satellite network as the control plane and the data plane, and takes the ground stations distributed all over the world as the application plane of SDN. As the application plane, the ground stations realize the development and deployment of the business application form of the algorithm in this paper, and manages the network resources. Through the northbound interface, the application plane can control the resource state of the whole satellite network by controlling LEO satellites. Via the southbound interface, every LEO satellite generates routing strategies and sends to internal data plane. The data plane in LEO satellites transmits and forwards packets in the light of corresponding policies, thus completing the process of packet routing. The overall system architecture is shown in Fig. 2.

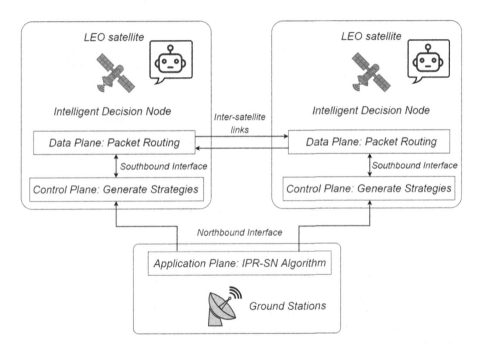

Fig. 2. SDN architecture in IPR-SN.

Under the above architecture, distributed control plane can give full play to the strengths of computing performance, make up for the shortcomings of on-board computing capacity, and then distribute routing strategies to satellites to complete the intelligent scheduling of packets. In terms of satellite communication network, this well-designed model is ingeniously applied to distributed DRL algorithm, achieving efficient and intelligent management of satellite network routing.

3.2 Reinforcement Learning Formulation

In the light of the above system model, we meticulously design RL framework in the satellite network in Fig. 3.

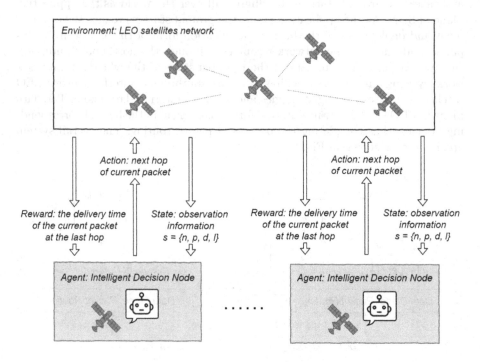

Fig. 3. RL framework in IPR-SN.

Environment: LEO Satellites Network. The environment needs to respond to actions given by the agent in RL. Satellite network is viewed as a RL environment with real time dynamic feedback. Packet delivery time varies in real time in accordance with link congestion and node queuing, reflecting the current state of nodes and links.

Agents: LEO Satellites. In this paper, LEO satellites constitute the multi-agent in RL. What the agent needs to do is to calculate the next action based on the state and reward of the environmental feedback. An intelligent decision node constructed by each LEO satellite is regarded as an agent, and these agents are used to judge the state of the nodes and packets fed back by LEO satellites network to calculate the next action.

State: Internal and External Information of Each Agent. Considering the dynamics of ISLs and network traffic, for each agent, the state that it can observe is defined as a quadruple $s = \{n, p, d, l\}$, where n is the destination of the current packet, p is the execution actions of the past n packets, d is the propagation delay of each link, and l is the queue length of each neighbor node.

Action: The Next Node of the Current Packet. After the agent observes the internal and external information, it needs to make the next hop decision for the current packet. Therefore, the next hop is one of the neighbor nodes of the agent, thus specifying its next hop for the current packet.

Reward: The Delivery Time of the Current Packet at the Last Hop. Because the algorithm of this paper is to reduce the packet delivery time, the design principle of the reward is that the smaller packet delivery time corresponds to the larger reward. For each action, the reward is defined as $r = -t$, where t is the delivery time of the current packet at the last hop. By virtue of this design, the goal of minimizing the packet delivery time is achieved, that is, selecting proper action to minimize the propagation delay and queuing time of each hop of the packet.

3.3 Intelligent Packet Routing in Satellite Networks

Inspired by some existing work [6,9,23], we propose a novel fully distributed deep reinforcement learning packet routing framework named Intelligent Packet Routing in Satellite Networks (IPR-SN). Next, the structure of DNN and IPR-SN specific design are introduced.

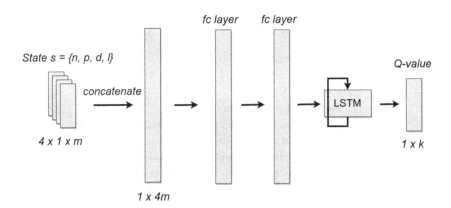

Fig. 4. The structure of DNN in IPR-SN.

First, we introduce the structure of DNN in IPR-SN. In accordance with the formula $s = \{n, p, d, l\}$, DNN input is the state of Dimension $1 \times 4\,\mathrm{m}$ concatenated by n, p, d and l. Before concatenating, the dimensions of n, p, d

and l are encoded into $1 \times m$. As shown in Fig. 4, the hidden layers consist of two fully connected (fc) layers and a LSTM layer. At the end of DNN is an output of dimension $1 \times k$, which represents Q-value for each possible action, where k is the number of neighbor nodes.

As far as the above DNN structure is concerned, we have designed a fully distributed multi-agent reinforcement learning framework. The pseudo code of the algorithm is shown in Table 1.

Because it is completely distributed, each agent has its own independent DNN to approximately calculate Q-value. In each step of the training of the model, each agent will first observe and choose the action that maximizes Q-value with the probability of ϵ, or act randomly with the probability of $1 - \epsilon$. After the execution of the action, the agent will get the new state and calculate the reward. Then a transition is stored in the replay buffer. If the packet has reached its destination, then $f = 1$, otherwise $f = 0$. Each agent samples a batch $(s_u^i, a_u^i, r_u^i, s_{u+1}^i, f_u^i)$ from its own replay buffer to update the network parameters by minimizing the loss function:

$$\mathcal{L}(\theta_i) \approx \theta_i + \alpha \nabla_{\theta_i}(y_u - Q_i(s_u^i, a_u^i|\theta_i))^2,$$

where

$$y_u = r_u + \gamma max_{a_{u+1}} Q_i(s_{u+1}, a_{u+1}|\theta_i)(1 - f_u^i)$$

for each agent i.

Table 1. The pseudo code of IPR-SN

Algorithm: IPR-SN	
1.	**For** agent i = 1 to N **do**
2.	Initialize deep Q-network Q_i randomly with weights θ_i
3.	Initialize replay buffer D_i
4.	**End For**
5.	**For** episode = 1 to M **do**
6.	Reset environment
7.	**For** step t = 1 to S **do**
8.	**For** agent i = 1 to N **do**
9.	Get the state $s_t^i = \{n_t^i, p_t^i, d_t^i, l_t^i\}$ through observation
10.	Select and execute an action a_t^i
11.	Calculate reward r_t^i and Get new state s_{t+1}^i
12.	Store transition $(s_t^i, a_t^i, r_t^i, s_{t+1}^i, f_t^i)$ in D_i
13.	Sample a batch $(s_u^i, a_u^i, r_u^i, s_{u+1}^i, f_u^i)$ from D_i
14.	Update Q_i with $\theta_i \leftarrow \theta_i + \alpha \nabla_{\theta_i}(y_u - Q_i(s_u^i, a_u^i|\theta_i))^2$, where $y_u = r_u + \gamma max_{a_{u+1}} Q_i(s_{u+1}, a_{u+1}|\theta_i)(1 - f_u^i)$
15.	**End For**
16.	**End For**
17.	**End For**

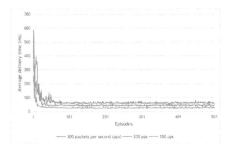 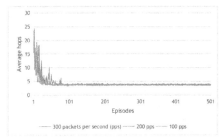

Fig. 5. Comparison of packets average delivery time at different packet generation rates.

Fig. 6. Comparison of packets average hops at different packet generation rates.

4   Evaluation

The following is the experimental evaluation of IPR-SN. This section mainly introduces the experimental environment and analyzes the results.

4.1   Experimental Environment

In this section, the convergency and performance of the algorithm of IPR-SN are tested, and the results are compared and analyzed with other algorithms. In this experiment, satellite tool kit (STK) is adopted to build the satellite constellation and extract the coordinate information of the satellites. Then, the satellite network is carried out the environment construction and simulated the network at the packet level. The whole algorithm is implemented by python 3.7 and tensorflow 1.15.0.

4.2   Experimental Results

In consideration of the number of satellites in LEO satellite constellation, 66 satellites are built as 66 intelligent decision nodes. The propagation delay of ISLs is based on the real time calculation of inter-satellite distance. To train the model, randomly generated packets are used as training sets, and the source point and destination of packets are randomly divided in the light of a certain proportion. Then, at different packet generation rates, the results of the training model are shown in Fig. 5 and Fig. 6. It can be concluded that the model can converge effectively at different generation rates, and remarkably reduce the average delivery time and the average hops of packets.

In order to better evaluate the performance, under the same network configuration, GBP [4] and centralized IPR-SN are added for comparison, and randomly generated packets are tested, where centralized IPR-SN is the single-agent RL version of IPR-SN. As can be seen from Fig. 7, compared with traditional routing algorithm GBP and centrally trained centralized IPR-SN, the trained IPR-SN

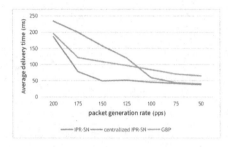 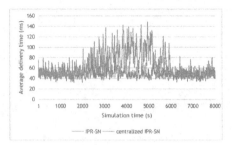

Fig. 7. Comparison of GBP, centralized IPR-SN and IPR-SN at different packet generation rates.

Fig. 8. Comparison between centralized IPR-SN and IPR-SN with changing network loads.

can effectively reduce the average delivery time of packets at different packet generation rates and its performance is better than centralized IPR-SN.

To test the adaptability of IPR-SN to the dynamic change of network load, we dynamically change the packet generation rate during the simulation period and observe the change of performance. In Fig. 8, in pace with the progress of satellite network simulation, when the network load increases dynamically at simulation time 2000 2000 s, IPR-SN has smaller delay jitter and stronger adaptability than centralized IPR-SN.

5 Conclusion

We propose a novel fully distributed DRL packet routing framework named Intelligent Packet Routing in Satellite Networks (IPR-SN). The fully distributed framework is designed to avoid problems caused by centralized training or centralized execution in IPR-SN. Through experimental analysis and comparison with other algorithms, the results show that this algorithm can effectively reduce the average delivery time of packets in satellite networks.

References

1. Alagoz, F., Korcak, O., Jamalipour, A.: Exploring the routing strategies in next-generation satellite networks. IEEE Wirel. Commun. **14**(3), 79–88 (2007). https://doi.org/10.1109/MWC.2007.386616
2. Alawe, I., Ksentini, A., Hadjadj-Aoul, Y., Bertin, P.: Improving traffic forecasting for 5G core network scalability: a machine learning approach. IEEE Netw. **32**(6), 42–49 (2018). https://doi.org/10.1109/MNET.2018.1800104
3. Bao, J., Zhao, B., Yu, W., Feng, Z., Wu, C., Gong, Z.: Opensan: a software-defined satellite network architecture. In: Bustamante, F.E., Hu, Y.C., Krishnamurthy, A., Ratnasamy, S. (eds.) ACM SIGCOMM 2014 Conference, SIGCOMM 2014, Chicago, IL, USA, 17–22 August 2014, pp. 347–348. ACM (2014). https://doi.org/10.1145/2619239.2631454

4. Chen, J., Liu, L., Hu, X.: Feasibility of backpressure algorithm for satellite networks. In: 2016 IEEE 12th International Conference on Wireless and Mobile Computing, Networking and Communications (WiMob), pp. 1–8 (2016). https://doi.org/10.1109/WiMOB.2016.7763247
5. Ferrús, R., et al.: SDN/NFV-enabled satellite communications networks: opportunities, scenarios and challenges. Phys. Commun. **18**, 95–112 (2016). https://doi.org/10.1016/j.phycom.2015.10.007
6. Foerster, J.N., Assael, Y.M., de Freitas, N., Whiteson, S.: Learning to communicate to solve riddles with deep distributed recurrent q-networks. CoRR abs/1602.02672 (2016). http://arxiv.org/abs/1602.02672
7. Georgiadis, L., Neely, M.J., Tassiulas, L.: Resource allocation and cross-layer control in wireless networks. Found. Trends Netw. **1**(1) (2006). https://doi.org/10.1561/1300000001
8. Goodfellow, I., Bengio, Y., Courville, A.: Deep Learning. MIT Press (2016). http://www.deeplearningbook.org
9. Hausknecht, M.J., Stone, P.: Deep recurrent q-learning for partially observable MDPS. CoRR abs/1507.06527 (2015). http://arxiv.org/abs/1507.06527
10. Hochreiter, S., Schmidhuber, J.: Long short-term memory. Neural Comput. **9**(8), 1735–1780 (1997). https://doi.org/10.1162/neco.1997.9.8.1735
11. Lillicrap, T.P., et al.: Continuous control with deep reinforcement learning. In: Bengio, Y., LeCun, Y. (eds.) 4th International Conference on Learning Representations, ICLR 2016, San Juan, Puerto Rico, 2–4 May 2016, Conference Track Proceedings (2016). http://arxiv.org/abs/1509.02971
12. Lowe, R., Wu, Y., Tamar, A., Harb, J., Abbeel, P., Mordatch, I.: Multi-agent actor-critic for mixed cooperative-competitive environments. In: Guyon, I., et al.(eds.) Advances in Neural Information Processing Systems 30: Annual Conference on Neural Information Processing Systems 2017, 4–9 December 2017, Long Beach, CA, USA, pp. 6379–6390 (2017). https://proceedings.neurips.cc/paper/2017/hash/68a9750337a418a86fe06c1991a1d64c-Abstract.html
13. Mnih, V., et al.: Human-level control through deep reinforcement learning. Nature **518**(7540), 529–533 (2015). https://doi.org/10.1038/nature14236
14. Mohorcic, M., Werner, M., Svigelj, A., Kandus, G.: Alternate link routing for traffic engineering in packet-oriented ISL networks. Int. J. Satell. Commun. Netw. **19**(5), 463–480 (2001). https://doi.org/10.1002/sat.712
15. Mohorčič, M., Švigelj, A., Kandus, G., Werner, M.: Performance evaluation of adaptive routing algorithms in packet-switched intersatellite link networks. Int. J. Satell. Commun. **20**(2), 97–120 (2002). https://doi.org/10.1002/sat.714, https://onlinelibrary.wiley.com/doi/abs/10.1002/sat.714
16. Niyaz, Q., Sun, W., Javaid, A.Y.: A deep learning based ddos detection system in software-defined networking (SDN). EAI Endorsed Trans. Secur. Safety **4**(12) (2017). https://doi.org/10.4108/eai.28-12-2017.153515
17. Qin, Z., Yao, H., Mai, T.: Traffic optimization in satellites communications: a multi-agent reinforcement learning approach. In: 2020 International Wireless Communications and Mobile Computing (IWCMC), pp. 269–273 (2020). https://doi.org/10.1109/IWCMC48107.2020.9148523
18. Stampa, G., Arias, M., Sanchez-Charles, D., Muntés-Mulero, V., Cabellos, A.: A deep-reinforcement learning approach for software-defined networking routing optimization. CoRR abs/1709.07080 (2017). http://arxiv.org/abs/1709.07080
19. Sutton, R., Barto, A.: Reinforcement Learning: An Introduction. MIT Press (1998)

20. Taleb, T., Mashimo, D., Jamalipour, A., Kato, N., Nemoto, Y.: Explicit load balancing technique for ngeo satellite ip networks with on-board processing capabilities. In: IEEE/ACM Transactions on Networking, vol. 17, no. 1, pp. 281–293 (2009). https://doi.org/10.1109/TNET.2008.918084
21. Tu, Z., Zhou, H., Li, K., Li, G., Shen, Q.: A routing optimization method for software-defined sgin based on deep reinforcement learning. In: 2019 IEEE Globecom Workshops (GC Wkshps), pp. 1–6 (2019). https://doi.org/10.1109/GCWkshps45667.2019.9024680
22. Yao, H., Mai, T., Jiang, C., Kuang, L., Guo, S.: AI routers & network mind: a hybrid machine learning paradigm for packet routing. IEEE Comput. Intell. Mag. 14(4), 21–30 (2019). https://doi.org/10.1109/MCI.2019.2937609
23. You, X., Li, X., Xu, Y., Feng, H., Zhao, J.: Toward packet routing with fully-distributed multi-agent deep reinforcement learning. In: International Symposium on Modeling and Optimization in Mobile, Ad Hoc, and Wireless Networks, WiOPT 2019, Avignon, France, 3–7 June 2019, pp. 1–8. IEEE (2019). https://doi.org/10.23919/WiOPT47501.2019.9144110

Author Index

Printed in the United States
by Baker & Taylor Publisher Services